Human Communication

Human Communication

THE BASIC COURSE

Sixth Edition

Joseph A. DeVito

Hunter College of the City University of New York

HarperCollins*College*Publishers

Project Editor: Thomas R. Farrell
Design Supervisor: Wendy A. Fredericks
Cover Design: John Callahan
Photo Researcher: Karen Koblik
Production Manager: Willie Lane
Compositor: Black Dot, Inc.
Printer and Binder: R. R. Donnelley & Sons Company
Cover Printer: R. R. Donnelley & Sons Company

For permission to use copyrighted material, grateful acknowledgment is made to the copyright holders on page C-1, which is hereby made part of this copyright page.

Human Communication: The Basic Course, Sixth Edition

Library of Congress Cataloging-in-Publication Data

DeVito, Joseph A., (date)–
      Human communication : the basic course / Joseph A. DeVito — 6th ed.
            p.   cm.
      Includes bibliographical references and index.
      ISBN 0-06-501879-6
      1. Communication.   I. Title
  P90.D485   1993
  302.2—dc20   93-23537

                                                                      CIP

    95 96   9 8 7 6 5 4 3

To Bernard J. Brommel
for his insightful and caring leadership
in the study of human communication,
for his friendship,
for his wise counsel

CONTENTS IN BRIEF

Contents in Detail   ix

Preface   xvii

To the Student   xxiii

PART 1   FOUNDATIONS   2

Unit 1 Preliminaries to Human Communication   4
Unit 2 Principles of Communication   24
Unit 3 The Self in Communication 41
Unit 4 Perception 58
Unit 5 Listening 76

PART 2   MESSAGES: VERBAL AND NONVERBAL   96

Unit 6 Preliminaries to Verbal and Nonverbal Messages   98
Unit 7 Verbal Message Barriers   112
Unit 8 Verbal Message Principles   125
Unit 9 Nonverbal Messages of Body and Sound   146
Unit 10 Nonverbal Messages of Space and Time   158
Unit 11 Messages in Conversation   178

PART 3   INTERPERSONAL COMMUNICATION,
              RELATIONSHIPS, AND INTERVIEWING   202

Unit 12 Preliminaries to Interpersonal Communication and
              Relationships   204
Unit 13 Relationship Development, Deterioration, and
              Repair   225
Unit 14 Interpersonal Conflict   241
Unit 15 Interviewing   259

PART 4   GROUP AND ORGANIZATIONAL
              COMMUNICATION   282

Unit 16 Preliminaries to Group Communication   284
Unit 17 Members and Leaders in Group Communication   302
Unit 18 Organizational Communication   322

PART 5 PUBLIC COMMUNICATION   348

Unit 19 Preliminaries to Public Communication   350
Unit 20 Principles of Public Communication   366
Unit 21 The Anatomy of the Audience and the Speech   388

PART 6 INTERCULTURAL COMMUNICATION   414

Unit 22 Preliminaries to Intercultural Communication:
         Importance, Difficulties, and Forms   416
Unit 23 Intercultural Communication: Principles, Barriers,
         and Gateways   431

PART 7 MASS COMMUNICATION   452

Unit 24 Preliminaries to Mass Communication: Components,
         Forms, and Functions   454
Unit 25 Theories of Mass Communication   471

Bibliography   B-1

Glossary   G-1

Credits   C-1

Index   I-1

CONTENTS IN DETAIL

Preface   xvii
To the Student   xxiii

PART 1 FOUNDATIONS   2

**UNIT 1 PRELIMINARIES TO HUMAN
COMMUNICATION   4**

The Areas of Human Communication   5
The Components of Human Communication   8
The Purposes of Communication   17
Summary   21
Applications   21

UNIT 2 PRINCIPLES OF COMMUNICATION   24

Communication Is a Package of Signals   25
Communication Is a Process of Adjustment   27
Communication Involves Content and Relationship
    Dimensions   28
Communication Involves Symmetrical and
    Complementary Transactions   30
Communication Sequences Are Punctuated   30
Communication Is a Transactional Process   32
Communication Is Inevitable, Irreversible, and
    Unrepeatable   34
Summary   36
Applications   36

UNIT 3 THE SELF IN COMMUNICATION   41

Self-concept   42
Self-awareness   43
Self-esteem   47
Self-disclosure   48
Summary   56
Application   56

UNIT 4 PERCEPTION   58

The Perception Process   59
Processes Influencing Perception   60
Critical Perception: Making Perceptions More Accurate   70

ix

Summary   73
Applications   73

UNIT 5 LISTENING   76

The Process of Listening   78
Listening Effectively   83
Active Listening   87
Summary   90
Applications   90

Part 1 Feedback   92
Questions and Activities   92
Skill Check   93
Suggested Readings   94

PART 2   MESSAGES: VERBAL AND NONVERBAL   96

**UNIT 6 PRELIMINARIES TO VERBAL AND NONVERBAL
         MESSAGES   98**

The Interaction of Verbal and Nonverbal
    Messages   99
Meanings and Messages   99
Message Characteristics   104
Summary   110
Applications   110

UNIT 7 VERBAL MESSAGE BARRIERS   112

Polarization   113
Intensional Orientation   114
Fact-Inference Confusion   115
Bypassing   116
Allness   118
Static Evaluation   119
Indiscrimination   120
Summary   122
Applications   122

UNIT 8 VERBAL MESSAGE PRINCIPLES   125

In-Group and Inclusive Talk   126
Downward and Equality Talk   127
Lying and Honesty   129
Gossip and Confidentiality   132
Disconfirmation and Confirmation   134

Summary 141
Applications 141

UNIT 9　NONVERBAL MESSAGES OF BODY AND SOUND　146

Body Movements　147
Facial Movements　149
Eye Movements　150
Sound　152
Summary 156
Applications 156

UNIT 10　NONVERBAL MESSAGES OF SPACE AND TIME 158

Proxemics　159
Artifactual Communication　162
Territoriality　166
Touch Communication　168
Temporal Communication　171
Summary 176
Applications 176

UNIT 11　MESSAGES IN CONVERSATION　178

The Conversational Process　179
Conversational Management　181
Conversational Effectiveness　186
Summary 195
Applications 195

Part 2 Feedback　197
Questions and Activities　197
Skill Check　198
Suggested Readings 201

PART 3　INTERPERSONAL COMMUNICATION, RELATIONSHIPS, AND INTERVIEWING　202

UNIT 12　PRELIMINARIES TO INTERPERSONAL COMMUNICATION AND RELATIONSHIPS　204

Interpersonal Communication　205
Interpersonal Relationships　206
Theories of Interpersonal Relationships　213
Summary 220
Applications 220

UNIT 13 RELATIONSHIP DEVELOPMENT, DETERIORATION, AND REPAIR   225

    Relationship Development   226
    Relationship Deterioration   229
    Relationship Repair and Self-repair   233
Summary   238
Applications   238

UNIT 14 INTERPERSONAL CONFLICT   241

    The Nature of Interpersonal Conflict   242
    Conflict Management   245
    Aggressiveness and Argumentativeness   250
    Before and After the Conflict   252
Summary   256
Applications   256

UNIT 15 INTERVIEWING   259

    Interviewing Defined   260
    The Information Interview   262
    The Employment Interview   265
Summary   274
Applications   274

Part 3 Feedback   277
    Questions and Activities   277
    Skill Check   279
Suggested Readings   280

PART 4   GROUP AND ORGANIZATIONAL COMMUNICATION   282

UNIT 16 PRELIMINARIES TO GROUP COMMUNICATION   284

    The Small Group   285
    Problem-solving Groups   289
    The Idea-Generation Group   294
    The Personal Growth Group   295
    Information-Sharing Groups   297
    Small Group Formats   299
Summary   300
Applications   301

UNIT 17 MEMBERS AND LEADERS IN GROUP COMMUNICATION   302

Members in Small Group Communication   303
Leaders in Small Group Communication   308
Factors That Work Against Small Group Effectiveness
     317
Summary   318
Applications 318

UNIT 18 ORGANIZATIONAL COMMUNICATION   322

Organization and Organizational Communication:
     Definitions   323
Approaches to Organizations   326
Communication Networks   331
Communication Flow in Organizations   334
Summary   341
Application   341

Part 4 Feedback   345
     Questions and Activities   345
     Skill Check   346
Suggested Readings   347

PART 5   PUBLIC COMMUNICATION   348

UNIT 19 PRELIMINARIES TO PUBLIC COMMUNICATION   350

The Nature of Public Speaking   351
Apprehension in Public Speaking   355
Criticism in Public Speaking   358
Summary   362
Application   362

UNIT 20 PRINCIPLES OF PUBLIC COMMUNICATION   366

Principles of Informative Speaking   367
Principles of Persuasion   368
Logic   371
Emotion   375
Credibility   380
Summary   383
Applications   383

UNIT 21 THE ANATOMY OF THE AUDIENCE AND THE
        SPEECH   388

          Anatomy of the Audience   389
          The Sociology of Audiences   390
          The Psychology of Audiences   393
          Anatomy of the Speech   395
    Summary   402
    Applications   402

Part 5 Feedback   408
  Questions and Activities   408
  Skill Check   410
Suggested Readings   411

PART 6   INTERCULTURAL COMMUNICATION   414

UNIT 22 PRELIMINARIES TO INTERCULTURAL
        COMMUNICATION: IMPORTANCE, DIFFICULTIES,
        AND FORMS   416

          The Importance of Intercultural
            Communication   417
          The Nature of Intercultural
            Communication   420
          The Difficulty in Mastering Intercultural
            Communication   426
    Summary   429
    Application   429

UNIT 23 INTERCULTURAL COMMUNICATION: PRINCIPLES,
        BARRIERS, AND GATEWAYS   431

          Principles of Intercultural Communication   433
          Barriers to Intercultural Communication   436
          Gateways to Intercultural Communication   442
    Summary   445
    Application   445

Part 6 Feedback   447
  Questions and Activities   447
  Skill Check   448
Suggested Readings   449

PART 7   MASS COMMUNICATION   452

UNIT 24 PRELIMINARIES TO MASS COMMUNICATION:
         COMPONENTS, FORMS, AND FUNCTIONS   454

A Definition of Mass Communication   455
Forms of Mass Communication   457
The Functions of Mass Communication   463

Summary   469
Application   469

UNIT 25 THEORIES OF MASS COMMUNICATION   471

Step Theories   472
Diffusion of Innovations Theory   474
Cultivation Theory   476
Uses and Gratification Theory   477
Agenda-setting Theory   478
RevStep Theories   472
Diffusion of Innovations Theory   474
Cultivation Theory   476
Uses and Gratification Theory   477
Agenda-setting Theory   478
Reversing the Process: Influencing the Media   480

Summary   482
Applications   482

Part 7 Feedback   485
Questions and Activities   485
Skill Check   486
Suggested Readings   487

Bibliography   B-1
Glossary   G-1
Credits   C-1
Index   I-1

PREFACE

It is a pleasure to write a preface to a book that is now in its sixth edition and that has proved so popular with both students and teachers. This edition continues in the same tradition as the previous editions, but with significant changes and updates.

Human Communication: The Basic Course is addressed to the introductory college course in communication that surveys the broad field of communication, including intrapersonal, interpersonal, small group and organizational, public, intercultural, and mass communication. It covers classic approaches and new developments; it covers research, theory, and skills.

The book is addressed to students who have little or no prior background in communication. For those students who will take this course as their only communication course, it will provide a broad background in both theory and skills in this essential liberal art. For those who will take additional and advanced courses or who are beginning their majors in communication, it will provide the essential theoretical foundation for their more advanced and specialized study.

The sixth edition, revised in the light of comments from a large number of instructors, builds on the successful features of previous editions and incorporates new materials that make the text even more useful and more enjoyable.

MAJOR FEATURES OF HUMAN COMMUNICATION

Among the major features of *Human Communication* are its

- comprehensive coverage of the field of human communication
- focus on research, theories, and skills
- unique treatment of public speaking
- intercultural consciousness
- interactive pedagogy

Comprehensive Coverage of Human Communication

Like its previous editions, this edition continues to survey the entire field—the preliminaries of human communication (axioms, perception, listening, verbal and nonverbal messages), interpersonal communication and relationships, interviewing, small group communication, organizational communication, intercultural communication, and mass communication.

Research, Theories, and Skills

The sixth edition emphasizes the research and theory in human communication but also considers the skills and practical implications to be drawn from this theory and research. Theories are extremely practical and skills—like examples and applications—clarify the theories. The two work together, each informing and enlarging upon the other.

Public Communication

The public communication section has been greatly reduced. The three units contained in this sixth edition focus on the theory and principles of public speaking, the information that every educated citizen needs to interact in a world so heavily influenced by public communication. An accompanying supplement, *The Public Speaking Guide,* available with this text at the option of the instructor and at no extra cost, focuses on the practical skills of effective public speaking. In this way, both theory and skills get to be covered in the depth they deserve.

Intercultural Consciousness

This edition reflects the growing importance of intercultual communication. There are few communications that are not intercultural in some way and to some extent. Thus, an intercultural consciousness is essential in any text in communication. In this sixth edition, this intercultural consciousness is seen in

- the numerous examples and illustrations identifying cultural variations in communication
- all interior photographs containing captions that focus attention on intercultural issues and that raise intercultural consciousness, ensuring that all major topics in the text get looked at through the influence of culture
- the two complete units (Units 22 and 23) that focus exclusively on intercultural communication—its research, theory, and skills—as a growing part of the communication discipline

Interactive Pedagogy

As in the previous edition, I continue to emphasize new and useful pedagogical aids, especially those that are interactive, to help the student master both the theory and the skills of human communication. Among those aids are the following.

Interactive Discussions (IDs)

Throughout the text are discussions that ask the reader to respond to issues just discussed or about to be discussed. These IDs—new to this edition and perhaps to textbooks generally—cover about 30 issues and appear throughout the text, highlighted by the icon and rule in the margin.

Self-tests

Throughout the text I have integrated 22 self-tests that encourage self-examination and increase self-awareness in such areas as listening, perception, self-monitoring, psychological time orientation, touch avoidance, interpersonal effectiveness, aggressiveness and argumentativeness, apprehension, and intercultural and mass communication awareness. These tests may be used to facilitate understanding the theories of human communication and acquiring the skills of effective communication. They may be done individually during normal study times or integrated into the class lecture-discussion.

New Application Exercises

In all, 52 applications (exercises) are included and appear at the ends of the units. Many of these are new to this edition.

Questions and Activities

An innovation introduced in the fifth edition and expanded here in the direction of fostering critical thinking about communication in all its forms is questions and activities for individuals and groups and lists of suggested readings.

Skill Checks

At the end of each of the seven parts is a skill check. These skill checks summarize the major skills to be learned and provide a convenient means for assessing the student's level of skill development. Instructors may want to use the skill checks as guidelines for selecting topics for class discussion. They can be used to identify areas of student weakness to extend skills to a higher level of complexity. They may also be used as discussion probes or stimuli for class discussion, for example, identifying specific behaviors that make up the skill or situations in which the application of the general skill should be modified.

THE SIXTH EDITION: WHAT'S NEW

Human Communication: The Basic Course is divided into seven parts (reduced from eight in the last edition). Each of these parts begins with a unit titled "Preliminaries," which provides an overview of the essential principles needed to understand the particular area and to ensure that all readers begin the study of each topic with comparable backgrounds. The 25 units (reduced from 30 in the last edition) cover the specifics of these seven major topics.

Part 1, Foundations (Units 1–5), covers the nature of human communication, the general principles of communication, the role of the self in communication, and the processes of receiving messages: perception and listening.

New to this section are the following:

- a reconceptualization of feedback (Unit 1)
- self-concept (Unit 3)
- self-esteem (Unit 3)
- a much revised discussion of attribution (Unit 4)
- a five-stage model of the listening process (Unit 5)

Part 2, Messages: Verbal and Nonverbal (Units 6–11), discusses the message codes—the nature of language, the barriers to effective interaction, principles to guide everyday communication, and the nonverbal codes of body, facial, and eye movements; sound; space, territoriality, and artifacts; and time communication.

New to this section are the following:

- a new unit stressing the commonalities between verbal and nonverbal message systems (Unit 6)
- racism, sexism, and heterosexism as disconfirmation (Unit 6)
- artifactual communication (Unit 10)
- a new unit on conversation, which includes thorough coverage of the process of conversation and its effective management (Unit 11)
- metaskills, the skills for regulating the more specific skills of interpersonal communication (flexibility, mindfulness, and cultural sensitivity) (Unit 11)

Part 3, Interpersonal Communication and Relationships (Units 12–15), covers two-person communication and emphasizes communication encounters between intimates and how those encounters, including conflict encounters, may be made more effective. How and why interpersonal relationships develop and deteriorate and how we can achieve greater control over them are the focal points. An entire unit on interviewing shows how effective interpersonal communication skills can make for effective interviewing.

New to this section are the following:

- theories of interpersonal relationships (Unit 12)
- relationship repair (Unit 13)
- a complete unit on conflict and conflict management, including aggressiveness and argumentativeness as modes of conflict resolution (Unit 14)
- a more comprehensive discussion of the information gathering interview (Unit 15)

Part 4, Group and Organizational Communication (Units 16–18), focuses on the nature and patterns of group interaction (membership and leadership) and how they may be made more effective. An entire unit on organizational communication focuses on the principles and techniques of communication within the organization.

New to this section are the following:

- power in the small group (Unit 16)
- focus groups (Unit 16)
- critical thinking in small groups (Unit 16)
- sexual harassment (Unit 18)
- guidelines for communicating upward, downward, laterally, and for dealing with the grapevine and with information overload (Unit 18)

Part 5, Public Communication (Units 19–21), focuses first on the nature of public speaking, speaker apprehension, and criticism. The principles of informative and persuasive communication are identified, as are the major issues involved in using logic, emotion, and credibility appeals in public speaking. Last, the anatomy of the audience (its sociological and psychological characteristics) and of the speech are explained.

New to this section are the following:

- the inclusion of a separate supplement, *The Public Speaking Guide,* which covers in depth the specific techniques for preparing and presenting a public speech
- an expanded discussion of speaker apprehension (Unit 19)
- criticism in public communication (Unit 19)
- an expanded discussion of the techniques of persuasion, including, for example, foot-in-the-door and door-in-the-face techniques (Unit 20)

Part 6, Intercultural Communication (Units 22–23), covers communication between members of different cultures and identifies some of the major forms of intercultural communication. In these units, primary attention is given to understanding the importance and role of intercultural communication in today's world and to examining the major barriers to intercultural communication and ways to make such communications more effective.

New to this section are the following:

- discussion of the ways cultures differ in individual versus collective orientation and high versus low context (Unit 22)
- the role of fear in intercultural communication (Unit 22)
- streamlining of the reasons why intercultural communication is so important (Unit 23)
- an expansion of the coverage of ethnocentrism (Unit 23)

Part 7, Mass Communication (Units 24–25), focuses on the structure and function of mass communication systems and especially on how consumers of the media may interact more effectively and intelligently with the media systems.

New to this section are the following:

- streamlining of the functions of mass communication (Unit 24)
- reversing the process of media influence; the ways in which we can influence the media (Unit 25)
- updating of the theories of mass communication (Unit 25)

SUPPLEMENTARY MATERIALS

This text comes with a variety of supplementary aids to make using this book more effective and for helping your students get the most out of their course experience.

Instructor's Manual

The *Instructor's Manual* prepared by Thomas Veenendall of Montclair State College includes unit planners containing suggested teaching approaches, sample syllabi, examination questions and answers, guidelines for using the application exercises, and transparency masters that highlight essential terms and principles.

TestMaster

The complete test bank (arranged by unit) is available on diskette for IBM PC and compatibles. TestMaster comes with a word-processing program that allows complete customizing capabilities.

Grades

A grade-keeping and classroom-management software program for IBM PC and compatibles that can maintain data for up to 200 students is available from the publisher.

The HarperCollins Communication Video Library

A wide variety of videos are available to users and cover such topics as effective listening, interpersonal relationships, interviewing, small group communication, and public speaking.

ACKNOWLEDGMENTS

It is a pleasure to thank the many people who have had an influence on the writing and production of this book. My major debt is to those colleagues who reviewed the manuscript for this edition and the previous editions and have given freely of their insights, suggestions, criticisms, time, and energy. Their input has resulted in substantial improvements for which I am most grateful. Thank you:

Steven A. Beebe, Southwest Texas State University
Ernest G. Bormann, University of Minnesota
Bernard Brommel, Northeastern Illinois University
Edward Brown, Abilene Christian University
Marcia L. Dewhurst, Ohio State University
Robert Dixon, St. Louis Community College at Meramac
Joseph R. Dominick, University of Georgia
Kenneth D. Frandsen, University of New Mexico
Fran Franklin, University of Arkansas
Ted Hindemarsh, Brigham Young University
Fred Jandt, California State University at San Bernardino
Stephen Johnson, Freed-Hardeman College
Robert Kastenbaum, Arizona State University
Albert M. Katz, University of Wisconsin, Superior
Kathleen Kendall, State University of New York
Elaine Klein, Westchester Community College
Joel Litvin, Bridgewater State College
Don B. Morlan, University of Dayton
John F. Nussbaum, University of Oklahoma
Dorman Picklesimer, Jr., Boston College
George Ray, Cleveland State University
Mark V. Redmond, Iowa State University
Armeda C. Reitzel, Humboldt State University
Thomas Ruddick, Edison State College
Robert M. Shuter, Marquette University
Gail Sorenson, California State University at Fresno
James S. Taylor, Houston Baptist University
Robert Worthington, New Mexico State University
Christopher Zahn, Cleveland State University

I also wish to thank the people at HarperCollins, especially Dan Pipp, Thomas Farrell, Claire Caterer, and Wendy Fredericks.

JOSEPH A. DEVITO

TO THE STUDENT

This course in human communication should prove one of your most enjoyable as well as the most practical of all college courses. It will provide you with a broad overview of the dynamic and exciting area of communication, its research and its theory. The course and text, however, are also significant because they deal with the skills of your communication effectiveness—skills that will lead to increasing self-awareness and that you will use in such activities as establishing, maintaining, and perhaps ending intimate relationships, interviewing for a job, solving a problem with co-workers, interacting in the workplace, delivering a prepared speech, talking with people from other cultures, and dealing with the ever-growing media influence.

THE PAYOFFS

For every course and for every textbook, you have the right to ask, What will I get out of this? I would like to identify here some of the major payoffs that you should derive from this text. These payoffs concern both the **understanding** of theory and the **acquisition of skills.** After reading this text, you should be able to

1. **understand** a wide variety of communication forms and the principles governing them and **acquire the skills** needed to apply these principles in a variety of situations as source, receiver, and critic
2. **understand** the role of self-concept, self-awareness, and self-esteem in communication and **acquire the skills** for increasing your own awareness and esteem
3. **understand** the ways you perceive others, the ways they perceive you, how these processes influence communication and interaction generally, and **acquire the skills** for making your own people perception more accurate
4. **understand** what listening is and how it can be made more effective and **acquire the skills** for listening more effectively and efficiently in a wide variety of communication situations
5. **understand** how language works in human communication and **acquire the skills** for making your language more effective in interpersonal, small group, and public communication settings
6. **understand** how nonverbal communication operates and **acquire the skills** for making your own nonverbal messages more effective
7. **understand** the nature of interpersonal relationships and the role of communication in their development, maintenance, and deterioration and **acquire the skills** to communicate more effectively to initiate relationships, to arrest relational deterioration, and to manage interpersonal conflict effectively
8. **understand** the nature of interviewing, the wide variety of interviewing situations, and **acquire the skills** for communicating more effectively in interview situations, especially in information gathering and employment

9. **understand** the wide variety of group encounters (including organizational settings) and the roles of members and leaders and **acquire the skills** for communicating more effectively as a group member and leader in, for example, learning, problem-solving, therapeutic, and idea-generation groups

10. **understand** the role of public speaking in a democracy and the varied benefits to be derived from its mastery and **acquire the skills** for constructing and delivering effective informative and persuasive speeches

11. **understand** the nature of intercultural communication and the difficulties involved in effective intercultural encounters and **acquire the skills** needed to improve your abilities to communicate in intercultural situations by overcoming the common barriers and by employing the principles of effectiveness

12. **understand** the nature and functions of the mass media in society, how you are influenced by and in turn influence the media, and **acquire the skills** for managing the ways the media influence you and for influencing the media

The most general payoff is this: increased understanding and control of human communication in interpersonal, group, public, intercultural, and mass communication situations. More specific payoffs in the form of learning goals preface each of the 25 units in the text. More specific skills-oriented goals are identified in the Skill Checks appearing at the end of each of the seven parts of the text.

READING THE TEXT

Let me offer a few suggestions for reading this text.

1. Get a broad overview of the book as a whole. Thumb through the book, getting a general idea of how it is organized and what topics are covered. This will give you a general frame for the specifics that will follow.

2. In reading a unit, read the goals first. These identify the main topics covered in the unit and identify what you should know after reading the unit.

3. Do the self-tests. These are included to increase your self-awareness. These self-tests will help you understand the material in the unit and will also help you identify your own strengths and weaknesses.

4. After you have read a unit, read the summary statements.

5. After you have read the summary, return to the goals at the beginning of the unit so that you can test your mastery of the unit's material. If anything is still not clear, reread the relevant sections of the unit.

6. If possible, do the applications suggested at the end of each unit. These will help you see the theory discussed in the unit in actual practice.

7. If possible, when you have completed a part, discuss the questions and do the suggested activities. These will help bring the varied topics of the several units together and extend the principles of communication effectiveness to your own unique world.

8. Check your skill mastery. Review each of the skills identified in the Skill Check. Refer back to the relevant units for those skills that may not be clear or that you do not feel you have mastered sufficiently.

9. Review the list of suggested readings. Try to read at least sections from one or two of these suggested sources. They will provide you with additional perspectives on the topics covered here and will also help you pursue topics, raised only briefly here, in more depth.

10. Refer to the glossary whenever terms may be unclear. All boldfaced italic terms are defined in the glossary. Add to this glossary any words that you come across in your other readings or in lectures.

J. A. D.

Human
Communication

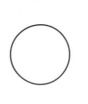

FOUNDATIONS

Unit 1. **Preliminaries to Human Communication**

Unit 2. **Principles of Communication**

Unit 3. **The Self in Communication**

Unit 4. **Perception**

Unit 5. **Listening**

Part 1. **Feedback**
Questions and Activities
Skill Check
Suggested Readings

This first part of *Human Communication* introduces the basic concepts and principles of communication. Unit 1 considers the nature and areas of communication, its most important components, and its purposes. Unit 2 covers the basic principles of human communication and further explains how communication works. Unit 3 focuses on the self: self-concept, self-awareness, self-esteem, and self-disclosure. Units 4 and 5 discuss the processes involved in receiving messages: perception and listening.

Approaching Human Communication

In approaching the study of human communication, keep the following in mind:

- The study of human communication involves not only theory and research but also practical skills for increasing communication effectiveness. Seek to understand the theories *and* to improve your skills.

- Effective communicators are made, not born. Regardless of the level of communication skills you now have, you can improve your effectiveness by applying the principles discussed here.

- The concepts and principles discussed throughout this book and this course directly relate to your everyday communications. Try, for instance, to recall examples from your own communications that illustrate the ideas considered here. This will help make the material more personal and easier to assimilate.

- The principles apply to you as both speaker and listener. See yourself and the principles from the perspectives of speaking *and* listening.

UNIT 1

PRELIMINARIES TO HUMAN COMMUNICATION

UNIT CONTENTS

The Areas of Human Communication

The Components of Human Communication

The Purposes of Human Communication

Summary

Applications

    1.1   Building Models of Human Communication

    1.2   Listening to Disclaimers

    1.3   Ethics in Human Communication

UNIT GOALS

After completing this unit, you should be able to

1. identify the major areas of human communication

2. define *communication* and its components: *communication context, sources-receivers, encoding-decoding, competence, messages, channel, feedback, feedforward, noise, communication effect,* and *ethics*

3. diagram the model of the universals of communication presented in this unit and label its parts

4. explain the five purposes of communication

Of all the knowledge and skills you have, those concerning communication are among the most important and useful. This unit introduces the areas of communication, the major components of the communication process, and its general purposes.

THE AREAS OF HUMAN COMMUNICATION

In **intrapersonal communication** you communicate with yourself. You talk with, learn about, and evaluate yourself; persuade yourself of this or that; reason about possible decisions to make; and rehearse the messages you intend to send to others.

Through **interpersonal communication** you interact with others, learn about them and about yourself, and reveal yourself to others. Whether with new acquaintances, old friends, lovers, or family members, it is through interpersonal communication that you establish, maintain, sometimes destroy (and sometimes repair) your personal relationships. Through **interviewing** you secure information from those with special knowledge and present yourself as a valuable potential employee.

In **small group and organizational communication** you interact with others, solving problems, developing new ideas, and sharing knowledge and experiences. From the employment interview to the executive board meeting, from the informal social group having coffee to the formal meeting discussing issues of international concern, your work and social life are lived largely in small groups.

Through **public communication**, others inform and persuade you. And you in turn inform and persuade others—to do, to buy, or to think in a particular way, or to change an attitude, opinion, or value.

In **intercultural communication** you learn about other cultures and about living with different customs, roles, and rules. Perhaps most important, you come to understand new ways of thinking and new ways of behaving. Intercultural cooperation begins with mutual understanding.

Through **mass communication** you are entertained, informed, and persuaded by the media—movies, television, radio, newspapers, and books. Likewise, through your viewing habits and buying patterns, you in turn influence the media's form and content.

This book, then, is about these types of communication and about your personal communications. It has two major goals: first, to explain the concepts and principles, the theory and research central to these varied areas of human communications; second, to explain the skills of human communication in order to help you increase your own communication competency.

The difference between effective and ineffective communication is evident in our everyday lives. It is the difference between

- the self-confident and the self-conscious speaker
- the person who is hired and the one who is passed over
- the couple who argue constructively and the couple who argue by hurting each other and eventually destroying their relationship
- the group member who is too self-focused to listen openly and contribute to the group's goals and the member who helps accomplish the group's task *and* satisfy the interpersonal needs of the members
- the public speaker who lacks credibility and persuasive appeal and the speaker audiences believe and follow

Table 1.1 Human Communication

	Areas of Human Communication	Some Common Purposes
	Intrapersonal: communication with oneself	To think, reason, analyze, reflect
	Interpersonal: communication between two persons	To discover, relate, influence, play, help
	Small group: communication within a small group of persons	To share information, generate ideas, solve problems, help
	Organizational: communication within a formal organization	To increase productivity, raise morale, inform, persuade
	Public: communication of speaker to audience	To inform, persuade, entertain
	Intercultural: communication between persons of different cultures	To learn, relate, influence, play, help
	Mass: communication addressed to an extremely large audience, mediated by audio and/or visual means	To entertain, persuade (reinforce, change, activate, ethicize), inform, confer status, narcotize, create ties of union

- the culturally isolated person and the one who enjoys, profits from, and grows from effective and satisfying intercultural experiences
- the person who is uncritically influenced by the media and the one who uses the media to grow and who in turn influences the media.

Some Theory-related Concerns	Some Skills-related Concerns
How does one's self-concept develop? How does one's self-concept influence communication? How can problem-solving and analyzing abilities be improved and taught? What is the relationship between personality and communication?	Enhancing self-esteem, increasing self-awareness, improving problem-solving and analyzing abilities; increasing self-control; reducing stress; managing interpersonal conflict
What is interpersonal effectiveness? Why do people develop relationships? What holds friends, lovers, and families together? What tears them apart? How can relationships be repaired?	Increasing effectiveness in one-to-one communication, developing and maintaining effective relationships (friendship, love, family), improving conflict resolution abilities
What makes a leader? What type of leadership works best? What roles do members serve in groups? What do groups do well and what do they fail to do well? How can groups be made more effective?	Increasing effectiveness as a group member, improving leadership abilities, using groups to achieve specific purposes (for example, solving problems, generating ideas)
What makes an effective organization? What needs must an organization meet to ensure worker morale and productivity? How does communication work in an organization?	Improving efficiency of upward, downward, and lateral communication; using communication to improve morale and increase productivity; reducing information overload; structuring networks to increase efficiency
What kinds of organizational structure work best in informative and persuasive speaking? How can audiences be most effectively analyzed and adapted to? How can ideas be best developed for communication to an audience?	Communicating information more effectively; increasing persuasive abilities; developing, organizing, styling, and delivering messages with greater effectiveness
How do different cultures treat communication? What prevents meaningful communication between persons of different cultures? How can persons of widely different cultures best communicate?	Avoiding the major barriers to intercultural communication, improving communication between members of different cultures, dealing with culture shock
What functions do the media serve? How do the media influence us? How can we influence the media? In what ways is information censored by the media for the public?	Improving our ability to use the media to greater effectiveness, increasing our ability to control the media, avoiding being taken in by advertisements and tabloid journalism

The areas of human communication, some common purposes of each area, and some theory- and skills-related concerns are summarized in Table 1.1.

This book is relatively long because communication is an enormous field and for many of you this is your first academic exposure to it. Fortunately, the time and effort that you will put into this book and this course will be more than repaid by the knowledge you will gain and the skills you will acquire and improve.

Before beginning your formal study of human communication, take the following self-test: "What Do You Know About Communication?"

THE COMPONENTS OF HUMAN COMMUNICATION

Communication refers to the act, by one or more persons, of sending and receiving messages that are distorted by noise, occur within a context, have some effect, and provide some opportunity for feedback.

Figure 1.1 illustrates what we might call the universals of communication. It contains the elements present in every communication act, regardless of whether it is intrapersonal, interpersonal, small group, public speaking, or mass communication.

Communication Context

The **context of communication** has at least four dimensions: physical, cultural, social-psychological, and temporal. The *physical context* is the tangible or concrete en-

---

SELF-TEST

What Do You Know About Communication?

Respond to each of the following statements with TRUE if you think the statement is usually true and FALSE if you think the statement is usually false.

_____ 1. Good communicators are born, not made.

_____ 2. The more a couple communicates, the better their relationship will be.

_____ 3. Unlike effective speaking, effective listening cannot be taught.

_____ 4. Opening lines such as "Hello, how are you?" or "Fine weather today" or "Have you got a light?" serve no useful communication purpose.

_____ 5. In interpreting the meaning of another person you should focus exclusively on the words used.

_____ 6. When verbal and nonverbal messages contradict each other, people believe the verbal message.

_____ 7. Complete openness should be the goal of any meaningful interpersonal relationship.

_____ 8. When there is conflict, your aim should be to win even at the expense of the other person.

_____ 9. Like good communicators, leaders are born, not made.

_____ 10. Fear of speaking in public is detrimental and must be eliminated.

Scoring: All 10 statements are false. As you read through the text, you'll discover not only why these statements are false but some of the problems that can arise when people act on the basis of such misconceptions about communication.

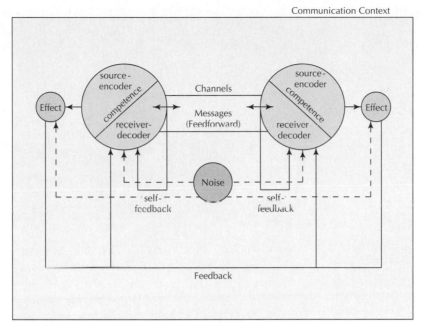

FIGURE 1.1 The universals of human communication.

vironment in which communication takes place—the room or hallway or park. This physical context exerts some influence on the content (what we say) as well as the form (how we say it) of our messages.

The *cultural context* refers to the communicators' rules and norms, beliefs and attitudes that are transmitted from one generation to another. For example, in some cultures it is considered polite to talk to strangers; in others, it is something to avoid. In some cultures, direct eye contact between child and adult signifies directness and honesty; in others it may signify defiance and a lack of respect.

The *social-psychological context* includes, for example, the status relationships among the participants, the roles and the games that people play, and the cultural rules of the society in which they are communicating. It also includes the friendliness or unfriendliness, formality or informality, and seriousness or humorousness of the situation. Communications are permitted at a graduation party that would not be permitted in a hospital.

The *temporal (or time) context* includes the time of day as well as the time in history in which the communication takes place. For many people, the morning is not a time for communication. For others, the morning is ideal. Historical context is no less important, because the appropriateness and impact of messages depend, in part, on the time in which they are uttered. Consider, for example, how messages on racial, sexual, or religious attitudes and values would be differently framed and responded to in different times in history.

Even more important is how a particular message fits into the temporal sequence of communication events. For example, consider the varied meanings a "simple" compliment paid to a friend would have depending on whether you said it immediately after

Why is it so important to include "culture" as part of the communication context? Would it be possible for communication to exist without a cultural component?

your friend paid you a compliment, immediately before you asked your friend for a favor, or during an argument.

These four dimensions of context interact with one another. Each influences and is influenced by the others. For example, arriving late for a date (temporal context) has a certain meaning influenced by the culture (cultural context) and may lead to changes in friendliness-unfriendliness (social-psychological context), which in turn may lead to changes in physical closeness and in the selection of the restaurant for dinner (physical context). And these changes may lead to a host of other changes. The communication process is never static.

Sources-Receivers

The hyphenated term *sources-receivers* emphasizes that each person involved in communication is both a source (or speaker) and a receiver (or listener). You send messages when you speak, write, gesture, or smile. You receive messages in listening, reading, smelling, and so on. As you send messages, however, you are also receiving messages. You are receiving your own messages (you hear yourself, you feel your own movements, you see many of your own gestures) and you are receiving the messages of the other person—visually, aurally, or even through touch or smell. You look at anyone you speak to for responses—approval, understanding, sympathy, agreement, and so on. As you decipher these nonverbal signals, you are performing receiving functions.

Source-Receiver Encoding-Decoding   In communication we refer to the act of producing messages—for example, speaking or writing—as **encoding**. By putting our ideas into sound waves we are putting these ideas into a code, hence *en*coding. We refer to the act of receiving messages—for example, listening or reading—as **decoding**. By translating sound waves or words on paper into ideas you take them out of the code they are in, hence *de*coding. Thus we refer to speakers or writers as *encoders*, and listeners or readers as *decoders*.

The hyphenated term *encoding-decoding* emphasizes that you perform these functions *simultaneously*. As you speak (encoding), you are also deciphering the responses of the listener (decoding).

Source-Receiver Communicative Competence   Communicative competence refers to a person's knowledge of the social aspects of communication (Rubin, 1982, 1985; Spitzberg and Cupach, 1989). It includes such knowledge as the role the context plays in influencing the content and form of communication messages—for example, the knowledge that in certain contexts and with certain listeners one topic is appropriate and another is not. Knowledge about the rules of nonverbal behavior—for example, the appropriateness of touching, vocal volume, and physical closeness—is also part of communicative competence.

You learn communicative competence by observing others, by explicit instruction, by trial and error, and so on. Some have learned better than others, though. These are the people we find interesting and comfortable to talk with. One of the major goals of this text and this course is to spell out the nature of communicative competence and to increase your own competence.

By increasing your competence, you will have available a broader range of options in your various communication activities. That is, the more you know about communication (the greater your competence), the more choices will be available for your day-to-day communications. The process is comparable to learning vocabulary: the more vocabulary you know, the more ways you have for expressing yourself.

Culture and Competence   Competence is specific to a given culture. The principles of effective communication will vary from one culture to another; what will prove effective in one culture may prove ineffective in another. For example, in the United States business executives will get right down to business during the first several minutes of a meeting. In Japan business executives interact socially for an extended period of time and try to find out something about each other. Thus, the small group communication principle influenced by United States culture would advise participants to get down to the meeting's agenda during the first five or 10 minutes. The principle influenced by Japanese culture would have participants avoid dealing with business until all members of the group had socialized sufficiently and felt they knew each other well enough to begin business negotiations.

Note that neither principle is right or wrong. Each is effective within its own culture and each is ineffective outside its own culture. When specific communication advice is given in this text, it is from the perspective of the general United States culture, though with clear recognition that "general United States culture" is in great part *multi*cultural.

Messages and Channels

Communication **messages** may take many forms. You send and receive them through any one or any combination of sensory organs. Although you may customarily

In many cultures it is important to be bilingual; the language of commerce and the language spoken within the family, for example, are often different. What arguments can you make for the importance of your knowing the communication patterns of other cultures?

think of messages as being verbal (oral or written), these are not the only kinds of messages. You also communicate nonverbally. For example, the clothes you wear as well as the way you walk, shake hands, cock your head, comb your hair, sit, and smile all communicate messages. In fact, everything about you communicates.

The communication **channel** is the medium through which the message passes. Communication rarely takes place over only one channel; you may use two, three, or four different channels simultaneously. For example, in face-to-face interactions you speak and listen (vocal channel), but you also gesture and receive these signals visually (visual channel). In addition you emit and detect odors (olfactory channel). Often you touch another person, and this too communicates (tactile channel).

Two special types of messages that should be explained more fully are *feedback* and *feedforward*.

Feedback   Throughout the listening process, a listener gives a speaker feedback—messages sent back to the speaker reacting to what is said (Clement and Frandsen, 1976). Feedback tells the speaker what effect he or she is having on the listener(s). On the basis of this feedback, the speaker may adjust the messages by strengthening, deemphasizing, or changing the content or form of the messages.

In the diagram of the universals of communication (Figure 1.1), the arrows from source-receiver to effect and from one source-receiver to the other source-receiver go in both directions to illustrate the notion of feedback. When you speak to another person you also hear yourself. That is, you get feedback from your own messages; you hear what you say, you feel the way you move, you see what you write.

In addition to this self-feedback, you get feedback from others, which can take many forms. A frown or a smile, a yea or a nay, a pat on the back or a punch in the mouth are all types of feedback.

Feedback can be looked at in terms of three important dimensions: immediate-delayed, low monitoring-high monitoring, and critical-supportive. To use feedback effectively, then, you need to make informed choices along these dimensions.

Immediate-Delayed   Generally, the most immediate feedback is the most effective. In interpersonal situations, feedback is most often sent immediately after the message is received, in, for example, a smile, a frown, a verbal response. In other communication situations, however, the feedback may be delayed. Instructor evaluation questionnaires completed at the end of the course provide feedback long after the first day of class. When you applaud or ask questions of a public speaker, the feedback is also delayed. In interview situations, the feedback may come weeks afterward. In the case of the media, some feedback comes immediately—for example, through Nielsen ratings—and other feedback comes much later, through viewing and buying patterns.

Low Monitoring-High Monitoring   Feedback varies from the spontaneous and totally honest reaction (low-monitored feedback) to the carefully constructed response designed to serve a specific purpose (high-monitored feedback). In most interpersonal situations you probably give feedback spontaneously; you allow your responses to show without any monitoring. At other times, however, you may be more guarded, as when your boss asks you how you like your job or when you write a letter to protest a newspaper editorial.

Critical-Supportive   Critical feedback is evaluative. When you give critical feedback you judge another person's performance as in, for example, evaluating a speech or coaching someone learning a new skill. Feedback can also be supportive, as when you console someone, encourage someone to talk, or affirm another person's self-definition.

These categories are not exclusive. Feedback does not have to be either critical or supportive; it can be both. Thus, in teaching someone how to become a more effective interviewer, you might critically evaluate a specific interview but you might also express support for the effort. Similarly, you might respond to a friend's question immediately and then after a day or two elaborate on your response. Each feedback opportunity will, then, present you with choice along at least these three dimensions. Consider, for example, how you would give feedback (immediate or delayed? low-monitoring or high-monitoring? critical or supportive?) in these varied situations:

- your mother asks how you like the dinner
- a stranger on a bus asks you for a date
- your instructor asks you to evaluate the course
- a telephone interviewer asks if you want a credit card
- a homeless person smiles at you on the street
- a friend tells a racist joke

Feedforward   Feedforward is information you provide before sending your primary messages (Richards, 1951), revealing something about the messages to come.

Feedforward includes such diverse examples as the preface or the table of contents to a book, the opening paragraph of a chapter, movie previews, magazine covers, and introductions in public speeches.

Feedforward messages are examples of *metamessages*—messages that communicate about other messages. Such information may be verbal ("Wait until you hear this one") or nonverbal (a prolonged pause or hands motioning for silence to signal that an important message is about to be spoken). Or, as is most often the case, it is some combination of verbal and nonverbal signals. Feedforward may refer to the content of the message to follow ("I'll tell you exactly what they said to each other") or to the form ("I won't spare you the gory details").

Feedforward has four major functions: (1) to open the channels of communication, (2) to preview the message, (3) to disclaim, and (4) to altercast.

To Open the Channels of Communication   Phatic communion refers to messages that open the channels of communication rather than communicate information (Malinowski, 1923). Phatic communion is a perfect example of feedforward. It is information that tells us that the normal, expected, and accepted rules of interaction will be in effect. It tells us another person is willing to communicate. The infamous "opening line" ("Have you got a match?" or "Haven't we met before?") is a clear example of phatic communion. When such phatic messages do not precede an initial interaction, you sense that something is wrong and may conclude that the speaker lacks the basic skills of communication.

To Preview Future Messages   Feedforward messages frequently preview other messages. Feedforward may, for example, preview the content ("I'm afraid I have bad news for you"), the importance ("Listen to this before you make a move"), the form or style ("I'll be brief"), and the positive or negative quality of subsequent messages ("You're not going to like this, but here's what I heard").

To Disclaim   The *disclaimer* is a statement that aims to ensure that your message will be understood and will not reflect negatively on you. Five types of disclaimers may be identified (Hewitt & Stokes, 1975). These, along with their definitions and examples, are presented in Table 1.2. As you can see, disclaimers try to persuade the listener to hear your message as you wish it to be heard.

To Altercast   Feedforward is often used to place the receiver in a specific role and to request that the receiver respond to you in terms of this assumed role. This process, known as *altercasting*, asks the receiver to approach your message from a particular role or even as someone else (McLaughlin, 1984; Weinstein & Deutschberger, 1963). For example, you might ask a friend, "As an advertising executive, what do you think of corrective advertising?" This question casts your friend into the role of advertising executive (rather than parent, Democrat, or Baptist, for example). It asks your friend to answer from a particular perspective.

Noise

Noise is a disturbance in communication that distorts the message. Noise prevents the receiver from getting the message the source is sending. Noise is present in a communication system to the extent that the message sent differs from the message received. The noise may be physical (others talking in the background), psychological

Table 1.2 Disclaimers		
Disclaimer	**Definition/Function**	**Examples**
Hedging	Speaker disclaims the importance of the message to his or her own identity; speaker makes it clear that listeners may reject the message without rejecting the speaker.	"I didn't read the entire report, but. . . " "I'm no physiologist, but that irregularity seems. . . " "I may be wrong here, but. . . "
Credentialing	Speaker knows that the message may be poorly received, but will say it nevertheless; speaker attempts to avoid any undesirable inference that may be drawn by listeners; speaker seeks to establish special qualifications.	"Don't get the wrong idea; I'm not sexist, but. . . " "I'm not homophobic. . . " "Some of my best friends are. . . "
Sin licenses	Speaker announces that he or she will commit a violation of some social or cultural rule but should be "forgiven" in advance (a "license to sin").	"I realize that this may not be the time to talk about money, but. . . " "I know you'll think this suggestion is out of order, but do consider. . . "
Cognitive disclaimers	Speaker seeks to reaffirm his or her cognitive abilities in anticipation of listeners doubting their capacity.	"You'll probably think I'm crazy, but let me explain the logic of the case." "I know you think I'm drunk but I'm as sober and as lucid as anyone here."
Appeals for the suspension of judgment	Speaker asks the listeners to delay making judgments until a more complete account is presented.	"Don't hang up on me until you hear my side of the story." "Don't say anything until I explain what really happened." "If you promise not to laugh, I'll tell you exactly what happened on that first date."

(preconceived ideas), or semantic (misunderstood meanings). Table 1.3 identifies these three major types of noise in more detail.

Noise is inevitable. All communications contain noise of some kind, and although you cannot eliminate noise completely, you can reduce noise and its effects. Making your language more precise, acquiring the skills for sending and receiving nonverbal messages, and improving your listening and feedback skills are some ways you can combat the interference of noise.

Communication Effects

Communication *always* has some effect on one or more persons involved in the communication act. For every communication act, there is some consequence. For example, you may gain knowledge or learn how to analyze, synthesize, or evaluate something. These are intellectual or cognitive effects. Or you may acquire or change your attitudes, beliefs, emotions, and feelings. These are affective effects. You may even learn new bodily movements, such as throwing a ball or painting a picture, as well as appropriate verbal and nonverbal behaviors. These are psychomotor effects.

Table 1.3 Three Types of Noise

Type	Definition	Example
Physical	Interference with the physical transmission of the message	Screeching of passing cars, hum of computer, sunglasses
Psychological	Cognitive or mental interference	Biases and prejudices in senders and receivers, closed-mindedness
Semantic	Speaker and listener assigning different meanings	People speaking different languages, use of jargon or overly complex terms not understood by listener

Ethics and Individual Choice

Because communication has consequences, it also involves *ethical* questions. There is a right-versus-wrong aspect to any communication act. For example, while it may be effective to exaggerate or even lie in selling a product or in getting elected, it would not be ethical to do so. Unlike principles of effective communication, principles of ethical communication are difficult to formulate (Bok, 1978; Jaksa & Pritchard, 1988). Often you can observe the effect of communication and, on the basis of the observations, formulate principles of effective communication. You cannot, however, observe the rightness or wrongness of a communication act.

The ethical dimension of communication is further complicated because ethics is so interwoven with one's personal philosophy of life that it is difficult to propose guidelines for everyone. Given these difficulties, ethical considerations are nevertheless integral to any communication act. The decisions you make concerning communication must be guided by what you consider right as well as what you consider effective.

Whether communications are ethical or unethical may be grounded in the notion of choice and the assumption that people have a right to make their own choices. Communications are ethical when they facilitate an individual's freedom of choice by presenting that person with accurate bases for choice. Communications are unethical when they interfere with an individual's freedom of choice by preventing that person from securing information relevant to the choice. Unethical communications, therefore, would be those that force people (1) to make choices they would not normally make or (2) to decline to make choices they would normally make.

For example, the corporate recruiter might exaggerate the benefits of working for General Dynamo and thus encourage you to make a choice you would not normally make (if you knew the true facts) and to decline to make a choice you would have made (for example, to work for National Widget).

The ethical communicator, then, provides others with the kind of information that helps them make their own choices. In this ethic based on choice, however, there are a few qualifications. We assume that these individuals are of an age and mental condition to allow the reasonable execution of free choice. For example, children of 5 or 6 years of age are not ready to make certain choices (for example, to choose their own menu, time for bed, or type of medication to take).

In addition, the circumstances under which one is living can restrict free choice. For example, persons in the military will at times have to give up free choice and eat hamburger rather than steak, wear uniforms rather than jeans, and march rather than stay in bed. Finally, these free choices must not prevent others from making their free choices. We cannot permit a thief to have the freedom of choice to steal, because the granting of that freedom effectively prevents the victims from exercising their free choice—to own property and to be secure in their possessions.

Ethical issues are integral to all forms and functions of communication. Here are just a few such questions that deal with issues we will consider throughout this text. You may find it interesting to review these questions from the perspective of choice or any other ethical principle or system.

Interpersonal Communication   Would it be ethical to exaggerate your virtues and minimize your vices in order to win someone's approval? To get a job? To get someone to love you? To what extent can you exaggerate before considering it unethical? Would it be ethical to lie to your relationship partner if by lying you could avoid an argument and ill feelings? How much of your past are you ethically obligated to reveal to your partner? How much of your present feelings are you obliged to reveal to this partner? Would it be ethical to reveal what someone else told you in confidence?

Small Group Communication   Would it be ethical to assume leadership of a group so that you can get the group to do as you wish? Do you have an ethical obligation to enhance the potential of group members?

Public Communication   Would it be ethical to present another's research as your own in a public speech? Are you morally responsible for informing your listeners of weaknesses in your evidence and arguments? Would it be ethical to persuade an audience to do something by scaring them? By threatening them?

Intercultural Communication   Do you have an ethical obligation for increasing intercultural understanding and communication? Are you morally responsible for responding to racist, sexist, or heterosexist language? Are you ethically obligated to protest negative cultural stereotypes?

Mass Communication   What ethical obligations do the media have? What are the ethical obligations of an advertiser? Do consumers of the mass media have ethical obligations to respond to the media's slanting of the truth or distortion of evidence?

THE PURPOSES OF COMMUNICATION

Five general purposes or motives of communication should be noted here. Purposes need not be conscious, nor must individuals agree about their purposes for communicating. Purpose may be subconscious or conscious, and unrecognizable or recognizable. Further, although communication technologies are changing rapidly and drastically—we send electronic mail, work at computer terminals, and telecommute, for example—the purposes of communication are likely to remain essentially the same throughout the electronic revolution and whatever revolutions follow (Arnold & Bowers, 1984; Naisbitt, 1984).

Figure 1.2 identifies just some of today's occupations that rely heavily on communication and where these purposes are served throughout the performance of these jobs.

FIGURE 1.2 Some occupations that rely on communication. (This flyer was prepared by HarperCollins College Publishers and was originally titled "What Can You Do with a Communication Degree?")

To Discover

One of the major purposes of communication concerns personal discovery. When you communicate with another person, you learn about yourself as well as about the other person. In fact, your self-perceptions result largely from what you have learned about yourself from others during communications, especially your interpersonal encounters.

By talking about yourself with another individual you gain valuable feedback on your feelings, thoughts, and behaviors. From this type of encounter you learn, for example, that your feelings are not so different from someone else's. This positive reinforcement helps you feel "normal."

Much as communication gives you a better understanding of yourself and the person with whom you are communicating, it also helps you discover the external world—the world of objects, events, and other people. Today, you rely heavily on the various communications media for information about entertainment, sports, war, economic developments, health and dietary concerns, and new products to buy. Much of what you acquire from the media interacts with what you learn from your interpersonal interactions. You gain a great deal of information from the media, discuss it with other people, and ultimately learn or internalize the material as a result of the interaction between these two sources.

To Relate

One of our strongest motivations is to establish and maintain close relationships with others. The vast majority of people want to feel loved and liked, and in turn want to love and like others. You probably spend much of your communication time and energy establishing and maintaining social relationships. You communicate with your close friends in school, at work, and probably on the phone. You talk with your parents, children, and brothers and sisters. You interact with your relational partner. All told, this takes a great deal of your time and attests to the importance of this purpose of communication.

Of course, you may also use communication to distance yourself from others, to argue and fight with friends and romantic partners, and even to dissolve relationships.

To Help

Therapists, counselors, teachers, parents, and friends are just a few categories of those who often—though not always— communicate to help. As is the case with therapists and counselors, entire professions are built around this communication function. But, there are few professions that do not make at least some significant use of this helping function. You also use this function when you constructively criticize, express empathy, work with a group to solve a problem, or listen attentively and supportively to a public speaker.

To Persuade

The mass media exist largely to persuade us to change our attitudes and behaviors. The media survive on advertisers' money, which is directed at getting us to buy a variety of items and services. Right now you probably spend much more time as consumers than originators of these mass-media messages. But in the not too distant future you will no doubt be originating messages. You may work on a newspaper or edit a magazine, or work in an ad agency, television station, or a variety of other communication-related fields.

You probably also, however, spend a great deal of your time in interpersonal persuasion, as both sources and receivers. In your everyday interpersonal encounters you try to change the attitudes and behaviors of others. You try to get them to vote a particular way, try a new diet, buy a particular item, see a movie, read a book, take a specific course, believe that something is true or false, value or devalue some idea, and so on. The list is endless. Few of your interpersonal communications, in fact, do *not* seek to change attitudes or behaviors.

To Play

You probably also spend a great deal of your communication behavior on play. As viewed here, communication as play includes motives of pleasure, escape, and relaxation (Barbata & Perse, 1992; Rubin, Perse, & Barbata, 1988). For example, you often listen to comedians as well as friends largely because it is fun, enjoyable, and exciting. You tell jokes, say clever things, and relate interesting stories largely for the pleasure it gives to you and your listeners. Similarly, you may communicate because it relaxes you, allowing you to get away from pressures and responsibilities.

Although no list of communication purposes can be exhaustive, these five are the major ones. Further, no communication act is motivated by just one factor; communication is motivated by a combination of purposes.

The discussions of the various contexts of communication—interpersonal, small group and organizational, public, intercultural, and mass communication—will identify more specific purposes that each of these forms fulfills.

Summary

1. *Communication* refers to the act, by one or more persons, of sending and receiving messages that are distorted by noise, occur within a context, have some effect (and some ethical dimension), and provide some opportunity for feedback.

2. The universals of communication—the elements present in every communication act—are: *context*, *source-receiver*, *message*, *channel*, *noise* (*physical*, *social-psychological*, and *semantic*), *sending* or *encoding processes*, *receiving* or *decoding processes*, *feedback* and *feedforward*, *effect*, and *ethics*.

3. The *communication context* has at least four dimensions: physical, cultural, social-psychological, and temporal.

4. *Communicative competence* refers to knowledge of the elements and rules of communication and is culture-specific.

5. Communication *messages* may be of varied forms and may be sent and received through any combination of sensory organs. The communication *channel* is the medium through which the messages are sent.

6. *Feedback* refers to messages or information that is sent back to the source. It may come from the source itself or from the receiver and may be indexed along such dimensions as immediate-delayed, low-monitored–high-monitored, and critical-supportive.

7. *Feedforward* refers to messages that preface other messages and may be used to open the channels of communication, to preview future messages, to disclaim, and to altercast.

8. *Noise* is anything that distorts the message; it is present to some degree in every communication transaction.

9. Communication always has an *effect*. Effects may be cognitive, affective, or psychomotor.

10. *Communication ethics* refers to the rightness or wrongness—the morality—of a communication transaction and is an integral part of every communication transaction.

11. Communication may serve at least five general *purposes*: discovery, relating to others, help, persuasion, and play.

Applications

1.1 BUILDING MODELS OF HUMAN COMMUNICATION

In this first exercise we explore the components of the human communication process. Examine Figure 1.1 and respond to the questions with reference to this diagram.

1. Who or what might be designated as a *source* of communication? Identify as many different types of communication sources as you can.

2. Who or what might be designated by the term *destination?* Identify as many different types of communication destinations as you can.

3. What forms might noise take? That is, what types of noise might enter or interfere with a communication system? From what sources might noise originate?

4. How can noise be reduced? Might a communication system ever be noise free? Explain.

5. What kinds of information can be fed back from the destination to the source? What kinds of information can be fed forward?

6. Of what value to the source is information fed back from the destination?

7. What kinds of information might sources receive from their own communications?

8. Of what value is information that sources receive from their own communications?

9. What forms can a message take? That is, what signals can be used to communicate information?

10. Over what channels might a message be communicated? That is, what senses can be used by the source and by the receiver in sending and receiving information? What advantages and limitations do each of the senses have in terms of communication?

11. What are the dimensions or significant aspects of the context of the communication act? That is, in analyzing the context of communication, what factors would have to be investigated?

12. How might *interpersonal communication, small group communication, public communication, intercultural communication,* and *mass communication* be defined and distinguished from one another on the basis of the elements noted in the diagram?

13. Construct an original diagram of one of these forms of communication. How does it differ from the one presented in this unit?

1.2 LISTENING TO DISCLAIMERS

Over a two-day period, collect examples of disclaimers from your interpersonal interactions as well as from the media. Try to find examples of all five types discussed here. Share these examples along with your analysis of the disclaimers with others in the class. Use the four questions presented here as guidelines for your analysis.

1. What is the nature of the disclaimer? What type of disclaimer is being used? Why is it being used?

2. Is the disclaimer appropriate? For example, to inappropriately preface remarks with "I'm no liar" may well lead listeners to think that perhaps the speaker is a liar. On the other hand, disclaimers are useful when the speaker thinks he or she might offend listeners by telling a joke (for example, "I don't usually like these types of jokes, but. . . ").

3. Does the disclaimer require a response? In responding to statements containing disclaimers, listeners should respond to both the disclaimer and the content message to let the speaker know that they heard the disclaimer. Appropriate responses might be: "I know you're no sexist but I don't agree that. . ." or "Well, perhaps we should discuss the money now even if it doesn't seem right."

4. Are disclaimers used to excess? Generally, disclaimers should be used sparingly. If they are overused, they weaken the impact of the message. This seems especially true of *hedging*.

1.3   ETHICS IN HUMAN COMMUNICATION

This exercise may be completed in small groups of five or six or by the class as a whole. Select a set of ethics questions from those presented in this unit's discussion of ethics (p. 17) and explain:

- What *would* you do?
- What do you feel you *should* do?
- What *general principle* of ethics are you using in making these would/should judgments?

Differences of opinions as to what another member would do or feels he or she should do or in the formulation of the general principles may be discussed.

The process is then repeated, with another group or class member responding to another set of ethics questions. After all questions have been discussed, members may share their most important insights and conclusions about the ethical dimension of human communication.

PRINCIPLES OF COMMUNICATION

UNIT CONTENTS

Communication Is a Package of Signals

Communication Is a Process of Adjustment

Communication Involves Content and Relationship Dimensions

Communication Involves Symmetrical and Complementary
  Transactions

Communication Sequences Are Punctuated

Communication Is a Transactional Process

Communication Is Inevitable, Irreversible, and Unrepeatable

  Summary

  Applications
      2.1   The Principles of Human Communication in Transaction
      2.2   What's Happening?

UNIT GOALS

After completing this unit, you should be able to

1. explain the packaged nature of communication and double-bind messages

2. explain the principle of adjustment in communication

3. distinguish between content and relationship dimensions of communication

4. distinguish between symmetrical and complementary transactions

5. define *punctuation*

6. explain the transactional nature of communication

7. explain the inevitability and irreversibility of communication

The previous unit defined communication and explained some of its components and characteristics. This unit continues to elaborate on the nature of communication by presenting seven principles of communication. These principles are essential to understanding communication in all its forms and functions.

COMMUNICATION IS A PACKAGE OF SIGNALS

Communication behaviors, whether they involve verbal messages, gestures, or some combination thereof, usually occur in "packages" (Pittenger, Hockett, & Danehy, 1960). Usually, verbal and nonverbal behaviors reinforce or support each other. All parts of a message system normally work together to communicate a particular meaning. You do not express fear with words while the rest of your body is relaxed. You do not express anger through your posture while your face smiles. Your entire body works together—verbally and nonverbally—to express your thoughts and feelings.

In any form of communication, whether interpersonal, small group, public speaking, or mass media, you probably pay little attention to its packaged nature. It goes unnoticed. But when there is an incongruity—when the weak handshake belies the verbal greeting, when the nervous posture belies the focused stare, when the constant preening belies the expressions of being comfortable and at ease—you take notice. Invariably you begin to question the credibility, the sincerity, and the honesty of the individual.

Double-Bind Messages

A particular type of contradictory message that deserves special mention is the **double-bind** message, one whose verbal and nonverbal injunctions contradict each other. Consider the following interpersonal interaction:

PAT: You're never affectionate anymore. You never hug me like you used to [that is, "love me"].

CHRIS: *(Makes advances of a loving nature.)*

PAT: *(Tenses, fails to maintain eye contact, and, in general, sends nonverbal messages that say, "Don't love me.")*

CHRIS: *(Withdraws.)*

PAT: See? You don't love me.

The following factors must be involved for an interaction to constitute significant double-binding (Brommel, 1990).

Intense Relationship   The two persons interacting must share a relatively intense relationship in which the messages and demands of one and the responses of the other are important. This kind of relationship can exist between various family members, between close friends and lovers, and in some instances between employer and employee.

Incompatible Responses   The two messages must demand different and incompatible responses. That is, the messages must be such that both cannot logically be verbalized. Usually, the positive message is communicated verbally; for example, "Love me." The accompanying negative message, usually communicated nonverbally, contradicts the first message, as in withdrawal and a general tenseness that communicates,

"Stay away." Both parties in a double-bind relationship are likely to send such messages, either both in the same conversation or separately on different occasions.

Inability to Escape   One of the persons in a double-bind situation must be unable to escape from the contradictory messages. People in double-bind situations feel trapped. Preventing a person's escape from the contradictory message may be a legal commitment (such as a marriage license) or, in the case of lovers, an unwritten but understood agreement that each is responsible for meeting the needs of the other. No matter what response is made, the person receiving the message is failing to comply with at least one of the demands. If, for example, Chris makes loving advances, the nonverbal injunction "Don't love me" is violated. If Chris does not make any loving advances, the verbal injunction "Love me" is violated.

Threat of Punishment   There must be some threat of punishment for the receiver's failure to comply with the sender's verbal or nonverbal demands. In our example, there is an implied threat of punishment for the failure to make loving advances but also for the failure to comply with the demand *not* to love. Regardless of how the lover responds, some form of punishment will follow. This is one reason why the relationship must be relatively intense; otherwise, the threat would not be significant.

Frequent Occurrences   For double-binding to be a serious communication problem, it must occur frequently. Such frequent exposure has the effect of setting up a response pattern in the person such that she or he comes to anticipate that whatever is done will be incorrect, that there is no escape from these confused and confusing communications, and that punishment will follow the inevitable noncompliance.

Double-bind messages are particularly damaging when children are involved. Children can neither escape from such situations nor communicate about the communications. They cannot talk about the lack of correspondence betweeen the verbal and the nonverbal. They cannot ask their parents why they do not hold them or hug them when they say they love them.

These double-bind messages may be the result of the desire to communicate two different emotions or feelings. For example, you may like a person and want to communicate a positive feeling, but you may also feel resentment toward this person and want to communicate a negative feeling as well. The result is that you communicate both feelings, one verbally and one nonverbally (Beier, 1974).

Listening to and confronting mixed messages or messages that do not seem to ring true is a difficult skill. Perhaps the most difficult aspect is to frame responses that are appropriate and supportive. Here are several statements that contain either mixed messages or messages that seem illogical or inconsistent with what you know about the individual. How would you respond to each of these statements?

- Even if I do fail the course, so what? I don't need it for graduation.
- I called three people. They all have something to do on Saturday night. I guess I'll just curl up with a good book or a good movie. It'll be better than a lousy date anyway.
- My parents are getting divorced after twenty years of marriage. My mother and father are both dating other people now so everything is going okay.

- My youngest child is going to need special treatments if he's going to walk again. The doctors are going to decide today on what kind of treatment. But all will end well in this, the best of all possible worlds.

COMMUNICATION IS A PROCESS OF ADJUSTMENT

Communication may take place only to the extent that the communicators use the same system of signals (Pittenger, Hockett, & Danehy, 1960). You will not be able to communicate with another person to the extent that your language systems differ. In reality, however, no two persons use identical signal systems, so this principle is relevant to all forms of communication. Parents and children, for example, not only have largely different vocabularies but also have different meanings for the terms they do share. Different cultures, even when they use a common language, often have greatly different nonverbal communication systems. To the extent that these systems differ, meaningful and effective communication will not take place.

Part of the art of communication is identifying the other person's signals, learning how they are used, and understanding what they mean. Those in close relationships will realize that learning the other person's signals takes a great deal of time and often a great deal of patience. If you want to understand what another person means (by a smile, by saying "I love you," by arguing about trivia, by self-deprecating comments), rather than simply acknowledging what the other person says or does, you have to learn that person's system of signals.

How does the principle of adjustment relate to cultural differences in the classroom? What benefits can students and teachers alike derive from cultural differences in the classroom? What problems might cultural differences create?

COMMUNICATION INVOLVES CONTENT
AND RELATIONSHIP DIMENSIONS

Communications, to a certain extent at least, refer to the real world, to something external to both speaker and hearer. At the same time, however, communications also refer to the relationships between the parties (Watzlawick, Beavin, & Jackson, 1967).

For example, an employer may say to a worker, "See me after the meeting." This simple message has a *content aspect* and a *relational aspect*. The content aspect refers to the behavioral responses expected—namely, that the worker see the employer after the meeting. The relational aspect tells how the communication is to be dealt with. Even the use of the simple command says that there is a status difference between the two parties: the employer can command the worker. This is perhaps seen most clearly when you imagine the worker giving this command to the employer; it appears awkward and out of place because it violates the expected communications between employer and worker.

In any communication situation the content dimension may stay the same but the relationship aspect may vary. Or, the relationship aspect may be the same while the content is different. For example, the employer could say to the worker either "You had better see me after the meeting" or "May I please see you after the meeting?" In each case the content is essentially the same; that is, the message being communicated about the behaviors expected is the same in both cases. But the relationship dimension is very different. In the first it signifies a definite superior-inferior relationship and even a put-down of the worker. In the second, the employer signals a more equal relationship and shows respect for the worker.

Similarly, at times the content may be different but the relationship essentially the same. For example, a teenager might say to his or her parents, "May I go away this weekend?" and "May I use the car tonight?" The content of the two messages is clearly very different. The relationship dimension, however, is essentially the same. It is clearly a superior-inferior relationship in which permission to do certain things must be secured.

Ignoring Relationship Dimensions

Problems may arise when the distinction between the content and relationship levels of communication is ignored. Consider a couple arguing over the fact that Pat made plans to study during the weekend with friends without first asking Chris if that would be all right. Probably both would have agreed that to study over the weekend was the right choice to make. Thus the argument is not at all related to the content level. The argument centers on the relationship level. Chris expected to be consulted about plans for the weekend. Pat, in not doing so, rejected this definition of the relationship.

Let me give you a personal example. My mother came to stay for a week at a summer place I had. On the first day she swept the kitchen floor six times, though I had repeatedly told her that it did not need sweeping since I would be tracking in dirt and mud from outside—all her effort would be wasted. But she persisted in sweeping, saying that the floor was dirty and should be swept. On the content level, we were talking about the value of sweeping the kitchen floor. But on the relationship level we were talking about something quite different. We were each saying, "This is my house."

When I realized this (though only after considerable argument), I stopped complaining about the relative usefulness of sweeping a floor that did not need sweeping and she stopped sweeping it.

Consider the following interchange:

Dialogue:	Commentary:
PAUL: I'm going bowling tomorrow. The guys at the plant are starting a team.	(He focuses on the content and ignores any relational implications of the message.)
JUDY: Why can't we ever do anything together?	(She responds primarily on a relational level and ignores the content-implications of the message, and expresses her displeasure at being ignored in his decision.)
PAUL: We can do something together anytime; tomorrow's the day they're organizing the team.	(Again, he focuses almost exclusively on the content.)

This example reflects research findings that show that men focus more on content messages, whereas women focus more on relationship messages (Pearson, Turner, & Todd-Mancillas, 1991). Once we recognize this gender difference, we may be able to develop increased sensitivity to the opposite sex.

Recognizing Relationship Dimensions

Here is essentially the same situation but with the added sensitivity to relationship messages:

Dialogue:	Commentary:
PAUL: The guys at the plant are organizing a bowling team. I'd sure like to be on the team. Would it be all right if I went to the organizational meeting tomorrow?	(Although he focuses on content, he shows awareness of the relational dimensions by asking if this would be a problem. He also shows this in expressing his desire rather than his decision to attend this meeting.)
JUDY: That sounds great, but I'd really like to do something together tomorrow.	(She focuses on the relational dimension but also acknowledges his content orientation. Note too that she does not respond as if she has to defend herself or her emphasis on relational aspects.)
PAUL: How about your meeting me at Luigi's for dinner after the organizational meeting?	(He responds to the relational aspect —without abandoning his desire to join the bowling team—and seeks to incorporate it into his communications. He attempts to negotiate a solution that will meet both Judy's and his needs and desires.)

JUDY: That sounds great. I'm dying   *(She responds to both messages, ap-*
        for spaghetti and meatballs.   *proving of both his joining the team*
                                           and their dinner date.)

Arguments over the content dimension are relatively easy to resolve. You may look something up in a book or ask someone what actually took place. Arguments on the relationship level, however, are much more difficult to resolve, in part because you (like me in the example of my mother) may not recognize that the argument is in fact a relationship one.

COMMUNICATION INVOLVES SYMMETRICAL AND COMPLEMENTARY TRANSACTIONS

Relationships can be described as either symmetrical or complementary (Watzlawick, Beavin, & Jackson, 1967). In a **symmetrical relationship** the two individuals mirror each other's behavior. The behavior of one person is reflected in the behavior of the other. If one member nags, the other member responds in kind. If one member expresses jealousy, the other member expresses jealousy. If one member is passive, the other member is passive. The relationship is one of equality, with the emphasis on minimizing the differences between the two individuals.

Note, however, the problems that can arise in this type of relationship. Consider the situation of a husband and wife, both of whom are aggressive. The aggressiveness of the husband fosters aggressiveness in the wife; the anger of the wife arouses anger in the husband. As this escalates, the aggressiveness can no longer be contained, and the relationship is consumed by aggression.

In a **complementary relationship** the two individuals engage in different behaviors. The behavior of one serves as the stimulus for the complementary behavior of the other. In complementary relationships the differences between the parties are maximized. One partner acts as the superior and the other the inferior, one passive and the other active, one strong and the other weak. At times cultures establish such relationships—as, for example, the complementary relationship between teacher and student or between employer and employee.

A problem in complementary relationships familiar to many college students is one created by extreme rigidity. Whereas the complementary relationship between a nurturing and protective mother and a dependent child was at one time vital and essential to the life of the child, that same relationship when the child is older becomes a handicap to further development. The change so essential to growth is not allowed to occur.

COMMUNICATION SEQUENCES ARE PUNCTUATED

Communicating events are continuous transactions. There is no clear-cut beginning or ending. As a participant in or an observer of the communication act, you divide up this continuous, circular process into causes and effects, or stimuli and responses. That is, you segment this continuous stream of communication into smaller pieces. You label some of these pieces causes or stimuli and others effects or responses.

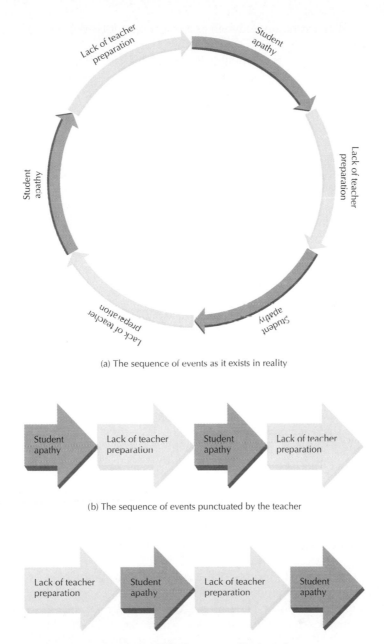

(a) The sequence of events as it exists in reality

(b) The sequence of events punctuated by the teacher

(c) The sequence of events punctuated by the students

FIGURE 2.1 The sequence of events.

Consider an example: The students are apathetic; the teacher does not prepare for classes. Figure 2.1(a) illustrates the sequence of events in which there is no absolute beginning and no absolute end. Each action (the students' apathy and the teacher's lack of preparation) stimulates the other. But there is no *initial* stimulus. Each of the events may be regarded as a stimulus and each as a response, but there is no way to determine which is which.

Consider how the teacher might divide up this continuous transaction. Figure 2.1(b) illustrates the teacher's perception of this situation. From this point of view, the teacher sees the students' apathy as the stimulus for his or her lack of preparation, and the lack of preparation as the response to the students' apathy. In Figure 2.1(c) we see how the students might divide up the transaction. The students might see this "same" sequence of events as beginning with the teacher's lack of preparation as the stimulus (or cause) and their own apathy as the response (or effect).

This tendency to divide up the various communication transactions in sequences of stimuli and responses is referred to as **punctuation** (Watzlawick, Beavin, & Jackson, 1967). People punctuate the continuous sequences of events into stimuli and responses for ease of understanding and remembering. And, as the example of the students and teacher illustrates, people punctuate communication in ways that allow them to look good and that are consistent with their own self-image.

If communication is to be effective, if you are to understand what another person means from his or her point of view, then you have to see the sequence of events as punctuated by the other person. Further, you have to recognize that your punctuation does not reflect what exists in reality. Rather, it reflects your own unique but fallible perception.

COMMUNICATION IS A TRANSACTIONAL PROCESS

Communication is a transaction (Barnlund, 1970; Watzlawick, 1977, 1978; Watzlawick, Beavin, & Jackson, 1967; Wilmot, 1987). One implication of viewing communication as transactional is that each person is seen as both speaker and listener, as simultaneously communicating and receiving messages. Figure 2.2 illustrates this transactional view and compares it with earlier views of communication that may still influence the way you see communication.

By transactional we also mean that communication is an ever-changing process. It is an ongoing activity all the elements of communication are in a state of constant change. You are constantly changing, the people with whom you are communicating are changing, and your environment is changing. Nothing in communication ever remains static.

In any transactional process, each element relates integrally to every other element. The elements of communication are interdependent (never independent). Each exists in relation to the others. For example, there can be no source without a receiver. There can be no message without a source. There can be no feedback without a receiver. Because of this interdependence, a change in any one element of the process produces changes in the other elements. For example, you are talking with a group of your friends and your mother enters the group. This change in "audience" will lead to other changes. Perhaps you or your friends will adjust what you are saying or how you say it. The new situation may also influence how often certain people talk, and so on. Regardless of what change is introduced, other changes will be produced as a result.

Each person in a communication transaction acts and reacts on the basis of the present situation influenced in great part by his or her history, past experiences, atti-

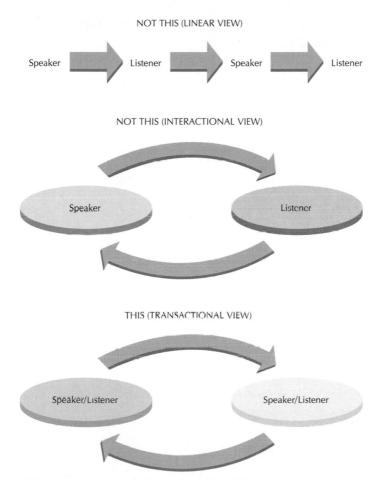

NOT THIS (LINEAR VIEW)

NOT THIS (INTERACTIONAL VIEW)

THIS (TRANSACTIONAL VIEW)

FIGURE 2.2 The transactional view of communication. The top figure represents a *linear* view of communication, in which the speaker speaks and the listener listens. The middle figure represents an *interactional* view, in which speaker and listener take turns speaking and listening; A speaks while B listens and then B speaks while A listens. The bottom figure represents a *transactional* view, in which each person serves simultaneously as speaker and listener; at the same time that you send messages, you are also receiving messages from your own communications and also from the reactions of the other person(s).

tudes, cultural beliefs, self-image, future expectations, and a host of related issues. One implication of this is that actions and reactions in communication are determined not only by what is said, but also by the way the person interprets what is said. Your responses to a movie, for example, do not depend solely on the words and pictures in the film but also on your previous experiences, present emotions, knowledge, physical well-being, and other factors.

Another implication is that two people listening to the same message will often derive two very different meanings. Although the words and symbols are the same, each person interprets them differently.

COMMUNICATION IS INEVITABLE, IRREVERSIBLE, AND UNREPEATABLE

In many instances communication takes place even though one of the individuals does not think he or she is communicating or does not want to communicate. Consider, for example, the student sitting in the back of the room with an expressionless face, perhaps staring out the window. Although the student might claim not to be communicating with the teacher, the teacher may derive any one of a variety of messages from this behavior. Perhaps the teacher assumes that the student lacks interest, is bored, or is worried about something. In any event, the teacher is receiving messages even though the student may not intend to communicate. In an interactional situation, you cannot *avoid* communicating (Watzlawick, Beavin, & Jackson, 1967); communication is inevitable.

This is not to say that all behavior is communication. For example, if the student looked out the window and the teacher failed to notice this, no communication would have taken place.

Further, when you are in an interactional situation you cannot *avoid* responding to the messages of others. For example, if you notice someone winking at you, you must respond in some way. Even if you do not respond actively or openly, that lack of response is itself a response, and it communicates. Again, if you don't notice the winking, then obviously communication has not occurred.

Communication is also irreversible. You can reverse the processes of some systems. For example, you can turn water into ice and then the ice back into water. And

What relevance do the principles of inevitability, irreversibility, and unrepeatability have for intercultural communication between, say, the people in this photo?

you can repeat this reversal process as many times as you wish. Other systems, however, are irreversible. You can turn grapes into wine but you cannot turn the wine back into grapes—the process can go in only one direction. Communication is such an irreversible process. <u>Once you communicate something, you cannot uncommunicate it</u>. You can of course try to reduce the effects of your message. You can say, for example, "I was angry; I really didn't mean what I said." But regardless of how you try to negate or somehow reduce the effects of your message, the message itself, once it has been sent and received, cannot be reversed.

This principle has several important implications for communication in all its forms. For example, in interpersonal interactions you need to be careful not to say things you may be sorry for later. Especially in conflict situations, when tempers run high, you need to avoid saying things you may later wish to withdraw. Commitment messages—the "I love you" messages and their variants—need to be similarly monitored. Otherwise, you may commit yourself to a position you may not be happy with later. In public and in mass communication situations, when the messages are heard by hundreds, thousands, or even millions of people, it is especially crucial to consider the irreversibility of your communications.

<u>Communication is also unrepeatable</u>. The reason for this is simple: <u>everyone and everything is constantly changing</u>. As a result, you can never recapture the exact same situation, frame of mind, or relationship dynamics that defined a previous communication act. For example, you can never repeat meeting someone for the first time, making a first impression in an interview, or resolving a specific group problem.

You can, of course, try again as when you say, "I'm sorry I came off so forward, can we try again?" But, notice that even when you say this you have not erased the initial impression. Instead you try to counteract this initial and perhaps negative impression by going through the motions again.

Summary

1. Communication is normally a package of *signals*, each reinforcing the other. Opposing communication signals from the same source result in contradictory messages.

2. The *double-bind*, a special kind of contradictory message, may be created when contradictory messages are sent simultaneously.

3. Communication is a process of *adjustment* and takes place only to the extent that the communicators use the same system of signals.

4. Communication involves both *content dimensions* and *relationship dimensions*.

5. Communication involves *symmetrical* and *complementary transactions*.

6. Communication sequences are *punctuated* for processing. Different people divide up the communication sequence into stimuli and responses differently.

7. Communication is *transactional*. Communicators serve simultaneously as speakers and listeners. Communication is an ever-changing process with interrelated components in which message effects are influenced by the individual, not only by the words and gestures.

8. In any interactional situation, communication is *inevitable*; you cannot *avoid* communicating nor can you *not* respond to communication.

9. Communication is *irreversible*. You cannot uncommunicate.

10. Communication is *unrepeatable*. You cannot duplicate a previous communication act.

Application

2.1 THE PRINCIPLES OF HUMAN COMMUNICATION IN TRANSACTION

The principles of human communication discussed in this unit should prove useful in analyzing any communication interaction. To help you understand these principles and give you some practice in applying them, here is a representation of a family dinner. Carefully study the interaction of the family members and respond to the questions that follow the dialogue.

Dinner with Margaret and Fred

Cast of Characters:
Margaret: mother, homemaker, junior high school history teacher; 41 years old
Fred: father, gas station attendant; 46 years old
Diane: daughter, receptionist in an art gallery; 22 years old
Stephen: son, college freshman; 18 years old

Margaret is in the kitchen finishing the preparation of dinner—lamb chops, Fred's favorite, though she does not care much for them. Diane is going through some records. Stephen is reading one of his textbooks. Fred comes in from work and throws his jacket over the couch; it falls to the floor.

FRED: *(bored but angry, looking at Stephen)*: What did you do with the car last night? It stunk like rotten eggs. And you left all your school papers all over the back seat.

STEPHEN: *(as if expecting the angry remarks)*: What did I do now?

FRED: You stunk up the car with your pot or whatever you kids smoke, and you left the car looking a mess. Can't you hear? (*Stephen says nothing; goes back to looking at his book but without really reading*)

MARGARET: All right, everybody, dinner's ready. Come on. Wash up and sit down.

(At dinner)

DIANE: Mom, I'm going to go to the shore for the weekend with some friends from work.

MARGARET: Okay. When will you be leaving?

DIANE: Friday afternoon, right after work.

FRED: Like hell you're going. No more going to the shore with *that* group.

MARGARET: Fred, they're nice people. Why shouldn't she go?

FRED: Because I said so, okay? Finished. Closed.

DIANE: *(mumbling)*: I'm 22 years old and he gives me problems. *(Turning to Fred)* You make me feel like a kid, like some stupid little kid.

FRED: Get married. Then you can tell your husband what to do.

DIANE: I wish I could.

STEPHEN: But nobody'll ask her.

MARGARET: Why should she get married? She's got a good life—good job, nice friends, good home. Listen, I was talking with Elizabeth and Cara this morning and they both feel they've just wasted their lives. They raised a family and what have they got? They got *nothing*. *(To Diane)* And don't think sex is so great either; it isn't, believe me.

FRED: Well, they're idiots.

MARGARET: *(snidely)*: They're idiots? Yeah, I guess they are.

DIANE: Joanne's getting married.

MARGARET: Who's Joanne?

STEPHEN: That creature who lives with that guy Michael.

FRED: Watch your mouth, Stephen. Don't be disrespectful to your mother or I'll teach you how to act *right*.

MARGARET: Well, how do you like the dinner?

(Prolonged silence)

DIANE: Do you think I should be in the wedding party if Joanne asks me? I think she will; we always said we'd be in each other's wedding.

MARGARET: Sure, why not? It'll be nice.

FRED: I'm not going to no wedding, no matter who's in it.

STEPHEN: Me neither.

DIANE: I hope you'll both feel that way when I get married.

STEPHEN: By then I'll be too old to remember I got a sister.

MARGARET: How's school?

STEPHEN: I hate it. It's so big. Nobody knows anybody. You sit in these big lecture halls and listen to some creep talk. I really feel lonely and isolated, like nobody knows I'm alive.

FRED: Listen to that college talk. You won't feel lonely if you get yourself a woman instead of hanging out with those pot-heads.

(Diane looks at Margaret, giving a sigh as if to say, "Here we go again")

MARGARET: *(to Diane, in a whisper)*: I know.

DIANE: Mom, do you think I'm getting fat?

STEPHEN: Yes.

FRED: Just don't get fat in the stomach or you'll get thrown out of *here.*

MARGARET: No, I don't notice it.

DIANE: Well, I just thought I might be.

STEPHEN: *(pushing his plate away)*: I'm finished; I'm going out.

FRED: Sit down and finish your supper. You think I work all day for you to throw the food away? You wanna go smoke your dope?

STEPHEN: No. I just want to get away from you—forever.

MARGARET: You mean we both work all day; it's just that I earn a lot more than you do.

FRED: *No,* I mean I work and you baby-sit.

MARGARET: Teaching junior high school history isn't baby-sitting.

FRED: Well, what is it then? You don't teach them anything.

MARGARET: *(to Diane)*: You see? You're better off single. I should've stayed single. Instead . . . Oh, well. I was young and stupid. It was my own fault for getting involved with a loser. Just don't you make the same mistake.

FRED: *(to Stephen)*: Go ahead. Leave the table. Leave the house. Who cares what you do?

1. Communication is a package of signals.
    a. What instances can you find in this dialogue of communication being a package of signals?
    b. Are there any examples of mixed or contradictory messages? Any examples of double-binding?
2. Communication is a process of adjustment.
    a. Can any of the failures to communicate be traced to the lack of adjustment?
    b. What suggestions would you offer this family for increasing their abilities to adjust to one another?
3. Communication involves content and relationship dimensions.

    a.   How does each of the characters deal with the self-definitions of the other characters? For example, how does Fred deal with the self-definition of Margaret? How does Margaret deal with the self-definition of Fred?

    b.   Are any problems caused by the failure to recognize the distinction between the content and the relationship levels of communication?

4. Communication involves symmetrical and complementary transactions.

    a.   What type of relationship do you suppose exists between Fred and Margaret? Between Fred and Diane? Between Fred and Stephen? Between Diane and Stephen? Between Margaret and Stephen?

    b.   What do you see as the major problems in each of these relationship pairs?

5. Communication sequences are punctuated for processing.

    a.   Select any two characters and indicate how they differ in their punctuation of any specific sequence of events. Do the characters realize that they are each arbitrarily dividing the sequence of events differently?

    b.   What problems might a failure to recognize the arbitrary nature of punctuation create?

6. Communication is transactional.

    a.   How is the process nature of communication illustrated in this interaction? Are there instances in which individual characters try to deny the process nature of interactions?

    b.   In what ways are the messages of the different characters interdependent?

    c.   In what ways do the characters demonstrate that they are serving simultaneously as speaker and listener?

7. Communication is inevitable, irreversible, and unrepeatable.

    a.   Do the characters communicate significant messages, even though they may not intend to? For example, do the characters communicate simply by their physical presence or by the role they occupy in the family?

    b.   Are any messages communicated that you think the characters would have (at a later date) wished they had not communicated? Why do you think so?

    c.   Can you detect any implications of the principle that communication is unrepeatable? How does unrepeatability relate to irreversibility?

As an alternative to analyzing this interaction, the entire class may watch a situation comedy show, television drama, or film and explore the communication principles in these presentations. The questions in this exercise should prove useful in formulating parallel questions for the television program or film. Another way of approaching this exercise is for all members of the class to watch the same television programs for an entire evening and have different groups concentrate on the way different principles operate. One group might focus on illustrations of the impossibility of not communicating, one group on the content and relationship dimensions of messages, and so on. Each group can then report its findings and insights to the entire class.

2.2   WHAT'S HAPPENING?

How would you use the principles of communication discussed in this unit to *describe* (not to solve) what is happening in each of the following situations? Do realize that these scenarios are extremely brief and are written only as exercises to stimulate you to think more concretely about the principles. Note, too, that the objective is not to select the one correct principle (each scenario can probably be elucidated by reference to several principles), but to provide an opportunity to think about the principles in reference to specific situations.

1. A couple, together for twenty years, argues constantly about the seemingly most insignificant things—who takes the dog out, who does the shopping, who decides where to go to dinner, and so on. It's to the point where they rarely have a day without argument; both are considering separating.

2. In teaching communication skills, Professor Jones frequently asks students to role play effective and ineffective communication patterns and offers criticism after each session. Although most students respond well to this instructional technique, Mariz has difficulty and has frequently left the class in tears.

3. Pat has sought the assistance of a family therapist. The problem is simple: whatever Pat says, Chris says the opposite. If Pat wants to eat Chinese, Chris wants to eat Italian; if Pat wants Italian, Chris wants Chinese. And on and on. The problem is made worse by the fact that Chris has to win; Pat's wishes are invariably dismissed.

4. In the heat of a big argument, Harry said he didn't want to ever see Peggy's family again: "They don't like me and I don't like them." Peggy reciprocated and said she felt the same way about his family. Now, weeks later, there remains a great deal of tension between them, especially when they find themselves with one or both families.

5. Grace and Tom, senior executives at a large advertising agency, are engaged to be married. Recently, Grace made a presentation that was not received positively by the other members of the team. Grace feels that Tom—in not defending her proposal—created a negative attitude and actually encouraged others to reject her ideas. Tom says that he felt he could not defend her proposal because others would have felt his defense was motivated by their relationship and not by an objective evaluation of her proposal. So, he felt it was best to say nothing.

6. Joe, a police detective, can't understand what happened. "All I did," he says, "was introduce myself and they refused to talk to me."

THE SELF IN COMMUNICATION

UNIT CONTENTS

Self-concept

Self-awareness

Self-esteem

Self-disclosure

Thinking Critically About Self-disclosure

   Summary

   Application

      3.1   Applying the Guidelines to Self-disclosure

UNIT GOALS

After completing this unit, you should be able to

1. define *self-concept* and explain how it develops

2. explain the Johari Window

3. explain self-awareness and suggestions for increasing it

4. explain self-esteem and the ways to raise it

5. define *self-disclosure* and the factors influencing it

6. explain self-disclosure's major rewards and dangers as well as the guidelines for self-disclosure and for responding to disclosures

Of all the components of the communication act, the most important is the self. Who you are and how you perceive yourself and others influence your communications and your responses to the communications of others. In this unit, we explore four aspects of the self: self-concept, self-awareness, self-esteem, and self-disclosure, the process of revealing yourself to others.

SELF-CONCEPT

Your image of who you are is your **self-concept** and is composed of your feelings and thoughts about your strengths and weaknesses, your abilities and limitations. Your self-concept develops from at least these three sources: the image that others have of you and that they reveal to you; the comparisons you make between yourself and others; and the way you interpret and evaluate your own thoughts and behaviors (Figure 3.1).

Others' Images of You

If you wanted to see how your hair looked, you would look in a mirror. But what would you do if you wanted to know how friendly or how assertive you are? According to Charles Horton Cooley's (1922) concept of the **looking-glass self**, you would look at the image of yourself that others reveal to you through their behavior—especially the way they treat you and react to you.

Of course, you would not look to just anyone, but rather to those who are most significant in your life—your *significant others*. As a child you would look to your parents and then to your schoolteachers, for example. As an adult you might look to your friends and romantic partners.

If these significant others think highly of you, you will see this positive image of yourself reflected in their behavior; if they think little of you, you will see a more negative image. These reflected images help form the view you develop of yourself.

Social Comparisons

Another way you develop your self-concept is to compare yourself with others. Again, when you want to gain insight into who you are and how effective or competent you are, you look to your peers. For example, after an examination you probably want to know how you performed relative to the other students in your class. This gives you a

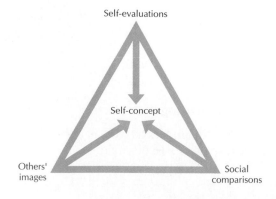

FIGURE 3.1 The sources of self-concept.

clearer idea of how effectively you performed. If you play on a baseball team, it's important to know your batting average in comparison with the batting average of others on your team or in your league. Absolute exam or batting scores may be helpful in telling you something about your performance, but you gain a different perspective when you see your score in comparison with those of your peers.

Your Own Interpretations and Evaluations

Just as others form images of you based on what you do, you interpret and evaluate your own behavior. These interpretations and evaluations help you form your self-concept. For example, suppose you were taught and came to believe that telling lies is wrong. If you lie, you will evaluate this behavior in terms of your internalized beliefs about lying and will react to your own behavior negatively. You will probably experience some degree of guilt as a result of your behavior contradicting your beliefs. On the other hand, let's say that you pulled someone out of a burning building at great personal risk. You will probably evaluate this behavior positively; you will feel good about this behavior and, as a result, about yourself.

Understanding the way your self-concept develops increases your *self-awareness*. The more you understand why you view yourself as you do, the better you will understand who you are. You can gain additional insight into yourself by looking more directly at self-awareness and especially at the Johari model of the self.

SELF-AWARENESS

If you listed some of the qualities you wanted to have, self-awareness would surely rank high. Self-awareness is eminently practical: you control our thoughts and behaviors largely to the extent that you understand yourself and are aware of who you are.

The Four Selves

Figure 3.2 explains self-awareness by the Johari Window (Luft, 1969, 1984). The window is broken up into four basic areas or quadrants, each of which contains a somewhat different self. Let's assume that this window and the four selves represent you.

The Open Self   The **open self** represents all the information, behaviors, attitudes, feelings, desires, motivations, ideas, and so on that you know about yourself and that others also know. The information included here might vary from your name, skin color, and sex to your age, political and religious affiliations, and job title. Your open self will vary in size depending on the individuals with whom you are dealing. Some people probably make you feel comfortable and support you. To them, you open yourself wide. To others you may prefer to leave most of yourself closed.

The size of the open self also varies from person to person. Some people tend to reveal their innermost desires and feelings. Others prefer to remain silent about both significant and insignificant details. Most of us, however, open ourselves to some people about some things at some times.

"The smaller the first quadrant," says Luft (1984), "the poorer the communication." Communication depends on the degree to which you open yourself to others and to yourself. If you do not allow others to know you, communication becomes extremely difficult, if not impossible. You can communicate meaningfully only when you know

How much emphasis does your native culture place on self-awareness? As you were growing up, what three people taught you the most about who you are? Can what those people taught you about self-awareness be traced to their own cultural traditions?

the other person, the other person knows you, and you each know yourself. To improve communication, you have to work first on enlarging the open self.

A change in the open area—or in any of the quadrants—will bring about a change in the other quadrants. Visualize the size of the entire window being constant, and the size of each pane being variable—sometimes small, sometimes large. As one pane becomes smaller, one or more of the others must become larger. Similarly, as one

	Known to self	Not known to self
Known to others	Open self	Blind self
Not known to others	Hidden self	Unknown self

FIGURE 3.2 The Johari Window. [*Source:* Joseph Luft, *Group Process: An Introduction to Group Dynamics,* 3rd ed. (Palo Alto, Calif.: Mayfield, 1989), p. 11.]

pane becomes larger, one or more of the others must become smaller. These several selves, then, are not separate and distinct from each other. Rather, each depends on the others.

The Blind Self   The **blind self** represents information about yourself that others know but you do not. This may vary from relatively insignificant habits—using the expression "you know," rubbing your nose when you get angry, or having a peculiar body odor—to something as significant as defense mechanisms, fight strategies, or repressed experiences.

Some people have a very large blind self and seem oblivious to their own faults and sometimes (though not as often) their own virtues. Others seem overly concerned with having a blind self. They seek therapy at every turn and join every consciousness-raising group. Some think they know everything about themselves—that they have reduced the blind self to zero.

Communication depends in great part on both parties having the same basic information about the other. Where blind areas exist, communication will be difficult. Yet blind areas will always exist for each of us. Although we may be able to shrink our blind areas, we can never eliminate them.

The Unknown Self   The **unknown self** represents those parts of yourself about which neither you nor others know. This is the information that is buried in your subconscious or that has somehow escaped notice.

You gain insight into the unknown self from a number of different sources. Sometimes this area is revealed through temporary changes brought about by drug experiences, special experimental conditions such as hypnosis or sensory deprivation, or various projective tests or dreams. The exploration of the unknown self through open, honest, and empathic interaction with trusted and trusting others—parents, friends, counselors, children, lovers—is an effective way of gaining insight.

The Hidden Self   The **hidden self** contains all that you know of yourself but keep hidden from others. This area includes all your successfully kept secrets about yourself and others. At the extremes, there are the overdisclosers and the underdisclosers. The overdisclosers tell all, keeping nothing hidden about themselves or others. They will tell you their family history, sexual problems, financial status, goals, failures and successes, and just about everything else.

The underdisclosers tell nothing. They will talk about you but not about themselves. You may feel that they are afraid of rejection; you may feel rejected yourself by their refusal to trust. When you refuse to reveal anything about yourself to others, you say something about how you feel with these people. On one level, at least, you are sending the message "I don't feel comfortable enough to reveal myself to you."

Most of us fall somewhere between these two extremes. We keep certain things hidden and we disclose other things. We disclose to some people and we do not disclose to others. We are, in effect, selective disclosers.

The variations in the relative sizes of the four selves can produce a variety of windows (Figure 3.3). You may find it interesting to review these four selves as if they were your windows when interacting with different people. With whom would you be interacting in each of these four windows?

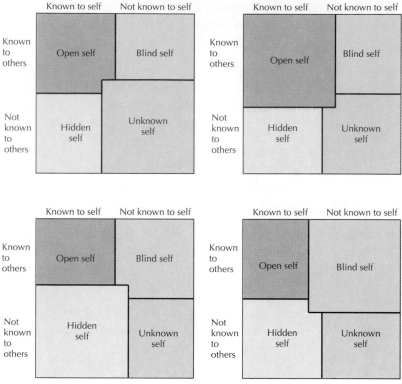

FIGURE 3.3 Johari Windows of varied structure.

Growing in Self-Awareness

Embedded in the foregoing discussion are suggestions on how to increase your own self-awareness. Some of these may now be made explicit.

Dialogue with Yourself No one knows you better than you do. The problem is that we seldom if ever ask ourselves about ourselves. It can be interesting and revealing. One way to do this is informally to take a "Who Am I?" test (Bugental and Zelen, 1950). Take a piece of paper, head it "Who Am I?" and write 10, 15, or 20 times, "I am. . ." Then complete the sentence each time. Try not to give only positive or socially acceptable responses; respond with what comes to mind first. Second, take another piece of paper and divide it into two columns. Head one column "Strengths" or "Virtues" and the other column "Weaknesses" or "Vices." Fill in each column as quickly as possible.

Remember too that you are constantly changing. Consequently, your self-perceptions and goals also change, often in drastic ways. Update them at regular and frequent intervals.

Listen You can learn about yourself from seeing yourself as others do. Conveniently, others are constantly giving you the very feedback you need to increase self-awareness. In every interpersonal interaction, people comment on you in some way—

on what you do, what you say, how you look. Sometimes these comments are explicit: "You really look washed-out today." Most often they are only implicit, such as a stare or averted eyes. Often they are "hidden" in the way others look, what they talk about, and the focus of their interest.

Reduce Your Blind Self   Actively seek information to reduce your blind self. People will reveal such information when you encourage them. Use some of the situations that arise every day to gain self-information: "Do you think I came down too hard on the instructor today?" "Do you think I was assertive enough when I asked for the raise?" Do not, of course, seek this information constantly. Your friends would quickly find others with whom to interact. But you can make use of some situations—perhaps those in which you are particularly unsure of what to do or how you appear—to reduce your blind self and increase self-awareness.

See Your Different Selves   To each of your friends and relatives, you are a somewhat different person. Yet you are really *all* of these. Try to see yourself as do the people with whom you interact. For starters, visualize how you are seen by your mother, your father, your teacher, your best friend, the stranger you sat next to on the bus, your employer, and your neighbor's child. Because you are, in fact, a composite of all of these views, it is important that you see yourself through the eyes of many people.

Increase Your Open Self   Self-awareness generally increases when you increase your open self. When you reveal yourself to others, you learn about yourself at the same time. You bring into clearer focus what you may have buried within. As you discuss yourself, you may see connections that you had previously missed. In receiving feedback from others, you gain still more insight.

Further, by increasing your open self, you increase the likelihood that a meaningful and intimate dialogue will develop. It is through such interactions that you best get to know yourself.

SELF-ESTEEM

Self-esteem refers to the way you feel about yourself. How much do you like yourself? How valuable a person do you think you are? How competent do you think you are? The answers to these questions reflect the value you place on yourself.

The major reason that self-esteem is so important is simply that success breeds success. When you feel good about yourself—about who you are and what you are capable of doing—you perform more effectively. When you think like a success, you are more likely to act like a success. When you think you're a failure, you're more likely to act like a failure. Increasing your self-esteem will help you function more effectively in school, in your interpersonal relationships, and in your career. Next we explore a few ways you can do this.

Engage in Self-affirmation   Remind yourself of your successes from time to time. Focus on your good deeds, strengths, and positive qualities. Also, look carefully at the good relationships you have with friends and relatives. Concentrate on your potential, not your limitations (Brody, 1991).

Seek Out Nurturing People   Seek out positive people who are optimistic and make you feel good about yourself. Avoid those who find fault with just about everything. Seek to build a network of supportive others (Brody, 1991).

Work on Projects That Will Result in Success   Success builds self-esteem. Each success makes achieving the next one a little easier. Remember that the failure of a project is not the failure of you as a person; failure is something that happens, not something inside you. Everyone faces defeat somewhere along the line. The attitude that distinguishes failures from successes is that successful people know how to deal with setbacks. Further, one defeat does not mean you will fail the next time. Put failure in perspective, and don't make it an excuse for not trying again.

You Do Not Have to Be Loved by Everyone   Many people believe that everyone should love them. This belief traps you into thinking you must always please others so they will like you.

SELF-DISCLOSURE

When you reveal information from your hidden self, you are engaging in self-disclosure (Jourard 1968, 1971a, b). In this section we look at self-disclosure from a number of vantage points: the nature of self-disclosure, the factors influencing self-disclosure, the rewards and dangers of self-disclosure, and some guidelines to consider before self-disclosing. But before reading about these rewards and dangers, explore your own feelings about how willing you are to self-disclose by taking the self-test on page 49.

The Nature of Self-Disclosure

Self-disclosure is communication in which you reveal information about yourself. Because self-disclosure is a type of communication, it includes not only overt statements but also, for example, slips of the tongue and unconscious nonverbal signals. It varies from whispering a secret to a best friend to making a public confession on *Oprah Winfrey.*

Self-disclosure concerns you—your thoughts, feelings, and behaviors—or about your intimates that has a significant bearing on yourself. Thus, self-disclosure could refer to your own actions or the actions of, say, your parents or children, since these have a direct relationship to who you are.

Although by definition self-disclosure may be any information about the self, it is in practice most often used to refer to information that you normally keep hidden rather than simply to information that you have not previously revealed.

Factors Influencing Self-Disclosure

Self-disclosure occurs more readily under certain circumstances than others. Here, we identify several factors influencing self-disclosure.

Group Size   Self-disclosure occurs more in small groups than in large groups. Dyads (groups of two people) are the most hospitable setting for self-disclosure. With one listener, you can attend carefully to the person's responses. On the basis of this

SELF-TEST

How Willing to Self-Disclose Are You?

Respond to each of the following statements by indicating the likelihood of your disclosing such information to, for instance, other members of this class. Use the following scale:

1 = would definitely self-disclose
2 = would probably self-disclose
3 = don't know
4 = would probably not self-disclose
5 = would definitely not self-disclose

_____   1. My religious beliefs.

_____   2. My attitudes toward other religions, nationalities, and races.

_____   3. My economic status.

_____   4. My parents' attitudes toward other religions, races, and nationalities.

_____   5. My feelings about my parents.

_____   6. My sexual fantasies.

_____   7. My ideal mate.

_____   8. My drinking and/or drug-taking behavior.

_____   9. My unfulfilled desires.

_____   10. My feelings about the people in this group.

After all the questionnaires are completed, discuss the responses in groups of five or six or with the class as a whole. Disclose what you wish to self-disclose and keep to yourself what you do not wish to disclose. Discussion might center on these issues:

1. Are there discrepancies between what you said you would disclose and what you actually chose to disclose? Why?
2. Can you classify the types of information that people are reluctant to disclose about themselves? What does this tell you about self-disclosure?
3. Self-disclosure is usually a two-way process and follows what is called the dyadic effect—what one person does, the other does as well. Did this dyadic effect occur in this group? Why or why not?
4. Would the results of this questionnaire have differed if the target audience of these disclosures was your parents? A stranger you would never see again? A best friend or lover? A teacher or counselor?
5. Do you notice gender differences in self-disclosing behavior? Are there cultural differences? Do some cultures reward self-disclosure more than others? Can you give specific examples of cultural variation?

support or lack of support, you can monitor the disclosures, continuing if the situation is supportive and stopping if it is not.

Liking People tend to disclose to people they like or love, and not to disclose to people they dislike (Derlega, Winstead, Wong, & Greenspan, 1987). This is not surprising, since people you like (and who probably like you) will be supportive and positive. Not only do you disclose to those you like, you probably also come to like those to whom you disclose (Berg & Archer, 1983). You probably also disclose more to those you trust (Wheeless & Grotz, 1977; Petronio, 1991).

At times self-disclosure is more likely to occur in temporary than permanent relationships—for example, between strangers on a train or plane, a kind of "in-flight intimacy" (McGill, 1985). In this situation, two people establish an intimate self-disclosing relationship during some brief travel period, knowing that they will never see each other again.

Dyadic Effect   You probably self-disclose in response to the self-disclosures of the other person. This **dyadic effect** probably leads you to feel more secure and, in fact, reinforces your own self-disclosing behavior. Not surprisingly, disclosures are more intimate when they are made in response to the disclosures of others (Berg & Archer, 1983). So strong is this dyadic effect that you may feel a pressure to respond with disclosures of your own that are within the same general topic area and at about the same level of depth or "personalness."

Competence   Competent communicators self-disclose more than less competent ones. "It may very well be," note James McCroskey and Lawrence Wheeless (1976), "that people who are more competent also perceive themselves to be more competent, and thus have the self-confidence necessary to take more chances with self-disclosure. Or, even more likely, competent people may simply have more positive things about themselves to disclose than less competent people."

Personality   Highly sociable and extroverted people self-disclose more than those who are less sociable and more introverted. Sometimes, anxiety increases self-disclosing and at other times it reduces it to a minimum. People who are apprehensive about talking in general also self-disclose less than do those who are more comfortable in oral communication.

Topics   If you are like the people studied by researchers, you are more likely to disclose about some topics than others. For example, you are more likely to self-disclose information about your job or hobbies than about your sex life or financial situation (Jourard, 1968, 1971a). You would also disclose favorable information more readily than unfavorable information. Generally, the more personal and the more negative the topic, the less likely you are to self-disclose (Nakanishi, 1986).

Culture   Different cultures view self-disclosure differently. People in the United States, for example, disclose more than do those in Great Britain, Germany, Japan, or Puerto Rico (Gudykunst, 1983). American students also disclose more than do students from nine different Middle East countries (Jourard, 1971). However, there are also important similarities across cultures. For example, people from Great Britain, Germany, the United States, and Puerto Rico are all more apt to disclose personal information—hobbies, interests, attitudes, and opinions on politics and religion—than information on finances, sex, personality, and interpersonal relationships (Jourard, 1971). Similarly, one study showed self-disclosure patterns between American males to be virtually identical to the patterns between Korean males (Won-Doornink, 1991).

Gender   Generally, men disclose less than do women (Naifeh & Smith, 1984; Rosenfeld, 1979) except in initial heterosexual encounters, in which men disclose more (Derlega, Winstead, Wong, & Hunter, 1985). Judy Pearson (1980) has argued that it is sex *role* rather than biological gender that accounts for the differences in self-disclosure. In Pearson's study, "masculine women" self-disclosed to a lesser extent than did women who scored low on masculinity scales. Further, "feminine men" self-disclosed to a greater extent than did men who scored low on femininity scales.

The major reason both men and women give for avoiding self-disclosure is the fear of projecting an unfavorable image. In addition men fear appearing inconsistent, losing control over the other person, and threatening the relationship. In addition, women fear revealing information that may be used against them, giving others the impression that they are emotionally disturbed, or hurting their relationships (Rosenfeld, 1979).

THINKING CRITICALLY ABOUT SELF-DISCLOSURE

Because self-disclosure and its effects can be so significant, think critically before deciding to disclose or not disclose. Specifically, weigh the rewards and dangers carefully. Also, think about the way you'll disclose and respond to the disclosures of others. In reading these topics, recall our earlier model of communication and the importance of

How might the rewards and dangers of self-disclosure differ from one culture to another? Are there cultures that consistently reward (or punish) disclosure? How would you describe your own culture in terms of the rewards and punishments it places on self-disclosure? Does it treat disclosures by men and women in the same way?

culture (Unit 1). Not all societies and cultures view self-disclosure in the same way. In some cultures, disclosing one's inner feelings is considered a weakness. Among Anglo-Saxon Americans, for example, it would be considered "out of place" if a man cried at a happy occasion like a wedding. That same behavior would go unnoticed, for example, in some Latin cultures. Similarly, in Japan it is considered undesirable to reveal personal information whereas in the United States it is considered desirable and is even expected (Barnlund, 1989; Hall, 1984).

The potential rewards and dangers of self-disclosure as well as any suggested guidelines, then, must be examined in terms of the specific culture and its rules. As with many such cultural rules, following them brings approval and violating them brings disapproval.

The Rewards of Self-Disclosure

One reason why self-disclosure is so significant is that its rewards are great. Self-disclosure may bring self-knowledge, increase your ability to cope, improve communication, and increase relationship depth.

Self-Knowledge   When you self-disclose you gain a new perspective on yourself and a deeper understanding of your own behavior. In therapy, for example, often the insight comes while the client is self-disclosing. He or she may recognize some previously unknown facet of behavior or relationship. Through self-disclosure, then, you may also come to understand yourself more thoroughly.

Coping Abilities   Self-disclosure may help you deal with your problems, especially guilt. One of the great fears many people have is that they will not be accepted because of some deep, dark secret, because of something they have done, or because of some feeling or attitude they have. By self-disclosing such feelings and receiving support rather than rejection, you may become better able to deal with any such guilt and perhaps reduce or even eliminate it (Pennebaker, 1990).

Even self-acceptance is difficult without self-disclosure. If you accept yourself, in part at least through the eyes of others, then it becomes essential that you give others the opportunity to know and to respond to the "real" you. Through self-disclosure and subsequent support, you put yourself in a better position to receive positive responses to who you really are, stripped of the facade that the failure to self-disclose erects.

Communication Efficiency   Self-disclosure may help to improve communication. You understand the messages of others largely to the extent that you understand the senders of those messages. You can understand what someone says better if you know that individual well. You can tell what certain nuances mean, when the person is serious and when joking, and when the person is being sarcastic out of fear and when out of resentment. Self-disclosure is an essential condition for getting to know another individual, for the process of adjustment considered in Unit 2.

Relational Depth   Self-disclosure is often helpful for establishing a meaningful relationship between two people. Research has found, for example, that marital satisfaction is higher for couples who are mid to high self-disclosers; satisfaction is significantly less in low disclosing relationships (Rosenfeld & Bowen, 1991). Without self-disclosure, relationships of any meaningful depth seem difficult if not impossible. By self-disclosing, you tell others that you trust them, respect them, and care enough about them and your relationship to reveal yourself to them. This in turn leads the other individual to self-disclose and forms at least the start of a meaningful relationship, one that is honest and open and goes beyond surface trivialities.

The Dangers of Self-Disclosure

The numerous advantages of self-disclosure should not blind us to its very real risks (Bochner, 1984). Here are a few of the major ones.

Personal and Social Rejection   Usually you self-disclose to someone whose responses you feel will be supportive of your disclosures. Of course, the person you think will be supportive may turn out to reject you. Parents, normally the most supportive of all interpersonal relations, have frequently rejected children who self-disclosed their homosexuality, their plans to marry someone of a different religion, their decision to avoid the draft, or their belief in a certain faith. Your best friends, your closest intimates, may reject you for similar self-disclosures.

Material Loss   Sometimes, self-disclosures result in material losses. Politicians who disclose that they have seen a psychiatrist may later find that their own political party no longer supports them and that voters are unwilling to vote for them. Teachers who disclose former or present drug-taking behavior or cohabitation with one of their students may find themselves being denied tenure, forced to teach undesirable schedules, and eventually becoming victims of "budget cuts." In the corporate world, self-disclosures of alcoholism or drug addiction are often met with dismissal, demotion, or transfer.

Intrapersonal Difficulties   When other people's reactions are not as predicted, intrapersonal difficulties may result. When you are rejected instead of supported, when your parents say that you disgust them instead of hugging you, and when your friends ignore you at school rather than seeking you out as before, you are in line for some intrapersonal difficulties. No one likes to be rejected, and those with fragile egos might well consider what damage such rejection could bring.

Remember that self-disclosure, like any communication, is irreversible (see Unit 2). Regardless of how many times you may try to qualify a self-disclosure or "take it back," once something is said it cannot be withdrawn. Nor can you erase the conclusions and inferences listeners have made on the basis of your disclosures.

Guidelines for Self-Disclosing

Each person has to make her or his own decisions concerning self-disclosure. Each decision will be based on numerous variables, many of which we considered in the previous discussion. The following guidelines will help you raise the right questions before making what must be *your* decision.

The Motivation for Self-Disclosure   Effective self-disclosure is motivated by a concern for the relationship, for the others involved, and for yourself. Some people self-disclose out of a desire to hurt the listener. For example, a daughter who tells her parents that they hindered rather than helped her emotional development may be disclosing out of a desire to hurt and punish rather than to improve the relationship. Nor, of course, should self-disclosure be used to punish yourself (perhaps because of some guilt feeling or unresolved conflict).

The Appropriateness of Self-Disclosure Effective self-disclosure should be appropriate to the context and to the relationship between speaker and listener. Before making any significant self-disclosure, ask yourself if the context is right. Could you arrange a better time and place? Is this self-disclosure appropriate to the relationship? Generally, the more intimate the disclosures, the closer the relationship should be. It is probably best to resist intimate disclosures with nonintimates and casual acquaintances, or in the early stages of a relationship. This suggestion applies especially to intimate negative disclosures, for example, financial or sexual difficulties or a history of drug dependency.

The Disclosures of the Other Person During your disclosures, give the other person a chance to reciprocate with his or her own disclosures. If the other person does not also self-disclose, then reassess your own decision to open up. The lack of reciprocity may be a signal that this person—at this time and in this context— does not welcome your disclosures. So disclose gradually and in small increments. When disclosures are made too rapidly and all at once, the normal reciprocity cannot operate. Further, you lose the ability to retreat if the responses are not positive enough.

The Possible Burdens Self-Disclosure Might Entail Carefully weigh any problems you may run into as a result of a disclosure. Can you afford to lose your job if you disclose your previous prison record? Are you willing to risk losing a relationship if you disclose previous relationship infidelities? Ask yourself whether you are making unreasonable demands on the listener. Parents often place unreasonable burdens on their children by self-disclosing marital problems, addictions, or self-doubts that children are too young or too emotionally involved to accept. Often such disclosures do not make the relationship a better one but instead add tension and friction. Sometimes the motivation is to ease one's own guilt without considering the burden this places on the other person.

Guidelines for Responding to Self-Disclosures

When someone discloses to you, it is usually a sign of trust and affection. In serving this most important receiver function, keep the following points in mind.

Use Effective and Active Listening Skills In Unit 5 we identify the skills of effective listening. These are especially important when listening to self-disclosures. Listen actively, listen for different levels of meaning, listen with empathy, and listen with an open mind. Paraphrase the speaker so that you can be sure you understand both the thoughts and the feelings communicated. Express understanding of the speaker's feelings to allow her or him the opportunity to see these more objectively and through the eyes of another individual. Ask questions to ensure your own understanding and to signal your interest and attention.

Support and Reinforce the Discloser   Express support for the person during and after the disclosures. Refrain from evaluation during the disclosures; don't say, "You shouldn't have done that" or "Did you really cheat that often?" Concentrate on understanding and empathizing with the person. Allow the speaker to set her or his own pace; don't rush the person with the too frequent "So how did it all end?" type of response. Make your supportiveness clear through your verbal and nonverbal responses. For example, consider maintaining eye contact, leaning toward the speaker, asking relevant questions, and echoing the speaker's thoughts and feelings.

Maintain Confidentiality   When a person confides in you, it is because she or he wants you to know these feelings and thoughts. If the discloser wishes others to share these details, then it is up to her or him to reveal them. If you tell others about these confidences, be prepared for all sorts of negative effects. Such indiscretion will likely inhibit future disclosures from this individual to anyone in general and to you in particular, and your relationship will probably suffer. Those to whom you reveal these disclosures will likely feel that since you have betrayed a confidence once, you will do so again, perhaps with their own personal details. A general climate of distrust is easily established. But most important, betraying a confidence debases what should be a significant and meaningful interpersonal experience.

Don't Use the Disclosures as Weapons   Many self-disclosures expose vulnerability or weakness. If you later turn around and use these against the person—called "hitting below the belt"—you betray that person's confidence and trust. The relationship is sure to suffer and may never fully recover.

Summary

1. *Self-concept* refers to the image you have of yourself. It is developed from the image others have of you and reveal, the comparisons you make between yourself and others, and the way you evaluate your own thoughts and behaviors.

2. In the Johari Window model of the self, there are four major areas: the *open self*, the *blind self*, the *hidden self*, and the *unknown self*.

3. To increase *self-awareness*, ask yourself about yourself, listen to others to see yourself as others do, actively seek information from others about yourself, see yourself from different perspectives, and increase your open self.

4. *Self-esteem* refers to the way you feel about yourself, the value you place on yourself, and the positive-negative evaluation you make of yourself. It may be increased by engaging in self-affirmation, seeking out nurturing people, working on projects that will result in success, and recognizing that you do not have to be loved by everyone.

5. *Self-disclosure* refers to a form of communication in which information about the self (usually information that is normally kept hidden) is communicated to another person.

6. Self-disclosure is more likely to occur when the potential discloser is with one other person, when the discloser likes or loves the listener, when the listener also discloses, when the discloser feels competent, when the discloser is highly sociable and extroverted, and when the topic of disclosure is fairly impersonal and positive.

7. The *rewards of self-disclosure* include increase in self-knowledge, a better ability to cope with difficult situations and guilt, more efficient communication, and a better chance for a meaningful relationship.

8. The *dangers of self-disclosure* include personal and social rejection, material loss, and intrapersonal difficulties.

9. Before self-disclosing, consider the motivation and appropriateness of the self-disclosure, the opportunity available for open and honest responses, the disclosures of the other person, and the possible burdens that your self-disclosure might impose on you and your listener.

10. When *listening to disclosures*, practice the skills of effective and active listening, support and reinforce the discloser, keep the disclosures confidential, and do not use the disclosures as weapons against the person.

Application

3.1   APPLYING THE GUIDELINES TO SELF-DISCLOSURE

Should you self-disclose or not self-disclose? Here are several instances of impending self-disclosure. For each, indicate whether or not you think the self-disclosure would be appropriate. Specify your reasons for each judgment. In making your decision, consider each of the guidelines identified in this unit.

1. A mother of two teen-aged children (one boy, one girl) has been feeling guilty for the past year over a romantic affair she had with her brother-in-law while her husband was in prison. The mother has been divorced for the last few months. She wants to disclose this affair and her guilt to her children.

2. A student plagiarized a term paper for an anthropology class. He is sorry for having done this and especially sorry that the plagiarized paper only earned a grade of C+. He wants to confess to his instructor and rewrite the paper.

3. Tom is engaged to Cathy, but has recently fallen in love with another woman. He wants to call Cathy on the phone, break his engagement, and disclose his new relationship.

4. Sam has been living in a romantic relationship with another man for the past several years. Sam wants to reveal his relationship to his parents, with whom he has been very close throughout his life, but he can't seem to get up the courage to do so. He decides to tell them in a long letter.

5. Mary and Jim have been married for twelve years. Mary has been honest about most things and has disclosed a great deal to Jim about her past romantic encounters, her fears, her insecurities, her ambitions, and so on. Yet Jim doesn't seem able to reciprocate. He almost never shares his feelings and has told Mary almost nothing about his life before they met. Mary wonders if she should continue to disclose or if she should begin to limit her disclosures.

PERCEPTION

UNIT CONTENTS

The Perception Process

Processes Influencing Perception

Critical Perception: Making Perceptions More Accurate

Summary

Applications

  4.1 Hearing the Barriers to Perception

  4.2 Critically Evaluating Causal Attributions

UNIT GOALS

After completing this unit, you should be able to

1. define *perception*

2. explain the three stages in the perception process

3. explain how the following processes influence perception: *primacy* and *recency*, the *self-fulfilling prophecy*, *perceptual accentuation*, *implicit personality theory*, *consistency*, *stereotyping*, and *attribution*.

Perception is the process by which you become aware of the many stimuli impinging on your senses. Perception influences what stimuli or messages you take in *and* what meanings you give them once they reach awareness. Perception is therefore central to the study of communication in all its forms and functions. Here we look at (1) the process of perception, identifying its three main stages; (2) the processes that influence perception; and (3) how you can make your perceptions more accurate.

THE PERCEPTION PROCESS

Perception is complex. There is no one-to-one relationship between the messages that occur "out there" in the world—in the vibrations of the air and in the black marks on paper—and the messages that eventually get to your brain. What occurs "out there" may differ greatly from what reaches your conscious mind. Examining how and why these messages differ is crucial to understanding communication. We can illustrate how perception works by explaining the three steps involved in the process. These stages are not discrete and separate; in reality they are continuous and blend into and overlap one another (Figure 4.1).

Sensory Stimulation Occurs

At this first stage the sense organs are stimulated. You hear a recording. You see someone you have not seen for years. You smell perfume on the person next to you. You taste a slice of pizza. You feel a sweaty palm as you shake hands.

Even when you have the sensory ability to perceive stimuli, you do not always do so. For example, when you are daydreaming in class, you do not hear what the teacher is saying until your own name is called. Then you wake up. You know you heard your name, but you do not know why. This is a clear example of perceiving what is meaningful to you and not perceiving what is not meaningful.

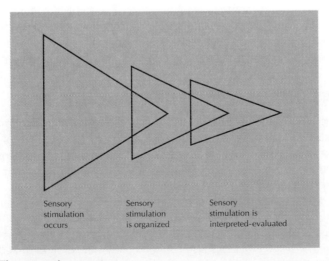

Sensory stimulation occurs

Sensory stimulation is organized

Sensory stimulation is interpreted-evaluated

FIGURE 4.1 The perception process.

Sensory Stimulation Is Organized

At the second stage, the sensory stimulations are organized according to various principles. One of the more frequently used principles is that of **proximity**: people or messages that are physically close to one another are perceived together, or as a unit. For example, you probably perceive people you often see together as a unit (such as a couple). Similarly, you perceive messages uttered one immediately after the other as a unit and assume that they are in some way related to each other. Another such principle is *closure*: you perceive as closed, or complete, a figure or message that is in reality unclosed or incomplete. For example, you see a broken circle as a circle even though part of it is missing. You would even perceive a series of dots or dashes arranged in a circular pattern as a circle. Similarly, you fill in the fragmented messages you hear with those parts that seem logically to complete the messages.

Proximity and closure are just two of the many organizing principles. In thinking about these principles, remember that whatever you perceive you also organize into a pattern that is meaningful to you. It is not a pattern that is necessarily true or logical in any objective sense.

Sensory Stimulation Is Interpreted-Evaluated

The third step in the perceptual process is *interpretation-evaluation*. This term is hyphenated to emphasize that its two parts cannot be separated. This third step is a subjective process involving evaluations on the part of the perceiver. Your interpretations-evaluations are not based solely on the external stimulus. Like communication, perception is a transactional process (Unit 2) and as a result is greatly influenced by your past experiences, needs, wants, value systems, beliefs about the way things are or should be, physical or emotional states at the time, expectations, and so on.

It should be clear from even this very incomplete list of influences that there is much room for individual interpretation of a given stimulus and hence disagreements. Although we may all be exposed to the same message, the way each person interprets-evaluates it will differ. The interpretation-evaluation will also differ for the same person from one time to another. The sound of a popular rock group may be heard by one person as terrible noise and by another as great music. The sight of someone you have not seen for years may bring joy to you and anxiety to someone else. The smell of perfume may be pleasant to one person and repulsive to another. A sweaty palm may be perceived by one person to show nervousness and by another to show excitement.

PROCESSES INFLUENCING PERCEPTION

Between the occurrence of the stimulus (the uttering of the message, presence of the person, a smile or wink of the eye) and the evaluation or interpretation of that stimulation, perception is influenced by a number of significant psychological processes. Before reading about these processes, take the following self-test to analyze your own customary ways of perceiving others.

Here we discuss seven major obstacles to accurate perception of others (Cook, 1971; Rubin, 1973; Rubin & McNeil, 1985): implicit personality theory, the self-fulfilling prophecy, perceptual accentuation, primacy-recency, consistency, stereotyping, and attribution. Each of these processes also contains potential barriers to accurate perception that can significantly distort your perceptions *and* your interpersonal interactions.

SELF-TEST

How Accurate Are You at People Perception?

Respond to each of the following statements with TRUE if the statement is usually accurate in describing your behavior. Respond with FALSE if the statement is usually inaccurate in describing your behavior.

F   1. I base most of my impressions of people on the first few minutes of our meeting.

T   2. When I know some things about another person I fill in what I don't know.

T   3. I make predictions about people's behaviors that generally prove to be true.

T   4. I have clear ideas of what people of different national, racial, and religious groups are really like.

T   5. I reserve making judgments about people until I learn a great deal about them and see them in a variety of situations.

T   6. On the basis of my observations of people, I formulate guesses about them (which I am willing to revise) rather than firm conclusions.

F   7. I pay special attention to people's behaviors that might contradict my initial impressions.

T   8. I delay formulating conclusions about people until I have lots of evidence.

T   9. I avoid making assumptions about what is going on in someone else's head on the basis of their behaviors.

T   10. I recognize that people are different, and I don't assume that everyone else is like me.

Scoring   This brief perception test was designed to raise questions we will consider in this and not to provide you with a specific "perception score." The first four questions represent distortions of some common process influencing perception. Ideally you would have responded "false" to these four questions. Questions 5–10 represent guidelines for increasing accuracy in perceptions. Ideally you would have responded with "true" to these six questions.

Implicit Personality Theory

Choose the characteristic in parentheses that best seems to complete each of these sentences:

John is energetic, eager, and (intelligent, unintelligent).
Mary is bold, defiant, and (extroverted, introverted).
Joe is bright, lively, and (thin, fat).
Jane is attractive, intelligent, and (likable, unlikable).
Susan is cheerful, positive, and (attractive, unattractive).
Jim is handsome, tall, and (flabby, muscular).

Certain choices in this list seem right and others seem wrong. What makes some seem right is implicit personality theory, the system of rules that tells you which characteristics go with other characteristics. Most people's theories tell them that a person who is energetic and eager is also intelligent. Of course, there is no logical reason why an unintelligent person could not be energetic and eager. Or is there?

Sitting on a park bench and people-watching is a favorite pastime for lots of us. As you watch people, how does your implicit personality theory operate? Do you have different theories for teenagers and for senior citizens? Do you have different theories for men and for women?

The widely documented "halo effect" is a function of the implicit personality theory. If you believe an individual has a number of positive qualities, you make the inference that she or he also has other positive qualities. The "reverse halo effect" operates in a similar way. If you know a person has a number of negative qualities, you are likely to infer that the person also has other negative qualities.

Potential Barriers   Two serious barriers may occur when you use implicit personality theories. Your tendency to develop personality theories and to perceive individuals as confirming your theory can lead you to

- perceive qualities in an individual that your "theory" tells you should be present when they actually are not. For example, you may see "goodwill" in the "charitable" acts of a friend when a tax deduction may be the real motive.
- ignore or distort qualities or characteristics that do not conform to your theory. You may ignore negative qualities in your friends that you would easily perceive in your enemies.

The use of implicit personality theories, with their halo and reverse halo effects, may lead to self-fulfilling prophecies, the second perceptual process.

The Self-Fulfilling Prophecy

A **self-fulfilling prophecy** occurs when you make a prediction or formulate a belief that comes true *because* you made the prediction and acted on it as if it were true (Insel & Jacobson, 1975; Merton, 1957). There are four basic steps in the self-fulfilling prophecy:

1. You make a prediction or formulate a belief about a person or a situation. *You predict that Pat is awkward in interpersonal situations.*
2. You act toward that person or situation as if that prediction or belief were true. *You act toward Pat as if Pat were awkward.*
3. Because you act as if the belief were true, it becomes true. *Because of the way you act toward Pat, Pat becomes tense and manifests awkwardness.*
4. You observe your effect on the person or the resulting situation, and what you see strengthens your beliefs. *You observe Pat's awkwardness, and this reinforces your belief that Pat is in fact awkward.*

If you expect people to act in a certain way or if you make a prediction about the characteristics of a situation, your predictions will frequently come true because of the self-fulfilling prophecy. Consider, for example, people who enter a group situation convinced that the other members will dislike them. Almost invariably they are proved right, perhaps because they act in a way that encourages people to respond negatively. Such people fulfill their own prophecies.

The Pygmalion Effect   A widely known example of the self-fulfilling prophecy is the Pygmalion effect (Rosenthal & Jacobson, 1992). In one study of this effect, teachers were told that certain pupils were expected to do exceptionally well, that they were late bloomers. The experimenters actually selected the students' names at random. The students whose names were selected actually did perform at a higher level than the other students. The expectations of the teacher probably generated extra attention to the students, thereby positively affecting their performance.

Potential Barriers   The self-fulfilling prophecy may create two potential barriers. Your tendency to fulfill your own prophecies can lead you to

- influence another's behavior so it confirms your prophecy.
- see what you predicted rather than what is really there; for example, it can lead you to perceive yourself as a failure because you have made this prediction rather than because of any actual setbacks.

Perceptual Accentuation

"Any port in a storm" is a phrase that appears in various guises throughout your communications. To the would-be actor, any part is better than no part at all. Spinach may taste horrible, but when you are starving, it can taste as good as pepperoni pizza. And so it goes.

This process, called *perceptual accentuation,* can lead you to see what you expect to see and what you want to see. You probably see people you like as being better-looking and smarter than people you do not like. The obvious counterargument to this is that you actually prefer good-looking and smart people and therefore seek them out. But perhaps that is not the entire story.

In a study reported by Zick Rubin (1973), male undergraduates participated in what they thought were two separate and unrelated studies that were actually two parts of a single experiment. In the first part, each subject read a passage. Half the subjects read an arousing sexual seduction scene. The other half read about sea gulls and herring gulls. In the second part of the experiment, subjects were asked to rate a female student on the basis of her photograph and a self-description. As predicted, the subjects who read the arousing scene rated the woman as significantly more attractive than did the other group. Further, the subjects who expected to go on a blind date with this woman rated her as more sexually receptive than did the subjects who were told that they had been assigned to date someone else. How can we account for such findings?

Although this experiment was a particularly dramatic demonstration of perceptual accentuation, this same general process occurs frequently. The thirsty person sees a mirage of water; the nicotine-deprived person sees a mirage of cigarettes and smoke.

Potential Barriers   Perceptual accentuation can create a variety of barriers. Your tendency to perceive what you want or need can lead you to

- distort your perceptions of reality; to make you perceive what you need or want to perceive rather than what is really there and to fail to perceive what you do not want to perceive. For example, people frequently perceive politeness and friendliness from a salesperson as demonstrating personal liking for them, not as a persuasive strategy. Similarly, you may not perceive that you are about to fail your chemistry course because you focus on what you want to perceive.
- filter out or distort information that might damage or threaten your self-image (for example, criticism of your writing or speaking) and thus make self-improvement extremely difficult.
- perceive in others the negative characteristics or qualities you have, a defense mechanism psychoanalysts refer to as *projection*.
- perceive and remember positive qualities better than negative ones (called the *Pollyanna effect*), and thus distort perceptions of others.

Primacy-Recency

Assume that you are taking a course in which half the classes are extremely dull and half are extremely exciting. At the end of the semester, you evaluate the course and the instructor. Would your evaluation be more favorable if the dull classes came during the first half of the semester and the exciting classes during the second half? Or would it be more favorable if the order were reversed? If what comes first exerts the most influence, the result is a **primacy effect**. If what comes last (or is the most recent) exerts the most influence, the result is a **recency effect**.

In an early study on the effects of primacy-recency in interpersonal perception, Solomon Asch (1946) read a list of adjectives describing a person to a group of subjects and found that the effects of sequence were significant. A person described as "intelligent, industrious, impulsive, critical, stubborn, and envious" was evaluated more positively than a person described as "envious, stubborn, critical, impulsive, industrious, and intelligent." The implication here is that you use early information to provide yourself with a general idea of what a person is like. You then use later information to make this general idea more specific. The obvious practical implication of primacy-recency is that the first impression you make is likely to be the most important. Through this first impression, others filter additional information to formulate a picture of who they perceive you to be.

Potential Barriers   Primacy-recency may lead to two major types of barriers. Your tendency to give greater weight to early information and to interpret later information in light of these early impressions can lead you to

- form a "total" picture of an individual on the basis of initial impressions that may not be typical or accurate. For example, you might form an image of someone as socially ill at ease. If this impression is based on watching this person at a stressful job interview, it is likely to be wrong.
- discount or distort later perceptions to avoid disrupting initial impressions. For example, you may fail to see signs of deceit in someone who made a good first impression.

Consistency

You have a strong tendency to maintain balance or consistency among your perceptions. **Consistency** represents people's need to maintain balance among their attitudes. You expect certain things to go together and other things not to go together. On a purely intuitive basis, for example, respond to the following sentences by noting the *expected* response.

1. I expect a person I like to (like, dislike) me.
2. I expect a person I dislike to (like, dislike) me.
3. I expect my friend to (like, dislike) my friend.
4. I expect my friend to (like, dislike) my enemy.
5. I expect my enemy to (like, dislike) my friend.
6. I expect my enemy to (like, dislike) my enemy.

According to most consistency theories, your expectations would be as follows: You would expect a person you liked to like you (Question 1) and a person you disliked to dislike you (2). You would expect a friend to like a friend (3) and to dislike an enemy (4). You would expect your enemy to dislike your friend (5) and to like your other enemy (6). All these expectations are intuitively satisfying. Or are they?

Further, you expect someone you like to have characteristics you like or admire. And you would expect your enemies not to possess characteristics you liked or admired. Conversely, you would expect persons you liked to lack unpleasant characteristics and persons you dislike to have unpleasant characteristics.

Potential Barriers   Consistency can create three major barriers. Your tendency to see consistency in an individual can lead you to

- ignore or distort your perceptions of behaviors that are inconsistent with your picture of the whole person. For example, you may misinterpret Karla's unhappiness because your image of Karla is "happy, controlled, and contented."
- perceive specific behaviors as emanating from positive qualities in people you like and from negative qualities in people you dislike. You therefore fail to see both positive and negative behaviors.
- see certain behaviors as positive if other behaviors were interpreted positively (the halo effect) or as negative if other behaviors were interpreted negatively (the reverse halo effect).

Stereotyping

A frequently used shortcut in perception is stereotyping. Originally **stereotype** was a printing term that referred to the plate that printed the same image over and over. A sociological or psychological stereotype is a fixed impression of a group of people. Everyone has attitudinal stereotypes—of national groups, religious groups, racial groups, or perhaps of criminals, prostitutes, teachers, or plumbers.

If you have these fixed impressions, you might, upon meeting a member of a particular group, see that person primarily as a member of that group. Initially, this may provide you with some helpful orientation. It creates problems when you apply to that person all the characteristics you assign to members of that group without examining this unique individual. If you meet a politician, for example, you may have a host of characteristics for politicians that you can readily apply to this person. To complicate matters further, you may see in this person's behavior the manifestation of various characteristics that you would not see if you did not know that this person was a politician. Although we often think of stereotypes as negative ("They're lazy, dirty, and only interested in getting high"), they may also be positive ("They're all smart, hardworking, and extremely loyal"). Whether negative or positive, stereotypes distort your ability to perceive other people accurately. They prevent you from seeing an individual as an individual rather than as a member of a group.

What stereotypes do you have about "the singles-scene people"? What stereotypes do you have about men? About women? About members of your own race? About members of races other than your own? How do those stereotypes influence your own communications with those who are similar to as well as those who are different from you?

Consider, however, another kind of stereotype: You're driving along a dark road and are stopped at a stop sign. A car pulls up besides you and three people jump out and rap on your window. There may be a variety of reasons for this: they need help, they want to ask directions, they want to tell you your trunk opened, or they may be in the process of carjacking. Your self-protective stereotype may help you decide on "carjacking" and may lead you to pull away and into the safety of a busy service station. In doing that, of course, you may have escaped being carjacked or you may have failed to help those who may have needed your help.

You may find it helpful to think critically about your own stereotypes. For example, what (if any) stereotypes do you have for:

- bodybuilders
- the opposite sex
- a racial group different from your own
- members of a religion very different from your own
- drug abusers or alcoholics
- college professors

What basis or evidence do you have for these stereotypes? How accurate generally are your stereotypes? What problems might these stereotypes lead to? Are there any benefits to these stereotypes?

Potential Barriers   Stereotyping can lead to two major barriers. Your tendency to group people into classes and to respond to individuals primarily as members of that class can lead you to

- perceive someone as having those qualities (usually negative) that you believe characterize the group to which he or she belongs (for example, all Venusians are lazy) and, therefore, fail to appreciate the multifaceted nature of all people and all groups.
- ignore the unique characteristics of an individual and therefore fail to benefit from the special contributions each can bring to an encounter.

Attribution

Attribution is a process through which you try to understand your own as well as others' behavior (Fiske & Taylor, 1984; Jones & Davis, 1965; Kelley, 1979). Especially important are the reasons or motivations for these behaviors.

Your task is to determine whether the cause of the behavior is *internal* or *external*. Internal behaviors are caused by the person's personality or some enduring trait. In this case you might hold the person responsible for his or her behaviors and you would judge the behavior and the person in light of this responsibility. External behaviors, on the other hand, are caused by a situational factor. In this case you might not hold the person responsible for his or her behaviors.

Consider an example. A teacher has given 10 students F's on a cultural anthropology examination. In an attempt to discover what this behavior (assignment of the 10 F's) reveals about the teacher, you have to determine whether the teacher was responsible for the behavior (the behavior was internally caused) or not (the behavior was externally caused). If you discover that a faculty committee made up the examination and that the committee set the standards for passing or failing, you could not attribute any particular motives to the teacher. You would have to conclude that the behavior was externally caused. In this case, it was caused by the department committee in conjunction with each student's performance on the examination.

On the other hand, assume that this teacher made up the examination and set the standards for passing and failing. Now you would be more apt to attribute the 10 F's to internal causes. You would be strengthened in your belief that something within this teacher (some personality trait, for example) led to this behavior if you discovered that (1) no other teacher gave nearly as many F's, (2) this particular teacher frequently gave F's in cultural anthropology, (3) this teacher frequently gave F's in other courses as well, and (4) this teacher was free to give grades other than F. These four bits of added information would lead you to conclude that something in this teacher motivated the behavior. Each of these new items of information represents one of the principles you use in making causal judgments, or attributions, in interpersonal perception: consensus, consistency, distinctiveness, and controllability.

Consensus   When you focus on the principle of **consensus**, you ask, "Do other people behave the same way as the person on whom I am focusing?" That is, does this person act in accordance with the general consensus? If the answer is no, you are more likely to attribute the behavior to some internal cause. In the previous example, you were strengthened in your belief that the teacher's behavior had an internal cause when you learned that other teachers did not follow this behavior—there was low consensus.

Consistency   When you focus on *consistency* you ask whether a person repeatedly behaves the same way in similar situations. If the answer is yes, there is high consistency, and you are likely to attribute the behavior to internal motivation. The fact that the teacher frequently gives F's in cultural anthropology leads you to attribute the cause to the teacher rather than to outside sources.

Distinctiveness   When you focus on the principle of **distinctiveness**, you ask if this person acts in similar ways in different situations. If the answer is yes, you are likely to conclude the behavior has an internal cause. Low distinctiveness indicates that this person acts in similar ways in different situations; it indicates that this situation is not distinctive.

Consider the alternative: Assume that this teacher gave all high grades and no failures in all other courses (that is, that the cultural anthropology class situation was distinctive). Then you would probably conclude that the motivation for the failures was external to the teacher and was unique to this class.

Controllability   Another principle to consider is whether the person was in control of the behavior. For example, let us say that you have invited your friend Desmond to dinner for seven o'clock and he arrives at nine. Consider how you would respond to the reasons he might give you for his lateness:

Reason No. 1: Oh, I got to watching this old movie and I wanted to see the end.
Reason No. 2: On my way here I witnessed a robbery and went to identify the thief in a lineup. The police phones were all tied up.
Reason No. 3: I got in a car accident and was taken to the hospital.

Assuming you would believe all three explanations, you would attribute very different motives to Desmond's behavior. With Reasons 1 and 2, you would conclude that Desmond was in control of his behavior; with Reason 3, you would conclude that Desmond was not in control of his behavior. Further, you would probably respond negatively to Reason 1 (Desmond was selfish and inconsiderate) and positively to Reason 2 (Desmond did his duty as a responsible citizen). Because Desmond was not in control of his behavior in Reason 3, you would probably not attribute either positive or negative motivation to Desmond's behavior. Instead you would probably feel sorry that he had an accident on the way to your house.

You probably make similar judgments based on controllability in numerous situations. Consider, for example, how you would respond to such situations as the following:

- Doris fails her midterm history exam.
- Sidney's car is repossessed because he failed to keep up with the payments.
- Margie is 150 pounds overweight and is complaining that she feels awful.
- Thomas's wife has just filed for divorce and he is feeling depressed.

Very probably you would be sympathetic to each of these people if you felt they were *not* in control of what happened—for example, if the examination was unfair, if Sidney lost his job because of employee discrimination, if Margie has a glandular problem, and if Thomas's wife is leaving him for a wealthy drug dealer. On the other hand, you might blame these people for their problems if you felt that they were in control of the situation—for example, if Doris partied instead of studied, if Sidney gambled his payments away, if Margie ate nothing but junk food and refused to exercise, and if Thomas had been repeatedly unfaithful and his wife finally gave up trying to change him.

In perceiving other people and especially in evaluating their behavior, you frequently ask if the person was in control of the behavior. Generally, research shows that if you feel people are in control of negative behaviors, you will come to dislike them. But you feel sorry for someone who you feel is not in control of negative behaviors, and you will not blame the person for his or her negative circumstances.

Low consensus, high consistency, low distinctiveness, and high controllability lead to an attribution of internal causes. As a result you praise or blame the person for his or her behaviors. High consensus, low consistency, high distinctiveness, and low controllability lead to an attribution of external causes. As a result you might consider this person lucky or unlucky. Table 4.1 summarizes these four principles of attribution.

Potential Barriers   Attribution of causality can lead to several major barriers. Your tendency to make judgments of others' behaviors can lead you to

- mind-read the motives of another person and confuse guesses with valid conclusions. This tendency is common in a wide variety of situations (attempts to mind-read are shown in italics): You forgot my birthday; *you don't love me.* You don't want to go to my parents' house for dinner; *you've never liked my parents.* You don't want to go to that interview; *you lack self-confidence.*
- fall into the **self-serving bias**, when you evaluate your own behaviors by taking credit for the positive and denying responsibility for the negative. You are

Table 4.1 A Summary of Causal Attribution

Situation: John was fired from a job he began a few months ago. On what basis will you decide whether this behavior is internally caused (and John is, therefore, responsible) or externally caused (and John is not responsible)?

Internal if:	External if:
No one else was fired. (low consensus)	Lots of others were fired. (high consensus)
John was fired from lots of other jobs. (high consistency)	John was never fired from any other job. (low consistency)
John has failed at lots of other things. (low distinctiveness)	John has always been successful. (high distinctiveness)
John could have been retained if he agreed to move to another shop. (high controllability)	John was not given any alternatives. (low controllability)

more likely to attribute your own negative behaviors to uncontrollable factors. For example, you are more likely to attribute getting a D on an exam to the difficulty of the test rather than to your failure to prepare adequately for it. And you are more likely to attribute your positive behaviors to controllable factors, to your own strength or intelligence or personality. For example, after getting an A on an exam, you are more likely to attribute it to your ability or hard work (Bernstein, Stephan, & Davis, 1979).

Figure 4.2 summarizes these seven influences and illustrates that any specific person perception may be influenced by these processes. You may find it interesting to identify your own people perceptions that have been influenced by each process.

CRITICAL PERCEPTION: MAKING PERCEPTIONS MORE ACCURATE

Communication and relational effectiveness depend in great part on your accuracy in interpersonal perception. You can improve accuracy by (1) employing strategies for reducing uncertainty, and (2) following some suggested guidelines.

General Strategies for Reducing Uncertainty

Communication is a gradual process during which people reduce uncertainty about each other. With each interaction, each person learns more about the other and gradually comes to know that person on a more meaningful level. Three major strategies help achieve this reduction in uncertainty: passive, active, and interactive strategies (Berger & Bradac, 1982).

Passive Strategies   When you observe another person without their being aware of it, you are employing *passive* strategies. One useful strategy is to observe the person in some active task, preferably interacting with other people in informal social situations.

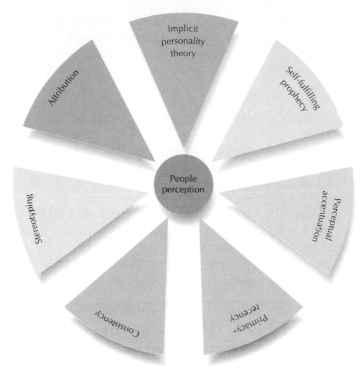

FIGURE 4.2 Processes influencing perception.

Active Strategies   Actively seeking information about a person in any way other than interacting with that person is to employ *active* strategies. For example, you can ask others about the person ("What is she like?" "Does he work out?" "Does she date guys younger than she is?"). You can also manipulate the environment in order to observe the individual in more specific and more revealing contexts. Employment interviews, theatrical auditions, and student teaching are examples of ways in which people manipulate situations to see how someone might act and react, hence reducing uncertainty about the person.

Interactive Strategies   When you interact with an individual, you are employing *interactive* strategies such as asking questions ("Do you enjoy sports?" "What did you think of that computer science course?" "What would you do if you got fired?").

You also gain knowledge of another by disclosing information about yourself. Self-disclosure creates a relaxed environment that encourages disclosures from the person about whom you wish to learn more (see Unit 3).

All three general strategies are useful for reducing your uncertainty about others. Unfortunately, many people feel they know a person well enough after employing only passive strategies. Active strategies are more revealing. Interactive strategies are more revealing still. Employing all three types of strategies will give you the most information.

Specific Strategies for Increasing Accuracy in Perception

In addition to avoiding the potential barriers in the various perceptual processes noted earlier and to employing all three general uncertainty-reduction strategies, here are a few more specific suggestions that will help you increase the accuracy of your interpersonal perceptions.

Look for a variety of cues pointing in the same direction. The more perceptual cues pointing to the same conclusion, the more likely that your conclusion will be correct.

Formulate hypotheses on the basis of your observations of behaviors. Test these against additional information and evidence. *Be especially alert to contradictory cues that will refute your initial hypotheses.* It is easier to perceive cues that confirm your hypotheses than to perceive contradictory evidence.

Delay drawing conclusions until you have had a chance to process a wide variety of cues. In drawing your conclusions, be sure to *recognize the diversity in people.* Do not assume that others are like you, that they think like you, or that they would act as you would. *Beware of your own biases*, for example, drawing positive conclusions about people you like and only negative conclusions about people you do not like.

Avoid mind reading ("You forgot my birthday because you don't really love me"). Remember that regardless of how many behaviors you observe and how carefully you examine these behaviors, you can only *guess* what is going on in another person's mind. A person's motives, attitudes, or values are not open to outside inspection. You can only make assumptions based on overt behaviors.

Check your perceptions. First seek validation. Compare your perceptions with those of others. Do others see Andrew as selfish and egocentric as you do? Second, check your perceptions with the person you are focusing on. For example, in response to a lukewarm agreement to go to your sister's house for dinner, you might ask your partner, "You don't seem anxious to go. Would you rather stay home?" A perception check, in its most basic form, consists of two steps:

- Describe (in tentative terms) what you think is happening as descriptively as you can: *You seem angry, You don't seem to want to go out this evening, You seemed disturbed when he said. . . , You sound upset with my plans.*
- Ask the other person for confirmation: *Are you angry? Do you feel like going out? Are you disturbed? Did my plans upset you?*

Summary

1. *Perception* refers to the process by which you become aware of the many stimuli impinging on your senses.

2. The *process* of perception consists of three stages: *sensory stimulation occurs*; *sensory stimulation is organized*; and *sensory stimulation is interpreted-evaluated*.

3. The following processes influence perception: (1) *implicit personality theory*, (2) *self-fulfilling prophecy*, (3) *perceptual accentuation*, (4) *primacy-recency*, (5) *consistency*, (6) *stereotyping*, and (7) *attribution*.

4. *Implicit personality theory* refers to the private personality theory that individuals hold and that influence how they perceive other people.

5. The *self-fulfilling prophecy* occurs when you make a prediction or formulate a belief that comes true *because* you have made the prediction and acted on it as if it were true.

6. *Perceptual accentuation* leads you to see what you expect and what you want to see.

7. *Primacy-recency* refers to the relative influence of stimuli as a result of the order in which you perceive them. If what occurs first exerts the greatest influence, you are influenced by the primacy effect. If what occurs last exerts the greatest influence, you are experiencing a recency effect.

8. *Consistency* refers to the tendency to perceive that which enables you to achieve psychological balance or comfort among various attitude objects and the connections between and among them.

9. *Stereotyping* is the tendency to develop and maintain fixed, unchanging perceptions of groups of people and to use these perceptions to evaluate individual members of these groups, ignoring their individual, unique characteristics.

10. *Attribution* is the process by which you try to understand your own and others' behaviors and the motivations for these behaviors. In this process you utilize four types of data: *consensus*, *consistency*, *distinctiveness*, and *controllability*.

11. Accuracy in perception can be increased by using the general strategies for reducing uncertainty (passive, active, and interactive) and the more specific strategies such as looking for a variety of cues, becoming alert to contradictory cues, and checking your perceptions.

Applications

4.1 HEARING THE BARRIERS TO PERCEPTION

Learning to hear the barriers to accurate perception in yourself and in others will help you avoid them or counteract them when used by others. For the next several days, record all personal examples of the four barriers to accurate perception. Record also the specific context in which these barriers occurred.

After you have identified the various barriers, share your findings in groups of five or six or with the entire class. As always, disclose what you wish to disclose and do not disclose what you do not want to disclose. You may find it profitable to discuss some or all of these questions:

1. Which barrier seems most frequent?

2. Which problems did the barrier cause?

3. What advantages do you gain when you avoid making first impressions? When you avoid using implicit theories? When you avoid making prophecies? When you avoid stereotyping?

4. What disadvantages are there in avoiding these shortcuts to people perception?

4.2   CRITICALLY EVALUATING CAUSAL ATTRIBUTIONS

For each of the following examples, indicate whether you think the behavior of the individual was due to *internal causes*—for example, personality characteristics and traits or various personal motives—or *external causes*—for example, the particular situation, the demands of others who might be in positions of authority, or the behaviors of others. The behavior in question appears in italics.

1. *Mita's performance in the race was disappointing.* For the last few days she had to tend to her sick grandfather and got too little sleep.

2. *Peter just quit his job.* No one else that you know has quit that job. Peter quit a number of jobs in the last five years and has in fact quit this same job once before.

3. *Karla just failed her chemistry test.* A number of other students (in fact, some 40 percent of the class) also failed the test. Karla has never failed a chemistry test before and, in fact, has never failed any other test in her life.

4. *Juan earned a substantial income from real estate.* His brother made the investment decisions for both of them.

5. *Liz tasted the wine, rejected it, and complained to the waiter.* No one else in the place complained about the wine. Liz has complained about the wine before and has frequently complained that her food was seasoned incorrectly, that the coffee was cold, and so on.

6. *Russell took the schoolchildren to the zoo.* Russell works for the board of education in a small town, and taking the students on trips is one of his major functions. All people previously on the job have taken the students to the zoo. Russell has never taken any other children to the zoo.

7. *John ran from the dog.* A number of other people also ran from this dog. I was surprised to see John do this because he has never run from other animals before and never from this particular dog.

8. *Donna received A's on all her speeches.* In fact, everyone in the class got

A's. This was the first A that Donna has ever received in public speaking and in fact the first A she has ever received in any course.

After you have responded to all eight examples, identify the information contained in the brief behavior descriptions that enabled you to make judgments concerning (1) consensus, (2) consistency, (3) distinctiveness, and (4) controllability. What combination of these principles would lead you to conclude that the behavior was internally motivated? What combination would lead you to conclude that the behavior was externally motivated?

LISTENING

UNIT CONTENTS

The Process of Listening

Listening Effectively

Active Listening

Summary

Applications

5.1 Listening for Message Distortions
5.2 Listening Actively

UNIT GOALS

After completing this unit, you should be able to

1. define *listening* and explain its five-part process

2. define and distinguish between *participatory* and *passive, empathic* and *objective, nonjudgmental* and *judgmental*, and *surface* and *deep* listening

3. define *active listening*, its functions and its techniques

There can be little doubt that we all listen a great deal. Upon awakening you listen to the radio. On the way to school you listen to friends, people around you, screeching cars, singing birds, or falling rain. In school you listen to the teacher, to other students, and sometimes even to yourself. You listen to friends at lunch and return to class to listen to more teachers. You arrive home and again listen to family and friends. Perhaps you listen to CDs, radio, or television. All in all, you listen for a good part of your waking day.

Before reading about this area of human communication, examine your own listening habits by taking the Listening Effectiveness Test.

SELF-TEST

How Good a Listener Are You?

Before you read about the barriers to listening and the guides to effective listening, examine your own listening habits and tendencies. Respond to each question using the following scale:

1 = always
2 = frequently
3 = sometimes
4 = seldom
5 = never

_____ 1. I focus on my own performance during an interaction, which results in my missing some of what the speaker has said.

_____ 2. I allow my mind to wander away from what the speaker is talking about.

_____ 3. I try to simplify messages I hear by omitting details.

_____ 4. I focus on a particular detail of what the speaker is saying instead of the general meaning the speaker wishes to communicate.

_____ 5. I allow my attitudes toward the topic or speaker to influence my evaluation of the message.

_____ 6. I hear what I expect to hear instead of what is actually being said.

_____ 7. I listen passively, letting the speaker do the work while I relax.

_____ 8. I listen to what others say but I don't feel what they are feeling.

_____ 9. I judge and evaluate what the speaker is saying before I fully understand the meaning intended.

_____ 10. I listen to the literal meaning that a speaker communicates but do not look for hidden or underlying meanings.

Scoring the Listening Effectiveness Test All statements describe ineffective listening tendencies. High scores, therefore, reflect effective listening and low scores reflect ineffective listening. If you scored significantly higher than 30, then you probably have better than average listening skills. Scores significantly below 30 represent lower than average listening skills. Regardless of your score, however, most people can significantly improve their listening skills. Each of the questions in this listening test refers to an obstacle or effectiveness principle discussed in this unit.

If we measured importance by the time we spend on an activity, then listening would be our most important communication activity. A glance at Figure 5.1, which diagrams the results of three studies, should illustrate this point. Figure 5.1(a) shows the percentage of time spent in four activities during the everyday lives of adults from a wide variety of occupations (Rankin, 1929). Figure 5.1(b) reflects the results from a similar study of adults as well as high school and college students done more recently (Werner, 1975). The results from a study on the communication activities of college students (Barker, Edwards, Gaines, Gladney, & Holley, 1980) is shown in Figure 5.1(c). These studies as well as others demonstrate that listening occupies more time than any other communication activity (Steil, Barker, & Watson, 1983; Wolvin & Coakley, 1982.

Another way to appreciate the importance of listening is to consider its many benefits. Table 5.1 presents six of these benefits.

THE PROCESS OF LISTENING

Because listening is often only vaguely and sometimes inaccurately understood, you need to examine the nature of listening more thoroughly. The process of **listening** can be described as a series of five steps: receiving, understanding, remembering, evaluating, and responding. The process is visualized in Figure 5.2. Note that the listening process is a circular one. The responses of Person A serve as the stimuli for Person B, whose responses in turn serve as the stimuli for Person A, and so on.

Receiving

Unlike listening, hearing begins and ends with this first stage of receiving. Hearing is something that just happens when you open your ears or when you get within earshot of some auditory stimuli. Listening, on the other hand, is quite different.

Listening begins (but does not end) with receiving the messages the speaker sends. The messages are both verbal and nonverbal; they consist of words as well as gestures, facial expressions, variations in volume and rate, and lots more as we will see when we discuss messages in more detail in Part 2.

At this stage you note not only what is said (verbally and nonverbally) but also what is omitted. Your friend's summary of good deeds as well as the omission of the broken promises are both received at this stage.

In receiving, you should try to

- focus your attention on the speaker's verbal and nonverbal messages, on what is said and on what is not said

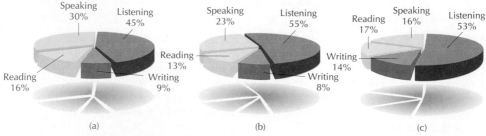

FIGURE 5.1 Amount of time spent listening.

Table 5.1 Six Benefits of Effective Listening

Effective listening increases:	Examples:
1. your ability to help others, because you'll hear more, empathize more, and come to understand others more deeply	1. If you listen to your child's complaints about her teacher (instead of responding with "now what did you do wrong?"), you'll be in a better position to help your child cope with school and with her teacher.
2. your social acceptance and popularity, because people come to like those who are attentive and supportive	2. Jack and Jill will increase their liking for you once they feel you have genuine concern attentive and supportive for them, a concern that is readily communicated through attentive and supportive listening.
3. your knowledge of others, the world, and yourself, because you will profit from the insights, experiences, and perceptions of others who have learned or seen what you have not	3. Listening to Peter talk about his travels to Moscow will help you understand more about Peter as well as more about life in Russia.
4. your ability to avoid problems and difficulties, because you will hear and be able to respond to warnings of impending problems before they develop or before they escalate and become impossible to control	4. Listening to student reactions (instead of responding with "students just don't want to work hard") will help the teacher plan more effective and relevant classes and be better able to respond to real student needs and concerns.
5. your power and influence, because people are more likely to respect and follow those who they feel have listened to them and understand them	5. Workers are more likely to follow your advice once they feel you have heard and really listened to their points of view, their concerns, and their insights.
6. your ability to make more reasoned and more reasonable decisions, because you'll acquire more information relevant to decisions you'll be called upon to make in business or in your personal life	6. Listening to the difficulties your sales staff has selling widgets (instead of responding with "you're just not trying hard enough") may help you design a more effective advertising campaign or offer more pertinent sales training.

- look for both feedback to your own previous messages as well as feedforward (Unit 1), which can tell you how the speaker would like his or her message viewed
- avoid distractions in the environment
- focus your attention on the speaker rather than on what you will say next
- maintain your role as listener and avoid interrupting the speaker until he or she is finished

Understanding

Understanding is the stage at which you learn what the speaker means. This understanding must take into consideration both the thoughts that are expressed as well as the emotional tone that accompanies these thoughts—the urgency or the joy or sorrow expressed in the message.

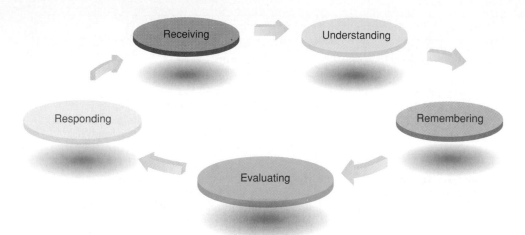

FIGURE 5.2 A five-stage model of listening. This model draws on a variety of previous models that listening researchers have developed (for example, Alessandra, 1986; Barker, 1990; Brownell, 1987; Steil, Barker, & Watson, 1983).

In understanding, try to

- relate the new information the speaker is giving to what you already know (in what way will your friend's information change your opinions of Pat and Chris?)
- see the speaker's messages from the speaker's point of view; avoid judging the message until it is fully understood as the speaker intended it
- ask questions for clarification, if necessary; ask for additional details or examples if these are needed
- rephrase (paraphrase) the speaker's ideas into your own words

Remembering

Messages that you receive and understand need to be retained for at least some period of time. In some small group and public-speaking situations you can augment your memory by taking notes or by tape-recording the messages. In most interpersonal communication situations, however, such note taking would be considered inappropriate, although you often do write down a phone number, an appointment, or directions.

What you remember is actually not what was said, but what you think (or remember) was said. Memory for speech is not reproductive; you don't simply reproduce in your memory what the speaker said. Rather, memory is reconstructive; you actually reconstruct the messages you hear into a system that seems to make sense to you—a concept noted in the discussion of perception. To illustrate this important concept, try to memorize the list of twelve words presented below (Glucksberg & Danks, 1975). Don't worry about the order of the words; only the number remembered counts. Don't read any further until you have tried to memorize the list of words. Take about 20 seconds to memorize as many words as possible.

Word List

bed	dream	comfort	awake	night	slumber
rest	wake	sound	tired	eat	snore

Now close the book and write down as many of the words from this list as you can remember. Don't read any further until you have tested your memory.

If you are like my students, you not only remembered a good number of the words on the list but you also "remembered" at least one word that was not on the list: sleep. Most people recall the word sleep being on the list—but it wasn't. What happens is that you do not simply reproduce the list but you reconstruct it. In this case you gave the list meaning, and part of that meaning included the word "sleep." You do this with all types of messages; you reconstruct the messages you hear into a meaningful whole and in the process often remember a distorted version of what was said.

In remembering, try to

- identify the central ideas and the major support advanced
- summarize the message in a more easily retained form but be careful not to ignore crucial details or qualifications
- repeat names and key concepts to yourself or, if appropriate, aloud

Evaluating

Evaluating consists of judging the messages in some way. At times you may try to evaluate the speaker's underlying intent. Often this evaluation process goes on without much conscious thought. For example, Elaine tells you that she is up for a promotion and is really excited about it. You may then try to judge her intention. Does she want you to use your influence with the company president? Is she preoccupied with her accomplishment and so tells everyone about it? Is she looking for a pat on the back? Generally, if you know the person well, you will be able to identify the intention and therefore be able to respond appropriately.

In other situations, the evaluation is more in the nature of critical analysis. For example, in listening to proposals advanced in a business meeting, you would at this stage evaluate them. Is there evidence to show that these proposals are practical and will increase productivity? Is there contradictory evidence? Are there alternative proposals that would be more practical and more productive?

In evaluating, try to

- resist evaluation until you fully understand the speaker's point of view
- assume that the speaker is a person of goodwill and give the speaker the benefit of any doubt by asking for clarification on issues that you feel you must object to (are there any other reasons for accepting this new proposal?)
- distinguish facts from inferences (see Unit 5), opinions, and personal interpretations by the speaker
- identify any biases, self-interests, or prejudices that may lead the speaker to slant unfairly what is presented

Responding

Responding occurs in two phases: (1) responses you make while the speaker is talking and (2) responses you make after the speaker has stopped talking. These responses are feedback—information that you send back to the speaker and which tells the speaker how you feel and think about his or her messages. Responses made while the speaker is talking should be supportive and should acknowledge that you are listening to the speaker. These include what nonverbal researchers call backchanneling cues, such as "I see," "yes," "uh-huh," and similar signals that let the speaker know that you are attending to the message.

Responses made after the speaker has stopped talking are generally more elaborate and might include expressing empathy ("I know how you must feel"), asking for clarification ("Do you mean that this new health plan is to replace the old one or will just be a supplement?"), challenging ("I think your evidence is weak here"), and agreeing ("You're absolutely right on this and I'll support your proposal when it comes up for a vote").

In responding, try to

- be supportive of the speaker throughout the speaker's talk by using and varying your backchanneling cues; using only one backchanneling cue—for example, saying "uh-huh" throughout will make it appear that you are not listening but are merely on automatic pilot
- express support for the speaker in your final responses
- be honest; the speaker has a right to expect honest responses, even if these express anger or disagreement
- respond to both the disclaimer (if there is one—see Unit 1) and the content message to let the speaker know that you heard the disclaimer and do retain a favorable impression of him or her. For example, appropriate responses might be: "I know you're not sexist, but I don't agree that. . . "
- state your thoughts and feelings as your own; use I-messages (for example, say "I think the new proposal will entail greater expense than you outlined" rather than "Everyone will object to the plan for costing too much.")

Do you find it easier to listen to and understand members of your own culture than members of other cultures? What specific elements of communication might you point out that make such listening easier or more difficult?

LISTENING EFFECTIVELY

Because you listen for different reasons and toward different ends, the principles you follow in listening effectively should vary from one situation to another. Here we identify four dimensions of listening and illustrate the appropriateness of different listening modes for different communication situations.

Participatory and Passive Listening

The key to effective listening is to participate. Perhaps the best preparation for participatory listening is to *act* like one who is participating (physically and mentally) in the communication act. This may seem trivial and redundant. In practice, however, it may be the most abused rule of effective listening. Students often, for example, put their feet up on a nearby desk, nod their head to the side, and expect to listen effectively. It just will not happen this way. To see why, recall how your body reacts to important news. Almost immediately you assume an upright posture, turn toward the speaker, focus your eyes on the speaker, and remain relatively still and quiet. You do this reflexively because this is how you listen most effectively. This is not to say that you should be tense and uncomfortable when listening, but your body should reflect your active mind.

Even more important than this physical alertness is mental alertness. As a listener, participate in the communication interaction as an equal partner with the speaker, as one who is emotionally and intellectually ready to engage in the mutual sharing of meaning.

Passive listening, however, is not without merit. Passive listening—listening without talking and without directing the speaker in any nonverbal way—is a powerful means for communicating acceptance. Passive listening allows the speaker to develop his or her thoughts and ideas in the presence of another person who accepts but does not evaluate, who supports but does not intrude. By listening passively, you provide a supportive and receptive environment. Once that has been established, you may wish to participate in a more active way, verbally and nonverbally.

Another form of passive listening is just to sit back, relax, and let the auditory stimulation massage you without exerting any significant energy or effort and especially without your directing the stimuli in any way. Listening to music for pure enjoyment (rather than as a music critic) is perhaps the best example.

In regulating participatory and passive listening, keep the following guidelines in mind:

- Work at listening. Listening is hard work, so be prepared to participate actively. Avoid what James Floyd (1985) calls "the entertainment syndrome": the expectation that a speaker will entertain you. Avoid daydreaming, the natural tendency to let your mind wander.
- Combat sources of noise as much as possible. Remove distractions or other interferences (newspapers, magazines, stereos), so your listening task will have less competition.
- Because you can process information more quickly than a speaker can speak, there is often time left over. Use this time to summarize the speaker's thoughts, formulate questions, and draw connections between what you have heard and what you already know.

- Assume there is value in what the speaker is saying. Resist assuming that what you have to say is more valuable than the speaker's remarks.

Empathic and Objective Listening

If you are to understand what a person means and what a person is feeling, you need to listen with empathy (Rogers, 1970; Rogers & Farson, 1981). To empathize with others is to feel with them, to see the world as they see it, to feel what they feel. Only when you achieve this can you understand another person's meaning fully.

There is no fast method for achieving empathy. But it is something you should work toward. It is important, for example, that a student see the teacher's point of view through the eyes of the teacher. And it is equally important for the teacher to see the student's point of view from the student's perspective. Popular students might understand intellectually the reasons why an unpopular student might feel depressed. But that will not enable them to understand the feelings of depression emotionally. To accomplish that, they must put themselves in the position of the unpopular student, to role play a bit and begin to feel that student's feelings and think that student's thoughts. Although for most communication situations, empathic listening is the preferred mode of responding, there are times when you need to go beyond it to measure the meanings and feelings against some objective reality. It is important to listen to Peter tell you how the entire world hates him and to understand how Peter feels and why he feels this way. But then you need to look a bit more objectively at Peter and perhaps see the paranoia or the self-hatred. Sometimes you have to put your empathic responses aside and listen with objectivity and detachment.

In adjusting your empathic and objective listening focus, keep the following recommendations in mind:

- Punctuate from the speaker's point of view. If you are to understand the speaker's perspective, you must see the sequence of events as the speaker does and ascertain how this can influence what the speaker says and does.
- Engage in dialogue, not monologue. View the speaker as an equal. Try to eliminate any physical or psychological barriers to equality to encourage openness and empathy (for example, step from behind the large desk separating you from your employees). Avoid interrupting the speaker—a sign that what you have to say is more important.
- Seek to understand both thoughts and feelings. Do not consider your listening task finished until you have understood what the speaker is feeling as well as thinking.
- Avoid "offensive listening," the tendency to listen to bits and pieces of information that will enable you to attack the speaker or find fault with something the speaker has said.
- Avoid focusing on yourself. For example, you may focus on your own performance in interaction, on whether you are communicating the right image or on assuming the role of speaker. During this time of self-focus, you inevitably miss what the speaker was saying.
- Strive especially to be objective when listening to friends or foes. Your attitudes may lead you to distort messages—to block out positive messages about a foe and negative messages about a friend. Guard against "expectancy hear-

ing," when you fail to hear what the speaker is really saying and instead hear what you expect.

Here, for example, are some typical situations. How would you respond empathically?

STEPHEN: I just can't seem to get my act together. Everything just falls apart as soon as I get involved.

PAT: I never felt so alone in my life. Chris left last night and said it was all over. We were together for three years and now—after a ten minute argument—everything is lost.

MARIA: I just got $20,000 from my aunt's estate. She left it to me! Twenty thousand! Now, I can get that car and buy some new clothes.

LIN: I just can't bear the thought of going into work today. I'm really fed up with the company. They treat us all like idiots.

Nonjudgmental and Critical Listening

Effective listening includes both nonjudgmental and critical responses. You need to listen nonjudgmentally—with an open mind with a view toward understanding. However, you also need to listen critically with a view toward making some kind of evaluation or judgment. Clearly, you should first listen for understanding and suspend judgment. Only after you have fully understood the relevant messages should you evaluate or judge. Listening with an open mind is extremely difficult. It is not easy, for example, to listen to arguments against some cherished belief or to criticisms of something you value. Further, you need to listen fairly, despite the red flag of an out-of-place expression or a hostile remark. Listening often stops when such a remark is made. Admittedly, to continue listening with an open mind is difficult. Yet it is particularly important in such situations that you do continue.

If meaningful communication is to take place, however, you need to supplement open-minded listening with critical listening. Listening with an open mind will help you understand the messages better. Listening with a critical mind will help you analyze that understanding and to evaluate the messages. As an intelligent and educated citizen, it is your responsibility to evaluate critically what you hear. This is especially true in the college environment. It is easy simply to listen to a teacher and take down what is said. Yet, it is perhaps even more important to evaluate and critically analyze what you hear. Contrary to what most students believe, most teachers appreciate the responses of critical listeners. They demonstrate that someone is listening and stimulate further examination of ideas.

In adjusting your nonjudgmental and critical listening, focus on the following guidelines:

- Keep an open mind. Avoid prejudging. Delay your judgments until you fully understand the intention and the content the speaker is communicating. Avoid both positive and negative evaluation until you have a reasonably complete understanding.
- Avoid filtering out difficult messages. Avoid oversimplification—the tendency to eliminate details and to simplify complex messages so they are easier to remember. Avoid filtering out undesirable messages. None of us wants to hear

that something we believe in is untrue, that people we care for are unkind, or that ideals we hold are self-destructive. Yet, it is important that educated people reexamine their beliefs by listening to these messages.

- Recognize your own biases. These may interfere with accurate listening and cause you to distort message reception through the process of **assimilation**—the tendency to integrate and interpret what you hear or think you hear with your own biases, prejudices, and expectations. For example, are your ethnic, national, or religious biases preventing you from appreciating a speaker's point of view?
- Judge content as delivered, not delivery as content. Although you should give attention to all aspects of the message (including delivery), do not focus on delivery to the exclusion of all else. For example, do not judge a speaker with a monotone as having nothing of interest to say, or a speaker with a foreign accent as being uninformed or uneducated.
- Avoid uncritical listening when you need to make evaluations and judgments.
- Recognize and combat the normal tendency to sharpen—a process in which one or two aspects of the message become highlighted, emphasized, and perhaps embellished. Often the concepts that are frequently sharpened are incidental remarks that somehow stand out from all the other messages.

Surface and Depth Listening

In Shakespeare's *Julius Caesar,* Marc Antony, in giving the funeral oration for Caesar, says: "I come to bury Caesar, not to praise him. / The evil that men do lives after them; / The good is oft interred with their bones." And later: "For Brutus is an honourable man; / So are they all, all honourable men." But Antony, as we know, did come to praise Caesar and to convince the crowd that Brutus was not an honorable man.

In most messages there is an obvious meaning that we can derive from a literal reading of the words and sentences. But there is often another level of meaning. Sometimes, as in *Julius Caesar,* it is the opposite of the literal meaning. At other times it seems totally unrelated. In reality, few messages have only one level of meaning. Most messages function on two or three levels at the same time. Consider some frequently heard messages: Carol asks you how you like her new haircut. On one level, the meaning is clear: Do you like the haircut? Do you like the painting? But there seems another level, perhaps a more important level: Carol is asking you to say something positive about her appearance. In the same way, the parent who complains about working hard at the office or in the home may in reality be asking for some expression of appreciation. The child who talks about the unfairness of the other children in the playground may be asking for affection and love, for some expression of caring. To appreciate these other meanings you need to engage in depth listening.

In listening, you have to be particularly sensitive to different levels of meaning. If you respond only to the surface-level communication (the literal meaning), you miss the opportunity to make meaningful contact with the other person's feelings and real needs. If you say to the parent, "You're always complaining. I bet you really love working so hard," you fail to respond to this call for understanding and appreciation.

In regulating your surface and depth listening, consider the following guidelines:

- Focus on both verbal and nonverbal messages. Recognize both consistent and inconsistent "packages" of messages and use these as guides for drawing inferences about the speaker's meaning. Ask questions when in doubt. Listen also to what is omitted. Remember that you communicate by what you leave out as well as by what you include. Listen, therefore, for omissions that may give you a clue to the speaker's meanings.

- Listen for both content and relational messages. The student who constantly challenges the teacher is on one level communicating disagreement over content. However, on another level—the relationship level—the student may be voicing objections to the instructor's authority or authoritarianism. To deal effectively with the student, the instructor must listen and respond to both types of messages.
- Listen carefully for disclaimers (Unit 1). What is the nature of the disclaimer? Why is it used here? What purpose does the speaker wish it to serve?
- Make special note of statements that refer back to the speaker. Remember that people inevitably talk about themselves. Whatever a person says is, in part, a function of who that person is. Listening for the different levels of meaning means attending to those personal, self-reference messages.
- See the forest, then the trees. Connect the specifics to the speaker's general theme rather than merely trying to remember isolated incidents.
- Do not disregard the literal meaning of interpersonal messages in trying to uncover the more hidden meanings. Balance your listening between surface and the underlying meanings. Respond to the various levels of meaning in the messages of others as you would like others to respond to yours—sensitively but not obsessively, readily but not overambitiously.

ACTIVE LISTENING

Active listening is a special kind of listening. It owes its development to Thomas Gordon (1975) who made it a cornerstone of his P-E-T (Parent-Effectiveness-Training) technique. Consider the following brief exchange:

SPEAKER: That creep gave me a C on the paper. I really worked on that project and I get a lousy C.

LISTENER 1: That's not too bad; most people got around the same grade. I got a C too.

LISTENER 2: So what? This is your last semester. Who cares about grades anyway?

LISTENER 3: You should be pleased with a C. Peggy and Michael both failed and John and Judy got D's.

LISTENER 4: You got a C on that paper you were working on for the last three weeks? You sound really angry and hurt.

All four listeners are probably anxious to make the speaker feel better. But they go about it in very different ways and, we can be sure, with very different results. The first three listeners give fairly typical responses. Listeners 1 and 2 both try to lessen the significance of a C grade. This is an extremely common response to someone who expresses displeasure or disappointment. It is also a most inappropriate response. It may be well-intended but it does little to promote meaningful communication and understanding. Listener 3 tries to make the C grade take on a more positive meaning. Note, however, that in the process these listeners are also saying a great deal more. All three listeners are also saying that the speaker should not be feeling as he or she does. They are saying the speaker's feelings are not legitimate and should be replaced with feelings that are more logical.

Listener 4, however, uses *active listening*. It is a process of sending back to the speaker what you as a listener think the speaker meant—both in content and in feelings. Active listening is not a process of merely repeating the speaker's exact words, but rather of putting together into some meaningful whole the listener's understanding of the speaker's total message.

The Functions of Active Listening

Active listening serves important functions. First, it enables the listener to check on his or her understanding of what the speaker said and, more important, what the speaker meant. When the listener reflects back to the speaker what he or she perceived to be the speaker's meaning, the listener gives the speaker an opportunity to clarify whatever needs clarification. In this way, future messages will have a better chance of being relevant and purposeful.

Second, through the process of active listening the listener expresses acceptance of the speaker's feelings. Note that in the sample responses given on page 87, the first three listeners challenged the speaker's feelings. The active listener, who reflected back to the speaker what he or she thought was said, gave the speaker acceptance. The speaker's feelings were not challenged. Rather, they were echoed in a sympathetic and empathic manner. Note too that in the first three responses the speaker's feelings are denied. Listener 4, however, not only accepts the speaker's feelings but identifies them explicitly ("You sound really angry and hurt"), again allowing an opportunity for correction.

Third, and perhaps most important, active listening stimulates the speaker to explore feelings and thoughts. With the response of listener 4, the speaker has an opportunity to elaborate on his or her feelings. Active listening encourages the speaker to explore and express thoughts and feelings. Active listening facilitates meaningful dialogue of mutual understanding. In stimulating this further exploration, active listening also encourages the speaker to solve his or her own problems by providing the opportunity to talk them through.

The Techniques of Active Listening

Three simple techniques may prove useful in learning active listening.

Paraphrase the Speaker's Thoughts   State in your own words what you think the speaker meant. This will help ensure understanding, since the speaker will be able to correct your restatement. It will also serve to show the speaker that you are interested in what is being said. Everyone wants to feel attended to, especially when angry or depressed.

The paraphrase also gives the speaker a chance to elaborate on or extend what was originally said. Thus, when Listener 4 echoes the speaker's thought, the speaker may next elaborate on why that C was an important one. Perhaps the speaker fears that the history paper will receive a similar grade.

Finally, in your paraphrase, be especially careful that you do not lead the speaker in the direction you think he or she should go. Paraphrases should be objective descriptions.

According to most research, men are less willing to communicate their inner feelings than are women. What implications might this have for active listening with men and with women?

Express Understanding of the Speaker's Feelings In addition to paraphrasing the content, echo the feelings you felt the speaker expressed or implied. ("I can imagine how you must have felt. You must have felt really horrible.") Just as the paraphrase enables you to check on your perception of the content, the expression of feelings will enable you to check on your perception of the speaker's feelings. This expression of feelings will also provide the speaker with the opportunity to see his or her feelings more objectively. It is helpful especially when the speaker feels angry, hurt, or depressed. We all need that objectivity; we need to see our feelings from a somewhat less impassioned perspective if we are to deal with them effectively.

When you echo the speaker's feelings, you also provide a stimulus for elaboration of these feelings. Most of us hold back our feelings until we are certain they will be accepted. When we feel they are accepted, we then feel free to go into more detail. Active listening gives the speaker this important opportunity. In echoing these feelings, however, be careful that you do not over- or understate the speaker's feelings. Just try to restate the feelings as accurately as you can.

Ask Questions Ask questions to ensure your own understanding of the speaker's thoughts and feelings and to secure additional information ("How did you feel when you read your job appraisal report?"). The questions should be designed to provide just enough stimulation and support for the speaker to express the thoughts and feelings he or she wants to express. Questions should not pry into unrelated areas or challenge the speaker in any way. These questions will further confirm your interest and concern for the speaker.

Summary

1. *Listening* is a five-part process that begins with receiving and continues through understanding, remembering, evaluating, and responding.

2. Effective listening involves adjusting our behaviors on the basis of at least four dimensions: *participatory and passive listening, empathic and objective listening, nonjudgmental and judgmental listening,* and *surface and deep listening.*

3. *Active listening* is listening in which you send back to the speaker what you think the speaker said and felt. Active listening enables the listener to check understanding, express acceptance, and stimulate the speaker to explore his or her feelings and thoughts.

4. Three major *techniques for active listening* are: (1) paraphrase the speaker's thoughts, (2) express understanding of the speaker's feelings, and (3) ask relevant questions.

Applications

5.1 LISTENING FOR MESSAGE DISTORTIONS

In this exercise, we listen to message interferences, especially omissions, additions, and distortions. The exercise involves serial communication and is similar to the old game of telephone. Six volunteers are selected, five of whom leave the room. The volunteer who is still in the classroom is read a message and instructed to repeat the message—as accurately and as completely as possible— to the second person. (It is helpful if class members have a copy of the verbal message so they can more completely identify the various distortions.) The second person likewise repeats the message to the third person. The process is continued until the sixth person repeats the message to the class. The class members may then address the following:

1. What kinds of information were *omitted*? At what point in the chain of communication were such omissions introduced? Did the omissions follow any pattern? That is, what kinds of information seemed more likely to be omitted?

2. What kinds of information were *added*? When? Can patterns be identified here, or are the additions totally random?

3. What kinds of information were *distorted*? When? Can the types of distortions be classified in any way? Were the distortions in the direction of increased simplicity? Increased complexity? Can you identify the reasons for the distortions?

Here is a message, modeled on one constructed by William Haney (1973), that will prove useful in this exercise:

> Every once in a while at George Washington Community College, the lions standing guard at the new Women's Political Center were sprayed with sexist graffiti. Whenever this happened, it cost the Center more

than $3000 to have them cleaned. The students from the Women's Center were promised by the president that if anyone was caught writing graffiti anywhere on campus, but especially on these lions, they would be expelled without any hope of ever returning.

5.2 LISTENING ACTIVELY

For each of the situations described below, supply at least one appropriate active listening response.

1. Your friend Phil has just broken up a love affair and is telling you about it. *I can't seem to get Chris out of my mind. All I do is daydream about what we used to do and all the fun we used to have.*

2. You and a fellow student are discussing the recent chemistry examination. *I know I failed the exam. What am I going to do now? I'll never get into medical school if I can't even pass Introductory Chemistry.*

3. Your cousin is bemoaning the lack of suitable relationship partners and the difficulties involved in forming long-lasting and productive relationships. He says, *I feel bad that I may never get married. I may never meet anyone I really care for and who would really care for me.*

4. Your mother has been having a difficult time at work. She was recently passed up for a promotion and received no merit raise. *I'm not sure what I did wrong. I do my work, mind my own business, and I don't take my sick days like everyone else. Maybe I should just quit and try to find something else.*

Questions and Activities

1. What area of communication will have the greatest role in your professional life? In your personal and social life?

2. In what other ways might you categorize feedback? What additional insights do the additional categories provide?

3. What other functions might feedforward serve? Have you heard any good examples of feedforward in the last few hours? Have you used feedforward? How does television use feedforward?

4. What ethical guideline do you use in judging whether communications are ethical or unethical?

5. What do you think is the single most important factor in communication effectiveness? In ineffective communication?

6. Which principle discussed in Unit 2 do you think is the most useful to effective family communication? To effective on-the-job communication? To effective teacher-student communication? To effective intercultural communication?

7. Can you identify specific relationships that you have that are generally symmetrical? Generally complementary?

8. Can you identify a specific example of a communication breakdown that was due to the failure to distinguish between content and relationship messages.

9. Can you identify a specific example of how the irreversibility of communication created problems for yourself or someone you know?

10. How would you describe your self-concept? What helps to make your self-concept more positive? More negative?

11. How would you describe your Johari Window with the following people:
    a. your parents (distinguish between mother and father if appropriate)
    b. your friends (distinguish among the types of friends if appropriate)
    c. your primary relational partner
    d. your dentist or doctor

12. How important to you is mutual self-disclosure in your close friendship or primary relationship? What would be the ideal self-disclosing situation between you and your friend or primary partner? What is the actual self-disclosing situation? What changes would you like to see in the self-disclosure that takes place in this relationship?

13. How accurate are you at interpersonal perceiving? Which perceptual processes discussed in Unit 4 influences you most? Does any of the seven processes not influence you at all? Which barriers influence you most?

14. Are you satisfied with the level of listening that others accord to you? What might you do to correct any dissatisfaction?

15. Write down the first impressions that you think people form of you. Next, interview a few of your friends and acquaintances and find out what first impressions these people formed of you. Are they similar? Different? What specific behaviors lead to these first impressions? Will you (should you) do anything on the basis of these findings?

Skill Check

_____ 1. I'm sensitive to **contexts** of communication. I recognize that changes in the physical, cultural, social-psychological, and/or temporal contexts will alter meaning. (Unit 1)

_____ 2. I look for **meaning** not only in words but in nonverbal behaviors as well. (Unit 1)

_____ 3. I am sensitive to the **feedback** that I give to others and that others give to me and regulate my own feedback on the basis of such dimensions as immediate-delayed, low-and high-monitoring, and critical-spontaneous. (Units 1)

_____ 4. I am sensitive to the **feedforward** that I give to others and that others give to me and use feedforward to open the channels of communication, preview future messages, disclaim, and altercast as appropriate. (Unit 1)

_____ 5. I combat the effects of physical, psychological, and semantic **noise** that distort messages. (Unit 1)

_____ 6. Because communication is a **package of signals**, I use my verbal and nonverbal messages to reinforce rather than contradict each other, and I respond to **contradictory messages** by identifying the dual meanings communicated and by discussing these openly. (Unit 2)

_____ 7. I listen to the **relational messages** that I and others communicate. I respond to the relational messages of others in order to increase meaningful interaction. (Unit 2)

_____ 8. I actively look for the **punctuation** pattern that I and others use in order to understand better the meanings communicated. (Unit 2)

_____ 9. Because **communication is inevitable**, I look carefully for meanings that may be hidden. (Unit 2)

_____ 10. Because **communication is irreversible**, I am especially cautious in communicating messages that I may later wish to withdraw. (Unit 2)

_____ 11. I actively seek to increase **self-awareness** by talking with myself, listening to others, reducing my blind self, seeing myself from different perspectives, and increasing my open self. (Unit 3)

_____ 12. I actively seek to increase my self-esteem by engaging in self-affirmation, seeking out nourishing people, working on projects that
will result in success, and realizing that I do not have to be loved by
everyone.

_____ 13. I self-disclose when appropriate. (Unit 3)

_____ 14. I respond to the disclosures of others appropriately. (Unit 3)

_____ 15. Recognizing the operation of primacy-recency, I actively guard
against first impressions that might prevent accurate perceptions of
subsequent events. (Unit 4)

_____ 16. To guard against the self-fulfilling prophecy, I take a second look at
my perceptions when they conform too closely to my expectations.
(Unit 4)

_____ 17. I guard against perceptual accentuation by being careful that my
perception of an event is not unduly influenced by what I expect or
want to see. (Unit 4)

_____ 18. I bring to consciousness my implicit personality theories. (Unit 4)

_____ 19. I understand how the need for balance or consistency can distort
my perceptions. (Unit 4)

_____ 20. I avoid stereotyping. (Unit 4)

_____ 21. In attempting to account for behavior, I apply the principles of attribution theory. (Unit 4)

_____ 22. In attempting to account for my own behavior, I take into consideration the possible operation of the self-serving bias. (Unit 4)

_____ 23. In seeking to understand others' behaviors I avoid mind reading.

_____ 24. I practice effective listening. (Unit 5)

_____ 25. I am especially careful to avoid prejudging messages or filtering out
messages that may appear too complex or too unpleasant. (Unit 5)

_____ 26. I use the skills of active listening when appropriate. (Unit 5)

SUGGESTED READINGS

Arnold, Carroll C. and John Waite Bowers, eds. *Handbook of Rhetorical and Communication Theory*. Boston, Mass.: Allyn & Bacon, 1984. A collection of 14 original
scholarly essays focusing on the functions of human communication.

Berger, Charles R. and Steven H. Chaffee, eds. *Handbook of Communication Science*.
Newbury Park, CA.: Sage, 1987. Twenty-eight original scholarly articles covering
the broad field of human communication.

DeVito, Joseph A. *The Communication Handbook: A Dictionary*. New York: Harper &
Row, 1986. A dictionary of terms used in the study of communication along with
brief essays on some of the more important terms. Also includes references for
more in-depth study of selected terms.

Infante, Dominic A., Andrew S. Rancer, and Deanna F. Womack. *Building Communication Theory*, 2nd ed. Prospect Heights, Il.: Waveland Press, 1993. An excellent

survey of the theoretical foundations of human communication.

Watzlawick, Paul, Janet Helmick Beavin, and Don D. Jackson. *Pragmatics of Human Communication: A Study of Interactional Patterns, Pathologies, and Paradoxes*. New York: Norton, 1967. One of the most influential works in the field of communication; established the transactional viewpoint and clarified many of the fundamental principles of communication.

Textbooks in human communication can provide much additional insight and perspective. Especially useful are Pearson and Nelson (1991), Williams (1989) and Rubin (1988). Adler (1989), Curtis, Floyd, and Winsor (1992), and O'Hair and Friedrich (1992) discuss many of the same areas within a business context. More advanced texts, centering on the theories of human communication, include Trenholm (1986), Stacks, Hickson, and Hill (1991), and Littlejohn (1992). Griffin's (1991) discussion of theory is interestingly presented in short separate chapters.

Popular works in human communication are plentiful and for the most part focus on improving communication skills. Some of the more useful general works include Adams (1989), Ailes (1988), Dawson (1992), Eisen (1984), and Schloff and Yudkin (1991).

MESSAGES: VERBAL AND NONVERBAL

Unit 6. **Preliminaries to Verbal and Nonverbal Messages**
Unit 7. **Verbal Message Barriers**
Unit 8. **Verbal Message Principles**
Unit 9. **Nonverbal Messages of Body and Sound**
Unit 10. **Nonverbal Messages of Space and Time**
Unit 11. **Messages in Conversation**
  Part 2. **Feedback**
    Questions and Activities
    Skill Check
    Suggested Readings

In this part we focus on the verbal and nonverbal message systems. In Unit 6, we cover some of the ways verbal and nonverbal messages interact and the nature of meaning and messages. The next two units focus on verbal messages and identify the major barriers to and principles of effective verbal interaction. In Units 9 and 10 we look at nonverbal messages. In Unit 9 we consider how you communicate with your body—for example, gestures, face, and eyes, and paralanguage (variations in, for example, rate, volume, and pausing). Unit 10 focuses on space (including territoriality, closeness to others, colors, and space decoration), touch, and time. In Unit 11 we bring verbal and nonverbal systems together and examine how they operate in everyday conversations.

Approaching Verbal and Nonverbal Messages

In approaching verbal and nonverbal messages, keep the following in mind:

- Your messages are combinations of verbal and nonverbal signals, and their effectiveness depends on how well you integrate them.
- Language is a social institution. It is a part of your culture and reflects that culture. See language within a social context, always inquiring into the social implications of language usage.
- Resist the temptation to draw conclusions about people on the basis of isolated bits of message behavior, whether verbal, nonverbal, or both.
- Observe. Observe. Observe. Look at your own communications and interactions and see the various verbal and nonverbal behaviors discussed here and in class. Learn to see in practice what you read about here in theory.

PRELIMINARIES TO VERBAL AND NONVERBAL MESSAGES

UNIT CONTENTS

The Interaction of Verbal and Nonverbal Messages

Meanings and Messages

Message Characteristics

Summary

Applications

6.1 Breaking Nonverbal Rules
6.2 Communicating Verbally and Nonverbally

UNIT GOALS

After completing this unit, you should be able to

1. diagram and explain Wendell Johnson's Model of Meaning

2. explain the major ways in which nonverbal and verbal messages interact

3. explain these principles of meaning: meanings are in people, meanings are more than words, meanings are unique; meanings are denotative and connotative; and meanings are context-based

4. explain these principles of messages: messages are rule-governed, messages vary in directness, messages vary in believability, and messages may metacommunicate

In this unit we introduce the message system, the system you use to communicate meaning to another person. The message system comprises both a verbal and a nonverbal part. The verbal portion is language—the words, phrases, and sentences you use. The nonverbal portion consists of a wide variety of elements—spatial relationships, time orientation, gestures, facial expressions, eye movements, touch, and variations in the rate and volume of your speech.

THE INTERACTION OF VERBAL AND NONVERBAL MESSAGES

In face-to-face communication you blend verbal and nonverbal messages to best convey your meanings. Here are six ways in which nonverbal messages are used with verbal messages; these will help you highlight this important verbal-nonverbal interaction.

Accenting   Nonverbal communication is often used to emphasize some part of the verbal message. You might, for example, raise your voice to underscore a particular word or phrase, bang your fist on the desk to stress your commitment, or look longingly into someone's eyes when saying "I love you."

Complementing   Nonverbal communication may add nuances of meaning not communicated by your verbal message. Thus, you might smile when telling a story (to suggest that you find it humorous) or frown and shake your head when recounting someone's deceit (to suggest your disapproval).

Contradicting   You may deliberately contradict your verbal messages with nonverbal movements—for example, by crossing your fingers or winking to indicate that you are lying.

Regulating   Movements may be used to control, or to indicate your desire to control, the flow of verbal messages, as when you purse your lips, lean forward, or make hand gestures to indicate that you want to speak. You might also put up your hand or vocalize your pauses (for example, with "um") to indicate that you have not finished and are not ready to relinquish the floor to the next speaker.

Repeating   You can repeat or restate the verbal message nonverbally. You can, for example, follow your verbal "Is that all right?" with raised eyebrows and a questioning look, or motion with your head or hand to repeat your verbal "Let's go."

Substituting   You may also use nonverbal communication to take the place of verbal messages. For instance, you can signal "OK" with a hand gesture. You can nod your head to indicate yes or shake your head to indicate no.

MEANINGS AND MESSAGES

Meaning is an active process created by cooperation between source and receiver—speaker and listener, writer and reader. This process is illustrated in the model developed by communication theorist Wendell Johnson (1951) and is illustrated in Figure

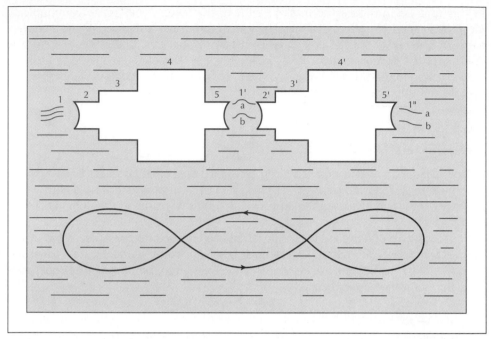

FIGURE 6.1 Johnson's model of communication. *Source:* Wendell Johnson, "The Spoken Word and the Great Unsaid," *Quarterly Journal of Speech* 37 (1951): 421.

6.1. Although it may seem complex, the model is actually simple when compared to the truly complex process of transmitting meaning from one person to another. The surrounding rectangle shows that communication takes place in a context external to both speaker and listener. The twisted loop indicates that the stages of communication are interrelated and interdependent.

The actual process begins at stage 1, which represents the occurrence of an event—-anything that can be perceived. This is the stimulus. At stage 2 the observer is stimulated through one or more sensory channels. The relatively small opening at 2 reflects the fact that out of all the possible stimuli in the world, only a small number actually stimulate the observer. At stage 3 organismic evaluations occur. Nerve impulses travel from the sense organs to the brain, causing certain bodily changes, for example, in muscular tension. At stage 4 the sensations aroused at stage 3 are beginning to be translated into verbal and nonverbal signals, a process that takes place in accordance with the individual's unique communication habits. At stage 5, from all the possible verbal and nonverbal symbols, certain ones are selected and arranged in a pattern.

At 1' the verbal and nonverbal behaviors emitted by the speaker by means of sound and light waves stimulate the receiver, much as the outside event at 1 stimulated the source. At 2' the receiver is stimulated. At 3' there are organismic evaluations. At 4' sensations begin to be translated into verbal and nonverbal symbols. At 5' certain of these symbols are selected and arranged. At 1" these symbols, in the form of sound or light waves, are emitted and stimulate another receiver. The process is continuous.

This model suggests several important principles of meaning and effective interpersonal interaction, to which we now turn.

Meanings Are in People

Meaning depends not only on messages (whether verbal, nonverbal, or both) but on the interaction of those messages and the receiver's own thoughts and feelings. You do not "receive" meaning; you create meaning. Words do not mean; people mean. Consequently, to uncover meaning, you need to look into people and not merely into words.

An example of the confusion that can result when this relatively simple fact is overlooked is provided by Ronald D. Laing, H. Phillipson, and A. Russell Lee in *Interpersonal Perception* (1966) and analyzed with insight by Paul Watzlawick in *How Real Is Real?* (1977): A couple on the second night of their honeymoon are sitting at a hotel bar. The woman strikes up a conversation with the couple next to her. The husband refuses to communicate with the couple and becomes antagonistic toward his wife as well as the couple. The wife then grows angry because he has created such an awkward and unpleasant situation. Each becomes increasingly disturbed, and the evening ends in a bitter conflict in which each is convinced of the other's lack of consideration. Eight years later, they analyze this argument. Apparently the idea of *honeymoon* had meant very different things to each of them. To the husband it had meant a "golden opportunity to ignore the rest of the world and simply explore each other." He felt his wife's interaction with the other couple implied there was something lacking in him. To the

As we explain in depth in Unit 22, members of some cultures make their meanings verbally explicit, whereas others leave a great deal implied. Members in those latter cultures are supposed to understand such implied meanings from the general context, from knowing the people, from understanding the social relationships among the people, and so on. Without reading about the specific differences between these two types of cultures, how would describe your own culture? How do those patterns relate to the principle that meanings are in people? What implications does this have for communication?

wife, *honeymoon* had meant an opportunity to try out her new role as wife. "I had never had a conversation with another couple as a wife before," she said. "Previous to this I had always been a 'girlfriend' or 'fiancee' or 'daughter' or 'sister.'"

Meanings Are More Than Words and Gestures

When you want to communicate a thought or feeling to another person, you do so with relatively few symbols. These represent just a small part of what you are thinking or feeling, much of which remains unspoken. If you were to try to describe every feeling in detail, you would never get on with the job of living. The meanings you seek to communicate are much more than the sum of the words and nonverbal behaviors you use to represent them.

Because of this, you can never fully know what another person is thinking or feeling. You can only approximate it on the basis of the meanings you receive, which, as already noted, are greatly influenced by who *you* are and what *you* are feeling. Conversely, others can never fully know you; they too can only approximate what you are feeling. Failure to understand another person or to be understood are not abnormal situations. They are inevitable, although you should realize that you can always understand another person a little better than you now do.

Meanings Are Unique

Because meanings are derived from both the messages communicated and the receiver's own thoughts and feelings, no two people ever derive the same meanings. Similarly, because people change constantly, no one person can derive the same meanings on two separate occasions. Who you are can never be separated from the meanings you create. As a result, you need to check your perceptions of another's meanings by asking questions, echoing what you perceive to be the other person's feelings or thoughts, and seeking elaboration and clarification—in general, practicing all the skills identified in the discussion on effective interpersonal perception and listening (Units 4 and 5).

Also recognize that as you change, you also change the meanings you created out of past messages. Thus, although the message sent may not have changed, the meanings you created from it yesterday and the meanings you create today may be quite different. Yesterday, when a special someone said, "I love you," you created certain meanings. But today, when you learn that the same "I love you" was said to three other people or when you fall in love with someone else, you drastically change the meanings you perceive from those three words.

Meanings Are Both Denotative and Connotative

To explain denotative and connotative meaning, consider a word like *death*. To a doctor this word might mean, or denote, simply the point at which the heart stops beating; that is, an objective description of a particular event. To a mother whose son has just died, on the other hand, the word means much more. It recalls the son's youth, his ambitions, his family, his illness, and so on. To her the word is emotional, subjective, and highly personal. These emotional, subjective, and personal reactions are the word's connotative meaning. The **denotation** of a word is its objective definition; the **connotation** is its subjective or emotional meaning.

Now consider a simple nod of the head in answer to the question, "Do you agree?" This gesture—in American culture—is largely denotative and simply says yes. What about a wink or a smile or a vigorous nod of the head? These nonverbal expressions are more connotative; they express feelings rather than communicate objective information.

Some words and nonverbal behaviors are primarily denotative, such as *perpendicular*, *parallel*, nodding the head, and the OK sign made with thumb and index finger. Other words and behaviors, such as derogatory racial names, curse words, smiles, and touches are primarily connotative and often have little denotative meaning. In short, your signals—whether words or nonverbal behaviors—may vary from highly denotative to highly connotative. A good way to determine whether a message has connotative meaning is to ask where it would fall on a good-bad scale. If *good* and *bad* do not seem to apply, then it has little, if any, connotative meaning for you. If, however, you can place the message on the good-bad scale with some conviction, it has connotative meaning for you.

Another distinction between the two types of meaning has already been implied: The denotative meaning of a message is more general or universal; most people would agree with the denotative meanings and would give similar definitions. Connotative meanings, however, are extremely personal, and few people would agree on the precise connotative meaning of a word or nonverbal behavior. Test this idea by trying to get a group of people to agree on the connotative meanings of such words as *religion*, *God*, *democracy*, *wealth*, and *freedom* or of such nonverbal behaviors as raised eyebrows, arms folded in front of one's chest, or sitting with one's legs crossed. Chances are very good that it will be impossible to reach an agreement.

Meanings Are Context-Based

Verbal and nonverbal communications exist in a context, and that context to a large extent determines the meaning of any verbal or nonverbal behavior. The same words or behaviors may have totally different meanings when they occur in different contexts. For example, the greeting, "How are you?" means "Hello" to someone you pass regularly on the street but means "Is your health improving?" when said to a friend in the hospital. A wink to an attractive person on a bus means something completely different from a wink that signifies a put-on or a lie. Similarly, the meaning of a given signal depends on the other behaviors it accompanies or is close to in time. Pounding a fist on the table during a speech in support of a politician means something quite different from that same gesture in response to news of a friend's death. Divorced from the context, it is impossible to tell what meaning was intended just from examining the signals. Of course, even if you know the context in detail, you still may not be able to decipher the meaning of the verbal or nonverbal message.

Here, for example, are "semantic differential" scales for rating the meanings of words. Take a few terms—*love, college, gay, parents, religion, abortion, racism*, and *happiness* will work well—and rate each term by writing the initial letter of each term in the space coresponding to *your* meaning on each of the bipolar scales. For example, if you feel that "love" is *extremely kind* or *extremely cruel* write "L" in the space next to "kind" or next to "cruel." If you feel that love is *quite kind* or *quite cruel* write "L" in the 2nd or 6th space. If *slightly kind* or *slightly cruel* use the 3rd or 5th space. If you feel it is neither kind nor cruel then use the middle (*neutral*) space. Compare your responses with others. Does this experience illustrate the five principles of meaning just considered: meanings are in people, more than words and gestures, unique, both denotative and connotative, and context-based?

kind	——:——:——:——:——:——:——	cruel
large	——:——:——:——:——:——:——	small
good	——:——:——:——:——:——:——	bad
pleasant	——:——:——:——:——:——:——	unpleasant
ugly	——:——:——:——:——:——:——	beautiful
active	——:——:——:——:——:——:——	passive
hot	——:——:——:——:——:——:——	cold
sharp	——:——:——:——:——:——:——	dull
light	——:——:——:——:——:——:——	heavy

MESSAGE CHARACTERISTICS

Interpersonal communication messages are governed by rules, vary in directness, vary in believability, and may refer to objects and events in the real world as well as to other messages. Reviewing these four message characteristics will enable you to understand better how interpersonal messages are transferred and how you can better control your own messages.

Messages Are Governed by Rules

The rule-governed nature of verbal communication is well known. All languages have rules that native speakers follow in producing and understanding sentences, although they may be unable to state them explicitly.

Nonverbal communication is also regulated by a system of rules or norms that state what is and what is not meaningful, appropriate, expected, and permissible in specific social situations. And of course these rules will vary greatly from one culture to another. Rules are cultural (and relative) institutions; they are not universal laws (see Units 22 and 23 on intercultural communication).

You learned the ways to communicate nonverbally *and* the rules of meaningfulness and appropriateness from observing the behaviors of the adult community. For example, you learned how to express sympathy along with the rules that your culture has established for expressing it appropriately. You learned that touch is permissible under certain circumstances but not under others and which types of touching are permissible and which are not. You learned that women may touch each other in public; for example, they may hold hands, walk arm in arm, engage in prolonged hugging, and even dance together. You also learned that men may not do this, at least not without inviting social criticism. And, perhaps most obvious, you learned that there are certain parts of the body that may not be touched and others that may. As a relationship changes, so do the rules of touching. As you become more intimate, the rules for touching become less restrictive.

In the United States, direct eye contact signals openness and honesty. But in various countries of Latin America and among some Native Americans, direct eye contact between, say, a teacher and a student is considered inappropriate, perhaps aggressive;

appropriate student behavior is to avoid eye contact with the teacher. From even this simple example it is easy to see how miscommunication can take place. To a teacher in the United States, avoidance of eye contact by a Latin American or Native American could signify guilt, disinterest, or disrespect, when in fact the student is following her or his own culturally established rules.

Messages Vary in Directness

Consider the following sentence sets:

1. I'm so bored; I have nothing to do tonight.
2. I'd like to go to the movies. Would you like to come?

1. Do you feel like hamburgers tonight?
2. I'd like hamburgers tonight. How about you?

The statements numbered 1 are indirect; they are attempts to get the listener to say or do something without committing the speaker. Number 2 statements are direct—-they state clearly the speaker's preferences and then ask the listeners if they agree. A more obvious example of an indirect message occurs when you glance at your watch to communicate that it is late and that you had better be going. Such messages serve at least two important functions.

Indirect messages allow you to express a desire without insulting or offending anyone; they allow you to observe the rules of polite interaction. So instead of saying,

In some cases, as in giving directions, you expect and want a very direct form of communication. In what situations would you prefer the other person to be more indirect? Why?

"I'm bored with this group," you say, "It's getting late and I have to get up early tomorrow," or you look at your watch and pretend to be surprised by the time. Instead of saying, "This food tastes like cardboard," you say, "I just started my diet" or "I'm stuffed." In each instance you are stating a preference but are saying it indirectly so as to avoid offending someone.

Sometimes indirect messages allow you to ask for compliments in a socially acceptable manner, such as saying, "I was thinking of getting a nose job." You hope to get the desired compliment: "A nose job? You? Your nose is perfect."

Indirectness, largely because it enables a person to avoid appearing criticized or contradicted and thereby losing face, is the preferred mode of address in many Asian and Latin American cultures. In Unit 22 we elaborate on this concept in the discussion of high and low context cultures.

Problems with Indirect Messages   Indirect messages, however, can also create problems. Consider the following dialogue in which an indirect request is made:

> PAT: You wouldn't like to have my parents over for dinner this weekend, would you?
> CHRIS: I really wanted to go to the shore and just relax.
> PAT: Well, if you feel you have to go to the shore, I'll make the dinner myself. You go to the shore. I really hate having them over and doing all the work myself. It's such a drag shopping, cooking, and cleaning all by myself.

Win-Lose and Win-Win Situations   Given this situation, Chris has two basic alternatives. One is to stick with the plans to go to the shore and relax. In this case Pat is going to be upset and Chris is going to be made to feel guilty for not helping with the dinner. A second alternative is to give in to Pat, help with the dinner, and not go to the shore. In this case Chris is going to have to give up a much-desired plan and is sure to resent Pat's manipulative tactics. Regardless of which decision is made, one person wins and one person loses. This is referred to as a win-lose situation—a situation that creates resentment, competition, and often an "I'll get even" mentality.

With direct requests, this type of situation is much less likely to develop. Consider:

> PAT: I'd like to have my parents over for dinner this weekend. What do you think?
> CHRIS: Well, I really wanted to go to the shore and just relax.

Regardless of what develops next, both individuals are starting out on relatively equal footing. Each has clearly and directly stated a preference. In this case, these preferences seem mutually exclusive. But it might be possible to meet both persons' needs. For example, Chris might say, "How about going to the shore this weekend and having your parents over next weekend? I'm really exhausted; I could use the rest." Here is a direct response to a direct request. Unless there is some pressing need to have Pat's parents over for dinner this weekend, this response may enable each to meet the other's needs.

With the use of indirect requests, win-win outcomes are difficult to see because of an implied inequality and an attempt to manipulate the other person from the outset. Direct requests, on the other hand, do not employ manipulation. The result is that win-

win solutions readily suggest themselves, and the defensiveness that makes accepting an alternative plan difficult or ego-threatening is avoided. Here both parties can get what they want; it is a win-win situation—a situation that creates supportiveness and a willingness to cooperate.

Responsibility and Honesty   Indirect requests can cause other problems. Note that in saying "You don't really want to have my parents over for dinner this weekend," Pat tries to shift the responsibility for the decision to Chris. With a statement like "I'd like to have my parents over for dinner this weekend," the speaker owns his or her own statements, thoughts, and feelings.

Perhaps the most obvious difference between direct and indirect requests is that direct requests are honest and open; indirect requests are often, though not always, dishonest and manipulative. Direct questions encourage open, honest, and supportive responses; indirect questions encourage responses that are resentful, dishonest, and defensive.

Messages Vary in Believability

For the most part, research shows that when verbal and nonverbal messages conflict, people believe the nonverbal. Nonverbal theorist Dale Leathers (1986), for example, reports that nonverbal cues are more than four times as effective as verbal cues in their impact on interpersonal impressions and 10 times more important in expressing confidence. For most messages, a good guess is that approximately 60 to 65 percent of meaning is communicated nonverbally (Burgoon, Buller, & Woodall, 1989).

Nonverbal cues help you to guess whether or not a person is lying. You also use them to help you discover the underlying truth that the lie is meant to conceal. Interestingly enough, as you become more and more intimate with a person, your ability to detect the underlying truth that your partner is trying to hide declines. Research also shows that women are better than men at discovering the underlying truth (McCormack & Parks, 1990).

Why do people believe the nonverbal message rather than the verbal one? It may be that verbal messages are easier to fake. Consequently, when there is a contradiction, you distrust the verbal and accept the nonverbal. Or it may be that nonverbal messages often function below the level of conscious awareness. You learned them without being aware of such learning, and you perceive them without conscious awareness. Thus, when such a conflict arises, you somehow get a "feeling" from the nonverbal messages. Since you cannot isolate its source, you assume that it is somehow correct.

Believability and Deception   Usually your verbal and nonverbal behavior is consistent; it comes as a package. When you lie verbally, you also try to lie nonverbally; you always strive for consistency. Yet both your verbal and your nonverbal behaviors often betray you. Researchers have identified a number of behaviors that often accompany deception. Generally, a liar moves less than a person who is telling the truth, talks more slowly (perhaps to give herself or himself the time needed to create the fabrication or mentally check on the consistency of the story), and makes more speech errors. The best indicator of lying, according to Albert Mehrabian (1978), is that the liar uses fewer words, particularly in answering questions. The liar gives monosyllabic answers and generally does not elaborate on them.

When compared with truth tellers, liars pause longer before answering questions and use longer pauses throughout their communications (Cody, Marston, & Foster, 1984). Further, they use more generalizing phrases, for example, adding "stuff like that" and "you know" to the ends of sentences. Liars also use less concrete terms, and they speak of nonspecific activities ("hung out," "had fun") more often than truth tellers. They refer less frequently to specific persons and places. You also use general categories to judge whether or not a person is telling the truth. Friendliness, attentiveness, and preciseness, for example, have been found to be good predictors of honesty (O'Hair, Cody, Goss, & Krayer, 1988).

Remember to interpret communication behaviors (verbal and nonverbal) within the context in which they occur. The examples just cited should be used to suggest hypotheses, not firm conclusions, about possible deceit. After reviewing the extensive literature on deception, Paul Ekman, in *Telling Lies* (1985), cautions: "Evaluating behavioral clues to deceit is hazardous . . . . The lie catcher must always estimate the *likelihood* that a gesture or expression indicates lying or truthfulness; rarely is it absolutely certain."

Messages May Metacommunicate

Metacommunication is communication that refers to other communications. All behavior, verbal and nonverbal, can be metacommunicational. Verbally, you can say, for example, "This statement is false" or "Do you understand what I am trying to tell you?" These refer to communication and are called *metacommunicational statements*.

Nonverbal behavior may also be metacommunicational. Obvious examples include crossing one's fingers behind one's back or winking when telling a lie. But the more subtle instances of metacommunication are more interesting: You end your blind date, but even as you say "I had a really nice time," the nonverbal messages—the lack of a smile, the failure to maintain eye contact, the extra-long pauses—contradict the verbal "really nice time" and tell your date that you did not enjoy the evening.

Nonverbal messages may also metacommunicate about other nonverbal messages. The individual who, upon meeting a stranger, both smiles and extends a totally lifeless hand shows how one nonverbal behavior may contradict another.

Usually when nonverbal behavior is metacommunicational, it reinforces other verbal or nonverbal behavior. You may literally roll up your sleeves when talking about cleaning up the room, smile when greeting someone, run to meet the person you say you are eager to see, greet your dentist with a frown, or arrive early for a party you verbally express pleasure in attending.

Here are just a few ways to use metacommunication to check that your message is understood as you wish it to be:

- Give clear feedforward. This will help the other person get a general picture of the message that will follow. It will provide a kind of schema that makes information processing and learning easier.
- Give specific examples. Many people talk in too many and too high abstractions. Thus, if you talk of "financial security"—a relatively high-level abstraction—your listener may think "job security" when you want to emphasize the importance of "insurance." Specific examples will help make your abstrac-

tions clearer and will help your listener focus on the specifics you wish him or her to focus on.

- Confront contradictory or inconsistent messages. At the same time, explain your own messages that may appear inconsistent to your listener. Refer to the discussion of mixed messages in Unit 2.

- Explain the feelings that go with the thoughts. Often people communicate only the thinking part of their message, resulting in listeners being unable to hear the other parts of their meaning. Communicate how you feel as well as what you think.

- Paraphrase your own complex messages. It will help listeners understand you if they hear the same idea phrased differently. Similarly, to check on your own understanding of another's message, try to paraphrase what you think the other person means.

- Ask questions. If you have doubts about another's meaning, don't assume you understand; instead, ask for clarification.

Summary

1. Verbal and nonverbal messages interact and accent, complement, contradict, regulate, repeat, and substitute for each other.

2. *Meaning* is an active process created by cooperation between source and receiver; it is a function of the interaction of messages and the receiver's previous experiences, expectations, attitudes, and so on.

3. Meanings are (a) in people, (b) more than words and gestures, (c) unique, (d) both *denotative* (objective) and *connotative* (subjective), and (e) *context-based*.

4. Messages are rule-governed: both verbal and nonverbal communication messages follow rules that are learned and known by native communicators.

5. Messages vary in *directness*.

6. Messages vary in *believability*: when verbal and nonverbal messages contradict each other, people are more apt to believe the nonverbal.

7. Messages may refer to objects in the world or to other messages (*metacommunication*).

Applications

6.1   BREAKING NONVERBAL RULES[1]

The general objective of this exercise is to become better acquainted with some of the rules of nonverbal communication (in this case, rules from North American culture) and to analyze some of the effects of breaking these rules. You learn nonverbal language much the same way you learn verbal language—without explicit instruction. Among such rules might be:

1. Upon entering an elevator, turn to the door and stare at it or at the numbers indicating which floor the elevator is on until your floor is reached.

2. When sitting next to or near someone, do not invade the person's private space with your body or belongings.

3. When strangers are talking, do not enter their group.

4. When talking with someone, do not stand too close or too far away. You may move closer when talking about intimate topics. Never stand so close that you can smell the other person's odor. This rule may be broken only under certain conditions, for example, when the individuals involved are physically attracted to each other, when one individual is consoling another, or when engaged in a game whose rules require this close contact.

5. When talking in an otherwise occupied area, lower your voice so that other people are not disturbed by your conversation.

[1]The idea for this exercise was suggested by Professor Jean Civikly, University of New Mexico.

Procedure

Form pairs, with one student in each pair designated as the rule breaker and the other the observer. The task of the rule breaker is simply to enter some campus situation in which one or more rules of nonverbal communication would normally be operative and to break one or more rules. The task of the observer is to record mentally (or in writing, if possible) what happens as a result of the rule breaking.

Each pair should return after a specified amount of time and report what happened to the entire class.

Note: No rules should be broken if it means infringing on the rights of others.

6.2 COMMUNICATING VERBALLY AND NONVERBALLY

To illustrate the integration of verbal and nonverbal, read each of the following statements and describe (rather than act out) the nonverbal messages that you would use in making these statements in normal conversation.

1. Hurry up; we're late already.
2. You look great!
3. Hold on. What did you say?
4. How many?
5. You talked to Madonna?
6. I'm not feeling well.
7. I don't agree with that.
8. I'm depressed.
9. I feel so satisfied and relaxed.
10. Well, what do you want to do?

VERBAL MESSAGE BARRIERS

UNIT CONTENTS

Polarization

Intensional Orientation

Fact-Inference Confusion

Bypassing

Allness

Static Evaluation

Indiscrimination

  Summary

  Applications
    7.1 I, You, and Them Talk
    7.2 Thinking in E-Prime
    7.3 Barriers in Language in Action

UNIT GOALS

After completing this unit, you should be able to

1. define *polarization, intensional orientation, fact-inference confusion, bypassing, allness, static evaluation,* and *indiscrimination*

2. explain how these barriers can be avoided

3. identify examples of these misevaluations in your own communications and in those of others (including the media)

4. explain the role of the *et cetera,* the date, and the index in reducing the barriers in language and verbal interaction

Communication may break down or encounter barriers at any point in the process from sender to receiver. Here we look at seven possible barriers in verbal messages (DeVito, 1974; Haney, 1973; Rothwell, 1982). These barriers may appear in intrapersonal, interpersonal, small group, public speaking, intercultural, and mass communications.

POLARIZATION

Polarization refers to the tendency to look at the world in terms of opposites and to describe it in extremes—good or bad, positive or negative, healthy or sick, intelligent or stupid. It is often referred to as the fallacy of "either-or" or "black and white." Although magnetic poles are either positive or negative and certain people are extremely rich while others are extremely poor, most people are in the middle. Most people exist somewhere between the extremes of good and bad, healthy and sick, intelligent and stupid, rich and poor. Yet people have a strong tendency to view only the extremes and to categorize other people, objects, and events in terms of these polar opposites.

This tendency is easily illustrated by the following example. In the second space after each of the following words, fill in the polar opposites for that word:

hot _____   _____
high _____   _____
good _____   _____
popular _____   _____
sad _____   _____

Filling in these opposites was probably easy for you. Also, the words you supplied were probably short. Further, if a number of people supplied opposites, you would find a high degree of agreement among them.

Now try to fill in the middle positions with words meaning, for example, "midway between high and low," "midway between hot and cold." You probably had greater difficulty here. And you probably took more time to think of these middle terms. You also probably used multiword phrases. Further, you would probably find less agreement among different people completing this same task.

Take a look at the familiar bell-shaped curve (Figure 7.1). Notice that few items exist at either of the two extremes. As you move closer to the center, however, more and more items are included. This is true of any random sample. If you selected a hundred people at random you would find that their intelligence, height, weight, income, age, health, and so on would, if plotted, fall into a bell-shaped or "normal" distribution. Yet the common tendency is to concentrate on the extremes at either end of this curve and ignore the middle, which contains the vast majority of cases.

You create problems, however, when you use the absolute form in inappropriate situations—for example, "The politician is either for us or against us." These options do *not* include all possibilities. The politician may be for you in some things and against you in other things, or may be neutral. During the Vietnam War people were categorized as either hawks or doves. But clearly there were many people who were neither and many who were hawks on certain issues and doves on others.

In correcting this tendency to polarize, beware of implying (and believing) that two extreme classes include *all* possible classes—that an individual must be a hawk or a dove, with no other alternatives. "Life is either a daring adventure or nothing," said

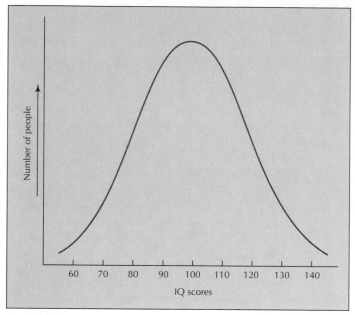

FIGURE 7.7 A bell-shaped curve.

Helen Keller. But for most people it is neither a daring adventure nor nothing, but something somewhere in between these two extremes.

INTENSIONAL ORIENTATION

Intensional orientation (the *s* in *intensional* is intentional) refers to the tendency to view people, objects, and events in the way they are talked about and the way they are labeled. For example, if Sally is labeled "uninteresting" you would, responding intensionally, evaluate her as uninteresting before listening to what she had to say. *Extensional orientation,* on the other hand, is the tendency to look first to the actual people, objects, and events and only afterward to their labels—for example, seeing Sally without any preconceived labels. It is the tendency to be guided by what you see happening rather than by the label used for what is happening.

Intensional orientation occurs when you act as if the labels are more important than the things they represent—as if the map is more important than the territory. An extreme form of intensional orientation is seen in the person who, afraid of dogs, begins to sweat when shown a picture of a dog or when hearing people talk about dogs. Here the person is responding to the label (a picture or verbal description) as if it were the actual thing (a dog).

Visualize yourself seated with a packet of photographs before you. Each photograph shows a person you have never seen before. You are asked to scratch out the eyes in each photograph. You are further told that this is simply an experiment and that the individuals whose pictures you have will not be aware of anything that has happened here. As you progress through the pictures, scratching out the eyes, you come upon a photograph of your mother. What do you do? Are you able to scratch out the eyes as you have done with the pictures of the strangers? Or have you somehow lost your ability to scratch out eyes? If, like many others, you are unable to scratch out the eyes, you are responding intensionally. You are, in effect, responding to the map (in this case the picture) as if it were the territory (your own mother).

Correcting Intensional Orientation

The way out of intensional orientation is to extensionalize. Give your main attention to the people, things, and events in the world as you see them and not as they are presented in words. For example, when you meet Jack and Jill, observe them, interact with them. Then form your impressions. Don't respond to them as "greedy, money-grubbing landlords" because Harry labeled them this way. Don't respond to Carmen as "lazy and inconsiderate" because Elaine told you she was.

FACT-INFERENCE CONFUSION

You can make statements about the world you observe, and you can make statements about what you have not observed. In form or structure these statements are similar, and you cannot distinguish them by any grammatical analysis. For example, you can say, "She is wearing a blue jacket," as well as "He is harboring an illogical hatred." If you diagrammed these sentences they would yield identical structures. Yet it is clear that these are very different types of statements. You can observe the jacket and the blue color, but how do you observe "illogical hatred"? Obviously, this is not a descriptive but an inferential statement. It is a statement made on the basis not only of what you observe, but of what you infer.

There is nothing wrong with making inferential statements. You must make them to talk about much that is meaningful. The problem arises when you act *as if* those inferential statements are factual, a phenomenon called **fact-inference confusion**. Consider, for example, the following anecdote (Maynard, 1963):

> A woman went for a walk one day and met a friend whom she had not seen, heard from, or heard of in 10 years. After an exchange of greetings, the woman said: "Is this your little boy?" and her friend replied, "Yes, I got married about six years ago." The woman then asked the child, "What is your name?" and the little boy replied, "Same as my father's." "Oh," said the woman, "then it must be Peter."

How did the woman know the boy's father's name when she had not seen, heard from, or heard of her friend in the last 10 years? The answer is obvious, but only after you recognize that in reading this short passage you have made an unconscious inference that is preventing you from answering a simple question. Specifically, you have inferred that the woman's friend is a woman. Actually, the friend is a man named Peter.

You may wish to test your ability to distinguish facts from inferences by taking the fact-inference test on page 116.

Correcting Fact-Inference Confusion

Table 7.1, based on Haney (1973), summarizes the differences between factual and inferential statements. Inferential statements need to be made tentatively. Recognize that such statements may prove to be wrong. Inferential statements should leave open the possibility of alternatives. If, for example, you treat the statement "Our biology

SELF-TEST

Can You Distinguish Facts from Inferences?

Instructions: Carefully read the following report, modeled on one developed by William Haney (1973), and the list of observations based on it. Indicate whether you think the observations are true, false, or doubtful on the basis of the information presented in the report. Write *T* if the observation is definitely true, *F* if the observation is definitely false, and *?* if the observation may be either true or false. Judge each observation in order. Do not reread the observations after you have indicated your judgment, and do not change any of your answers.

A well-liked college teacher had just completed making up the final examinations and had turned off the lights in the office. Just then a tall, broad figure appeared and demanded the examination. The professor opened the drawer. Everything in the drawer was picked up and the individual ran down the corridor. The dean was notified immediately.

_____ 1. The thief was tall and broad.

_____ 2. The professor turned off the lights.

_____ 3. A tall figure demanded the examination.

_____ 4. The examination was picked up by someone.

_____ 5. The examination was picked up by the professor.

_____ 6. A tall figure appeared after the professor turned off the lights in the office.

_____ 7. The man who opened the drawer was the professor.

_____ 8. The professor ran down the corridor.

_____ 9. The drawer was never actually opened.

_____ 10. Three persons are referred to in this report.

Scoring   This test was designed to sensitize you to the difficulty to making factual statements. In small groups of five or six discuss your responses. What conclusions are you willing to draw from this discussion and this test? Your instructor will provide the "correct" answers.

teacher was fired for poor teaching" as factual, you eliminate the possibility of any alternatives. When making inferential statements, be psychologically prepared to be proved wrong. If you are thus prepared, you will be less hurt if you are shown to be incorrect.

BYPASSING

Bypassing is a pattern of misevaluation in which people fail to communicate their intended meanings. It is "the miscommunication pattern which occurs when the *sender* (speaker, writer, and so on) and the *receiver* (listener, reader, and so forth) *miss each other with their meanings*" (Haney, 1973).

Bypassing can take one of two forms. One type of bypassing occurs when two people use different words but give them the same meaning. On the surface there is disagreement but at the level of meaning there is agreement. Consider the following dialogue:

Table 7.1 Differences Between Factual and Inferential Statements

Factual Statements	Inferential Statements
1. May be only after observation	1. May be made at any time.
2. Are limited to what has been observed	2. Go beyond what has been observed
3. May be made only by the observer	3. May be made by anyone
4. May only be about the past or the present	4. May be about any time—past, present, future
5. Approach certainty	5. Invove varying degrees of probability
6. Are subject to verifiable standards	6. Are not subject to verifiable standards

PAT: I want a permanent relationship. I'm not interested in one-night stands. [*Meaning: I want to date you exclusively and I want you to date me exclusively*].

CHRIS: I'm not ready for that. [*Thinking and meaning: marriage*]. Let's keep things the way they are. [*Meaning: let's continue dating only each other.*]

This scenario illustrates a situation in which two people agree but assume, because they use different words (some of which may actually never be verbalized), that they disagree.

The second type is more common. This form of bypassing occurs when two people use the same words but give the words different meanings. On the surface it looks

How would you define "cultural bypassing"? What relevance might this concept have for communication around your college campus? For communication in your professional life?

like the two people agree (simply because they are using the same words). But if you look more closely you see that the apparent agreement masks real disagreement. Consider this brief dialogue:

> PAT: I don't really believe in religion. [Meaning: I don't really believe in God.]
> CHRIS: Neither do I. [Meaning: I don't really believe in organized religions.]

Here Pat and Chris assume they agree, but actually they disagree. At some later date the implications of these differences may well become crucial.

Numerous other examples could be cited. Couples who say they are "in love" may mean very different things; one person may mean "a permanent and exclusive commitment" while the other may mean "a sexual involvement." "Come home early" may mean one thing to an anxious parent and quite another to a teenager.

The underlying assumption in bypassing is that words have intrinsic meanings. You incorrectly assume that when two people use the same word they mean the same thing, and when they use different words those words have different meanings. But words do not have meaning; meaning is in the people who use those words.

Correcting Bypassing

One obvious corrective for this misevaluation, as Haney (1973) points out, is to look for meaning in the person and not in the words. Remember, as pointed out in the discussion of Johnson's (1951) model of meaning, that words may be assigned a wide variety of meanings by different people and, alternatively, people may use different words to communicate the same meaning.

A second corrective is to use the active listening techniques discussed in Unit 5. By paraphrasing the speaker you can verify whether there is agreement or disagreement, not in the words but in the communicators. By reflecting back the speaker's thoughts and feelings, you can see whether you understand the speaker. You also provide the speaker with an opportunity to clarify any misunderstanding or ambiguity. At the same time you can verify your own perception of the speaker's meanings.

ALLNESS

Because the world is infinitely complex, you can never know all or say all about anything. The poem by John Saxe about the six blind men and the elephant is an excellent example of an **allness** orientation and its problems. You may recall from elementary school that in Saxe's poem, six blind men come from Indostan to examine an elephant, an animal they have only heard about. From their different vantage points around the elephant's body— the side, tusk, trunk, knee, ear, and tail—the six men draw six different conclusions about what the elephant is like: a wall, a spear, a snake, a tree, a fan, and a rope, respectively. Each man reaches his own conclusion regarding what this marvelous beast is really like. Each argues that he is correct and that the others are wrong. Each, of course, is correct; but at the same time each is wrong.

Each of us is in the position of the six blind men. You never see all of anything. You never experience anything fully. You see part of an object, an event, a person. On that limited basis you then conclude what the whole is like. Of course, you have to draw conclusions on the basis of insufficient evidence (you always have insufficient evidence). And yet you must also recognize that when you make judgments based only on a part, you are actually making inferences that can later be proved wrong.

Disraeli, the famous British prime minister, once said that "to be conscious that you are ignorant is a great step toward knowledge." That observation is an excellent example of a **nonallness** attitude. If you recognize that there is more to learn, more to see, and more to hear, you will leave yourself open to finding additional information.

Correcting Allness

A useful device to help you remember your nonallness orientation is to end each statement, verbally or mentally, with an *et cetera*—a reminder that there is more to learn, more to know, and more to say, and that every statement is inevitably incomplete.

Some people overuse the *et cetera*. They use it not to mentally remind themselves that there is more to know and more to say but rather as a substitute for being specific. This, of course, defeats the purpose of the *et cetera*.

STATIC EVALUATION

When you form an abstraction of something or someone or you make a verbal statement about an event or person, that abstraction or statement remains static. But notice that the object or person to whom it originally referred may change enormously. Alfred Korzybski (1933), the founder of the study of language called General Semantics, used an interesting illustration in this connection: In a tank are a large fish and many small fish, which are the natural food for the large fish. Given freedom in the tank, the large fish will eat the small fish. The tank is then partitioned, with the large fish on one side and the small fish on the other, divided only by a clear piece of glass. For a considerable time the large fish will attempt to eat the small fish but will fail each time. Each time it will knock into the glass partition. After some time it learns that trying to eat the small fish is impossible and will no longer go after them. Now, however, the partition is removed and the little fish swim all around the big fish. But the big fish does not eat them and in fact will die of starvation. The large fish has learned a pattern of behavior, and even though the actual territory has changed, the map remains static.

While you would probably agree that everything is in a constant state of flux, the relevant question is whether you act as if you know this. Do you act in accordance with the notion of change, instead of just accepting it intellectually? Do you treat your little sister as if she were 10 years old, or do you treat her like the 20-year-old woman she has become? Your evaluations of yourself and others must keep pace with the rapidly changing real world. Otherwise you will be left with attitudes and beliefs about a world that no longer exists—what are called **static evaluations**.

Correcting Static Evaluation

To guard against static evaluation, date your statements and especially your evaluations. Remember that Pat Smith$_{1994}$ is not Pat Smith$_{1990}$; academic abilities$_{1993}$ are not academic abilities$_{1995}$. T. S. Eliot, in *The Cocktail Party*, said that "what we know of other people is only our memory of the moments during which we knew them. And they have changed since then . . . at every meeting we are meeting a stranger."

How has the perception of members of your nationality, gender, religion, or race changed over the past 100 years among members of the city in which you now live? Over the past 25 years? Over the past 5 years?

INDISCRIMINATION

Nature seems to abhor sameness at least as much as a vacuum, for nowhere in the universe will you find two things that are identical. Everything is unique. Everything is unlike everything else.

Our language, however, provides you with common nouns, such as *teacher, student, friend, enemy, war, politician,* and *liberal,* which lead you to focus on similarities. Such nouns lead you to group all teachers together, all students together, and all friends together. At the same time, these terms divert attention away from the uniqueness of each person, each object, and each event. **Indiscrimination** occurs when you focus on classes of people, objects, or events and fail to see that each is unique and needs to be looked at individually.

This misevaluation is at the heart of the common practice of stereotyping national, racial, and religious groups. A *stereotype* (Unit 4) is a fixed mental picture of some group that you apply to each individual of the group without regard to his or her unique qualities. Regardless of whether your stereotypes are positive or negative, the problem they create is the same. They provide you with shortcuts that are often inappropriate. For example, when you meet a particular person, your first reaction may be to pigeonhole him or her into some category—perhaps religious, national, or academic. Regardless of the type of category you use, you fail to give sufficient attention to the unique characteristics of the individual before you. Although two people may both be Christian, for example, each will be different from the other. Indiscrimination is a denial of another person's uniqueness.

Correcting Indiscrimination

A useful antidote to indiscrimination is the index, a verbal or mental subscript that identifies each individual as an individual even though two individuals may be covered by the same label: $politician_1$ is not $politician_2$, $teacher_1$ is not $teacher_2$. The index helps you to discriminate *among* without discriminating *against*.

Summary

1. *Polarization* occurs when you divide reality into two unrealistic extremes—for example, black and white, or good and bad.

2. *Intensional orientation* occurs when you respond to the way something is talked about or labeled rather than to its true nature. *Extensional orientation* is the tendency to respond to things as they are rather than as they are labeled or talked about.

3. *Fact-inference confusion* occurs when you treat inferences as if they were facts.

4. *Bypassing* occurs when speaker and listener miss each other with their meanings. It may occur when different words are used but are given the same meaning or when the same word is used but is given two different meanings.

5. *Allness* refers to the tendency to assume that one knows all there is to know, or that what has been said is all that there is to say.

6. *Static evaluation* occurs when you ignore change and assume that reality is static.

7. *Indiscrimination* occurs when you group unlike things together and assume that because they have the same label, they are all alike.

Applications

7.1   I, YOU, AND THEM TALK

The way you phrase something often influences the way you perceive it. This is especially true when dealing with and talking about people. Notice that you do not talk about yourself the same way you talk about the people you are with or the people you know but who aren't present.

Recognizing this simple language habit, Bertrand Russell, the British philosopher and mathematician, proposed a conjugation of "irregular" verbs. One example he used was:

> I am firm.
>
> You are obstinate.
>
> He is a pig-headed fool.

The *New Statesman* and *The Nation* picked up on this and offered prizes for contributions in the style of these irregular verbs. One of the best ones was:

> I am sparkling.
>
> You are unusually talkative.
>
> He is drunk.

Here are 10 sentences phrased in the first person. Following Russell's lead, "conjugate" these irregular verbs.

1. I speak my mind.

2. I believe in what I say.

3. I take an occasional drink.

4. I smoke.

5. I like to talk with people about people.

6. I am frugal.

7. I am concerned with what other people do.

8. I have been known to get upset at times.

9. I am concerned with my appearance.

10. I will put off certain things for a few days.

7.2 THINKING IN E-PRIME

The expression *E-prime* (E') refers here to the mathematical equation E – e – E' where E = the English language and e = the verb *to be*. E', therefore, stands for normal English without the verb *to be*. D. David Bourland, Jr. (1965–1966; Wilson and Klein, 1992) argued that if you wrote and spoke without the verb *to be*, you would describe events more accurately. The verb *to be* often suggests that qualities are in the person or thing rather than in the observer making the statement. It is easy to forget that these statements are evaluative rather than purely descriptive. For example, when you say, "Johnny is a failure," you imply that failure is somehow within Johnny instead of a part of someone's evaluation of Johnny. This type of thinking is especially important in making statements about yourself. When you say, for example, "I'm not good at mathematics" or "I'm unpopular" or "I'm lazy," you imply that these qualities are *in* you. But these are simply evaluations that may be incorrect or that, if partly accurate, may change. The verb *to be* implies a permanence that is simply not true of the world in which we live.

To appreciate further the difference between statements that use the verb *to be* and those that do not, try to rewrite the following sentences without using the verb *to be* in any of its forms—*is*, *are*, *am*, *was*, and so on.

1. I'm a poor student.

2. They are inconsiderate.

3. What is meaningful communication?

4. Is this valuable?

5. Happiness is a dry nose.

6. Love is a useless abstraction.

7. Is this book meaningful?

8. Was the movie any good?

9. Dick and Jane are no longer children.

10. This class is boring.

7.3   BARRIERS IN LANGUAGE IN ACTION

Here is a brief dialogue illustrating the various barriers to communication discussed in this unit. Read over the dialogue and identify the barriers illustrated. Also consider why these statements establish barriers and how the people in the dialogue might have avoided the barriers.

PAT: Look, do you care about me or don't you? If you do then you'll go away for the weekend with me like we planned originally.

CHRIS: I know we planned to go, but I got this opportunity to put in some overtime and I really need the extra money.

PAT: Look, a deal is a deal. You said you'd go and that's all that really matters.

CHRIS: Pat! You never give me a break, do you? I just can't go; I have to work.

PAT: All right, all right. I'll go alone.

CHRIS: Oh, no you don't. I know what will happen.

PAT: What will happen?

CHRIS: You'll go back to drinking again. I know you will.

PAT: I will not. I don't drink anymore.

CHRIS: Pat, you're an alcoholic and you know it.

PAT: I am not an alcoholic.

CHRIS: You drink, don't you?

PAT: Yes, occasionally.

CHRIS: Occasionally? Yeah, you mean two or three times a week, don't you?

PAT: That's occasionally. That's not being an alcoholic.

CHRIS: Well, I don't care how much you drink or how often you drink. You're still an alcoholic.

PAT: Anyway, what makes you think I'll drink if I go away for the weekend?

CHRIS: All those weekend ski trips are just excuses to drink. I've been on one of them—remember?

PAT: Well, see it your way, my dear. See it your way. I'll be gone right after I shower. *(Thinking: I can't wait to get away for the weekend.)*

CHRIS: *(Thinking: Now, what have I done? Our relationship is finished.)*

VERBAL MESSAGE PRINCIPLES

UNIT CONTENTS

In-Group and Inclusive Talk

Downward and Equality Talk

Lying and Honesty

Gossip and Confidentiality

Disconfirmation and Confirmation

  Summary

  Applications
     8.1   Confirmation, Rejection, and Disconfirmation
     8.2   Inclusive Language
     8.3   Gender Differences in Language

UNIT GOALS

After completing this unit, you should be able to

1. define *in-group talk* and the *principle of inclusion* and provide examples of each

2. define *downward talk* and the *principle of equality* and provide examples of each

3. explain some of the disadvantages of lying from a communication point of view

4. define *gossip* and explain how the principle of confidentiality should operate

5. define *disconfirmation* and *confirmation* and provide examples of each

6. define *racism*, *sexism*, and *heterosexism*

The effects people have on each other come largely from the verbal messages they send and receive. In this unit, we consider five "turnoffs"—ways in which you may create negative effects—and their corresponding opposites—the principles that should be followed to avoid such negative reactions. These principles should enable you to create a more positive environment for communication in all its forms.

IN-GROUP AND INCLUSIVE TALK

An annoying and destructive verbal habit is the use of **in-group talk** in the presence of some out-group member—someone who is not a member of this in-group. When doctors get together and discuss medicine, there is no problem. But when they get together with someone who is not a doctor, they often fail to adjust to this new person. Instead, they simply continue with discussions of prescriptions, symptoms, medication, and all the in-group talk that could interest only another doctor.

A variant of this habit occurs when people of the same nationality get together within a larger, more heterogeneous group and use the language of their nationality, sometimes just isolated words, sometimes sentences, and sometimes even entire conversations. This is not merely a question of comprehension; the use of these terms in the presence of a nonmember emphasizes that person's status as an outsider. In almost every instance, the foreign term could easily be translated. The use of the foreign expression does not aid communication. It serves no purpose other than to mark the in-group members as united and the out-group members as outsiders.

Instead of trying to emphasize the exclusion of one or more members, consider the *principle of inclusion*. Regardless of the type of communication situation, you need to engage in **inclusive talk**—include everyone in the interaction. Even when you have to "talk shop" in the presence of a nonmember, you can include that person in a variety of ways. You can seek a nonmember's perspective on the issue or perhaps draw an analogy with that person's field. When inclusion is practiced, everyone gains a great deal more satisfaction from the interaction.

A variation of in-group talk is self-talk. We are an egocentric society. Although we have long since learned that the sun does not revolve around the earth, we apparently have yet to learn that the world does not revolve around us. For most children their every wish is responded to before they even learn to express it. Fortunately, most of us grow up. Yet many people still act as if the world and its people existed only for their pleasure (Addeo & Burger, 1973). They talk constantly about themselves—their jobs, accomplishments, families, love lives, problems, successes, and sometimes even failures. Rarely do they ask how you are, what you think (except perhaps about them), or what your plans are.

There are other people who go to the opposite extreme and never talk about themselves. These are the underdisclosers we discussed in Unit 3. These are the people who want to learn everything about you but do not want to reveal anything about themselves that might make them vulnerable. As a result, you leave the interaction with the feeling that they did not like or trust you. Otherwise, you feel, they would have revealed something of themselves.

The majority of interactions need to be characterized by the *principle of balance*—some self-talk, some other-talk, and never all of one or the other. Communication is a two-way process. Each person needs to function as source and as receiver. Each person needs a chance to function as subject. Balanced communication interactions are more satisfying and result in much more interesting interactions (Hecht, 1978a, 1978b). You get bored hearing too much about the other person—and, let's face it, others get bored with too much of you. The principle of balance is a sorely needed guide.

DOWNWARD AND EQUALITY TALK

You hear downward talk from the teacher who says, "This may be beyond your reach, but try to grasp it anyway" or the friend who puts himself or herself above others by using phrases such as "You probably didn't realize this, but. . . " or "I know you don't keep up with the computer literature, but. . . " Regardless of who is doing the talking, you get the feeling that somehow the speaker is above you for a multitude of reasons—intelligence, experience, knowledge, position, wealth, or whatever. You are put into the position of learner and subordinate.

Another way some people talk down to others is by telling them how to feel. "Don't be silly, you'll pass the course." "Forget about the louse. You'll meet someone else." "Lots of people are worse off than you. Don't feel so sorry for yourself." Usually, people resent this intrusion into their private world of feelings.

Still another way to talk down is to interrupt the other person. People who interrupt you are stating that their communications are more important than yours; therefore they have a right to interrupt you, but you do not have a right to interrupt them.

A somewhat different form of talking down occurs when people use gobbledygook—double-talk, or language that is needlessly complex and confusing (Lambdin, 1981; Rank, 1984). Semanticist J. Dan Rothwell (1982) calls it "verbosity and circumlocution that buries a message in an avalanche of verbal rubble." Originally coined by Maury Maverick, a representative from Texas, the term *gobbledygook* refers to much around us, particularly in government documents, legal and medical contracts, and, unfortunately, much academic writing. You can gain perspective on this type of noncommunication by viewing it as a form of talking down.

Power Plays

A special type of talking down occurs in **power plays** (Steiner, 1981), verbal maneuvers that put you down and allow the other person to get what he or she wants. Consider a few power plays analyzed by Steiner. In "Nobody Upstairs" the other person refuses to acknowledge your request. The game takes the form of not listening to what you are saying, regardless of how you say it or how many times you say it. One common form is to refuse to take no for an answer. We see this clearly in the stereotypical man who persists in making advances to a woman despite her repeated refusals.

Sometimes "Nobody Upstairs" takes the form of ignoring socially and commonly accepted (but unspoken) rules such as knocking when you enter a person's office, not opening another person's desk drawers, or not going through another person's office mailbox. The power play takes the form of expressing ignorance of the rules: "I didn't know you didn't want me to look in your mailbox" or "Do you want me to knock the next time I come into your office?"

Another power play is "You Owe Me." Here the person does something for you and then demands something in return. The maneuver puts you in the position of owing this person something. This game is played frequently by men who take a woman on an expensive date. The objective is to make the woman owe something, usually sex. Another common example is the boss who hires you at an entry-level position and expects you to stay in that position out of gratitude for being hired. Whenever you ask for a promotion or begin looking for a new job, the boss reminds you of how much he or she has done for you: "How can you think of leaving Rawley after all we've done for you?"

In "Metaphor" the other person uses metaphors to express some negative opinion or impression. For example, let's say you are going out with someone your coworkers do not like. The coworkers may make such comments as "How can you go out with her? She's a real dog" or "How can you date him? He's such a pig." *Dog* and *pig* are metaphors. *Metaphors* are figures of speech in which one word is used in the place of another. In these examples, *dog* and *pig* are used in place of the persons referred to with the intention of identifying the most obvious characteristics of these animals (ugliness and sloppiness, for example) with the people. The object here is to deny you the chance to defend your choice. After all, it is difficult to defend dating a dog or a pig!

Management Strategy   What do you do when confronted by such power plays? Claude Steiner (1981) recommends that you follow a three-part strategy.

1. Express your feelings. Tell the person that you are angry or annoyed or disturbed by his or her behavior.
2. Describe the behavior you object to. Tell the person—in language that describes rather than evaluates—the specific behavior that you object to, for example, reading your mail, reminding you of how much you owe him or her, or calling your date names.
3. State a cooperative response that you both can live with comfortably. Tell the person—in a cooperative tone—what you want, for example: "I want you to knock before coming into my office. I want you to stop reminding me of how much I owe you. I want you to stop calling my dates names."

Table 8.1 presents specific examples of these management strategies.

Table 8.1 Power Plays and Management Strategies

Nobody Upstairs

"I'm angry *(statement of feeling)* that you persist in opening my mail. You have opened my mail four times this past week alone *(description of the behavior that you object to)*. I want you to allow me to open my own mail. If there is anything in it that concerns you, I will let you know immediately *(statement of cooperative response)*."

You Owe Me

"I'm angry that you're doing this to me *(statement of feelings)*. I'm angry that when you want me to do something, you preface it by reminding me of my obligations to you. You tell me all you did for me and then tell me that I should therefore do what you want me to do *(description of behavior you object to)*. Please don't do things for me because you want something in return. I don't want to feel obligated. I want to do what I want because I think it is best for me and not because I would feel guilty about not paying you back for what you've done for me *(statement of cooperative response)*."

Metaphor

"I resent your calling Jane a dog. I'm very attracted to Jane and she to me. I feel like a real loser *(statement of feelings)* when you refer to my dates as pigs or dogs. You've referred to the last three women I've dated with these insulting names *(description of the behavior you object to)*. If you don't like the women I'm dating, please tell me. But please don't insult them or me by using terms like *pig* or *dog (statement of cooperative response)*."

When used unfairly to intimidate or to manipulate, downward talk creates problems for all involved. Although the three-part management strategy is useful for power plays, the most general antidote is the *principle of equality*. If you receive messages that talk down to you or attempt to strip you of power, you need to recognize that all parties in the communication act are equal in the sense that each person's communications are worthwhile and each person has something to contribute. Some people use power plays and manipulations without being aware of them. Perhaps keeping the principle of equality in mind will lessen the likelihood of their doing this in the future. As a receiver, recognize your own responsibility in these situations. When you allow people to interrupt you or somehow to treat your communications as unimportant, you are encouraging and reinforcing this behavior. Demand communication equality. The simple statement "Excuse me, but you're interrupting me; I'd like to finish my thought" is usually effective.

LYING AND HONESTY

According to the *Random House Dictionary,* a *lie* is "a false statement made with deliberate intent to deceive; a falsehood; something intended or serving to convey a false impression." As this definition makes clear, lying may also be committed by omission as well as commission. When you omit something relevant to the issue at hand, and this omission leads others to draw incorrect inferences, you have lied just as surely as if you had made a false statement (Bok, 1978).

Most cultures, if not all, respond negatively to lying. Yet, within each culture, members of small cultures often develop their own ethic about lying, especially about lying to members of other cultural groups. With reference to one group of which you are a member, are there certain "lies" that are not viewed negatively? Are there certain lies that are viewed positively?

Similarly, although most lies are verbal, some are nonverbal and most seem to involve at least some nonverbal elements. The innocent facial expression—despite the commission of some punishable act—and the knowing nod instead of the honest expression of ignorance are common examples of nonverbal lying. Lies may range from the white lie that stretches the truth to the big lie in which one formulates falsehoods so elaborate that everyone comes to believe they are true.

Reasons for Lying

There are probably as many reasons for lying as there are lies—each situation is different. But most lies are told for two main reasons: (1) to gain some reward or (2) to avoid some punishment. Lying to gain a reward is motivated by four major reasons (Camden, Motley, & Wilson, 1984):

- *Basic needs:* Lies told to gain or to retain objects that fulfill basic needs—for example, money or various material possessions.
- *Affiliation:* Lies told to increase desired affiliations or to decrease undesired affiliations—for example, lies told to prolong desirable social interactions, avert interpersonal conflicts, or avoid granting some request to halt undesirable interaction.
- *Self-esteem:* Lies told to protect or increase the self-esteem of oneself, the person one is interacting with, or some third party—for example, lies told to increase one's perceived competence, taste, or social desirability.

- *Self-gratification:* Lies told to achieve some personal satisfaction—for example, lies told for the sake of humor or to exaggerate for some desired effect.

Although usually people lie for their own benefit, some lies are motivated by a desire to benefit another person. An analysis of 322 lies revealed that 75.8 percent benefited the liar, 21.7 percent benefited the person who was told the lie, and 2.5 percent benefited some third party (Camden, Motley, & Wilson, 1984).

Generally, you know when you are lying and when you are not lying. No one has to tell you. And yet there are many gray areas where it is not clear when a statement is a lie. For example, sometimes it is difficult to tell when someone is asking for an honest opinion or merely asking for a compliment. "What do you think of my new apartment?" may be designed to get a needed pat on the back and not an honest opinion of the decoration. Sometimes there is a tacit agreement between people to avoid telling the truth about certain issues. A couple, for example, may agree that extrarelational affairs are not to be disclosed and that the acceptable procedure is to make up some kind of innocent excuse—working late at the office and its variants—to cover up. In these instances, the context and the intent of the message would define whether something is or is not a lie. Thus, if in response to the question about the apartment, you said "It's really beautiful" because of the belief that the question was asking for a compliment, your statement may not be considered a lie. Similarly, if the individuals have made it known that they do not want to deal with the truth about certain issues, then it is probably not a lie to conform to this expectation or wish.

Is Lying Effective?

Lies have both ethical and effectiveness dimensions. The ethical dimension concerns what is right and what is wrong. Lying is unethical simply because each person has a right to base his or her choices on the best information available. By lying you withhold at least part of that information and contribute to decisions based on incorrect assumptions and falsehoods. The effectiveness dimension concerns whether the lie succeeds or fails to gain the reward or avoiding the punishment. Many lies are effective; people have risen to the top of their professions and have amassed fortunes built on lies and deceit. There can be little doubt that in many instances lying works. And yet lying has enough problems and disadvantages to make you pause and reconsider any decision to lie.

Lies and Inconsistent Packages   As already noted, communication messages are sent and received as packages. Lies are no exception (Burgoon, Buller, & Woodall, 1989). It is often difficult to lie nonverbally with any degree of conviction (Ekman, 1985). Often lies are betrayed nonverbally. It is far easier to lie with your mouth than with your face and body. And when the contradiction is observed, it is the nonverbal message that people believe. The result is that you have lied to no avail. Your reputation may suffer without your having achieved the reward or avoided the punishment.

Lying influences who you are and what you think of yourself. When you believe that lying is wrong and yet lie yourself, you are creating psychological imbalance and intrapersonal conflict. You seem to be designed to function as a consistent whole, with your thinking and your behavior echoing each other. When you believe one thing and do something else, you begin to develop various internal conflicts.

Lies and Interpersonal Disapproval   Perhaps the most obvious disadvantage to lying is that there will be social disapproval when the lie is discovered. Although the vast majority of people lie—at some times and with some issues—the vast majority dislike and condemn it. Consequently, when your lie is discovered, you incur social disapproval. It may range from mild disapproval to total ostracism from a group or organization. The upshot of all this is that the liar's communication effectiveness will be drastically impaired. A person who is known to have lied is seldom believed, even when telling the truth. You not only disbelieve the proven liar, you also give no persuasive force to his or her arguments, frequently discounting them as lies. Even more important is that a liar's relational messages and relational interactions generally become less meaningful. The most important messages an individual can communicate—the "I love you," "I enjoy being with you" messages—are discounted, since the listener can no longer ascertain whether or not they are true.

The alternative to lying is honesty. Honesty, of course, does not mean hurting other people or destroying their illusions. Honesty can serve effectively only as a means for relating more closely, for exchanging feelings, sharing, and responding to the deeper levels of communication. When viewed in this way, there is little chance that honesty will be confused with forcing others to see what they may not wish to see or what they may not be ready to see.

GOSSIP AND CONFIDENTIALITY

There can be no doubt that everyone spends a great deal of time gossiping. According to the *Random House Dictionary, gossip* is defined as "idle talk or rumor, especially about the personal or private affairs of others." A gossiper, then, is a person who engages in this idle talk.

Gossip is an inevitable part of your daily interactions; to advise anyone not to gossip would be absurd. Not gossiping would eliminate one of the most frequent and enjoyable forms of communication. Ogden Nash put it this way: "There are two kinds of people who blow through life like a breeze / And one kind is gossipers, and the other kind is gossipees."

Some Problems of Gossip

Nevertheless, gossip does create serious problems when it is not managed correctly or fairly, and it is to this point that your attention should be directed. When you tell someone that you fear you are falling out of love with your fiancé, you expect the conversation to be held in confidence. If you wanted it relayed to a third party or to your fiancé, you probably would have done that yourself. When such a conversation is relayed without your knowledge or approval, you feel that your confidence has been betrayed.

Quite often the person who repeats such remarks is, perhaps subconsciously, seeking to create friction. And this motivation is usually recognized, sooner or later, by all parties involved. To claim—as some do—that they didn't realize the information was confidential is absurd. It is usually obvious from the context what should and what should not be held in confidence. You have little trouble in deciding when something is said in confidence, and it does not seem unreasonable to expect others to be equally discerning.

Do you find a gender difference in gossiping behavior? Do men and women both label the same behavior "gossiping"? Do men and women "gossip" about the same things? What gender differences can you identify in this general type of communication?

Ethical Implications

In some instances gossip is unethical. In the book *Secrets* (1983), Sissela Bok identifies three kinds of gossip that she considers unethical. First, it is unethical to reveal information that you have promised to keep secret. When you promise to keep something confidential, you should do so. When that is impossible (Bok offers the example of the teenager who confides a suicide plan), the information should be revealed only to those who must know it, not to the world at large.

Second, gossip is unethical when you know it to be false and nevertheless pass it on. Third, gossip is unethical when it invades the privacy that everyone has a right to. More specifically, gossip is invasive when it concerns matters that are properly considered private and when the gossip can hurt the individuals involved.

Bok does not argue that these conditions are easy to identify in any given instance of gossip. But they do provide you with excellent starting points for asking yourself, "Is this talk about another person ethical?"

The *principle of confidentiality* presents a good guideline for dealing with gossip: Keep confidential all private conversations about third parties. Messages that begin with "He said. . . " or "She thinks that you. . . " should be automatically suspect as potential violators of the principle of confidentiality. Remember too the *principle of irreversibility*—you cannot take messages back; once you say something, you cannot uncommunicate it.

DISCONFIRMATION AND CONFIRMATION

Before reading about these important concepts, take this self-test to examine your own behavior.

Pat arrives home late one night. Chris is angry and complains about Pat's coming home so late. Consider some responses Pat might make:

1. Stop screaming. I'm not interesting in what you're babbling about. I'll do what I want when I want. I'm going to bed.
2. What are you so angry about? Didn't you get in three hours late last Thursday, when you went to that office party? So knock it off.
3. You have a right to be angry. I should have called when I was going to be late, but I got involved in an argument at work and I couldn't leave until it was resolved.

In (1), Pat dismisses Chris's anger and even indicates a dismissal of Chris as a person. In (2), Pat rejects the validity of Chris's reasons for being angry but does not dismiss Chris's feelings of anger or Chris as a person. In (3), Pat acknowledges Chris's anger and the reasons for being angry. In addition Pat provides some kind of explanation and in doing so shows that Chris's feelings are valid, that Chris as a person is important, and that Chris deserves to know what happened. The first response is an example of disconfirmation, the second of rejection, and the third of confirmation.

The psychologist William James once observed that "no more fiendish punishment could be devised, even were such a thing physically possible, than that one should be turned loose in society and remain absolutely unnoticed by all the members thereof." In this often-quoted observation James identifies the essence of disconfirmation (Veenendall & Feinstein, 1990; Watzlawick, Beavin, & Jackson, 1967).

Disconfirmation is a communication pattern in which you ignore someone's presence as well as that person's communications. You say, in effect, that this person and what this person has to say are not worth serious attention or effort—that this individual and her or his contributions are so unimportant or insignificant that there is no reason to concern yourself with them.

Note that disconfirmation is not the same as **rejection**. To reject someone is to disagree with him or her; you indicate your unwillingness to accept something the other person says or does. In disconfirming someone, however, you deny that person's significance; you claim that what this person says or does simply does not count.

Confirmation is the opposite communication pattern. In confirmation you not only acknowledge the presence of the other person but you indicate your acceptance of this person, of this person's definition of self, and of your relationship as defined or viewed by her or him.

Disconfirmation and confirmation may be communicated in a wide variety of ways. Table 8.2 shows just a few and parallels the self-test presented on page 135 so that you can see clearly not only the confirming but also the opposite, disconfirming behaviors. As you review this table, try to imagine a specific illustration for each of the ways of communicating disconfirmation and confirmation (Galvin & Brommel, 1991; Pearson, 1993).

We can gain insight into a wide variety of offensive language practices by viewing

How Confirming Are You?

In your typical communications, how likely are you to display the following behaviors? Use the following scale in responding to each statement:

5 = always
4 = often
3 = sometimes
2 = rarely
1 = never

_____ 1. I acknowledge the presence of another person both verbally and nonverbally.

_____ 2. I acknowledge the contributions of the other person— for example, by supporting or taking issue with what the person says.

_____ 3. During the conversation, I make nonverbal contact by maintaining direct eye contact, touching, hugging, kissing, and otherwise demonstrating acknowledgment of the other person.

_____ 4. I communicate as both speaker and listener with involvement, and with a concern and respect for the other person.

_____ 5. I signal my understanding of the other person both verbally and nonverbally.

_____ 6. I reflect the other person's feelings as a way of showing that I understand these feelings.

_____ 7. I ask questions when appropriate concerning the other person's thoughts and feelings.

_____ 8. I respond to the other person's requests, for example, by returning phone calls and answering letters within a reasonable time.

_____ 9. I encourage the other person to express his or her thoughts and feelings.

_____ 10. I respond directly and exclusively to what the other person says.

Scoring All 10 statements are phrased so that they express confirming behaviors. Therefore, high scores (above 35) reflect a strong tendency to engage in confirmation. Low scores (below 25) reflect a strong tendency to engage in disconfirmation.

them as types of disconfirmation, as language that alienates and separates. The three obvious practices are racism, sexism, and heterosexism.

Racism

According to Andrea Rich (1974), "any language that, through a conscious or unconscious attempt by the user, places a particular racial or ethnic group in an inferior position is racist." **Racist language** expresses racist attitudes. It also, however, contributes to the development of racist attitudes in those who use or hear the language.

Racist terms are used by members of one culture to disparage members of other cultures—their customs or their accomplishments. Racist language emphasizes differ-

Table 8.2 Confirmation Versus Disconfirmation

Confirmation	Disconfirmation
1. Acknowledge the presence of the other verbally or nonverbally	1. Ignore the presence of the other person
2. Acknowledge the contributions of the other by either supporting or taking issue with what the other says	2. Ignore what the other says: express (nonverbally and verbally) indifference to anything the other says
3. Make nonverbal contact by maintaining direct eye contact, touching, hugging, kissing, and otherwise demonstrating acknowledgment of the other	3. Make no nonverbal contact; avoid direct eye contact; avoid touching other person
4. Engage in dialogue—communication in which both persons are speakers and listeners, both are involved, and both are concerned with and have respect for each other	4. Engage in monologue—communication in which one person speaks and one person listens, there is no real interaction, and there is no real concern or respect for each other
5. Demonstrate understanding of what the other says and means	5. Jump to interpretation or evaluation rather than working at understanding what the other means
6. Reflect the other's feelings to demonstrate your understanding of these feelings	6. Express your own feelings, ignore feelings of the other, or give abstract intellectualized responses
7. Ask questions of the other concerning both thoughts and feelings	7. Make statements about yourself, ignore any lack of clarity in the other's remarks
8. Acknowledge the other's requests; answer the other's questions, return phone calls, and answer letters	8. Ignore the other's requests; fail to answer questions, return phone calls, and answer letters
9. Encourage the other to express thoughts and feelings	9. Interrupt or otherwise make it difficult for the other to express himself or herself
10. Respond directly and exclusively to what the other says	10. Respond tangentially by acknowledging the other's comment but then shifting the focus of the message in another direction

ences rather than similarities and separates rather than unites members of different cultures. Generally, racist language is used by the dominant group to establish and maintain power over other groups. The social consequences of racist language in terms of employment, education, housing opportunities, and general community acceptance are well known.

Many people feel that it is permissible for members of a culture to refer to themselves with the same racist terms. That is, Asians may use the negative terms referring to Asians, Italians may use the negative terms referring to Italians, and so on. The reasoning seems to be that groups should be able to laugh at themselves. One possible problem, though, is that these terms may just reinforce the negative stereotypes that society has already assigned this group. By using these terms, members may come to accept these labels with their negative connotations and thus contribute to their own stereotyping.

It is interesting to note that the terms denoting some of the major movements in art—for example, *impressionism* and *cubism*—were originally applied negatively. The terms were taken on by the artists and eventually became positive. A parallel can be seen in the use of the word *queer* by some of the more militant lesbian and gay organizations. Their purpose in using the term is to dispel its negative connotation.

It has often been pointed out (Bosmajian, 1974; Davis, 1967) that there are aspects of language that may be inherently racist. For example, in one examination of English there were found 134 synonyms for *white*. Of these, 44 have positive connotations (for example, "clean," "chaste," and "unblemished") and only 10 has negative connotations (for example, "whitewash" and "pale"). The remaining were relatively neutral. Of the 120 synonyms for *black*, 60 had unfavorable connotations ("unclean," "foreboding," and "deadly") and none had positive connotations.

Consider such phrases as the following:

- the Korean doctor
- the Latino prodigy
- the African-American mathematician
- the white nurse

In some cases, of course, the racial identifier may be relevant, for instance, "The American doctor argued for hours with the French doctors over the patent." Here the aim might be to identify the nationality of the doctor or the specific doctor (as you would if you forgot her or his name).

Often, however, such identifiers are used to emphasize that the combination of race and occupation (or talent or accomplishment) is rare and unexpected. It emphasizes that this combination is out of the ordinary and that the racial member is an exception. It also implies that somehow racial factors are important in the context. As noted, there are times when this may be true but most often race is irrelevant.

Sexism

Consider some of the **sexist language** used to refer to women. A woman loses her last name when she marries and in certain instances loses her first name as well. She changes from "Ann Smith" to "Mrs. John Jones."

You say that a woman "marries into" a man's family and that a family "dies out" if there are no male children. You do not speak of a man marrying into a woman's family (unless the family is extremely prestigious or wealthy or members of royalty), and a family can still "die out," even if there are ten female children. In the traditional marriage ceremony, you hear "I now pronounce you man and wife," not "man and woman" or "husband and wife." The man retains his status as man, but the woman changes hers from woman to wife. Barrie Thorne, Cheris Kramarae, and Nancy Henley, in their *Language, Gender and Society* (1983), summarize this line of research by noting that "women tend to be defined by their relation to men." "The available and 'approved' titles, pronouns, lexicons, and labels," they note, "reflect the fact that women (as well as other subordinates) have been named by others."

Julia Stanley researched terms indicating sexual promiscuity and found 220 terms referring to a sexually promiscuous woman but only 22 terms for a sexually promiscuous man (Thorne, Kramarae, & Henley, 1983). Surely, there are as many promiscuous men as there are promiscuous women, yet our language fails to reflect this. If you assume that the number of terms indicates the importance of a concept to a culture, then you might argue that promiscuity among women *is* significant (that is, "abnormal" or "beyond the norm") and something to take special notice of, but that promiscuity among men *is not* significant (it is "normal") and therefore no special notice need be taken of it. Since a volume could be written on the implications and consequences of such a double standard, you can draw your own conclusions.

The National Council of Teachers of English has proposed guidelines for nonsexist (gender-free or gender-neutral) language. These concern the use of generic *man*, the use of the generic *he* and *his*, and sex role stereotyping (Penfield, 1987).

Generic Man   The word man refers clearly to an adult male. To use the term to refer to both men and women emphasizes maleness at the expense of femaleness. Similarly the terms *mankind* or *the common man* or even *cavemen* imply a primary focus on adult males. Gender-neutral terms can easily be substituted. Instead of *mankind,* you can say *humanity, people,* or *human beings.* Instead of *the common man,* you can say *the average person* or *ordinary people.* Instead of *cavemen,* you can say *prehistoric people* or *cave dwellers.*

Similarly, the use of such terms as *policeman, fireman, salesman, chairman, mailman,* and other terms that presume maleness as the norm and femaleness as a deviation are clear and common examples of sexist language. Consider using nonsexist alternatives for these and similar terms; make these alternatives (for example, *police officer* and *firefighter*) a part of your active vocabulary.

Here are a few other terms that are not inclusive: *man, mankind, countryman, manmade, the common man, caveman, manpower, repairman, doorman, stewardess, waitress, salesman, mailman,* and *actress*. What alternatives can you offer for each of these terms? What advantages or disadvantages do these alternative expressions have as compared with the terms given here?

Generic He and His   The use of the masculine pronoun to refer to any individual regardless of sex further illustrates the extent of linguistic sexism. There seems to be no legitimate reason why the feminine pronoun could not alternate with the masculine pronoun in referring to hypothetical individuals, or why such phrases as *he and she* or *her and him* could not be used in place of *he* or *him*. Alternatively, you can restructure your sentences to eliminate any reference to gender. Here are a few examples from the NCTE Guidelines (Penfield, 1987):

Sexist	*Gender-Free*
The average student is worried about his grades.	The average student is worried about grades.
Ask the student to hand in his work as soon as he is finished.	Ask students to hand in their work as soon as they are finished.
When a teacher asks his students for an evaluation, he is putting himself on on the spot.	When you ask your students for an evaluation, you are putting yourself on the spot.

Sex Role Stereotyping   The words you use often reflect a sex role bias, the assumption that certain roles or professions belong to men and others belong to women. To eliminate sex role stereotyping, avoid making the hypothetical elementary school teacher female and the college professor male. Avoid referring to doctors as male and nurses as female. Avoid noting the sex of a professional with terms such as "female doctor" or "male nurse." When you are referring to a specific doctor or nurse, the person's sex will become clear when you use the appropriate pronoun: *Dr. Smith wrote the prescription for her new patient* or *The nurse recorded the patient's temperature himself.*

Heterosexism

A close relative of sexism is heterosexism. The term is a relatively new addition to our list of linguistic prejudices. As the term implies, heterosexist language is used to disparage gay men and lesbians. As with racist language, you see heterosexism in the derogatory terms used for lesbians and gay men. As with racist language, you hear these terms on the street. Unlike racist language, however, you also hear these terms in the media and on college campuses. In the media's use of such terms, you have a clear example of the institutionalization of prejudice against a minority group.

As with sexism, however, you also see the occurrence of heterosexism in more subtle forms of language usage. For example, when you qualify a profession—as in "gay athlete" or "lesbian doctor"—you are in effect stating that athletes and doctors are not normally gay or lesbian. Further, you are highlighting the affectional orientation of the

Is it heterosexist to presume that an unknown athlete, senator, or scientist is heterosexual (assuming that you don't know anything about the individual's affectional orientation)? Is it sexist to presume, for example, that an unknown doctor, nurse, or lawyer is of a particular sex?

athlete and the doctor in a context where it may have no relevance. This practice, of course, is the same as qualifying by race or gender, which we have already noted.

Still another instance of heterosexism—and perhaps the most difficult to deal with—is the presumption of heterosexuality. Simple questions like "Are you married?" or "Have you met the right young man yet?" (when speaking to a woman) assume that the person is heterosexual.

Another way in which a heterosexist bias is shown is in not using relational terms like "aunt" or "uncle" for the relationship partners of your gay or lesbian relatives. A similar bias is shown in ignoring anniversaries between gay or lesbian partners or the birthday of a gay or lesbian partner. Such linguistic devices—though perhaps unintentionally—exclude rather than include and are monocultural rather than multicultural. Usually, people assume the person they are talking to or about is heterosexual. Usually they are correct, as the majority of the population is heterosexual. At the same time, however, note that it denies lesbians and gay males their real identity. The practice is very similar to the presumption of whiteness and maleness, which we have made significant inroads in eliminating.

Summary

1. *In-group talk* occurs when members belonging to a particular group talk about their group concerns or use their group's language in the presence of outsiders. A variation of in-group talk is *self-talk*, which, when extreme, creates communication problems by distorting the normal give and take.

2. *Downward talk* refers to the tendency to talk down to others, rather than talking as equals.

3. *Lying* creates communication problems by lessening credibility, by creating psychological imbalance, and by engendering social disapproval of the liar.

4. *Gossip*, although inevitable, creates problems when it betrays a confidence, is false and known to be false, or is used to hurt another person.

5. *Disconfirmation* refers to the process whereby you ignore the presence and the communications of others. *Confirmation* refers to the process whereby you accept, support, and acknowledge the importance of the other person.

6. *Racist, sexist,* and *heterosexist language* are specific cases of disconfirmation, of language that separates and distances rather than unites and bonds.

Applications

8.1 CONFIRMATION, REJECTION, AND DISCONFIRMATION

Classify the following responses as confirmation (C), rejection (R), or disconfirmation (D):

Enrique receives this semester's grades in the mail; they are a lot better than previous semesters' grades but are still not great. After opening the letter, Enrique says: "I really tried hard to get my grades up this semester." Enrique's parents respond:

_____ Going out every night hardly seems like trying very hard.

_____ What should we have for dinner?

_____ Keep up the good work.

_____ I can't believe you've really tried your best; how can anyone study with the stereo blasting in his ears?

_____ I'm sure you've tried real hard.

_____ That's great.

_____ What a rotten day I had at the office.

_____ I can remember when I was in school; got all B's without ever opening a book.

Peter, who has been out of work for the past several weeks, says: "I feel like such a failure; I just can't seem to find a job. I've been pounding the pavement for the last five weeks and still nothing." Peter's friend responds:

_____ I know you've been trying real hard.

_____ You really should get more training so you'd be able to sell yourself more effectively.

_____ I told you a hundred times: you need that college degree.

_____ I got to go to the dentist on Friday. Boy, do I hate that.

_____ The employment picture is real bleak this time of the year but your qualifications are really impressive. Something will come up soon.

_____ You are not a failure. You just can't find a job.

_____ What do you need a job for? Stay home and keep house. After all, John makes more than enough money to live in style.

_____ What's five weeks?

_____ Well, you'll just have to try harder.

For each of the following situations, write an example or provide an illustration of confirmatory, rejecting, and disconfirmatory responses.

Situation 1: *Pat: "I haven't had a date in the last four months. I'm getting really depressed over this." A friend responds:*

Confirmation:
Rejection:
Disconfirmation:

Situation 2: *Pat and Chris have just had another fight. Pat is telling a friend about what has been going on. "We just can't seem to get along anymore. Every day is a hassle. Every day, there's another conflict, another battle. I feel like walking away from the whole mess." The friend responds:*

Confirmation:
Rejection:
Disconfirmation:

8.2 INCLUSIVE LANGUAGE

Rewrite each of the following sentences—which purposely recall the popular stereotypes—into more inclusive language so that they do not limit the referent to one sex and so that they punch holes in these limiting and discriminating stereotypes. In eliminating the stereotypes do be sure to retain the intended meaning, however. What advantages or disadvantages do you see in the rewritten versions?

1. You really should get a second doctor's opinion. Just see what he says.

2. Johnny went to school today and met his kindergarten teacher. I wonder who she is.

3. Everyone needs to examine his own conscience.

4. No one can tell what his ultimate fortune will be.

5. The effective communicator is a selective self-discloser; he discloses to some people about some things some of the times.

6. I wonder who the new chairman will be.

7. The effective waitress knows when her customers need her.

8. Advertisers don't care what the intellectual thinks; they want to know what the man in the street thinks.

9. What do you think the ideal communicator should be like? How should he talk? How should he gesture?

10. The history of man is largely one of technology replacing his manual labor.

8.3 GENDER DIFFERENCES IN LANGUAGE

This exercise focuses on male and female speech. We look at the results of research examining specific language elements as used by men and women and at some generalizations concerning the speech of women and men.

Research on Male and Female Speech

Examine the information, adapted from the research summary provided by Mulac and colleagues (1988), presented below. Here some of the differences between male and female language usage are identified. Not all researchers agree that men interrupt more than women (Dindia, 1987; Wiemann et al., 1987). Further, not all interruptions are negatively perceived. Some interruptions, as we discuss in Unit 16, are actually supportive expressions that communicate an interest and involvement in what the other person is saying.

Males use more:

Interruptions	Break into the sentences of the other speaker before the person has indicated that she or he has finished speaking
Conjunctions/fillers to begin sentences	For example, "well," "OK, so what else happened?"
Directives	Tell the other person what to do
Justifiers	Give reasons or evidence for assertion, as in, "I believe...," "because..."

Females use more:

Fillers	Words that have no reference to other things, such as *you know, well, like*

Adverbials to begin sentence	As in *really, actually, truly*
Negations	Stating what something is not, for example, "It's not that I am against. . ."
Questions	Asking for information
Hedges, softeners	"It's *probably* not right," "It *may be* okay"
Intensive adverbs	*really, quite, exactly*
Action verbs	Verbs that indicate movement or action
Personal pronouns	*I, you, he, she, they, we*

For the next two days collect examples of male and female language that illustrate the differences noted here as well as examples that contradict these findings. Share your examples in small groups or with the class as a whole. Also consider the following:

1. What are the implications of male-female language differences for general interpersonal effectiveness? What are the implications of these differences for success in the business world?

2. What other differences did you notice that might distinguish male and female language?

3. On the basis of your analysis, what principles for language effectiveness would you recommend men follow? What principles would you recommend women follow?

Generalizations About Men's and Women's Speech

Here are 10 statements about the "differences" between the speech of women and men. For each of the following statements, indicate whether you think the statement describes women's speech (WS), men's speech (MS), or women's and men's speech equally (W-MS).

_____ 1. This speech is logical rather than emotional.

_____ 2. This speech is vague.

_____ 3. This speech is endless, less concise, and jumps from one idea to another.

_____ 4. This speech is highly businesslike.

_____ 5. This speech is more polite.

_____ 6. This speech uses weaker forms (for example, the weak intensifiers like *so* and *such*) and fewer exclamations.

_____ 7. This speech contains more tag questions (for example, questions appended to statements that ask for agreement, such as "Let's meet at ten o'clock, *OK?*").

_____ 8. This speech is more euphemistic (contains more polite words as substitutes for some taboo or potentially offensive terms) and uses fewer swear terms.

_____ 9. This speech is generally more effective.

_____ 10. This speech is less forceful and less in control.

After responding to all 10 statements, consider the following:

1. On what evidence did you base your answers?

2. How strongly do you believe that your answers are correct? Give each of your statements a certainty rating (1 = absolutely certain; 2 = pretty certain; 3 = fairly certain; 4 = pretty uncertain; 5 = very uncertain).

3. What do you think might account for sex differences in verbal behavior? That is, how did the language differences that might distinguish the sexes come into existence?

4. What effect might these language differences (individually or as a group) have on communication (and relationships generally) between the sexes?

Do not read any further until you have responded to the preceding statements and questions.

The 10 statements were drawn from the research of Cheris Kramarae (1974a, 1974b, 1977, 1981; also see Arliss, 1991; Coates, 1986; Pearson, Turner, & Todd-Mancillas, 1991; and Stewart, Stewart, Friedley, & Cooper, 1990), who argues that these "differences"—with the exception of statements 5 and 8 (women's speech is often more "polite")—are actually stereotypes of women's and men's speech that are not in fact confirmed in analyses of actual speech. According to Kramarae, then, you should have answered "Women's and Men's Speech Equally" for statements 1, 2, 3, 4, 6, 7, 9, and 10 and "Women's Speech" for statements 5 and 8. Perhaps you see these "differences" in cartoons or on television, and this teaches you that they actually characterize real speech.

Reexamine your answers to the 10 statements. For those that you indicated were characteristic of either women's or men's speech, were your answers based on your actual experience with the speech of women and men or might they have been based on popular beliefs about women's and men's speech?

Reconciling Research Findings and Popular Generalizations

How might some of the research findings be interpreted to support the generalizations? In what ways might the research findings be interpreted to support contradictory generalizations? For example, research finds that hedges and softeners are more common in women's speech. Can this be interpreted to support the generalization that women's speech is less forceful? At the same time, the finding that women use more action verbs could be interpreted to support the generalization that women's speech is more forceful.

Both women and men use a wide variety of language forms and adapt their speech to the unique communication situations in which they find themselves. How might the communication situation lead to differences in some of the language forms identified by research?

NONVERBAL MESSAGES OF BODY AND SOUND

UNIT CONTENTS

Body Movements

Facial Movements

Eye Movements

Sound

  Summary

  Applications
    9.1 Praising and Criticizing
    9.2 Dysfunctional Nonverbals

UNIT GOALS

After completing this unit, you should be able to

1. define and provide examples of *emblems*, *illustrators*, *affect displays*, *regulators*, and *adaptors*

2. identify the types of information communicated by the face and the problems in judging the meanings of facial expressions

3. define *micromomentary expressions*

4. identify the functions of eye movements

5. explain the types of information communicated by pupil dilation and constriction

6. define *paralanguage* and explain its role in making judgments about people and about communication

First among all the avenues of nonverbal communication is the body. You communicate your thoughts and feelings frequently and accurately, through body movements, facial movements, and eye movements. In this unit we look at body communication and examine the many ways in which body, face, and eyes communicate meaning.

BODY MOVEMENTS

Five types of body movement may be identified (Ekman & Friesen, 1969). Through these movements you communicate a wide variety of thoughts and feelings (Table 9.1).

Emblems

Emblems are nonverbal behaviors that directly translate words or phrases. Emblems include, for example, the signs for "okay," "peace," "come here," "I'm hitchhiking and I need a lift," "up yours," and so on. Emblems are nonverbal substitutes for specific words or phrases. You probably learn them in essentially the same way you learned words—without conscious awareness or explicit teaching and largely through a process of imitation.

Table 9.1　The Five Body Movements

	Name and Function	Examples
	Emblems directly translate words or phrases	"Okay" sign, "come here" wave, hitchhiker's sign
	Illustrators accompany and literally "illustrate" verbal messages	Circular hand movements when talking of a circle; hands far apart when talking of something large
	Affect displays communicate emotional meaning	Expressions of happiness, surprise, fear, anger, sadness, disgust/contempt
	Regulators monitor, maintain, or control the speaking of another	Facial expressions and hand gestures indicating "keep going," "slow down," or "what else happened?"
	Adaptors satisfy some need	Scratching one's head

Although emblems seem natural and inherently meaningful, they are as arbitrary as any word in any language. Thus our present culture's emblems are not necessarily the same as the emblems of three hundred years ago or the emblems of other cultures.

Illustrators

Illustrators are nonverbal behaviors that accompany and literally "illustrate" verbal messages. In saying, "Let's go up," for example, you may move both your head and hands in an upward direction. In describing a circle or a square you are likely to make circular or square movements with your hands. So well learned are these movements that it is difficult to reverse them or to employ inappropriate ones.

You are only partially aware of the illustrators you use. At times they have to be brought to your attention. Illustrators are more natural, less arbitrary, and more universal than emblems. It is likely that they include some innate component as well as some learning.

Affect Displays

Affect displays are those facial movements that convey emotional meaning; they show anger and fear, happiness and surprise, eagerness and fatigue. Such facial expressions "give us away" when you try to present a false image and lead people to say, "You look angry today, what's wrong?" You can, however, consciously control affect displays, as actors do when they play a role. Affect displays depend less on verbal messages than do illustrators. Further, you do not consciously control affect displays as much as you do emblems and illustrators. Affect displays may be unintentional—as when they give you away—but they may also be intentional. You may want to show anger, love, hate, or surprise and, usually, you do a credible job.

Regulators

Regulators are nonverbal behaviors that "regulate," monitor, maintain, or control another individual's speech. When you listen to another person, you are not passive; you nod your head, purse your lips, adjust your eye focus, and make various paralinguistic sounds such as "mm-mm" or "tsk." Regulators are clearly culture-bound and are not universal.

Regulators tell speakers what you expect or want them to do as they are talking—for example, "Keep going," "What else happened?" "I don't believe that," or "Slow down." Speakers in turn receive these nonverbal behaviors unconsciously. Depending on the speaker's degree of sensitivity, he or she will change their behavior according to the directions the regulators supply.

Adaptors

Adaptors are nonverbal behaviors that when performed in private—or in public but without being seen—serve some kind of need and occur in their entirety. For example, when you are alone you might scratch your head until you put the itch to rest. In public, when people are watching you, you perform these adaptors only partially. You might, for example, put your fingers to your head and move them around a bit, but you probably would not scratch enough to eliminate the itch.

FACIAL MOVEMENTS

Facial messages communicate types of emotion as well as selected qualities or dimensions of emotion. Most researchers agree with Paul Ekman, Wallace V. Friesen, and Phoebe Ellsworth (1972) in claiming that facial messages may communicate at least the following "emotion categories": happiness, surprise, fear, anger, sadness, and disgust/contempt. Nonverbal researcher Dale Leathers (1986) proposes that facial movements may also communicate bewilderment and determination.

The six emotions identified by Ekman and his colleagues are generally called **primary affect displays.** These are relatively pure, single emotions. Other emotional states and other facial displays are combinations of these various primary emotions and are called *affect blends.* Approximately 33 affect blends have been identified. These blends are consistently recognized by trained nonverbal analysts. You can communicate these affects by different parts of your face. Thus, for example, you may experience both fear and disgust at the same time. Your eyes and eyelids may signal fear, and movements of your nose, cheek, and mouth area may signal disgust.

Encoding-Decoding Accuracy

Considerable research has addressed the issue of how accurately you can encode and decode facial emotions. One problem in answering this question is that it is difficult to separate the ability of the encoder from the ability of the decoder. Thus, a person may be quite adept at communicating emotions, but the receiver may prove insensitive. On the other hand, the receiver may be good at deciphering emotions, but the sender may be inept.

Accuracy also varies with the emotions themselves. Some emotions are easier to encode and decode than others. Ekman, Friesen, and Ellsworth (1972), for example, report that people judge happiness with an accuracy ranging from 55 to 100 percent, surprise from 38 to 86 percent, and sadness from 19 to 88 percent. Try to communicate surprise using only facial movements. Do this in front of a mirror and try to describe the specific movements of the face that make up surprise. If you signal surprise like most people, you probably employ raised and curved eyebrows, long horizontal forehead wrinkles, wide-open eyes, a dropped-open mouth, and lips parted with no tension.

Paul Ekman (Ekman, Friesen, & Tomkins, 1971) has developed what he calls FAST—the Facial Affect Scoring Technique. In this technique, the face is broken up into three main parts: eyebrows and forehead, eyes and eyelids, and the lower face, from the bridge of the nose down. Judges then try to identify various emotions by observing the different parts of the face and writing descriptions like the one for surprise given above. Certain areas of the face seem best suited to communicating certain emotions. For example, the eyes and eyelids are best for communicating fear. The nose, cheek, and mouth area are best for communicating disgust.

Micromomentary Expressions

Researchers have long been interested in whether you can really hide emotions or whether they somehow reveal themselves below the level of conscious awareness. Is your contempt encoded facially without your being aware of it or even without observers being aware of it? Although we do not have a complete answer to this question, some indication that you do communicate these emotions without awareness comes from research on micromomentary expressions. Slow-motion films of therapy patients show that therapy patients' expressions often change dramatically during the therapy session (Haggard & Isaacs, 1966). For example, a frown would change to a smile and then quickly back to a frown. If the film was played at normal speed, the smile would go unnoticed. We call these extremely brief movements, which last for less than 0.4 second, **micromomentary expressions**. These expressions, some theorists argue, indicate a person's real emotional state.

EYE MOVEMENTS

From Ben Jonson's poetic observation "Drink to me only with thine eyes, and I will pledge with mine" to the scientific observations of contemporary researchers (Hess, 1975; Marshall, 1983), the eyes are regarded as the most important nonverbal message system.

The messages communicated by the eyes vary depending on the duration, direction, and quality of the eye behavior. For example, in every culture there are rather strict, though unstated, rules for the proper duration for eye contact. In our culture the average length of gaze is 2.95 seconds. The average length of mutual gaze (two persons

Do men and women use eye contact and eye avoidance to communicate the same meanings? Can you give specific examples to support your position?

gazing at each other) is 1.18 seconds (Argyle, 1988; Argyle & Ingham, 1972). When eye contact falls short of this amount, you may think the person is uninterested, shy, or preoccupied. When the appropriate amount of time is exceeded, you generally perceive this as showing unusually high interest.

The direction of the eye also communicates. Your cultural rule in communicating with another person states that you glance alternatively at the other person's face, then away, then again at the face, and so on. When these directional rules are broken, different meanings are communicated—abnormally high or low interest, self-consciousness, nervousness over the interaction, and so on. The quality—how wide or how narrow your eyes get during interaction—also communicates meaning, especially interest level and such emotions as surprise, fear, and disgust.

Functions of Eye Communication

Researchers note four major functions of eye communication (Knapp & Hall, 1992).

To Seek Feedback   You frequently use your eyes to seek feedback from others. In talking with someone, you look at her or him intently, as if to say, "Well, what do you think?" As you might predict, listeners gaze at speakers more than speakers gaze at listeners. Research shows that the percentage of interaction time spent gazing while listening was between 62 and 75 percent. However, the percentage of time spent gazing while talking was between 38 and 41 percent (Argyle, 1988; Knapp & Hall, 1992).

Women make eye contact more and maintain it longer (both in speaking and in listening) than do men. This holds true whether the woman is interacting with other women or with men. This difference in eye behavior may result from women's tendency to display their emotions more than men; eye contact is one of the most effective ways of communicating emotions. Another possible explanation, as Evan Marshall (1983) argues, is that women have been conditioned more than men to seek positive feedback from others. Women may thus use eye contact in trying to seek this visual feedback.

To Inform Others to Speak   A second function of eye contact is to inform the other person that the channel of communication is open and that he or she should now speak. This is evident in the college classroom, when the instructor asks a question and then locks eyes with a student. Without saying anything, the instructor clearly expects that student to answer the question.

To Signal the Nature of the Relationship   Eye contact is also used to signal the nature of the relationship between two people—for example, a focused attentive glance indicates a positive relationship, but avoiding eye contact shows one of negative regard. You may also signal status relationships with your eyes. This is particularly interesting, because the same movements of the eyes may signal either subordination or superiority. The superior individual, for example, may stare at the subordinate or may glance away. Similarly, the subordinate may look directly at the superior or perhaps to the floor.

We signal power through *visual dominance behavior* (Exline, Ellyson, & Long, 1975). The average speaker maintains a high level of eye contact while listening and a lower level while speaking. When powerful individuals want to signal dominance, they may reverse this pattern. They may, for example, maintain a high level of eye contact while talking but a much lower level while listening. Eye movements may also signal whether the relationship between two people is an amorous one, a hostile one, or one of indifference. Because some of the eye movements expressing these different relationships are so similar, you often utilize information from other areas, particularly the rest of the face, to decode the message before making any final judgments.

To Compensate for Increased Physical Distance   Last, eye movements may compensate for increased physical distance. By making eye contact you overcome psychologically the physical distance between us. When you catch someone's eye at a party, for example, you become psychologically close even though separated by a large physical distance. Not surprisingly, eye contact and other expressions of psychological closeness, such as self-disclosure, are positively related; as one increases, so does the other.

Eye Contact Avoidance Functions

Sociologist Erving Goffman, in *Interaction Ritual* (1967), observed that the eyes are "great intruders." When you avoid eye contact or avert your glance, you help others maintain their privacy. You frequently do this when a couple argues in public. You turn your eyes away (though your eyes may be wide open) as if to say, "I don't mean to intrude; I respect your privacy." Goffman refers to this behavior as **civil inattention**.

Eye contact avoidance can signal lack of interest—in a person, a conversation, or some visual stimulus. At times, like the ostrich, you hide your eyes in an attempt to cut off unpleasant stimuli. Notice, for example, how quickly people close their eyes in the face of some extreme unpleasantness. Interestingly enough, even if the unpleasantness is auditory, you tend to shut it out by closing your eyes. Sometimes you close your eyes to block out visual stimuli and thus heighten your other senses. For example, you often listen to music with your eyes closed. Lovers often close their eyes while kissing, and many prefer to make love in a dark or dimly lit room.

Pupil Dilation

In addition to eye movements, considerable research has been done on pupil dilation, or pupillometrics, largely as a result of the impetus of psychologist Ekhard Hess (1975). In Italy during the fifteenth and sixteenth centuries, women used to put drops of belladonna (which literally means "beautiful woman") into their eyes to dilate the pupils so they would look more attractive. Contemporary research supports the logic of these women; dilated pupils are in fact judged to be more attractive.

Pupil size also indicates your interest and level of emotional arousal. Your pupils enlarge when you are interested in something or when you are emotionally aroused. Perhaps we judge dilated pupils as more attractive because we judge an individual's dilated pupils to indicate interest in us. More generally, Ekhard Hess has argued—with both experimental and intuitive support—that pupils dilate in response to positively evaluated attitudes and objects, and constrict in response to negatively evaluated attitudes and objects.

SOUND

An old exercise to increase the student's ability to express different emotions, feelings, and attitudes was to have the student repeat a sentence while accenting or stressing different words. One popular sentence was, "Is this the face that launched a thousand ships?" Significant differences in meaning are easily communicated depending on where the stress is placed. Consider, for example, the following variations:

1. *Is* this the face that launched a thousand ships?
2. Is *this* the face that launched a thousand ships?
3. Is this the *face* that launched a thousand ships?
4. Is this the face that *launched* a thousand ships?
5. Is this the face that launched a *thousand ships?*

Each of the five sentences communicates something different. Each, in fact, asks a totally different question, even though the words used are the same. All that distinguishes the sentences is stress, one of the aspects of **paralanguage**. Paralanguage refers to the vocal (but nonverbal) dimension of speech. It refers to the *manner* in which you say something rather than to *what* you say.

In addition to stress or pitch, paralanguage includes such vocal characteristics as rate, volume, and rhythm. Paralanguage also includes the vocalizations you make in crying, whispering, moaning, belching, yawning, and yelling (Argyle, 1988; Trager 1958, 1961). A variation in any of these features communicates. The speaker who talks quickly, for example, communicates something different from the one who speaks slowly. Even though the words might be the same, if the speed (or volume, rhythm, or pitch) differs, the meanings you receive will also differ.

Judgments About People

We are a diagnostically oriented people. We are quick to make judgments about another's personality based on paralinguistic cues. Sometimes our judgments turn out to be correct, and sometimes not. You may, for example, conclude that those who speak very softly feel inferior—that they feel no one wants to listen and that nothing they say is significant, so they speak softly. Similarly, you may judge that people who speak loudly have overinflated egos and think that everyone in the world wants to hear them. Those who speak with no variation, in a complete monotone, seem uninterested in what they are saying. You might perceive such people as having a lack of interest in life in general. All these conclusions are, at best, based on little evidence. Yet, this does not stop us from making them.

Among the interesting research findings is one showing that listeners can accurately judge the socioeconomic status (whether high, middle, or low) of speakers from 60-second voice samples (Davitz, 1964). In fact, many listeners reported that they made their judgments in fewer than 15 seconds. Speakers judged to be of high status were also rated as being of higher credibility than speakers rated middle and low in status.

Listeners can also judge with considerable accuracy the emotional states of speakers from vocal expression alone. In these studies, speakers recite the alphabet or numbers while expressing emotions with their voices. Some emotions, of course, are easier to identify than others. For example, it is easy to distinguish between hate and sympathy but more difficult to distinguish between fear and anxiety. And, of course, listeners vary in their ability to decode and speakers vary in their ability to encode emotions (Scherer, 1986).

What judgments would you make about these people before you had the opportunity to talk with them? For example, would you make judgments (perhaps mindlessly) about their education, occupation, political affiliation, religiousness, or affectional orientation?

Judgments About Communication

The rate or speed at which people speak is the aspect of paralanguage that has received the most attention (MacLachlan, 1979). It is of interest to the advertiser, the politician, and in fact, anyone who tries to convey information or to influence others. It is especially important when time is limited or expensive.

Persuasiveness and Credibility   The research conducted on the rate of speech shows that in one-way communication (when one person is doing all or most of the speaking and the other person is doing all or most of the listening), those who talk fast are more persuasive and are evaluated more highly than those who talk at or below normal speeds. This finding holds true regardless of whether the speech is naturally fast or electronically speeded up.

In one experiment, for example, subjects listened to taped messages and then indicated their degree of agreement with the message and their opinion of the speaker's intelligence and objectivity. Speaking rates of 111, 140 (the average speaking rate), and 191 words per minute were used. Subjects agreed most with the fastest speech and least with the slowest speech. Further, they rated the fastest speaker as the most intelligent and objective. They rated the slowest speaker as the least intelligent and objective. Even when the speaker was shown to have something to gain personally from persuasion (as would a used-car dealer), the fastest speaking rate was the most persuasive.

Comprehension   When we look at comprehension, rapid speech shows an interesting effect. Subjects who listened to speeches at different speeds had their comprehension measured by multiple-choice tests (MacLachlan, 1979). Researchers used 141 words per minute as the average and considered comprehension at this rate to be 100 percent. When they increased the rate to 201 words per minute the comprehension was 95 percent. When they further increased the rate to 282 words per minute (double the normal rate), comprehension was still 90 percent. Even though the rates increased dramatically, the comprehension rates fell only slightly. These 5 and 10 percent losses are more than offset by the increased speed and thus make the faster rates much more efficient in communicating information. If the speeds are increased more than twice normal speech, however, comprehension begins to fall dramatically.

Preferences   Most listeners prefer a somewhat faster than normal speed. For example, when subjects were able to adjust the speed at which they heard a message, they adjusted it to approximately 25 percent faster than normal speed. Similarly, persons find commercials presented at 25 percent faster than normal more interesting than those presented at normal speeds. Further, the level of attention (indexed by the amount of electrical activity in the brain) is greater for fast speeds.

We need to be cautious, however, in applying this research to the field of interpersonal communication. As John MacLachlan (1979) points out, during the time the speaker is speaking, the listener is generating and framing a reply. If the speaker talks too rapidly, there may not be enough time to compose this reply. As a result, the listener may become resentful. Furthermore, the increased rate may seem so unnatural that the listener may focus on the speed of speech rather than the thought expressed. But with one-way communication, especially mass communication, it is clear that increased speech rates will become more and more popular (see Units 24 and 25).

Summary

1. *Emblems* are nonverbal behaviors that rather directly translate words or phrases.

2. *Illustrators* are nonverbal behaviors that accompany and literally "illustrate" the verbal messages.

3. *Affect displays* are nonverbal movements that communicate emotional meaning.

4. *Regulators* are nonverbal movements that coordinate, monitor, maintain, or control the speaking of another individual.

5. *Adaptors* are nonverbal behaviors that are emitted without conscious awareness and that usually serve some kind of need, as in scratching an itch.

6. *Facial movements* may communicate a wide variety of emotions. The most frequently studied are happiness, surprise, fear, anger, sadness, and disgust/contempt. Communications of these six emotions are referred to as *primary affect displays*.

7. *Micromomentary expressions* are extremely brief movements that are not consciously perceived and that are thought to reveal a person's real emotional state.

8. *Eye movements* may serve to seek feedback, to inform others to speak, to signal the nature of a relationship, and to compensate for increased physical distance.

9. *Pupil size* seems indicative of one's interest and one's level of emotional arousal. Pupils enlarge when you are interested in something or when you are emotionally aroused in a positive way.

Applications

9.1 PRAISING AND CRITICIZING

The aim of this exercise is to show that the same verbal statement can communicate praise and criticism depending on the paralinguistic cues that accompany the statement. Read each of the 10 statements first to communicate praise and second to communicate criticism. One procedure is to have the entire class seated in a circle and to go around the room with the first student reading statement No. 1 with a praising meaning, the second student reading statement No. 1 with a criticizing meaning, and so on until all 10 statements are read.

After all 10 statements are read from both the praising and criticizing perspective, consider these questions:

1. What paralinguistic cues communicate praise? What paralinguistic cues communicate criticism?

2. What one paralinguistic cue was most helpful in enabling the speaker to communicate praise or criticism?

3. Most people would claim that it is easier to decode the praise or criticism than to encode these meanings. Was this true in this experience? Why or why not?

4. Although this exercise focused on paralanguage, the statements were probably read with different facial expressions, eye movements, and body postures. How would you describe these other nonverbals when communicating praise and criticism?

Statements

1. Now that looks good on you.
2. You lost weight.
3. You look younger than that.
4. You're gonna make it.
5. That was some meal.
6. You really know yourself.
7. You're an expert.
8. You're so sensitive. I'm amazed.
9. Your parents are really something.
10. Are you ready? Already?

9.2 DYSFUNCTIONAL NONVERBALS

This experience is desinged to highlight some of the nonverbal behaviors that get in the way of effective communication. Describe one or more nonverbal behaviors (along with appropriate real or hypothetical situations in which these nonverbals have occurred or might occur) that can create each of the following communication problems or difficulties:

1. Draws attention away from what is being said to a concentration on the nonverbal behavior
2. Unintentionally contradicts the meaning of the verbal message
3. Conveys the imperssion that the speaker is unconcerned with communicating or is uninterested in the other person
4. Gives the impression that the speaker does not like the person he or she is talking with
5. Conveys the imperssion that the speaker is not enjoying the interaction
6. Gives the impression that the speaker is not being honest or candid

NONVERBAL MESSAGES OF SPACE AND TIME

UNIT CONTENTS

Proxemics

Artifactual Communication

Territoriality

Touch Communication

Temporal Communication

    Summary

    Application

        10.1 Nonverbal Dating Behaviors

        10.2 The Meanings of Color

UNIT GOALS

After completing this unit, you should be able to

1. explain the four spatial distances and give examples of the kinds of communication that take place at each distance

2. define *territoriality*

3. explain the types of territorial encroachment and possible reactions to it

4. define *marker* and distinguish among central, boundary, and ear-markers

5. explain the meanings communicated by touch

6. explain the factors that influence whom one touches and where

7. explain the nature of touch avoidance and its relationship to apprehension, self-disclosure, age, and sex

8. define *cultural* and *psychological time*

In addition to communicating with words and with our hands, face, and eyes, we communicate with space, territoriality, and touch. These forms of nonverbal communication figure in almost every communication transaction. In this unit, we focus on how these systems operate in human communication.

PROXEMICS

Our use of space speaks as surely and as loudly as words and sentences. A speaker who stands close to her listener, with her hands on the listener's shoulders and her eyes focused directly on those of the listener, communicates something very different from the speaker who sits crouched in a corner with his arms folded and his eyes on the floor. Similarly, the executive office suite on the top floor with huge windows, private bar, and plush carpeting communicates something very different from the 6-foot-square cubicle occupied by the rest of the workers.

This area of communication is often called **proxemics**, a term coined by anthropologist Edward T. Hall (1963). In our discussion we focus first on the four major spatial distances that people maintain when they communicate. Second, we examine some of the influences on these spatial distances.

Spatial Distances

Edward Hall (1959, 1966) distinguishes four distances that define the type of relationship permitted. Each of these four has a close phase and a far phase, making a total of eight clearly identifiable distances (see Figure 10.1).

Intimate Distance Intimate distance ranges from the close phase of actual touching to the far phase of 6 to 18 inches; from this distance, the presence of the other individual is unmistakable. Each person experiences the sound, smell, and feel of the other's breath. You use the *close phase* for lovemaking and wrestling, for comfort-

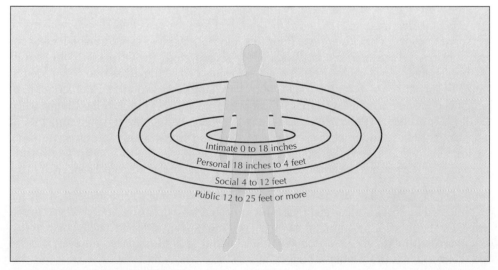

Intimate 0 to 18 inches
Personal 18 inches to 4 feet
Social 4 to 12 feet
Public 12 to 25 feet or more

FIGURE 10.1 Proxemic distances.

ing and protecting. In the close phase the muscles and the skin communicate, while actual verbalizations play a minor role. In this close phase, even whispering has the effect of increasing the psychological distance between the two individuals.

The *far phase* allows you to touch another person by extending your hands. This distance is still so short that it is not considered proper in public. Because this distance feels inappropriate and uncomfortable (at least for Americans), the eyes seldom meet. They remain fixed on some remote object.

Personal Distance   Each of us, says Hall, carries around with us a protective bubble defining our **personal distance**. This bubble keeps you protected and untouched by others. In the *close phase* of personal distance (one and a half to two and a half feet), you can still hold or grasp another person but only by extending your arms. You take into your protective bubble only certain individuals—for example, loved ones. In the *far phase* (two and a half to four feet), two people can touch each other only if they *both* extend their arms. This far phase represents the extent to which you can physically get your hands on people. As a result, it defines, in one sense, the limits of our physical control over others.

Even at this distance you can see many details of an individual—the gray hairs, tooth stains, clothing lint, and so on. However, you can no longer detect body heat. At times you may detect breath odor, but at this distance etiquette demands that you direct your breath to some neutral corner so as not to offend (as television commercials warn that you might do).

When personal space is invaded, you often become uncomfortable and tense. Your speech may become disrupted, unsteady, jerky, and staccato. You may have difficulty maintaining eye contact and may frequently look away from the person. This discomfort may also reveal itself in excessive body movement. At other times you do not mind the invasion of personal space—for example, when others enter your personal space bubble at a crowded party. Similarly, when people you like come close to you, you perceive the situation as being less crowded than when less-liked people enter the same space. People you like crowd you psychologically less than people you do not like.

Social Distance   At the **social distance** you lose the visual detail you have in the personal distance. The *close phase* (four to seven feet) is the distance at which you conduct impersonal business and interact at a social gathering. The *far phase* (7 to 12 feet) is the distance at which you stand when someone says, "Stand back so I can look at you." At this distance, business transactions have a more formal tone. In offices of high officials desks are positioned so that the official is assured of at least this distance when dealing with clients. Unlike intimate distance, where eye contact is awkward, the far phase of social distance makes eye contact essential. Otherwise, communication would be lost. The voice is generally louder than normal at this distance. Shouting or raising the voice, however, has the effect of reducing the social distance to a personal distance.

Public Distance   In the *close phase* of **public distance** (12 to 15 feet), a person is protected by space. At this distance a person could take defensive action when threatened. On a public bus or train, for example, you might keep at least this distance from a drunkard. Although at this distance you lose fine details of the face and eyes, you are still close enough to see what is happening.

How culturally universal do you think these four distances are? Can you think of a culture which does not make these same distinctions? In what ways do they differentiate spatial distances? Do these four distances apply equally to communication among women and among men?

At the *far phase* (more than 25 feet), you see people not as separate individuals but as part of the whole setting. You automatically allow about 30 feet of space around important public figures. And, it seems, you do this whether or not there are guards preventing you from entering this space. This far phase is of course the distance from which actors perform on stage. At this distance, actions and voices have to be somewhat exaggerated to convey detail.

Influences on Space Communication

Several factors influence the way you treat space in communication, and a number of generalizations are especially important to communication (Burgoon, Buller, & Woodall, 1989).

Status   People of equal status maintain a shorter distance between themselves than do people of unequal status. When the status is unequal, the higher-status person may approach the lower-status person more closely than the lower-status person may approach the higher-status person.

Culture   Americans stand fairly far apart when conversing, at least compared with people in certain European and Middle Eastern cultures. Arabs, for example, stand much closer to each other than do Americans. Italians and Spaniards likewise maintain less distance in their interactions than many northern Europeans.

In the United States, if you live next door to someone, then you are almost automatically expected to be friendly and to interact with that person. But this is a cultural expectation not shared by all cultures. In Japan, for example, the fact that your house is next to another person's house does not imply that you should become close or that you should visit each other. Consider, therefore, the situation in which a Japanese buys a house next to an American. The Japanese may well see the American as overly familiar and as taking friendship for granted. The American may see the Japanese as distant, unfriendly, and unneighborly. Yet each person is merely fulfilling the expectations of his or her own culture (Hall & Hall, 1987).

Context   Generally, the larger the physical space you are in, the smaller the interpersonal space. Thus, for example, the space between two people conversing will be smaller in the street than in an apartment. The larger the space, the more you seem to need to close it off to make the immediate communication context manageable.

Subject Matter   If you talk about personal matters or share secrets, you maintain a short distance. When you talk about impersonal, general matters, the space is generally larger. Psychologically, it seems you are trying to exclude others from hearing even though physically there may be no one within earshot. You maintain a shorter distance if you are being praised than if you are being blamed. Perhaps you want to move in closer to the praise lest it fall on someone else. And perhaps you try to remove yourself (physically) from blame.

Sex and Age   Women stand closer to one another than do men. Opposite-sex pairs stand the farthest apart. Similarly, our culture allows women to touch each other more than men and more than unacquainted opposite-sex pairs. Children stand closer to each other than do adults, showing that maintained distance is a learned behavior.

Positive and Negative Evaluation   You stand farther from enemies, authority figures, and higher-status individuals than from friends and peers; you maintain a greater distance from the physically handicapped and from people of a different racial group than from the nonhandicapped and those of your own race. Typically, you maintain more distance between yourself and people you may subconsciously evaluate negatively.

ARTIFACTUAL COMMUNICATION

Artifactual messages are those made by human hands. Thus, color, clothing, jewelry, and the decoration of space would be considered artifactual. We look at each of these here briefly.

Color Communication

Henry Dreyfuss, in his *Symbol Sourcebook* (1971), reminds us of some of the positive and negative meanings associated with various colors. Some of these are presented in Table 10.1. Dreyfuss also notes some cultural comparisons for some of these colors. For example, red in China is used for joyous and festive occasions, whereas in Japan it signifies anger and danger. Blue signifies defeat for the Cherokee, but virtue and truth for the Egyptian. In the Japanese theater, blue is the color for villains. Yellow signifies happiness and prosperity in Egypt, but in tenth-century France, yellow colored the doors of criminals. Green communicates femininity to certain Native Americans, fertility and strength to Egyptians, and youth and energy to the Japanese. Purple signifies virtue and faith in Egypt, grace and nobility in Japan.

There is some evidence that colors affect you physiologically. For example, when subjects are exposed to red light, respiratory movements increase; blue light decreases

Table 10.1 Some Positive and Negative Messages of Colors

Color	Positive Messages	Negative Messages
red	warmth	death
	passion	war
	life	revolution
	liberty	devil
	patriotism	danger
blue	religious feeling	doubt
	devotion	discouragement
	truth	
	justice	
yellow	intuition	cowardice
	wisdom	malevolence
	divinity	impure love
green	nature	envy
	hope	jealousy
	freshness	opposition
	prosperity	disgrace
purple	power	mourning
	royalty	regret
	love of truth	penitence
	nostalgia	resignation

Source: Adapted from Henry Dreyfuss, *Symbol Sourcebook* (New York: McGraw-Hill, 1971).

respiratory movements. Similarly, eye blinks increase in frequency when eyes are exposed to red light and decrease when exposed to blue. This seems consistent with our intuitive feelings about blue being more soothing and red being more arousing. After changing a school's walls from orange and white to blue, the blood pressure of the students decreased while their academic performance increased (Mella, 1988).

Colors also influence your perceptions and behaviors (Kanner, 1989). Consumers' acceptance of a product, advertisers find, is largely determined by its package. For example, the very same coffee taken from a yellow can was described by subjects as weak, from a dark brown can too strong, from a red can rich, and from a blue can mild. Even your acceptance of a person may depend on the colors worn. Consider, for example, the comments of one color expert (Kanner, 1989): "If you have to pick the wardrobe for your defense lawyer heading into court and choose anything but blue, you deserve to lose the case." Black is so powerful it could work against the lawyer with the jury. Brown lacks sufficient authority. Green would probably elicit a negative response.

Clothing and Body Adornment

Clothing serves a variety of functions. It *protects* you from the weather and, in sports like football, from injury. It helps you conceal parts of your body and thus serves a *modesty* function. Clothing also serves as a *cultural display* (Morris, 1977) by communicating your cultural affiliations. In the United States, where there are a number of different ethnic groups, you regularly see examples of dress that tell you the wearers' country of origin.

People make inferences about who you are in part by the way you dress. Whether these inferences prove to be accurate or inaccurate, they will nevertheless influence what people think of you and how they react to you. Your social class, your seriousness, your attitudes (for example, whether you are conservative or liberal), your concern for convention, and your sense of style and perhaps even your creativity will all be judged partly from the way you dress. In fact, the very popular *Dress for Success* and *The Woman's Dress for Success Book* by John Molloy (1975, 1977, 1981) instructs men and women in how to dress so that they can communicate a number of desirable images—for example, efficiency, reliability, or authoritativeness.

Similarly, college students will perceive an instructor dressed informally as friendly, fair, enthusiastic, and flexible and the same instructor dressed formally as prepared, knowledgeable, and organized (Malandro, Barker, & Barker, 1989).

Your jewelry likewise communicates messages about you. Wedding and engagement rings are obvious examples of jewelry that communicates very specific messages. College rings and political buttons also send specific messages. If you wear a Rolex watch or large precious stones, others are likely to infer that you are rich. Men with earrings will be judged differently from men without earrings.

The way you wear your hair says something about who you are. Your hair may communicate a concern for being up to date, a desire to shock, or perhaps a lack of concern for appearances. Men with long hair will generally be judged as less conservative than will men with shorter hair.

Space Decoration

The way your private spaces are decorated also communicates who you are. The office with mahogany desk and bookcases and oriental rugs communicates the occu-

There seems to be no cultural group that has not been affected by AIDS. How have the cultures of which you are a member been affected by AIDS? How do those cultural groups react to AIDS and to people with AIDS? What is your college doing to increase AIDS awareness?

Can you identify the sex of the person who occupies this office solely on the basis of the way the space is decorated? What specific items would identify the office as belonging to a man? To a woman?

pant's importance and status within the organization, just as the metal desk and bare floors distinguishes a worker who is much further down in the hierarchy. Similarly, people will make inferences about you on the basis of the way you decorate your home. The luxuriousness of the furnishings may communicate your status and wealth; their coordination may communicate your sense of style. The magazines display your interests. The arrangement of chairs around a television set show how important watching television is to you. Bookcases lining the walls reveal the importance of reading. In fact, there is probably little in your home that does not send messages to others and that others do not use for making inferences about you. Computers, wide-screen televisions, well-equipped kitchens, and oil paintings of great grandparents, for example, all say something about the people who display them.

The lack of certain items will communicate something else about you. Consider, for example, what messages you would get from a home without a television, or one without a telephone or books.

Smell Communication

Smell communication, or *olfactics*, is extremely important in a wide variety of situations and is now "big business" (Kleinfeld, 1992). Without smell, taste would be severely impaired. For example, it would be extremely difficult to taste the difference between a raw potato and an apple without the sense of smell. In communication smell also holds much influence. Advertisers and manufacturers, convinced of the influence of smell, spend millions of dollars each year creating scents for cleaning products and toothpastes, which have *nothing* to do with their cleaning power.

More obviously, of course, are perfumes, colognes, aftershave lotions, and deodorants. In 1989, for example, women in the United States spent $1.8 billion and men spent $85 million on perfumes, colognes, and other fragrances. Your own behaviors of ritual bathing with scented soap, wearing cologne (or some such scent), and using mouthwash and scented toothpaste may reveal your own beliefs in the power of smell communication.

Perhaps the most obvious message that smell communicates is that of attraction. People use perfumes, colognes, aftershave lotions, powders, and the like to make themselves smell more attractive to others. Sophia Loren, Elizabeth Taylor, Dionne Warwick, Cher, and, most recently, Billy Dee Williams, all sell perfumes by associating their own attractiveness with the fragrance. The implication is that others can smell likewise and can therefore appear equally attractive.

You also use odors to make yourself feel better; after all, you also smell yourself. When the smells are pleasant, you feel better about yourself; when the smells are unpleasant, you feel less good about yourself and probably (and hopefully) shower and perhaps put on some cologne.

TERRITORIALITY

One of the most interesting concepts in ethology (the study of animals in their natural surroundings) is **territoriality**. For example, male animals will stake out a particular territory and consider it their own. They will allow prospective mates to enter but will defend it against entrance by others, especially other males of the same species. Among deer, the size of the territory signifies the power of the buck, which in turn determines how many females he will mate with. Less powerful bucks will be able to control only small parcels of land and so will mate with only one or two females. This is a particularly adaptive measure, since it ensures that the stronger members will produce most of the offspring. When the "landowner" takes possession of an area—either because it is vacant or because he gains it through battle—he marks it, for example, by urinating around the boundaries. The size of the animal's territory, then, indicates the status of the animal within the herd.

The size and location of human territory also say something about status (Mehrabian, 1976; Sommer, 1969). An apartment or office in midtown Manhattan or downtown Tokyo, for example, is extremely high-status territory. The cost of the territory restricts it to those who have lots of money.

Status is also signaled by the unwritten law granting the right of invasion. Higher-status individuals have more of a right to invade the territory of others than vice versa. The boss of a large company, for example, can invade the territory of a junior executive by barging into her or his office, but the reverse would be unthinkable.

Some researchers claim that territoriality is innate and demonstrates the innate aggressiveness of humans. Others claim that territoriality is learned behavior and is culturally based. Most, however, agree that a great deal of human behavior can be understood and described as territorial, regardless of its origin.

SELF-TEST

What's Wrong with the Gift?

One aspect of nonverbal communication that is frequently overlooked is that of giving gifts. Each culture follows somewhat different rules and customs when it comes to giving and receiving gifts. Here are a few situations (largely from the excellent work of Roger Axtell, 1990a, 1990b) where gift giving backfired and created barriers rather than bonds. These examples are designed to heighten your awareness of both the importance of gift giving and of recognizing intercultural differences. What might have gone wrong in each of these situations?

1. An American brings chrysanthemums to a Belgian colleague and a clock to a Chinese colleague. Both react negatively.

2. Upon meeting an Arab businessman for the first time—someone with whom you wish to do considerable business—you present him with a gift. He becomes disturbed.

3. When visiting an Arab family in Oman, you bring a bottle of your favorite brandy for drinking after dinner. Your host seems annoyed.

4. When arriving for dinner at the home of a Kenya colleague you bring flowers as a dinner gift. Your host accepts them politely but looks puzzled.

5. In arriving for dinner at the home of a Swiss colleague, you bring 14 red roses. Your host accepts them politely but looks strangely at you.

Possible reasons

1. Chrysanthemums in Belgium and clocks in China are both reminders of death.
2. Gifts given at the first meeting may be interpreted as a bribe and so should be avoided.
3. Alcohol is prohibited by Islamic law and so should be avoided when selecting gifts for most Arabs.
4. In Kenya flowers are only brought to express your condolence.
5. In Switzerland red roses are a sign of romantic interest. Also, an even number of flowers is generally considered bad luck and so should be avoided.

Territorial Encroachment

Look around your home. You probably see certain territories that different people have staked out and where invasions are cause for at least mildly defensive action. This is perhaps seen most clearly with siblings who each have (or "own") a specific chair, room, radio, and so on. Father has his chair and Mother has her chair.

In classrooms where seats are not assigned, territoriality can also be observed. When a student sits in a seat that has normally been occupied by another student, the regular occupant will often become disturbed and resentful.

Following Lyman and Scott (1967; DeVito & Hecht, 1990), Table 10.2 identifies the three major types of territorial encroachment: violation, invasion, and contamination.

You can react to encroachment in several ways (DeVito & Hecht, 1990; Lyman & Scott, 1967). The most extreme form is **turf defense**. When you cannot tolerate the in-

Table 10.2 Three Types of Territorial Encroachment

Name	Definition	Example
Violation	Unwarranted use of another's territory	Entering another's office or home without permission
Invasion	Entering the territory of another and thereby changing the meaning of that territory	Parents entering a teen's social group
Contamination	Rendering a territory impure	Smoking a cigar in a kitchen

truders, you may choose to defend the territory against them and try to expel them. This is the method of gangs who defend "their" streets and neighborhoods by fighting off members of rival gangs (intruders) who enter the territory.

A less extreme defense is **insulation,** a tactic in which you erect some sort of barrier between yourself and the invaders. Some people do this by wearing sunglasses to avoid eye contact. Others erect fences to let others know that they do not welcome interpersonal interaction.

Linguistic collusion, another method of separating yourself from unwanted invaders, involves speaking in a language unknown to these outsiders. Or you might use professional jargon to which they are not privy. Linguistic collusion groups together those who speak that language and excludes those who do not know the linguistic code. Still another type of response is **withdrawal;** you leave the territory altogether.

Markers

Much as animals mark their territory, humans mark theirs with three types of markers: central, boundary, and earmarkers (Hickson & Stacks, 1993). **Central markers** are items you place in a territory to reserve it. For example, you place a drink at the bar, books on your desk, and a sweater over the chair to let others know that this territory belongs to you.

Boundary markers set boundaries that divide your territory from "theirs." In the supermarket checkout line, the bar placed between your groceries and those of the person behind you is a boundary marker. Similarly, the armrests separating your chair from those of the people on either side, and the molded plastic seats on a bus or train are boundary markers.

Earmarkers—a term taken from the practice of branding animals on their ears—are those identifying marks that indicate your possession of a territory or object. Trademarks, nameplates, and initials on a shirt or attaché case are all examples of earmarkers.

TOUCH COMMUNICATION

Touch communication, also referred to as **haptics,** is perhaps the most primitive form of communication (Montagu, 1971). Developmentally, touch is probably the first sense to be used. Even in the womb the child is stimulated by touch. Soon after birth the child is fondled, caressed, patted, and stroked. In turn, the child explores its world through touch. In short time, the child learns to communicate a wide variety of meanings through touch.

The Meanings of Touch

We discuss here five of the major meanings of touch, identified in an extensive study (Jones & Yarbrough, 1985). We consider these functions largely to illustrate the great number of messages that touch can communicate.

Positive Affect   Touch often communicates positive emotions. This occurs mainly between intimates or others who have a relatively close relationship. "Touch is such a powerful signalling system," notes Desmond Morris (1972), "and it's so closely related to emotional feelings we have for one another that in casual encounters it's kept to a minimum. When the relationship develops, the touching follows along with it." Among the most important of these positive emotions are support, appreciation, inclusion, sexual interest or intent, and affection.

Playfulness   Touch often communicates our intention to play, either affectionately or aggressively. When you communicate affection or aggression in a playful manner, the playfulness lessens the emotion and tells the other person not to take it seriously. Playful touch lightens an interaction.

Control   Touch may also direct the behaviors, attitudes, or feelings of the other person. Such control may communicate a number of messages. In compliance, for example, you touch the other person to communicate "move over," "hurry," "stay here," and "do it." You might also touch a person to gain his or her attention, as if to say "look at me" or "look over here."

Touching to control sometimes communicates dominance as well. Consider, as Nancy Henley suggests in her *Body Politics* (1977), who would touch whom—say, by putting an arm on the other person's shoulder or by putting a hand on the other person's back—in the following dyads: teacher and student, doctor and patient, master and servant, manager and worker, minister and parishioner, police officer and accused, business executive and secretary. Most people brought up in our culture would say that the first-named person in each dyad would more likely touch the second-named person than the other way around—the higher-status person is permitted to touch the lower-status person. In fact, it would be a breach of etiquette for the lower-status person to touch the person of higher status.

Henley further argues that in addition to indicating relative status, touching demonstrates the assertion of male power and dominance over women. Men may, says Henley, touch women in the course of their daily routine. In the restaurant, office, and school, for example, men touch women and thus indicate their "superior status." When women touch men, on the other hand, the interpretation that it designates a female-dominant relationship is not acceptable (to men). Men may therefore explain and interpret this touching as a sexual invitation.

Ritual   Ritualistic touching centers on greetings and departures. Shaking hands to say "hello" or "good-bye" is a clear example of ritualistic touching. Ritualistic touching also includes hugging, kissing, or putting your arm around another's shoulder when greeting or saying farewell.

Task-Relatedness   Task-related touching is associated with the performance of some function. This ranges from removing a speck of dust from another person's face to helping someone out of a car or checking someone's forehead for fever.

Who Touches Whom Where

A great deal of research has been directed at the question of who touches whom where. Most of it has addressed two basic questions: First, are there gender differences? Do men and women communicate through touch in the same way? Are men and women touched in the same way? Second, are there cultural differences? Do people in widely different cultures communicate through touch in the same way?

Gender Differences and Touch   Early research reported that touching and being touched differ little between men and women (Jourard, 1968). Men touch and are touched as often and in the same places as women. The major exception to this finding is the touching behavior of mothers and fathers. Mothers touch children of both sexes and of all ages more than do fathers. In fact, many fathers go no further than touching the hands of their children. More recent research has found differences and show that women touch adults as well more than men do. Research shows that women initiate touch more than men and that women touch and are touched more than men (Jones, 1986).

Opposite-sex friends report more touching than do same-sex friends. Both male and female college students report that they touch and are touched more by their opposite-sex friends than by their same-sex friends. No doubt the strong societal bias against same-sex touching accounts for these generalizations.

Culture Differences and Touch   Students from the United States reported being touched twice as much as did students from Japan (Barnlund, 1975). In Japan there is a strong taboo against touching between strangers. The Japanese are therefore especially careful to maintain sufficient distance.

Another obvious cross-cultural contrast is presented by the Middle East, where same-sex touching in public is extremely common. Men, for example, walk with their arms around each other's shoulders—a practice that would cause many raised eyebrows in the United States. Middle Easterners, Latin Americans, and southern Europeans touch each other while talking a great deal more than do people from "noncontact cultures"—Asia and northern Europe, for example.

Even such seemingly minor nonverbal differences as these can create difficulties when members of different cultures interact. Southern Europeans may perceive northern Europeans and Japanese as cold, distant, and uninvolved. Southern Europeans in turn may be perceived as pushy, aggressive, and inappropriately intimate (see Units 22 and 23).

Touch Avoidance

Much as you have a need and desire to touch and be touched, you also have a tendency to avoid touch from certain people or in certain circumstances (Andersen & Leibowitz, 1978). Touch avoidance is positively related to communication apprehension. If you have a strong fear of oral communication then you probably also have strong touch avoidance tendencies. Touch avoidance is also high with those who self-disclose less.

Both touch and self-disclosure are intimate forms of communication. People who are reluctant to get close to another person by self-disclosing also seem reluctant to get close by touching.

Older people avoid touch with opposite-sex persons more than do younger people. As people get older they are touched less by members of the opposite sex; this decreased frequency of touching may lead them to avoid touching.

Males avoid same-sex touch more than do females. This accords well with current stereotypes. Men avoid touching other men, but women may and do touch other women. Women, however, avoid opposite-sex touching more than do men.

TEMPORAL COMMUNICATION

Temporal communication (**chronemics**) concerns the use of time—how you organize it, how you react to it, and the messages it communicates (Bruneau, 1985, 1990). Cultural and psychological time are two aspects of particular interest in human communication.

Cultural Time

We can distinguish three types of cultural time. *Technical time* is precise, scientific time. Milliseconds and atomic years are examples of technical or scientific time. This time system is used only in the laboratory, so it has little relevance to our daily lives.

Formal time refers to how a culture defines and teaches time. In our culture time is divided into seconds, minutes, hours, days, weeks, months, and years. Other cultures may use phases of the moon or the seasons to delineate time periods. We divide college courses into 50- or 75-minute periods that meet two or three times a week for 14-week periods called semesters. Eight semesters of 15 or 16 periods per week equal a college education. As these examples illustrate, formal time units are arbitrary. The culture establishes them for convenience.

Informal time refers to a rather loose use of time terms—for example, *forever, immediately, soon, right away, as soon as possible*. This is the area of time that creates the most communication problems because the terms have different meanings for different people.

Displaced and Diffused Time Orientations   An important distinction is between displaced and diffused time orientations. In a displaced time orientation, time is viewed exactly. Persons with this orientation will be exactly on time. In a diffused time orientation, people see time as approximate rather than exact. People with this orientation are often late for appointments because they understand, for example, a scheduled time of 8 P.M. as meaning anywhere from seven forty-five to eight fifteen or eight thirty.

In one study, researchers examined the accuracy of the clocks in different cultures and found considerable variation (LeVine & Bartlett, 1984). Clocks in Japan were the most accurate, while clocks in Indonesia were the least accurate. Clocks in England, Italy, Taiwan, and the United States fell between these two extremes in accuracy. Not surprisingly, when the speed of pedestrians in these cultures were measured, the researcher found that the Japanese walked the fastest and the Indonesians the slowest.

Here is a photo of the Mud Men of the Solomon Islands in a ceremonial dance. If you knew nothing about this culture, what guesses would you make about their concept of time? Would it differ from your own? Is your own view of time consistent with your achieving your personal and professional goals?

Such differences reflect the different ways in which cultures treat time and their general attitude toward the importance of time in their everyday lives.

Psychological Time

Psychological time refers primarily to the importance you place on the past, present, and future. If you have a *past orientation*, you relive old times and regard the old methods as the best. You see events as circular and recurring, so the wisdom of yesterday is applicable also to today and tomorrow. Having a *present orientation* means you live in the present; for now, not tomorrow. If you have a *future orientation* you look toward and live for the future. You save today, work hard in college, and deny yourself luxuries because you are preparing for the future.

Recent research has provided some interesting conclusions about ourselves on the basis of the way we view time (Gonzalez & Zimbardo, 1985). Before reading these conclusions take the time test on page 173.

SELF-TEST

What Time Do You Have?

For each statement, indicate whether the statement is true (T) of your general attitude and behavior, or false (F) of your general attitude and behavior. (A few statements are purposely repeated to facilitate scoring and analyzing your responses.)

_T_   1. Meeting tomorrow's deadlines and doing other necessary work comes before tonight's partying.

_T_   2. I meet my obligations to friends and authorities on time.

_T_   3. I complete projects on time by making steady progress.

_F_   4. I am able to resist temptations when I know there is work to be done.

_T_   5. I keep working at a difficult, uninteresting task if it will help me get ahead.

_F_   6. If things don't get done on time, I don't worry about it.

_F_   7. I think that it's useless to plan too far ahead because things hardly ever come out the way you planned anyway.

_F_   8. I try to live one day at a time.

_F_   9. I live to make better what is rather than to be concerned about what will be.

_____ 10. It seems to me that it doesn't make sense to worry about the future, since fate determines that whatever will be, will be.

_____ 11. I believe that getting together with friends to party is one of life's important pleasures.

_____ 12. I do things impulsively, making decisions on the spur of the moment.

_____ 13. I take risks to put excitement in my life.

_____ 14. I get drunk at parties.

_____ 15. It's fun to gamble.

_____ 16. Thinking about the future is pleasant to me.

_____ 17. When I want to achieve something, I set subgoals and consider specific means for reaching these goals.

_____ 18. It seems to me that my career path is pretty well laid out.

_____ 19. It upsets me to be late for appointments.

_____ 20. I meet my obligations to friends and authorities on time.

_____ 21. I get irritated at people who keep me waiting when we've agreed to meet at a given time.

_____ 22. It makes sense to invest a substantial part of my income in insurance premiums.

_____ 23. I believe that "a stitch in time saves nine."

Continued on page 174

SELF-TEST (continued)

_____ 24. I believe that "a bird in the hand is worth two in the bush."

_____ 25. I believe it is important to save for a rainy day.

_____ 26. I believe a person's day should be planned each morning.

_____ 27. I make lists of things I must do.

_____ 28. When I want to achieve something, I set subgoals and consider specific means for reaching those goals.

_____ 29. I believe that "a stitch in time saves nine."

Scoring   This psychological time test measures seven different factors. If you scored True for all or most of the questions within any given factor, then you are probably high on that factor. If you scored False for all or most of the questions within any given factor, then you are probably low on that factor's scale.

The first factor, measured by questions 1 through 5, is a future, work motivation, perseverance orientation. People with this orientation have a strong work ethic and are committed to completing a task despite difficulties and temptations.

The second factor, measured by questions 6 through 10, is a present, fatalistic, worry-free orientation. People who score high on this factor live one day at a time, not necessarily to enjoy the day but to avoid planning for the next day and to avoid the anxiety about a future that seems determined by fate rather than by anything they can do themselves.

The third factor, measured by questions 11 through 15, is a present, hedonistic, pleasure-seeking, partying orientation. These people seek to enjoy the present, take risks and engage in a variety of impulsive actions. Teenagers score particularly high on this factor.

The fourth factor, measured by questions 16 through 18, is a future, goal-seeking, and planning orientation. These people derive special pleasure from planning and achieving a variety of goals.

The fifth factor, measured by questions 19 through 21, is a time sensitivity orientation. People who score high on this factor are especially sensitive to time and its role in social obligations.

The sixth factor, measured by questions 22 through 25, is a future, pragmatic action orientation. These people do what they have to do to achieve the future they want. They take practical actions for future gain.

The seventh factor, measured by questions 26 through 29, is a future, somewhat obsessive daily planning orientation. People who score high on this factor make daily "to do" lists, devoting great attention to specific details and subordinate goals.

Source: From "Time in Perspective" by Alexander Gonzalez and Philip G. Zimbardo in *Psychology Today,* March 1985. Reprinted by permission.

Consider some of the findings relevant to psychological time orientation found by Gonzalez and Zimbardo (1985). Future income is positively related to future orientation. The more future oriented a person is, the greater that person's income is likely to be. Present orientation is strongest among lowest-income males.

The time orientation that people develop depends a great deal on their socioeconomic class and their personal experiences. Gonzalez and Zimbardo (1985) observe: "A child with parents in unskilled and semiskilled occupations is usually socialized in a way that promotes a present-oriented fatalism and hedonism. A child of parents who are managers, teachers or other professionals learns future-oriented values and strategies designed to promote achievement."

Different time perspectives also account for much intercultural misunderstanding (see Units 22 and 23) since different cultures will often teach their members drastically different time orientations. The future-oriented person who works for tomorrow's goals will frequently look down on the present-oriented person who avoids planning and focuses on enjoying today as lazy and poorly motivated. In turn the present-oriented person may see those with strong future orientations as obsessed with accumulating wealth or rising in status.

Time and Status

Time is especially linked to status considerations. For example, the importance of being on time varies directly with the status of the individual you are visiting. If the person is extremely important, you had better be there on time. In fact, you had better be there early just in case he or she is able to see you before schedule. As the individual's status decreases, it is less important for you to be on time. Students, for example, must be on time for conferences with teachers, but it is more important to be on time for deans and still more important to be on time for the president of the college. Teachers, on the other hand, may be late for conferences with students but not for conferences with deans or the president. Deans, in turn, may be late for teachers but not for the president. Business organizations and other hierarchies have similar rules.

Even the time of dinner and the time from the arrival of guests to eating varies on the basis of status. Among lower-status individuals, dinner is served relatively early. If there are guests, they eat soon after they arrive. For higher-status people, dinner is relatively late, and a longer time elapses between arrival and eating.

Time and Appropriateness

Promptness or lateness in responding to letters, returning telephone calls, acknowledging gifts, and returning invitations all communicate significant messages to others. We can analyze these messages on such scales as interest-disinterest, organized-disorganized, considerate-inconsiderate, sociable-unsociable, and so on.

Also, there are times when certain activities are considered appropriate and other times when they are considered inappropriate. Thus, it is permissible to make a social phone call during the late morning, afternoon, and early evening, but not before eight or nine o'clock in the morning, during dinnertime, or after eleven o'clock at night. Similarly, in making dates, an appropriate amount of notice is customary. When you give that acceptable amount of notice, you communicate a recognition of the accepted standards, respect for the individual, and perhaps a certain social grace. Should you violate any of these time conventions, however, you would communicate other meanings. For example, a phone call at an abnormal hour will almost surely communicate urgency of some sort. You begin to worry as you race toward the phone.

Summary

1. *Proxemics* refers to the communicative function of space and spatial relationships.

2. Four major proxemic distances are: (1) *intimate distance*, ranging from actual touching to 18 inches; (2) *personal distance*, ranging from one and a half to four feet; (3) *social distance*, ranging from 4 to 12 feet; and (4) *public distance*, ranging from 12 to more than 25 feet.

3. Our treatment of space is influenced by such factors as *status, culture, context, subject matter, sex, age,* and *positive or negative evaluation* of the other person.

4. *Territoriality* refers to one's possessive reaction to an area of space or to particular objects.

5. *Territorial encroachment* may take any of three major forms: *violation, invasion,* and *contamination.*

6. You may react to territorial encroachment by *turf defense, insulation, linguistic collusion,* and *withdrawal.*

7. *Markers* are devices that identify a territory as yours; these include *central markers, boundary markers,* and *earmarkers.*

8. *Touch communication* (*haptics*) may communicate a variety of meanings, the most important being positive affect, playfulness, control, ritual, and task-relatedness.

9. *Touch avoidance* refers to our desire to avoid touching and being touched by others; it has been found to be related to *apprehension, self-disclosure, age,* and *sex.*

10. Generally, women touch more and are touched more than men. Touching patterns vary greatly from one culture to another. Both *gender* and *culture differences* in touch behavior are learned rather than innate.

11. Time may be viewed from at least two perspectives: cultural and psychological. *Cultural time* is concerned with how our culture defines and teaches time, and with the difficulties created by the different meanings people have for informal time terms. *Psychological time* is concerned with people's time orientations, whether past, present, or future.

12. The messages that time communicates are greatly influenced by *status considerations* and by the *social rules* for appropriateness and inappropriateness.

Applications

10.1 NONVERBAL DATING BEHAVIORS

Assume that a friend of yours (male or female) is having trouble dating. Your friend generally communicates a cold, unemotional, and unromantic image. What advice for nonverbal communication could you give your friend to make him or her a more attractive, more appealing date? What common nonverbals would you tell your friend to avoid? Organize your advice around the areas of nonverbal communication as covered in this chapter. For each area be sure to include both nonverbals to use as well as nonverbals to avoid.

1. Body communication
2. Facial communication
3. Eye communication
4. Space communication
5. Artifactual communication
6. Touch communication
7. Paralanguage communication

10.2   THE MEANINGS OF COLOR

This exercise is designed to raise questions about the meanings that colors communicate and focuses on the ways in which advertisers and marketers use colors to influence our perceptions of a particular product. Assume that you are working for an advertising agency and that your task is to select colors for the various objects listed below. For each object select the major color as well as the secondary colors you would use in its packaging.

1. Coffee can for rich Columbian coffee
2. A children's cereal
3. An especially rich ice cream
4. Freshly squeezed and expensive orange juice
5. Packaging for up-scale jewelry store
6. Dietetic TV dinners
7. Microwave popcorn
8. Shampoo for grey hair
9. Liquid detergent for heavy duty washing
10. A textbook in human communication

After each person has recorded his or her decisions, discuss these in small groups of five or six or with the class as a whole. You may find it helpful to consider the following:

1. What meanings did you wish to communicate for each of the objects for which you chose colors? How effectively do the colors communicate these desired meanings?
2. What colors would communicate meanings opposite to those you would want to communicate? That is, what colors would be obviously wrong choices?
3. Pool the insights of all group members and re-color the products. Are these group designs superior to those developed individually? If a number of groups are working on this project at the same time, it may be interesting to compare and evaluate the final group colors for each of the products.

MESSAGES IN CONVERSATION

UNIT CONTENTS

The Conversational Process

Conversational Management

Conversational Effectiveness

Summary

Applications

11.1 Opening a Conversation
11.2 Closing a Conversation

UNIT GOALS

Upon completion of this unit, you should be able to

1. explain the five-step model of conversation

2. explain the processes involved in managing conversations: opening, maintaining, and closing them

3. explain the skills for conversational effectiveness

Looking at conversation will give you an opportunity to look at verbal and nonverbal messages as you use them in your day-to- day communications, as interconnected signaling systems. In this unit, then, we look at the conversational process—what it is, how we manage a conversation, and how we can be most effective. This unit will also serve as an introduction to the process of interpersonal communication, to which we devote the next four units.

THE CONVERSATIONAL PROCESS

The process of conversation takes place in five steps: opening, feedforward, business, feedback, and closing (Figure 11.1).

Step One: The Opening   The first step is to open the conversation, usually with some kind of greeting: "Hi," "How are you?" "Hello, this is Joe."

Greetings can be verbal or nonverbal and are usually both (Krivonos & Knapp, 1975; Knapp and Vangelisti, 1992). Verbal greetings include, for example, verbal salutes ("Hi," "Hello"), initiation of the topic ("The reason I called. . ."), making reference to the other ("Hey, Joe, what's up?"), and personal inquiries ("What's new?" "How are you doing?"). Nonverbal greetings include waving, smiling, shaking hands, and winking. Usually, you greet another person both verbally and nonverbally: You smile when you say "Hello."

Greeting can serve three major functions (Knapp & Vangelisti, 1992; Krivonos & Knapp, 1975). First, the greeting *signals a stage of access*; it opens up the channels of communication for more meaningful interaction and is a good example of **phatic communion**. Phatic communion opens the channels of communication; it's the "small talk" that paves the way for the "big talk." Phatic communion, a clear example of feedforward, tells you that the normal, expected, and accepted rules of interaction will be in effect. It tells you that there is a willingness to communicate, an openness, and a receptivity.

Second, the greeting *reveals important information about the relationship between the two persons*. For example, a big smile and a warm "Hi, it's been a long time" signals that the relationship is still a friendly one.

Third, the greeting *helps maintain the relationship*. You see this function served between workers who pass each other frequently. This greeting-in-passing assures you

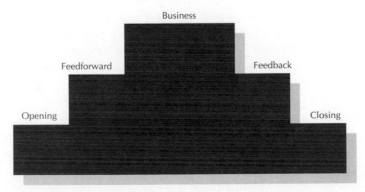

FIGURE 11.1 The process of conversation.

that even though you do not stop and talk for an extended period, you still have access to each other.

In normal conversation, your greeting is reciprocated with a greeting from the other person that is similar in degree of formality or informality and in intensity. When it isn't—when the other person turns away or responds coldly to your friendly "good morning"—you know that something is wrong. Openings are also generally consistent in tone with the main part of the conversation; a cheery "How ya doing today, big guy?" is not normally followed by news of a family death.

Step Two: Feedforward   At the second step, there is usually some kind of feedforward (see Unit 1). Here you give the other person a general idea of what the conversation will focus on: "I've got to tell you about Jack," "Did you hear what happened in class yesterday?" or "We need to talk about our vacation plans."

Feedforward may also identify the tone of the conversation ("I'm really depressed and need to talk with you") or the time required ("This will just take a minute") (Frentz, 1976; Reardon, 1987). One of the most interesting types of feedforward is the *disclaimer*—a statement that attempts to ensure that your message will be understood and will not reflect negatively on you (Unit 1).

Step Three: Business   The third step is the "business," the substance or focus of the conversation. "Business" is a good term to use for this stage because it emphasizes that most conversations are goal-directed. You converse to fulfill one or several of the general purposes of interpersonal communication: to learn, relate, influence, play, or help (Unit 1). The term is also sufficiently general to incorporate all kinds of interactions.

The business is conducted through an exchange of speaker and listener roles. Usually, brief (rather than long) speaking turns characterize most satisfying conversations. Here you talk about Jack, what happened in class, or your vacation plans. This is obviously the longest part of the conversation and the reason for both the opening and the feedforward.

Step Four: Feedback   The fourth step is the reverse of the second. Here you reflect back on the conversation to signal that as far as you're concerned, the business is completed: "So, you may want to send Jack a get well card," "Wasn't that the craziest class you ever heard of?" or "I'll call for reservations while you shop for what we need."

Of course, the other person may not agree that the business is completed and may therefore counter with, for example, "But what hospital is he in?" When this happens, you normally go back a step and continue the business.

Step Five: The Closing   The fifth and last step, the opposite of the first step, is the closing, the good-bye (Knapp, Hart, Friedrich, & Shulman, 1973; Knapp & Vangelisti, 1992). Like the opening, the closing may be verbal or nonverbal but is usually a combination of both verbal and nonverbal. Most obviously, the closing signals the end of accessibility. Just as the opening signaled access, the closing signals the end of access. The closing usually also signals some degree of supportiveness, for example, you express your pleasure in interacting: "Well, it was good talking with you." The closing may also summarize the interaction.

Reflections on the Model

Not all conversations will be easily divided into these five steps. Often the opening and the feedforward are combined, as when you see someone on campus and say "Hey, listen to this" or when in a work situation, someone says, "Well, folks, let's get the meeting going." In a similar way, the feedback and the closing might be combined: "Look, I've got to think more about this commitment, okay?"

As already noted, the business is the longest part of the conversation. The opening and the closing are usually about the same length and the feedforward and feedback are usually about equal in length. When these relative lengths are severely distorted, you may feel that something is wrong. For example, when someone uses a long feedforward or a too-short opening, you might suspect that what is to follow is extremely serious.

This model may also help identify skill deficiencies and distinguish effective and satisfying from ineffective and unsatisfying conversations. Consider, for example, the following violations. What meanings might each communicate?

- Using openings that are insensitive.
- Using overly long feedforwards.
- Omitting feedforward entirely.
- Doing business without the normally expected greeting.
- Omitting the feedback stage entirely.
- Omitting an appropriate closing.

Of course, each culture will alter these basic steps in different ways. In some cultures, the openings are especially short whereas in others the openings are elaborate, lengthy, and, in some cases, highly ritualized. It is easy in intercultural communication situations to violate another culture's conversational rules. Being overly friendly, too formal, or too forward may easily hinder the remainder of the conversation.

The reasons such violations may have significant consequences is that you may not be aware of these rules and hence may not see violations as cultural differences but rather as aggressiveness, stuffiness, or pushiness—and almost immediately dislike the person and put a negative cast on the future conversation.

CONVERSATIONAL MANAGEMENT

Speakers and listeners have to work together to make conversation an effective and satisfying experience. We can look at the management of conversations in terms of initiating, maintaining, and closing conversations.

Initiating Conversations

Opening a conversation is especially difficult. At times you may not be sure of what to say or how to say it. You may fear being rejected or having someone not understand your meaning.

One way to develop opening approaches is to focus on some of the elements of the communication process discussed in Unit 1. From these we can derive several avenues for opening a conversation:

How universal do you think these five steps are in describing conversation in other cultures? Can you identify a culture that views conversation very differently?

1. Self-references. Say something about yourself. Such references may be of the name, rank, and serial number type of statement, for example: "My name is Joe; I'm from Omaha." On the first day of class students might say "I'm worried about this class" or "I took this instructor last semester; she was excellent."
2. Other references. Say something about the other person or ask a question: "I like that sweater," "Didn't we meet at Charlie's?"
3. Relational references. Say something about the two of you, for example, "May I buy you a drink?" "Would you like to dance?" or simply "May I join you?"
4. Context references. Say something about the physical, social-psychological, or temporal context. The familiar "Do you have the time?" is of this type. But, you can be more creative, for example, "This place seems real friendly" or "That painting is just great."

Keep in mind two general rules. First, be positive. Lead off with something positive rather than something negative. Say, for example, "I really enjoy coming here" instead of "Don't you just hate this place?" Second, do not be too revealing; don't self-disclose too early in an interaction. If you do, you risk making the other person feel uncomfortable.

The Opening Line   Another way of looking at the process of initiating conversations is to examine the infamous "opening line," which can be of three basic types (Kleinke, 1986).

Cute-flippant openers are humorous, indirect, and ambiguous as to whether or not the one opening the conversation really wants an extended encounter. Examples include: "Is that really your hair?" "Bet I can outdrink you." "I bet the cherries jubilee isn't as sweet as you are."

Innocuous openers are highly ambiguous as to whether these are simple comments that might be made to just anyone or whether they are in fact openers designed to initiate an extended encounter. Examples include: "What do you think of the band?" "I haven't been here before. What's good on the menu?" "Could you show me how to work this machine?"

Direct openers clearly demonstrate the speaker's interest in meeting the other person. Examples include: "I feel a little embarrassed about this, but I'd like to meet you." "Would you like to have a drink after dinner?" "Since we're both eating alone, would you like to join me?"

According to Kleinke (1986), the most preferred opening lines by both men and women are generally those that are direct or innocuous. The least preferred lines by both men and women are those that are cute-flippant; women, however, dislike these openers more than men.

Men generally underestimate how much women dislike the cute-flippant openers and probably continue to use them because they are indirect enough to cushion any rejection. Men also underestimate how much women actually like innocuous openers.

Women prefer men to use openers that are relatively modest and to avoid coming on too strong. Women generally underestimate how much men like direct openers. Most men prefer openers that are very clear in meaning, which may be because men are not used to having a women initiate a meeting. Women also overestimate how much men like innocuous lines.

Maintaining Conversations

The defining feature of conversation is that the roles of speaker and listener are exchanged throughout the interaction. You accomplish this by using a wide variety of verbal and nonverbal cues to signal conversational turns—the changing (or maintaining) of the speaker or listener role during the conversation. Combining the insights of a variety of communication researchers (Burgoon, Buller, & Woodall, 1989; Duncan, 1972; Pearson & Spitzberg, 1990), we can look at conversational turns in terms of speaker cues and listener cues.

Speakers regulate the conversation through two major types of cues: turn-maintaining cues and turn-yielding cues.

Turn-maintaining Cues   These are designed to enable the speaker to maintain the role of speaker and may be communicated in a variety of ways (Burgoon, Buller, & Woodall 1989; Duncan, 1972):

- audibly inhaling breath to show that the speaker has more to say
- continuing a gesture or series of gestures to show that the thought is not yet complete
- avoiding eye contact with the listener so there is no indication that the speaker is passing the speaking turn on to the listener
- sustaining the intonation pattern to indicate that more will be said

- vocalizing pauses (*er, umm*) to prevent the listener from speaking and to show that the speaker is still talking

In most cases you expect the speaker to maintain relatively brief speaking turns and to willingly turn over the speaking role to the listener (when so signaled by the listener). Those who don't are likely to be evaluated negatively.

Turn-yielding Cues   These cues tell the listener that the speaker is finished and wishes to exchange the role of speaker for the role of listener. They tell the listener (and sometimes they are addressed to a specific listener rather than to just any listener) to take over the role of speaker. For example, you may at the end of a statement add some paralinguistic cue such as "eh?" which asks one of the listeners to assume the role of speaker. You can also indicate that you have finished speaking by dropping your intonation, by a prolonged silence, by making direct eye contact with a listener, by asking some general question, or by nodding in the direction of a particular listener.

In much the same way that you expect a speaker to yield the role of speaker, you also expect the listener to willingly assume the speaking role. Those who don't may be regarded as reticent or unwilling to involve themselves and take equal responsibility for the conversation. For example, in an analysis of turn-taking violations in the conversations of married couples, the most common violation found was that of no response (DeFrancisco, 1991). Forty-five percent of the 540 violations identified involved a lack of response to an invitation to take on the role of speaker. Of these "no response" violations, 68 percent were committed by men and 32 percent by women. Other turn-taking violations include interruptions, delayed responses, and inappropriately brief responses. DeFrancisco argues that with these violations, all of which are committed more frequently by men, men silence women in marital interactions.

As a listener you can regulate the conversation by using three types of cues: turn-requesting cues, turn-denying cues, and backchanneling cues.

Turn-requesting Cues   These cues let the speaker know that you would like to say something, that you would like to take a turn as speaker. Sometimes you can do this by simply saying, "I'd like to say something," but often it is done more subtly through some vocalized *er* or *um* that tells the speaker that you would now like to speak. This request to speak is also often made with facial and mouth gestures. Frequently a listener will indicate a desire to speak by opening his or her eyes and mouth wide as if to say something, by beginning to gesture with a hand, or by leaning forward.

Turn-denying Cues   You would use turn-denying cues to indicate your reluctance to assume the role of speaker, for example, intoning a slurred "I don't know" or by giving some brief grunt that signals you have nothing to say. Often turn denying is accomplished by avoiding eye contact with the speaker who wishes you to now take on the role of speaker, or by engaging in some behavior that is incompatible with speaking—for example, coughing or blowing your nose.

Backchanneling Cues   These are used to communicate various types of information back to the speaker without assuming the role of the speaker. You can send a variety of messages with backchanneling cues (Burgoon, Buller, & Woodall, 1989; Pearson & Spitzberg, 1990). You can indicate your *agreement* or disagreement with the speaker through smiles or frowns, gestures of approval or disapproval, brief comments such as "right" or "never," or a vocalization such as *uh-huh*.

You can also indicate your degree of *involvement* or boredom with the speaker. Attentive posture, forward leaning, and focused eye contact will tell the speaker that you are involved in the conversation just as an inattentive posture, backward leaning, and avoidance of eye contact will communicate your lack of involvement.

Giving the speaker *pacing* cues helps regulate the speed of speech. You can, for example, ask the speaker to slow down by raising your hand near your ear and leaning forward and to speed up by continuously nodding your head. You can also do this verbally by simply asking the speaker to slow down ("Slow down, I want to make sure I'm getting all this"). Similarly, you can tell the speaker to speed up by saying something like "and. . . " or "go on, go on. . . "

A request for *clarification* is still another function of backchanneling cues. A puzzled facial expression, perhaps coupled with a forward lean, will probably tell most speakers that you want some clarification. Similarly, you can ask for clarification by interjecting some interrogative: Who? When? Where?

Some of these backchanneling cues are actually interruptions. These interruptions, however, are generally confirming rather than disconfirming. They tell the speaker that you are listening and are involved (Kennedy & Camden, 1988).

Figure 11.2 provides an illustration of the various turn-taking cues and how they correspond to the conversational wants of speaker and listener.

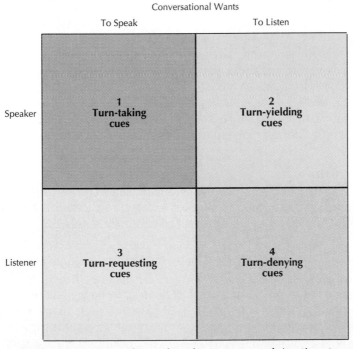

FIGURE 11.2 Quadrant 1 represents the speaker who wants to speak (continue to speak) and uses turn-maintaining cues; Quadrant 2 the speaker who wants to listen and uses turn-yielding cues; Quadrant 3 the listener who wants to speak and uses turn-requesting cues; and Quadrant 4 the listener who wants to listen (continue listening) and uses turn-denying cues. Backchanneling cues would appear in Quadrant 4, since they are cues that listeners use while they continue to listen.

Closing Conversations

Closing a conversation is almost as difficult as opening a conversation. It is frequently an awkward and uncomfortable part of interpersonal interaction. Here are a few ways you might consider for closing a conversation.

- Reflect back on the conversation and briefly summarize it so as to bring it to a close. For example, "I'm glad I ran into you and found out what happened at that union meeting. I'll probably be seeing you at the meetings."
- State the desire to end the conversation directly and to get on with other things. For example, "I'd like to continue talking but I really have to run. I'll see you around."
- Refer to future interaction. For example, "Why don't we get together next week sometime and continue this discussion?"
- Ask for closure. For example, "Have I explained what you wanted to know?"
- State that you enjoyed the interaction. For example, "I really enjoyed talking with you."

With any of these closing, it should be clear to the other person that you are attempting to end the conversation. Obviously, you will have to use more direct methods with those who don't take these subtle hints—those who don't realize that *both* persons are responsible for the interpersonal interaction and for bringing it to a satisfying closing.

CONVERSATIONAL EFFECTIVENESS

In developing conversational effectiveness we need to look at interpersonal skills on two levels. On one level there are the skills of effectiveness such as openness and supportiveness. On another level, however, are skills that guide us in regulating our openness and our supportiveness. They are skills about skills, or metaskills. These qualities will provide a good foundation for communicating interpersonally, in small groups, in public speaking, and especially in intercultural communication.

Metaskills

Because each conversation is unique, the qualities of interpersonal effectiveness cannot be applied indiscriminately. You need to know how the skills themselves should be applied. You should be mindful, flexible, and culturally sensitive.

Mindfulness   After you have learned a skill or a rule you often apply it without thinking; you apply it "mindlessly," without considering the novel aspects of this unique situation. Instead, conversational skills need to be applied mindfully (Langer, 1989). For example, after learning the skills of active listening, many will respond to all situations with active listening responses. Some of these responses will be appropriate but others will prove inappropriate and ineffective. Before responding, think about the unique communication situation you face and consider your alternatives. Be alert and responsive to small changes in the situation that may cue which behaviors will be effective and which ineffective. Be especially mindful of the cultural differences among people, as outlined in the section "Cultural Sensitivity."

Flexibility   Respond to each of the following statements using the following scale:

A = almost always true
B = frequently true
C = sometimes true
D = infrequently true
E = almost never true

_____ 1. People should be frank and spontaneous in conversation.

_____ 2. When angry, a person should say nothing rather than say something he or she will be sorry for later.

_____ 3. When talking to your friends, you should adjust your remarks to suit them.

_____ 4. It is better to speak your gut feelings than to beat around the bush.

_____ 5. If people would open up to each other the world would be better off.

The preferred answer to all five of these statements is "C" and underscores the importance of flexibility in all interpersonal encounters (Hart & Burks, 1972; Hart, Carlson, & Eadie, 1980). Although here we provide general principles for conversational effectiveness, be flexible and sensitive to the unique factors present in every situation. You may need to be frank and spontaneous when talking with a close friend about your feelings but you may not want to be so open when talking with your grandmother about the dinner she prepared that you disliked.

Cultural Sensitivity   In applying the skills for interpersonal effectiveness be sensitive to the cultural differences among people. What may prove effective for upper income people working in the IBM subculture of Boston or New York may prove ineffective for lower-income people working as fruit pickers in Florida or California. What works in Japan may not work in Mexico. The direct eye contact that signals immediacy in most of the United States may be considered rude or too intrusive in other cultures. The specific skills discussed in the next section are considered to be generally effective in the United States and among most people living in the United States; but do be aware that these skills and the ways you communicate them may not apply to other cultures (Kim, 1991).

Effectiveness in intercultural settings, according to Kim, requires that you be

- *open* to new ideas and to differences among people
- *flexible* in ways of communicating and in adapting to the communications of the culturally different
- *tolerant* of other attitudes, values, and ways of doing things
- *creative* in seeking varied ways to communicate

These qualities—along with some knowledge of the other culture and the general skills of effectiveness—"should enable a person to approach each intercultural encounter with the psychological posture of an interested learner . . . and to strive for the communication outcomes that are as effective as possible under a given set of relational and situational constraints" (Kim, 1991).

Skills in Conversational Effectiveness

The skills of conversational effectiveness discussed here are (1) openness, (2) empathy, (3) positiveness, (4) immediacy, (5) interaction management, (6) expressiveness, and (7) other-orientation. As you read the discussions of these concepts, keep in mind that the most effective communicator is one who is flexible and who adapts to the individual situation. To be always open or empathic, for example, will probably prove ineffective. Although these qualities are generally appropriate to most interpersonal interactions, do remember that the ability to control these qualities—rather than exhibiting them reflexively—should be your aim.

Openness Openness refers to three aspects of interpersonal communication. First, you should be willing to self-disclose—to reveal information about yourself. Of course, these disclosures need to be appropriate to the entire communication act (see Unit 3). There must also be an openness in regard to listening to the other person; you should be open to the thoughts and feelings of the person with whom you're communicating.

A second aspect of openness refers to your willingness to react honestly to the situations that confront you. You want people to react openly to what you say, and you have a right to expect this. You demonstrate openness by responding spontaneously and honestly to the communications and the feedback of others.

Third, openness calls for the "owning" of feelings and thoughts. To be open in this sense is to acknowledge that the feelings and thoughts you express are yours and

The characteristics of effective conversation identified here are positively valued throughout much of the general American culture. Can you identify characteristics discussed here that would be negatively evaluated in other cultures?

that you bear the responsibility for them; you do not try to shift the responsibility for your feelings to others. For example, consider these comments:

1. Your behavior was grossly inconsiderate.
2. Everyone thought your behavior was grossly inconsiderate.
3. I was really disturbed when you told my father he was an old man.

Comments 1 and 2 do not evidence ownership of feelings. In 1, the speaker accuses the listener of being inconsiderate without assuming any of the responsibility for the judgment. In 2, the speaker assigns responsibility to the convenient but elusive "everyone" and again assumes none of the responsibility. In comment 3, however, a drastic difference appears. Note that here the speaker is taking responsibility for his or her own feelings ("*I* was really disturbed").

When you own your own messages you use I-messages instead of you-messages. Instead of saying, "You make me feel so stupid when you ask what everyone else thinks but don't ask my opinion," the person who owns his or her feelings says "I feel stupid when you ask everyone else what they think but don't ask me." When you own your feelings and thoughts, when you use I-messages, you say in effect, "This is how *I* feel," "This is how *I* see the situation," "This is what *I* think," with the *I* always paramount. Instead of saying, "This discussion is useless," one would say, "*I'm* bored by this discussion," or "*I* want to talk more about myself," or any other such statement that includes a reference to the fact that *I* am making an evaluation and not describing objective reality. By doing so, you make it explicit that your feelings are the result of the interaction between what is going on in the world outside your skin (what others say, for example) and what is going on inside your skin (your preconceptions, attitudes, and prejudices, for example).

Empathy   When you *empathize* with someone, you are able to experience what the other is experiencing from that person's point of view. Empathy does *not* mean that you agree with what the other person says or does. You never lose your own identity or your own attitudes and beliefs. To *sympathize,* on the other hand, is to feel *for* the individual—to feel sorry for the person. To empathize is to feel the same feelings in the same way as the other person does. Empathy, then, enables you to understand, emotionally and intellectually, what another person is experiencing.

Of course, empathy will mean little if you are not able to communicate this empathic understanding back to the other person. You must use this empathy to achieve increased understanding and to adjust your communications appropriately.

Most people find it easier to communicate empathy in response to a person's positive statements (Heiskell & Rychiak, 1986). So perhaps you will have to exert special effort to communicate empathy for negative statements. Here are a few suggestions for communicating empathy both verbally and nonverbally:

- Confront mixed messages. Confront messages that seem to be communicating conflicting feelings to show you are trying to understand the other person's feelings. For example, *You say that it doesn't bother you but I seem to hear a lot of anger coming through.*
- Avoid judgmental and evaluative (nonempathic) responses. Avoid should- and ought-statements that try to tell the other person how he or she *should* feel.

For example, avoid expressions such as "Don't feel so bad," "Don't cry," "Cheer up," "In time you'll forget all about this," and "You should start dating others; by next month you won't even remember her name."

- Use reinforcing comments. Let the speaker know that you understand what the speaker is saying and encourage the speaker to continue talking about this issue. For example, use comments such as "I see," "I get it," "I understand," "Yes," and "Right."
- Demonstrate interest by maintaining eye contact (avoid scanning the room or focusing on objects or persons other than the person with whom you are interacting), maintaining physical closeness, leaning toward (not away from) the other person, and showing your interest and agreement with your facial expressions, nods, and eye movements.

Positiveness   You can communicate positiveness in interpersonal communication in at least two ways. First, you can state positive attitudes. Second, you can "stroke" the person with whom you interact.

People who feel negatively about themselves invariably communicate these feelings to others, who in turn probably develop similar negative feelings. On the other hand, people who feel positively about themselves convey this feeling to others, who then return the positive regard.

Positiveness in attitudes also refers to a positive feeling for the general communication situation. A negative response to a communication makes you feel almost as if you are intruding, and communication is sure to break down.

Positiveness is most clearly evident in the way you phrase statements. Consider these two sentences:

1.   You look horrible in stripes.
2.   You look your best, I think, in solid colors.

The first sentence is critical and will almost surely encourage an argument. The second sentence, on the other hand, expresses the speaker's thought clearly and positively and should encourage responses that are cooperative.

You also communicate positiveness through "stroking." *Stroking* behavior acknowledges the importance of the other person. It is the opposite of indifference. When you stroke someone, whether positively or negatively, you acknowledge him or her as a person, as a significant human being.

Stroking may be verbal, as in "I like you," "I enjoy being with you," or "You're a pig." Stroking may also be nonverbal. A smile, a hug, or a slap in the face are also examples of stroking. Positive stroking generally takes the form of compliments or rewards. Positive strokes bolster your self-image and make you feel a little bit better than you did before you received them. Negative strokes, on the other hand, are punishing. Sometimes, like cruel remarks, they hurt you emotionally. Sometimes, like a punch in the mouth, they hurt you physically.

Immediacy   Immediacy refers to the joining of the speaker and listener, the creation of a sense of togetherness. The communicator who demonstrates immediacy conveys a sense of interest and attention, a liking for and an attraction to the other person. People respond favorably to immediacy. Immediacy joins speaker and listener.

Nonverbally you can communicate immediacy in several ways:

- maintain appropriate eye contact and limit looking around at others
- maintain a physical closeness which suggests a psychological closeness
- use a direct and open body posture, for example, by arranging your body to keep others out
- smile and otherwise express that you are interested in and care about the other person

Likewise you can communicate immediacy verbally in a variety of ways:

- Use the other person's name; for example, say "Joe, what do you think?" instead of "What do you think?" Say, "I like that, Mary" instead of "I like that."
- Focus on the other person's remarks. Make the speaker know that you heard and understood what was said and will base your feedback on it. For example, use questions that ask for clarification or elaboration, such as "Do you think the same thing is true of baseball?" or "How would your argument apply to the Midwest?" Also, refer to the speaker's previous remarks, as in "I never thought of that being true of all religions" or "Colorado does sound like a great vacation spot."
- Reinforce, reward, or compliment the other person. Make use of such expressions as "I like your new outfit" or "Your comments were really to the point."
- Incorporate self-references into evaluative statements rather than depersonalizing them. Say, for example, "I think your report is great" rather than "Your report is great" or "Everyone likes your report."

Interaction Management   The effective communicator controls the interaction to the satisfaction of both parties. In effective **interaction management,** neither person feels ignored or on stage. Each contributes to the total communication interchange. Maintaining your role as speaker or listener and passing back and forth the opportunity to speak are interaction management skills. If one person speaks all the time and the other listens all the time, effective conversation becomes difficult if not impossible. Depending on the situation, one person may speak more than the other person. This imbalance, however, should be a function of the situation and not that one person is a "talker" and another a "listener."

Effective interaction managers also avoid interrupting the other person. Interruption signals that what you have to say is more important than what the other person is saying and puts the other person in an inferior position. The result is dissatisfaction with the conversation.

Similarly, keeping the conversation flowing and fluent without long and awkward pauses that make everyone uncomfortable are signs of effective interaction management.

One of the best ways to look at interaction management is to take the self-test on page 192, developed by Mark Snyder (1987), "Are You a High Self-Monitor?" This test will help you to identify the qualities that make for the effective management of interpersonal communication situations.

Self-monitoring, the manipulation of the image that you present to others in your interpersonal interactions, is integrally related to interpersonal interaction man-

SELF-TEST

Are You a High Self-Monitor?

These statements concern personal reactions to a number of different situations. No two statements are exactly alike, so consider each statement carefully before answering. If a statement is true, or mostly true, as applied to you, mark it T. If a statement is false, or not usually true, as applied to you, mark it F.

_____ 1. I find it hard to imitate the behavior of other people.

_____ 2. At parties and social gatherings, I do not attempt to do or say things that others will like.

_____ 3. I can only argue for ideas which I already believe.

_____ 4. I can make impromptu speeches even on topics about which I have almost no information.

_____ 5. I guess I put on a show to impress or entertain people.

_____ 6. I would probably make a good actor.

_____ 7. In a group of people I am rarely the center of attention.

_____ 8. In different situations and with different people, I often act like very different persons.

_____ 9. I am not particularly good at making other people like me.

_____ 10. I'm not always the person I appear to be.

_____ 11. I would not change my opinions (or the way I do things) in order to please someone or win their favor.

_____ 12. I have considered being an entertainer.

_____ 13. I have never been good at games like charades or improvisational acting.

_____ 14. I have trouble changing my behavior to suit different people and different situations.

_____ 15. At a party I let others keep the jokes and stories going.

_____ 16. I feel a bit awkward in company and do not show up quite as well as I should.

_____ 17. I can look anyone in the eye and tell a lie with a straight face (if for a right end).

_____ 18. I may deceive people by being friendly when I really dislike them.

Scoring   Give yourself one point for each True response you gave to questions 4, 5, 6, 8, 10, 12, 17, and 18 and give yourself one point for each False response you gave to questions 1, 2, 3, 7, 9, 11, 13, 14, 15, and 16. According to Snyder (1987), scores may be interpreted roughly as follows: 13 or higher = very high self-monitoring;   11–12 = high self-monitoring;   8–10 = low self-monitoring;   0–7 = very low self-monitoring.

Source: From Mark Snyder, *Public Appearances/Private Realities* (New York: W. H. Freeman and Company, 1987), p. 179.

agement. High self-monitors carefully adjust their behaviors on the basis of feedback from others so that they produce the most desirable effect. Low self-monitors are not concerned with the image they present to others. Rather, they communicate their thoughts and feelings with no attempt to manipulate the impressions they create. Most of us lie somewhere between the two extremes.

When you compare high and low self-monitors, you find several interesting differences. For example, high self-monitors are more apt to take charge of a situation, are more sensitive to the deceptive techniques of others, and are better able to detect self-monitoring or impression management techniques when used by others. High self-monitors prefer to interact with low self-monitors, over whom they are able to assume positions of influence and power.

Although there seem to be two clear-cut types of persons—high and low self-monitors—we all engage more or less in selective monitoring, depending on the situation. If you go to a job interview, you are likely to monitor your behaviors very carefully. On the other hand, you are less likely to monitor your performance with a group of friends.

Expressiveness   The *expressive* speaker communicates genuine involvement in the interpersonal interaction. He or she plays the game instead of just watching it as a spectator. **Expressiveness** is similar to openness in its emphasis on involvement. It includes taking responsibility for your thoughts and feelings, encouraging expressiveness or openness in others, and providing appropriate feedback.

This quality also includes taking responsibility for both talking and listening and in this way is similar to equality. In conflict situations, expressiveness involves fighting actively and stating disagreement directly. Expressiveness means using I-messages in which you accept responsibility for your thoughts and feelings, for example, "I'm bored when I don't get to talk" or "I want to talk more," rather than you-messages ("you ignore me," "you don't ask my opinion"). It is the opposite of fighting passively, withdrawing from the encounter, or attributing responsibility to others.

More specifically, expressiveness may be communicated in a wide variety of ways. Here are a few guidelines:

- Practice active listening by paraphrasing, expressing understanding of the thoughts and feelings of the other person, and asking relevant questions (as explained in Unit 5).
- Avoid clichés and trite expressions that signal a lack of personal involvement and originality.
- Address mixed messages—messages (verbal or nonverbal) that are communicated simultaneously but that contradict each other.
- Address messages that somehow seem unrealistic to you (for example, statements claiming that the breakup of a long-term relationship is completely forgotten or that failing a course doesn't mean anything).
- Use I-messages to signal personal involvement and a willingness to share your feelings. Instead of saying "You never give me a chance to make any decisions," say "I'd like to contribute to the decisions that affect both of us."

Nonverbally you communicate expressiveness by using appropriate variations in vocal rate, pitch, volume, and rhythm to convey involvement and interest, and by allowing your facial muscles to reflect and echo this inner involvement. Similarly, the appropriate use of gestures communicates involvement. Too few gestures signal disinterest, while too many may communicate discomfort, uneasiness, and awkwardness. The monotone and motionless speaker who talks about sex, winning the lottery, and fatal illness all in the same tone of voice, with a static posture and an expressionless face, is the stereotype of the ineffective interaction manager.

Other Orientation   Some people are primarily self-oriented and talk mainly about themselves, their experiences, their interests, and their desires. They do most of the talking, and pay little attention to verbal and nonverbal feedback from the other person. **Other-orientation** is the opposite of self-orientation. It involves the ability to communicate attentiveness and interest in the other person and in what is being said. Without other-orientation each person pursues his or her own goal instead of cooperating and working together to achieve a common goal.

Other-orientation is especially important (and especially difficult) when you are interacting with people who are very different from you as in, for example, talking with people from other cultures.

You communicate other-orientation nonverbally through focused eye contact, smiles, head nods, leaning toward the other person, and displaying feelings and emotions through appropriate facial expression. You avoid focusing on yourself (as in preening, for example) or on anyone other than the person to whom you're speaking (through frequent or prolonged eye contact or body orientation).

Verbally, you can communicate other-orientation in several ways:

- Ask the other person for suggestions, opinions, and clarification as appropriate. Statements such as "How do you feel about it?" or "What do you think?" will go a long way toward focusing the communication on the other person.
- Express agreement when appropriate. Comments such as "You're right" or "That's interesting" help to focus the interaction on the other person, which encourages greater openness.
- Use minimal responses to encourage the other person to express himself or herself. Minimal responses are those brief expressions that encourage another to continue talking without intruding on their thoughts and feelings or directing them to go in any particular direction. For example, "yes," "I see," or even "aha" or "hmm" are minimal responses that tell the other person that you are interested in his or her continued comments.
- Use positive affect statements to refer to the other person and to his or her contributions to the interaction; for example, "I really enjoy talking with you" or "That was a clever way of looking at things" are positive affect statements that are often felt but rarely expressed.

Other-orientation demonstrates consideration and respect—for example, asking if it's all right to dump your troubles on someone before doing so or asking if your phone call comes at an inopportune time before launching into your conversation. Other-orientation involves acknowledging others' feelings as legitimate: "I can understand why you're so angry; I would be too."

Summary

1. *Conversation* consists of five general stages: *opening, feedforward, business, feedback,* and *closing*.

2. *Initiating conversations* can be accomplished in various ways, for example, with self, other, relational, and context references.

3. Conversations are maintained by the passing of speaking and listening turns; *turn-maintaining* and *turn-yielding cues* are used by the speaker, and *turn-requesting, turn-denying,* and *backchanneling cues* are used by the listener.

4. *Conversational closure* may be achieved through a variety of methods; for example: reflect back on the conversation as in summarizing, directly state your desire to end the conversation, refer to future interaction, ask for closure, and state your pleasure with interaction.

5. The *metaskills* of conversational effectiveness need to be applied with *mindfulness, flexibility,* and *cultural sensitivity* (as appropriate).

6. Among the skills of *conversational effectiveness* are *openness, empathy, positiveness, immediacy, interaction management, expressiveness,* and *other-orientation.*

Applications

11.1 OPENING A CONVERSATION

This exercise provides experience in the difficult but essential process of opening a conversation and should help make this difficult act a bit easier. Working individually, indicate two appropriate ways in which you might initiate a conversation with the persons described in each of these situations. Then, in small groups or with the class as a whole, discuss your responses. What general approaches seem favored? What general approaches seem frowned on?

1. On the first day of class, you and another student are the first to come into the classroom and are seated in the room alone.

2. You are a guest at a friend's party. You are one of the first guests to arrive and are now there with several other people to whom you have only just been introduced. Your friend, the host, is busy with other matters.

3. You have just started a new job in a large office where you are one of several computer operators. It seems as if most of the other people know each other.

4. You are in the college cafeteria eating alone. You see another student who is also eating alone and who you have seen in your English Literature class. You're not sure if this person has noticed you in class.

11.2 CLOSING A CONVERSATION

The following experiences should help make the process of closing a conversation more effective. Working individually, indicate two ways in which you might go about closing each of the following conversations. Then, in small groups or with the class as a whole, share your closing. What types of closing seem most effective? Which seem least effective?

1. You and a friend have been talking on the phone for the last hour but not much new is being said. You have a great deal of work to get to and would like to close the conversation. Your friend just doesn't seem to hear your subtle cues.

2. You are at a party and are anxious to meet a person with whom you have exchanged eye contact for the last 10 minutes. The problem is that a friendly and talkative former teacher of yours is demanding all your attention. You don't want to insult the instructor but at the same time want to make contact with this other person.

3. You have had a conference with a teacher and have learned what you needed to know. This teacher, however, doesn't seem to know how to end the conversation, seems very ill at ease, and just continues to go over what has already been said. You have to get to your next class and must close the conversation.

4. You are at a party and notice a person you would like to get to know. You initiate the conversation but after a few minutes realize that this person is not the kind of person with whom you would care to spend any more time. You want to close this conversation as soon as possible.

Messages: Verbal and Nonverbal

Questions and Activities

1. Each member of the class should look up the meaning of any *noun* in a standard dictionary. Note that this definition is (almost) exclusively denotational. Try writing a dictionary entry for the connotative meaning of that same noun. Share your connotative dictionary entries in small groups or with the class as a whole. On the basis of the discussion, rewrite your entry. What factors or characteristics does your connotative meaning entry include?

2. In what ways do you respond intensionally? (Note that we make the assumption that most people respond intensionally at some time and in some situations.) What consequences did this intensional orientation have?

3. Members of the class should cite one specific instance in which they were disconfirmed or in which they witnessed the disconfirmation of others. What were the effects of such disconfirmation? How might it have been avoided?

4. What role does taboo language play in your social group? In your family? At work? What effects does this use of taboo have on interpersonal interactions? On the people using the taboo language?

5. Watch television for one evening (dramas and situation comedies work best) and record all the examples of the barriers to language and verbal interactions that are considered in Unit 7 (polarization, intensional orientation, fact-inference confusion, bypassing, allness, static evaluation, and indiscrimination). You will probably find many examples and in some instances entire plots that revolve around one or more characters making a misevaluation. Share these with other members of the class.

6. The following situations—or similar ones—seem to cause difficulty for many people. What, if anything, should you do in each scenario?
   a. You see your best friend's spouse in a romantic liaison with another person.
   b. You see two students cheating on an examination.
   c. Your friend dresses so badly (though not for any financial reason) that everyone else laughs and pokes fun.
   d. You're doing badly in a required course. A friend offers you a term paper that earned an A+.

7. Describe at least three specific nonverbal behaviors that you usually find:
   a. annoying
   b. friendly
   c. hostile

d.   loving
e.   neutral

Share these descriptions and meanings with others in small groups of five or six or with the class as a whole.

8.   Write out one rule of nonverbal behavior that a Martian would find helpful to know when interacting with Earthlings. Write this rule for any one area of nonverbal communication. Share these with others in small groups of five or six or with the class as a whole.

9.   Identify at least five specific examples of your own territorial behavior.

10. For a period of one day (admittedly much too short a time period), keep a record of all examples of your touching others and of others touching you. What general conclusions can you draw about the following questions:

a.   Who do you touch the most?
b.   Who touches you the most?
c.   What meanings do you communicate through touch?
d.   What meanings did you derive from the touching of others?

11. What is your own psychological time orientation? Are you satisfied? Dissatisfied? If dissatisfied, what do you intend to do about it?

12. What mistakes in nonverbal communication do men and women frequently make in their dating behavior? What advice would you give these people to eliminate these mistakes?

13. Research shows that women smile more than men even when making negative comments or expressing negative feelings. What implications does this have for male-female communication? What implications might this have for childrearing? For teaching?

14. What nonverbal cues do you find generally reliable in showing that someone likes you? In showing that someone dislikes you?

15. What other methods seem to work for opening a conversation? Which openers do you especially resent? Why?

16. Do you find gender differences in the use of the qualities of conversational effectiveness? What evidence can you offer to support your conclusions?

17. Which quality of conversational effectiveness do you find most important? Most often violated? Most important for a successful, long-term romantic relationship?

Skill Check

_____   1.   I take special care to make **spoken messages clear and unambiguous**. (Unit 6)

_____   2.   I **ask questions** whenever intended meaning is in doubt. (Unit 6)

_____   3.   I **connect my words and meanings** to the real world. (Unit 6)

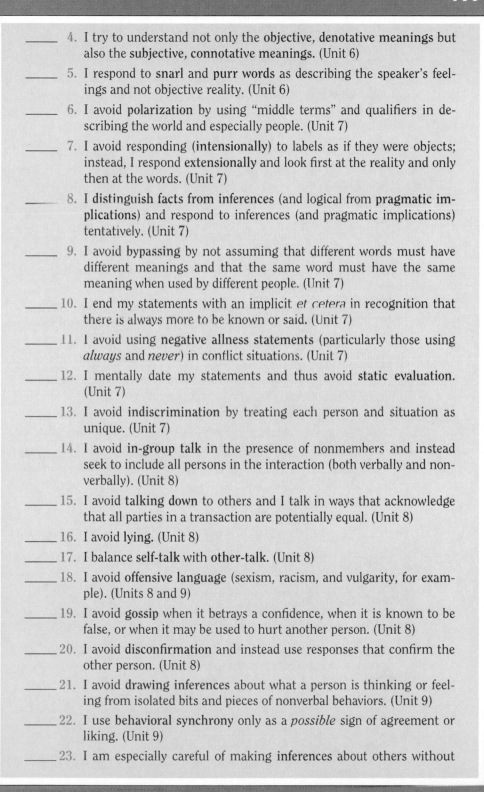

_____ 4. I try to understand not only the **objective, denotative meanings** but also the **subjective, connotative meanings.** (Unit 6)

_____ 5. I respond to **snarl** and **purr words** as describing the speaker's feelings and not objective reality. (Unit 6)

_____ 6. I avoid **polarization** by using "middle terms" and qualifiers in describing the world and especially people. (Unit 7)

_____ 7. I avoid responding (**intensionally**) to labels as if they were objects; instead, I respond **extensionally** and look first at the reality and only then at the words. (Unit 7)

_____ 8. I **distinguish facts from inferences** (and logical from **pragmatic implications**) and respond to inferences (and pragmatic implications) tentatively. (Unit 7)

_____ 9. I avoid **bypassing** by not assuming that different words must have different meanings and that the same word must have the same meaning when used by different people. (Unit 7)

_____ 10. I end my statements with an implicit _et cetera_ in recognition that there is always more to be known or said. (Unit 7)

_____ 11. I avoid using **negative allness statements** (particularly those using _always_ and _never_) in conflict situations. (Unit 7)

_____ 12. I mentally date my statements and thus avoid **static evaluation.** (Unit 7)

_____ 13. I avoid **indiscrimination** by treating each person and situation as unique. (Unit 7)

_____ 14. I avoid **in-group talk** in the presence of nonmembers and instead seek to include all persons in the interaction (both verbally and nonverbally). (Unit 8)

_____ 15. I avoid **talking down** to others and I talk in ways that acknowledge that all parties in a transaction are potentially equal. (Unit 8)

_____ 16. I avoid **lying.** (Unit 8)

_____ 17. I balance **self-talk** with **other-talk.** (Unit 8)

_____ 18. I avoid **offensive language** (sexism, racism, and vulgarity, for example). (Units 8 and 9)

_____ 19. I avoid **gossip** when it betrays a confidence, when it is known to be false, or when it may be used to hurt another person. (Unit 8)

_____ 20. I avoid **disconfirmation** and instead use responses that confirm the other person. (Unit 8)

_____ 21. I avoid **drawing inferences** about what a person is thinking or feeling from isolated bits and pieces of nonverbal behaviors. (Unit 9)

_____ 22. I use **behavioral synchrony** only as a _possible_ sign of agreement or liking. (Unit 9)

_____ 23. I am especially careful of making **inferences** about others without

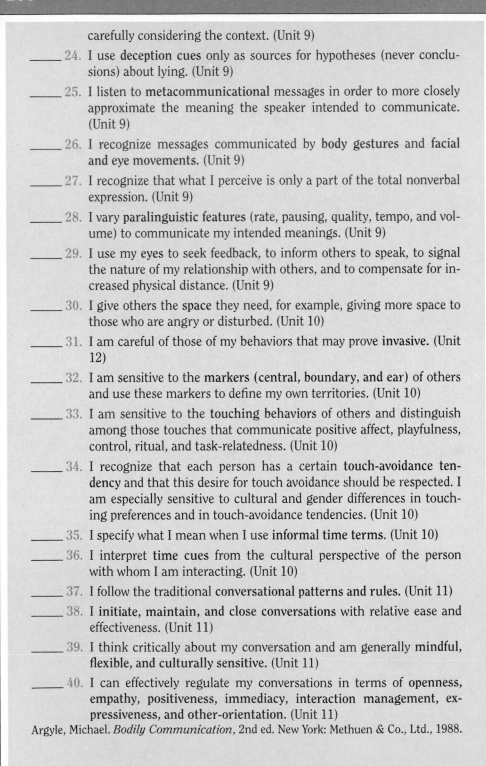

carefully considering the context. (Unit 9)

_____ 24. I use **deception cues** only as sources for hypotheses (never conclusions) about lying. (Unit 9)

_____ 25. I listen to **metacommunicational** messages in order to more closely approximate the meaning the speaker intended to communicate. (Unit 9)

_____ 26. I recognize messages communicated by **body gestures** and **facial and eye movements.** (Unit 9)

_____ 27. I recognize that what I perceive is only a part of the total nonverbal expression. (Unit 9)

_____ 28. I vary **paralinguistic features** (rate, pausing, quality, tempo, and volume) to communicate my intended meanings. (Unit 9)

_____ 29. I use my **eyes** to seek feedback, to inform others to speak, to signal the nature of my relationship with others, and to compensate for increased physical distance. (Unit 9)

_____ 30. I give others the **space** they need, for example, giving more space to those who are angry or disturbed. (Unit 10)

_____ 31. I am careful of those of my behaviors that may prove **invasive.** (Unit 12)

_____ 32. I am sensitive to the **markers (central, boundary, and ear)** of others and use these markers to define my own territories. (Unit 10)

_____ 33. I am sensitive to the **touching behaviors** of others and distinguish among those touches that communicate positive affect, playfulness, control, ritual, and task-relatedness. (Unit 10)

_____ 34. I recognize that each person has a certain **touch-avoidance tendency** and that this desire for touch avoidance should be respected. I am especially sensitive to cultural and gender differences in touching preferences and in touch-avoidance tendencies. (Unit 10)

_____ 35. I specify what I mean when I use **informal time terms.** (Unit 10)

_____ 36. I interpret **time cues** from the cultural perspective of the person with whom I am interacting. (Unit 10)

_____ 37. I follow the traditional **conversational patterns and rules.** (Unit 11)

_____ 38. I **initiate, maintain, and close conversations** with relative ease and effectiveness. (Unit 11)

_____ 39. I think critically about my conversation and am generally **mindful, flexible, and culturally sensitive.** (Unit 11)

_____ 40. I can effectively regulate my conversations in terms of **openness, empathy, positiveness, immediacy, interaction management, expressiveness, and other-orientation.** (Unit 11)

Argyle, Michael. *Bodily Communication*, 2nd ed. New York: Methuen & Co., Ltd., 1988.

SUGGESTED READINGS

A popular and scholarly summary of research in nonverbal communication.

Burgoon, Judee K., David B. Buller, and W. Gill Woodall. *Nonverbal Communication: The Unspoken Dialogue*. New York: Harper & Row, 1989. A thorough and scholarly survey of research and theory in nonverbal communication.

DeVito, Joseph A. *The Nonverbal Communication Workbook*. Prospect Heights, Ill.: Waveland Press, 1989. Contains brief overviews of the various areas of nonverbal communication and 75 exercises to increase awareness of and control over nonverbal communication.

DeVito, Joseph A. and Michael L. Hecht, eds. *The Nonverbal Communication Reader*. Prospect Heights, Ill.: Waveland Press, 1990. Contains 47 readings in all areas of nonverbal communication.

Gordon, Thomas. *P.E.T.: Parent Effectiveness Training*. New York: New American Library, 1975. This groundbreaking book tells us more than how to talk with children. Everyone can benefit from its insights, which are useful in just about any communication situation.

Rothwell, J. Dan. *Telling It Like It Isn't: Language Misuse & Malpractice/What We Can Do About It*. Englewood Cliffs, N.J.: Prentice-Hall (Spectrum), 1982. An excellent introduction to the barriers to language and how we can eliminate them.

Tannen, Deborah (1990). *You Just Don't Understand: Women and Men in Conversation*. New York: William Morrow. A popular yet scholarly discussion of a wide variety of communication differences between men and women.

Wardhaugh, Ronald. *How Conversation Works*. New York: Basil Blackwell, 1985. An enjoyable and scholarly introduction to the language of conversations.

Popular books on language include Schaefer (1984); Faber and Mazlish (1980) (two books in the tradition of Gordon's *P.E.T.*); Eisen (1984); Wells (1979); Nierenberg and Calero (1973); Miller, Wackman, Nunnally, and Saline (1982); Albrecht (1980); and Hamlin (1988). Popular works by Nierenberg and Calero (1971); Davis (1973); and Morris (1977, 1985) provide fun reading along with considerable insight into nonverbal communication.

Textbooks on language include Borisoff and Merrill (1985); Penfield (1987); Thorne, Kramarae, and Henley (1983); Berger and Bradac (1982); and Infante (1986). Excellent textbooks in nonverbal communication abound. Any of the following will provide a wealth of additional insight: Knapp and Hall (1992); Leathers (1986); Malandro, Barker, and Barker (1989); Hickson and Stacks (1993); and Richmond, McCroskey, and Payne (1987).

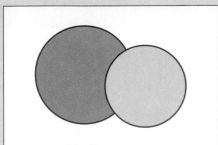

INTERPERSONAL COMMUNICATION, RELATIONSHIPS, AND INTERVIEWING

Unit 12. **Preliminaries to Interpersonal Communication and Relationships**

Unit 13. **Relationship Development, Deterioration, and Repair**

Unit 14. **Interpersonal Conflict**

Unit 15. **Interviewing**

Part 3. **Feedback**
Questions and Activities
Skill Check
Suggested Readings

In Part 3 we deal with interpersonal communication, relationships, and interviewing—forms of communication held together by the one-on-one nature of the interaction. In Unit 12 we consider the nature of interpersonal communication and relationships and in Unit 13 relationship development, deterioration, and repair.

Unit 14 focuses on interpersonal conflict and how we can manage conflict so that it strengthens relationships. In Unit 15 we examine interviewing, its nature and skills.

Approaching Interpersonal Communication, Relationships, and Interviewing

In approaching the study of interpersonal communication, keep the following in mind:

- Each person and each relationship is unique. What is true of the majority of people or of some large group is not necessarily true of you.

- Interpersonal relationships are dynamic, living things. They are always in the process of becoming. Although we artificially stop the process to discuss specific issues, remember that relationships and the people who are part of the relationship are never static. They are always changing.

- Culture influences not only the way you communicate but also the way you think about communication and especially about the way you are expected to communicate in developing and maintaining relationships, in managing conflict, and in presenting yourself in an interview. Violating even arbitrary customs may have important consequences.

PRELIMINARIES TO INTERPERSONAL COMMUNICATION AND RELATIONSHIPS

UNIT CONTENTS

Interpersonal Communication

Interpersonal Relationships

Theories of Interpersonal Relationships

Summary

Applications

12.1   The Greeting Card and the Popular Song

12.2   Analyzing a Relationship

UNIT GOALS

After completing this unit, you should be able to

1. define the three approaches to interpersonal communication

2. describe the six-stage model of interpersonal relationships and the movement between the stages

3. describe attraction theory and the factors that increase interpersonal attractiveness

4. define affinity-seeking strategies and identify at least six strategies

5. describe social penetration theory

6. describe social exchange theory

7. describe equity theory

In this unit we look at some preliminaries to interpersonal communication. First, we explore its nature and definition. Second, we consider the nature and growth of interpersonal relationships. Finally, we focus on several theories that try to explain how and why relationships develop.

INTERPERSONAL COMMUNICATION

Communication theorists define interpersonal communication in different ways (Bochner, 1978; Cappella, 1987). Each of the three following main approaches add a different perspective on the nature of interpersonal communication.

A Componential Definition

A componential definition explains interpersonal communication by noting its major components—here, the sending of messages by one person and the receiving of messages by another person or small group of persons, with some effect and with some opportunity for immediate feedback. These components were discussed in Unit 1. The model of the universals of human communication is essentially a model of the interpersonal communication process.

A Relational (Dyadic) Definition

In a relational definition, interpersonal communication is viewed as communication that takes place between two persons who have a clearly established relationship. Thus, for example, interpersonal communication would include what takes place between a waiter and a customer, a son and his father, two people in an interview, and so on. Under this definition it is almost impossible to have dyadic (two-person) communication that is not interpersonal. Not surprisingly, this definition is also referred to as the *dyadic* definition. Almost inevitably, there is some relationship between two persons. Even the stranger in the city who asks directions from a resident has a clearly defined relationship with the resident as soon as the first message is sent. Sometimes this relational definition is extended to include small groups of persons, such as family members or groups of three or four friends.

A Developmental Definition

In the developmental approach, interpersonal communication is seen as the end of a progression from impersonal communication at one extreme to highly personal or intimate communication at the other end. This progression signals or defines the development of interpersonal communication. According to communicologist Gerald Miller's (1978) analysis, interpersonal communication is characterized by and distinguished from impersonal communication on the basis of at least three factors.

Psychologically Based Predictions   In *im*personal encounters you respond to another person on the basis of sociological data—the classes or groups to which the person belongs. For example, you respond to a particular college professor the way you respond to college professors in general. Similarly, the college professor responds to a particular student in the way professors respond to students generally. As the relationship becomes more personal, however, both the professor and the student begin to respond to each other not as members of their groups but as individuals. You respond to another person on the basis of psychological data, on the ways this person differs from the members of his or her group.

Explanatory Knowledge   In interpersonal interactions you base your communications on *explanatory knowledge* of each other. When you know a particular person, you can predict how that person will act in a variety of situations. As you get to know that person better, however, you can predict not only how a person will act but also why the person behaves as he or she does. The college professor may, in an impersonal relationship, know that Pat will be five minutes late to class each Friday. That is, the professor is able to predict Pat's behavior. In an interpersonal situation, however, the professor can also offer explanations for the behavior (giving reasons for Pat's lateness).

Personally Established Rules   Society sets up rules for interaction in impersonal situations. As noted in the previous example of the student and professor, the social rules of interaction set up by the culture lose importance as the relationship becomes more personal. In the place of these social rules, the individuals set up rules of their own. When individuals establish their own rules for interacting with each other rather than using the rules set down by the society, the situation is interpersonal.

These three characteristics vary in degree. You respond to another on the basis of psychological data *to some degree*. You can explain another's behavior *to some degree*. And you interact on the basis of mutually established rules rather than on socially established norms *to some degree*. A developmental approach to communication implies a continuum ranging from highly impersonal to highly intimate. "Interpersonal communication" occupies a part of this continuum, though each person might draw its boundaries a bit differently.

Communication theorists are divided among these three definitions. Each instructor and each text will define interpersonal communication somewhat differently. My own feeling is that interpersonal communication is best defined, in its broadest sense, to include any interaction in which there is a relationship established between or among the participants. At the same time, recognize that interpersonal communication changes as it becomes more intimate—a progression clearly explained in the developmental definition. Thus, all three definitions are helpful in explaining what interpersonal communication is and how it develops.

INTERPERSONAL RELATIONSHIPS

Interpersonal relationships are established in stages. You do not become intimate friends with someone immediately upon meeting. Rather, you grow into an intimate relationship gradually, through a series of steps from the initial contact, through intimacy, and perhaps on to dissolution. And the same is probably true with most other relationships as well. In all, six major stages are identifiable (see Figure 12.1): contact, involvement, intimacy, deterioration, repair, and dissolution. Each stage can be divided into an early and a late phase, as noted in the diagram. For each specific relationship, you might wish to modify and revise the basic model in various ways. As a general description of relationship development, however, the stages seem fairly standard.

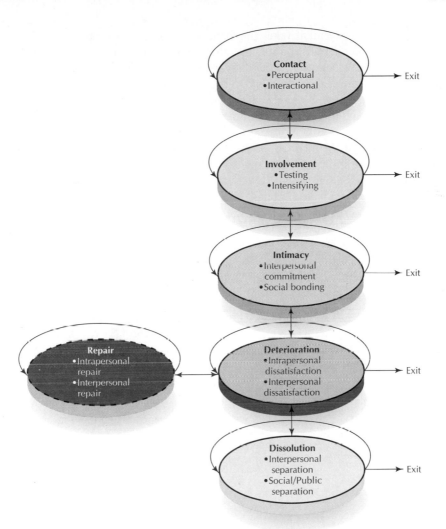

FIGURE 12.1 A six-stage relationship model.

Contact   At the first stage you make **contact.** At first, the contact is *perceptual;* you see what the person looks like, you hear what the person sounds like. You get a physical picture of the person—sex, approximate age, height, and so on. After this perception, there is usually *interactional contact.* According to some researchers (Zunin & Zunin, 1972), it is during this stage—within the first four minutes of initial interaction—that you decide whether you want to pursue the relationship. It is at this stage that physical appearance is so important, because the physical dimensions are most open to easy inspection. Yet qualities such as friendliness, warmth, openness, and dynamism are also revealed at this stage. If you like the individual and want to pursue the relationship, you proceed to the second stage.

Involvement   The **involvement** stage is the stage of acquaintance, when you commit yourself to getting to know the other person better and also to revealing yourself. At first, this involvement takes the form of testing the other person and the relationship. In the later phase, you may intensify your involvement. If this is to be a romantic relationship, then you might date at this stage. If it is to be a friendship, you might share your mutual interests—go to the movies or to some sports event together.

Dating couples use a variety of strategies, identified in Table 12.1, to intensify their relationship and to move close to intimacy (Tolhuizen, 1989).

Intimacy   At the **intimacy** stage, you commit yourself still further to the other person. Usually the intimacy stage divides itself neatly into two phases: an *interpersonal commitment* phase in which you commit yourselves to each other in a kind of private way and a *social bonding* phase in which the commitment is made public—perhaps to family and friends, perhaps to the public at large through, say, a legal or religious ceremony. This stage is reserved for very few people—sometimes just one and sometimes two, three, or perhaps four. Rarely do people have more than four intimates, except in a family situation.

When the intimacy stage involves marriage, people are faced with three main premarital anxieties (Zimmer, 1986):

Table 12.1   Dating Strategies: Fifteen Ways to Intensify Relationships

Social Rewards and Attraction

Increase rewards	increase giving partner rewards
Tokens of affection	give partner gifts
Behavioral adaptation	do things to impress or increase partner's favorable impression
Personal appearance	increase personal attractiveness
Social enmeshment	interact with partner's network of friends or family

Implicitly Expressed Intimacy

Suggestive actions	declare interest indirectly through suggestions
Nonverbal expressions of affection	use nonverbal communication to convey the desire for increased intimacy
Sexual intimacy	become more intimate sexually

Passive and Indirect

Accept definitional bid	say "yes" to partner's invitation to increase intimacy
Social support and assistance	ask others for relationship advice

Verbal Directness and Intimacy

Relationship negotiation	talk about the relationship and desires for the future
Direct definitional bid	directly request a more intimate relationship
Personalized communication	disclose personal information, use terms to reflect the intimacy of the relationship
Verbal expression of affection	declare love or caring
Increased contact	increase interaction with partner

What reasons might you give in support of the proposition that intimacy is easier to achieve between members of the same culture? What reasons might you give for the proposition that intimacy is easier to achieve when members come from different cultures? How might you go about testing which of those propositions has greater validity?

- the security anxiety: Will my mate leave me for someone else? Will my mate be sexually unfaithful?
- the fulfillment anxiety: Will we be able to achieve a close, warm, and special rapport? Will we be able to have an equal relationship?
- the excitement anxiety: Will boredom and routine set in? Will I lose my freedom and become trapped?

Of course, not everyone strives for intimacy (Bartholomew, 1990). Some may consciously desire intimacy, but are so fearful of its consequences that they avoid it. Others dismiss intimacy and defensively deny their need for more and deeper interpersonal contact. To some people relational intimacy is extremely risky. To others, it involves only low risk.

For example, how true of your attitudes are the following statements?

- It is dangerous to get really close to people.
- I'm afraid to get really close to someone because I might get hurt.
- I find it difficult to trust other people.
- The most important thing to consider in a relationship is whether I might get hurt.

People who agree with these statements (and similar statements not included here), which come from recent research on risk in intimacy (Pilkington & Richardson,

1988), perceive intimacy to involve great risk. Such people, it has been found, have fewer close friends, are less likely to be involved in a romantic relationship, have less trust in others, have a low level of dating assertiveness, and are generally less sociable than those who see intimacy as involving little risk.

In the popular mind the intimacy stage is the stage of falling in love. This is the time you "become lovers" and commit yourselves to being romantic partners. It is interesting and important to note, however, that loving means very different things to different people. To illustrate this important concept, take the love test on page 212, "What Kind of Lover Are You?"

Eros: Beauty and Sensuality   Erotic love focuses on beauty and physical attractiveness, sometimes to the exclusion of qualities you might consider more important and more lasting. The erotic lover has an idealized image of beauty that is unattainable in reality. Consequently, the erotic lover often feels unfulfilled.

Ludus: Entertainment and Excitement   Ludus love is seen as fun, a game to be played. To the ludic lover, love is not to be taken too seriously; emotions are to be held in check lest they get out of hand and make trouble. Passions never rise to the point at which they get out of control. A ludic lover is self-controlled; this lover is consciously aware of the need to manage love rather than allowing it to control him or her.

Storge Love: Peaceful and Slow   Like ludus, storge lacks passion and intensity. Storgic lovers do not set out to find lovers but to establish a companion-like relationship with someone they know and can share interests and activities. Storgic love develops over a period of time rather than in one mad burst of passion. Sex in storgic relationships comes late, and when it comes it assumes no great importance. Storgic love is sometimes difficult to separate from friendship; it is often characterized by the same qualities that characterize friendship: mutual caring, compassion, respect, and concern for the other person.

Pragma: Practical and Traditional   The pragma lover is practical and wants compatibility and a relationship in which important needs and desires will be satisfied. In its extreme, pragma may be seen in the person who writes down the qualities wanted in a mate and actively goes about seeking someone who matches up. The pragma lover is concerned with the social qualifications of a potential mate even more than personal qualities; family and background are extremely important to the pragma lover, who relies not so much on feelings as on logic. The pragma lover views love as a necessity—or as a useful relationship—that makes the rest of life easier. So the pragma lover asks such questions of a potential mate as "Will this person earn a good living?" "Can this person cook?" and "Will this person help me advance in my career?"

Manic Love: Elation and Depression   The quality of mania that separates it from other types of love is the extremes of its highs and lows, its ups and downs. The manic lover loves intensely and at the same time intensely worries about and fears the loss of the love. With little provocation, for example, the manic lover may experience extreme jealousy. Manic love is obsessive; the manic lover has to possess the beloved completely—in all ways, at all times. In return, the manic lover wishes to be possessed, to be loved intensely. It seems almost as if the manic lover is driven to these extremes by some outside force or perhaps by some inner obsession that cannot be controlled.

Agape: Compassionate and Selfless   *Agape* (uh-GAH-pay) is a compassionate, egoless, self-giving love. Agape is nonrational and nondiscriminative. Agape creates value and virtue through love rather than bestowing love only on that which is valuable and virtuous. The agapic lover loves even people with whom he or she has no close ties. This lover loves the stranger on the road, and the fact that they will probably never meet again has nothing to do with it. Jesus, Buddha, and Gandhi practiced and preached this unqualified love. Agape is a spiritual love, offered without concern for personal reward or gain. The agapic lover loves without expecting that the love will be returned or reciprocated.

Deterioration   Although many relationships become stabilized at one of the previous stages, some relationships experience **deterioration**. The first phase of deterioration is usually *intrapersonal dissatisfaction*. You begin to feel that this relationship may not be as important as you had thought before. You grow further and further apart. You share less of your free time, and when you are together there are awkward silences, fewer self-disclosures, and a self-consciousness in your exchanges. If this dissatisfaction continues or grows, you may pass to the second phase, *interpersonal dissatisfaction*, when you discuss these dissatsfactions with your partner. During this stage, Some people may seek to repair their relationship.

Repair   The *repair* stage is optional, and so is indicated in the model as a broken circle. Some relational partners may pause during deterioration and try to repair their relationship. Others, however, may progress—without stopping or thinking—to dissolution. Repair usually occurs in at least two stages: intrapersonal and interpersonal. At the *intrapersonal level* you analyze what went wrong and consider ways to solve your difficulties. At this stage you might consider changing your behaviors or perhaps your expectations of your partner. You might also evaluate the rewards of continuing your relationship as it is now and those of ending it. At the *interpersonal level,* you might discuss with your partner the problems that you see in the relationship, the corrections you want to see, and perhaps what you are willing to do and what you want the other person to do. You and your partner might try to solve your problems yourselves, seek the advice of friends or family, or perhaps enter professional counseling. A wide variety of repair strategies are considered in Unit 13.

Dissolution   If repair is not successful, you might enter the stage of **dissolution**. The early phase of dissolution takes the form of *interpersonal separation;* you might move into separate apartments and begin to lead lives apart from each other. If the relationship is marriage, you might seek a legal separation. If the separation period proves workable and if the original relationship is not repaired, you may enter the *social* or *public separation* phase. If the bond was marriage, the dissolution is symbolized by a divorce, although the actual relational dissolution takes the form of establishing separate lives away from each other. Sometimes there is relief and relaxation. At other times there is intense anxiety and frustration. There may be recriminations and hostility and resentment over time ill-spent and now lost.

SELF-TEST

What Kind of Lover Are You?

Respond to each of the following statements with T (if you believe the statement to be a generally accurate representation of your attitudes about love) or F (if you believe the statement does not adequately represent your attitudes about love).

_T_ 1. My lover and I have the right physical "chemistry" between us. _T_

_T_ 2. I feel that my lover and I were meant for each other. _T_

_F_ 3. My lover and I really understand each other. _T_

_T_ 4. My lover fits my ideal standards of physical beauty/handsomeness. _T_

_F_ 5. I try to keep my lover a little uncertain about my commitment to him/her. _T_

_T_ 6. I believe that what my lover doesn't know about me won't hurt him/her. _T_

_F_ 7. My lover would get upset if he/she knew of some of the things I've done with other people. _T_

_F_ 8. When my lover gets too dependent on me, I want to back off a little. _T_

_T_ 9. To be genuine, our love first required *caring* for a while. _T_

_T_ 10. I expect to always be friends with my lover. _T_

_T_ 11. Our love is really a deep friendship, not a mysterious, mystical emotion. _T_

_T_ 12. Our love relationship is the most satisfying because it developed from a good friendship. _T_

_F_ 13. In choosing my lover, I believed it was best to love someone with a similar background. _F_

_F_ 14. A main consideration in choosing my lover was how he/she would reflect on my family. _T_

Movement Among the Stages Figure 12.1 contains three types of arrows. The **exit arrows** indicate that each stage offers the opportunity to exit the relationship. After saying "hello," you can say "good-bye" and exit. The vertical or **movement arrows** going to the next stage and back again (including the horizontal arrow from dissolution to repair) represent the ability to move to another stage. You can move to a stage that is more intense (from involvement to intimacy) or less intense (from intimacy to deterioration). You can also go back to a previously established stage. For example, you may have established an intimate relationship but no longer want to maintain it at that level. At the same time, you are relatively pleased with the relationship, so it is not really deteriorating. You just want it to be less intense. So, you might go back to the involvement stage and reestablish the relationship at that more comfortable level.

The **self-reflexive arrows** return to the same level or stage. These signify that any relationship may become stabilized at any point. You may, for example, maintain a relationship at the intimate level without the relationship's deteriorating or going back to the less intense stage of involvement. Or you might remain at the "Hello, how are you" stage—the contact stage—without getting involved any further.

SELF-TEST (continued)

__T__ 15. An important factor in choosing a partner is whether or not he/she would be a good parent.

__F__ 16. One consideration in choosing my lover was how he/she would reflect on my career.

__F__ 17. When things aren't right with my lover and me, my stomach gets upset.

__F__ 18. Sometimes I get so excited about being in love with my lover that I can't sleep.

__F__ 19. When my lover doesn't pay attention to me, I feel sick all over.

__T__ 20. I cannot relax if I suspect that my lover is with someone else.

__T__ 21. I try to always help my lover through difficult times.

__T__ 22. I would rather suffer myself than let my lover suffer.

__/__ 23. When my lover gets angry with me, I still love him/her fully and unconditionally.

__T__ 24. I would endure all things for the sake of my lover.

Scoring   This scale is designed to enable you to identify those styles that best reflect your own beliefs about love. The statements refer to the six types of love discussed on pages 210 and 211: eros, ludus, storge, pragma, mania, and agape. "True" answers represent your agreement and "false" answers represent your disagreement with the type of love to which the statements refer. Statements 1 through 4 are characteristic of the eros lover. If you answered "true" to these statements, you have a strong eros component to your love style. If you answered "false," you have a weak eros component. Statements 5 through 8 refer to ludus love; 9 through 12 to storge love, 13 through 16 to pragma love, 17 through 20 to manic love, and 21 through 24 to agapic love.

Source: "A Relationship-Specific Version of the Love Attitudes Scale" by Susan S. Hendrick and Clyde Hendrick. Reprinted by permission of the authors.

THEORIES OF INTERPERSONAL RELATIONSHIPS

You can gain considerable insight into interpersonal relationships by looking at the theories that try to explain what happens when you enter a relationship and your reasons for entering or exiting such relationships. Here we look at four general theories: social penetration, attraction, social exchange, and equity. Each offers a different perspective; each provides different insight.

Social Penetration Theory

Social penetration theories describe relationships in terms of the number of topics that people talk about and their degree of "personalness" (Altman & Taylor, 1973; Taylor & Altman, 1987). This theory is not so much concerned with why relationships develop but with what happens when they do develop; it provides an additional step on the six-stage model just discussed.

Breadth and Depth of Relationships   In social penetration theory, relationships are described by the number of topics the two people talk about and the degree of "personalness" to which they pursue these topics. The number of topics about which

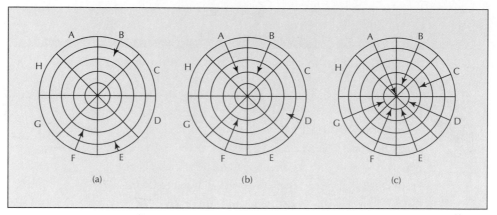

FIGURE 12.2 Social penetration with (a) acquaintance, (b) friend, and (c) intimate.

you communicate is referred to as **breadth**. The degree to which the inner personality—the core of an individual—is penetrated is referred to as depth.

Let us represent an individual as a circle and divide that circle into parts as in Figure 12.2 (Altman & Taylor, 1973). These parts represent the topics or areas that people talk about (breadth). Further, let's visualize the circle and its parts as consisting of concentric inner circles. These represent the different levels of communication, or the depth. Note that in circle (a) only three of the topic areas are penetrated. Two are penetrated only to the first level and one is penetrated to the second level. In this type of interaction, three topic areas are talked about and they are discussed at rather superficial levels. This is the type of relationship you might have with an acquaintance.

Circle (b) represents a more intense relationship, both broader (here four topics are discussed) and deeper. This is the type of relationship you might have with a friend. Circle (c) shows a still more intense relationship. Here seven of the eight areas are penetrated and most of the areas are penetrated to the deepest levels. This is the type of relationship you might have with a lover, a parent, or a sibling.

We can describe relationships—friendships, loves, families—in terms of breadth and depth. In its initial stage, a relationship is normally characterized by narrowness (few topics are discussed) and shallowness (the topics discussed are discussed only superficially). If early in a relationship topics are discussed to a depth which is normally reserved for intimates, you would probably experience considerable discomfort. As already noted (Unit 3), when intimate disclosures are made early in a relationship, you may feel something is wrong with the disclosing individual. As the relationship grows in intensity and intimacy, both the breadth and the depth increase and these increases are seen as comfortable, normal, and natural.

Depenetration When a relationship begins to deteriorate, the breadth and depth often (but not always) reverse themselves—a process of **depenetration** (Baxter, 1983). For example, while terminating a relationship, you might stop talking about certain topics. At the same time you might discuss the remaining topics in less depth. You would reduce the level of your self-disclosures and reveal less of your innermost feelings.

Attraction Theory

You are no doubt attracted to some people and not attracted to others. In a similar way, some people are attracted to you and some people are not. If you are like most people, then you are probably attracted to others on the basis of a variety of factors: physical appearance and personality, proximity, reinforcement, similarity, complementarity, and their use of affinity-seeking strategies.

Physical Appearance and Personality   When you say, "I find that person attractive," you probably mean either that (1) you find that person physically attractive or (2) you find that person's personality or behavior attractive. For the most part you probably like physically attractive people rather than physically unattractive people, and you like people who have a pleasant rather than an unpleasant personality. Of course, we each define "attractive" differently.

Generally, people attribute positive characteristics to people they find attractive and negative characteristics to people they find unattractive. Numerous studies have supported this commonsense observation (Aronson, 1980). When photographs of men and women varying in attractiveness were viewed by both men and women who were asked to assess these persons, the more attractive persons were judged to be sexually warmer and more responsive, more sensitive, kinder, more interesting, stronger, more

What physical and personality characteristics make a person attractive and what characteristics make a person unattractive to you? Did you learn to like or dislike those characteristics as a result of your cultural upbringing? If so, how?

poised, more modest, more sociable, more outgoing, more competent husbands and wives, to have happier marriages, and to secure more prestigious jobs. Those who are perceived as attractive are also perceived as more competent generally. Interestingly enough, those who are perceived as more competent in communication are also perceived as more attractive—both socially and physically, and in terms of working on a task (Duran & Kelly, 1988)

Proximity If you look around at people you find attractive, you would probably find that they are the people who live or work close to you. This aspect is referred to as **proximity**. People who become friends are the people who have the greatest opportunity to interact with each other.

Physical closeness is most important in the early stages of interaction, for example, during the first days of school or the first days on a new job. It decreases (but always remains significant) as the opportunity to interact with more distant others increases.

Reinforcement Not surprisingly, you are probably attracted to people who give you rewards or reinforcements. These may be social, as in the form of compliments or praise, or they may be material, as in the case of the suitor whose gifts eventually win the hand of the beloved. When overdone, however, rewards can lose their effectiveness and may even lead to negative responses. The people who reward you constantly soon become too sweet to take, and in a short period you probably learn to discount whatever they say. Also, if the reward is to work, it must be perceived as genuine and not motivated by selfish concerns. The salesperson who compliments your taste in clothes, your eyes, your complexion, and just about everything else is not going to have the effect that someone without ulterior motives would have. Interestingly enough, you are probably also attracted to people *you* reward (Aronson, 1980; Jecker & Landy, 1969). You come to like people for whom you do favors. For example, you may have noticed that in your own interactions you have increased your liking for persons after buying them an expensive present or going out of your way to do them a special favor. In these and numerous similar instances, you justify your behavior by believing that the person was worth your efforts; otherwise, you would have to admit to being a poor judge of character and to spending your money and effort on people who do not deserve it.

Similarity If you could construct your mate, it is likely that your mate would look, act, and think very much like you do. By being attracted to people like yourself, you validate yourself; you tell yourself, in effect, that you are worthy of being liked, that you are attractive. Although there are exceptions, you probably like people who are similar to yourself in nationality, race, ability, physical characteristics, intelligence, attitudes, and so on.

If you were to ask a group of friends, "To whom are you attracted?" they would probably name very attractive people; in fact, they would probably name the most attractive people they know. But if you were to observe these friends, you would find that they go out with and establish relationships with people who are quite similar to themselves in terms of physical attractiveness. This is known as the **matching hypothesis**: people date and mate with people who are similar to themselves in physical attractiveness (Walster & Walster, 1978).

Complementarity   Although many people would argue that "birds of a feather flock together," others would argue that "opposites attract." This latter concept is the principle of **complementarity**. Take, for example, the individual who is extremely dogmatic. Would this person be attracted to people who are equally dogmatic or to those who are much less so? The similarity principle predicts that this person will be attracted to those who are like him or her (that is, very dogmatic), while the complementarity principle predicts that this person will be attracted to those who are unlike him or her (that is, not dogmatic).

Affinity-Seeking Strategies   In addition to the five factors noted already, attractiveness also depends on a broad class of behaviors known as **affinity-seeking strategies** (Bell & Daly, 1984). Several of these strategies are presented in Table 12.2. In the definitions, the term *Other* is used as shorthand for "other person or persons."

As you read through these strategies, consider such issues as these:

- Are there other strategies that you would add to this list?
- Do you find some of these strategies ineffective?
- Which strategies work best for you? Which strategies work best *on* you?
- What are the ethical implications of these strategies? When is the use of a given strategy unethical?

Table 12.2 Affinity-Seeking Strategies: How to Get People to Like Us and Feel Positively Toward Us

Altruism	Be of help to Other.
Assume control	Appear "in control," as a leader, as one who takes charge.
Assume equality	Present yourself as socially equal to Other.
Comfortable self	Present yourself as comfortable and relaxed when with Other.
Dynamism	Appear active, enthusiastic, and dynamic.
Elicit Other's disclosures	Stimulate and encourage Other to talk about himself or herself; reinforce disclosures and contributions of Other.
Inclusion of Other	Include Other in your social activities and groupings.
Listening	Listen to Other attentively and actively.
Openness	Engage in self-disclosure with Other.
Optimism	Appear optimistic and positive rather than pessimistic and negative.
Self-concept confirmation	Show respect for Other and help Other to feel positively about himself or herself.
Self-inclusion	Arrange circumstances so that you and Other come into frequent contact.
Sensitivity	Communicate warmth and empathy to Other.
Similarity	Demonstrate that you share significant attitudes and values with Other.
Trustworthiness	Appear to Other as honest and reliable.

Social Exchange Theory

Social exchange theory claims that you develop relationships that will enable you to maximize your profits (Chadwick-Jones, 1976; Gergen, Greenberg, & Willis, 1980; Thibaut & Kelley, 1986), a theory based on an economic model of profits and losses. The theory begins with the following equation:

$$\text{Profits} = \text{Rewards} - \text{Costs}$$

Rewards are anything that you would incur costs to obtain. For example, in order to acquire the reward of financial gain, you might have to work rather than play. To earn an A in interpersonal communication, you might have to write a term paper or study more than you might want to. Love, affection, status, money, gifts, security, social acceptance, companionship, friendship, and intimacy are just a few examples of the rewards for which you might be willing to work.

Costs are those things that you normally try to avoid, the things you consider unpleasant or difficult. Working overtime, washing dishes and ironing clothes, watching your partner's favorite television show (which you find boring), and doing favors for those you dislike might all be considered costs.

Using this basic economic model, social exchange theory claims that you seek to develop relationships (friendship and romantic) which will give you the greatest profits; that is, relationships in which the rewards are greater than the costs. The most preferred relationships, according to this theory, are those that give you the greatest rewards with the least costs.

If you think about your current or past relationships, you will probably see that the relationships you pursued and maintained were those that provided you with prof-

How would you apply social exchange and equity theories to explain the development, maintenance, and deterioration of relationships in the culture of professional sports?

its, with rewards that were greater than costs. Equally important, the relationships that you did not pursue or that you ended were probably those where there was no profit, that is, those whose costs exceeded the rewards. These were the relationships in which there was more dissatisfaction than satisfaction, more unhappiness than happiness, more problems than pleasures.

When you enter a relationship, you bring a certain *comparison level*—a general idea of the kinds of rewards and profits that you feel you ought to get out of such a relationship. It is your realistic expectations concerning what you feel you deserve from a relationship. For example, in a study of married couples it was found that most people expect reasonably high levels of trust, mutual respect, love, and commitment. Their expectations are significantly lower for time spent together, privacy, sexual activity, and communication (Sabatelli & Pearce, 1986). When the rewards that you get equal or surpass this comparison level, you feel satisfied with your relationship.

However, you also have a *comparison level for alternatives*. That is, you compare the profits that you get from your current relationships with the profits you think you can get from alternative relationships. Thus, if you see that the profits from your present relationship are below the profits that you could get from an alternative relationship, you might decide to leave your current relationship and enter this new, more profitable relationship.

Equity Theory

Equity theory uses the concepts of social exchange but goes a step further and claims that you develop and maintain relationships in which the *ratio* of your rewards compared to costs is approximately equal to your partner's (Messick & Cook, 1983; Walster, Walster, & Berscheid, 1978). An equitable relationship, then, would be one in which each of you derives rewards that are proportional to your costs. If you work harder for the relationship than your partner, then equity demands that you should get greater rewards. If you each work equally hard, then equity demands that you should each get approximately equal rewards.

Conversely, inequity exists in a relationship if you pay more of the costs (for example, you do more of the unpleasant tasks) but your partner enjoys more of the rewards, or if you and your partner work equally hard, but your partner gets more of the rewards.

Equity theory puts into clear focus the sources of relational dissatisfaction seen every day. For example, in a relationship both partners may have full-time jobs but one may also be expected to do the major share of the household chores. Thus, although both may be deriving equal rewards—they have equally good cars, they live in the same three-bedroom house, and so on—one partner is paying more of the costs. According to equity theory, this partner will be dissatisfied because of this lack of equity.

Equity theory claims that you will develop and maintain relationships and will be satisfied with relationships that are equitable. You will not develop, will terminate, and will be dissatisfied with relationships that are inequitable. The greater the inequity, the greater the dissatisfaction.

Summary

1. A *componential* definition of interpersonal communication identifies the components or elements in the interpersonal communication act.

2. A *relational* or *dyadic* definition defines interpersonal communication as that which takes place between two persons who have a clearly established relationship.

3. A *developmental* definition defines interpersonal communication as a development or progression from impersonal communication at one extreme to personal communication at the other. Interpersonal communication is distinguished from other types in that (1) predictions are based on psychological rather than sociological data; (2) predictions are based on explanatory knowledge of each other; and (3) behaviors are based on personally established rules.

4. *Relationships are established in stages.* At least the following six stages should be recognized: *contact, involvement, intimacy, deterioration, repair*, and *dissolution*.

5. *Social penetration theory* describes relationships in terms of *breadth* (the number of topics talked about) and *depth* (the degree of "personalness" to which the topics are pursued). As relationships develop, the breadth and depth increase. When a relationship deteriorates, the breadth and depth will often (but not always) decrease, a process referred to as *depenetration*.

6. *Interpersonal attraction* depends on such factors as *physical appearance* and *personality, proximity, reinforcement, similarity, complementarity,* and the use of *affinity-seeking strategies*.

7. The *matching hypothesis* holds that you would probably date and mate with those who are about equivalent to yourself in physical attractiveness.

8. *Social exchange theory* claims that you seek and maintain relationships in which the rewards exceed the costs. Conversely, relationships deteriorate and dissolve when the costs exceed the rewards.

9. *Equity theory* builds on social exchange theory and asserts that people also want an equitable distribution of the rewards based on the costs paid by each person.

Applications

12.1 THE GREETING CARD AND THE POPULAR SONG

The aims of this exercise are (1) to familiarize you with some of the popular conceptions and sentiments concerning interpersonal relationships, and (2) to introduce a wide variety of concepts important in the study of interpersonal relationships.

Methods and Procedures

1. Bring to class one greeting card or one song that expresses a sentiment that is significant for any one of the following reasons. This list is not exhaustive and the items are not mutually exclusive.

    a. it expresses a popular sentiment that is true or that is false
    b. it expresses a sentiment that incorporates a concept or theory that can assist us in understanding interpersonal relationships
    c. it illustrates a popular problem in interpersonal relationships
    d. it illustrates a useful strategy for relationship development, maintenance, repair, or dissolution
    e. it illustrates a significant concept or theory in interpersonal relationships
    f. it suggests a useful question (or hypothesis for scientific study) that should be asked in the study of interpersonal relationships
    g. it supports or contradicts some currently accepted theory in interpersonal relationships

2. Be prepared to explain the greeting card or song sentiment as it relates to the study of interpersonal relationships in a brief discussion (three to five minutes).

3. Identify one principle of interpersonal communication that is suggested by your card or song.

Remember: Sentiments in greeting cards and songs are communicated through a number of different channels. Therefore, consider the sentiments communicated through the verbal message but also consider the messages communicated through the illustrations, the colors, the physical form of the card, the type of print, the tempo of the song, the volume of the music, and so on.

12.2   ANALYZING A RELATIONSHIP

The dialogue that follows is an abbreviated account of the development and dissolution of a relationship. Consequently, the stages of relationships, for example, are easy to see and are clearly differentiated. In reality and in longer dialogues, these divisions would not be so obvious. The main purpose of this dialogue is to provide a focus for the discussion of interpersonal relationships. Examine the dialogue, taking into consideration some or all of the following questions:

1. *Stages in Interpersonal Relations.* Identify the stages in the dialogue. What specific phrases in the dialogue cue you to the stages of the relationships? What conversational cues signal movement from one stage to another? Look especially for the following types of messages:

    a. messages of contact
    b. messages of involvement
    c. messages of intimacy

    d.   messages of deterioration

    e.   messages of repair

    f.   messages of dissolution

2. *Social Penetration Theory*. What would you expect the breadth and depth of the relationship to be at each of the six stages? At what stage is there greatest breadth? The least? At what stage is there greatest depth? The least?

3. *Attraction Theory*. What do you suppose accounted for the attraction between Pat and Chris? Can you use attraction theory to explain the deterioration and dissolution of the relationship?

4. *Social Exchange Theory*. What are the rewards and costs in this relationship? To whom does the relationship seem more profitable? On what basis do you assume this?

5. *Equity Theory*. How equitable does this relationship seem? Can equity help explain the relationship's difficulties?

The Saga of Chris and Pat

PAT: Hi. Didn't I see you in English last semester?

CHRIS: Yeah. I'm surprised you noticed me. I cut that class more than I attended. I really hated it.

PAT: So did I. Higgins never did seem to care much about whether you learned anything or not.

CHRIS: That's why I think I cut so much. Your name's Pat, isn't it?

PAT: Yes. And you're Chris. Right?

CHRIS: Right. What are you doing in Interpersonal Communication?

PAT: I'm majoring in communication. I want to go into advertising or public relations or something like that. I'm not really sure. What about you?

CHRIS: It's required for engineering. I guess they figure engineers should learn to communicate.

PAT: You gonna have lunch after this class?

CHRIS: Yeah. You?

PAT: Yeah. How about going over to the Union for a burger?

(At the Union Cafeteria)

CHRIS: I'm not only surprised you noticed me in English, I'm really flattered. Everyone in the class seemed to be interested in you.

PAT: Well, I doubt that, but it's nice to hear.

CHRIS: No, I mean it. Come on. You know you're popular.

PAT: Well, maybe . . . but it always seems to be with the wrong people. Today's the exception, of course.

CHRIS: You sure know the right things to say.

PAT: OK, then let me try another. What are you doing tonight? Want to go to a movie? I know it's late and all, but I thought just in case you had nothing to do.

CHRIS: I'd love to. Even if I had something else planned, I'd break it.

PAT: That makes me feel good.

CHRIS: That makes me feel good, too.

(Six months later)

PAT: I hope that this doesn't cause problems, but I got you some-
           thing.

CHRIS: What is it?

PAT: Take a look. I hope you like it.

CHRIS   *(Opens the package and finds a ring)*: I love it. I can't believe
           it! You know, a few weeks ago when we had to write up a recent
           fantasy for class, I wrote one I didn't turn in. And this was it. My
           very own fantasy coming true. I love you.

PAT: I love you . . . very much.

(Chris and Pat have now been together for about two years)

PAT: It's me. I'm home.

CHRIS: So am I.

PAT: That's not hamburgers I smell, is it?

CHRIS: Yes, it is. I like hamburgers. We can afford hamburgers. And I
           know how to cook hamburgers. Make something else if you
           don't want to eat them.

PAT: Thanks. It's nice to know that you go to such trouble making
           something I like. I hate these damn hamburgers. And I espe-
           cially hate them four times a week.

CHRIS: Eat out.

PAT: You know I have work to do tonight. I can't go out.

CHRIS: So shut up and eat the burgers. I love them.

PAT: That's good. It's you for you. Whatever happened to *us* and *we*?

CHRIS: It died when I found out about your little side trips upstate.

PAT: But I told you I was sorry about that. That was six months ago
           anyway. I got involved, I know, but I'm sorry. What do you want
           to do, punish me for the rest of my life? I'm sorry, damn it. *I'm
           sorry!*

CHRIS: So am I. But I'm the one who was left at home alone while you
           were out fooling around.

PAT: Is that why you don't want to make love? You always have some
           kind of excuse.

CHRIS: It's not an excuse. It's a reason. And the reason is that I've been
           lied to and cheated on. How can I make love to someone who
           treats me like dirt?

PAT: But I don't. I love you.

CHRIS: But I don't love you. Maybe I never have.

PAT: I *will* eat out.

(Two weeks later)

PAT: *(Thinking)* I really don't want this relationship to end. What can
           I do to make it the way it was?

CHRIS: *(Thinking)* Maybe it's better to break up. I really don't want to
           go through another one of Pat's affairs.

PAT: *(On phone)* Chris? It's me. It's been two weeks. I'd really like to talk. Can I come over and talk about this?

CHRIS: There really isn't anything to talk about. I really think it's better this way. You go your way and I'll go mine.

PAT: But, most of the time everything was fine. Okay, we've had differences, but can't we put these aside?

CHRIS: I can't. I just can't do it. I can't forget. And I guess maybe I don't want to. It's over, Pat. Maybe we can be friends at a later time. Right now, I think it's best we just don't see each other.

PAT: Can I call you tomorrow? I really want to resolve this and get back to the way we were.

CHRIS: Call if you want, but there really is no reason to.

(The next day)

PAT: Chris, it's me again. Chris, is there any hope? Did you mean what you said when you said you didn't love me?

CHRIS: I think I did. I just lost my feelings. I can't explain it. When I learned about your upstate trips, I just couldn't deal with it. And I guess I tried to protect myself and, in the process, lost my feelings for you.

PAT: Then why did you stay with me? Why didn't you leave?

CHRIS: I don't know. Maybe I was afraid to be alone. I wasn't sure I could do it alone.

PAT: So you stayed with me because you were afraid to be alone? That's crazy. Crazy. I would have rather seen us break up long ago than live like this—a loveless relationship where you go out on Tuesdays and I go out on Wednesdays. What kind of life is that?

CHRIS: Not much.

PAT: Then I guess we should separate. There's no point in living with someone who stays out of fear of being alone, who doesn't want to be touched, who doesn't want to love me. Let's try to live apart and see what happens. Maybe we need some distance. Maybe you'll want to try it again.

CHRIS: I won't, but I guess separation is the best thing.

PAT: Why don't you stay here and I'll go to my brother's place tonight. I'll pick up my things tomorrow when you're at work. I don't think I can bear to do it when you're here.

CHRIS: Good-bye.

RELATIONSHIP DEVELOPMENT, DETERIORATION, AND REPAIR

UNIT CONTENTS

Relationship Development

Relationship Deterioration

Relationship Repair and Self-repair

    Summary

    Applications

        13.1 Cherishing Behaviors

        13.2 Asking for Positive Behaviors

        13.3 Male and Female

UNIT GOALS

After completing this unit, you should be able to

1. explain the reasons for relationship development

2. identify the process of initiating relationships and the suggestions for communicating (nonverbally and verbally) during the first encounter

3. explain the reasons for relationship deterioration

4. describe the changes in communication that take place during relationship deterioration

5. explain the suggestions for relationship repair and for self-repair

In this unit we look at the relationship process in more detail. First, we examine the process of relationship development—why we seek relationships and how we initiate them. Second, we consider relationship deterioration: its nature and causes, and the changes in communication that take place during relationship deterioration. Third, we look at how a relationship might be repaired and offer some suggestions for dealing with relationships that do end.

RELATIONSHIP DEVELOPMENT

There is probably nothing as important to most people than contact with others. So important is this contact that when it is absent for prolonged periods, depression sets in, self-doubt surfaces, and people find it difficult to conduct even the basics of daily living.

Reasons for Relationship Development

Of course, each person pursues a relationship for unique reasons. Yet there are also some general reasons for developing relationships: to lessen loneliness, to secure stimulation, to acquire self-knowledge, and to maximize pleasures and minimize pain.

Lessening Loneliness   Contact with another human being helps lessen loneliness. At times you may experience loneliness because you are physically alone, although being alone does not necessarily lead to loneliness (Perlman & Peplau, 1981). At other times you may be lonely because, although you may be with another person, you may

How influential was your own culture in teaching you about relationships and particularly about the reasons for relationship development? What values did your culture teach you about relationships?

have an unfulfilled need for close contact—sometimes physical, sometimes emotional, but most often both (Peplau & Perlman, 1982; Rubenstein & Shaver, 1982).

Securing Stimulation   Human beings need stimulation. If we do not get stimulation, we withdraw and sometimes die. Human contact provides one of the best ways to be stimulated. You are a composite of many different dimensions, and all your dimensions need stimulation. You are an intellectual creature, and so you need intellectual stimulation. You talk about ideas, attend classes, and argue about different interpretations of a film or novel. You are also a physical creature who needs physical stimulation. You need to touch and be touched, to hold and be held. In addition, you are an emotional creature who needs emotional stimulation. You need to laugh and cry, feel hope and surprise, and experience warmth and affection.

Acquiring Self-knowledge   It is largely through contact with other human beings that you learn about yourself. In the discussion of self-awareness you learned that you see yourself in part through the eyes of others. If your friends see you as warm and generous, you will probably also see yourself as warm and generous. Your self-perceptions are greatly influenced by what you believe others think of you.

Maximizing Pleasures, Minimizing Pain   The most general reason to establish relationships, and one that could include all the others, is that you seek human contact to maximize your pleasures and minimize your pain. You need to share with others both your good fortune and your emotional or physical pain. Perhaps this latter need began in childhood, when you ran to your mother so that she could kiss your wounds or share your joy. You now find it difficult to run to your mother, so you go to others, generally to friends who will provide you with the same kind of support Mother did.

Initiating Relationships: The First Encounter

Perhaps the most difficult and yet the most important aspect of relationship development is the beginning. Meeting the person, presenting yourself, and somehow moving to another stage is a difficult process. Three major phases can be identified in the first encounter: examining the qualifiers, determining clearance, and communicating your desire for contact.

Before reading about this first encounter you may wish to take the apprehension test on page 228, which measures your fear of communication in interpersonal conversations.

Examining Qualifiers   *Qualifiers* are those qualities that make the individual you wish to meet an appropriate choice (Davis, 1973). Some qualifiers are obvious, such as beauty, style of clothes, jewelry, and the like. Others are hidden, such as personality, health, wealth, talent, and intelligence. These qualifiers tell you something about who the person is and help you to decide if you wish to pursue this initial encounter.

Determining Clearance   Your second step is to determine if the person is available for the type of meeting you are interested in (Davis, 1973). If you are inter-

SELF-TEST

How Apprehensive Are You in Interpersonal Conversations?

Although we often think of apprehension or fear of speaking in connection with public speaking, each of us has a certain degree of apprehension in all forms of communication. The following brief test is designed to measure your apprehension in interpersonal conversations.

This questionnaire consists of six statements concerning your feelings about interpersonal conversations. Indicate in the space provided the degree to which each statement applies to you by marking whether you (1) Strongly Agree, (2) Agree, (3) Are Undecided, (4) Disagree, or (5) Strongly Disagree with each statement. There are no right or wrong answers. Some of the statements are similar to other statements. Do not be concerned about this. Work quickly; just record your first impression.

_____ 1. While participating in a conversation with a new acquaintance, I feel very nervous.

_____ 2. I have no fear of speaking up in conversations.

_____ 3. Ordinarily I am very tense and nervous in conversations.

_____ 4. Ordinarily I am very calm and relaxed in conversations.

_____ 5. While conversing with a new acquaintance, I feel very relaxed.

_____ 6. I'm afraid to speak up in conversations.

Scoring   To obtain your apprehension score, use the following formula: Add 18 to your score for items 2, 4, and 5; then subtract your scores for items 1, 3, and 6. A score above 18 shows some degree of apprehension.

Source: From *An Introduction to Rhetorical Communication*, 4th ed. by James C. McCroskey. Reprinted by permission of the author.

ested in a date, then you might look to see if the person is wearing a wedding ring. Does the person seem to be waiting for someone else?

Communicating Contact   The next stage is communicating your desire for contact. You need to open the encounter nonverbally and verbally. Nonverbally you might signal this desire for contact in a variety of ways. Here are just a few:

- Establish eye contact first. The eyes communicate awareness of and interest in the other person.
- While maintaining eye contact, smile and further signal your interest in and positive response to this other person.
- Concentrate your focus. Nonverbally shut off from awareness the rest of the room. Be careful, however, that you do not focus so directly that you make the person uncomfortable.
- Establish physical closeness or at least lessen the physical distance between the two of you. Approach the other person, but not to the point of discomfort, so your interest in making contact is obvious.
- Maintain an open posture. Throughout this encounter, maintain a posture that communicates a willingness to enter into interaction with the other per-

son. Hands crossed over the chest or clutched around your stomach are exactly the kinds of postures you want to avoid. These often signal an unwillingness to let others enter your space.

- Reinforce positive behaviors—what the other person does to signal interest and a reciprocal willingness to make contact. Respond positively. Again, nod, smile, or somehow communicate your favorable reaction.

Although nonverbal contact is signaled first, much of the subsequent nonverbal contact takes place at the same time that you are communicating verbally. Here are some methods for making verbal contact:

- Introduce yourself. Try to avoid trite opening lines, such as "Haven't I seen you here before?" It is best simply to say, "Hi, my name is Pat."
- Focus the conversation on the other person. Get the other person talking about himself or herself. No one enjoys talking about any topic more than this one. Also, you will gain an opportunity to learn something about the person you want to get to know.
- Exchange favors and rewards. Compliment the other person; be sincere but complimentary and positive. If you can't find anything to compliment, then you might want to reassess your interest in this person.
- Stress the positives. Positiveness contributes to a good first impression simply because people are more attracted to a positive than to a negative person.
- Avoid negative or too intimate self-disclosures. Enter a relationship gradually and gracefully. Disclosures should come slowly and should be reciprocal. Anything too intimate or too negative revealed early in the relationship will create a negative image. If you cannot resist self-disclosing, try to stick to the positives and to issues that are not overly intimate.
- Establish commonalities. Seek to discover in your interaction those things you have in common with the other person—attitudes, interests, personal qualities, third parties, places: anything that will stress a connection.

RELATIONSHIP DETERIORATION

The other end of relationship development is deterioration and possible dissolution. *Relational deterioration,* the weakening of the bonds that hold people together, may be gradual or sudden, slight or extreme.

Murray Davis (1973), in his *Intimate Relations,* uses the terms *passing away* to designate gradual deterioration and *sudden death* to designate immediate or sudden deterioration. An example of passing away occurs when one of the parties develops close ties with a new intimate and this new relationship gradually pushes out the old. An example of sudden death occurs when one or both of the parties break a rule that was essential to the relationship (for example, the rule of fidelity). As a result, both realize that the relationship must be terminated.

Although you may be accustomed to thinking of relationship breakup as negative, this is not necessarily so. At times a relationship may be unproductive for one or both parties, and a breakup is often the best thing that could happen. Such a termination may provide a period for the individuals to regain their independence and self-reliance. Some relationships are so absorbing that there is little time available for reflection about oneself, others, and the relationship itself. Some distance often helps. For the most part, it is up to the individual to draw out of any decaying relationship some positive characteristics and some learning that can be used later on.

Causes of Relationship Deterioration

The causes of relationship deterioration are as numerous as the individuals involved. All these causes may also be seen as effects of relational deterioration. For example, when things start to go sour, the individuals may remove themselves physically from one another in response to the deterioration. This physical separation may in turn cause further deterioration by driving the individuals farther apart emotionally and psychologically or may encourage them to seek other partners. We can, however, examine some of the major causes.

Reasons for Establishing the Relationship Have Diminished   When the reasons you developed the relationship change drastically, your relationship may deteriorate. For example, when loneliness is no longer lessened, the relationship may be on the road to decay. When the stimulation is weak, one or both may begin to look elsewhere. If self-knowledge and self-growth prove insufficient you may become dissatisfied with yourself, your partner, and your relationship. When attractiveness has faded you may lose one of the most important reasons for establishing the relationship in the first place. When relationships break up, it is usually the more attractive partner who leaves (Blumstein & Schwartz, 1983). In short, when the pleasures don't exceed the pain (when there is no profit), the relationship is likely to deteriorate.

Third-Party Relationships   Relationships are established and maintained largely because within them, pleasures are maximized and pains are minimized. When this ceases to be the case, the relationship stands little chance of survival. The need for pleasure—and the avoidance of pain—is so great that when it is not met within the existing relationship, satisfaction and fulfillment will be sought elsewhere. When a new relationship serves these needs better, the old relationship may deteriorate.

Relational Changes   Relational changes in one or both parties may encourage relational deterioration. Psychological changes such as the development of different intellectual interests or incompatible attitudes may create relational problems. Behavioral changes such as preoccupation with business or schooling may strain the relationship and create problems. Status changes may also create difficulties for a couple.

Undefined Expectations   Sometimes each person's expectations of the other are unrealistic. This often occurs early in a relationship when, for example, the individuals think that they will want to spend all their time together. When they discover that neither one does, each resents this "lessening" of feeling in the other. The resolution of such conflicts lies not so much in meeting these unrealistic expectations as in discovering why they were unrealistic and substituting more attainable expectations.

Sex   Few sexual relationships are free of problems. In fact, sexual problems rank among the top three problems in almost all studies of newlyweds (Blumstein &

Schwartz, 1983). Although sexual frequency is not related to relational breakdown, sexual satisfaction is. It is the quality and not the quantity of a sexual relationship that is crucial. When the quality is poor, the partners may seek sexual affairs outside the primary relationship. Extrarelational affairs contribute significantly to breakups for all couples, whether married or cohabiting, whether heterosexual or homosexual. Even "open relationships"—ones which are based on sexual freedom outside the primary relationship—experience these problems and are more likely to break up than the traditional "closed" relationship.

Work   Unhappiness with work often leads to difficulties in relationships. Most people cannot separate problems with work from their relationships (Blumstein & Schwartz, 1983). Dissatisfaction with work is often associated with relationship breakup. This is true for all types of couples. With heterosexual couples (both married and cohabiting), if the man is disturbed over the woman's job—for example, if she earns a great deal more than he does or devotes a great deal of time to the job—the relationship is in for considerable trouble. And this is true whether the relationship is in its early stages or is a well-established one. A study conducted by Staines, Pottick, and Fudge (1986) demonstrated that husbands whose wives worked were less satisfied with their own jobs and lives than were men whose wives did not work. Often the man expects the woman to work but does not reduce his expectations concerning her household responsibilities. The man becomes resentful if the woman does not fulfill these expectations, and the woman becomes resentful if she takes on both outside work and full household duties.

Financial Difficulties   In surveys of problems among couples, financial difficulties loom large. Money is perhaps the most taboo topic for couples beginning a relationship. Yet it proves to be one of the major problems faced by all couples as they settle into their relationship. Dissatisfaction with money usually leads to dissatisfaction with the relationship. This is true for married and cohabiting heterosexual couples and gay male couples. It is not true for lesbian couples, who seem to care a great deal less about financial matters. This difference has led some researchers to speculate that concern over money and its equation with power and relational satisfaction are largely male attitudes.

Money is so important in relationships largely because of its close connection with power. Money brings power. This is true in business and in relationships. The power that money brings quickly generalizes to nonfinancial issues as well.

The unequal earnings of men and women create further problems, regardless of who earns more. In most relationships, the man earns more money than the woman, and because of this he controls a disproportionate share of power. When the woman earns more than the man, the problems are different. Although our society has finally allowed women to achieve success in business and the professions, it has not taught men to accept this very well. As a result, the higher-earning woman is often resented by the lower-earning man. This is true for both married and cohabiting couples.

Money also creates problems in heterosexual relationships because men and women view it differently. To men, money is power. To women, it is security and independence. Conflicts over how the couple's money is to be spent or invested can easily result from such different perceptions (Blumstein & Schwartz, 1983).

Inequitable Distribution of Rewards and Costs   Generally, and as predicted by social exchange theory, you stay in relationships that are rewarding, and leave relationships that are punishing. Further, you expect and desire equity in your relationships (Berscheid & Walster, 1978; Hatfield & Traupman, 1981). Equitable relationships are those in which the rewards and the costs are almost equally distributed between the two individuals. When partners see their relationship as equitable, they will continue building it. When the relationship is not equitable, it may deteriorate.

Communication in Relationship Deterioration

Like relational development, relational deterioration involves unique and specialized communication. In this section, we describe and analyze some of the ways in which people communicate during relational deterioration. These communication patterns are in part a response to the deterioration itself. However, these patterns are also causative. The way you communicate will influence the course of a relationship.

Withdrawal   Nonverbally, withdrawal is seen in the greater space each person seems to require and the ease with which tempers are aroused when that space is encroached on. When people are close emotionally, they can occupy close physical quarters, but when they are growing apart, they need wider spaces. Withdrawal of another kind may be seen in the decrease in similarities in clothing and in the display of "intimate trophies" such as bracelets, photographs, and rings (Knapp & Vangelisti, 1992). Other nonverbal signs include the failure to engage in eye contact, to look at each other generally, and to touch each other (Miller & Parks, 1982).

Verbally, withdrawal is seen in a number of ways. Where once there was a great desire to talk and listen, there is now less desire—perhaps none. At times phatic communion is also severely limited, since the individuals do not want any of the regular functions it serves. At other times, however, phatic communion is engaged in as an end in itself. Whereas phatic talk is usually a preliminary to serious conversation, here phatic communion is used as an alternative to or a means of forestalling serious talk. Thus people in the throes of dissolution may talk a great deal about insignificant events—the weather, a movie on television, a neighbor down the hall. By focusing on these topics, they avoid confronting serious issues.

Self-Disclosure   Self-disclosing communications decline significantly when a relationship deteriorates. Self-disclosure may not be thought worth the effort if the relationship is dying. You may also limit self-disclosures because you feel that the other person may not be supportive or may use the disclosures against you.

Deception   Deception increases as relationships break down. Lies may be seen as a way to avoid arguments over staying out all night, not calling, or being seen in the wrong place with the wrong person. At other times lies are used because of some feeling of shame. Perhaps you want to save the relationship and do not want to add another obstacle or you may not want to appear to be the cause of any further problems—and you lie. Sometimes deception takes the form of avoidance—the lie of omission. You talk about everything except the crux of the difficulty. Whether by omission or commission, deception has a way of escalating and creating a climate of distrust and disbelief.

Do men and women communicate similarly in relationship deterioration? If not, what are some of the major differences? Can you identify racial or national differences in the ways people communicate during deterioration?

Evaluative Responses   Relational deterioration often brings an increase in negative evaluations and a decrease in positive evaluations. Where once you praised the other's behaviors, talents, or ideas, you now criticize them. Often the behaviors have not changed significantly. What has changed is your way of looking at them. Negative evaluation frequently leads to outright fighting and conflict. And although conflict is not necessarily bad (Unit 14), in relationships that are deteriorating, the conflict (often coupled with withdrawal) is often not resolved.

Exchange of Favors   When a relationship deteriorates, the costs begin to exceed the rewards. When the costs get too high (and the rewards too low), the relationship may be ended. During relational deterioration there is little favor exchange. Compliments, once given frequently and sincerely, are now rare. Positive stroking is minimal. Nonverbally, eye contact, smiling, touching, caressing, and holding each other occur less frequently.

RELATIONSHIP REPAIR AND SELF-REPAIR

If you wish to salvage a relationship, you may try to do so by changing your communication patterns and, in effect, putting into practice the insights and skills learned in this course. First, let's look at ways to repair the relationship and then we can consider some self-repair strategies if the relationships ends.

Relationship Repair

We can look at the strategies for repairing a relationship in terms of the following six suggestions, which conveniently spell out the word REPAIR (Figure 13.1), a useful reminder that repair is not a one-step but a multistep process:

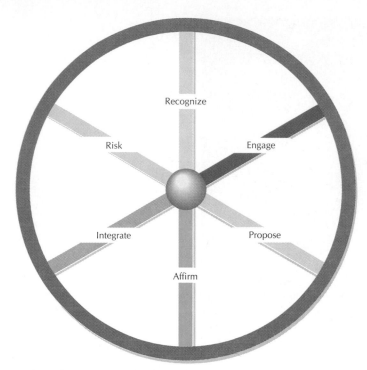

FIGURE 13.1 The Relationship Repair Wheel. This metaphorical wheel is designed to suggest that (1) relationship repair consists of several processes, (2) that must work together, (3) so that the relationship can move from one place to another, and (4) works best when another wheel (propelled by the other person) is moving in the same direction. You may find it interesting to create your own metaphor for identifying the steps involved in relationship repair and how the general process of repair works.

> Recognize the problem
> Engage in productive conflict resolution
> Propose possible solutions
> Affirm each other
> Integrate solutions into normal behavior
> Risk

Recognize the Problem Your first step is to identify the problem and to recognize it both intellectually and emotionally. Specify what is wrong with your present relationship (in concrete, specific terms) and what changes would be needed to make it better (again, in specific terms). Without this first step there is little hope for improving any interpersonal relationship. Create a picture of your relationship as you would want it to be and compare that picture to the way the relationship looks now. Specify the changes that would have to take place to have the idealized picture replace the present picture.

If the relationship is to be repaired and become rewarding once again, then the withdrawal and deception that characterize communication during the stage of deterioration must give way to open and honest communication. As is true of alcohol or drug

Do men and women think about and approach relationship repair in the same way? If not, what kinds of differences do you observe?

addiction, you must admit you have a problem before you can work on a cure. And you have to be honest about what the problem is.

Try to see the problem from your partner's point of view and to have your partner see the problem from yours. Exchange these perspectives, empathically and with open minds. Try to be descriptive when discussing grievances, being especially careful to avoid such troublesome terms as *always* and *never*. Also, own your own feelings and thoughts; use I-messages and take responsibility for your feelings instead of blaming your partner.

Engage in Productive Conflict Resolution   Interpersonal conflict is an inevitable part of relationship life. It is not so much the conflict that causes relationship difficulties but rather the way in which the conflict is dealt with. If it is confronted with productive strategies, the conflict may be resolved and the relationship may actually emerge stronger and healthier. If, however, unproductive and destructive strategies are used, the relationship may well deteriorate further. Because this topic is so crucial, the next unit is devoted exclusively to the process of conflict and especially to the ways to engage in productive interpersonal conflict.

Propose Possible Solutions   After the problem is identified, you need to discuss ways to lessen or eliminate the difficulty. Look for solutions that will enable both of you to win. Try to avoid "solutions" where one person wins and the other person loses, in which case, resentment and hostility are likely to fester. The suggestions offered in our discussion of the problem-solving group (Unit 16) are especially applicable to this phase of relationship repair.

Affirm Each Other   Any strategy of relationship repair should incorporate supportiveness and positive evaluations. For example, it has been found that happily married couples engage in greater positive behavior exchange; they communicate more agreement, approval, and positive affect than do unhappily married couples (Dindia & Fitzpatrick, 1985). Clearly, these behaviors result from the positive feelings these spouses have for each other. But it can also be argued that these expressions help to increase the positive regard that each person has for his or her partner. Other affirming messages are also needed, such as the exchange of favors, compliments, positive stroking, and all the nonverbals that say "I care."

One especially insightful way to increase favor exchange is to use cherishing behaviors (Lederer, 1984). Cherishing behaviors are those small gestures that you enjoy receiving from your relational partner (a smile, a wink, a squeeze, a kiss). Cherishing behaviors should be (1) specific and positive, (2) focused on the present and future rather than related to issues about which the partners have argued in the past, (3) capable of being performed daily, and (4) easily executed.

People can make a list of the cherishing behaviors they each wish to receive and then exchange lists. Each person then performs the cherishing behaviors desired by the partner. At first these behaviors may seem self-conscious and awkward. In time, however, they will become a normal part of interaction.

Integrate Solutions into Normal Behavior   Often solutions that are reached after an argument are followed for only a very short time; then the couple goes back to their previous unproductive behavior patterns. Instead, solutions need to be integrated into your normal behavior; they need to become integral to your everyday relationship behavior. Exchanging favors, compliments, and cherishing behaviors need to become a part of your everyday relational behaviors.

Risk   Take risks in trying to improve your relationship. Risk giving favors without any certainty of reciprocity. Risk rejection; make the first move to make up or say you are sorry. Be willing to change, to adapt, and to take on new tasks and responsibilities.

Self-Repair (What to Do If the Relationship Ends)

Of course, some relationships end. Sometimes there is simply not enough to hold the couple together or there are problems that cannot be resolved. Sometimes the costs are too high and the rewards too few, or the relationship is recognized as destructive and escape seems the only alternative. Given the inevitability that some relationships will break up, here are some suggestions to ease the difficulty that is sure to follow. These suggestions can apply to the termination of any type of relationship, between friends or lovers, through death, separation, or breakup. We use the language of romantic breakups because these are the ones we deal with most frequently.

Break the Loneliness-Depression Cycle   Loneliness and depression, the two most experienced feelings following the ending of a relationship, are serious. Depression, for example, may lead to physical illness. Ulcers, high blood pressure, insomnia, stomach pains, and sexual difficulties frequently accompany or are seriously aggravated by depression. In most cases loneliness and depression are temporary. Your task then is to eliminate or lessen these uncomfortable and potentially dangerous feelings by changing the situation. When depression does last or proves particularly upsetting, it is time to seek professional help.

Take Time Out   Take time out for yourself. Renew your relationship with yourself. If you were in a long-term relationship, you probably saw yourself as part of a team, as part of a couple. Now get to know yourself as a unique individual, standing alone now but fully capable of entering a meaningful relationship in the near future.

Bolster Self-Esteem   When relationships fail, self-esteem often falls. You may feel guilty for having been the cause of the breakup; you may feel inadequate for not holding on to a permanent relationship. You may feel unwanted and unloved. All of these feelings contribute to a lowering of self-esteem. Your task here is to regain the positive self-image that you need to function effectively as an individual and as a member of another relationship.

Take positive action to raise your self-esteem. Oddly enough, helping others is one of the best ways to do this. When you do things for others, either informally for people you know or by volunteer work in some community agency, you get the positive stroking from others that helps you feel better about yourself. Positive and successful experiences are extremely helpful in building self-esteem, so engage in activities that you enjoy, that you do well, and that are likely to result in success.

Seek Support   Although many people feel they should bear their burdens alone (men, in particular, have been taught that this is the only "manly" way to handle things), seeking the support of others is one of the best antidotes to the unhappiness caused when a relationship ends. Avail yourself of your friends and family for support. Tell your friends of your situation—in only general terms, if you prefer—and make it clear that you need support now. Seek out people who are positive and nurturing. Make the distinction between seeking support and seeking advice. If you feel you need advice, seek out a professional. For support, friends are best.

Avoid Repeating Negative Patterns   Many people enter second and third relationships with the same blinders, faulty preconceptions, and unrealistic expectations with which they entered earlier relationships. It is possible, however, to learn from failed relationships and not repeat the same patterns. Ask yourself at the start of a new relationship if you are entering a relationship modeled on the previous one. If the answer is yes, be especially careful not to repeat the same problems.

At the same time, do not become a prophet of doom. Do not see in every new relationship vestiges of the old. Treat the new relationship as the unique relationship it is and do not evaluate it through past experiences. Past relationships and experiences should be guides, not filters.

Summary

1. *Relationships develop for a variety of reasons,* of which some of the most important are to *lessen loneliness, secure stimulation, acquire self-knowledge,* and *maximize pleasures and minimize pain.*

2. Three main phases in *initiating relationships* may be noted: examining the qualifiers, determining clearance, and communicating your desire for contact.

3. The following nonverbal behaviors are useful in initiating relationships: establish eye contact, signal positive response, concentrate your focus, establish proximity, maintain an open posture, respond visibly, reinforce positive behaviors, and avoid overexposure.

4. The following verbal behaviors are helpful in initiating relationships: introduce yourself, focus the conversation on the other person, exchange favors and rewards, be energetic, stress the positives, avoid negative or too intimate self-disclosures, and establish commonalities.

5. *Relationship deterioration*—the weakening of the bonds holding people together—may be gradual or sudden and may have positive as well as negative effects.

6. Among the *causes for relationship deterioration* are diminution of the reasons for establishing the relationship, third-party relationships, relational changes, undefined expectations, sex, work, financial difficulties, and the inequitable distribution of rewards and costs.

7. Among the *communication changes* that take place during relationship deterioration are general withdrawal, a decrease in self-disclosure, an increase in deception, a decrease in positive and an increase in negative evaluative responses, and a decrease in the exchange of favors.

8. A useful approach to *relationship repair* is first to recognize the problem, engage in productive conflict resolution, pose possible solutions, affirm each other, integrate solutions into relationship behaviors, and take risks.

9. If the relationship does end, engage in *self-repair*. Break the loneliness-depression cycle, take time out, bolster self-esteem, seek emotional support, and avoid repeating negative patterns.

Applications

13.1 CHERISHING BEHAVIORS

Cherishing behaviors (Lederer, 1984) are those small favors that you enjoy receiving from your relational partner. It's the phone call to say "I love you," the card for no reason, the flowers, the tight squeeze, the specially prepared meal, and the prolonged kiss.

Cherishing behaviors should be (1) specific and positive, (2) focused on the present and future rather than on issues about which the partners have argued, (3) capable of being performed daily, and (4) easily executed.

As noted earlier in this unit, William Lederer suggests that partners exchange lists of the cherishing behaviors they each wish to receive. Compile a list of cherishing behaviors that you would like to receive and exchange lists with your friend or partner. Agree to exchange a fixed number of cherishing behaviors per day. Continue your cherishing behavior exchange for at least five days. Report back your experiences.

13.2 ASKING FOR POSITIVE BEHAVIORS

One of the ways in which you can improve communication during relational deterioration is to ask for positive behaviors rather than asking your partner to stop behaviors you consider negative. Listed below are 10 requests for the cessation of negative behaviors. Rewrite these requests so that they request positive behaviors, but be sure to retain the basic or general meaning of the statements. The first statement is done as an example.

1. Don't even think of coming to class without having read the assigned chapter.

You'll find next week's class a lot more meaningful if you first read Chapter 4. In that way we'll all have a common background and we'll be able to argue about some of the more significant issues raised in that chapter.

2. Don't just leave the house without telling me where you're going.
3. Don't ever again bring home a guest for dinner without calling me first.
4. I hate it when you ignore me at business functions.
5. I can't stand going to these cheap restaurants. When are you going to start spending a few bucks?
6. I think you look lousy in pink.
7. Lower that damn stereo.
8. Get rid of that punk hairdo. You look ridiculous—after all, 53 is a little late to go punk.
9. If you make another tuna casserole I'm going to go to a soup kitchen for a decent meal.
10. Stop talking so negatively. You criticize just about everything and everyone you come into contact with.

13.3 MALE AND FEMALE

This exercise is designed to increase your awareness of matters that may prevent meaningful interpersonal communication between the sexes. It is also designed to encourage meaningful dialogue among class members.

Separate the women and the men in the class and have one group go into another classroom. The task of each group is to write on the blackboard all the things that they dislike having the other sex think, believe, do, or say about them in general. Group members should especially note those behaviors that prevent meaningful interpersonal communication from taking place.

After this is done, the groups should change rooms. The men discuss what the women have written and the women discuss what the men have written. After satisfactory discussion has taken place, the groups should get together in the original room. Discussion might center on the following questions:

1. Were there any surprises?

2. Were there any disagreements? That is, did the members of one sex write anything that the members of the other sex argued that they do not believe, think, do, or say?

3. How do you suppose the ideas about the other sex got started?

4. Is there any reliable evidence in support of the beliefs of the men about the women or the women about the men?

5. What is the basis for the things that are disliked? Why was each statement written on the blackboard?

6. What kind of education or training program (if any) do you feel is needed to eliminate these problems?

7. In what specific ways do these beliefs, thoughts, actions, and statements prevent meaningful interpersonal communication?

8. How do you feel now that these matters have been discussed?

INTERPERSONAL CONFLICT

UNIT CONTENTS

The Nature of Interpersonal Conflict

Conflict Management

Aggressiveness and Argumentativeness

Before and After the Conflict

Summary

Applications

14.1 Dealing with Conflict Starters
14.2 Analyzing Conflict in Action

UNIT GOALS

After completing this unit, you should be able to

1. define *interpersonal conflict* and distinguish between content and relationship conflict

2. explain the strategies of conflict management

3. distinguish between verbal aggressiveness and argumentativeness

4. describe the suggestions for preparing for and following up an interpersonal conflict

In this unit we consider interpersonal conflict, what it is, how it can go wrong, and how it can be used to improve relationships.

THE NATURE OF INTERPERSONAL CONFLICT

Pat wants to go to the movies with Chris; Chris wants to stay home. Pat's insisting on going to the movies interferes with Chris's staying home and Chris's determination to stay home interferes with Pat's going to the movies.

Jim and Bernard own a small business. Jim wants to expand the business and open a branch in California. Bernard wants to sell the business and retire. Each has opposing goals and each interferes with each other's attaining these goals.

As experience teaches us, relational conflicts can be of various types:

- goals to be pursued ("We want you to go to college and become a teacher or a doctor, not a disco dancer")
- allocation of resources such as money or time ("I want to spend the tax refund on a car, not on new furniture")
- decisions to be made ("I refuse to have the Jeffersons over for dinner")
- behaviors that are considered appropriate or desirable by one person and inappropriate or undesirable by the other ("I hate it when you get drunk/pinch me/ridicule me in front of others/flirt with others/dress provocatively")

Content and Relationship Conflicts

Using concepts developed earlier (Unit 2), we may distinguish between content conflict and relationship conflict. *Content conflict* centers on objects, events, and persons in the world that are usually, but not always, external to the parties involved in the conflict. These include the millions of issues that you argue and fight about every day—the value of a particular movie, what to watch on television, the fairness of the last examination or job promotion, and the way to spend your savings.

Relationship conflicts are equally numerous and include such conflict situations as a younger brother who does not obey his older brother, two partners who each want an equal say in making vacation plans, and the mother and daughter who each want to have the final word concerning the daughter's life-style. Here the conflicts are concerned not so much with some external object as with the relationships between the individuals, with such issues as who is in charge, the equality of a primary relationship, and who has the right to set down rules of behavior.

Myths About Conflict

One of the problems in studying and in dealing with interpersonal conflict is that you may be operating with false assumptions about what conflict is and what it means. Such assumptions often have their origins in the communications we witnessed in our family as we were growing up. For example, do you think the following are true or false?

- If two people are in a relationship fight, it means their relationship is a bad one.
- Fighting damages an interpersonal relationship.

What myths about conflict do you think are most prevalent among members of your culture? Do men and women entertain the same myths? Do teenagers and, say, persons in their 50s view relationship conflict in the same general way? If not, how do those groups differ from each each?

- Fighting is bad because it reveals our negative selves—our pettiness, our need to be in control, our unreasonable expectations.

Simple answers are usually wrong. The three assumptions above may all be true or may all be false. It depends. In and of itself, conflict is neither good nor bad. Conflict is a part of every interpersonal relationship, between parents and children, brothers and sisters, friends, lovers, coworkers. If it isn't, then the relationship is probably dull, irrelevant, or insignificant. Conflict is inevitable in any meaningful relationship.

It is not so much the conflict that creates the problem as the way in which you approach and deal with the conflict. Some ways of approaching conflict can resolve difficulties and actually improve the relationship. Other ways can hurt the relationship; they can destroy self-esteem, create bitterness, and foster suspicion. Your task, therefore, is not to try to create relationships that will be free of conflict but rather to learn appropriate and productive ways of managing conflict.

Similarly, it is not the conflict that will reveal your negative side but the fight strategies you use. Thus if you personally attack the other person, use force, or use personal rejection or manipulation you will reveal your negative side. But in fighting you can also reveal your positive self—your willingness to listen to opposing points of view, your readiness to change unpleasant behaviors, and your willingness to accept imperfection in others.

The Negatives and Positives of Conflict

The kind of conflict focused on here is conflict among or between "connected" in-dividuals. Interpersonal conflict occurs frequently between lovers, best friends, siblings, and parent and child. Interpersonal conflict is made all the more difficult because, un-like many other conflict situations, you often care for, like, even love the individual with whom you are in disagreement. There are both negative and positive aspects or di-mensions to interpersonal conflict, and each of these should be noted.

Negative Aspects   Conflict often leads to increased negative regard for the op-ponent, and when this opponent is someone you love or care for very deeply, it can cre-ate serious problems for the relationship. One problem is that many conflicts involve unfair fighting methods that aim largely to hurt the other person. When one person hurts the other, increased negative feelings are inevitable; even the strongest relation-ship has limits.

Conflict frequently leads to a depletion of energy better spent on other areas. This is especially true when unproductive conflict strategies are used.

At times conflict leads you to close yourself off from the other individual. Though it would not be to your advantage to reveal your weaknesses to your "enemy," when you hide your true self from an intimate, you prevent meaningful communication from tak-ing place. One possible consequence is that one or both parties may seek intimacy else-where. This often leads to further conflict, mutual hurt, and resentment—qualities that add heavily to the costs carried by the relationship. As these costs increase, exchanging rewards may become difficult—perhaps impossible. The result is a situation in which the costs increase and the rewards decrease—a situation that often results in relation-ship deterioration and eventual dissolution.

Positive Aspects   The major value of interpersonal conflict is that it forces you to examine a problem and work toward a potential solution. If productive conflict strategies are used, the relationship may well emerge from the encounter stronger, healthier, and more satisfying than before.

Conflict enables you to state what you each want and—if the conflict is resolved effectively—perhaps to get it. For example, let's say that I want to spend our money on a new car (my old one is unreliable) and you want to spend it on a vacation (you feel the need for a change of pace). Through our conflict and its resolution, we hopefully learn what each really wants—in this case, a reliable car and a break from routine. We may then be able to figure out a way for us each to get what we want. I might accept a good used car or a less expensive new car and you might accept a shorter or less expensive vacation. Or we might buy a used car and take an inexpensive motor trip. Each of these solutions would satisfy both of us—they are win-win solutions.

Conflict also prevents hostilities and resentments from festering. Suppose I'm an-noyed at your talking with your colleague from work for two hours on the phone in-stead of giving that time to me. If I say nothing, my annoyance and resentment are likely to grow. Further, by saying nothing I have implicitly approved of such behavior and so it is likely that such phone calls will be repeated.

Through our conflict and its resolution we stop resentment from increasing. In the process we also let our own needs be known—that I need lots of attention when I come home from work and that you need to review and get closure on your day's work.

If we both can appreciate the legitimacy of these needs, then solutions may be easily identified. Perhaps the phone call can be made after my attention needs are met or perhaps I can delay my need for attention until you get closure about work. Or perhaps I can learn to provide for your closure needs and in doing so get may attention needs met. Again, these are win-win solutions that meet both of our needs.

Consider too that when you try to resolve conflict within an interpersonal relationship, you are saying in effect that the relationship is worth the effort; otherwise you would walk away from such a conflict. Although there may be exceptions—as when you confront conflict to save face or to gratify some ego need—usually confronting a conflict indicates concern, commitment, and a desire to preserve the relationship.

CONFLICT MANAGEMENT

Throughout the process of resolving conflict, avoid the common but damaging strategies that can destroy a relationship. At the same time, consciously apply those strategies that will help to resolve the conflict and even improve the relationship.

Do realize that different cultures view conflict management techniques differently. For example, in one study (Collier, 1991) it was found that African American men preferred clear argument and a focus on problem-solving. African American women, however, preferred assertiveness and respect. Mexican American men emphasized mutual understanding achieved through discussing the reasons for the conflict while women focused on support for the relationship. Anglo American men preferred direct and rational argument while women preferred flexibility. These, of course, are merely examples, but the underlying principle is that techniques for dealing with interpersonal conflict will be viewed differently by different cultures. The productive and unproductive strategies identified here, and previewed in Table 14.1, have been defined as such by American culture and by many others as well.

Avoidance and Fighting Actively   Avoidance may involve actual physical flight. You may leave the scene of the conflict (walk out of the apartment or go to another part of the office), fall asleep, or blast the stereo to drown out all conversation. It

Table 14.1 Conflict Management Strategies

Unproductive	Productive
Avoid the conflict.	Fight actively.
Use force.	Talk.
Blame the other person.	Empathize with the other person.
Use silencers.	Facilitate open expression.
Gunnysack.	Focus on the present.
Strategically manipulate the other person.	Act spontaneously and honestly.
Stress personal rejection.	Stress acceptance.
Hit below the belt.	Hit only above the belt.

may also take the form of emotional or intellectual avoidance. Here you may leave the conflict psychologically by not dealing with any of the arguments or problems raised.

Nonnegotiation is a special type of avoidance. Here you refuse to discuss the conflict or to listen to the other person's argument. At times this nonnegotiation takes the form of hammering away at one's own point of view until the other person gives in, called *steamrolling.*

Instead of avoiding the issues, take an active role in your interpersonal conflicts. Don't close your ears (or mind), blast the stereo, or walk out of the house during an argument. This is not to say that a cooling-off period is not at times desirable. But if you wish to resolve conflicts, you need to confront them actively.

Involve yourself on both sides of the communication exchange. Participate actively as a speaker-listener; voice your own feelings and listen carefully to the voicing of your opponent's feelings. Although periodic moratoriums are sometimes helpful, be willing to communicate as both sender and receiver—to say what is on your mind and to listen to what the other person is saying.

Another part of active fighting involves taking responsibility for your thoughts and feelings. For example, when you disagree with your partner or find fault with her or his behavior, take responsibility for these feelings. Say, for example, "I disagree with. . ." or "I don't like it when you. . ." Avoid statements that deny your responsibility, as in, "Everybody thinks you're wrong about. . ." or "Even Chris thinks you shouldn't. . ."

Force and Talk   When confronted with conflict, many people prefer not to deal with the issues but rather to physically force their position on the other person. The force may be emotional or physical. In either case, the issues are avoided and the person who "wins" is the one who exerts the most force. This is the technique of warring nations, children, and even some normally sensible and mature adults. This is surely one of the most serious problems confronting relationships today, but many approach it as if it were of only minor importance or even something humorous.

Over 50 percent of both single and married couples reported that they had experienced physical violence in their relationship. If we add symbolic violence (for example, threatening to hit the other person or throwing something), the percentages are above 60 percent for singles and above 70 percent for marrieds (Marshall & Rose, 1987). In another study, 47 percent of a sample of 410 college students reported some experience with violence in a dating relationship (Deal & Wampler, 1986). In most cases the violence was reciprocal— each person in the relationship used violence. In cases where only one person was violent, the research results are conflicting. For example, Deal and Wampler (1986) found that in cases were one partner was violent, the aggressor was significantly more often the female partner. Earlier research found similar sex differences (for example, Cate et al., 1982). These findings contradict our popular belief that males are more violent in heterosexual partnerships. One possible explanation for this, according to interpersonal researchers Deal and Wampler (1986, p. 468; Gelles, 1981), is that "in our society women are more likely to accept victimization as 'normal,' the implication being that they are therefore less likely to report it .... Aggression by women, on the other hand, being 'unnatural,' would stand out more and be remembered more. Since women are traditionally (or stereotypically) seen as less aggressive than men, it may take less aggression on the part of a woman for her to be labelled aggressive. This may then lead to an over-reporting of the woman's aggressive acts." Other research, however, has found that the popular conception of men being more likely to use force than women is indeed true (Deturck, 1987): Men are more apt than women to use violent methods to achieve compliance.

One form of relational force is, of course, rape. Studies on rape show alarming findings. According to Karen Kersten and Lawrence Kersten (1988), "forced sex on a date is probably one of the most common forms of all types of rape." In a study of force and violence on one college campus, more than half of the women students reported that they were verbally threatened, physically coerced, or physically abused. And over 12 percent indicated that they had been raped (Barrett, 1982; Kersten & Kersten, 1988). In another investigation of sexual assault on college campuses, 45 percent of the women surveyed reported being victims of criminal sexual assault, criminal sexual abuse, and battery/intimidation (Coalition Commentary, 1990).

One of the most puzzling findings is that many victims of violence interpret it as a sign of love. For some reason, they see being beaten, verbally abused, or raped as a sign that their partner is fully in love with them. Many victims, in fact, accept the blame for contributing to the violence instead of blaming their partners (Gelles & Cornell, 1985).

Equally puzzling but more frightening is the finding from at least one study that of the college-aged men surveyed, 51 percent said that they would rape a woman if they knew they would never get caught (Coalition Commentary, 1990).

Findings such as these point to problems well beyond the prevalence of unproductive conflict strategies that you want to identify and avoid. They demonstrate the existence of underlying pathologies that we are discovering are a lot more common than were thought previously, when issues like these were never mentioned in college textbooks or lectures. Awareness, of course, is only a first step in understanding and eventually combatting such problems.

The only real alternative to force is talk. Instead of using force, you need to talk and listen. The qualities of openness, empathy, and positiveness, for example, discussed in Unit 11 are suitable starting points.

Blame and Empathy   Conflict is rarely caused by a single, clearly identifiable problem or by only one of the parties. Usually, conflict is caused by a wide variety of factors, in which both individuals play a role. Any attempt to single out one person for blame is sure to fail. Yet, a frequently used fight strategy is to blame the other person. Consider, for example, the couple who fight over their child's getting into trouble with the police. The parents may—instead of dealing with the conflict itself—blame each other for the child's troubles. Such blaming, of course, does nothing to resolve the problem or to help the child.

Often when you blame someone you attribute motives to the person, a process often referred to as *mind reading*. Thus, if the person forgot your birthday and this disturbs you, fight about the forgetting of the birthday (the actual behavior). Try not to presuppose motives: "Well, it's obvious you just don't care about me. If you really cared, you could never have forgotten my birthday!"

Empathy is an excellent alternative to blame. Try to feel what the other person is feeling and to see the situation as does the other person. Try to see the situation as punctuated by the other person and how this differs from your own punctuation.

Demonstrate empathic understanding (Unit 11). Once you have empathically understood your opponent's feelings, validate those feelings where appropriate. If your partner is hurt or angry, and you feel that such feelings are legitimate and justified (from the other person's point of view), say so; say, "You have a right to be angry; I shouldn't have called your mother a slob. I'm sorry. But I still don't want to go on vacation with her." In expressing validation you are not necessarily expressing agreement on the issue in conflict; you are merely stating that your partner has feelings that are legitimate and that you recognize them as such.

Silencers and Facilitating Open Expression   **Silencers** cover a wide variety of fighting techniques that literally silence the other individual. One frequently used silencer is crying. When a person is unable to deal with a conflict or when winning seems unlikely, he or she may begin to cry and thus silence the other person.

Another silencer is to feign extreme emotionalism—to yell and scream and pretend to be losing control of yourself. Still another is to develop some "physical" reaction—headaches and shortness of breath are probably the most popular. One of the major problems with silencers is that you can never be certain that they are strategies to win the argument. They *may* be real physical reactions that you should pay attention to. Regardless of what you do, the conflict remains unexamined and unresolved.

Grant the other person permission to express himself or herself freely and openly, to be himself or herself. Avoid power tactics that suppress or inhibit freedom of expression. Avoid, for example, the tactics such as "Nobody Upstairs" or "You Owe Me" identified in Unit 8. Such tactics are designed to put the other person down and to subvert real interpersonal equality.

Gunnysacking and Present Focus   A gunnysack is a large bag usually made of burlap. As a conflict strategy, **gunnysacking** refers to the practice of storing up grievances so you may unload them at another time. The immediate occasion may be relatively simple (or so it might seem at first), such as someone's coming home late without calling. Instead of arguing about this, the gunnysacker unloads all past grievances. The birthday you forgot, the time you arrived late for dinner, the hotel reservations you forgot to make are all noted. As you probably know from experience, gunnysacking begets gunnysacking. When one person gunnysacks, the other person gunnysacks. The result is two people dumping their stored-up grievances on one another. Frequently the original problem never gets addressed. Instead, resentment and hostility escalate.

Focus your conflict on the here and now rather than on issues that occurred two months ago. Similarly, focus your conflict on the person with whom you are fighting, and not on the person's mother, child, or friends.

Manipulation and Spontaneity   **Manipulation** involves an avoidance of open conflict. The individual attempts to divert the conflict by being especially charming (disarming, actually). The manipulator gets the other individual into a receptive and noncombative frame of mind. Then the manipulator presents his or her demands to a weakened opponent. The manipulator relies on your tendency to give in to people who are especially nice to you.

Instead, try expressing your feelings with spontaneity, with honesty. Remember that in interpersonal conflict situations there is no need to plan a strategy to win a war. The objective is not to win but to increase mutual understanding and to reach a decision that both parties can accept.

Personal Rejection and Acceptance   A person practicing **personal rejection** withholds love and affection from his or her opponent in conflict. He or she seeks to win the argument by getting the other person to break down in the face of this withdrawal. The individual acts cold and uncaring in an effort to demoralize the other person. In withdrawing affection, the individual hopes to make the other person question his or her own self-worth. Once the other is demoralized and feels less than worthy, it is relatively easy for the "rejector" to get his or her way. The renewal of love and affection is held out as a reward for resolving the conflict in the manipulator's favor.

Instead, express positive feelings for the other person and for the relationship between the two of you. Throughout any conflict, many harsh words will probably be exchanged, later to be regretted. The words cannot be unsaid or uncommunicated, but they can be partially offset by the expression of positive statements. If you are engaged in combat with someone you love, remember that you are fighting with a loved one and express that feeling. "I love you very much, but I still don't want your mother on vacation with us. I want to be alone with you."

Fighting Below and Above the Belt   Much like fighters in a ring, each of us has a "beltline." When you hit someone below it, a tactic called **beltlining**, you can

Would you be willing to guess which of the conflict strategies discussed in this uint the couple pictured here would be most likely to use? On what basis would you make that judgment? For example, would the strategies differ on the basis of education? Age? Sex?

inflict serious injury. When you hit above the belt, however, the person is able to absorb the blow. With most interpersonal relationships, especially those of long standing, we know where the belt line is. You know, for example, that to hit Pat with the inability to have children is to hit below the belt. You know that to hit Chris with the failure to get a permanent job is to hit below the belt. Hitting below the beltline causes everyone involved added problems. Keep blows to areas your opponent can absorb and handle.

Remember that the aim of a relationship conflict is not to win and have your opponent lose. Rather, it is to resolve a problem and strengthen the relationship. Keep this ultimate goal always in clear focus, especially when you are angry or hurt.

AGGRESSIVENESS AND ARGUMENTATIVENESS

An especially interesting perspective on conflict is emerging from the work on verbal aggressiveness and argumentativeness (Infante, 1988; Infante & Rancer, 1982; Infante & Wigley, 1986). Understanding these two concepts will help in understanding some of the reasons why things go wrong and some of the ways in which you can use conflict to actually improve your relationships.

Verbal Aggressiveness

Verbal aggressiveness is a method of winning an argument by inflicting psychological pain, by attacking the other person's self-concept. The technique relies on many of the unproductive conflict strategies just considered. It is a type of disconfirmation in

Do you find cultural differences in the tendency to be aggressive and argumentative? For example, are members of some cultures more likely to practice aggressiveness and others argumentativeness in their conflict management? What did your culture teach you about aggressiveness and argumentativeness?

that it seeks to discredit the individual's view of self (see Unit 8). To explore this tendency further, take the test of verbal aggressiveness on page 252.

In reviewing your score, make special note of the characteristics identified in the 20 statements that refer to the tendency to act verbally aggressive. Note those inappropriate behaviors that you are especially prone to commit. Review your previous encounters when you acted verbally aggressive. What effect did such actions have on your subsequent interaction? What effect did they have on your relationship with the other person? What alternative ways of getting your point across might you have used? Might these have proved more effective?

Argumentativeness

Contrary to popular belief, argumentativeness is a quality to be cultivated rather than avoided. **Argumentativeness refers to your willingness to argue for a point of view, your tendency to speak your mind on significant issues.** It is the mode of dealing with disagreements that is the preferred alternative to verbal aggressiveness. Before reading about ways to increase your argumentativeness, take the heavily researched test on page 254.

Generally, those who score high in argumentativeness have a strong tendency to state their position on controversial issues and argue against the positions of others. A high scorer sees arguing as exciting, intellectually challenging, and as an opportunity to win a kind of contest.

The moderately argumentative person possesses some of the qualities of the high argumentative and some of the qualities of the low argumentative. The person who scores low in argumentativeness tries to prevent arguments. This person experiences satisfaction not from arguing, but from avoiding arguments. The low argumentative sees arguing as unpleasant and unsatisfying. Not surprisingly, this person has little confidence in his or her ability to argue effectively.

The researchers who developed this test note that both high and low argumentatives may experience communication difficulties. The high argumentative, for example, may argue needlessly, too often, and too forcefully. The low argumentative, on the other hand, may avoid taking a stand even when it seems necessary.

Persons scoring somewhere in the middle are probably the most interpersonally skilled and adaptable, arguing when it is necessary but avoiding the many arguments that are needless and repetitive.

Here are some suggestions for cultivating argumentativeness and for preventing it from degenerating into aggressiveness (Infante 1988):

- Treat disagreements as objectively as possible; avoid assuming that because someone takes issue with your position or your interpretation that they are attacking you as a person.
- Avoid attacking the other person (rather than the person's arguments) even if this would give you a tactical advantage—it will probably backfire at some later time and make your relationship more difficult. Center your arguments on issues rather than personalities.
- Reaffirm the other person's sense of competence; compliment the other person as appropriate.
- Avoid interrupting; allow the other person to state her or his position fully before you respond.

SELF-TEST

How Verbally Aggressive Are You?

This scale is designed to measure how people try to obtain compliance from others. For each statement, indicate the extent to which you feel it is true for you in your attempts to influence others. Use the following scale:

1 = almost never true
2 = rarely true
3 = occasionally true
4 = often true
5 = almost always true

_____ 1. I am extremely careful to avoid attacking individuals' intelligence when I attack their ideas.

_____ 2. When individuals are very stubborn, I use insults to soften the stubbornness.

_____ 3. I try very hard to avoid having other people feel bad about themselves when I try to influence them.

_____ 4. When people refuse to do a task I know is important, without good reason, I tell them they are unreasonable.

_____ 5. When others do things I regard as stupid, I try to be extremely gentle with them.

_____ 6. If individuals I am trying to influence really deserve it, I attack their character.

_____ 7. When people behave in ways that are really in very poor taste, I insult them in order to shock them into proper behavior.

_____ 8. I try to make people feel good about themselves even when their ideas are stupid.

_____ 9. When people simply will not budge on a matter of importance, I lose my temper and say rather strong things to them.

_____ 10. When people criticize my shortcomings, I take it in good humor and do not try to get back at them.

_____ 11. When individuals insult me, I get a lot of pleasure out of really telling them off.

- Stress equality (see Unit 11) and stress the similarities that you have with the other person; stress your areas of agreement before attacking the disagreements.
- Express interest in the other person's position, attitude, and point of view.
- Avoid presenting your arguments too emotionally; using an overly loud voice or interjecting vulgar expressions will prove offensive and eventually ineffective.
- Allow the other person to save face; never humiliate the other person.

BEFORE AND AFTER THE CONFLICT

If you are to make conflict truly productive you will need to consider a few suggestions for preparing for the conflict and for using the conflict as a method for relational growth.

SELF-TEST (continued)

_____ 12. When I dislike individuals greatly, I try not to show it in what I say or how I say it.

_____ 13. I like poking fun at people who do things which are very stupid in order to stimulate their intelligence.

_____ 14. When I attack a person's ideas, I try not to damage their self-concepts.

_____ 15. When I try to influence people, I make a great effort not to offend them.

_____ 16. When people do things which are mean or cruel, I attack their character in order to help correct their behavior.

_____ 17. I refuse to participate in arguments when they involve personal attacks.

_____ 18. When nothing seems to work in trying to influence others, I yell and scream in order to get some movement from them.

_____ 19. When I am not able to refute others' positions, I try to make them feel defensive in order to weaken their positions.

_____ 20. When an argument shifts to personal attacks, I try very hard to change the subject.

Scoring   In order to compute your verbal aggressiveness score, follow these steps:

1. Add your scores on items 2, 4, 6, 7, 9, 11, 13, 16, 18, 19.
2. Add your scores on items 1, 3, 5, 8, 10, 12, 14, 15, 17, 20.
3. Subtract the sum obtained in step 2 from 60.
4. To compute your verbal aggressiveness score, add the total obtained in step 1 to the result obtained in step 3.

If you scored between 59 and 100, you are high in verbal aggressiveness; if you scored between 39 and 58, you are moderate in verbal aggressiveness; and if you scored between 20 and 38, you are low in verbal aggressiveness.

Source: From "Verbal Aggressiveness" by Dominic Infante and C. J. Wigley, *Communication Monographs 53*, 1986. Copyright © 1986 by the Speech Communication Association. Reprinted by permission of the publisher and authors.

Before the Conflict

Try to fight in private. When you air your conflicts in front of others you create a wide variety of other problems. You may not be willing to be totally honest when third parties are present; you may feel you have to save face and therefore must win the fight at all costs. This may lead you to use strategies to win the argument rather than strategies to resolve the conflict. Also, of course, you run the risk of embarrassing your partner in front of others, which will incur resentment and hostility.

Be sure you are both ready to fight. Although conflicts arise at the most inopportune times, you can choose the time when you will try to resolve them. Confronting your partner when she or he comes home after a hard day of work may not be the right time for resolving a conflict. Make sure you are both relatively free of other problems and ready to deal with the conflict at hand.

Know what you're fighting about. Sometimes people in a relationship become so hurt and angry that they lash out at the other person just to vent their own frustration. The "content" of the conflict is merely an excuse to express anger. Any attempt at re-

SELF-TEST

How Argumentative Are You?

This questionnaire contains statements about controversial issues. Indicate how often each statement is true for you personally according to the following scale:

1 = almost never true
2 = rarely true
3 = occasionally true
4 = often true
5 = almost never true

_____ 1. While in an argument, I worry that the person I am arguing with will form a negative impression of me.

_____ 2. Arguing over controversial issues improves my intelligence.

_____ 3. I enjoy avoiding arguments.

_____ 4. I am energetic and enthusiastic when I argue.

_____ 5. Once I finish an argument, I promise myself that I will not get into another.

_____ 6. Arguing with a person creates more problems for me than it solves.

_____ 7. I have a pleasant, good feeling when I win a point in an argument.

_____ 8. When I finish arguing with anyone, I feel nervous and upset.

_____ 9. I enjoy a good argument over a controversial issue.

_____ 10. I get an unpleasant feeling when I realize I am about to get into an argument.

_____ 11. I enjoy defending my point of view on an issue.

_____ 12. I am happy when I keep an argument from happening.

solving this "problem" will of course be doomed to failure since the problem addressed is not what gave rise to the conflict. Instead, it may be the underlying hostility, anger, and frustration that needs to be dealt with.

At other times, people argue about general and abstract issues that are poorly specified, for example, the person's lack of consideration or failure to accept responsibility. Only when you define your differences in specific terms can you begin to understand them and hence resolve them.

Fight about problems that can be solved. Fighting about past behaviors or about family members or situations over which you have no control solves nothing; instead, it creates additional difficulties. Any attempt at resolution is naturally doomed to failure since the problems cannot be solved. Often such conflicts are concealed attempts at expressing one's frustration or dissatisfaction.

After the Conflict

After the conflict is resolved, there is still work to be done. Learn from the conflict and from the process you went through in trying to resolve the conflict. For example, can you identify the fight strategies that aggravated the situation? Does your partner need a cooling off period? Do you need extra space when upset? Can you identify

SELF-TEST (continued)

_____ 13. I do not like to miss the opportunity to argue a controversial issue.

_____ 14. I prefer being with people who rarely disagree with me.

_____ 15. I consider an argument an exciting intellectual challenge.

_____ 16. I find myself unable to think of effective points during an argument.

_____ 17. I feel refreshed and satisfied after an argument on a controversial issue.

_____ 18. I have the ability to do well in an argument.

_____ 19. I try to avoid getting into arguments.

_____ 20. I feel excitement when I expect that a conversation I am in is leading to an argument.

Scoring   To compute your argumentativeness score follow these steps:

1. Add your scores on items 2, 4, 7, 9, 11, 13, 15, 17, 18, and 20.
2. Add 60 to the sum obtained in step 1.
3. Add your scores on items 1, 3, 5, 6, 8, 10, 12, 14, 16, 19.
4. To compute your argumentativeness score, subtract the total obtained in step 3 from the total obtained in step 2.

Interpreting Your Score

Scores between 73 and 100 indicate high argumentativeness.
Scores between 56 and 72 indicate moderate argumentativeness.
Scores between 20 and 55 indicate low argumentativeness.

Source: From *Arguing Constructively* by Dominic Infante. Copyright © 1988 by Waveland Press, Inc. Reprinted by permission of the author.

when minor issues are going to escalate into major arguments? Does avoidance make matters worse? What issues are particularly disturbing and likely to cause difficulties? Can these be avoided?

Keep the conflict in perspective. Be careful not to blow it out of proportion, defining your relationship in terms of conflict. Avoid the tendency to see disagreement as inevitably leading to major blowups. Conflicts in most relationships actually occupy a very small percentage of the couple's time, and yet in recollection they often loom extremely large. Also, don't allow the conflict to undermine your own or your partner's self-esteem. Don't view yourself, your partner, or your relationships as failures just because you had an argument or even lots of arguments.

Negative feelings frequently arise after an interpersonal conflict, most often because unfair fight strategies were used to undermine the other person—for example, personal rejection, manipulation, or force.

Resolve surely to avoid such unfair tactics in the future, but at the same time let go of guilt and blame for yourself and your partner. If you think it would help, discuss these feelings with your partner or even a therapist.

Increase the exchange of rewards and cherishing behaviors to demonstrate your positive feelings and that you are over the conflict. It's a good way of saying you want the relationship to survive and to flourish.

Summary

1. *Relationship conflict* refers to a situation in which two persons have opposing goals and interfere with each other's attaining these goals.

2. *Content conflict* centers on objects, events, and persons in the world that are usually, but not always, external to the parties involved in the conflict. *Relationship conflicts* are concerned not so much with some external object as with the relationships between the individuals, with such issues as who is in charge, the equality of a primary relationship, and who has the right to set down rules of behavior.

3. Unproductive and productive conflict strategies include: *avoidance and fighting actively, force and talk, blame and empathy, silencers and facilitating open expression, gunnysacking and present focus, manipulation and spontaneity, personal rejection and acceptance*, and *fighting below and above the belt*.

4. Additional perspectives on conflict can be achieved from understanding *verbal aggressiveness* (fighting for your position by personally attacking the other person) and *argumentativeness* (fighting for your position by focusing on the issues and expressing respect for the other person).

5. To cultivate argumentativeness, *treat disagreements objectively* and avoid attacking the other person; *reaffirm* the other's sense of competence; *avoid interrupting*; *stress equality* and similarities; *express interest* in the other's position; avoid presenting your arguments too *emotionally*; and allow the other to *save face*.

Applications

14.1   DEALING WITH CONFLICT STARTERS

The purpose of this exercise is to review some of the issues considered in this unit and to give you some practice in responding to potential interpersonal conflicts. In this exercise use your own conflict experiences as a guide. For each situation: (a) Write an unproductive response; that is, a response that will aggravate the potential conflict. Why do you assume this response will intensify the conflict? (b) Write a productive response that will lessen the potential conflict. Why do you assume this response will help resolve the conflict?

Conflict "Starters"

1. You're late again. You're always late. Your lateness is so inconsiderate of my time and my interests.

2. I just can't bear another weekend of sitting home watching television. I'm just not going to do that again.

3. Who forgot to phone for reservations?

4. Well, there goes another anniversary that you forgot.

5. You think I'm fat, don't you?

6. Just leave me alone.

7. Did I hear you say your mother knows how to dress?

8. We should have been more available when he needed us. I was always at work.

9. Where's the pepper? Is there no pepper in this house?

10. The Romeros think we should spend our money and start enjoying life.

14.2   ANALYZING CONFLICT IN ACTION

The following brief dialogue was written to illustrate unproductive conflict and to provide a stimulus for the consideration of alternative and more productive methods of conflict management.

Locate examples of each unproductive strategy and write or discuss alternative responses that represent more effective and more productive approaches to conflict management.

PAT: It's me. Just came in to get my papers for the meeting tonight.

CHRIS: You're not going to another meeting tonight, are you?

PAT: I told you last month that I had to give this lecture to the new managers on how to use some new research methods. What do you think I've been working on for the past two weeks? If you cared about what I do, you'd know that I was working on this lecture and that it was especially important that it go well.

CHRIS: What about shopping? We always do the shopping on Friday night.

PAT: The shopping will have to wait; this lecture is important.

CHRIS: Shopping is important, too, and so are the children and so is my job and so is the leak in the basement that's been driving me crazy for the past week and that I've asked you to look at every day since then.

PAT: Get off it. We can do the shopping anytime. Your job is fine and the children are fine and we'll get a plumber just as soon as I get his name from the Johnsons.

CHRIS: You always do that. You always think only you count, only you matter. Even when we were in school, your classes were the important ones, your papers, your tests were the important ones. Remember when I had that chemistry final and you had to have your history paper typed? We stayed up all night typing *your* paper. I failed chemistry, remember? That's not so good when you're pre-med! I suppose I should thank you for my not being a doctor? But you got your A in history. It's always been that way. You never give a damn about what's important in my life.

PAT: I really don't want to talk about it. I'll only get upset and bomb out with the lecture. Forget it. I don't want to hear any more about it. So just shut up before I do something I should do more often.

CHRIS: You hit me and I'll call the cops. I'm not putting up with another black eye or another fat lip—never, never again.

PAT: Well, then, just shut up. I just don't want to talk about it anymore. Forget it. I have to give the lecture and that's that.

CHRIS: The children were looking forward to going shopping. Johnny wanted to get a new record, and Jennifer needed to get a book for school. You promised them.

PAT: I didn't promise anyone anything. You promised them and now you want me to take the blame. You know, you promise too much. You should only promise what you can deliver—like fidelity. Remember you promised to be faithful? Or did you forget that promise? Why don't you tell the kids that? Or do they already know? Were they here when you had your sordid affair? Did they see their loving parent loving some stranger?

CHRIS: I thought we agreed not to talk about that. You know how bad I feel about what happened. And anyway, that was six months ago. What has that to do with tonight?

PAT: You're the one who brought up promises, not me. You're always bringing up the past. You live in the past.

CHRIS: Well, at least the kids would have seen me enjoying myself—one enjoyable experience in eight years isn't too much, is it?

PAT: I'm leaving. Don't wait up.

INTERVIEWING

UNIT CONTENTS

Interviewing Defined

The Information Interview

The Employment Interview

  Summary

  Applications

    15.1 Interview Skills in Action

    15.2 Responding to Unlawful Questions

    15.3 Experiencing and Analyzing Interviews

UNIT GOALS

After completing this unit, you should be able to

1. define *interviewing*

2. describe the major types of interviews

3. describe the sequence of steps recommended for an information interview

4. explain the principles suggested for the employment interview

5. distinguish between lawful and unlawful questions

Interviewing includes a wide range of communication situations. Here are just a few examples:

- A salesperson tries to sell a client a new car.
- A teacher talks with a student about the reasons the student failed the course.
- A counselor talks with a family about their communication problems.
- A recent graduate applies to IBM for a job in the product development division.
- A building owner talks with a potential apartment renter.
- A priest talks with a parishioner about marital problems.
- A lawyer examines a witness during a trial.
- A theatrical agent talks with a potential client.
- A client discusses with a dating service employee some of the qualities desired in a potential mate.
- A boss talks with an employee about some of the reasons for terminating a contract.

INTERVIEWING DEFINED

Interviewing is a particular form of interpersonal communication. In an **interview** two persons interact largely through a question-and-answer format to achieve specific goals. Interviews *usually* involve two persons. Some, however, involve more people. At conventions, for example, where many people apply for the few available jobs, interviewers may interview several people at once. Similarly, therapy frequently involves entire families, groups of coworkers, or other related individuals. Nevertheless, the two-person interview is certainly the most common and is the one we will be referring to throughout this unit.

The interview is distinctly different from other forms of communication because it proceeds through questions and answers. Both parties in the interview ask and answer questions, but most often the interviewer asks the questions and the interviewee answers them.

The interview has specific goals. These goals guide and structure the interview in both content and format. In an employment interview, for example, the goal for the interviewer is to find an applicant who can fulfill the tasks of the position. The interviewee's goal is to get the job, if it seems desirable. These goals guide the behaviors of both parties, are relatively specific, and are usually clear to both parties.

We can gain added insight into the nature of the interview by looking at their general structures. Interviews vary from relatively informal talks that resemble everyday conversations to those that ask rigidly prescribed questions in a set order. Table 15.1 presents the major types of general interview structures (Hambrick, 1991). Depending on your specific purpose, you would select the interview structure that best fits your needs. And, of course, you can also combine the various types and create an interview structure that will best suit your needs.

We can distinguish the different types of interviews on the basis of the goals of interviewer and interviewee. Here we identify briefly the persuasive, appraisal, exit, and counseling interview (Stewart & Cash, 1988; Zima, 1983). The information and employment interviews are probably the most important for most college students and so these are covered in considerable length.

Table 15.1 General Interview Structures	
Interview Structure	**Characteristics and Uses**
Informal interview	Resembles conversation; general theme for interview is chosen in advance but the specific questions arise from the context; useful for obtaining information informally.
Guided interview	Topics are chosen in advance but specific questions and wordings are guided by the ongoing interaction; useful in assuring maximum flexibility and responsiveness to the dynamics of the situation.
Standard open interview	Open-ended questions and their order are selected in advance; useful when standardization is needed, for example, when interviewing several candidates for the same job.
Quantitative interview	Questions and their order are selected in advance as are the possible response categories, for example, A, B, C, D; agree-disagree; check from 1 to 10. Useful when statistical analyses are to be performed and when large amounts of information (which can be logically categorized) are to be collected.

The Persuasive Interview

In the **persuasive interview** the goal is to change an individual's attitudes, beliefs, or behaviors. The interviewer may either ask questions that will lead the interviewee to the desired conclusion or answer questions in a persuasive way. For example, if you go into a showroom to buy a new car, you interview the salesperson. The salesperson's goal is to get you to buy a particular car. He or she attempts to accomplish this by answering your questions persuasively. You ask about mileage, safety features, and finance terms. The salesperson discourses eloquently on the superiority of this car above all others.

All interviews contain elements of both information and persuasion. When, for example, a guest appears on *The Tonight Show* and talks about a new movie, information is communicated. But the performer is also trying to persuade the audience to see the movie. Informing and persuading usually go together in actual practice.

The Appraisal Interview

In the appraisal or evaluation interview, the interviewee's performance is assessed by management or more experienced colleagues. The general aim is to discover what the interviewee is doing well (and to praise this), and not doing well and why (and to correct this). These interviews are important because they help new members of an organization see how their performance matches up with the expectations of those making promotion and firing decisions.

The Exit Interview

The exit interview is used widely by organizations in the United States and throughout the world. All organizations compete in one way or another for superior workers. When an employee leaves a company voluntarily, it is important to know why, to prevent other valuable workers from leaving as well. Another function of this interview is to provide a way of making the exit as pleasant and as efficient as possible for both employee and employer.

The Counseling Interview

Counseling interviews are given to provide guidance. The goal here is to help the person deal more effectively with problems; to work more effectively; to get along better with friends or lovers; or to cope more effectively with day-to-day living. For the interview to be of any value, the interviewer must learn a considerable amount about the person—habits, problems, self-perceptions, goals, and so on. With this information, the counselor then tries to persuade the person to alter certain aspects of his or her thinking or behaving. The counselor may try to persuade you, for example, to listen more attentively when your spouse argues or to devote more time to your classwork.

THE INFORMATION INTERVIEW

In the information interview, the interviewer tries to learn something about the interviewee, usually a person of some reputation and accomplishment. The interviewer accomplishes this goal by asking a series of questions designed to elicit his or her views, beliefs, insights, perspectives, predictions, life history, and so on. Examples of the information interview are those published in popular magazines. The TV interviews conducted by Jay Leno, Ted Koppel, and Barbara Walters as well as those conducted by a

If you wanted to see a counselor to help you with some personal problems, all other things being equal, what (if any) cultural characteristixs—for example, race, nationality, sex, affectional orientation, age—would influence your decision in selecting a counselor? Why?

If you were conducting a research project to secure information about work, sex, and money would the culture of your interviewers be a factor in your selecting them to work on this project? Why or why not?

lawyer during a trial are also information interviews. All aim to elicit specific information from someone who supposedly knows something others do not know. In this discussion we concentrate on your role as the interviewer, since that is the role you are likely to find yourself serving now and in the near future.

Let us say that your interview is designed to get information about a particular field, for example, desktop publishing. You want to know about the available job opportunities and the preparation you would need to get into this field. Here are a few guidelines for conducting such information-gathering interviews.

Select the Person You Wish to Interview

You might, for example, look through your college catalogue for a course in desktop publishing and interview the instructor. Or you might call a local publishing company and ask if there is someone in charge of desktop publishing. You are now on your first step; you've selected one of the people you hope to interview. But don't stop there. Before you pursue the interview try to learn something about the people you will interview. For example, has the instructor written a book or articles in the field? Look at the book catalogue and at the indexes to periodicals.

Secure an Appointment

Phone the person or send a letter requesting an interview. In your call or letter, identify the purpose of your request and that you would like a brief interview. For example, you might say: "I'm preparing for a career in desktop publishing and I would appreciate it if I could interview you to learn more about the subject. The interview would take about 15 minutes." (It is helpful to let the person know it will not take overly long; he or she is more likely to agree to being interviewed.) Generally, it is best to be available at the interviewee's convenience. So indicate flexibility on your part, for example, "I can interview you any day after 12 noon."

You may find it necessary to conduct the interview by phone. In this case, call to set up a time for a future call. For example, you might say: "I'm interesting in a career in desktop publishing and I would like to interview you on the job opportunities in this field. If you agree, I can call you back at a time that's convenient for you." In this way, you don't run the risk of asking the person to hold still for an interview while eating lunch, talking with colleagues, or running to class.

Prepare Your Questions

This will ensure that you will use the time available to your best advantage. Of course, as the interview progresses other questions will come to mind and should be asked. But having a prepared list of questions will help you obtain the information you need most easily.

Establish Rapport with the Interviewer

Open the interview with an expression of thanks for making the time available to you. Many people receive lots of requests and it helps if you also remind the person of your specific purpose. You might say something like this: "I really appreciate your making time for this interview. As I mentioned, I'm interesting in learning about the job opportunities in desktop publishing and your expertise and experience in this area will help a great deal."

Ask Permission to Tape the Interview

Generally, it is a good idea to tape the interview. But ask permission first. Some people prefer not to have informal interviews taped. Even if the interview is being conducted by phone, ask permission if you intend to tape the conversation.

Ask Open-ended Questions

Use questions that provide the interviewee with room to discuss the issues you want to raise. Thus, instead of asking "Do you have formal training in desktop publishing?" (a question which requires a simple "yes" or "no" and will not be very informative), you might ask, "Can you tell me something of your background in this field?" (a question which is open-ended and allows the person greater freedom). You can then ask follow-up questions to pursue more specifically the topics considered in the answers to your open-ended questions.

Close the Interview with an Expression of Appreciation

Thank the person for making the time available for the interview, for being informative, cooperative, helpful, or whatever. Showing your appreciation will make it a great deal easier if you want to return for a second interview.

Follow Up the Interview

Follow up the interview with a brief note of thanks in which you might express your appreciation for the time given you, your enjoyment in speaking with the person, and your accomplishing your goal of getting the information you needed.

THE EMPLOYMENT INTERVIEW

Perhaps of most concern to college students is the employment or selection interview. In this type of interview, a great deal of information and persuasion will be exchanged. The interviewer will learn about you, your interests, your talents— and, if clever enough, some of your weaknesses and liabilities. You will be informed about the nature of the company, its benefits, its advantages—and, if you are clever enough, some of its disadvantages and problems. Although these principles will prove useful for all interviews, we use the employment interview with you as the interviewee for illustration.

Prepare Yourself

This is perhaps the most difficult aspect of the entire interview process. It is also the step that is most often overlooked. At the most obvious level, *prepare yourself intellectually*. Educate yourself as much as possible about relevant topics. Learn something about the company and its specific product or products. Call the company and ask them to send you any company brochures or newsletters or perhaps a quarterly report. If it's a publishing company, familiarize yourself with their books. If it's an advertising agency, familiarize yourself with their major clients and their major advertising campaigns.

If you are applying for a job, both you and the company want something. You want a job that will meet your needs. The company wants an employee who will meet its needs. In short, you each want something that perhaps the other has. View the interview as an opportunity to engage in a joint effort to gain something beneficial to both. If you go into the interview in this cooperative frame of mind, you are much less likely to become defensive in your communications, which in turn will make you a more appealing potential colleague.

Would you find it easier to interview for a job with a same-sex or an opposite-sex interviewer or would there be no difference? Why?

A great number of jobs are won or lost on the basis of physical appearance alone, so give attention also to *physical preparation.* Dress in a manner that shows that you care enough about the interview to make a good impression. At the same time, dress comfortably. To avoid extremes is perhaps the most specific advice to give you. When in doubt, it is probably best to err on the side of formality: Wear the tie, high heels, or dress.

Bring with you the appropriate materials, whatever they may be. At the very least bring a pen and paper, an extra copy or two of your résumé and, if appropriate, a business card. If you are applying for a job in an area where you have worked before, you might bring samples of your previous work.

The importance of your résumé cannot be stressed too much. The résumé is a summary of essential information about your experience, goals, and abilities, and it is often the first contact a potential employer has with you. If it is thought interesting by the employer, the candidate is asked in for an interview. Because of the importance of the résumé and its close association with the interview, a sample résumé is provided in Figure 15.1, along with some guidelines to assist you in preparing your own.

1   Pat Jefferson
166 Josen Road
Accord, New York 12404
(914) 555-1221

2 **Objective**
To secure a position with a college textbook publisher as a sales representative

3 **Education**
A.A., Bronx Community College, 1988
B.A., Hunter College, 1996 [expected]
Major: Communications, with emphasis in interpersonal and public communication
Minor: Psychology
Courses included: Interpersonal Communication, Public Speaking, Small Group Communication, Interviewing, Organizational Communication, Public Relations, Persuasion: Theory and Practice, Psychology of Attitude Change
Extracurricular activities: Debate team (2 years), reporter on student newspaper (1 year)

4 **Work Experience**
Two years, salesclerk in college bookstore (part-time)
Six years in retail sales at Macy's; managed luggage department for last three years

5 **Special Competencies**
Working knowledge of major word processing and spreadsheet programs
Basic knowledge of college bookstore operation
Speaking and writing knowledge of Spanish

6 **Personal**
Enjoy working with computers and people; willing to relocate and travel

7 **References**
References from the following people are on file in the Office of Student Personnel, Hunter College (695 Park Avenue, New York, NY 10021):
Dr. Martha Hubbard (Hunter College), major advisor and instructor for three courses
Mr. Jack Sprat (Hunter College Bookstore), manager
Professor Mary Contrari (Hunter College), debate coach
Dr. Robert Hood (Bronx Community College), communication instructor

8

FIGURE 15.1 A sample résumé.

Establish Goals

All interviews have specific objectives. As part of your preparation, fix these goals firmly in mind. Use them as guides to the remainder of your preparation and also to your behavior during and even after the interview.

After establishing your objectives clearly in your own mind, relate your preparation to these goals. For example, in considering how to dress, what to learn about the specific company, and what questions to ask during the interview, ask yourself how your goals might help you answer these questions.

Prepare Answers and Questions

If the interview is at all important to you, you will probably think about it for some time. Use this time productively by rehearsing the predicted course of the interview. Try also to predict the questions that will be asked and the answers you will most likely give.

Think about the questions that are likely to be asked and how you will answer them. Table 15.2 presents a list of questions commonly asked in employment interviews

1. Your name, address, and phone number are generally centered at the top of the résumé.
2. For most people just getting out of college, career goals are tentative. Although this career goal description may seem a bit general, it is probably realistic. Of course, if you do have more limited career goals, put them down. In setting your career goals, do not imply that you will take just anything. At the other extreme, do not be too specific or demanding.
3. It will be helpful to potential employers if you give a bit more information than simply your educational degree. Even the major department in which you earned your degree might be too vague. For example, in a communication arts and sciences department you could have concentrated on speech pathology, speech science, audiology, public communication, journalism, interpersonal communication, mass media theory, media production, film criticism, and so on. The same is true for many other departments as well, so identify your emphasis. If you earned honors or awards, list these if they are relevant to your educational experience or to your job experience. Note, for example, that you were on the Dean's List, received departmental honors, or won awards for working in your field. If the awards are primarily educational (for example, Dean's List), put them under the Education heading. If they are job-related, then put them under the Work Experience heading.
4. List your work experience in reverse chronological order, beginning with the most recent position and working backward. Depending on your work experience, you may have a great deal to write and hence will have to pare it down. Or you may have little or nothing to write and so you will want to search through your history for some relevant experience. The example given here focuses on work experience during college that relates specifically to the position. This reflects my own preference to put down only what is relevant to your career goals.
5. The section on special competencies is an often overlooked area, but one where college students and recent graduates actually have a great deal to say. Do you have some foreign language ability? Do you know how to perform statistical analyses? Do you know how to write a computer program? Do you know how to keep profit-and-loss statements? If you do, put it down. Such competencies are relevant to a wide variety of jobs.
6. Include any personal information that is relevant to the position you seek.
7. References may be handled in a number of different ways. Here, the specific names of people the potential employer may write to are listed. Sometimes phone numbers are included. If your school maintains personnel files for its students, you may simply note that references may be obtained by writing to the relevant department. (Be sure you keep your file up to date.) It is sometimes helpful to identify briefly the relationship between you and the person named as reference. Three references are generally considered enough. Note that the people listed should have special knowledge about you that is relevant to the job.
8. Give special care to the form of your résumé. Typographical errors, incorrect spelling, poorly spaced headings and entries, and generally sloppy work will not produce the effect you want.

organized around the major topics on the résumé and draws from a variety of interviewing experts (Seidman, 1991; Sincoff & Goyer, 1984; Skopec, 1986; Stewart & Cash, 1988; Zima, 1983). You may find it helpful to rehearse with this list before going into the interview. Although not all of these questions would be asked in any one interview, be prepared to answer all of them.

Table 15.2 Common Interview Questions

Questions About Objectives and Career Goals

What made you apply to Datacomm?

Do you know much about Datacomm?

What do you like most about Datacomm?

If you took a job with us, where would you like to be in 5 years? Ten years?

What benefits do you want to get out of this job?

Questions About Education

What do you think of the education you got at Hunter?

Why did you major in communication?

What was majoring in communication at Hunter like? What kinds of courses did you take? Which courses did you enjoy most? Which did you gain the most from?

Did you do an internship? What were your responsibilities?

Previous Work Experience

Tell me about your previous work experience. What did you do exactly? Did you enjoy working at Happy Publications? Why did you leave?

How does this previous experience relate to the work you'd be doing here at Datacomm?

What kinds of problems did you encounter at your last position?

Special Competencies

I see here you have a speaking and writing knowledge of Spanish. Could you talk with someone on the phone who speaks only Spanish? Would you be able to write letters in Spanish to our customers?

Do you know any other languages—even slightly?

How much do you know about computers? Do you know anything about desktop publishing? Accessing databases? Using spreadsheets to make predictions?

Personal

Tell me: Who is Pat Jefferson? What do you like? What do you dislike?

To what extent are you willing to relocate? To another state? To another country? If you were to relocate, where would be your ideal place? Where would you definitely not consider going?

Do you think you'd have any trouble giving orders to others? How about taking orders?

Do you have difficulty working under deadlines or under pressure?

References

Do the people you listed here know you personally or just professionally or academically?

Which of these people know you the best? Who would give you the best reference? The weakest?

Who else might know about your abilities that we might contact?

Even though the interviewer will ask most of the questions, you too will want to ask questions. In addition to rehearsing some answers to predicted questions, fix firmly in mind the questions you want to ask the interviewer.

After the preparations, you are ready for the interview proper. Several suggestions may guide you through this sometimes difficult procedure.

Make an Effective Presentation of Self

This is probably the most important part of the entire procedure. If you fail here and make a bad initial impression, it will be difficult to salvage the rest of the interview. So devote special care to the way in which you present yourself.

Arrive on Time   In interview situations this means five to 10 minutes early. This will allow you time to relax, to get accustomed to the general surroundings, and perhaps to fill out any forms that may be required. And it gives you a cushion should something delay you on the way.

Be sure you know the name of the company, the job title, and the interviewer's name. Although you will have much on your mind when you go into the interview, the interviewer's name is not one of the things you can afford to forget (or mispronounce).

In presenting yourself, be sure that you do not err on the side of too much casualness or too much formality. When there is doubt, act on the side of increased formality. Slouching back in the chair, smoking, and chewing gum or candy are obvious behaviors to avoid when you are trying to impress an interviewer.

Demonstrate Effective Interpersonal Communication   Throughout the interview, be certain that you demonstrate the skills of interpersonal communication that are spelled out in this book. The interview is the ideal place to put into practice all the skills you have learned. Table 15.3 shows seven characteristics of conversational effectiveness that we considered in Unit 11 with special reference to the interview situation. In addition to demonstrating these qualities of effectiveness, avoid those behaviors that create negative impressions during employment interviews (Table 15.4).

Demonstrate Confidence   A special type of communication skill is that of communicating confidence. Make the interviewer see you as someone who can get the job done, who is confident. Here are some suggestions for communicating confidence that are not limited in their application to interviewing but have relevance of all forms of communication.

- Control your emotions. Once your emotions get the best of you, you will have lost your power and influence and will appear to lack the confidence necessary to deal with the relevant issues.
- Admit mistakes. Attempting to cover up obvious mistakes communicates a lack of confidence. Only a confident person can openly admit her or his mistakes and not worry about what others will think.
- Take an active role in the interview. Initiate topics or questions when appropriate. Avoid appearing as a passive participant, waiting for some stimulus.

Table 15.3 Effective Conversational Behavior in an Interview

Characteristic	Behaviors
Openness	Answer questions fully. Avoid one-word answers that may signal a lack of interest or knowledge.
Empathy	See the questions from the asker's point of view. Focus your eye contact and orient your body toward the interviewer. Lean forward as appropriate.
Positiveness	Emphasize your positive qualities. Express positive interest in the position. Avoid statements critical of yourself and others.
Immediacy	Connect yourself with the interviewer throughout the interview, for example, by using the interviewer's name, focusing clearly on the interviewer's remarks, and expressing responsibility for your thoughts and feelings.
Interaction Management	Ensure the interviewer's satisfaction by being positive, complimentary, and generally cooperative.
Expressiveness	Let your nonverbal behaviors (especially facial expression and vocal variety) reflect your verbal messages and your general enthusiasm. Avoid fidgeting and excessive moving about.
Other-orientation	Focus on the interviewer and on the company. Express agreement and ask for clarification as appropriate.

- Don't ask for agreement from the interviewer by using tag questions, for example, "That was appropriate, don't you think?" or by saying normally declarative sentences with a rising intonation and thereby turning them into questions, for example, "I'll arrive at nine?" By asking for agreement you communicate a lack of confidence in making decisions and in expressing opinions.

Table 15.4 Why People Fail at Interviews

Trait	Examples
Unprepared	They forget to bring their résumé, don't show that they know anything about the company.
Poor communication skills	They avoid looking at the interviewer, slouch, slur their words, speak in an overly low or rapid voice; give one-word answers, fidget, dress inappropriately.
Unpleasant personality	They appear defensive, cocky, lacking in assertiveness, extremely introverted, overly aggressive.
Lack of initiative	They fail to pick up on ramifications of interviewer's questions, give one-word answers, don't ask questions as would be appropriate.
Poor listening skills	They are easily distracted, need to have questions repeated, fail to maintain appropriate eye contact.

- Avoid excessive movements, especially self-touching movements. Tapping a pencil on a desk, crossing and uncrossing your legs in rapid succession, or touching your face or hair all communicate an uneasiness, a lack of social confidence.
- Maintain eye contact with the interviewer. People who avoid eye contact are often judged to be ill at ease, as if they are afraid to engage in meaningful interaction.
- Avoid vocalized pauses—the *ers* and *ahs*—that frequently punctuate conversations and that communicate that you lack certainty and are hesitating, not quite sure what to say.

Mentally Review the Interview

By reviewing the interview, you will fix it firmly in your mind. What questions were asked? How did you answer them? Review and write down any important information the interviewer gave. Ask yourself what you could have done more effectively. Consider what you did effectively that you could repeat in other interviews. Ask yourself how you might correct your weaknesses and capitalize on your strengths.

Follow Up

In most cases, follow up an interview with a thank-you note to the interviewer. In this brief, professional letter, thank the interviewer for his or her time and consideration. Reiterate your interest in the company and perhaps add that you hope to hear from him or her soon. Even if you did not get the job, you might in a follow-up letter ask to be kept in mind for future openings.

This letter provides you with an opportunity to resell yourself—to mention again those qualities you possess and wish to emphasize, but may have been too modest to discuss at the time. It will help to make you stand out in the mind of the interviewer, since not many interviewees write thank-you letters. It will help to remind the interviewer of your interview. It will also tell the interviewer that you are still interested in the position. It is a kind of pat on the back to the interviewer that says, in effect, that the interview was an effective one.

Consider the Lawfulness of Questions

Through the Equal Employment Opportunity Commission, the federal government has classified some interview questions as unlawful. These are federal guidelines and therefore apply in all 50 states; individual states, however, may have added further restrictions. You may find it interesting to take the following self-test (constructed with the good help of Stewart and Cash, 1988, and Zincoff and Goyer, 1984) to see if you can identify which questions are lawful and which are unlawful.

Some of the more important areas in which unlawful questions are frequently asked concern age, marital status, race, religion, nationality, citizenship, physical condition, and arrest and criminal records. For example, it is legal to ask applicants whether they meet the legal age requirements for the job and could provide proof of that. But it is unlawful to ask their exact age, even in indirect ways as illustrated in question 2 in the self-test. It is unlawful to ask about a person's marital status (question 1) or about family matters that are unrelated to the job (question 7). An interviewer

SELF-TEST

Can You Identify Unlawful Questions?

For each question write L (Lawful) if you think the question is legal for an interviewer to ask in an employment interview and U (Unlawful) if you think the question is illegal. For each question you consider unlawful, indicate why you think it is so classified.

_____ 1. Are you married, Tom?

_____ 2. When did you graduate from high school, Mary?

_____ 3. Do you have a picture so I can attach it to your résumé?

_____ 4. Will you need to be near a mosque (church, synagogue)?

_____ 5. I see you taught courses in "gay and lesbian studies." Are you gay?

_____ 6. Is Chinese your native language?

_____ 7. Will you have difficulty getting a baby-sitter?

_____ 8. I notice that you walk with a limp. Is this a permanent injury?

_____ 9. Where were you born?

_____ 10. Have you ever been arrested for a crime?

Scoring   All ten questions are unlawful. The remaining discussion illustrates why each of these and similar questions are unlawful.

may ask you, however, to identify a close relative or guardian if you are a minor, or any relative who currently works for the company.

Questions concerning your race (questions 3 and 6), religion (question 4), national origin (question 9), affectional orientation (question 5), age (question 2), handicaps unrelated to job performance (question 8), or even arrest record (question 10) are unlawful, as are questions that get at this same information in oblique ways. (Note, for example, that requiring a picture may be a way of discriminating against an applicant on the basis of sex, race, and age.)

Thus, for example, the interviewer may ask you what languages you are fluent in but may not ask what your native language is (question 6), what language you speak at home, or what language your parents speak. The interviewer may ask you if you if are in this country legally but may not ask if you were born in this country or naturalized (question 9).

The interviewer may inquire into your physical condition only insofar as the job is concerned. For example, the interviewer may ask, "Do you have any physical problems that might prevent you from fulfilling your responsibilities at this job?" But the interviewer may not ask about any physical disabilities (question 8). The interviewer may ask you if you have been convicted of a felony but not if you've been arrested (question 10).

These are merely examples of some of the lawful and unlawful questions that may be asked during an interview. Note that even the questions used as examples here might be lawful in specific situations. The test to apply is simple: Is the information related to your ability to perform the job? Such questions are referred to as BFOQ—bona fide occupational qualification—Questions.

Once you have discovered what questions are unlawful, consider how to deal with them if they come up during an interview.

Possible Strategies   Your first strategy should be to deal with such questions by answering the part you do not object to and omitting any information you do not want to give. For example, if you are asked the unlawful question concerning what language is spoken at home, you may respond with a statement such as "I have some language facility in German and Italian," without specifying a direct answer to the question. If you are asked to list all the organizations of which you are a member (an unlawful question in many states, since it is often a way of getting at political affiliation, religion, nationality, and various other areas), you might respond by saying something like: "The only organizations I belong to that are relevant to this job are the International Communication Association and the Speech Communication Association."

This type of response is preferable to the one that immediately tells the interviewer he or she is asking an unlawful question. In many cases, the interviewer may not even be aware of the legality of various questions and may have no intention of trying to get at information you are not obliged to give. For example, the interviewer may recognize the nationality of your last name and simply want to mention that he or she is also of that nationality. If you immediately take issue with the question, you will be creating problems where none really exist.

On the other hand, do recognize that in many employment interviews, the unwritten intention is to keep certain people out, whether it is people who are older or those of a particular marital status, affectional orientation, nationality, religion, and so on. If you are confronted by questions that are unlawful and that you do not want to answer, and if the gentle method described above does not work and your interviewer persists—saying, for example, "Is German the language spoken at home?" or "What other organizations have you belonged to?"—you might counter by saying that such information is irrelevant to the interview and to the position you are seeking. Again, be courteous but firm. Say something like "This position does not call for any particular language skill and so it does not matter what language is spoken in my home." Or you might say, "The organizations I mentioned are the only relevant ones; whatever other organizations I belong to will certainly not interfere with my ability to perform in this company at this job."

If the interviewer still persists—and I doubt that many would after these rather clear and direct responses—you might note that these questions are unlawful and that you are not going to answer them.

Summary

1. *Interviewing* is a form of interpersonal communication in which two persons interact largely through a question-and-answer format to achieve specific goals.

2. Six types of interviewing are the *persuasive interview,* the *appraisal interview,* the *exit interview,* the *counseling interview,* the *information interview,* and the *employment interview.*

3. In the *informative interview* the following guidelines should prove useful: select the person you wish to interview, secure an appointment, prepare your questions, establish rapport with the interviewer, ask permission to tape the interview, ask open-ended questions, and follow up the interview.

4. In the *employment interview* the following guidelines should prove useful: prepare yourself intellectually and physically for the interview, establish your objectives, prepare answers to predicted questions, make an effective presentation of yourself, mentally review the interview, and follow up the interview with a brief letter.

5. Interviewees should familiarize themselves with possible *unlawful questions* and develop strategies for dealing with these questions.

Applications

15.1 INTERVIEW SKILLS IN ACTION

Presented below is a brief dialogue that might take place during an initial interview for a job. Read through the transcript and identify the elements that demonstrate a lack of interview skills. Indicate how the applicant might have better represented himself as a more effective and competent individual.

MR. ROSS: And you are?

PHIL SNAP: Me? Oh, I'm Phil. Mr. Snap. Phil Snap.

MR. ROSS: So, Mr. Snap, what can I do for you?

PHIL SNAP: I'm here for, I mean I'm applying for that job.

MR. ROSS: **So, you'd like a job with Datacomm. Is that right?**

PHIL SNAP: Well, er, yes. Don't you think that's a good idea? I mean it's a good company, no?

MR. ROSS: Tell me what you know about communications.

PHIL SNAP: Well, I guess, I mean I took lots of courses in college. Here's my transcript.

MR. ROSS: I can read your transcript. I want to hear from you exactly what you know about communications.

PHIL SNAP: Well, I took courses in interpersonal communication, television production, organizational communication, nonverbal communication.

MR. ROSS: Don't tell me your courses. Tell me what you know.

PHIL SNAP: Excuse me. I guess I'm a little nervous. This is my first interview and I really don't know what to say.

MR. ROSS:	*(Smiling)* Are you sure you were a communications major?
PHIL SNAP:	Oh, yes, I was. See, it's on the transcript.
MR. ROSS:	Yes, I know. Let me put it this way: Do you think you can do anything for Datacomm?
PHIL SNAP:	Oh, yes. Yes.
MR. ROSS:	Okay, Mr. Snap, now exactly what can you do for Datacomm that the next applicant can't do better?
PHIL SNAP:	Oh, well, I really don't know much about Datacomm. I mean, I may be wrong about this, but I thought I would assist someone and learn the job that way.
MR. ROSS:	Right. What skills can you bring to Datacomm? Why would you make such a good learner?
PHIL SNAP:	Shit, this isn't as easy as I thought it would be. Well, I'm not very good at giving speeches. But I guess that's not too important anyway, right?
MR. ROSS:	Everything is important, Mr. Snap. Tell me what you are especially good at.
PHIL SNAP:	Well, I guess I'm kind of good at group stuff—you know, working with people in groups.
MR. ROSS:	No, I'm not sure I know what that means. Tell me.
PHIL SNAP:	Like, I mean I'm pretty good at just working with people. People think I'm kind of a neat guy.
MR. ROSS:	I don't doubt that, Mr. Snap, but do you have any other talents—other than being a neat guy?
PHIL SNAP:	I can operate a Showpro system. Is that important?
MR. ROSS:	Mr. Snap, I told you that everything is important.
PHIL SNAP:	Is there anything else?
MR. ROSS:	I don't know, Mr. Snap, is there anything else?
PHIL SNAP:	I don't know.
MR. ROSS:	I want to thank you for your time, Mr. Snap. We'll be in touch with you.
PHIL SNAP:	Oh, I got the job?
MR. ROSS:	Not exactly. If we decide on you, we will call you.
PHIL SNAP:	Okay.

15.2   RESPONDING TO UNLAWFUL QUESTIONS

In dealing with unlawful questions, your first task is to recognize which questions are lawful and which are unlawful. Your second task is to respond to the question, to the unlawfulness of the question, to some unrelated issue as a way of avoiding the question, or in some other way. This exercise is designed to provide you with practice in developing responses that are effective in protecting your privacy (should you wish to protect it) and at the same time maintaining a positive relationship with the interviewer. Review the questions in the self-test on unlawful questions and indicate how you would deal with each of them. Write your responses and then compare them with those of others, either in groups or with the class as a whole.

Another alternative is to form two-person groups and role-play the interviewer-interviewee situation. To make this more realistic, the person playing the interviewer should press for an answer to the question, while the interviewee should continue to avoid answering the question, yet respond positively and cordially. As you will discover, this is not always easy; tempers are frequently lost in this type of interaction.

15.3 EXPERIENCING AND ANALYZING INTERVIEWS

Three-person groups should be formed, preferably among people who do not know each other well or who have had relatively little interaction. One person should be designated the interviewer, another the interviewee, and the third the interview analyst. One of the following situations should be chosen by the interview analyst:

1. an interview for the position of camp counselor for orphans
2. an interview for a part in a new Broadway musical
3. a therapy interview to focus on communication problems in relating to superiors
4. an interview between teacher and student in which the teacher is trying to discover why the course taught last semester was such a dismal failure
5. an interviewer for the position of professor of human communications

After the situation is chosen, the interviewer should interview the interviewee for approximately 10 minutes. During this time, the analyst should observe the interview but not interfere in any way, verbally or nonverbally. After the interview is over, the analyst should offer a thorough and detailed analysis, considering each of the following questions:

1. What happened during the interview (essentially a description of the interaction)?
2. What was well handled?
3. What went wrong? What aspects of the interview were not handled as effectively as they might have been?
4. What could have been done to make the interview more effective?

The analysts for each interview may then be called upon to report their major findings to the class as a whole. A list of "common faults" or "suggestions for improving interviews" may then be developed by the instructor or group leader in response to these analyses.

Interpersonal Communication, Relationships, and Interviewing

Questions and Activities

1. Can you identify how a close friendship or romantic relationship has progressed to psychologically based predictions, explanatory knowledge, and personally established rules? Who initiated the move toward greater intimacy? What effect did the changes have on your relationship and on your interpersonal behaviors? Which of these three changes was the most important for you?

2. What are your most important interpersonal relationships? What needs do each of these satisfy?

3. How long does it take you to decide whether to pursue a relationship with someone you just met? Is the four-minute limit that some researchers have proposed too short? Too long?

4. Have you or a partner used any of the dating strategies discussed in Unit 12 to intensify your relationship? Which ones? Were they effective? Ineffective? Are there any strategies that you would resent someone using on you? Do you notice men and women using the same or different strategies?

5. Are the three anxieties—security, fulfillment, and excitement—that people experience when contemplating marriage realistic? That is, are there good reasons for such anxieties?

6. Does the six-stage model adequately describe the development of relationships as you have experienced them? If not, how would you reconstruct the six-stage model?

7. With what stage of the relationship process do you experience the most difficulties? Why? What communication skills would be especially important here?

8. Comedian Henny Youngman once said "The first part of our marriage was very happy. But then, on the way back from the ceremony. . . " Why is this observation funny? Is there at least partial truth in this?

9. On a hierarchy of the important things in your life, where are your friendship relationships? Your romantic relationships? Your family relationships?

10. What makes others attractive to you? What makes you attractive to others?

11. Which of the affinity-seeking strategies have you witnessed (either as sender or receiver)? How were they used? What effects did they have? Are there some strategies that you would resent others using on you? Why?

12. How might you describe three or four of your current relationships in terms of breadth and depth? Are breadth and depth related to your degree of satisfaction with these relationships?

13. How might you describe three or four of your current relationships in terms of profit, costs, and rewards? Do these concepts help you explain the development, maintenance, and deterioration of these relationships?

14. How equitable are your own present interpersonal relationships? How equitable were your previous interpersonal relationships? What part do you think equity (and inequity) plays in maintaining and breaking down interpersonal relationships?

15. Why do you have your current relationships? Why do you maintain the relationships you are in?

16. Have you had a relationship that ended? Why did it end? Do the factors discussed in Unit 13 cover the major reasons? If not, what other factors would you add?

17. Have you ever tried to repair a deteriorating relationship? What strategies did you use? Were they effective?

18. Do you believe any of the myths about conflict discussed in Unit 14? What effect does this have on your own interpersonal and conflict behavior?

19. Review the productive and unproductive conflict strategies discussed in Unit 14. Which of these conflict strategies have you used in the past two weeks? Which have been used by others in conflicts with you? What effects did these strategies have? Does your analysis support or refute the discussion presented in the text?

20. Which of the unproductive conflict strategies causes you the most difficulty? Why?

21. What role will interviewing have in your professional life?

22. In what way is a date like an interview? In what way is the first day of class like an interview?

23. Examine the résumé on page 266. How might you tailor this to your own needs? What general categories would be especially appropriate for your résumé?

24. What would be your three greatest strengths as a prospective employee? How would you communicate these to the interviewer?

25. What skills of interviewing can you apply to other areas of human communication?

26. Using any of the insights presented in this section on interpersonal communication, describe the interpersonal communication and the interpersonal relationships of one of the following: (a) the gang in *Cheers,* (b) Roseanne and Dan from *Roseanne,* (c) the *FYI* team on *Murphy Brown,* (d) the nurses and doctors on *Nurses,* (e) Vivian and Phil on *Fresh*

Prince, (f) the Russos on *Blossom,* (g) Al and Peg on *Married . . . with Children,* or (h) Urkel and any other character on *Family Matters.*

Skill Check

_____ 1. I adjust my communication patterns on the basis of the intimacy of the relationship. (Unit 12)

_____ 2. I increase the breadth and depth of a relationship gradually. (Unit 12)

_____ 3. I can effectively manage physical proximity, reinforcement, and the emphasizing of similarities as ways of increasing interpersonal attractiveness. (Unit 12)

_____ 4. I can follow the basic steps in initiating relationships. (Unit 13)

_____ 5. I make use of both the nonverbal and verbal guidelines in initiating relationships. (Unit 13)

_____ 6. I can recognize the causes of relationship deterioration. (Unit 13)

_____ 7. I can recognize and control the communication patterns that may be symptomatic of relational deterioration. (Unit 13)

_____ 8. I can apply the repair strategies to relationships I wish to improve. (Unit 13)

_____ 9. I can take care of myself when I experience relationship problems or dissolution. (Unit 13)

_____ 10. I can recognize the popular myths about conflict in my own belief system. (Unit 14)

_____ 11. I avoid using unproductive methods of conflict resolution such as avoidance, force, blame, silencers, gunnysacking, manipulation, personal rejection, and beltlining. (Unit 14)

_____ 12. I make use of the productive conflict strategies such as fighting actively, talking, empathy, facilitating open expression, present focus, spontaneity, acceptance, and fighting above the belt. (Unit 14)

_____ 13. In interviewing for information I follow the recommended guidelines, for example, making an appointment, preparing questions, establishing rapport, taping the interview (with permission), closing with an expression of appreciation, and following up the interview. (Unit 15)

_____ 14. In interviewing for a job I follow the recommended guidelines, for example, preparing myself intellectually and physically, establishing my objectives as clearly as I can, preparing answers to predicted questions, making an effective presentation of self, establishing a relationship with the interviewer, demonstrating effective interpersonal communication skills, reviewing the interview, and following up with a letter. (Unit 15)

PART 4

GROUP AND ORGANIZATIONAL COMMUNICATION

Unit 16. Preliminaries to Group Communication: Types, Procedures, and Formats

Unit 17. Members and Leaders in Group Communication

Unit 18. Organizational Communication

  Part 4. Feedback
    Questions and Activities
    Skill Check
    Suggested Readings

In this part we examine groups and group communication in a variety of contexts. We begin in Unit 16 by looking at what a small group is and at some of the major types of small groups in which you participate regularly, for example, problem solving, brainstorming, personal growth, and information sharing. In Unit 17 we look at the productive and destructive roles of members and at the functions and styles of small group leaders. Unit 18 focuses on communication within the organizational setting and seeks to provide a broad overview of this rapidly developing area. Here we survey the nature of organizations, the types of organizational communications, and how communication flows within an organization—the problems created and guidelines for greater effectiveness.

Approaching Small Group and Organizational Communication

In approaching the study of small group and organizational communication, keep the following in mind:

- The skills of small group communication are largely the skills of leadership generally. Look at this section as a guide to improving your own leadership skills.

- Small groups and organizations are much like cultures. Each develops its own code of behavior for what a member should and should not do. And each fixes the price that a member pays for violating these rules.

- Small groups are usually more effective in solving problems than are individuals working alone. Creative solutions emerge from a combination of thoughts. Therefore, approach small group situations with flexibility.

- Organizations of all kinds depend on communication even more than on hardware; when the communication is poor, the health of the organization is in trouble.

U N I T 16

PRELIMINARIES TO GROUP COMMUNICATION

UNIT CONTENTS

The Small Group

Problem-solving Groups

The Idea-Generation Group

The Personal Growth Group

Information-Sharing Groups

Small Group Formats

   Summary

   Applications
     16.1   The Problem-solving Group
     16.2   Brainstorming

UNIT GOALS

After completing this unit, you should be able to

1. describe the nature of a small group
2. identify the steps that should be followed in problem-solving discussions
3. explain the four principles of brainstorming
4. describe the types and nature of personal growth groups
5. explain the function of the learning group and the focus group
6. distinguish among the round table, panel, symposium, and symposium-forum

Everyone is a member of a wide variety of small groups. The family is the most obvious example, but you also function as members of a team, a class, a collection of friends, and so on. Some of your most important and most personally satisfying communications take place within small groups.

In this unit we look into the nature of the small group and identify its characteristics. With this as a foundation, we examine four major types of small groups (problem-solving, brainstorming, personal growth, and information-sharing) and the procedures you may follow in participating in these groups. Last, we examine four popular small group formats.

THE SMALL GROUP

A *small group* is a relatively small collection of individuals who are related to each other by some common purpose and have some degree of organization among them. Each of these characteristics needs to be explained a bit further.

A small group is, first, a collection of individuals, few enough in number so all members may communicate with relative ease as both senders and receivers. Generally, a small group consists of approximately 5 to 12 people. The important point to keep in mind is that each member should be able to function as both source and receiver with relative ease. If the group gets much larger than 12 this becomes difficult.

Second, the members of a group must be connected to one another in some way. People on a bus would not constitute a group, since they are not working at some common purpose. Should the bus get stuck in a ditch, the riders may quickly become a group and work together to get the bus back on the road. In a small group the behavior of one member is significant for all other members. This does not mean that all members must have exactly the same purpose in being members of the group. But generally there must be some similarity in the individuals' reasons for interacting.

Third, the members must be connected by some organizing rules or structure. At times the structure is rigid—as in groups operating under parliamentary procedure, where each comment must follow prescribed rules. At other times, as in a social gathering, the structure is very loose. Yet in both groups there is some organization and some structure: Two people do not speak at the same time, comments or questions by one member are responded to by others rather than ignored, and so on.

Before beginning your study of small group communication, examine how apprehensive you are in group discussions and in meetings by taking the self-test on page 286.

Small Group Norms

Most groups develop **group norms** or rules for appropriate behavior. Sometimes these rules are explicitly stated as, for example, in a company contract or policy: all members must attend all department meetings. Sometimes the rules are only implicit: members must be well-groomed. Regardless of whether these norms are explicitly or only implicitly stated, they are powerful regulators of members behaviors.

These norms or rules may apply to individual members as well as to the group as a whole and, of course, will differ from one group to another. For example, a norm in a family might be that financial matters are never discussed outside the immediate family. A norm for a college faculty might be that members may dress as they like during

SELF-TEST

How Apprehensive Are You in Group Discussions and Meetings?

Just as you have apprehension in interpersonal interactions (see Unit 13) and public speaking (see Unit 19), you have some degree of apprehension in group discussions and in meetings. This brief test is designed to measure your apprehension in these small group communication situations.

This questionnaire consists of 12 statements concerning your feelings about communication in group discussions and meetings. Please indicate in the space provided the degree to which each statement applies to you by marking whether you (1) Strongly Agree, (2) Agree, (3) Are Undecided, (4) Disagree, or (5) Strongly Disagree. There are no right or wrong answers. Some of the statements are similar to other statements. Do not be concerned about this. Work quickly; just record your first impression.

_____ 1. I dislike participating in group discussions.

_____ 2. Generally, I am comfortable while participating in group discussions.

_____ 3. I am tense and nervous while participating in group discussions.

_____ 4. I like to get involved in group discussions.

_____ 5. Engaging in a group discussion with new people makes me tense and nervous.

_____ 6. I am calm and relaxed while participating in group discussions.

_____ 7. Generally, I am nervous when I have to participate in a meeting.

_____ 8. Usually, I am calm and relaxed while participating in meetings.

_____ 9. I am very calm and relaxed when I am called upon to express an opinion at a meeting.

_____ 10. I am afraid to express myself at meetings.

_____ 11. Communicating at meetings usually makes me uncomfortable.

_____ 12. I am very relaxed when answering questions at a meeting.

Scoring: This test will enable you to obtain two subscores, one for group discussions and one for meetings. To obtain your scores use the following formulas:

For Group Discussions

18 plus scores for items 2, 4, and 6
minus scores for items 1, 3, and 5

For Meetings

18 plus scores for items 8, 9, and 12
minus scores for items 7, 10, and 11

Scores above 18 show some degree of apprehension.

Source: From James C. McCroskey, _An Introduction to Rhetorical Communication_, 4th ed. (Englewood Cliffs, N.J.: Prentice-Hall, 1982) Reprinted by permission of the author.

In what ways are cultural norms similar to (or different from) small group norms? Can you identify two or three cultural norms that influence your communication behavior in the classroom?

normal teaching days, but when meeting with the president a more formal dress code is expected.

    Norms that regulate a particular member's behavior are called *role expectations:* the new person in an organization is expected to play the role of secretary; Mary, who knows a lot about photography, is expected to play the role of photographer at the company parties; John, whose family owns a bakery, is expected to bring rolls and coffee to early-morning group meetings.

    Some norms govern the behavior of the group as a whole: all members of the family must contribute to helping a member in trouble; the group gets its work done as quickly as possible and doesn't party until afterward.

    According to Napier and Gershenfeld (1989), you are more likely to accept group norms when you

- want to continue your membership in the group
- feel your group membership is important
- are in a group that is cohesive, when you and the other members are closely connected, are attracted to each other, and depend on each other to meet your needs
- would be punished by negative reactions or exclusion from the group for violating the group norms

Power in the Small Group

Power permeates all small groups and in fact all relationships. It influences what you do, when, and with whom. It influences the employment you seek and the employment you get. It influences the friends you choose and do not choose and those who choose you and those who do not. It influences your romantic and family relationships—their success, failure, and level of satisfaction or dissatisfaction.

Power is what enables one person (the one with power) to control the behaviors of the others. Thus, if A has power over B and C, then A, by virtue of this power and through the exercise of this power (or the threat of its being exercised), can control the behaviors of B and C. Differences in the amount and type of power influence who makes important decisions, who will prevail in an argument, and who will control the finances.

Although all relationships are the same in that they all involve power, they differ in the types of power that the people use and to which they respond. It is useful to distinguish among six types of power (French & Raven, 1968; Raven, Centers, & Rodrigues, 1975): referent, legitimate, reward, coercive, expert, and information or persuasion power.

As you read through these types of power, keep the following questions in mind:

- Do you hold this kind of power over anyone? What is the specific basis of the power?
- Does anyone hold this kind of power over you? What are the specific reasons for this power relationship?
- How satisfied are you with your own levels of power? For example, are you satisfied with those situations in which others hold power over you? Are you satisfied with the power that you hold over others? How might you go about changing your levels of power?

The **referent power** holder wields power over "Other" because Other wishes to be like the power holder. Often the referent power holder is attractive, has considerable prestige, is well-liked, and well-respected; as these increase, so does power. For example, an older brother may have power over a younger brother because the younger brother wants to be like him.

The **legitimate power** holder wields power because Other believes that the power holder has a right—by virtue of his or her position—to influence or control Other's behavior. Usually legitimate power derives from the roles people occupy and from the belief that because they occupy these roles, they have a right to influence others. For example, employers, judges, managers, and police officers are usually seen to hold legitimate power. You give these people power because you believe they have the right to regulate your behaviors.

The **reward power** holder controls the rewards that Other wishes to receive. Rewards may be material (for example, money, promotion, jewelry) or social (love, friendship, respect). The degree of power wielded is directly related to the desirability of the reward as seen by Other. For example, teachers have reward power over students because they control grades, letters of recommendation, and social approval.

The **coercive power** holder has the ability to administer punishments to or remove rewards from Other if Other does not do as the power holder wishes. Usually, people who have reward power also have coercive power. For example, parents may deny extended privileges concerning time or recreation or withhold money.

The **expert power** holder wields power over Other because Other believes the power holder has expertise or knowledge. Expert power increases when the expert is seen as unbiased with nothing personally to gain from exerting this power. Expert power decreases if the expert is seen as biased and as having something to gain from securing Other's compliance. For example, lawyers have expert power in legal matters and doctors have expert power in medical matters.

The **information or persuasion power** holder wields power over Other because Other attributes to the power holder the ability to communicate logically and persuasively. For example, researchers and scientists may be given information power because of the perception that they are informed, critical thinkers.

PROBLEM-SOLVING GROUPS

A problem-solving group is a collection of individuals who meet to solve a particular problem or to reach a decision. In one sense this is the most exacting kind of group to participate in. It requires not only a knowledge of small group communication techniques, but a thorough knowledge of the particular problem. And it usually demands faithful adherence to a somewhat rigid set of rules. We look at this group first in terms of the classic and still popular problem solving approach, whereby we identify the steps you would go through in solving a problem. Next we look at two approaches popular in organizations today: the nominal group and the Delphi method.

The Problem-solving Sequence

The problem-solving approach, which owes its formulation to the philosopher John Dewey's steps in reflective thinking, identifies six steps (see Figure 16.1). These steps are designed to make problem solving more efficient and effective.

Define and Analyze the Problem   In many instances the nature of the problem is clearly specified. For example, a group of designers might discuss how to package the new soap project. In other instances, however, the problem may be vague, and it remains for the group to define it in concrete terms. Thus, for example, the general problem may be poor campus communications. But such a vague and general topic is difficult to tackle in a problem-solving discussion, so it is helpful to specify the problem clearly. So, for purposes of discussion, a group might specify the problem as "How can we improve the student newspaper?"

Generally, it is best to define the problem as an open-ended question ("How can we improve the student newspaper?") rather than as a statement ("The student newspaper needs to be improved") or a yes/no question ("Does the student newspaper need improvement?"). The open-ended question allows for greater freedom of exploration. It does not restrict the ways in which the group may approach the problem.

The problem should also be limited in some way so that it identifies a manageable area for discussion. A question such as, "How can we improve the university?" is too broad and general. Rather, it would be more effective to limit the problem and to identify one subdivision of the university on which the group might focus. You might

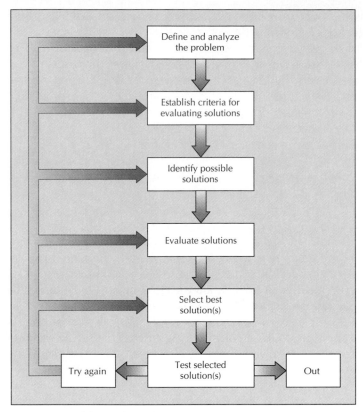

FIGURE 16.1 Steps in problem-solving discussion.

choose one of the following categories for discussion: the student newspaper, student-faculty relationships, registration, examination scheduling, or student advisory services.

In defining the problem, the group seeks to identify its dimensions. Appropriate questions (for most problems) revolve around the following issues: (1) *duration*—How long has the problem existed? Is it likely to continue in the future? What is the predicted course of the problem? For example, will it grow or lessen in influence? (2) *causes*—What are the major causes of the problem? How certain can we be that these are the actual causes? (3) *effects*—What are the effects of the problem? How significant are they? Who is affected by this problem? How significantly are they affected? Is this problem causing other problems? How important are these other problems?

Applied to our newspaper example, the specific questions might look something like this:

- *Duration:* How long has there been a problem with securing advertising? Does it look as though it will grow or lessen in importance?
- *Causes:* What seems to be causing the newspaper problem? Are there specific policies (editorial, advertising, or design) that might be causing the problem?
- *Effects:* What effects is this problem producing? How significant are these effects? Who is affected? Students? Alumni? Faculty? People in the community?

Establish Criteria for Evaluating Solutions   Before any solutions are proposed, you need to decide how to evaluate the solutions. At this stage you identify the standards or criteria that you will use in evaluating the solutions or in selecting one solution over another. Generally, two types of criteria need to be considered. First, there are the *practical criteria*. For example, you might decide that the solutions must not increase the budget, must lead to a higher number of advertisers, must increase the readership by at least 10 percent, and so on. Second, there are the *value criteria*. These are more difficult to identify. These might include, for example, that the newspaper must be a learning experience for all those who work on it, that it must reflect the attitudes of the board of trustees, the faculty, or the students. One school of thought would advise that you keep these criteria in mind as you generate possible solutions in your next step and that you return to these criteria to more thoroughly evaluate each of the proposed solutions. Another school of thought, however, would advise you to generate solutions first (without any discussion of how they will be evaluated) and consider how they will be evaluated only after these solutions are proposed (Brilhart & Galanes, 1986). The advantage of this second approach is that you are likely to generate more creative solutions since you won't be restricted by standards of evaluation. The disadvantage is that you might spend a great deal of time generating very impractical solutions that would never meet the standards you'll eventually propose. Depending on the topic and the inclination of the group, then, you may wish to identify possible solutions before or after establishing criteria for evaluating the solutions.

Identify Possible Solutions   At this stage identify as many solutions as possible. Focus on quantity rather than quality. Brainstorming may be particularly useful at this point (see discussion of idea-generation groups). Solutions to the student newspaper problem might include incorporating reviews of faculty publications; student evaluations of specific courses; reviews of restaurants in the campus area; outlines for new courses; and employment information.

Evaluate Solutions   After all the solutions have been proposed, you would go back and evaluate each according to the criteria established for evaluating solutions. For example, to what extent does incorporating reviews of area restaurants meet the criteria for evaluating solutions? Would it increase the budget? Would it lead to an increase in advertising revenue? Each potential solution should be matched against the criteria for evaluating solutions.

The Six Critical Thinking Hats Technique   Critical thinking pioneer Edward deBono (1987) suggests that in defining and analyzing problems, you use six thinking hats. With each hat you look at the problem from a different perspective. The technique provides a convenient and interesting way to further explore a problem from a variety of different angles.

- The *fact hat* focuses attention on the data, the facts and figures that bear on the problem. For example, What are the relevant data on the newspaper? How can you get more information on the paper's history? How much does it cost to print? How much advertising revenue can you get?
- *The feeling hat* focuses attention on our feelings, emotions, and intuitions

concerning the problem. How do you feel about the newspaper and about making major changes?

- *The negative argument* hat asks that you become the devil's advocate. Why might this proposal fail? What are the problems with publishing reviews of courses? What is the worst-case scenario?
- *The positive benefits hat* asks that you look at the upside. What are the opportunities that this new format will open up? What benefits will reviewing courses provide for the students? What would be the best thing that could happen?
- *The creative new idea hat* focuses attention on new ways of looking at the problem and can be easily combined with the techniques of brainstorming discussed later in this chapter. What other ways can you use to look at this problem? What other functions can a student newspaper serve that have not be thought of? Can the student paper provide a service to the nonacademic community as well?
- *The control of thinking hat* helps you analyze what you have done and are doing. It asks that you reflect on your own thinking processes and synthesize the results of your thinking. Have you adequately defined the problem? Are you focusing too much on insignificant issues? Have you given enough attention to the possible negative effects?

Select the Best Solution(s)   At this stage the best solution or solutions are selected and put into operation. Thus, for example, if "reviews of faculty publications" and "outlines for new courses" best met the criteria for evaluating solutions, the group might then incorporate these two new items in the next issue of the newspaper.

Test Selected Solution(s)   After the solution(s) are put into operation, test their effectiveness. The group might, for example, poll students about the new newspaper or examine the number of copies purchased. Or you might analyze the advertising revenue or see if readership did increase 10 percent.

If these solutions prove ineffective, you would go back to one of the previous stages and repeat part of the process. Often this takes the form of selecting other solutions to test. But, it may also involve going further back to, for example, a reanalysis of the problem, an identification of other solutions, or a restatement of criteria.

The Nominal Group

The nominal group is a group in "name only" and can best be described by following its procedures as it deals with a specific problem (Huseman, 1977). Let's say the task is to decide if a communications department should be established at ABC, Inc. First, each member of the nominal group writes down the major advantages and disadvantages of establishing the communications department. Second, a chairperson collects the responses and records them on a board so that all can see them. Third, members study the list and rank-order each advantage and disadvantage in terms of its importance. These rank-orders are then collected and tabulated.

At this point you would have a composite rank-ordered list of the advantages and disadvantages of establishing a communications department at ABC, Inc. The task of the nominal group is now complete. A regular discussion, perhaps using the problem-solving approach discussed earlier, may then follow.

One disadvantage of this approach is that the members do not profit from the stimulation of other members. An advantage to this approach is that there is likely to be great openness and honesty and less inhibition, since the lists are constructed privately. Further, since criticism and evaluation are postponed, all facets of the problem can be identified quickly.

The Delphi Method

In the Delphi method, originally developed by the RAND Corporation, a pool of experts is established but there is no interaction among them (Tersine & Riggs, 1980). Unlike the nominal group, where all members sit around a table, the members of a Delphi group may be scattered throughout the world. A Delphi questionnaire is distributed to all members asking them to respond to what they feel are, for example, the communication problems the organization will have to face in the next 25 years. Members record their predictions, and the questionnaires are sent back anonymously.

Responses are tabulated, recorded, and distributed to the experts, who then revise their predictions in light of the composite list. They then submit their revised predictions. These are again tabulated, recorded, and returned. The process continues until the responses no longer change significantly. The composite or final list represents the predictions or forecast of this group of experts.

With this approach, personality conflicts are eliminated. Status differences that might inhibit open and honest responses are also eliminated. Although it takes a great deal of time to construct the questionnaire and to tabulate the responses, the process uses very little of the experts' time. Physical distance is no problem here; the post office or the fax machine does the work.

Decision-making Methods

Groups may use different decision-making methods in deciding, for example, which criterion to use or which solution to accept. Generally, groups use one of three methods.

Authority   In decision making by authority, members voice their feelings and opinions but the leader, boss, or CEO makes the final decision. This is surely an efficient method; it gets things done quickly and the amount of discussion can be limited as desired. Another advantage is that experienced and informed members (for example, those who have been with the company longest) will probably exert a greater influence on the decision maker.

The great disadvantage is that members may not feel the need to contribute their insights and may become distanced from the power within the group or organization. Another disadvantage is that it may lead members to give the decision maker what they feel she or he wants to receive, a condition that can easily lead to groupthink.

Majority Rule   With this method the group agrees to abide by the majority decision and may vote on various issues as the group progresses to solve its problem. Majority rule is efficient since there is usually an option to call for a vote when the majority are in agreement. This is a useful method for issues that are relatively unimportant (What company should service the water cooler?) and where member satisfaction and commitment is not needed.

One disadvantage is that it can lead to factioning, where various minorities align against the majority. The method may also lead to limiting discussion once a majority has agreed and a vote is called.

Consensus   The group operating under consensus reaches a decision only when all group members agree, as in the criminal jury system. This method is especially important when the group wants the satisfaction and commitment of each member, to the decision and to the decision-making process as a whole (DeStephen & Hirokawa, 1988; Rothwell, 1992).

Consensus obviously takes longest and can lead to a great deal of wasted time if members wish to prolong the discussion process needlessly or selfishly. This method may also put great pressure on the person who honestly disagrees but who doesn't want to prevent the group from making a decision.

THE IDEA-GENERATION GROUP

Many small groups exist solely to generate ideas and often follow a formula called *brainstorming* (Beebe & Masterson, 1990; Osborn, 1957). **Brainstorming** is a technique for bombarding a problem and generating as many ideas as possible. In this system the process occurs in two phases. The first is the brainstorming period proper; the second is the evaluation period.

The procedures are simple. A problem is selected that is amenable to many possible solutions or ideas. Group members are informed of the problem to be brainstormed before the actual session, so they can think about the topic. When the group meets, each person contributes as many ideas as he or she can think of. All ideas are recorded either in writing or on tape. During this idea-generating session, four general rules are followed.

No Negative Criticism Is Allowed   All ideas are recorded. They are not evaluated nor even discussed. Any negative criticism—whether verbal or nonverbal—is itself criticized by the leader or the members.

Quantity Is Desired   The more ideas the better. Somewhere in a large pile of ideas will be one or two good ones. The more ideas generated, the more effective the brainstorming session.

Combinations and Extensions Are Desired   While you may not criticize a particular idea, you may extend it or combine it in some way. The value of a particular idea may well be in the way it stimulates someone to combine or extend it.

Freewheeling Is Desired   The wilder the idea the better. It is easier to tone an idea down than to spice it up. A wild idea can easily be tempered, but it is not so easy to elaborate on a simple or conservative idea.

At times, the brainstorming session may break down with members failing to contribute new ideas. At this point, the moderator may prod the members with statements such as the following:

- Let's try to get a few more ideas before we close this session.
- Can we piggyback any other ideas or extensions on the suggestion to . . .
- Here's what we have so far. As I read the list of contributed suggestions, additional ideas may come to mind.
- Here's an aspect we haven't focused on . . . . Does this stimulate any ideas?

After all the ideas are generated—a period lasting no longer than 15 or 20 minutes—the entire list of ideas is evaluated. The ones that are unworkable are thrown out; the ones that show promise are retained and evaluated. During this phase negative criticism is allowed.

THE PERSONAL GROWTH GROUP

Some personal growth groups, sometimes referred to as support groups, aim to help members cope with particular difficulties, such as drug addiction, having an alcoholic parent, being an ex-convict, or having an overactive child or a promiscuous spouse.

The personal growth group grew out of 1960s culture—in large part the feminist movement—that valued openness and honesty and believed that the average person can (and wants to) help another average person. Could this type of group have grown out of 1990s culture? What types of groups are emerging today? What kinds of personal growth groups (if any) would you be likely to join?

Other groups are more clearly therapeutic and are designed to change significant aspects of one's personality or behavior.

Some Popular Personal Growth Groups

There are many varieties of support or personal growth groups. The *encounter group* tries to facilitate personal growth and the ability to deal effectively with other people (Rogers, 1970). One of its assumptions is that the members will be more effective psychologically and socially if they get to know and like themselves better. Consequently, the atmosphere of the encounter group is one of acceptance and support. Freedom to express one's inner thoughts, fears, and doubts is stressed.

The *assertiveness training group* aims to increase the willingness of its members to stand up for their rights and to act more assertively in a wide variety of situations (Adler, 1977).

The *consciousness-raising group* aims to help people cope with the problems society confronts them with. The members of a consciousness-raising group all have one characteristic in common (for example, they are all women, all unwed mothers, all new fathers, or all gay). It is this commonality that leads the members to join together and assist one another. In the consciousness-raising group the assumption is that similar people are best equipped to assist each other's personal growth. Structurally, the consciousness-raising group is leaderless. All members (usually ranging from 6 to 12) are equal in their control of the group and in their presumed knowledge.

Some Rules and Procedures

Let's look at how one consciousness-raising group operates. In this group, the procedures are rather rigidly formulated and enforced. Other consciousness-raising groups operate with more flexible rules.

A topic is selected, usually by majority vote of the group. This topic may be drawn from a prepared list or suggested by one of the group members. But regardless of what topic is selected, it is always discussed from the point of view of the larger topic that brings these particular people together—let's say, sexual harassment. Whether the topic is men, employment, or family, it is pursued in light of the issues and problems of sexual harassment.

After a topic is selected, a starting point is established through some random procedure. That member speaks for about 10 minutes on his or her feelings, experiences, and thoughts. The focus is always on oneself. No interruptions are allowed. After the member has finished, the other group members may ask questions of clarification. The feedback from other members is to be totally supportive.

After questions of clarification have been answered, the next member speaks. The same procedure is followed until all members have spoken. After the last member has spoken, a general discussion follows. During this time members may relate different aspects of their experience to what the others have said. Or they may tell the group how they feel about some of the issues raised by others.

With this procedure your consciousness is raised by formulating and verbalizing your thoughts on a particular topic, hearing how others feel and think about the same topic, and formulating and answering questions of clarification.

INFORMATION-SHARING GROUPS

The purpose of information-sharing groups is to acquire new information or skill through a sharing of knowledge. In most information-sharing groups, all members have something to teach and something to learn. In others, the interaction takes place because some have information and some do not.

Learning Groups

In learning groups, the members pool their knowledge to the benefit of all. Members may follow a variety of discussion patterns. For example, a historical topic might be developed chronologically, with the discussion progressing from the past into the present and perhaps predicting the future. Issues in developmental psychology such as language development in the child or physical maturity might also be discussed chronologically. Some topics lend themselves to spatial development. For example, the development of the United States might take a spatial pattern going from east to west or a chronological pattern going from 1776 to the present. Other suitable patterns, depending on the nature of the topic and the needs of the discussants, might be developed in terms of causes and effects, problems and solutions, or structures and functions.

Perhaps the most popular is the topical pattern. A group might discuss the problems in raising a hyperactive child by itemizing and discussing each of the major problems. The structure of a corporation might also be considered in terms of its major divisions. As can be appreciated, each of these topics may be further systematized, for instance, by ordering the problems of hyperactivity in terms of their importance or complexity and ordering the major structures of the corporation in terms of decision-making power.

These patterns are essentially the same ones we consider under the structures of public speaking (in Part 5). They are actually patterns for organizing all sorts of communications. Some pattern or prearranged agenda should be developed if the discussion is to progress productively and if each of the major topics is to be given adequate time.

Focus Groups

A different type of learning group is the focus group, a kind of depth interview of a small group. The aim here is to discover what people think about an issue or product; for example, what do men between 18 and 25 think of the new aftershave lotion and its packaging? What do young executives earning over $70,000 think of buying a foreign luxury car?

In the focus group the leader tries to discover the beliefs, attitudes, thoughts, and feelings that members have so as to better guide decisions on changing the scent or redesigning the packaging or constructing advertisements for luxury cars. It is the leader's task to prod members to analyze their thoughts and feelings on a deeper level and to use the thoughts of one member to stimulate the thoughts of others.

For example, in one study the researcher tried "to collect supplementary data on the perceptions graduates have of the Department of Communication at ABC University" (Lederman, 1990). Two major research questions, taken directly from Lederman's study, motivated this focus group:

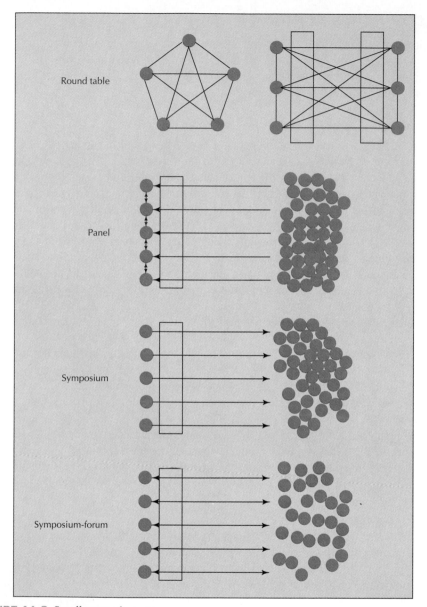

FIGURE 16.2 Small-group formats.

- What do graduates of the program perceive the educational effectiveness of their major to be at ABC?
- What would they want implemented in the program as it exists today?

Group participants then discussed their perceptions, organized around such questions as these (Lederman, 1990):

- The first issue to discuss is what the program was like when you were a major in the department. Let's begin by going around the table and making introductions. Will you tell me your name, when you graduated from ABC, what you are doing now, and what the program was like when you were here, as you remember it?

* Based on what you remember of the program and what you have used from your major since graduating, what kinds of changes, if any, would you suggest?

SMALL GROUP FORMATS

Small groups serve their functions in a variety of formats. Among the most popular are the panel or round table, the colloquy, the symposium, and the symposium-forum (Figure 16.2).

The Round Table In the round table format, group members arrange themselves in a circular or semicircular pattern. They share the information or solve the problem without any set pattern of who speaks when. Group interaction is informal and members contribute as they see fit. A leader or moderator may be present who may, for example, try to keep the discussion on the topic or encourage more reticent members to speak up.

The Panel In the panel, group members are "experts" and participate informally and without any set pattern of who speaks when. The difference is that there is an audience whose members may interject comments or ask questions. Many talk shows, such as *Donahue* and *Oprah Winfrey*, use this format.

A variation is the two-panel format, with an expert panel and a lay panel. The lay panel discusses the topic but when in need of technical information, additional data, or direction, they may turn to the expert panel members to provide the needed information.

The Symposium In the symposium, each member delivers a prepared presentation, much like a public speech. All speeches are addressed to different aspects of a single topic. In the symposium, the leader introduces the speakers, provides transitions from one speaker to another, and may provide periodic summaries.

The Symposium-Forum The symposium-forum consists of two parts: a symposium, with prepared speeches, and a forum, with questions from the audience and responses by the speakers. The leader introduces the speakers and moderates the question-and-answer session.

Summary

1. A *small group* is a collection of individuals that is small enough for all members to communicate with relative ease as both senders and receivers. The members are related to each other by some common purpose and have some degree of organization or structure among them.

2. Most small groups develop *norms* or *rules* identifying what is considered appropriate behavior for its members.

3. *Power* operates in all groups. Six types of power may be identified: *referent, legitimate, reward, coercive, expert,* and *information* or *persuasion.*

4. The *problem-solving group* attempts to solve a particular problem or at least to reach a decision that may be a preface to the problem solving itself.

5. The six steps in the *problem-solving approach* are: define and analyze the problem; establish criteria for evaluating solutions; identify possible solutions; evaluate solutions; select best solution(s); and test solution(s).

6. The *six hats technique* is especially useful in analyzing problems and consists of focusing on different aspects of the problem: facts, feelings, negative arguments, positive benefits, creative or new ways of viewing the problem, and your thinking processes.

7. Decision-making methods include *authority, majority rule,* and *consensus.*

8. The *nominal group* rank-orders significant issues by pooling members' contributions and rankings them without evaluation or discussion.

9. In the *Delphi method* experts respond to questionnaires until a final composite list is obtained that represents the opinions of these experts.

10. The *idea-generation or brainstorming group* attempts to generate as many ideas as possible.

11. The *personal growth group* helps members to deal with personal problems and to function more effectively. Popular personal growth groups are the encounter group, the assertiveness training group, and the consciousness-raising group.

12. The *educational or learning group* attempts to acquire new information or skill through a mutual sharing of knowledge or insight.

13. The *focus group* aims to discover what people think about an issue or product through a kind of in-depth group interview.

14. Small groups make use of four major formats: the *round table*, the *panel*, the *symposium*, and the *symposium-forum*.

Applications

16.1 THE PROBLEM-SOLVING GROUP

Together with four, five, or six others, form a problem- solving group and discuss one of the following questions:

- What should we do about the homeless?
- What should we do to improve student morale?
- What should we do to better prepare ourselves for the job market?
- What should we do to improve student-faculty communication?
- What should be the college's responsibility concerning AIDS?

Before beginning the discussion, each member should prepare a discussion outline, answering the following questions:

- What is the problem? How long has it existed? What caused it? What are the effects of the problem?
- What criteria should be used to evaluate possible solutions?
- What are some possible solutions?
- What are the advantages and disadvantages of each of these possible solutions?
- What solution seems best (in light of the advantages and disadvantages)?
- How might we put this solution to a test?

16.2 BRAINSTORMING

Together with a small group of students or with the class as a whole, sitting in a circle, brainstorm one of the topics identified in Application 16.1: The Problem-Solving Group. Be sure to appoint someone to write down all the contributions or use a recorder.

After this brainstorming session, consider these questions:

1. Did any members give negative criticism (even nonverbally)?
2. Did any members hesitate to contribute really wild ideas? Why?
3. Was it necessary to restimulate the group members at any point? Did this help?
4. Did possible solutions emerge in the brainstorming session that were not considered by members of the problem-solving group?

MEMBERS AND LEADERS IN GROUP COMMUNICATION

UNIT CONTENTS

Members in Small Group Communication

Leaders in Small Group Communication

Factors that Work Against Small Group Effectiveness

Summary

Applications

17.1   Using the IPA System of Analysis
17.2   Small Group Roles

UNIT GOALS

After completing this unit, you should be able to

1. identify the three major types of member roles and give examples of each type

2. define *groupthink* and identify its major symptoms

3. explain the situational theory of leadership

4. define the three leadership styles and the occasions when each would be most appropriate

5. explain at least four functions of leaders in small group communication

In this unit we consider the roles or functions of small group members and leaders. By gaining insight into the roles of both members and leaders, you will be in a better position to analyze your own small group behavior and to modify it as you wish.

MEMBERS IN SMALL GROUP COMMUNICATION

What are the major roles that members serve in small group communication? How can you become more effective participants in small groups?

Member Roles

Member roles can be divided into three general classes: group task roles, group building and maintenance roles, and individual roles (Benne & Sheats, 1948). You might serve each of these general roles by different specific behaviors. These roles are, of course, frequently served by leaders as well.

Group Task Roles   Group task roles are those that help the group focus more specifically on achieving its goals. In performing any of these roles, you do not act as an isolated individual, but rather as a part of the larger whole. The needs and goals of the group dictate the roles you would serve. As an effective group member you would serve several of these functions.

Some people, however, lock into a few specific roles. For example, one person may almost always seek the opinions of others, another may concentrate on elaborating de-

What member roles would your culture reward most? Reward least? Can you identify any general cultural principles that govern what is valued and what is not valued in group membership?

tails, still another on evaluating suggestions. Usually, this single focus is counterproductive. It is usually better for the roles to be spread more evenly among the members so that each may serve many group task roles. The twelve specific group task roles are described in Table 17.1.

Group Building and Maintenance Roles   Most groups focus not only on the task to be performed but on interpersonal relationships among members. If the group is to function effectively, and if members are to be both satisfied and productive, these relationships must be nourished. When these needs are not met, group members may become irritable when the group process gets bogged down, engage in frequent conflicts, or find the small group process unsatisfying. The group and its members need the same kind of interpersonal support that individuals need. The group building and maintenance roles serve this general function. Group building and maintenance are broken down into seven specific roles (Table 17.2).

Individual Roles   The group task and the group building and maintenance roles are all productive. They aid the group in achieving its goal. The roles are group oriented. The roles we discuss here are counterproductive. They hinder the group's achieving its goal and are individual rather than group oriented. Such roles, often

Table 17.1   Group Task Roles

Initiator-contributor	Presents new ideas or new perspectives on old ideas; suggests new goals, or new procedures or organizational strategies.
Information seeker	Asks for facts and opinions; seeks clarification of the issues being discussed.
Opinion seeker	Tries to discover the values underlying the group's task.
Information giver	Presents facts and opinions to the group members.
Opinion giver	Presents values and opinions and tries to spell out what the values of the group should be.
Elaborator	Gives examples and tries to work out possible solutions, trying to build on what others have said.
Coordinator	Spells out relationships among ideas and suggested solutions; coordinates the activities of the different members.
Orienter	Summarizes what has been said and addresses the direction the group is taking.
Evaluator-critic	Evaluates the group's decisions; questions the logic or practicality of the suggestions and thus provides the group with both positive and negative feedback.
Energizer	Stimulates the group to greater activity.
Procedural technician	Takes care of the various mechanical duties such as distributing group materials and arranging the seating.
Recorder	Writes down the group's activities, suggestions, and decisions; serves as the memory of the group.

Table 17.2 Group Building and Maintenance Roles	
Encourager	Supplies members with positive reinforcement in the form of social approval or praise for their ideas.
Harmonizer	Mediates the various differences between group members.
Compromiser	Tries to resolve conflict between his or her ideas and those of others; offers compromises.
Gatekeeper-expediter	Keeps the channels of communication open by reinforcing the efforts of others.
Standard setter	Proposes standards for the functioning of the group or for its solutions.
Group observer and commentator	Keeps a record of the proceedings and uses this in the group's evaluation of itself.
Follower	Goes along with the members of the group; passively accepts the ideas of others and functions more as an audience than as an active member.

termed *dysfunctional*, hinder the group's productivity and member satisfaction. Eight specific types are identified in Table 17.3.

Interaction Process Analysis

Another way of looking at the contributions group members make is through interaction process analysis, developed by Robert Bales (1950). In this system we analyze the contributions of members in four general categories: (1) social-emotional positive

Table 17.3 Individual Roles	
Aggressor	Expresses negative evaluation of the actions or feelings of the group members; attacks the group or the problem being considered.
Blocker	Provides negative feedback, is disagreeable, and opposes other members or suggestions regardless of their merit.
Recognition seeker	Tries to focus attention on oneself;, boasts about self-accomplishments rather than the task at hand.
Self-confessor	Expresses his or her own feelings and personal perspectives rather than focusing on the group.
Playboy/playgirl	Jokes around without any regard for the group process.
Dominator	Tries to run the group or the group members by pulling rank, flattering members of the group, or acting the role of the boss.
Help seeker	Expresses insecurity or confusion or deprecates oneself and thus tries to gain sympathy from the other members.
Special-interest pleader	Disregards the goals of the group and pleads the case of some special group.

contributions, (2) social-emotional negative contributions, (3) attempted answers, and (4) questions. Each of these four areas contains three subdivisions giving us a total of twelve categories into which we can classify group members' contributions (Table 17.4). Note that the categories under social-emotional positive are the natural opposites of those under social-emotional negative, and those under attempted answers are the natural opposites of those under questions.

Both the three-part member role and interaction process analysis categories are useful in viewing the contributions that members make in small group situations. When you look at member contributions through these systems, you can see, for example, if one member is locked into a particular role or if the group process breaks down because too many people are serving individual rather than group goals or because social-emotional negative comments dominate the discussion. These systems are designed to help you see more clearly what is going on in a group and what specific contributions may mean to the entire group process.

Member Participation

Another perspective on group membership may be gained from looking at the recommendations for effective participation in small group communication. Look at these suggestions as an elaboration and extension of the characteristics of effective conversation (Unit 11).

Be Group-Oriented   In the small group you are a member of a team, a larger whole. Your participation is of value to the extent that it advances the goals of the group and promotes member satisfaction. Your task is to pool your talents, knowledge, and insight so that the group may arrive at a better solution than any one person could have developed. Solo performances hinder the group.

This call for group orientation is not to be taken as a suggestion that members abandon their individuality or give up their personal values or beliefs for the sake of the group. Individuality with a group orientation is what is advocated here.

Table 17.4 Interaction Process Analysis Categories

Social-emotional positive	Shows solidarity
	Shows tension release
	Shows agreement
Social-emotional negative	Shows disagreement
	Shows tension
	Shows antagonism
Attempted answers	Gives suggestions
	Gives opinions
	Gives information
Questions	Asks for suggestions
	Asks for opinions
	Asks for information

Center Conflict on Issues   Conflict in small group situations is inevitable and its management should follow the general rules for dealing with conflict already covered (Unit 14). As in interpersonal communication, conflict is a natural part of the small group process.

It is particularly important in the small group to center conflict on issues rather than on personalities. When you disagree, make it clear that your disagreement is with the solution suggested or the ideas expressed, and not with the person who expressed them. Similarly, when someone disagrees with what you say, do not take this as a personal attack. Rather, view this as an opportunity to discuss issues from an alternative point of view.

When conflict does center on personalities, members have a responsibility to redirect that conflict to the significant issues. For example, right before Chris and Pat come to blows, you might say: "Then, Chris, you disagree with Pat's proposal mainly because it ignores the needs of the handicapped, right?" Then, you might go on to suggest that perhaps the group might focus on how the proposal might be altered to deal with the needs of the handicapped. When a more direct approach is necessary, you might say, for example: "Let's stick to the issue," "Can we get back to the proposal?" or perhaps, "Let's hear from a third point of view."

Be Critically Open-Minded   One common but unproductive development occurs when members come to the group with their minds already made up. When this happens, the small group process degenerates into a series of individual debates in which each person argues for his or her own position. Instead, members should come to the group equipped with relevant information that will be useful to the discussion. They should not have decided on the solution or conclusion they will accept. Any solutions or conclusions should be advanced tentatively rather than with certainty. Members should be willing to alter their suggestions and revise them in light of the discussion.

Listen openly but critically to the comments of all other members. Do not accept or reject any member's suggestions without critically evaluating them. Be *judiciously* open-minded. Be *judiciously* critical of your own contributions as well as of the contributions of others.

Ensure Understanding   Make sure that your ideas and information are understood by all participants. If something is worth saying, it is worth making it clear. When in doubt, ask: "Is that clear?" "Did I explain that clearly?"

Make sure, too, that you understand fully the contributions of the other members, especially before you take issue with them. In fact, it is often wise to preface any extended disagreement with some kind of paraphrase. For example, you might say "As I understand you, you want to exclude freshmen from playing on the football team. Is that correct? I disagree with that idea and I'd like to explain why I think that would be a mistake." Then you would go on to state your objections. In this way you give the other person the opportunity to clarify, deny, or otherwise alter what was said.

Groupthink

Groupthink is "the mode of thinking that persons engage in when *concurrence seeking* becomes so dominant in a cohesive ingroup that it tends to override realistic appraisal of alternative courses of action" (Janis, 1983). The term itself is meant to signal a "deterioration in mental efficiency, reality testing, and moral judgments as a result of group pressures."

Many specific behaviors of group members can lead to groupthink. One of the most significant occurs when the group limits its discussion to only a small number of alternative solutions, overlooking other possibilities. Another occurs when the group does not reexamine its decisions even when there are indications of possible dangers. Another is when the group spends little time discussing why certain initial alternatives were rejected. For example, if the group rejected a certain alternative because it was too costly, members will devote little time, if any, to the ways in which the cost may be reduced.

In groupthink, the group members are extremely selective in the information they consider seriously. Facts and opinions contrary to the position of the group are generally ignored. Facts and opinions that support the position of the group, however, are easily and uncritically accepted.

The following list of symptoms should help you recognize the existence of groupthink in the groups you observe or participate in (Janis, 1983):

- Group members think the group and its members are invulnerable to dangers.
- Members create rationalizations to avoid dealing directly with warnings or threats.
- Group members believe their group is moral.
- Those opposed to the group are perceived in simplistic, stereotyped ways.
- Group pressure is put on any member who expresses doubts or who questions the group's arguments or proposals.
- Group members censor their own doubts.
- Group members believe all members are in unanimous agreement, whether such agreement is stated or not.
- Group members emerge whose function it is to guard the information that gets to other members of the group, especially when such information may create diversity of opinion.

Figure 17.1 presents an evaluation form I use in my course in small group communication. It provides a convenient summary of the member's roles and responsibilities discussed here.

LEADERS IN SMALL GROUP COMMUNICATION

In many small groups, one person serves as leader. In others, leadership may be shared by several persons. In some groups, a person may be appointed the leader or may serve as leader because of her or his position within the company or hierarchy. In other groups, the leader may emerge as the group proceeds in fulfilling its functions or may be voted as leader by the group members. In any case the role of the leader or leaders is vital to the well-being and effectiveness of the group. (Even in leaderless groups, where all members are equal, leadership functions must still be served.)

Not surprisingly, leadership has been the focus of considerable attention from theorists and researchers who have identified a number of approaches, three of which are summarized in Table 17.5.

GROUP MEMBERSHIP EVALUATION FORM

Circle those roles played by the group member and *indicate the specific behaviors that led to these judgments.*

Group task roles: initiator-contributor, information seeker, opinion seeker, information giver, opinion giver, elaborator, coordinator, orienter, evaluator-critic, energizer, procedural technician, recorder

Group building and maintenance roles: encourager, harmonizer, compromiser, gatekeeper-expediter, standard setter or ego ideal, group observer and commentator, follower

Individual roles: aggressor, blocker, recognition seeker, self-confessor, playboy/playgirl, dominator, help seeker, special-interest pleader

Interaction process analysis: shows solidarity, shows tension release, shows agreement, shows disagreement, shows tension, shows antagonism, gives suggestions, gives opinions, gives information, asks for suggestions, asks for opinions, asks for information

GROUP PARTICIPATION

Is group-oriented	YES!	YES	yes	?	no	NO	NO!
Centers conflict on issues	YES!	YES	yes	?	no	NO	NO!
Is critically open-minded	YES!	YES	yes	?	no	NO	NO!
Ensures understanding	YES!	YES	yes	?	no	NO	NO!

IMPROVEMENT SUGGESTIONS

FIGURE 17.1 Group membership evaluation form.

Table 17.5 What Is a Leader?		
Approach	**Definition**	**Qualities Identified**
Traits approach	a leader is one who possesses those characteristics (or **traits**) that contribute to leadership	achievement, popularity, higher status, intelligence
Functional approach	a leader is one who behaves (or **functions**) as a leader	serves task roles, ensures member satisfaction, energizes group members
Situational approach	a leader is one who balances task accomplishment and member satisfaction on the basis of the unique **situation**	delegates, participates, sells, and tells depending on the members and the situation

are summarized in Table 17.5. Although contemporary theorists favor the situational approach, the traits and the functional approach continue to have merit.

The **traits approach** merits consideration because it emphasizes that leaders must possess certain qualities if they are to function effectively. The problem with the traits approach is that these qualities will vary with the situation, with the members, and with the culture in which the leader functions. Thus, for example, the leaders' knowledge or personality are generally significant factors. But, for some groups a knowledge of financial issues and a humorous personality might be effective, whereas for other groups a knowledge of design and a more serious personality might be effective.

The **functional approach** is significant because it helps identify what the leader should do in a given situation. Some of these functions have already been examined in the discussion of group membership where group roles, roles were identified. Additional functions are identified in the discussion of "Leadership's Functions: Task and People".

The **situational approach** deserves attention because it focuses on the two major tasks of the leader—accomplishing the task at hand and ensuring the satisfaction of the members—and because it recognizes that the leader's style must vary on the basis of the specific situation. Just as you adjust your interpersonal style in conversation or your motivational appeals in public speaking on the basis of the uniqueness of the situation, so must leadership style be adjusted.

Before examining this situational approach to leadership in more detail, you should find it interesting to take the T/P Leadership Test.

Situational Leadership: The Concern for Task and People

Leaders must be concerned with getting the task accomplished (the task dimension) *and* with ensuring that members are satisfied (the people dimension). The situational theory of leadership visualizes these two dimensions as in the figure in the leadership self-test (Hersey & Blanchard, 1988). (If you took the T-P Leadership Test, the following discussion will elaborate on the theory behind that test.) The vertical axis is the people dimension. The higher you go on this axis, the greater your concern for the members' social and emotional satisfaction. The horizontal axis is the task dimension. The more you move to the right, the greater your concern for accomplishing the task.

SELF-TEST

What Kind of Leader Are You?

The following items describe aspects of group member behavior. Respond to each item according to the way you would be most likely to act if you were in a problem-solving group. Circle whether you would be likely to behave in the described way always (A), frequently (F), occasionally (O), seldom (S), or never (N).

If I were a member of a problem solving group:

A F O S N A 1. I would be very likely to act as the spokesperson of the group.

A F O S N S 2. I would encourage overtime work.

A F O S N S 3. I would allow members complete freedom in their work.

A F O S N F 4. I would encourage the use of uniform procedures.

A F O S N O F 5. I would permit the others to use their own judgment in solving problems.

A F O S N × F 6. I would stress being ahead of competitive groups.

A F O S N F 7. I would speak as a representative of the group.

A F O S N O F 8. I would encourage members toward greater effort.

A F O S N × F 9. I would try out my ideas in the group.

A F O S N O 10. I would let the others do their work the way they think best.

A F O S N O 11. I would be working hard for personal recognition.

A F O S N O 12. I would be able to tolerate postponement and uncertainty.

A F O S N F 13. I would speak for the group when visitors were present.

A F O S N × F 14. I would keep the work moving at a rapid pace.

A F O S N O 15. I would help to identify a task and let the others do it.

A F O S N F 16. I would settle conflicts when they occur in the group.

A F O S N O 17. I would be likely to get swamped by details.

A F O S N F 18. I would represent the group at outside meetings.

A F O S N F 19. I would be reluctant to allow the others freedom of action.

A F O S N O 20. I would decide what should be done and how it should be done.

A F O S N × F 21. I would push for better results.

A F O S N × F 22. I would let other members have some authority.

A F O S N F 23. Things would usually turn out as I predicted.

A F O S N O 24. I would allow the others a high degree of initiative.

A F O S N × F 25. I would try to assign group members to particular tasks.

A F O S N O F 26. I would be willing to make changes.

A F O S N × F 27. I would ask the others to work harder.

A F O S N O F 28. I would trust the group members to exercise good judgment.

A F O S N F 29. I would try to schedule work to be done.

A F O S N N 30. I would refuse to explain my actions when questioned.

A F O S N × N 31. I would persuade others that my ideas are to their advantage.

A F O S N S 32. I would permit the group to set its own pace.

A F O S N × A 33. I would urge the group to beat its previous record.

A F O S N ✗ N 34. I would act without consulting the group.

A F O S N A 35. I would ask that group members follow standard rules and regulations.

Scoring

A. Circle the *item letter* for 1, 4, 7, 13, 16, 17, 18, 19, 20, 23, 29, 30, 31, 34, and 35.
B. Put an X *in front of only those circled item numbers* for items to which you responded S (seldom) or N (never).
C. Put an X *in front of those items whose numbers were not circled* only when you responded to such items with A (always) or F (frequently).
D. Circle any X that you have put *in front of any of the following item numbers:* 3, 5, 8, 10, 12, 15, 17, 19, 22, 24, 26, 28, 30, 32, and 34.
E. Count the circled Xs. This is your Person Orientation (P) Score. 7
F. Count the uncircled Xs. This is your Task Orientation (T) Score. 8

An individual's T and P scores are then plotted on the grid and are interpreted in terms of the descriptive elements given in the appropriate cell.

Name Group

Locating oneself on the grid:

To locate yourself on the grid below, find your score on the Person dimension (P) on the horizontal axis of the graph. Next, start up the column above your P score to the cell that corresponds to your Task score (T). Place an X in the cell that represents your two scores:

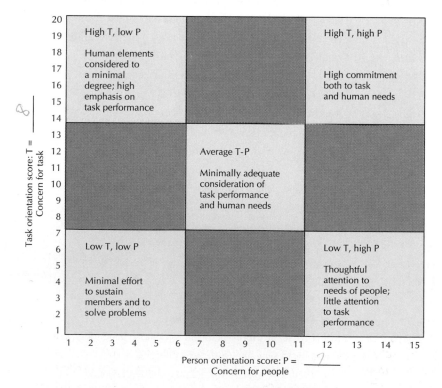

Source: Reprinted from B. R. Patton, K. Giffin, and E. N. Patton, *Decision-Making: Group Interaction,* 3rd ed. New York: Harper & Row, 1989, pp. 179–181. Originally developed by J. W. Pfeiffer and J. E. Jones, *Structured Experiences for Human Relations Training,* Iowa City, Iowa: University Associates Press, 1969, pp. 9–10.

Leaders in Quadrant 1 have little concern for people but great concern for accomplishing the task. Those in Quadrant 2 have high concern for both people and task. Those in Quadrant 3 have high concern for people but little concern for task. Those in Quadrant 4 have little concern for either people or task.

The general idea of this theory is that although both task and people are significant concerns, each situation will call for a somewhat different combination of task and people concerns. Some situations, for example, will call for high concentration on task issues but will need little in the way of people encouragement. For example, a group of scientists working on AIDS research would probably need a leader who provides them with the needed information to accomplish their task. They would be self-motivating and would probably need little in the way of social and emotional encouragement. On the other hand, a group of recovering alcoholics might require leadership that stresses the social and emotional needs of the members.

In this view, leadership effectiveness depends on combining the concerns for task and people according to the specifics of the situation—hence, the "situational theory of leadership." The most successful leader is the leader who is flexible and who can adapt his or her leadership style to the unique demands of the situation.

Leadership Styles

In addition to looking at the concerns of leadership for both task and function, as we did with the situational theory of leadership, we can also look at leadership in terms of its three major styles: laissez-faire, democratic, and authoritarian (Bennis & Nanus, 1985; Shaw, 1981).

Laissez-Faire Leader   As a laissez-faire leader you would take no initiative in directing or suggesting alternative courses of action. Rather, you would allow the group to develop and progress on its own, even allowing it to make its own mistakes. You would in effect give up or deny any real authority. As a laissez-faire leader you would answer questions or provide relevant information, but only when specifically asked. You would give little if any reinforcement to the group members. At the same time you would not punish members either. As a result you would be seen as nonthreatening.

Democratic Leader   As a democratic leader you would provide direction but allow the group to develop and progress the way its members wish. You would encourage group members to determine their own goals and procedures. You would stimulate self-direction and self-actualization of the group members. Unlike the laissez-faire leader, a democratic leader would give members reinforcement and contribute suggestions for direction and alternative courses of action. Always, however, you would allow the group to make its own decisions.

Authoritarian Leader   As an authoritarian leader you would be the opposite of the laissez-faire leader. You would determine the group policies or makes decisions without consulting or securing agreement from the members. You would be impersonal and would encourage communication that goes to you and from you but not from member to member; you would seek to minimize intragroup communication. In this way, you would enhance your own importance.

As an authoritarian leader you assume the greatest responsibility for the progress of the group and would not want interference from members. You would be concerned with getting the group to accept your decisions rather than making its own decisions. You might satisfy the group's psychological needs. You would reward and punish the group much as a parent does.

Effectiveness and Leadership Styles   A number of important studies have examined the relative effectiveness of these various leadership styles. For example, in one classic investigation groups of boys led by the three different styles were studied (White & Lippitt, 1960). The researchers found that in the laissez-faire group, the discussion was member-centered but the boys were inefficient. In the democratic group, cohesiveness was greatest, as was member satisfaction. The work completed, however, was less than that produced by the authoritarian group. In the authoritarian group, the boys were most productive and efficient. However, morale and satisfaction were lower than in the democratic group. It has also been found that groups led by an authoritarian leader make fewer errors, take less time, and communicate with fewer messages in solving mathematical problems than democratic groups (Shaw, 1955).

Cecil Gibb (1969), in summarizing the results of a series of studies on democratic as opposed to authoritarian leadership, notes that the authoritarian group produced "(1) a greater quantity of work, but (2) less work motivation and (3) less originality in work; (4) a greater amount of aggressiveness expressed both toward the leader and other group members; (5) more suppressed discontent; (6) more dependent and submissive behavior; (7) less friendliness in the group; and (8) less 'group mindedness.'"

Each of these leadership styles has its place; one style should not be considered superior to the others. Each is appropriate for a different purpose and for a different situation. In a social group at a friend's house, any leadership other than laissez-faire would be difficult to tolerate. But, when speed and efficiency are paramount, authoritarian leadership may be more appropriate.

Authoritarian leadership may also be more appropriate when group members continue to show lack of motivation toward the task despite democratic efforts to move them. When all members are about equal in their knowledge of the topic or when the members are very concerned with their individual rights, the democratic leadership style seems more appropriate.

Leader's Functions: Task and People

With this situational view of leadership and the three general styles of leadership in mind, we can look at some of the major functions leaders serve. In relatively formal small group situations, as when politicians plan a strategy, advertisers discuss a campaign, or teachers consider educational methods, the leader has several specific functions.

These functions are not the exclusive property of the leader. Nevertheless, when there is a specific leader, he or she is expected to perform them. Leadership functions are performed best when they are performed unobtrusively—in a natural manner. Leaders carry out both task and people functions.

Activate Group Interaction   Many groups need some prodding and stimulation to interact. Perhaps the group is newly formed and the members feel a bit uneasy with one another. As the group leader you would stimulate the members to interact. You would also serve this function when members act as individuals rather than as a group. In this case you would want to focus the members on their group task.

Maintain Effective Interaction   Even after the group is stimulated to group interaction, you would strive to see that members maintain effective interaction. When the discussion begins to drag, you would prod the group to effective interaction: "Do we have any additional comments on the proposal to eliminate required courses?" "What do those of you who are members of the college curriculum committee think about the English Department's proposal to restructure required courses?" "Does anyone want to make any additional comments on eliminating the minor area of concentration?" As the leader you would want to ensure that all members have an opportunity to express themselves.

Keep Members on the Track   Many individuals are egocentric and will pursue only their own interests and concerns. As the leader it would be your task to keep all members reasonably on track. You might accomplish this by asking questions, by interjecting internal summaries as the group goes along, or by providing transitions so that the relationship of an issue just discussed to one about to be considered is clear. In some problem-solving and educational groups, a formal agenda may be used to assist you in serving this function.

Ensure Member Satisfaction   Members have different psychological needs and wants, and many people enter groups to satisfy these personal concerns. Even though a group may, for example, deal with political issues, the members may have come together for reasons that are more psychological than political. If a group is to be effective, it must meet not only the surface purposes of the group, but also the underlying or interpersonal purposes that motivated many of the members to come together in the first place.

One sure way to meet these needs is for you as the leader to allow digressions and personal comments, assuming they are not too frequent or overly long.

Encourage Ongoing Evaluation and Improvement   Most groups encounter obstacles as they try to solve a problem, reach a decision, or generate ideas. Most groups could use some improvement. If the group is to improve, it must focus on itself. Along with trying to solve some external problem, it must try to solve its own internal problems as well, for example, personal conflicts, failure of members to meet on time, or members who come unprepared. As the leader you would try to identify any such difficulties and encourage and help the group to resolve them.

Prepare Members for the Discussion   Groups form gradually and need to be eased into meaningful discussion. As the leader you may need to prepare group members for the discussion. This may involve preparing the members for the small group interaction as well as for the discussion of a specific issue or problem.

Diverse members should not be expected to sit down and discuss a problem without becoming familiar with each other. Similarly, if members are to discuss a specific problem, it is necessary that a proper briefing take place. Perhaps materials need to be distributed before the actual discussion. Or perhaps you would tell members to read certain materials or view a particular film or television show. Whatever the preparations, you would need to organize and coordinate them.

LEADERSHIP EVALUATION FORM

Introductory Remarks							
Introduces topic(s)	YES!	YES	yes	?	no	NO	NO!
Introduces members	YES!	YES	yes	?	no	NO	NO!
Explains procedures	YES!	YES	yes	?	no	NO	NO!
Gets group going	YES!	YES	yes	?	no	NO	NO!
Maintenance of Interaction							
Keeps members on schedule	YES!	YES	yes	?	no	NO	NO!
Keeps to agenda	YES!	YES	yes	?	no	NO	NO!
Communication Guidance							
Encourages conflict resolution	YES!	YES	yes	?	no	NO	NO!
Ensures member understanding	YES!	YES	yes	?	no	NO	NO!
Involves all members	YES!	YES	yes	?	no	NO	NO!
Encourages expression of differences	YES!	YES	yes	?	no	NO	NO!
Uses transitions	YES!	YES	yes	?	no	NO	NO!
Development of Effective Interpersonal Climate							
Works for member satisfaction	YES!	YES	yes	?	no	NO	NO!
Builds open atmosphere	YES!	YES	yes	?	no	NO	NO!
Encourages supportiveness	YES!	YES	yes	?	no	NO	NO!
Ongoing Evaluation and Improvement							
Encourages process suggestions	YES!	YES	yes	?	no	NO	NO!
Accepts disagreements	YES!	YES	yes	?	no	NO	NO!
Directs group self-evaluation	YES!	YES	yes	?	no	NO	NO!
Encourages improvement	YES!	YES	yes	?	no	NO	NO!
Concluding Remarks							
Summarizes	YES!	YES	yes	?	no	NO	NO!
[Involves audience]	YES!	YES	yes	?	no	NO	NO!
Closes discussion	YES!	YES	yes	?	no	NO	NO!
Improvement Suggestions							

FIGURE 17.2 Leadership evaluation form

Table 17.6 Qualities of the Effective Leader

An effective leader:	
Values people	Acknowledges the importance of and the contributions of others
Listens actively	Works hard at understanding the wants and concerns of others.
Is tactful	Criticizes sparingly, constructively, and courteously.
Gives credit	Praises others and their contributions publicly.
Is consistent	Controls personal moods; treats others similarly; does not play favorites.
Admits mistakes	Willingly admits errors
Has a sense of humor	Maintains a pleasant disposition and an approachable manner.
Sets a good example	Does what others are expected to do.

In addition to these six functions—a mixture of task and people functions—as an effective leader you would relate to group members in ways that encourage effective interaction. Nido Qubein (1986) provides a useful analysis of the general qualities of the effective leader (Table 17.6). These qualities, together with the six functions already considered, should round out what makes an effective leader the specific functions the leader should serve and the qualities that the leader should demonstrate.

Figure 17.2 presents a form I use in small group communication courses to evaluate the effectiveness of the group leader. As with the group member evaluation form, this leadership form should serve to summarize the wide variety of functions a group leader is expected to serve.

FACTORS THAT WORK AGAINST SMALL GROUP EFFECTIVENESS

Small group communication researchers Bobby Patton, Kim Giffin, and Eleanor Patton (1989) have identified those factors that limit the effectiveness of the small group. These factors are presented here in brief. In examining these factors you will get an additional perspective on the roles and functions of both members and leaders.

Procedural problems include *role conflicts* (where members might compete for leadership positions or where members are unclear as to their functions), *problem analysis* (where members short-circuit the process of analyzing the problem), and *evaluating proposals* (where members evaluate proposals without agreement on the criteria for judging proposals and solutions).

Process problems include *too little cohesion* (when members lack affiliation with each other and may leave the group), *too much cohesion* (when members may ignore problems in the interest of maintaining group interpersonal relationships), *conformity pressures* (when members seek to conform and may not voice legitimate differences of opinion and disagreements), and *logical process problems* (when members might misunderstand the nature of the problem or reject accurate information).

Personality problems involve *members who are reticent to express themselves* or *disagreements that are taken personally*.

Summary

1. A popular classification of small group *member roles* divides them into *group task roles, group building and maintenance roles,* and *individual roles.*

2. Twelve *group task roles* are: initiator-contributor, information seeker, opinion seeker, information giver, opinion giver, elaborator, coordinator, orienter, evaluator-critic, energizer, procedural technician, and recorder.

3. Seven *group building and maintenance roles* are: encourager, harmonizer, compromiser, gatekeeper-expediter, standard setter or ego ideal, group observer and commentator, and follower.

4. Eight *individual roles* are: aggressor, blocker, recognition seeker, self-confessor, playboy or playgirl, dominator, help seeker, and special-interest pleader.

5. Interaction process analysis categorizes contributions into four areas: social-emotional positive, social-emotional negative, attempted answers, and questions.

6. *Member participation* should be group-oriented, should center conflict on issues, should be critically open-minded, and should ensure understanding.

7. *Groupthink* may be defined as "the mode of thinking that persons engage in when *concurrence seeking* becomes so dominant in a cohesive ingroup that it tends to override realistic appraisal of alternative courses of action."

8. In the *situational theory of leadership,* leadership is seen as concerned with accomplishing the task and serving the interpersonal needs of the members. The degree to which either concern is emphasized should depend on the specific group, on the unique situation.

9. Three major *leadership styles* are: *laissez-faire, democratic,* and *authoritarian.*

10. Among the *leader's functions* are: to activate the group interaction, maintain effective interaction, keep members on the track, ensure member satisfaction, encourage ongoing evaluation and improvement, and prepare members for the discussion.

11. The effective leader values people, listens actively, is tactful, gives credit, is consistent, admits mistakes, has a sense of humor, and sets a good example.

Applications

17.1   USING THE IPA SYSTEM OF ANALYSIS

The aim of this experience is to gain some practice in using Bales's system of interaction process analysis. Five or six students should engage in a problem-solving discussion. The rest of the class should carefully observe the group interaction and record the types of contributions each person makes using the form presented below. In the column under each participant's name, place a slash mark for each contribution in one of the twelve categories. An alternative procedure is to have the entire class watch a film such as *Twelve Angry Men* or *The Breakfast Club* and classify the contributions of the characters in the film. After the discussion, a general discussion should center on the following:

1. Does IPA enable you to identify the different types of contributions that individual members make during a discussion?

2. Can you offer suggestions for individual members based on this interaction process analysis?

3. Are the members of the discussion group surprised at the types of contributions they made?

Interaction Process Analysis Form	P	W	R	D	L
Social-Emotional Positive					
shows solidarity	✓✓	✓			
shows tension release					
shows agreement	✓✓	✓			
Social-Emotional Negative					
shows disagreement		✓✓		✓✓	✓✓✓
shows tension	✓		✓	✓✓✓	
shows antagonism				✓	
Attempted Answers					
gives suggestions	✓✓	✓✓			
gives opinions		✓✓✓✓	✓	✓✓	✓
gives information	✓	✓✓✓✓	✓	✓	
Questions					
asks for suggestions		✓	✓		
asks for opinions			✓		✓
asks for information	✓✓✓		✓	✓✓	✓

17.2 SMALL GROUP ROLES

The following dialogue was written to illustrate the general types of roles that members and leaders may serve in a small group situation. Read through the dialogue, paying special attention to the functions served by each member's comments. Then, alone or in small groups consider the questions following the dialogue.

TASKER: Well, we'd better get down to designing a package for this new aftershave lotion. Does anyone have any suggestions?

GROTASK: I understand the lotion is especially addressed to men in their 20s and 30s. Is that right?

TASKER: Yes, and the manufacturer especially wants the product targeted to the young executive and middle-management types.

GREETING: Oh, right; that's important to know.

SELFORD: Yuppies, I can't stand yuppies.

PEARSON: How do think we should attack this problem?

SELFORD: Yeah, I have an idea; let's go to work for a real ad agency.

GREETING: Well, we're a great creative team; we'll come up with the right solution. I think it really has to be unique; I mean it's got to look totally different from anything else on the market.

SELFORD: Are we really going to be able to do this? I don't think we're going to be able to accomplish this by the end of this week. I mean it's an impossible (not to say meaningless) task.

TASKER: Let's get to the task. First, we need to define the image we want to create for the lotion and then we can consider colors, the structure of the main dispenser, the material for the dispenser, the packaging, and so on. Another team will handle the ad copy and media buying.

PEARSON: Does anyone want coffee before we begin?

TASKER: I think we'd better get to the work instead of the coffee. Let's go around the group and identify what we each think would be a good image to present for the lotion. Selford, let's start with you.

SELFORD: How about "homelessness."

TASKER: How about being serious and not so flippant? You know, I'm really getting tired of your always degrading what we do. If you don't want to participate then let us know and get out.

PEARSON: Tasker, you want a general type of attitude or personality characteristic. Is that right?

TASKER: Yes, that's exactly what we want.

SELFORD: Okay, okay. How about "intellectualism." Instead of the typical image of the strong macho type, how about appealing to the intellectual side of man?

GREETING: That's a great idea.

GROTASK: I'll write that down.

PEARSON: Now we're starting to get going.

TASKER: Grotask, you're next.

GROTASK: How about "sensitive and brooding"?

GREETING: Yes, I like that. That's a fabulous idea.

TASKER: Okay, Greeting what do you think?

GREETING: I like the two suggestions already made. Either one is good with me.

TASKER: Greeting, you really have to contribute specific ideas or we'll never get this job done. At any rate, Pearson, what do you think?

PEARSON: I was going to say "intellectualism" myself. But, I like the "sensitive and brooding" too.

TASKER: All right, let's go with the intellectualism at least for now.

The second task is to develop ideas for packaging. Let's look at color.

GROTASK: What's the name of this lotion? Isn't that going to influence the colors we use?

TASKER: The name is chosen after the image is created and part of that image is the general packaging. Talk to me about color. Think color. What should the dominant colors of the package be?

GROTASK: How about different shades of blue? It's masculine but not too much so.

SELFORD: Blue? Blue? No, blue is ugly. Anything but blue.

GREETING: Blue is a good color, but it may be wrong.

TASKER: Let's go through the spectrum and see what we think of each of the primary colors. Okay? ROY G BIV. What about red?

SELFORD: Red's inappropriate; it's not masculine. Besides, red was my last boss's favorite color and I've come to hate anything red.

GROTASK: Isn't Marlboro directed at men? And that's red.

SELFORD: If you people want red, pick red. But, it's wrong; not intellectual.

GROTASK: What about gray?

TASKER: Gray isn't a primary color and anyway we need to go in order. Red is the first color. How do you others feel about red?

GREETING: I like it. But, it may not be intellectual enough. But, I think it's a good color.

PEARSON: That may be true. Do you want to consider orange?

SELFORD: No.

GROTASK: Does anyone know the meanings for the different colors?

TASKER: Maybe this is a good time to take lunch. I'll get the studies on the meanings of color and we can look at them after lunch. Let's meet back here at 1:30 sharp.

Questions for Thought and Discussion

1. What types of roles are each of the members playing? Cite specific elements of dialogue to support your decisions. Compare your findings and conclusions with those of other analysts. On which do you agree? On which do you differ? Can you come to a general consensus?

2. If you were a member of a similar discussion group, what member would your own behavior most resemble? Least resemble?

3. Can you identify the productive and the destructive contributions of each member? How would you justify your conclusions as to which specific behavior is productive or destructive?

4. What advice for increasing small group effectiveness would you give to each group member? Why?

ORGANIZATIONAL COMMUNICATION

UNIT CONTENTS

Organization and Organizational Communication: Definitions

Approaches to Organizations

Communication Networks

Communication Flow in Organizations

  Summary

  Application
    18.1   Communication Networks

UNIT GOALS

After completing this unit, you should be able to

1. define an *organization* and *organizational communication*

2. describe the scientific, behavioral, systems, and cultural approaches to organizations

3. define and describe five communication network structures and describe the ways in which these structures influence communication

4. define *upward, downward, lateral,* and *grapevine communication* and *information overload,* and identify the major problems and effectiveness guidelines for dealing with each

In his landmark book, *The Functions of the Executive* (1938), Chester Barnard observed: "In an exhaustive theory of organization, communication would occupy a central place, because the structure, extensiveness, and scope of organization are almost entirely determined by communication techniques." In this unit we explain this central position of communication by covering a number of interrelated topics of an area now called "organizational communication." First, we define organizations and organizational communication. Second, we explore four approaches to organizations, looking specifically at the role communication plays in each. Third, we examine communication patterns (networks) and their influence on productivity and morale. Fourth, we consider the issue of communication flow: upward, downward, lateral, and grapevine communication, and information overload.

ORGANIZATION AND ORGANIZATIONAL COMMUNICATION: DEFINITIONS

To understand organizational communication, we need to define what an organization is and what characterizes the communication within organizations.

The Organization

An **organization** may be defined as a group of individuals organized for the achievement of specific goals. The number of individuals varies greatly from one organization to another. Some have three or four members working in close contact. Others have thousands of workers scattered throughout the world. What is important is that these individuals operate within a defined structure.

The level of structure also varies greatly from one organization to another. In rigidly structured organizations, each person's role and position within the hierarchy is clearly defined. In more loosely structured organizations, roles may be interchanged, and hierarchical status may be unclear and relatively unimportant. Figure 18.1 depicts a representative organizational chart of a publishing company, which clearly shows the hierarchical structure of an organization and how the varied functions of the organization are related and coordinated. The organizational chart is a kind of road map for message travel; it visualizes the routes that messages—at least the formal ones—generally take. It also, of course, visualizes the power structure and identifies who is in charge of whom and where the decision-making power lies.

Within any organization, there are both formal and informal structures. For example, in a college there is the formal academic structure, with the president at the top, the provost at the next level, deans at the next, department chairpersons at the next, and faculty at the next. Through this structure the work of the university is accomplished; the president communicates to the provost who communicates to the deans, and so on. But, there are also informal structures throughout the university, and in many cases these cross hierarchical lines. These might include, for example, the four math professors who bowl together, the sociology instructor and the dean of arts who attend AA meetings together, and the graduate assistants and junior faculty members who study together. These informal structures serve the human needs of the individuals and keep the workers together as a unit.

The goal of most organizations is to make money. A variety of subordinate goals, however, must be achieved if this ultimate goal is to be reached. Thus, for example, in

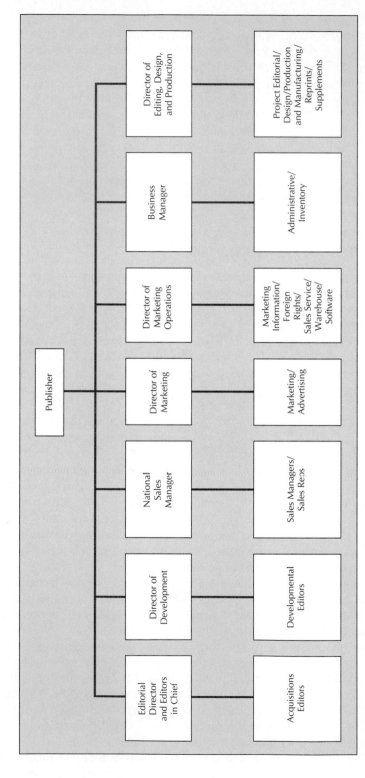

FIGURE 18.1 Organization of HarperCollins College Publishers.

order to make money, the organization must maintain an effective work force. To do this, it is necessary to have satisfied workers. To have satisfied workers, it may be necessary to have adequate parking facilities, merit bonuses, clean and safe working conditions, and so on.

A nonprofit organization, on the other hand, would have as its ultimate goal something other than making money. For example, the goal may be to disseminate information, offer legal counsel to the poor, or defend animal rights. In these cases, the goal of obtaining funds would probably be a subordinate one, necessary to achieve if these other goals are to be realized.

Each worker in each organization will naturally have different goals. The ultimate goal for most people is to earn a salary. Like organizations, workers, too, have subordinate goals that are usually consistent with this general goal. So workers may have such goals as to perform a job well, to get a promotion, to interact with others in pleasant surroundings, or to develop a network of friends.

The goals of the organization and the worker are often compatible. For example, performing a job well and thus earning a promotion is consistent with the organization's goal of increasing productivity and earning more money. But sometimes these goals are incompatible. For example, workers may want raises, which means less profit for the organization. These goals of both the organization as a whole and the individual workers—and their frequent reconciliation—are achieved largely through the formal and informal communication that takes place within the organization.

Organizational Communication

Organizational communication refers to the messages sent and received within the organization's formal and informal groups. As the organization becomes larger and more complex, so do the communications. In a three-person organization communication is relatively simple, but in an organization of thousands it becomes highly complex. Organizational communication includes such varied activities as giving directions, counseling workers, interviewing new employees, evaluating personnel, motivating people, analyzing problems, resolving conflicts, and establishing and monitoring work groups. As can be appreciated organizational communication relies upon the skills of interpersonal, small group, and public communication discussed throughout this text.

Organizational communication may be both formal and informal. The *formal communications* are those that are sanctioned by the organization itself and are organizationally oriented. They deal with the workings of the organization, with productivity, and with the various jobs done throughout the organization: memos, policy statements, press releases, employee newsletters. The *informal communications* are socially sanctioned. They are oriented not to the organization itself, but to the individual members.

Sexual Harassment   A special kind of communication, most often considered within the organizational context, though it can also occur outside this context—for example, in the classroom or on the street—is sexual harassment.

Ellen Bravo and Ellen Cassedy (1992) define sexual harassment as "bothering someone in a sexual way. The harasser offers sexual attention to someone who didn't ask for it and doesn't welcome it. The unwelcome behavior might or might not involve touching. It could just as well be spoken words, graphics, gestures or even looks (not any look—but the kind of leer or stare that says, 'I want to undress you')."

As Bravo and Cassedy point out, sexual harassment is most often directed against women by men but it may also be directed against women by other women or against men by either men or women. Insulting, ridiculing, or intimidating someone because of his or her sex constitutes sexual harassment. Note that for behavior to constitute sexual harassment, it need not be intentional.

For example, Fred may think his sexual jokes are very funny and that everyone in the office enjoys them and so he continues to tell such jokes. But if Maria finds such repeated behavior offensive (and, legal experts like to add, if Maria is a reasonable person or represents the judgment of reasonable people), the behavior constitutes sexual harassment. Simply informing Fred that his sexual jokes are not appreciated and are seen as offensive may be sufficient to make him stop this joke telling. Unfortunately, in some instances such criticism goes unheeded and the offensive behavior continues.

The Civil Rights Act of 1964 made sexual harassment illegal in its prohibition of discrimination on the basis of religion, color, race, national origin, or sex. The Civil Rights Act of 1991 made harassment victims eligible to collect damages.

Three suggestions for avoiding behaviors that might be considered as sexual harassment will help to further clarify the concept and to prevent its occurrence (Bravo & Cassedy, 1992):

- Begin with the assumption that others at work are not interested in your sexual advances, sexual stories and jokes, or sexual gestures.
- Listen and watch for negative reactions to any sexually related discussion. Use the suggestions and techniques discussed throughout this book to discover any such reactions. And, of course, when in doubt, ask questions.
- Avoid behaviors that you think would/might prove offensive to your parent, partner, or child should they be working with someone who engages in such behavior.

Mary Gill and William Wardrope (1992) suggest that you consider such nonverbal behaviors as looking a person with "elevator eyes" (up and down), displaying sexually graphic pictures, making hand and body gestures that are sexual in nature, hugging or patting another, or rubbing up against another.

Although we have defined organizational communication as occurring *within* the organization, organizations also spend considerable time, energy, and money on securing information from outside and on disseminating information to other organizations and to the general public. Although these outgoing messages are organizationally motivated, they are probably best treated as examples of public, mass, or even interpersonal communication, depending on the situation.

APPROACHES TO ORGANIZATIONS

We can approach organizations from at least four perspectives: the scientific management or classical approach, the behavioral or human relations approach, the systems approach, and the cultural approach (Goldhaber, 1990).

The Scientific Approach

This approach holds that organizations should make use of scientific methods to increase productivity. Scientifically controlled studies help management identify the ways and means for increasing productivity and ultimately profit.

In this view productivity is viewed in terms of the physical demands of the job and the physiological capabilities of the workers. Time-and-motion studies are perhaps the most characteristic type of research. These studies are designed to enable the organization to reduce the time it takes to complete a specific task—to cut down the motion and to best fit the person to the task. Frederick Taylor (1911), to whom the scientific management approach owes much of its development and from which industrial engineering grew, for example, conducted time-and-motion studies of coal shoveling. He analyzed and compared different sizes of shovels and the various tasks to be accomplished. As a result, he was able to reduce the number of workers needed to do the same work from between 400 and 600 to 140.

In this approach, communication is viewed as the giving of orders and the explaining of procedures and operations. Only the formal structure of the organization and the formal communication system are recognized.

Today the scientific management approach is held in disfavor largely because it emphasizes productivity over the needs of the workers and also because it was an approach better suited to manufacturing than to our present information technologies. As one management expert puts it: "The acquisition, storage, handling, and retrieval of information has become the main industry in the United States, with well over 65 percent of the workforce employed in information-related jobs" (Montana, 1991).

The Behavioral Approach

The **behavioral approach** (also referred to as *the humanistic, organic,* or *human relations approach*) developed as a reaction against the exclusive concern with physical factors in measuring organizational success. One of the principal assumptions of this approach is that increases in worker satisfaction lead to increases in productivity: A happy worker is a productive worker. Management's function, therefore, is to keep the workers happy.

Since leaders establish the norms that group members follow, control of leadership is considered one of the best ways to increase satisfaction and production. Management tries to influence the leaders, who then influence the workers to be happy and hence productive. The behavioral approach strongly favors the democratic leader. This leader encourages members to participate in the running of the organization by offering suggestions, giving feedback, and sharing their problems and complaints. What is desired is "participatory management" (Likert, 1971). All members of the organization are to participate in the decisions that ultimately affect them. Communication is one of the main tools in this endeavor.

Another reason for the importance of communication was advanced by Chester Barnard's (1938) "acceptance theory of authority"—a principle that held that workers will perform effectively and accept management's directives if they feel these are acceptable to their personal needs and goals. Hence, a prime task of management was to communicate this acceptability to its workers, to persuade them to see that the company's goals would advance their personal goals.

The behavioral approach acknowledges the importance of the social, informal groups within the organization and gives special consideration to the interpersonal communications within the subgroups of these organizations.

But even in this seemingly best of all possible worlds, where the communication is free and the leadership democratic, the human relations school encountered difficulties. The major problem was that the approach was based on an invalid assumption—namely, that satisfaction and productivity were positively related. They are in some cases, but certainly not in all. As you know from your own courses, there are some classes in which you are very productive, learn a great deal, and do well, but that you simply do not enjoy. And there are others you enjoy, but from which you gain little. Another problem with the human relations approach is that it gives too much attention to agreement. It fails to recognize the very important contribution played by conflict and competition. Some authorities go so far as to claim that "the relationship between productivity and satisfaction is close to zero" (Strauss & Sayles, 1980).

At this point you may wish to take the self-test, "What Kind of Manager Are You?" It will provide an additional perspective on some of the issues we have just discussed.

The Systems Approach

The systems approach combines the best elements of the scientific and behavioral approaches. It views an organization as a system in which all parts interact and in which each part influences every other part. This view is the same view we take of communication (see Unit 1). The organization is viewed as an open system—open to new information, responsive to the environment, dynamic and ever-changing.

The systems approach argues that both the physical and physiological factors of the scientific management approach and the social and psychological factors of the behavioral approach are important. Each influences the others. All must be taken into consideration if a fully functioning organization is to be achieved.

In this approach, communication keeps the system vital and alive. If a system is to survive, its parts to be coordinated, and its activities synchronized, communication is essential. Communication relates the various parts to each other and brings in the new ideas.

The Cultural Approach

A contemporary approach to organizations holds that a corporation should be viewed as a society or a culture (Pilotta, Widman, & Jasko, 1988; Putnam & Pacanowsky, 1983). Much as a social group or culture has rules of behaviors, roles, rituals, heroes, and values, for example, so does an organization. In this approach, then, an organization is studied to identify the type of culture it is and its specific norms or values. The aim of such an analysis is to enable us to understand the ways the organization functions and how it influences and is influenced by the members (workers) of that organizational culture.

We can make educated guesses about what makes a successful corporation by examining those qualities that make for a successful social group or society. For example, heroes are important to a social group and successful corporations can sometimes create their own. If an organization can create a hero—perhaps like Thomas Edison to General Electric, Henry Ford to Ford Motors, and Lee Iacocca to Chrysler—it may succeed in developing a dominant culture (or corporation).

SELF-TEST

X or Y? What Kind of Manager Are You?

Respond to each of the following statements with T (true) if you believe the statement is generally or usually true and F (false) if you believe the statement is generally or usually false.

The average worker:

T   1. will avoid work if possible.

T   2. will accept and even seek responsibility.

F   3. must be persuaded, even motivated by fear, to do work.

T   4. feels that physical and mental effort exerted in work is as natural as play.

_____ 5. has little real ambition.

_____ 6. will direct herself or himself to achieve objectives she or he accepts.

_____ 7. wants to be directed as a way of avoiding responsibility.

_____ 8. is creative and imaginative.

_____ 9. dislikes work.

_____ 10. is capable (and willing) to learn new tasks.

Scoring These statements refer to the theories labeled theory X and theory Y by Douglas McGregor (1980). Theory X holds that the worker is unmotivated and really does not want to work; theory Y holds that the worker is motivated and responsible and is represented by the behavioral or humanistic view of management. The odd-numbered statements (1, 3, 5, 7, 9) all refer to a belief in theory X and the even-numbered statements (2, 4, 6, 8, 10) to a belief in theory Y. To which statements did you give more true responses? If to odd-numbered statements, then you have a strong belief in theory X; if to even-numbered statements, then you have a strong belief in theory Y.

There is also a theory Z, identified most clearly by William Ouchi (1981), which characterizes Japanese management style. Some of the major features of theory Z is a focus on the entire organization rather than on just one's own department, group rather than individual decision making and responsibility, and the expansion of career opportunities (rather than specialization) within the organization.

The cultural perspective views both the organization and the workers as having a similar set of values and goals. Much like citizens of a country, workers contribute to the growth and prosperity of the organization. Workers also, however, reap the benefits of this growth and prosperity. Worker morale and productivity, therefore, go hand in hand. They are not separate and isolated goals but integrally related ones.

In this view, communication is not simply messages that are sent from one member to another through one or more channels (as conceived in some network analyses). Rather, communication is seen as integral to the very definition of an organization. Communication, in fact, defines and constructs the organization, its divisions, and its functions. The organization is not something apart from its workers and its communications. Rather, the organization is created and takes its form from its workers and their communication interactions.

How would you describe your college as a culture? What are its accepted rules of behavior? What roles does it expect you to serve? Who are its heroes? What are its values?

The characteristics of an effective organizational culture include, for example, teamwork, pride in work and in accomplishment, commitment to high standards and to the organization, honesty, and a willingness to change in order to grow despite difficulties from competition or regulations (Uris, 1986).

In one of the most popular books on the topic of organizations, *In Search of Excellence: Lessons from America's Best-Run Companies,* Thomas Peters and Robert Waterman make great use of this view of corporations as cultures—though they use other approaches and perspectives as well—and propose that excellent corporations are characterized by eight qualities. A review of these qualities should effectively round out our discussion of approaches to organizations. In reviewing these qualities, try to identify the organizational approach each derives from or supports and how communication can foster each. Excellent companies do the following:

1. *They have a bias for action.* These companies prefer action to lengthy surveys, reports, and committee meetings.
2. *They stay close to the customer.* These companies listen to their customers and try to provide the quality and service that the customers want.
3. *They encourage leaders who are autonomous and entrepreneurial.* These companies encourage practical risk taking and creativity in their workers.
4. *They achieve productivity through people.* These companies regard the rank-and-file members as the major source of productivity; sharp divisions between management and labor are discouraged.

5. *They encourage hands-on management.* In these companies management knows what is going on because management stays close to the main operations of the company, for example, visiting the stores and inspecting the plants.

6. *They stick to what they know.* These companies know the business the company is in and do not attempt to involve themselves in operations about which they are not expert.

7. *They have simple organizational structures and are lean at the top.* These companies are structured very simply, without a complicated organizational structure to create problems, and with a relatively small staff at the top of the hierarchy.

8. *They are decentralized (loose) and centralized (tight).* These companies are generally decentralized in that the workers are relatively autonomous but they are highly centralized in terms of their goals and their values.

COMMUNICATION NETWORKS

Because of their rigidly structured hierarchies, the large physical distances between people, the great differences in competence, and the specialized tasks that must be accomplished, organizations have evolved a number of different communication networks (Baird, 1977; Kreps, 1990). By a *network*, we mean the channels through which messages pass from one person to another. These networks may be viewed from two perspectives. First, small groups left to their own resources will develop communication patterns resembling these several network structures. These networks, then, represent some of the most commonly used systems of communication that groups use to send messages from one person to another. Second, these networks may be viewed as formalized structures established by an organization for communication within the company.

With either perspective, recognize that these networks represent general types of group communication patterns and can be found in most groups and in most organizations. Five major networks are examined briefly, first in terms of structure and second in terms of their actual operation within an organization.

The Network Structures

The five network structures are presented in Figure 18.2. Each diagram shows five individuals, although each network may include any number of people. The arrows indicate the direction the messages may travel.

The Circle The circle has no leader. There is total equality. All members of the circle have exactly the same authority or power to influence the group. Each member may communicate with the two members on either side.

The Wheel The wheel has a clear leader (central position). This person is the only one who can send and receive messages to all members. Therefore, if one member wishes to communicate with another member, the message must go through the leader.

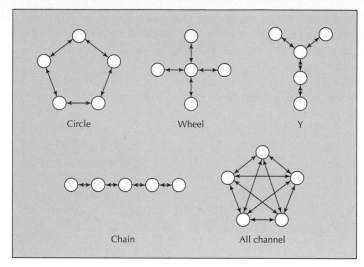

FIGURE 18.2 Five network structures.

The Y   The Y pattern is less centralized than the wheel but more centralized than some of the other patterns we'll look at. In the Y there is also a clear leader (the third person from the bottom in Figure 18.2). But one other member plays a type of secondary leadership role (the second person from the bottom). This member can send and receive messages from two others. The remaining three members are restricted to communicating with only one other person.

The Chain   The chain is similar to the circle except that the members on the ends may communicate with only one person each. There is some centrality here. The middle position is more leaderlike than any of the other positions.

The All-Channel   The all-channel or star pattern is like the circle in that all members are equal and all have exactly the same amount of power to influence others. In the all-channel, however, each member may communicate with any other member. This pattern allows for the greatest member participation.

Messages may be transmitted face to face, by telephone, or written in informal memos or in formal reports. Messages may be sent and responded to by computer. Groups may also communicate in a teleconference, wherein several members are simultaneously connected by telephone, or in a video teleconference, wherein each member can both see and hear the other members although they may be in separate offices, buildings, or cities.

Network Productivity and Morale

No network is good or bad in itself. They are all better viewed as useful or useless for specific tasks. For example, the highly centralized patterns—the wheel and the Y—are most efficient for dealing with relatively simple and repetitive tasks, such as those in which information must be collected in one place and disseminated to others. Information overload, to be discussed later, is most likely to occur in the highly centralized groups, since all information is coming to one person. These central individuals often become gatekeepers and prevent information from getting to the various members. Sometimes this may be due simply to information overload. At other times the leader may decide not to pass information along to the group.

Those in the central positions seem to have relatively high morale. They do a lot of work, have the most power, and are the most satisfied. The others in these centralized groups, however, develop low morale since they do little and have little or no influence on the group. Members of an all-channel group, in contrast, usually have high morale.

All highly centralized groups depend on the effectiveness of the person in the central position. If that person is an effective leader-communicator, the success of the group as a whole is almost ensured. Conversely, if that person is ineffective, the entire group will suffer. In the all-channel pattern, however, the effectiveness or ineffectiveness of any one individual will not make or break the group.

Even the relationship between morale and participation or power may be oversimplified. For example, although morale is high when participation is high, as in the all-channel group, this group is inefficient in dealing with relatively simple and repetitive tasks. This inefficiency may well lead to a decline in morale, since few people want to be associated with an inefficient organization.

Some groups seem to adapt well to change, whereas others do not. Groups in the wheel pattern, for example, have difficulty adapting to changing tasks and changing

How does your college culture view productivity versus morale? How does your family culture view those concepts? Are you comfortable with these relative emphases, or would you like them to be different? In what ways?

conditions. But in the circle, where everyone is equal, the group adapts well. It accepts new ideas readily.

COMMUNICATION FLOW IN ORGANIZATIONS

It is useful to discuss communication in organizations in terms of the direction in which it flows. Upward and downward (also called vertical) communication and lateral communication are the formal channels, those that can be found in an organization chart, for example, and which are officially sanctioned by the organization. In addition, we also need to look at the grapevine—the informal channel that no organization seems to be without. Last, we look at information overload, a problem that is becoming more and more prevalent.

In most organizations, management controls the communication system. The managers have the time, the expertise, and the facilities to improve the communication that takes places in an organization. And it seems logical to assign the responsibility for an effective communication system to management. This is not to say that the workers are absolved of their responsibility; effective communication is a two-way process. Nevertheless, management bears the larger responsibility for establishing and maintaining an effective and efficient internal communication system.

Upward Communication

Upward communication refers to messages sent from the lower levels of the hierarchy to the upper levels—for example, line worker to manager, faculty member to dean. This type of communication is usually concerned with (1) job-related activities—that is, what is going on at the job, what was accomplished, what remains to be done, and similar issues; (2) job-related problems and unresolved questions; (3) ideas for change and suggestions for improvement; and (4) job-related feelings about the organization, about the work, about other workers, and similar issues.

Upward communication is vital to the maintenance and growth of the organization. It gives management the necessary feedback on worker morale and possible sources of dissatisfaction. It gives subordinates a sense of belonging to and being a part of the organization. And it provides management with the opportunity to acquire new ideas from line workers.

Problems with Upward Communication   Despite its importance to the organization, upward communication is difficult to handle. One problem is that messages that travel up the ladder are often messages that higher-ups want to hear. Workers are often reluctant to send up a negative message for fear that they will be viewed as troublemakers.

Often the messages that do get sent up, especially those concerning worker dissatisfaction, are not heard or responded to by management because of its preoccupation with productivity. When these messages are ignored, workers feel there is no point to sending them. Then dissatisfactions fester and become major problems.

Sometimes the messages never get through. Gatekeepers may be so rigid that certain types of messages are automatically rerouted. When the issues concern clarification of job assignments, many workers prefer to go to other workers rather than to management for fear that they will be thought incompetent. Students often do the

Here are two photos of Melanie Griffith in the movie *Working Girl*. In the photo on the left she is dressed as a secretary, and on the right as a top executive. Did the director and costume designer accurately reflect the way people in these two roles might appear in today's corporate culture? If you were the costume designer, what other distinctions, if any, would you seek to make?

same thing. Rather than ask the teacher to clarify something, they ask other students, who probably do not understand any better.

Still another problem is that management, preoccupied with sending messages down the ladder, may have lost some capacity for receiving messages. Managers are so used to serving as sources for messages that they become poor listeners. Workers easily sense this and, quite logically, don't waste their time on upward communication.

One further barrier is the purely physical one. Management is often physically separated from the workers. Usually management offices are on separate floors of the building; not infrequently, they are in other cities. It becomes difficult in such situations to go to management with a work-related problem that needs immediate attention.

Guidelines for Upward Communication   Important guidelines for improving upward communication can be easily derived from an analysis of the problems already identified. Here are the major ones:

- Some nonthreatening system for upward communication should be established. Many organizations, for example, have suggestion boxes that enable workers to voice their opinions and complaints anonymously. Another system is to actively seek out and reward workers' comments and to respond to these comments to show that they are received and are considered.

- Management must be open to hearing worker comments and must eliminate unnecessary gatekeepers that prevent important messages from traveling up the organizational hierarchy.
- Management must listen; management must receive, understand, remember, evaluate, and respond to worker messages.
- Convenient channels must be established for workers to communicate to management.

Downward Communication

Downward communication refers to messages sent from the higher levels of the hierarchy to the lower levels. For example, messages sent by managers to workers, or from deans to faculty members are examples of downward communication. Orders are the most obvious example of downward communication: "Type this in duplicate," "Send these crates out by noon," "Write the advertisement copy," and so on. Along with these order-giving messages are the accompanying explanations of procedures, goals, and the like. Managers are also responsible for giving appraisals of workers and for motivating them, all in the name of productivity and for the good of the organization as a whole.

Problems with Downward Communication Management and labor often speak different languages. Many managers simply do not know how to make their messages understandable to workers. Most managers, for example, have more education and a greater command of the technical language of the business than their workers do. Another problem is that many managers do not distinguish between information that workers need and do not need. Providing too little information will prevent the worker from functioning effectively. Providing too much information will bog the worker down and contribute to information overload.

Guidelines for Downward Communication Downward communication can be made more effective with the following suggestions:

- Management needs to use a vocabulary known to the workers. Technical jargon, for example, must be kept to a minimum. At the same time, many workers throughout the industrialized world are not native speakers of the managers' language and this needs to be taken into consideration.
- Provide workers with sufficient information for them to function effectively. At the same time, avoid contributing to information overload.

Lateral Communication

Lateral communication refers to messages between equals—manager to manager, worker to worker. Such messages may move within the same subdivision or department of the organization or across divisions. Lateral communication refers to the communication that takes place between two history professors at Illinois State University. It also refers to communication between the psychologist at Ohio State and the communicologist at Kent State.

Lateral communication facilitates the sharing of insights, methods, and problems. It helps the organization avoid some problems and to solve others. Lateral communication also builds morale and worker satisfaction. Good relationships and meaningful communication between workers are among the main sources of worker satisfaction. More generally, lateral communication serves the purpose of coordinating the various activities of the organization and enabling the various divisions to pool insights and expertise.

Problems with Lateral Communication   One obvious problem with lateral communication is the specialized languages that divisions of an organization may develop. Such languages are often unintelligible to receivers. To communicate with the psychologist, for example, it is essential to speak the language of psychology—to know the meaning of such terms as *reinforcement schedules, egoism, catharsis, STM,* and *free association.* Not everyone does. And as knowledge becomes increasingly specialized, it becomes increasingly difficult for the behavioral psychologist to understand the clinical psychologist and, even within clinical psychology, for the Freudian to understand the Jungian.

Another problem is the tendency of workers in a specialized organization to view their area as the one that is most important to the health and success of the company. This is often the case within a university. Each faculty member sees her or his department as the most important for the education of the student. This attitude prevents us from seeing the value in the work of others and often precludes a meaningful exchange of ideas.

Another barrier is that while effective lateral communication is a sharing and pooling of insights and resources, we work in competitive organizations. If there is only one promotion available and that promotion is to be made on the basis of quality of work accomplished, it really does not benefit workers to share their best insights.

Guidelines for Lateral Communication   To improve lateral communication, the following suggestions should prove helpful:

- Recognize that your own specialty has a technical jargon that others outside your specialty might not know. Clarify when and as needed.
- See the entire organizational picture and recognize the importance of all areas. Seeing one's own area as important and all others as unimportant does little to foster meaningful communication.
- Balance the needs of an organization that relies on cooperation and a system that rewards competition. In most cases it seems that cooperation can be increased without doing any individual damage.

Informal Communication: The Grapevine

The types of communication discussed so far follow the formal structure of the organization. **Grapevine** messages do not follow such formal lines. Rather, they seem to have a life of their own and are concerned with personal and social matters rather than with the organization itself. Grapevine communications grow along with the formal communications; the more active the formal communication system, the more active the information system. Not surprisingly, the grapevine also grows as the size of the organization increases.

The term *grapevine* seems to have originated during the Civil War, when telegraph wires were hung from tree to tree and resembled grapevines. Messages that travel through no organized structure also resemble the physical grapevine, with its unpredictable pattern of branches.

According to organizational theorist Keith Davis (1977, 1980), the grapevine seems most likely to be used when (1) there is great upheaval or change within the organization; (2) the information is new—no one likes to spread old and well-known information; (3) face-to-face communication is physically easy; and (4) workers "cluster in clique-groups along the vine." The grapevine is most active immediately after the happening that is to be communicated and is most likely to be activated when the news concerns one's intimates, friends, and associates. Although the grapevine is part of every large organization's informal communications, it is not used as frequently as folklore would have us believe (Baird, 1977). It is unlikely to grow in climates that are stable and comfortable. Change, ambiguity, and organizational secrecy nourish the grapevine.

Even more surprising than its relative infrequency of usage, however, is its reported accuracy. Approximately 75 to 95 percent of grapevine information is correct (Davis, 1980; Hellweg, 1992). Even though many details are omitted, the stories are basically true.

Problems with Grapevine Communication   One obvious problem with the grapevine is that it is difficult to discover the source of the original message because the message's route is so circuitous and cannot be easily traced. For this reason it is also often difficult to discover the truth or falsity of grapevine information.

What cultural rules do the people in this photo seem to be following? Would you be comfortable working for this type of organization?

Grapevine information is often incomplete (Hellweg, 1992) and may easily be distorted as it passes through its many users. The distortions we discussed earlier (Listening, Unit 5) can all damage the fidelity of the information as it passes from one receiver to another.

Grapevine information can often lead to morale problems because it may be leaked before the necessary groundwork has been laid or explanation offered. For example, the grapevine might report that the department will be reduced by five workers. The assumption that may be made is that five people will be fired, which logically enough could cause severe morale problems. But it may be that five workers are taking early retirement.

Guidelines for Grapevine Communication   Among the useful suggestions for dealing with the inevitable grapevine are these:

- Understand the role of the grapevine in the organization. For example, many managers view the grapevine as a great inconvenience. Actually, it serves useful purposes. "A lively grapevine," notes Davis (1980), "reflects the deep psychological need of people to talk about their jobs and their company as a central life interest. Without it, the company would literally be sick." Its speed and general accuracy make it an ideal medium to carry a great deal of the social communications that so effectively bind workers together in an organization.
- Although grapevine information is generally accurate, it is usually incomplete and may contain crucial distortions. Therefore, treat grapevine information as tentative, as possibly true, not necessarily true.
- Tap into the grapevine. Whether worker or management, it is important that you hear grapevine information. It may clue you in to events that will figure into your future with the organization. And, of course, it will help you bond and network with others in the organization.

Information Overload

Today, with the explosion of technology, information overload is one of our greatest problems. Information is generated at such a rapid rate that it is impossible to keep up with all that is relevant to one's job. Invariably, each person must select certain information to attend to and other information to omit.

Information is so easily and quickly generated and disseminated throughout an organization that we often forget that it still takes time to digest the information and to make use of it in a meaningful way. The junk mail that seems to grow every day is a perfect example. Technological advances make it easy, quick, and inexpensive to send information. Now what we need is the corresponding technology to enable us to read and use the information just as quickly.

Another major cause of overload is that many managers disseminate information about a problem instead of solving it. A department head confronted with a problem may write a memo or set up a study group. The manager has thus bought time, but has also added to the information overload.

Information overload has probably crept into all organizations—the major reason why so many organizations have computerized their operations. Putting everything on computer is a relatively easy and efficient way to deal with vast amounts of information, but it isn't the whole answer. Some human being must still do something about the information—at least usually. And under conditions of information overload, errors are more likely simply because the person cannot devote the needed time to any one item. The more rushed you are, the more likely you are to make mistakes. There are also likely to be great delays between sending a message and taking a required action. And delays are inefficient and costly to an organization.

Problems with Information Overload   Information overload, by definition, is a problem for any organization. One of the specific problems it creates is that it absorbs an enormous amount of time for workers at all levels of the hierarchy. The more messages you have to deal with, the less time you have for those messages or tasks that are central to your organizational functions.

Another problem is that the overabundance of messages may make it difficult for a worker to determine efficiently which messages need immediate attention and which don't, which messages may be discarded and which must be retained.

Guidelines for Dealing with Information Overload   Several suggestions should prove useful in dealing with information overload:

- Think before passing on messages. Not all messages must be passed on; not everyone needs to know everything.
- Consider the suggestions for "wastebasketry" offered by Auren Uris (1986):

  1. Use the messages as they come to you and then throw them out; for example, write the relevant dates for a meeting on your calendar and then throw out the announcement.
  2. Get rid of extra copies. When you receive multiple copies get rid of all but the one you need, if you need it.
  3. Summarize the material you need from lengthy reports and retain the summary and file or throw out the rest. I have a friend who saves the entire *New York Times* when she wants to save an article. My pleas to cut out the article and throw the rest away have had no effect.
  4. Distinguish between material that you should save and material that is only cluttering up your space.
  5. Throw out materials that can be easily located elsewhere. Data posted on nearby bulletin boards usually do not have to be on your desk as well.

Summary

1. An *organization* is a group of individuals organized for the achievement of specific goals.

2. *Organizational communication* refers to the messages sent and received within the organization, within both its formally structured and informally established groups.

3. *Sexual harassment* occurs frequently in the organizational setting and may be defined, broadly, as unwelcome sexual communication.

4. Four major *approaches to organizations* have been identified: the *scientific management* or classical approach, the *behavioral* or *human relations approach*, the *systems approach*, and the *cultural approach*.

5. *Communication networks* refer to the channels that messages pass through from one person to another.

6. *Upward communication* refers to messages sent from the lower levels of the hierarchy to the upper levels.

7. *Downward communication* refers to messages sent from the higher levels of the hierarchy to the lower levels.

8. *Lateral communication* refers to messages sent by equals to equals.

9. The *grapevine* refers to the informal channels that messages pass through in an organization.

10. *Information overload* refers to the situation in which the information sent to any person exceeds that person's capacity to process it.

Application

18.1 COMMUNICATION NETWORKS

In this exercise we explore the efficiency and satisfaction of communicating through the five basic network structures indentified earlier:

1. the circle in which each person communicates only with the person next to him or her

2. the wheel in which the leader may communicate with all others but the others may only communicate with the leader

3. the Y, similar to the wheel, except that there is a kind of secondary leader who can communicate with two others

4. the chain, similar to the wheel, except that the members at the end of the chain may only communicate with one other person

5. the all-channel in which each person may communicate with any other person

These paterns are more clearly identified in the diagram on page 342. Groups of equal numbers are formed according to these five patterns.

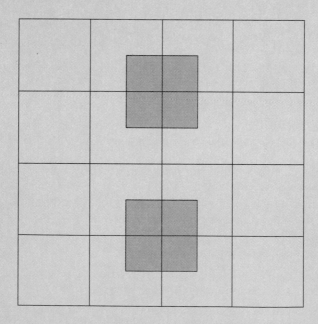

Arrows connecting two individuals indicate that communication may take place between them. Individuals not connected by arrows may communicate only indirectly through the individual(s) with whom they are connected. The problem is the same for all groups. Each group is to reach *unanimous* agreement on how many squares are contained in the following diagram:

All messages are to be written on individual pieces of paper. Members may pass to other members only those messages they themselves have written. Thus, if members receive a message they wish to pass on to another member, they must rewrite the message.

Efficiency and Satisfaction Indexes

The efficiency of the groups should be indexed in at least two ways. First, the time necessary for completion should be carefully noted. Second, the messages sent should be saved and counted. Efficiency will thus be indexed by the time it took to arrive at the correct answer and by the number of messages needed for communicating.

The satisfaction of the group members should be indexed by responses on the following scales:

Rate your *participation in the task* on the following scales:

```
interesting ___ : ___ : ___ : 4 : ___ : ___ : ___ boring
  enjoyable ___ : ___ : 5 : 4 : ___ : ___ : ___ unenjoyable
    dynamic ___ : 6 : ___ : ___ : 4 : ___ : ___ static
     userful ___ : ___ : 5 : ___ : ___ : ___ : ___ useless
       good ___ : ___ : ___ : 4 : ___ : ___ : ___ bad
```

Compute your mean score for these scales as follows: (1) number the scales from 7 to 1 from left to right; (2) total the scores from all five scales (this number should range from 5 to 35); and (3) divide by 5 to get your mean score.

Efficiency and Satisfaction Scores

Channel Patterns	Efficiency		Satisfaction
	Time	Number of Messages	Group Mean Scores
Circle	15.24	20	_____
Wheel	_____	_____	_____
Y	_____	_____	_____
Chain	_____	_____	_____
All-channel	13:24	35	6

Each group should then compute the group mean score by totaling the individual mean scores and dividing the sum by the number of participants.

For Discussion

1. Which patterns are most effective in ensuring rapid and accurate communication? Which patterns are least effective? Would this be true with all problems? With what types of problems would it be different? Why?

2. Which patterns result in the greatest degree of member satisfaction? Which patterns result in least satisfaction? How is this related to the leader's role in the group?

3. Are there realistic counterparts to these five communication structures? Do we find these communication structures and patterns in the "real world"? Where? What are some of the consequences of these various patterns?

4. How does structure influence function? Examine your own group situa-

tion and consider how the structure of the group (the positioning of the members, for example) influenced the functions the members played. Does this have a realistic counterpart? In what ways do you function differently as a result of the structure in which you find yourself?

5. What implications would you be willing to draw from this experience for improved communication in the classroom?

6. What implications can you draw from this exercise that might apply to family communication? For example, which of these five patterns most resembles the communication patterns in your family? What effects does your family communication pattern have on your own satisfaction? On your efficiency?

Group and Organizational Communication

Questions and Activities

1. What groups are you a member of? What needs do these groups serve for you?

2. In what ways is your family a small group? Does it serve problem solving, idea generation, personal growth, and information sharing functions? Might any of the principles and guidelines discussed in these units be useful in your family communication?

3. In what situations might you use the brainstorming concepts intrapersonally? That is, is there a personal problem or issue that might be approached with the techniques of brainstorming?

4. What roles do you normally serve in small groups? Are you satisfied or dissatisfied with your playing these roles? If dissatisfied, what do you plan to do about it?

5. Of all the individual roles identified in Unit 17, which one are you most likely to play? Least likely? Why?

6. What style of leadership are you most likely to use when you lead small groups? Which style of leadership do you respond to best when you are a group member?

7. What situations seem to bring out the leader in you? What situations seem to inhibit your leadership emergence?

8. How will the skills of leadership figure into your professional life? If such skills will figure prominently, what do you intend to do to master leadership skills more fully?

9. Have you ever witnessed "groupthink"? What were the consequences?

10. Create an evaluation form for group membership or group leadership that includes what you consider the most important elements in evaluating the effectiveness of a group member or leader.

11. If you work in an organization, how would you describe the orientation of the company? Does management approach the organization from the scientific approach, the human relations approach, the systems approach, the cultural approach, or some combination? Is this generally effective in accomplishing the goals of management? The goals of labor?

12. How do the problems involved in upward, downward, and lateral communication apply to student-teacher-administration communication in your college?

13. Are you likely to be "on the grapevine" in your social or work group? What kinds of information do these grapevines carry? Is the information

generally accurate? When it is inaccurate, what types of inaccuracies can be identified?

14. Auren Uris (1986) identifies three major types of rumors that are carried by the grapevine: (1) rumors of fear and anxiety, for example, people will be fired; (2) pipedreams or wishful thinking; and (3) character assassination. Do you notice these in the grapevines that you are familiar with? What effects do these rumors have on the group?

15. Using the language introduced in these three units on small group and organizational communication, how would you describe the communication that goes on in your human communication course?

Skill Check

This itemized list should help you review the skills covered in this part of the text. Check those skills that you feel you have mastered. Refer back to the relevant units for those skills that may not be clear or that you have not yet mastered.

_____ 1. I follow the six steps when in group problem-solving situations. (Unit 16)

_____ 2. I follow the general rules when brainstorming. (Unit 16)

_____ 3. I respond with supportiveness in consciousness-raising experiences. (Unit 16)

_____ 4. I avoid playing the popular but dysfunctional individual roles in a small group: aggressor, blocker, recognition seeker, self-confessor, playboy-playgirl, dominator, help seeker, or special interest pleader. (Unit 17)

_____ 5. In participating in a small group, I am group- rather than individually oriented, center conflict on issues rather than on personalities, am critically open-minded, and make sure that my meanings and the meanings of others are clearly understood. (Unit 17)

_____ 6. I adjust my leadership style on the basis of the task at hand and on the needs of the group members. (Unit 17)

_____ 7. As a small group leader, I activate group interaction, maintain effective interaction throughout the discussion, keep members on the track, ensure member satisfaction, encourage ongoing evaluation and improvement, and prepare members for the discussion as necessary. (Unit 17)

_____ 8. As a leader, I show that I value people, listen actively, am tactful, give credit to others, am consistent, admit mistakes, have a sense of humor, and set a good example. (Unit 17)

_____ 9. I adjust the communication patterns (for example, the wheel, Y, circle, chain, and all-channel) in an organizational group so that they are most effective in accomplishing the desired goals. (Unit 18)

_____ 10. I adjust my upward communication messages so as to avoid the common barriers and to employ the effectiveness guidelines. (Unit 18)

_____ 11. I adjust my downward communication so that I can discover problems that are not verbalized and learn the language of groups I will deal with or represent and at the same time use the guidelines for effective downward communication. (Unit 18)

_____ 12. In my lateral communications, I learn the relevant specialized languages and acknowledge the importance of areas other than my own to the well-being of the organization. (Unit 18)

_____ 13. I understand the role of the grapevine in organizations of which I'm a member, treat such information as tentative rather than absolutely true, and tap into the various grapevine messages.

_____ 14. I combat the tendency toward creating information overload by not presenting others with information that is irrelevant to them or beyond their processing capacity. (Unit 18)

_____ 15. I deal with information overload by throwing out unnecessary messages as appropriate. (Unit 18)

SUGGESTED READINGS

Bennis, Warren and Burt Nanus. *Leaders: The Strategies for Taking Charge.* New York: Harper & Row, 1985. A popular and useful guide to becoming an effective leader in a wide variety of situations.

Goldhaber, Gerald. *Organizational Communication,* 5th ed. Dubuque, Iowa: Wm. C. Brown, 1990. The most comprehensive introduction to the growing field of organizational communication.

Peters, Thomas J. and Robert H. Waterman, Jr. *In Search of Excellence: Lessons from America's Best-Run Companies.* New York: Harper & Row, 1982. Useful information based on the actual workings of America's best run companies.

Ulschak, Francis L., Leslie Nathanson, and Peter G. Gillan. *Small Group Problem Solving: An Aid to Organizational Effectiveness.* Reading, Mass.: Addison-Wesley, 1981. An excellent presentation of problem-solving and brainstorming techniques with specific application to the organization.

Uris, Auren. *101 of the Greatest Ideas in Management.* New York: Wiley, 1986. An introduction to the areas of management and especially the role of communication within management. For each of these great ideas, Uris defines the concept, explains how the concept operates within the organization, and offers suggestions for using the concept effectively.

Walters, J. Donald. *The Art of Supportive Leadership.* Nevada City, CA: Crystal Clarity, 1987. A brief (103 pages) handbook for the kind of leadership that emphasizes relationship considerations rather than getting a task accomplished.

Popular books include Williams (1985), Qubein (1986), Rogers (1970), Gratus (1988), and Schatzki (1981).

Useful textbooks are plentiful. Especially recommended are Beebe and Masterson (1990); Patton, Giffin, and Patton (1989); and Tubbs (1988).

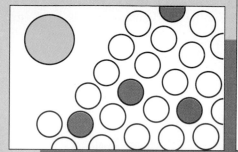

PUBLIC COMMUNICATION

Unit 19. **Preliminaries to Public Communication**
Unit 20. **Principles of Public Communication**
Unit 21. **The Anatomy of the Audience and the Speech**
 Part 5. **Feedback**
  Questions and Activities
  Skill Check
  Suggested Readings

In this part we cover public communication, that form of communication in which a speaker addresses a relatively large audience with a relatively continuous speech. In Unit 19 we introduce the nature of public speaking, speaker apprehension (or stage fright) and the role and standards of speech criticism. In Unit 20 we examine the principles of informative and persuasive speaking and the three forms of "proof"—logic, emotion, and speaker credibility. In Unit 21 we focus on the audience, and the major parts of the speech: body, introduction, and conclusion.

These units cover the foundations of public speaking. The pamphlet "A Practical Guide to Public Speaking," which accompanies this text, covers the more practical aspects of how to prepare and deliver a public speech.

Approaching Public Communication

In approaching the study of public communication, keep the following in mind:

- The principles for communicating information and for persuading are not limited to public speaking but are applicable to all forms of communication—to interpersonal and interviewing, to small group and organization, and to mass communication.

- In all types of communication, but especially in public speaking, fear is present. In public speaking, it is perhaps present to an uncomfortable degree. The insights into speaker apprehension presented here (and the suggestions offered in "A Practical Guide to Public Speaking") will help reduce apprehension.

- As you read about these principles, try to see them in operation (and in violation) in the speeches you hear every day—in classroom lectures, in political and religious speeches, and in television commercials.

PRELIMINARIES TO PUBLIC COMMUNICATION

UNIT CONTENTS

The Nature of Public Speaking

Apprehension in Public Speaking

Criticism in Public Speaking

Summary

Application
19.1 Thinking Critically About the Public Speech

UNIT GOALS

After completing this unit, you should be able to

1. define and diagram the *public speaking* process

2. define each of the following aspects of public speaking: speaker, listeners (audience), noise, effect, context, messages and channels, delivery, ethics, and language

3. define *speaker apprehension*

4. explain the influence on speaker apprehension of perceived novelty, subordinate status, conspicuousness, dissimilarity, and prior history

5. define *criticism* and explain its values

6. explain the major standards for criticism in public speaking

In this unit we introduce public communication. We consider the nature of public speaking and its major parts or components, apprehension in public speaking situations, and the criticism of public speaking.

THE NATURE OF PUBLIC SPEAKING

In **public communication** a speaker addresses a relatively large audience with a relatively continuous discourse, usually in a face-to-face situation. You deliver an oral report in your economics class, you ask your coworkers to elect you shop steward, you try to convince your neighbors to clean up the streets or other students to donate blood. These are all public speaking situations.

Unlike conversation, where the "audience" is one listener, the public speaking audience is "relatively large," ranging from groups of 10 or 12 to audiences of hundreds of thousands. During conversation, the role of speaker shifts repeatedly from one person to another. In public speaking, the speaker gives a relatively continuous talk. This does not mean that only the speaker communicates. Both speaker and audience communicate throughout the public speaking situation. The speaker communicates by delivering the speech and the audience by responding to the speech with feedback.

Figure 19.1 shows what public speaking is and how it works. Its major elements are: speaker, listener, noise, effect, context, messages and channels, language and style, delivery, and ethics.

Speaker

As a public speaker you bring to the public speaking situation all that you are and all that you know. Further, you bring with you all that the audience *thinks* you are and *thinks* you know. Everything about you becomes significant and contributes to the total effect of your speech. Your knowledge, your speech purpose, your speaking ability, your attitudes toward your audience, and other factors tell the audience who you are. These factors interact both during and after the public speaking event. As the public speaker you are the center of the transaction. The audience members look to you as the speaker; you and your speech are the reason for the gathering.

Listeners

Listeners are separate individuals and are symbolized as such in the diagram to emphasize that each is unique. Although we often speak of "the audience" as a collective body, it actually consists of separate and often very different individuals. Each of these listeners comes to the public speaking situation with different purposes, motives, expectations, attitudes, beliefs, and values. Each listener is going to respond differently to you and to the entire public speaking act.

Noise

Noise is interference—whether audible or not—that interferes with your listeners' receiving the messages you wish them to receive. The "noise band" around the speaker (Figure 19.1) shows how noise interferes with your messages. As discussed in Unit 1, noise may be physical, psychological, or semantic.

As a speaker you may cut out some noise sources or lessen their effects, but you cannot cut out all noise. Therefore, learn to combat its effects by speaking louder, re-

In what ways would public speaking be different in a dictatorship and in a democracy?

peating important assertions, organizing your ideas so they are easy to follow, gesturing to reinforce your spoken messages, or defining technical or complex terms.

Effect

As a public speaker, you design and deliver your speeches to influence your listeners. Politicians give campaign speeches to secure your vote. Advertisers and salespersons give sales pitches to get you to buy their products. Teachers give lectures to influence your thinking about history, psychology, or communication. The model of public speaking in Figure 19.1 shows each effect separately to emphasize that, as each listener is unique, each effect is also unique. To the very same speech, one listener may agree completely, another may disagree, and still another may misunderstand the entire message.

Context

Like all communicators, speaker and listeners operate in a physical, social-psychological, temporal, and cultural context (Unit 1). The context influences you as the speaker, the audience, the speech, and the effects of the speech. Therefore, analyze the context with care and prepare your speech with this specific context in mind. For example, you cannot treat a speech in a small intimate room and one in a sports arena in the same way (physical context). You couldn't treat similarly a supportive and a hostile audience (social-psychological context). Your speech at a protest rally will have to differ depending on whether you are the first speaker or the twentieth; the previous speeches—and even the anticipated speeches—will influence how the audience sees

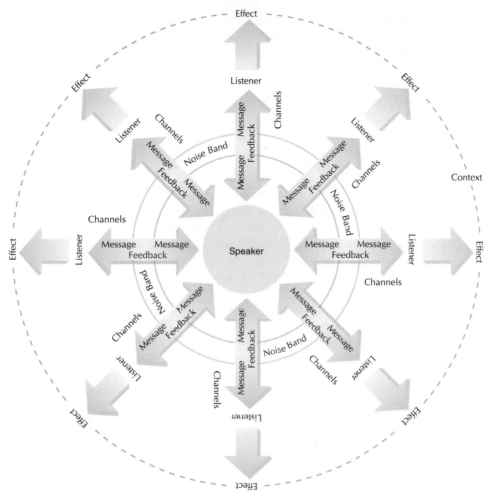

FIGURE 19.1 The public speaking transaction.

your speech (temporal context). Appealing to the "competitive spirit" and "financial gain" may prove effective with Wall Street executives but may insult Buddhist missionaries (cultural context).

Messages and Channels

In Unit 1 we stressed that messages are the signals sent by the speaker and received by the listener. These signals pass through one or more channels on their way from speaker to listener and from listener to speaker. The channel is the medium that carries the message signals from sender to receiver. Both the auditory and the visual channels are significant in public speaking. Through the auditory channel you send your spoken messages—your words and your sentences. At the same time, you also send messages through the visual channel, through eye contact (and the lack of it), body movement, hand and facial gestures, and clothing.

Language and Style

In conversation you vary your language on the basis of the person with whom you are speaking. When speaking with friends, for example, you would use your normal, everyday language. You would speak to them in much the same language you would use when you talk to yourself. When talking with children, you might use easier words and shorter sentences. If you were trying to impress someone, you might use a different style.

In public speaking situations, you adjust your language to your audience in the same way you do in conversation. In public speaking, however, your listeners cannot interrupt you to ask, for example, what a particular word means. So you need to make sure that your language is free of any terms that might not be instantly clear to your listeners. You don't want your listeners to stop listening to what you are saying while they try to figure out what "maximize the latter" or "unauthorized bribery" refers to. In public speaking, your language must be instantly intelligible.

"Oral style" is a quality of spoken language that clearly separates it from written language. You do not speak as you write. The words and grammatical constructions you use differ in written and spoken language. The major explanation for this difference is that you compose speech instantly. You select your words and construct your sentences as you think. When you write, however, you compose your thoughts after considerable reflection. Even then you may rewrite and edit as you go along.

Another explanation for the differences between speaking and writing style is that the listener hears a speech only once and it must therefore be instantly intelligible. The reader can reread an essay or look up an unfamiliar word. Temporary attention lapses may force the reader to reread a sentence or paragraph, but the listener can never make up for such lapses.

Researchers who have examined a great body of speech and writings have found several important differences (Akinnaso, 1982; DeVito, 1965, 1980). Generally, spoken language consists of shorter, simpler, and more familiar words than does written language. There is more qualification in speech than in writing. For example, speakers make greater use of such expressions as *although, however,* and *perhaps.* Writers edit out such expressions before their work is published and read.

Spoken language also contains a greater number of self-reference terms and a greater number of "allness" terms (for example, *all, none, every, always, never*). Spoken language contains more concrete terms; written language contains more abstract terms. Also more common spoken language are pseudo-quantifying terms (for example, *many, much, very,* and *lots*). Spoken language also contains more expressions that incorporate the speaker as part of the observation (for example, "It seems to me that. . ." or "As I see it. . ."). Further, spoken language uses more verbs and adverbs; writing contains more nouns and adjectives.

In large part, effective speeches retain this spoken style. But since the public speech is composed much as is a written essay—with considerable thought, deliberation, editing, and restyling—special consideration must be given to retain and polish the style that seems most appropriate to the spoken mode and that is most effective in communicating meaning to listeners.

Delivery

In conversation you don't even think of delivery. You don't ask yourself how you should sit or stand or gesture. If public speaking is a relatively new experience, you will probably feel uncomfortable at first. You may find yourself wondering what to do with your hands or whether or not you should move about. With time and experience, you will find that your delivery will follow naturally from what you are saying, just as it does in conversation.

Ethics

Public speaking, and in fact all forms of communication, have an ethical dimension (Bok, 1978; Jaksa & Pritchard, 1988; Johannesen, 1991). Communications can vary from highly ethical to highly unethical. Speakers may, for example, argue for a position because they believe it is right, even if it means they will be censured and criticized. Whistleblowers, critics of the rich and powerful, and social reformers are generally good examples of people who risk considerable losses to say what they feel has to be said. At the other extreme are speakers who will use the audience for their own gain—the advertising hucksters, con artists, and liars.

Between these extremes are the vast majority—those who exaggerate or slant the findings of a study to support their own position, emphasize their positive and hide their negative qualities, or lead others to think their motives are altruistic when they are actually selfish.

The questions that need to be asked regarding all communication are "To what extent is this message ethical? To what extent is the message morally responsible?" For some messages, the answers are easy. Thus, most would probably agree that to take someone else's work and pass it off as your own is plagiarism and that this is unethical. For other situations, however, the answers are not so easy, nor would everyone agree on what is ethical and what is unethical. For example:

Here, for example, are a few questions that raise ethical issues. These are similar to those raised in Unit 1 but are especially applicable to public speaking.

- Is it ethical to exaggerate the merits of your proposal to secure acceptance?
- Is it ethical to take phrases or ideas from others without telling your audience where these come from?
- Is it ethical to leave out negative aspects of your proposal and just reveal the positive aspects?
- Is it ethical to spread negative rumors about your opposition if you know these are true?
- Is it ethical to persuade an audience to do something by scaring them? By threatening them? By making them feel guilty?

Ethics is a crucial consideration in all communications. In public speaking, ethics is especially important because there are so many listeners and the potential effects of unethical messages are so wide ranging.

APPREHENSION IN PUBLIC SPEAKING

As explained throughout this text, apprehension is a normal part of most communication interactions. But it is in public speaking that it is usually most prominent. Apprehension is experienced not only by the beginning public speaker; it is also felt by even the most experienced speakers. You don't seem to get rid of apprehension but rather learn to deal with it and control it (Richmond & McCroskey, 1992).

Can you articulate a theory that would attribute speaker apprehension to cultural values and beliefs?

"Communication apprehension," note researchers James McCroskey and Lawrence Wheeless (1976), "is probably the most common handicap that is suffered by people in contemporary American society." According to a nationwide survey conducted by Bruskin Associates, speaking in public ranked as the number one fear of adult men and women. It ranks above fear of heights and even fear of snakes. According to surveys of college students by McCroskey and Wheeless, between 10 and 20 percent suffer "severe, debilitating communication apprehension." Another 20 percent "suffers from communication apprehension to a degree substantial enough to interfere to some extent with their normal functioning."

You may wish to pause here and take the Apprehension Test.

Speaker apprehension affects the way you feel and the way you act. Many people develop negative feelings about their ability to communicate orally. They predict that their communication efforts will fail. They feel that whatever gain they would make as a result of engaging in communication is not worth the fear they would experience. As a result apprehensive speakers avoid communication situations and, when forced to participate, participate as little as possible.

General and Specific Apprehension

If you have a general apprehension that manifests itself in all communication situations, you have *trait apprehension*—a fear of communication generally, regardless of the specific situation. Your fear would appear in conversations, small group settings, and public speaking situations.

If you are like most people and experience apprehension in only certain communication situations, you would have *state apprehension*—a fear that is specific to a

SELF-TEST

How Apprehensive Are You in Public Speaking?*

Instructions   This questionnaire is composed of six statements concerning your feelings about public speaking. Indicate in the space provided the degree to which each statement applies to you by marking whether you: 1 = strongly agree, 2 = agree, 3 = are undecided, 4 = disagree, 5 = strongly disagree. There are no right or wrong answers. Many of the statements are similar to other statements; do not be concerned about this. Work quickly; record your first impression.

_*1*_   1. I have no fear of giving a speech.

_*4*_   2. Certain parts of my body feel very tense and rigid while giving a speech.

_*2*_   3. I feel relaxed while giving a speech.

_*2*_   4. My thoughts become confused and jumbled when I am giving a speech.

_*2*_   5. I face the prospect of giving a speech with confidence.

_*4*_   6. While giving a speech, I get so nervous that I forget facts I really know.

Scoring   To obtain your public speaking apprehension score, use the following formula: 18 plus the scores for items 1, 3, and 5; minus scores for items 2, 4, and 6. A score above 18 indicates some degree of apprehension. Most people score above 18 in the public speaking context, so if you scored relatively high, you are among the vast majority of people.

Source: James C. McCroskey, *An Introduction to Rhetorical Communication*, 5th ed. (Englewood Cliffs, N.J.: Prentice-Hall, 1986).

given communication situation. For example, you may fear public speaking but have no difficulty in talking with two or three other people. Or, you may fear job interviews but have no fear of public speaking. State apprehension is extremely common. Most people experience it for some situations. As you probably guessed, public speaking provokes the most apprehension.

Degrees of Apprehension

Speaker apprehension exists on a continuum. Some people are extremely apprehensive and are unable to function in communication. They suffer greatly in a society oriented around communication where success often depends on the ability to communicate effectively. Other people are so mildly apprehensive that they appear to experience no fear at all. They actively seek out communication experiences and rarely experience even the slightest apprehension. Most of us fall between these two extremes.

For some people, apprehension is debilitating and hinders personal effectiveness in professional and social relationships (Comadena & Prusank, 1988). For others, apprehension is motivating and may actually help in achieving one's goals.

Normal Apprehension

Apprehension in public speaking is normal. The vast majority of people experience some fear in the relatively formal public speaking situation. In public speaking you are the sole focus of attention and are usually being evaluated on your performance. Therefore, experiencing fear or anxiety is not strange or unique. Once you recognize that you are not unique in experiencing speaker apprehension, you will have taken an important first step in managing your own apprehension.

Positive Apprehension

Although you may at first view apprehension as harmful, it is not necessarily so. In fact, apprehension can work for you. Fear can energize you. It may motivate you to work a little harder to produce a speech that will be better than it might have been. Further, the audience cannot see the apprehension symptoms that you might experience. Even though you may think that the audience can hear your heart beat faster and faster, they cannot. They cannot see your knees tremble. They cannot sense your dry throat—at least not most of the time.

Factors Influencing Public Speaking Apprehension

Five factors influence students' public speaking anxiety (Beatty, 1988; Ayres, 1990). Understanding how these factors may operate in your specific situation will help you control them and ultimately help you reduce your apprehension.

- *Perceived novelty*. Situations that are new and different from those with which you are familiar, contribute to anxiety. As the novelty of the situation is reduced (as you gain experience in public speaking), your anxiety is also reduced.
- *Subordinate status*. When you feel that others are better speakers than you or that they know more about the topic than you do, anxiety increases. Thinking more positively about yourself and being thorough in your preparation are helpful techniques for reducing this particular cause of anxiety.
- *Conspicuousness*. When you feel you are the center of attention, as you normally do in public speaking, your anxiety may increase. Thinking of public speaking as a type of conversation may help reduce this feeling of conspicuousness.
- *Dissimilarity*. The more different you feel from your listeners, the more apt you are to experience fear in public speaking. Therefore, emphasize your similarity with your listeners as you think of your public speeches as well as during the presentation of the actual speech.
- *Prior history*. A prior history of apprehension is likely to increase anxiety. Your positive public speaking experiences should help reduce this cause of anxiety.

CRITICISM IN PUBLIC SPEAKING

You can increase your understanding of public speaking from examining the criticism of public speaking. Consider some of the values of criticism and some of the standards for evaluating a speech.

The Value of Criticism

The term *criticism* comes from the Latin *criticus*, which means "able to discern," "to judge." There is nothing inherently negative about criticism; rather, **criticism** is a process of judging and evaluating a work of art, a movie, or a public speech. Hugh Blair, the great eighteenth-century rhetorical theorist and critic whose theories are still used today, noted that criticism teaches us "to admire and to blame with judgment, and not to follow the crowd blindly." Critics and criticism are thus essential parts of any art.

The major purpose of criticism in the classroom is to improve students' public speaking abilities. Constructive criticism is an effective way of teaching and learning the principles of public speaking. Through criticism, you will be better able to see what works and what doesn't work. You'll be able to see what should be kept, enlarged upon, modified, or eliminated. By observing what works and what doesn't work and then going beyond that to identify more effective alternatives, the critic offers specific suggestions for achieving greater effectiveness.

Criticism also helps develop standards for evaluating the wide variety of speeches you'll hear throughout your life. This critical frame of mind will prove useful in assessing all communications: the salesperson's pitch to buy the new car, the advertiser's plea to buy Tylenol rather than Excedrin, and the newspaper's or network's editorial.

When you give criticism, you are telling the speaker that you have listened carefully and that you care enough about the speech and the speaker to offer suggestions for improvement.

Standards of Criticism

What standards do you use when you criticize a speech (Foss, 1989)? How do you measure the excellence of a speech? On what basis do you say that one speech is weak, another is good, and still another is great? Two major standards quickly suggest themselves: effectiveness and conformity to the principles of the art.

Effectiveness   The effectiveness standard judges the speech in terms of whether or not it achieves its purpose. If the purpose is to sell soap, then the speech is effective if it sells soap and is ineffective if it fails to sell soap. Increased sophistication in measuring communication effects make this standard tempting to apply.

There are, however, problems with this approach. In many instances—in the classroom, for example—the effects of a speech cannot always be measured. Sometimes the effect of a speech is long term and you may not be present to see it take hold. Also, some effects are simply not measurable; you cannot always measure changes in attitude and belief. Sometimes audiences may be so opposed to a speaker's position that even the greatest speech will have no observable effect. It may take an entire campaign to get such an audience to change its position even slightly. At other times audiences may agree with the speaker and even the weakest speech will secure their compliance. In situations like these the effectiveness standard will produce intuitively inaccurate and inappropriate judgments.

Furthermore, a speech interacts with so many other factors that it is difficult to attribute a change in behavior to it. To isolate the effects of the speech is extremely difficult, often impossible. How, for example, do you isolate the effects of a speech from the influences of newspapers, television, and interpersonal interaction?

But perhaps more important is that there is more to a speech than its effect; for example, there are ethical obligations. A speech that violates ethical standards may be effective but doesn't deserve a positive evaluation.

Conformity to the Principles of the Art   A more useful standard (and one which I and most instructors and coaches use in teaching public speaking) is to evaluate the speech on the basis of its conformity to the principles of the art. With this standard a speech is positively evaluated when it follows the principles of public speaking established by critics, theorists, and practitioners of public speaking (and as described in a text on public speaking) and negatively evaluated as it deviates from these principles. Here you would ask such questions as these:

- Did the speaker analyze and adapt the speech to this specific audience?
- Did the speaker use convincing supporting materials?
- Did the speaker maintain the attention of the audience throughout the speech?
- Did the speaker use the available means of persuasion?
- Did the speaker use evidence that was recent, unbiased, accurate, and directly relevant to the thesis being advocated?
- Did the speaker use language and a style of delivery that was appropriate to the topic and audience?

This standard is of course not totally separate from the effectiveness standard since the principles of public speaking are largely principles of effectiveness. When you follow the principles of the art, your speech will in all likelihood be effective.

The great advantage of this standard is that it contributes to the learning of the principles of public speaking. When your speech is measured for its adherence to these principles, you will be learning the principles by applying them to your unique situation as well as through the critic's feedback.

Additional Standards Of course there are other standards that critics have applied. The *universality standard* (Murphy, 1957) asks to what extent the speech addresses values and issues that have significance for all people in all times. This standard is often the one used in evaluating literature. By this standard Martin Luther King, Jr.'s "I Have a Dream" (see Application 21.3 for the complete text) would be judged positively because it argues for beliefs, values, and actions most of the civilized world accepts as fundamental.

The *historical justification* standard asks to what extent was the speech's thesis and purpose justified by subsequent historical events. By this standard William Jennings Bryan's famous "Cross of Gold" speech (delivered in 1896)—although it won Bryan the Democratic nomination for president—would be judged negatively because it argued for a rejected monetary standard and against a monetary standard (gold) that the entire world had accepted.

The *ethical merit* standard asks to what extent does the speech argue for what is true, moral, humane, or good (Cooper, 1989). By this standard the speeches of Hitler, despite their effectiveness in persuading millions, would be judged negatively because they supported ideas most people find repugnant.

Despite their obvious appeal each of these standards creates problems. Consider how you would use each of these standards in evaluating, for example:

- a speech on how to program a VCR
- a speech against legalizing abortion
- a speech for legalizing abortion
- a speech against eating beef
- a speech advocating that all married couples be required to sign prenuptial agreements

As you can see, each topic presents somewhat different problems. Take the first example. Applying the universality standard, the speech would be judged negatively. In a few years VCRs will be so simple that current programming procedures will be useless. How will the speech be justified historically? History, it seems, won't care very much. Does the speech have ethical merit? Programming a VCR seems neither ethical nor unethical. Try your hand at identifying the problems inherent in applying these three standards to each of the other topics.

Summary

1. *Public speaking* consists of a speaker addressing a relatively large audience with a relatively continuous discourse usually in a face-to-face situation.

2. The essential components of a public speech are *speaker, listeners (audience), noise, effect, context, messages and channels, language and style, delivery,* and *ethics.*

3. The preferred style in public speaking is oral style. Compared with written style, oral style contains shorter, simpler, and more familiar words; greater qualification; more self-referential, allness, concrete, and pseudo-quantifying terms; more terms indicative of consciousness of projection; and more verbs and adverbs.

4. *Speaker apprehension* refers to a fear of communication and is extremely common in public speaking.

5. *Trait apprehension* refers to a fear that manifests itself in all communication situations and thus is a type of personality trait; *state apprehension* refers to a fear that is unique to specific situations, for example, public speaking or employment interviewing.

6. *Speech criticism* refers to making a judgment or evaluating (both positively and negatively) a public speech.

7. The major standards for speech criticism are effectiveness and the extent to which the speech conforms to the principles of the art.

8. Additional standards for criticism include the universality standard, the historical justification standard, and the ethical merit standard.

Application

19.1   THINKING CRITICALLY ABOUT THE PUBLIC SPEECH

This speech, given by William Fort, a student from California State University at Chico, is presented here as a kind of summary of the basic elements of public speaking. Read the speech all the way through first. Then glance over the questions to get a general idea of the areas highlighted. Then, reread the speech while considering each of the questions on the left. These questions should encourage you to think about the principles of public speaking (before we cover them formally in the next two units) and also provide experience in formulating and expressing criticism.

1. How effective was the opening quotation? Did it gain attention?

2. Did it introduce the importance of the topic?

"What is so terrible as war? I will tell you what is ten times and ten thousand times more terrible than war—outraged nature. I see that three persons out of every four are utterly unaware of the general causes of their own ill-health, and that is to stupid neglect, or what is just bad, stupid ignorance."

In 1859, Reverend Charles Kingsley used these powerful words to address the cholera epidemic. Which

3. How would members of your class respond to this topic? Would they see it as important? As relevant to their everyday lives?

4. How might you relate this topic to members of your class?

5. What method did Fort use to orient his listeners? How effective was this?

6. What is the thesis? How would members of your class respond to this thesis?

7. What is the specific purpose? Was the purpose sufficiently limited?

8. Did the speaker effectively weave in relevant research? Was the research appropriate? Sufficient?

created a 40 percent infant mortality rate in England, simply because of a lack of sanitation. Today we face a similar situation. There is a problem that most are unaware of, which is causing influenza, smallpox, pneumonia, tuberculosis, meningitis, airborne lead poisoning, and most fatally, legionnaire's disease. This problem? Sick Building Syndrome. Sick Building Syndrome describes any building with actual or potential health hazards due to contaminated air. The incidence of SBS is rising, partially because buildings have been planned with maximum energy savings in mind since the energy crisis of the 1970s. Dr. Tony Pickering, who is currently studying SBS, states in the May 1987 issue of *World Press Review* that "SBS affects 90 percent of supersealed buildings, and in some cases sickens up to 70 percent of the building occupants." Supersealed buildings describe any building which uses mechanical ventilation. In basic terms, a building whose windows cannot open or close.

SBS is a serious problem that we need to become aware of, because if we don't do something to cure this disease today, then like England in the 1860s, thousands of Americans will die in the 1990s. So today we will investigate SBS by first examining the general causes of the problem, then looking at the symptoms of SBS, and finally, we will find ways to end the outraged nature of SBS.

There are three major causes of SBS. The first is that buildings are using ineffective heating, ventilation, and air-conditioning systems, also known as HVAC systems. Architect William Heineman describes these systems in the December 1985 issue of *National Safety and Health News:* "Once we enter these air-tight buildings, we are completely dependent upon its support systems for survival. The quality and quantity of air we breathe are totally contained within the system."

Not only do these systems pick up fungus and bacteria and recirculate it throughout a system, but also airborne viruses, germs from coworkers, and cigarette smoke. "Microbiological health hazards are the most widespread of the many hazards in mechanically ventilated buildings," declares environmentalist Sandy Moretz in the February 1988 issue of *Occupational Hazards* magazine. Ms. Moretz goes on to state, "The vast majority of this microbial growth is caused by stagnant water and dirt build-up in air filters, and condensation drainage trays that are not regularly cleaned." Or, in Kingsley's words, "stupid neglect and stupid ignorance."

The third major cause of SBS is the lack of governmental support. The Environmental Protection Agency's Eileen Claussen states in the June 6, 1988, issue of *Time* magazine that "Some Americans spend an estimated

9. What additional research would you have wanted to be convinced of the importance of this topic?

10. Does the speaker use sufficient guide phrases or transitions to help listeners follow his development?

11. How effective is this internal summary?

12. Are these statistics convincing to you? Would you want additional information before accepting the importance of SBS?

13. How important would this argument be to members of your class?

14. How might the speaker have made these deaths more dramatic?

15. How effectively did the speaker use humor? Was this appropriate?

16. Note that the speaker discussed the causes of SBS before identifying the problems it creates. Was this pattern effective? How would you have arranged this speech?

90 percent of their time indoors, however no specific federal regulations have been adopted for control of air in offices, even though the air in some buildings is 100 times as polluted as the air outside the buildings."

Ineffective HVAC systems, lack of maintenance on existing systems, and no governmental support all perpetuate the problems associated with Sick Building Syndrome. And those problems are significant. The symptoms of SBS don't start out with our building throwing up or your elevator doors getting a fever, rather as minor annoyances such as a dry throat, headaches, or drowsiness. In fact, the May 1987 issue of *Occupational Health and Safety* printed a survey of over 1,000 office workers, half of which worked in naturally ventilated buildings, and half worked in mechanically ventilated buildings. The results showed that while only 15.7 percent of those in naturally ventilated buildings had frequent headaches, 37.4 percent of those in mechanically ventilated buildings did. When it comes to drowsiness, 13.8 percent in naturally ventilated buildings, and 51.4 percent, four times as many in mechanically ventilated buildings were frequently drowsy on the job.

These lopsided figures translate into a monetary loss by building owners. James Repace, an indoor air specialist with the EPA, states in the January 1989 issue of *Discover* magazine, "The millions of workdays lost each year [due to SBS] translate into billions of dollars in medical expense, diminished productivity, and compensation claims." In May 1988, 70 workers boycotted their office building, claiming that the air inside the building was so contaminated it caused frequent headaches, dizziness, eye irritation, chest pains, and breathing difficulties. The Washington, D.C., building is the National Headquarters of the Environmental Protection Agency.

Although usually the symptoms of SBS are the ones I've previously mentioned, sometimes just one visit into any supersealed building can be fatal. In May 1985, 37 men, women and children who stayed on the fourth floor of Stafford General Hospital mysteriously died. Later the cause was found to be Legionnaires' disease, a harmful bacterium which originated in an air-conditioning system which blew the deadly disease through the air ducts right into the unsuspecting patients' rooms. The HVAC system hadn't been cleaned in over a year. This incident outlined in the *Air Conditioning, Heating and Refrigeration News* is not an isolated one. In fact, the September 2, 1985, issue of *U.S. News and World Report* says "Legionnaires' disease strikes 25 to 50,000 Americans a year, and about 15 percent of the victims die." Translating these figures, we can see that the outraged nature of SBS causes around 5,000 deaths annually.

17. Are these calls to action effective? Should the speaker have been more specific (less specific) in his recommendations?

18. If you heard this speech would you be willing to do as requested? Why?

19. What organizational pattern did the speaker use? Was this pattern effective given the speaker's specific purpose?

20. Do you believe that "Sick building syndrome will be one of the major problems in the 1990s" and that we can "save thousands of lives lost each year to SBS"? If not, what might the speaker have done to make you believe these statements?

21. How effective was the conclusion? Did the speaker summarize his major points? Did he bring the speech to a definite close?

Hospitals, hotels, the Environmental Protection Agency, and school buildings are places where we should be able to go and feel safe and secure. However, until we, as individuals and as a nation, do something to stop the enraged nature of Sick Building Syndrome, then each and every trip into a supersealed building will be potentially life threatening.

Once this awareness is achieved, please act. Pick up the phone and call your local building inspector and ask him or her to examine your sick building, and let the building owner know what actual or potential health hazards are there due to contaminated air. Another practical step we can all take is to tell others about the problem so they can also help find these sick buildings and pressure building owners to start a preventative program against SBS.

On a larger level, we can see the need to attack the number one cause of SBS, which is microbial growth in HVAC systems. David Custer, the Vice President of Environmental Management Systems, says in the February 1987 issue of *Buildings,* "Microbiological health hazards are the most preventable of the many hazards in supersealed buildings. They can be virtually eliminated through simple maintenance." The types of simple maintenance which Mr. Custer speaks of include replacing all dirty air filters, emptying all condensation drainage trays, and treating the entire system with an inexpensive antimicrobial solution. By spending a few dollars today, they can save millions tomorrow, and end their stupid neglect. This is a simple and logical solution which will be easy and inexpensive to implement.

Finally, federal legislation which (a) requires building owners to use certain types of tested, effective HVAC sytems, and (b) which requires them to clean and maintain their existing systems, would be a great help in calming the outraged nature of SBS.

In 1859, one of England's major problems was a cholera epidemic which created a 40 percent infant mortality rate. This could have been solved by taking simple preventative measures and being more sanitary. Unfortunately, most ignored Reverend Kingsley, and because of it, hundreds of thousands needlessly died. Research scientist Michael McCawley said in the June 6, 1988, issue of *Time* that "unless we realize the severity of the problem today, Sick Building Syndrome will be one of the major problems of the 1990s." If we follow the simple steps which I've outlined, we can learn from the English mistakes of the 1860s, and end the stupid neglect, stupid ignorance, and outraged nature associated with SBS, and in the process we can all play doctor and save the thousands of lives lost each year to SBS.

PRINCIPLES OF PUBLIC COMMUNICATION

UNIT CONTENTS

Principles of Informative Speaking

Principles of Persuasion

Logic

Emotion

Credibility

  Summary

  Applications

     20.1 Reasoning Adequacy

     20.2 Constructing Motivational Appeals

     20.3 Credibility and the Famous Person

UNIT GOALS

After completing this unit, you should be able to

1. Explain the principles for informative speaking: information load, relevance, appropriateness, new to old, several senses, and levels of abstraction

2. Explain the principles of persuasion: selective exposure, audience participation, inoculation, and magnitude of change

3. Explain the foot-in-the-door and the door-in-the-face techniques

4. Define *argument* and *evidence* and the three general tests of reasoning

5. Explain the nature of reasoning from specific instances to a generalization, by analogy, by cause and effect, and by sign

6. Explain the role of emotion and motivational appeals in motivating behavior

7. Define *speaker credibility* and the ways in which credibility impressions may be formed

8. Explain the three components of credibility

In this unit we present some principles of public speaking for communicating information and persuasion. These principles are actually applicable to all forms of communication but seem especially appropriate in the public speaking context.

PRINCIPLES OF INFORMATIVE SPEAKING

When you communicate information you tell your listeners something they do not know, something new. You may tell them of a new way of looking at old things or an old way of looking at new things. You may discuss a theory not previously heard of or a familiar one not fully understood. You may talk about events that the audience may be unaware of or may have misconceptions about. Regardless of the type of informative speech, the following principles should help.

The Information Load Principle

There is a limit to the amount of information that a listener can take in at one time. Resist the temptation to overload your listeners with information. Limit the amount of information that you communicate and expand its presentation. It is better to present two new items of information and explain these with examples, illustrations, and descriptions, than to present five items without the needed amplification.

The Relevance Principle

Listeners remember information best when they see it as relevant and useful to their own needs or goals. Notice that as a listener you follow this principle all the time. In class, you attend to and remember information if you feel it is relevant to you, for example, if it's a skill that you can use at work or something that will be on the test. If you want the audience to listen, relate the information to their needs, wants, or goals, *throughout your speech*.

The Appropriateness Principle

Listeners best retain information when you present it on an appropriate level. Steer a middle course between being too simple—thus boring or insulting the audience—and being too sophisticated—thus confusing the audience. Remember that the audience hears the speech only once and must grasp on first hearing what you may have taken weeks to learn. For example, if you are a psychology major don't assume that terms that are part of your active vocabulary—like *conditioning, stimulus-response*, and *short-term memory*—will be immediately understood by your listeners.

The New to Old Principle

Listeners will learn information more easily and retain it longer when you relate it to what they already know. Relating the new to the old, the unfamiliar to the familiar, the unseen to the seen, the untasted to the tasted will help your listeners see more clearly what they have never experienced before.

The Several Senses Principle

You will impress your information on your audience if you reveal it to them through several senses—through hearing, seeing, smelling, tasting, feeling. Use as many of your listeners' senses as you can. If you are describing the layout of a football field (presenting information through hearing), also show them a picture of the field (presenting information through seeing as well). If you are giving a speech on stress and you are talking about muscular tension, make the audience feel their own muscle tension by asking them to tighten their leg or stomach muscles.

The Levels of Abstraction Principle

You can discuss freedom of the press in the abstract by talking about the importance of getting information to the public, by referring to the Bill of Rights, and by relating a free press to the preservation of democracy—all on a relatively high level of abstraction. But you can also talk about freedom of the press by citing specific examples, about how a local newspaper was prevented from running a story critical of the town council or about how Lucy Rinaldo was fired from the *Accord Sentinel* after she wrote a story critical of the mayor—all on a relatively low level of abstraction, a level that is specific and concrete. Too many high abstractions without the specifics or too many specifics without the high abstractions will prove less effective than the combination of abstract and specific.

PRINCIPLES OF PERSUASION

Most of the speeches you hear are persuasive speeches. The speeches of politicians, advertisers, and religious leaders are perhaps the clearest examples. In most of your own speeches, you too will aim at persuasion. You will try to change your listeners attitudes and beliefs or perhaps change their behaviors. In school you might try to persuade others to (or not to) expand the core curriculum, use a plus-minus or a pass-fail grading system, disband the basketball team, allocate increased student funds for the school newspaper, establish competitive majors, or eliminate fraternity hazing. On your job you may be called upon to speak in favor of (or against) having a union, a wage increase proposal, a health benefit package, or Pat Williams for shop steward.

Success in strengthening or changing attitudes or beliefs and in moving listeners to action will depend on the degree to which the speaker follows the principles of persuasion.

The Selective Exposure Principle

Listeners follow the "law of selective exposure." It has at least two parts:

1. Listeners actively seek out information that supports their opinions, beliefs, values, decisions, and behaviors.

2.   Listeners actively avoid information that contradicts their existing opinions, beliefs, attitudes, values, and behaviors.

Of course, if you are very sure that your opinions and attitudes are logical and valid, then you might not bother seeking supporting information. And, you may not actively avoid nonsupportive messages. Generally, you would exercise selective exposure when your confidence in your opinions and beliefs is weak.

The Audience Participation Principle

Persuasion is greatest when the audience participates actively in your presentation. In experimental tests, for example, the same speech is delivered to different audiences. The attitudes of each audience are measured before and after the speech. The difference between their attitudes before and after the speech is taken as a measure of the speech's effectiveness. For one audience the sequence consists of (1) pretest of attitudes, (2) presentation of the persuasive speech, and (3) posttest of attitudes. For another audience the sequence consists of (1) pretest of attitudes, (2) presentation of the persuasive speech, (3) audience paraphrases or summarizes the speech, and (4) posttest of attitudes. We consistently find that those listeners who participated actively (as in paraphrasing or summarizing) are more persuaded than those who receive the message passively. Demagogues and propagandists who succeed in arousing huge crowds often have the crowds chant slogans, repeat catch phrases, and otherwise participate actively in the persuasive experience.

The Inoculation Principle

The principle of inoculation is best explained with the biological analogy on which it is based. Suppose that you lived in a germ-free environment. Upon leaving this germ-free environment and upon exposure to germs, you would be particularly susceptible to infection because your body would not have built up an immunity—it would have no resistance. Resistance, the ability to fight off germs, might be achieved by the body through some form of inoculation if not naturally. You could, for example, be injected with a weakened dose of the germ so that your body begins to fight the germ by building up antibodies that create an immunity to this type of infection. Your body, because of the antibodies it produces, is now able to fight off even powerful doses of this germ.

The situation in persuasion is similar to this biological process. Some of your attitudes and beliefs have existed in a "germ-free" environment. These attitudes and beliefs have never been attacked or challenged. For example, you may have lived in an environment in which the values of a democratic form of government, the importance of education, and the traditional family structure were never challenged. Consequently, you have not been "immunized" against attacks on these values and beliefs. You have no counterarguments (antibodies) prepared to fight off possible attacks on your beliefs. So if someone were to come along with strong arguments against these beliefs, you might be easily persuaded.

Contrast these "germ-free" beliefs with issues that have been attacked and for which you have a ready arsenal of counterarguments. Your attitudes on gays and lesbians in the military, deforestation, abortion, nuclear weapons, and thousands of other issues have been challenged in the press, on television, and in our interpersonal interactions. As a result of this exposure, we have counterarguments ready for any attacks on our beliefs concerning these issues. We have been inoculated and immunized against attacks should someone attempt to change our attitudes or beliefs.

The Magnitude of Change Principle

The greater and more important the change you want to produce in your audience, the more difficult your task will be. The reason is simple: people demand a great number of reasons and lots of evidence before making important decisions—career changes, moving families to another state, or investing life savings in certain stocks.

On the other hand, they may be more easily persuaded (and demand less evidence) on relatively minor issues—whether to take the course Small Group Communication rather than Persuasion, or to give to the United Heart Fund instead of the American Heart Fund.

People change gradually, in small degrees over a long period of time. And although there are cases of sudden conversions, this general principle holds true more often than not. Persuasion, therefore, is most effective when it strives for small changes and works over a considerable period of time. For example, a persuasive speech stands a better chance when it tries to get the alcoholic to attend just one AA meeting rather than to give up alcohol for life. If you try to convince your audience to change their attitudes radically or to engage in behaviors to which they are violently opposed, your attempts may backfire.

When you have the opportunity to try to persuade your audience on several occasions—rather than simply delivering one speech—two strategies will prove relevant: the foot-in-the-door and the door-in-the-face techniques.

Do you find that women and men are likely to use different principles of persuasion? If so, which principles are women more likely to use? Which principles are men more likely to use?

Foot-in-the-Door Technique   This technique involves getting your foot in the door first. You first request something small, something that your audience will easily comply with. Once this compliance has been achieved, you then make your real request (Cialdini, 1984; DeJong, 1979; Freedman & Fraser, 1966; Pratkanis & Aronson, 1991). People are more apt to comply with a large request after they have complied with a similar but much smaller request. For example, in one study the objective was to get people to put a "Drive Carefully" sign on their lawn. When this (large) request was made first, only about 17 percent of the people were willing to comply. However, when this request was preceded by a much smaller request, in this case to sign a petition, between 50 and 76 percent complied with granting permission to install the sign.

For this strategy to work, the first request must be small enough to gain compliance. If it isn't, then the chance to gain compliance with the desired and larger request will be lost.

Door-in-the-Face Technique   This technique is the opposite of foot-in-the-door (Cialdini, 1984; Cialdini & Ascani, 1976). In this strategy you first make a large request that you know will be refused (for example, "We're asking most people to donate 100 dollars for new school computers"). Later, you make a more moderate request, the one you really want your listeners to comply with (for example, "Might you be willing to contribute 10 dollars?"). In changing from the large to the more moderate request, you demonstrate your willingness to compromise and your sensitivity to your listeners. The general idea here is that your listeners will feel that since you have made concessions, they will also make concessions and at least contribute something. Listeners will probably also feel that 10 dollars is actually quite little, considering the initial request and, research shows, are more likely to comply and donate the $10.

For this technique to work, the first request must be significantly larger than the desired request but not so large that it seems absurd and is rejected out of hand.

LOGIC

The logical aspect of public speaking consists basically of arguments which consist of evidence (for example, facts) and a conclusion. *Evidence* together with the *conclusion* that the evidence supports equal an argument. "Reasoning" is the process you go through in forming conclusions on the basis of evidence. For example, you might reason that since college graduates earn more money than non-graduates (*evidence*), Jack and Jill should go to college if they wish to earn more money (*conclusion*).

The same principles of logic will prove useful to the speaker in constructing the speech, to the listener in receiving and responding to the speech, and to the speech critic or analyst in analyzing and evaluating the speech. A poorly reasoned argument, inadequate evidence, and stereotypical thinking, for example, must be avoided by the speaker, recognized and responded to by the listener, and negatively evaluated by the critic.

General Test of Evidence
Before getting to the specific forms of argument or reasoning, let's review some general tests of support applicable to all forms of argument. We state these general tests

(and, in fact, all the tests of adequacy) as questions so that you may use them to evaluate your evidence and test the adequacy of your argument.

- *Recency.* We live in a world of rapid change. Economic strategies that worked for your parents will not work for you. Political strategies in place 10 years ago are now considered inappropriate. As the world changes, so must our strategies for coping with it. Therefore, it is important that your supporting materials be as recent as possible. Recency alone, obviously, does not make an effective argument. Yet, other things being equal, the more recent the evidence and support, the better.

- *Corroboration.* In drawing a conclusion (or in supporting a thesis) gather evidence and argument from numerous and diverse sources. When all or most of the evidence points in the same direction, you are on pretty firm ground. If some evidence points to yes and some evidence points to no, then perhaps you should reevaluate your conclusion. Just as you would be convinced by evidence all pointing in the same direction, so will your listeners.

- *Fairness.* You see the world through your own individual filters. You see the world, not objectively, but through your prejudices, biases, preconceptions, and stereotypes. Others see the world through their own filters. No one is totally objective. Consequently, in evaluating evidence, establish how fair or biased the sources are and in what direction they may be biased. A tobacco company and an impartial medical research institutes report on the connection between smoking and lung cancer should obviously be treated very differently. Question research conducted and disseminated by any special interest group. It is always legitimate to ask: To what extent might this source be biased? Might this source have a special interest that leads her or him to offer this evidence or this conclusion?

In reasoning from evidence to conclusion, four general forms of argument are used: reasoning from specific instances to a generalization, from analogy, from causes and effects, and from sign.

Reasoning from Specific Instances and Generalizations

In reasoning from specific instances (or examples), you examine several specific instances and then conclude something about the whole. This form of reasoning is useful when you want to develop a general principle or conclusion but cannot examine the whole. For example, you sample a few communication courses and conclude something about communication courses in general. You visit several Scandinavian cities and conclude something about the whole of Scandinavia.

You probably follow this same general process in dealing with other persons. For example, you see Samantha in several situations and conclude something about Samantha's behavior in general. You date Pat a few times, or maybe even for a period of several months, and on that basis draw a general conclusion about Pat's suitability as a spouse.

Technically, you may also argue in the other direction—namely, from a general principle to some specific instance. That is, you begin with some general statement or axiom that is accepted as true by the audience and argue that since something is true of the entire class, it must also be true of the specific instance, which is a member of that class. For example, listeners may all accept the general principle that Martians are lazy, uncooperative, and dull-witted. The argument from generalization would then apply this general principle to a specific instance, for example, "Obviously we should not hire Delta X since we do not want a lazy, uncooperative, stupid colleague."

In evaluating reasoning from specific instances use the following tests.

- *Were enough specific instances examined?* The larger the group you wish covered by your conclusion, the greater the number of specific instances you should examine. Also, the greater the diversity of items in the class, the more specific instances you will have to examine.
- *Were the specific instances examined representative?* If you wish to draw conclusions about an entire class, examine specific instances coming from all areas or subclasses within the major class.
- *Are there significant exceptions?* When you examine specific instances and attempt to draw a conclusion about the whole, take into consideration the exceptions.

Reasoning from Analogy

In reasoning from analogy, you compare like things and conclude that since they are alike in so many respects, they are also alike in some as yet unknown or unexamined respect. For example, you reason that since the meat at the Grand Union supermarket is fresh, the fish will be also. In this simple bit of reasoning, you compared two like things (the two foods, meat and fish) and concluded that what was known to be true about one item (that the meat was fresh), would also be true of the unknown item (the fish).

Analogies may be literal or figurative. In a *literal analogy* the items being compared are from the same class—foods, cars, people, countries, cities, or whatever. For example, in a literal analogy we might argue that (1) New York, Philadelphia, London, and Paris are like Los Angeles in all essential respects—they are all large cities and all have a few million people; (2) these cities have all profited from low-cost subway transportation; (3) therefore, Los Angeles would also profit from the construction of a subway system. Here, then, we have taken a number of like items belonging to the same class (large cities), have pointed out a number of similarities (large in area and having large populations), and then reasoned that the similarity would also apply to the unexamined item (the subway system).

In a *figurative analogy*, the items compared are from different classes. These analogies are useful for amplification but do not constitute logical proof.

In testing the adequacy of an analogy—here of literal analogies—ask yourself two general questions.

- *Are the two cases being compared alike in essential respects?* The more significant the differences, the less validity the analogy will have.
- *Do the differences make a difference?* In any analogy, the items being compared will be different: no two things are exactly the same. But in reasoning with analogies, ask yourself if the differences are significant enough to destroy the validity of your comparison.

Reasoning from Causes and Effects

In reasoning from causes and effects, you may go in either of two directions. You may reason from cause to effect (from observed cause to unobserved effect) or from effect to cause (from observed effect to unobserved cause).

Causal reasoning would go something like this. You would argue that X results from Y; and since X is undesirable, Y should be eliminated. In an actual speech, the reasoning might be presented like this:

> The Surgeon General and all the available evidence shows unmistakably that cancer [X] results from smoking [Y]. Smoking is personally destructive [X]; we have no choice but to do everything we can to eliminate smoking entirely [Y].

Alternatively, of course, you might argue that X results from Y; and since X is desirable, Y should be encouraged. In a speech, you might say something like this:

> We know that general self-confidence [X] results from positively reinforcing experiences [Y]. Therefore, if you wish to encourage the development of self-confidence in your children [X], give them positively reinforcing experiences [Y].

In testing reasoning from cause to effect or from effect to cause, ask yourself the following questions.

- *Might other causes be producing the observed effect?* Ask yourself if causes other than the one you are postulating might be producing these effects. Thus, you might postulate that poverty leads to high crime, but there might be other factors actually causing the high crime rate. Or poverty might be one cause, but it might not be the most important cause.
- *Is the causation in the direction postulated?* If two things occur together, it is often difficult to determine which is the cause and which is the effect. For example, a lack of interpersonal intimacy and a lack of self-confidence are often seen in the same person. The person who lacks self-confidence seldom has intimate relationships with others. But which is the cause and which is the effect? Of course, it might also be that some other previously unexamined cause (a history of negative criticism, for example) might be producing both the lack of intimacy and the low self-confidence.
- *Is there evidence for a causal rather than merely a time-sequence relationship?* Two things might vary together, but they may not be related in a cause-effect relationship. Divorce frequently results after repeated instances of infidelity, but infidelity itself may not be the cause of the divorce rate. Rather, some other factor may be leading to both infidelity and divorce. Thus, even though infidelity may precede divorce, it may not be the cause of it. When you assume that a temporal relationship implies a causal relationship, you are committing a fallacy of reasoning called *post hoc ergo propter hoc* ("after this, because of this").

Reasoning from Sign

Some years ago I went to my doctor because of some minor skin irritation. Instead of looking at my skin, the doctor focused on my throat, noticed that it was enlarged, felt around a bit, and began asking me a number of questions. Did I tire easily?

Yes. Did I drink lots of liquids? Yes. Did I always feel thirsty? Yes. Did I eat a great deal without gaining any weight? Yes. She then had me stretch out my hand and try to hold it steady. I couldn't do it. Lastly, she took a close look at my eyes and asked if I had noticed that they had expanded. I hadn't been aware of it, but when it was pointed out I realized that they had expanded.

These indicators were signs of a particular illness. Based on these signs, she made the preliminary diagnosis that I had a hyperthyroid condition. The results from blood and other tests confirmed the preliminary diagnosis. I was promptly treated, and the thyroid condition was corrected.

Medical diagnosis is a good example of reasoning by sign. The general procedure is simple. If a sign and an object, event, or condition are frequently paired, the presence of the sign is taken as proof of the presence of the object, event, or condition. Thus, the tiredness, extreme thirst, and overeating without weight gain were taken as signs of hyperthyroidism since they frequently accompany the condition.

In reasoning from sign, ask yourself these questions.

- *Do the signs necessitate the conclusion drawn?* Given the extreme thirst, overeating, and the like, how certain may I be of the hyperthyroid conclusion? With most medical and legal matters we can never be absolutely certain, but we can be "reasonably" certain.
- *Are there other signs that point to the same conclusion?* In the thyroid example, the extreme thirst could have been brought on by any number of factors. Similarly, the swollen throat and the overeating could have been attributed to other causes. Yet, taken together they seemed to point to only one reasonable diagnosis. This was later confirmed with additional and more sophisticated signs in the form of blood tests and thyroid scans. Generally, the more signs that point toward the conclusion, the more confidence you can have that it is valid.
- *Are there contradictory signs?* Are there signs pointing toward contradictory conclusions? If, for example, "Higgins" had a motive and a history of violence (signs that would support the conclusion that Higgins was the murderer), but Higgins also had an alibi for the time of the murder (a sign pointing to the conclusion of innocence), the conclusion of guilt would have to be reconsidered or discarded.

EMOTION

Emotional or psychological appeals—appeals to needs, desires, and wants—are the most powerful means of persuasion you possess. Because of their importance, we devote this entire section to explaining what psychological appeals are and how you can use them effectively. Specifically, we look at three issues: (1) the nature of psychological appeals; (2) the principles of motivation that apply to public speaking; and (3) specific motivational appeals that are widely used in public speaking.

When you use psychological appeals you direct your appeals to your listeners' needs and desires. Although psychological appeals are never totally separate from logical appeals, we consider them separately here. We are concerned here with motives, with those forces that energize or move or motivate a person to develop, change, or

Effective public speaking techniques vary widely from one culture to another. In some cultures, speakers are expected to present their arguments logically and dispassionately, whereas in others speakers are expected to present their case with great emotion. Do the principles covered here adequately convey the expectations of your own culture? Can you identify a culture for which these principles would need to be revised?

strengthen particular attitudes or ways of behaving. For example, one motive might be the desire for status. This desire might motivate you to develop certain attitudes about what occupation to enter, the importance of saving and investing money, and so on. It may move you to behave in certain ways—to buy Gucci shoes, a Rolex watch, or a Tiffany diamond. As these examples illustrate, appeals to status (or to any motive) may motivate different persons in different ways. Thus, the status motive may lead one person to enter the poorly paid but respected occupation of nursing. It may influence another to enter the well-paid but often disparaged real estate or diamond business.

One of the most useful analyses of motives is Abraham Maslow's fivefold classification, reproduced in Figure 20.1. One of the assumptions here is that you would seek to fulfill the need at the lowest level first and only then the need at the next higher level. Thus, for example, you would not concern yourself with the need for security or freedom from fear if you were starving (that is, if your need for food had not been fulfilled). Similarly, you would not be concerned with friendship or affectional relationships if your need for protection and security had not been fulfilled.

In this system certain needs have to be satisfied before other needs can motivate behavior. Thus, you need to determine what needs of the audience have been satisfied and, therefore, what needs might be used to motivate them. In most college classrooms, for example, you may assume that the two lowest levels—physiological needs and safety needs—have been reasonably fulfilled. For many students, however, the third level (love

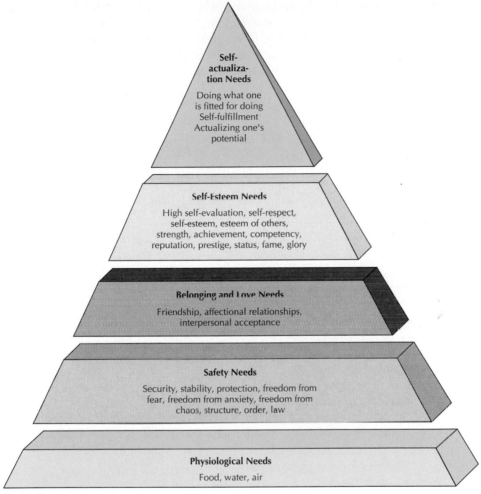

FIGURE 20.1 Maslow's Hierarchy of Needs. (*Source:* Based on Abraham Maslow, *Motivation and Personality,* New York: Harper & Row, 1970.)

needs) is not fulfilled, and propositions may be linked to these with great effectiveness. Thus, to assure the audience that what you are saying will enable them to achieve more productive interpersonal relationships or greater peer acceptance will go a long way toward securing their attention and receptiveness.

According to this system, satisfied needs do not motivate. For example, if the safety need of an individual is satisfied, that individual will not be motivated to seek further safety. Therefore, appeals to satisfied needs will not be persuasive. The insights of Maslow—as well as of various other theorists—underlie the principles of motivation that follow.

Motive Differences

Motives are not static, nor do they operate in the same way with different people. Motives differ from one time to another and from one person to another. Motives change with time. Think of the motives that are crucial to you at this time in your life and that motivate your current thinking and behavior. These motives, however, may not be significant 10 or even two years from now. They may fade and others may take their place. Now, for example, attractiveness may be one of the more dominant motives in your life. You have a strong need to be thought attractive by your peers. Later in life this motive may be replaced by, for example, the desire for security, for financial independence, for power, or for fame.

Motives also function differently with different people. This is simply a specific application of the general principle: people are different. Consequently, different people will respond differently to the very same motive. Further, different motives in different people may lead to the same behavior. Thus, three persons may choose to become college professors—one because of its security, one because of its relative freedom, and one because of its status. The resulting behavior in all three cases is essentially the same, but the motivational histories are very different.

Motive Ordering

Not all motives are equal in intensity. Some motives are strong. Some are weak. And the vast majority are somewhere in between. To complicate matters a bit more, the intensity of the various motives will vary from one time to another and from one communication situation to another.

Since motives vary in intensity and strength, they vary in the influence they have on the individual. It is obvious that people will be influenced more by motives that are strong and less by motives that are weak. Determining which motives your audience holds strongly and which weakly may be one of your most difficult tasks. But if you can identify those motives that will strongly influence the audience, you need not waste time on motives that are ineffective in influencing behavior.

Generally, the more specific the appeal, the more effective it will be. Consider, for example, the difference between the teacher's appeal to read this book because it will help to make you an educated person versus the appeal to read this book because it will help you to pass this course or the next test.

Motive Interaction

Motives rarely operate in isolation; usually a collection of motives operate together. Sometimes these motives operate in the same direction, all influencing behavior in the same way. At other times, motives may conflict with one another and each may stimulate behavior in different directions.

In cases where a number of motives influence behavior in the same direction, effective appeals need to be directed to several motives rather than limited to just one. For example, if you want an audience to contribute money to AIDS research, appeal to a variety of influential motives—safety for oneself and one's family and friends, altruism, control over the environment, and so on.

In cases where motives conflict with one another, your task is a more difficult one. Let us say that humanitarian motives would lead your audience to give money to AIDS research, but their desire for self-gain or for using their money to do other things would lead them not to donate funds. In this case you might propose that the humanitarian motives are more noble or perhaps that the amount of money involved is not so great as to prevent them from achieving their other goals.

Motive Complexity

The ways in which motives interact with attitudes and behaviors are not simple. Nor are they easy to predict. Two corollaries related to motive complexity may be noted here. First, there is no one-to-one correspondence between motive on the one hand and attitude and behavior on the other. You cannot examine attitudes and behaviors, for example, and conclude with any degree of certainty what an individual's motives are. Conversely, you cannot examine motivation and conclude that, therefore, such-and-such behaviors or attitudes will be manifested. The relationship between attitudes and behavior on the one hand and motivations on the other do not allow a simple cause-effect explanation.

Second, motivation does not guarantee action. A person may be motivated to engage in a specific behavior and yet may not do so. There are factors other than motives that influence attitudes and behaviors. Behaviors that are highly motivated may be inhibited, for example, by fear or anxiety. Behavior that is socially unacceptable is clearly of this type. You may, for example, be motivated to speak out against the management in your company because you fear losing your job.

Motive Appeals

Motivational appeals come in many forms. Each audience is different, and motives that are appropriately appealed to in one situation might be inappropriate or ineffective in another. You will always have to exercise judgment. With these qualifications in mind, here are some motives that persuaders rely upon. As you read through the list, you may find it interesting to recall a recent print or television advertisement that makes use of each of these motive appeals.

- *Altruism.* People want to do what they consider the right thing—to help others, to contribute to worthy causes, to help the weak, feed the hungry, and cure the sick.
- *Fear.* People are motivated in great part by a desire to avoid fear, fear of the loss of those things desired, for example, money, family, friends, love, attractiveness, health, job, and just about everything now possessed and valued. People also fear punishment, rejection, failure, the unknown, the uncertain, and the unpredictable.
- *Individuality and conformity.* People want to stand out from the crowd and may fear being lost in the crowd, being indistinguishable from everyone else. Yet many also want to conform, to be one of the crowd, to be "in."
- *Power, control, and influence.* People want power, control, and influence over themselves and over their own destinies. People also want control over other persons, to be influential, and to be opinion leaders.
- *Self-esteem and approval.* People want to see themselves as self-confident, as worthy and contributing human beings. Because of this need, inspirational speeches, speeches of the "you are the greatest" type, never seem to lack receptive and suggestive audiences.
- *Love and affiliation.* People are strongly motivated to love and be loved, to be assured that someone (preferably lots of people) loves them and at the same time to be assured they are capable of loving in return.
- *Achievement.* People want to achieve in whatever they do. You want to be a

successful student. As a teacher and writer I too want to be successful. You want to achieve as friends, as parents, as lovers. This is why you read books and listen to speeches that purport to tell you how to be better achievers.

- *Financial gain.* Most people seem motivated by the desire for financial gain— for what it can buy, for what it can do. Advertisers know this motive well and frequently get us interested in their messages by using such key words as *sale, 50 percent off, save now,* and the like. All of these are appeals to the desire for money.
- *Status.* In our society our status is measured by our occupation and wealth, but also by competence on the athletic field, from excelling in the classroom, or from superiority on the dance floor.
- *Self-actualization.* According to Maslow, the self-actualization motive only influences attitudes and behaviors after all other needs are satisfied. Yet we all have in some part a desire to self-actualize, to become what we feel we are fit for. If we see ourselves as poets, we must write poetry.

CREDIBILITY

How believable are you as a speaker? How believable are you apart from any evidence or argument you might advance? What is there about you as a person that makes us believe or not believe you? These are questions of **credibility**.

You have probably made judgments of speakers apart from any arguments, evidence, or motivational appeals they offered. Often you believe or disbelieve a speaker because of who the speaker is, not because of anything the speaker said. You may, for example, believe certain information or take certain action solely by virtue of Lee Iacocca's or Shirley MacLaine's reputation, personality, or character. Alexander Pope put it more poetically in his "Essay on Criticism":

> Some judge of author's names, not works, and then
> Nor praise nor blame the writings, but the men.

We call this quality of believability *speaker credibility.* Credibility is not something the speaker has or does not have in any objective sense. In reality the speaker may be a stupid, immoral person. If the audience perceives the speaker as intelligent and moral, then that speaker has high credibility. Further, research tells us, the audience will believe this speaker.

Much contemporary research focuses on what makes a person believable. Advertisers are interested because it relates directly to the effectiveness or ineffectiveness of their ad campaigns. Is Michael Jackson an effective spokesperson for Pepsi Cola? Is Bill Cosby an effective spokesperson for Jell-O?

Credibility is important to the politician because it determines in great part how people vote. It influences education, since the students' perception of teacher credibility will determine the degree of influence the teacher has on a class. There seems to be no communication situation that credibility does not influence.

We form a *credibility impression* of a speaker on the basis of two sources of information (Figure 20.2). First, we assess the reputation of the speaker as we know it. This is initial or what theorists call "extrinsic credibility." Second, we evaluate how that

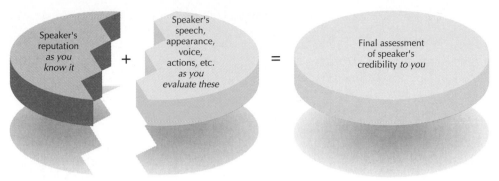

FIGURE 20.2 How we form credibility impressions.

reputation is confirmed or refuted by what the speaker says and does during the speech. This is derived or "intrinsic credibility." In other words, we combine what we know about the speaker's reputation with the more immediate information we get from present interactions. Information from these two sources—reputation and present encounters—interact and the audience forms some collective final assessment of credibility.

We can identify three major qualities of credibility. **Competence** refers to the knowledge and expertise the audience thinks the speaker has. **Character** refers to the intentions and concern of the speaker for the audience. **Charisma** refers to the personality and dynamism of the speaker. Figure 20.3 presents a sample rating scale for evaluating a speaker's credibility. It will serve as a visual summary of some of the more essential qualities we discuss next.

Competence

Competence refers to the knowledge and expertise a speaker is thought to have. The more knowledge and expertise the audience perceives the speaker as having, the more likely the audience will be to believe the speaker. For example, we believe a teacher to the extent that we think he or she is knowledgeable on the subject.

Competence is logically subject-specific. Usually, competence is limited to one specific field. A person may be competent in one subject and totally incompetent in another. Your political science instructor, for example, may be quite competent in politics but quite incompetent in mathematics or economics.

Often, however, we do not make the distinction between areas of competence and incompetence. Thus, we may see a person who we think competent in politics as competent in general. We will, therefore, perceive this person as credible in many fields. We refer to this as the *halo effect*—when listeners generalize their perception of competence to all areas. Listeners see the speaker's competence as a general trait of the individual.

This halo effect also has a counterpart—the *reverse halo effect*. Here the person, seen as incompetent in, say, mathematics, is perceived to be similarly incompetent in most other areas as well. As a critic of public speaking, be particularly sensitive to competence being subject-specific. Be sensitive to both halo and reverse halo effects.

Speaker

Knowledgeable	7	6	5	4	3	2	1	Unknowledgeable
Experienced	7	6	5	4	3	2	1	Inexperienced
Confident	7	6	5	4	3	2	1	Not confident
Informed	7	6	5	4	3	2	1	Uninformed
Fair	7	6	5	4	3	2	1	Unfair
Concerned	7	6	5	4	3	2	1	Unconcerned
Consistent	7	6	5	4	3	2	1	Inconsistent
Similar	7	6	5	4	3	2	1	Dissimilar
Positive	7	6	5	4	3	2	1	Negative
Assertive	7	6	5	4	3	2	1	Unassertive
Enthusiastic	7	6	5	4	3	2	1	Unenthusiastic
Active	7	6	5	4	3	2	1	Passive

The first four qualities refer to *competence*; the second four to *character*; the last four to *charisma*.

FIGURE 20.3 Rating scale for evaluating a speaker's credibility.

Character

We perceive a speaker as credible if we perceive that speaker as having high moral *character*. Here our concern is with the individual's honesty and basic nature. We want to know if we can trust that person. We believe a speaker we can trust. An individual's motives or intentions are particularly important in judging character.

When the audience perceives your intentions as good for them (rather than for your personal gain), they will think you credible. And, they will believe you.

Charisma

Charisma is a combination of the speaker's personality and dynamism as seen by the audience. We perceive as credible or believable speakers we like rather than speakers we do not like. We perceive as credible speakers who are friendly and pleasant rather than aloof and reserved. Similarly, we favor the dynamic over the hesitant, nonassertive speaker. We perceive as less credible the shy, introverted, soft-spoken individual than the extroverted and forceful individual. The great leaders in history have been dynamic people. Perhaps we feel that the dynamic speaker is open and honest in presenting herself or himself. The shy, introverted individual may be seen as hiding something. As speakers there is much that we can do to increase our charisma and hence our perceived credibility.

Summary

1. Among the *principles for communicating information* effectively are to: limit the amount of information, stress relevance and usefulness, present information at the appropriate level, relate new information to old, present information through several senses, and vary the level of abstraction.

2. Among the *principles of persuasion* are the principles of: selective exposure, audience participation, inoculation, and magnitude of change.

3. *Logical appeals* consist of evidence and argument which leads to a conclusion. General tests of evidence include recency, corroboration, and fairness.

4. The four *forms of reasoning* are from specific instances to a generalization, from analogy, from causes and effects, and from sign.

5. *Emotional appeals* are directed at the motives that energize people to behave in a certain way. Important characteristics of motives include their differences, ordering, interaction, and complexity.

6. *Speaker credibility* refers to the audience's perception of the speaker's believability and consists of judgements of competence, character, and charisma.

Applications

20.1 REASONING ADEQUACY

Here are, in brief, a few arguments. Read each of them carefully and (1) identify the type of reasoning used, (2) apply the tests of adequacy discussed in Unit 16, and (3) indicate what could be done to make the reasoning more logical *and* more persuasive.

1. Last year, the three campus theater productions averaged 250 paid admissions. In a college of 12,000 students and with a theater that seats 1,000, the record is not particularly good. It seems clear that students are apathetic and simply don't care about theater or about campus activities in general. Something should be done about this—to encourage an appreciation for the arts and support for college-sponsored activities in general.

2. Students are apathetic. This is true of high school as well as college students, at urban as well as campus schools. We see it all around us. So, why bother to build a new theater; the students are not going to attend the productions. Let's direct that money to something that will be used, something that will be useful to the students and to the community as a whole.

3. Dr. Manchester should be denied tenure for being an ineffective teacher. Two of my friends are in Manchester's statistics course and they hate it; they haven't learned a thing. Manchester's student evaluation ratings are way below the department and college average, and the readings Manchester assigns are dull, difficult, and of little relevance to students.

4. The lack of success among the Martians who have settle on Earth is not difficult to explain. They simply have no ambition, no drive, no desire to

excel. They're content to live on welfare, drink cheap wine, and smoke as much grass as they can get their hands on.

5. I went out with three people I met at clubs—they were all duds. In the club they were fine but once we got outside I couldn't even talk with them. All they knew how to do was wear freaky clothes and dance. So when Pat asked me out I said, "No." I decided it would be a waste of time.

6. College professors are simply not aware of the real world. They teach their courses in an atmosphere that is free of all the problems and complexities of real life. How could they possibly advise me as to how to go about preparing for and finding a job?

7. I took Smith's course in rhetorical theory and it was just great—and easy. In fact, only one test was given and it was simple. Everybody got an A or B+. We didn't even have a term paper, and the lectures were all really interesting and relevant. This semester I have room for an elective so I'm taking Smith's psycholinguistics course.

8. One recent sociological report indicates some interesting facts about Theta Three. In Theta Three there are, as most of us know, few restrictions on premarital sexual relations. Unlike in our country, the permissive person is not looked down on. Social taboos in regard to sex are few. Theta Three also has the highest suicide rate per 100 inhabitants. Suicide is not infrequent among teenagers and young adults. This condition must be changed. But before it is changed, life must be accorded greater meaning and significance. Social, and perhaps legal, restrictions on premarital sexual relations must be instituted if the individual is to have self-respect. Only in this way will the suicide rate—Theta Three's principal problem today—be significantly reduced.

9. In 1936 the *Literary Digest* took a poll to predict whether Landon or Roosevelt would win the presidential election. The *Digest* sent pre-election ballots to 10 million people, chosen at random from telephone directories and from lists of registered owners of automobiles. Two million ballots were returned and the *Digest* concluded that Landon would win the election.

10. Pat and Chris are unhappy and should probably separate. The last time I visited, Pat told me that they just had a big fight and mentioned that they now fight regularly. Chris spends more time with the kids than with Pat and frequently goes out after work with people from the office. Often, Chris has told me, they sit for hours without saying a word to each other.

20.2 CONSTRUCTING MOTIVATIONAL APPEALS

The *New York Post* (September 17, 1979, p. 19) reported that, according to "exhaustive studies," the 10 greatest sources of fear, in order of importance, are

1. Fear of losing money or not making enough; 80 percent noted this financial fear.

2. Fear of losing their jobs; 74 percent noted this.

3. Fear of ill health; 69 percent cited fear of real or imaginary ailments.

4. Fear of negative personal appearance; 59 percent feared that their personal appearance might handicap their chances for success.

5. Fear of political developments; 56 percent cited the fear of taxes and various government trends.

6. Fear of incompatibility; 44 percent feared marital difficulties and general incompatibility.

7. Fear of lack of self-confidence; 40 percent feared not having enough self-confidence.

8. Fear of religious confusion; 37 percent worried about what they should believe in terms of religious and philosophical convictions.

9. Fear of sexual matters; 34 percent worried about sexual temptations or transgressions.

10. Fear of trouble with relatives; 33 percent feared difficulties with relatives.

Select one of the specific purposes and audiences noted below and on page 386, and develop a motivational appeal based on one or more of these fears. After constructing these appeals, share the results of your labors with others, either in small groups or in the class as a whole. In your discussion you may wish to consider some or all of the following questions:

1. Why did you select the specific motivational appeal(s) you did?

2. Why did you assume that this (these) appeal(s) would prove effective with the topic and the audience selected?

3. How effective do you think such an appeal would be if actually presented to such an audience?

4. Might some of the appeals backfire and stimulate resentment in the audience? Why might such resentment develop? What precautions might be taken by the speaker to prevent such resentment from developing?

5. What are the ethical implications of using these motivational appeals?

6. What appeals to fear might prove more effective than the 10 noted here?

7. Where in the speech do you think you would place this (these) appeal(s)? In the beginning? Middle? End? Why?

Purposes

1. Marijuana should (not) be made legal for all those over 18 years of age.

2. Cigarette smoking should (not) be banned in all public places.

3. Capital punishment should (not) be law in all states.

4. Social Security benefits should be increased (decreased) by at least one-third.

5. Retirement should (not) be mandatory at age 65 for all government employees.

6. Police personnel should (not) be permitted to strike.

7. National health insurance should (not) be instituted.

8. Athletic scholarships should (not) be abolished.

9. Property taxes should (not) be abolished.

10. Required courses in college should (not) be abolished.

11. Teachers should (not) be paid according to performance rather than (but according to) seniority, degrees earned, or publications.

12. Divorce should (not) be granted immediately when the parties request it.

Audiences

1. Senior citizens of Metropolis

2. Senior Club of DeWitt Clinton High School

3. Small Business Operators Club of Accord

4. American Society of Young Dentists

5. Council for Better Housing

6. Veterans of Vietnam

7. Los Angeles Society of Interior Designers

8. Catholic Women's Council

9. National Council of Black Artist

10. Parent–Teachers Association of New Orleans Elementary Schools

11. Midwestern Council of Physical Education Instructors

12. Society for the Rehabilitation of Ex-Offenders

20.3 CREDIBILITY AND THE FAMOUS PERSON

Listed here are 28 famous personalities. For each person, identify the subject matter area(s) in which he or she would be perceived as credible and give at least one reason why you think so. Use your public speaking class as the target audience.

Ted Koppel	Edward Kennedy	Woody Allen
Al Gore	Michael Jackson	Martin Scorsese
Bill Clinton	Abigail Van Buren	Superman
Elizabeth Taylor	Coretta King	Dr. Ruth
Boris Yeltsin	Calvin Klein	Henry Kissinger
Bill Gates	Al Sharpton	Leo Buscaglia
George Lucas	Oprah Winfrey	Billy Graham
Hillary Clinton	Yoko Ono	Bill Cosby
Phil Donahue	David Brinkley	Madonna
Michael Jordon	Janet Reno	Ross Perot

After completing this exercise, discuss your responses with others, either in small groups or in the class as a whole. From an analysis of these responses, the following should be clear and may also serve as springboards for further discussion:

1. Each individual will be perceived in a somewhat different way by each other individual.

2. Each person—regardless of "expertise" or "sophistication"—will be perceived as credible on some topics by some audiences.

3. Credibility exists in the perception of the audience rather than in the person-speaker.

THE ANATOMY OF THE AUDIENCE AND THE SPEECH

UNIT CONTENTS

Anatomy of the Audience

The Sociology of Audiences

The Psychology of Audiences

Anatomy of the Speech

  Summary

  Applications
    21.1 Analyzing a Specific Audience
    21.2 Identifying Audience Attitudes
    21.3 The Anatomy of a Persuasive Speech

UNIT GOALS

After completing this unit, you should be able to

1. define *audience*

2. define *attitude*, *belief*, and *value*

3. identify the basic characteristics of the audience

4. identify the basic characteristics of the context

5. explain the four psychological dimensions of an audience

6. explain the anatomy of the public speech

In this unit we look at the audience and the speech. In public speaking—as in other forms of communication—the audience and the speech (the message and the listener) are really inseparable.

ANATOMY OF THE AUDIENCE

Public speaking audiences vary greatly. Thousands of people at Yankee Stadium listening to Billy Graham, 30 students in a classroom listening to a lecture, and five people listening to a street orator are all audiences. The characteristic that seems best to define such an audience is *common purpose*. An *audience* is a group of individuals gathered together to hear a speech.

You deliver a speech to inform or persuade your audience. A teacher lectures on Gestalt psychology to increase understanding. A minister talks against adultery to influence behaviors and attitudes. A football coach gives a pep talk to motivate the team to improve. All of these persons are trying to produce change. If they are to be successful, then they must know their audience. If you are to be successful, you must know your audience. This knowledge will help you in a variety of ways; here are just a few:

- selecting your topic
- phrasing your purpose
- establishing a relationship between yourself and your audience
- choosing examples and illustrations
- the words you use
- stating your thesis, whether directly or indirectly
- the arguments you use and the motives you appeal to
- choosing sources that will prove credible

Your first step in audience analysis is to construct an audience profile in which you analyze the sociological or demographic characteristics of your audience. These characteristics help you to estimate the attitudes, beliefs, and values of your audience. If you want to effect changes in these attitudes, beliefs, and values, you have to know what they are.

Attitudes, Beliefs, and Values

Attitude refers to your tendency to act for or against a person, object, or position. If you have a positive attitude toward the death penalty, you are likely to act in favor of instituting the death penalty (for example, vote for a candidate who supports the death penalty) or argue in favor of the death penalty. If you have a negative attitude toward the death penalty, then you are likely to act against it or argue against it. Attitudes influence how favorable or unfavorable listeners will be toward speakers who support or denounce the death penalty.

Belief refers to the confidence or conviction you have in the existence or truth of some proposition. For example, you may believe that there is an afterlife, that education is the best way to rise from poverty, that democracy is the best form of government, or that all people are born equal. If your listeners believe that the death penalty is a deterrent to crime, for example, then they will be more likely to favor arguments for (and speakers who support) the death penalty than would listeners who do not believe in the connection between death penalty and deterrence.

Value refers to the relative worth you place on an object, person, or position. Technically, value can refer to either positive or negative worth. In popular usage, however, we often reserve the term for positive evaluation. If your listeners place a high positive value on crime deterrence, then they will also positively view arguments that will help achieve this goal.

As you can readily see from this example of the death penalty, the attitudes, beliefs, and values that your listeners have will greatly influence how receptive they will be to your topic, your point of view, and your evidence and arguments.

Caution: All Generalizations Are False

The generalizations noted here seem true in most cases but may not hold for any specific audience. *Beware of using these generalizations as stereotypes.* Don't assume that all women or all older people or all highly educated people think or believe the same things. They do not. Nevertheless, there are characteristics that seem to be more common among one group than another. And it is these characteristics that we attempt to capture in these generalizations. Use these to stimulate your thinking about your specific and unique audience. Most important, test what is said here against your own experience.

THE SOCIOLOGY OF AUDIENCES

Six sociological or demographic variables are especially important: (1) age; (2) gender; (3) cultural factors; (4) educational and intellectual levels; (5) occupation, income, and status; and (6) religion.

Age

Different age groups have different attitudes, beliefs, and values simply because they have had different experiences. Take these differences into consideration in preparing your speeches.

For example, let us say that you are an investment counselor and you want to persuade your listeners to invest their money to increase their earnings. Your speech would have to be very different if you were addressing an audience of retired people (say, in their 60s) and an audience of young executives (in their 30s).

Here are some questions about age that you might find helpful in analyzing and in adapting to your audience.

1. *Do the age groups differ in the goals, interests, and day-to-day concerns that may be related to your topic and purpose?*
2. *Do the age groups differ in liberal-conservative views on matters relating to your topic and purpose?*
3. *Do the groups differ in their respect for tradition and the past or in the degree to which they are motivated by their peer group?*

Gender

Gender is one of the most difficult audience variables to analyze. The rapid social changes taking place today make it difficult to pin down the effects of gender. Although we use the shorthand "men" and "women," remember that psychological sex roles may be more significant than biological sex in accounting for these differences.

Here are some questions to guide your analysis of this very difficult audience characteristic.

1. *Do men and women differ in the values they consider important and that are related to your topic and purpose?*
2. *Will your topic be seen as more interesting by men? By women? Will men and women have different attitudes toward these topics?*
3. *Will men or women feel uncomfortable with your topic or purpose?*

Cultural Factors

Nationality, race, and cultural identity and identification are crucial in audience analysis. Largely because of different training and experiences, the interests, values, and goals of different cultural groups will also differ.

1. *Are the differences within cultures relevant to your topic and purpose?*
2. *Are the attitudes, beliefs, and values—about education, employment, or life in general—held by different cultures relevant to your topic and purpose?*
3. *Will the varied cultures differ in their goals or suggestions to change their lives?*

What other reasons might you offer for the importance of cultural characteristics? Can you give an example of how insight into the culture of your audience might benefit you as a public speaker in some specific way?

Educational and Intellectual Levels

An educated person may not be very intelligent. Conversely, an intelligent person may not be very well educated. In most cases, however, the two go together. Further, they seem to influence the reception of a speech in similar ways and so we consider them together. We use the shorthand "educated" to refer to both qualities.

In looking at the education and intelligence of your audience, consider asking questions such as the following.

1. *Are the educational levels related to the audience's level of social or political activism; for example, will the interests and concerns of the audience differ on the basis of their educational level?*
2. *Will the educational levels influence how critical the audience will be of your evidence and argument?*
3. *Will the educational levels relate to what the audience knows about your topic?*

Occupation, Income, and Status

Occupation, income, and status, although not the same, are most often positively related. Therefore, we can deal with them together.

1. *How will job security and occupational pride be related to your topic and purpose?*
2. *Will people from different status levels view long-range planning and goals differently?*
3. *Will the different status groups have different time limitations?*

Religion

Today there is great diversity within each religion. Almost invariably there are conservative, liberal, and middle-of-the-road groups within each religion. As the differences within each religion widen, the differences between and among religions seem to narrow. Different religions are coming closer together on various social and political, as well as moral, issues. Generalizations here, as with sex, are changing rapidly.

1. *Will the religious see your topic or purpose from the point of view of religion?*
2. *Does your topic or purpose attack the religious beliefs of any segment of your audience?*
3. *Do the religious beliefs of your audience differ in any significant ways from the official teachings of their religion?*

Other Factors

No list of audience characteristics can possibly be complete, and the list presented here is no exception. You will need another category—"other factors"—to identify any additional characteristics that might be significant to your particular audience. Such factors might include the following.

Expectations   How will your audience's expectations about you influence their reception of your speech?

Relational Status   Will the relational status of your audience members influence the way in which they view your topic or your purpose?

Special Interests   Do the special interests of your audience members relate to your topic or purpose?

Organizational Memberships   How might the organizational memberships of your audience influence your topic or purpose? Might you use these organizational memberships in your examples and illustrations?

Political Affiliation   Will your audience's political affiliations influence the ways in which they view your topic or purpose?

Context Characteristics

In addition to analyzing specific listeners, devote attention to the specific context in which you will speak. Consider the size of the audience, the physical environment, and the occasion, the time of your speech, and where your speech fits into the sequence of events.

How might the size of your audience influence your speech presentation? Generally, the larger the audience, the more formal the speech presentation should be. With a small audience, you may be more casual and informal.

How will the physical environment influence your speech presentation?

How might the occasion influence the nature and the reception of your speech?

How might the time during which you are to give your speech influence your presentation?

Where your speech fits into the general events of the time, for example, political events of the day but also the immediately preceding events such as the previous speakers.

THE PSYCHOLOGY OF AUDIENCES

Now that you have a firm grasp on the sociological characteristics of audiences, let's look into some additional ways in which audiences differ. We may view audiences along such scales as those in Figure 21.1. By indicating on each scale where a particular audience is (or where you think it is), you may construct an audience profile. Since each audience is unique, each audience will have a unique profile.

How Willing Is Your Audience?

Audiences gather with varying degrees of willingness to hear a speaker. Some are anxious to hear the speaker and might even pay substantial admission prices. The "lecture circuit," for example, is a most lucrative aspect of public life. Public figures often earn substantially more from speaking than they do from their regular salaries.

While some audiences are willing to pay to hear a speaker, others do not seem to care one way or the other. Still other audiences need to be persuaded to listen (or at least to sit in the audience). A group of people who gather to hear Shirley MacLaine talk about supernatural experiences are probably there willingly. They want to be there and

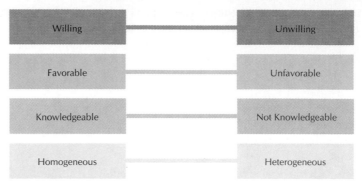

FIGURE 21.1 The dimensions of an audience.

they want to hear what MacLaine has to say. On the other hand, some groups gather because they have to. For example, the union contract may require members to attend meetings.

How Favorable Is Your Audience?

Audiences may or may not agree with your thesis or point of view. One group may be in agreement with your speech advocating comprehensive health insurance while another group may be totally against it. If you intend to change your audiences' attitudes, beliefs, or behaviors, you must understand their present position.

Audiences also differ in their attitudes toward you and toward your topic. At times the audience may have no real feeling, positive or negative. At other times they will have very clear feelings that must be confronted. Thus, when Richard Nixon addressed the nation after Watergate, it was impossible to avoid the audience's unfavorable attitude toward him as a person. Sometimes the degree of favorableness will depend not only on the specific speaker but on certain of the speaker's characteristics. Thus, a group of police officers may resent listening to a convicted felon argue against unlawful search and seizure. On the other hand, they might be quite favorable toward essentially the same speech given by a respected jurist or criminologist.

Similarly, audiences may have favorable or unfavorable responses to you because of your racial or ethnic origin, religion, or social status.

How Knowledgeable Is Your Audience?

Listeners differ greatly in the knowledge they have. Some listeners will be quite knowledgeable about the topic. Others will be almost totally ignorant. Mixed audiences are the really difficult ones. If you are unaware of the audience's knowledge, you will not know what to assume and what to explain. You will not know how much information will overload the channels and how much will bore the audience to sleep.

How Homogeneous Is Your Audience?

Audiences vary in homogeneity—the degree to which they have similar characteristics, for example, values, attitudes, knowledge, willingness, and so on. Homogeneous audiences consist of individuals who are very much alike. Heterogeneous audiences consist of widely different individuals.

Obviously, it is easier to address a homogeneous group than a heterogeneous group. If your listeners are alike, your arguments will be as effective for one as for another. The language appropriate to one will be appropriate to another, and so on, through all the elements of the public speaking transaction.

With a heterogeneous group, however, this does not hold. The argument that works with one subgroup will not work with another. The language that is appropriate to the educated members will not be appropriate to the uneducated. So, when you address a heterogeneous audience you will have to make some tough decisions.

ANATOMY OF THE SPEECH

Perhaps the best way to conclude these units on public speaking is to look at the anatomy of the speech, its parts and their functions. In the *Phaedrus* the ancient Greek philosopher Plato said that a speech is composed like a human, with a body (the main substance of the speech), a head (the introduction), and extremities (the conclusion). This provides a good starting place to examine the anatomy of the public speech.

Taking into consideration all the factors discussed here, how would you describe the easiest and the most difficult audience to persuade of each of the following propositions? (1) The death penalty should be declared illegal in all states. (2) Elementary school children should be taught about lesbian and gay families. (3) The federal government should provide free health care for all its citizens. (4) Immigration laws should be changed so that anyone who wishes to settle in this country should be allowed. (5) Condoms should be distributed to all students above the fourth grade in all public and private schools.

The Body

The main substance of a public speech is referred to as the body and is best viewed in terms of its thesis and the ways in which the support for this thesis may be arranged.

The Thesis   The thesis is the essence of your speech; it states what you want your audience to get out of your speech. It's the single idea you want them to go away with. If your speech is an informative one, then your thesis is the main idea that you want your audience to understand. Examples of such theses would be: "Human blood consists of four major elements," or "The new computerized billing system has three components."

If your speech is to be a persuasive one, then your thesis is the central idea that you wish your audience to accept or follow. Examples of such theses would be: "We should support Grace Moore for Union Representative" or "We should contribute to the college athletic fund."

Once you word the thesis statement, ask yourself—as would an audience—questions about the thesis to identify its major components. For an informative speech, the most helpful questions are *What?* or *How?* So, to the thesis "Human blood consists of four major elements," the logical question seems to be: *What are they?* To the thesis "The new computerized billing system has three components" the logical question would be: *What are they?* The answers to these questions identify the major propositions that you should cover in your speech. The answer to the question *What are the major elements of the blood?,* in the form of a brief speech outline, would look like this:

Thesis: "There are four major elements in the human blood." (What are they?)

   I.   Plasma
  II.   Red blood cells (erythrocytes)
 III.   White blood cells (leukocytes)
 IV.   Platelets (thrombocytes)

In a persuasive speech, the questions an audience would ask would be more often of the *Why?* type. If your thesis is "We should support Grace Moore for Union Representative," then the inevitable question is: *Why should we support Grace Moore?* Your answers to this question will then enable you to identify the major parts of the speech, which might look like this:

Thesis: "We should support Grace Moore" (Why should we support Grace Moore?)

   I.   Grace Moore is honest.
  II.   Grace Moore is knowledgeable.
 III.   Grace Moore is an effective negotiator.

Organizational Patterns   A speech that is clearly organized is easier to remember and will very likely better achieve its purpose. There are many organizational patterns that speakers use; we will discuss several.

Topical Pattern   This involves dividing your topic into its logical subdivisions or subtopics. Each subtopic becomes a main point (a major proposition) of your speech and each is treated approximately equally. You would then organize the supporting materials under each of the appropriate items. The body of the speech, then, might look like this:

I. Main point I
   A. Supporting material for I
   B. Supporting material for I
II. Main point II
   A. Supporting material for II
   B. Supporting material for II
   C. Supporting material for II
III. Main point III
   A. Supporting material for III
   B. Supporting material for III

Problem-Solution Pattern   For a persuasive speech you may wish to consider the problem-solution pattern. Let us say you want to persuade your listeners that medical schools should require communication courses. Your speech in outline form might look like this.

I. Doctors cannot communicate. (problem)
   A. They are inarticulate in expressing ideas. (problem 1)
   B. They are ineffective listeners. (problem 2)
   C. They do not see beyond the literal meaning. (problem 3)
II. Medical schools should require communication courses. (solution)
   A. Communication courses will train doctors to express themselves. (solution 1)
   B. Communication courses will train doctors in listening skills. (solution 2)
   C. Communication courses will train doctors to listen for meaning beyond the literal. (solution 3)

Temporal Pattern   Organizing propositions on the basis of some temporal (time) relationship is a popular and easy-to-use organizational pattern. It is also a pattern that listeners will find easy to follow. Generally, when you use this pattern, you organize your speech into two, three, or four major parts, beginning with the past and working up to the present or the future, or beginning with the present or the future and working back to the past.

The temporal (sometimes called chronological) pattern is especially appropriate for informative speeches in which you wish to describe events or processes that occur over time. It is also useful when you wish to demonstrate how something works or how to do something.

Most historical topics lend themselves to organization by time. The events leading up to the Civil War, the steps toward a college education, the history of writing, and the like would all be appropriate for temporal patterning. A time pattern would also be appropriate in describing the essential steps in a multistep process in which temporal order is especially important, for example, the steps involved in making interpersonal contact or in solving a problem.

Spatial Pattern   A spatial pattern is especially useful when you wish to describe objects or places. Like the temporal pattern it is an organizational pattern that listeners will find easy to follow as you progress, from top to bottom, left to right, inside to outside, or from east to west, for example.

Geographical topics generally fit well into organization by spatial patterning. Similarly, the structure of a place, object, or even animal is easily placed into a spatial pattern. You might describe the layout of a hospital, school, skyscraper, or perhaps even the structure of a dinosaur with a spatial pattern of organization.

Cause-Effect/Effect-Cause Pattern   Similar to the problem-solution pattern is the cause-effect or effect-cause pattern. This pattern is useful in persuasive speeches in which you want to convince your audience of the causal connection existing between two events or two elements. In the cause-effect pattern you divide the speech into two major sections, causes and effects.

For example, a speech on the reasons for highway accidents or birth defects might lend itself to a cause-effect pattern. Here you might first consider, say, the causes of highway accidents or birth defects and then some of the effects, for example, the number of deaths, the number of accidents, and so on.

Motivated Sequence Pattern   Developed by Alan H. Monroe in the 1930s and widely used in all sorts of oral and written communications, the motivated sequence is a pattern of arranging your information so as to motivate your audience to respond positively to your purpose (Gronbeck, McKerrow, Ehninger, & Monroe, 1990). In fact, it may be reasonably argued that all effective communications follow this basic pattern whether it is called the motivated sequence or given some other name.

The motivated sequence is especially appropriate for speeches designed to move an audience to action (to persuade your listeners to do something). However, it is also useful for a wide variety of informative speeches.

The previous organizational patterns provided ways of organizing the main ideas in the body of the speech. The motivated sequence is a pattern for organizing the entire speech. Here the speech (introduction, body, and conclusion) is divided into five parts or steps: attention, need, satisfaction, visualization, and action.

The attention step makes the audience give you their undivided attention. If you execute this step effectively, your audience should be anxious and ready to hear what you have to say. You can gain audience attention through a variety of means (more fully identified in the discussion of the introduction, which follows.)

The need step demonstrates that a need exists and that the audience should feel that something has to be learned or something has to be done because of this demonstrated need.

The satisfaction step presents the "answer" or the "solution" to satisfying the need that you demonstrated in Step 2. On the basis of this satisfaction step, the audience should now believe that what you are informing them about or persuading them to do will effectively satisfy the need. In this step you answer the question: How will the need be satisfied by what I am asking the audience to learn, to believe, to do? *The visualization step* intensifies the audience's feelings or beliefs. In this step you take the audience beyond the present time and place and enable them to imagine the situation as it would be if the need were satisfied as you suggested in Step 3.

The action step tells the audience what they should do to ensure that the need (as demonstrated in Step 2) is satisfied (as stated in Step 3). That is, what must the audience do to satisfy the need? Here you want to move the audience in a particular direction, for example, to speak in favor of additional research funding for AIDS or against cigarette advertising, to attend the next student government meeting, to contribute free time to read to the blind. You can accomplish this step by stating exactly what the audience members should do, using an emotional appeal, or giving the audience guidelines for future action.

Introductions

The introduction can serve three major functions: gain attention, establish a speaker-audience-topic connection, and orient the audience as to what is to follow.

Gain Attention   The introduction must gain the attention of the audience and focus it on the speech topic (Hashimoto, 1986). (And, of course, that attention must be maintained throughout your speech as well.) Attention is secured in a number of ways.

Questions are effective because they are a change from declarative statements and we automatically pay attention to change. *Rhetorical questions,* questions to which you don't expect an answer, are especially helpful in focusing the audience's attention on your subject: "Do you want to live a happy life?" "Do you want to succeed in college?" "Do you want to meet the love of your life?" Also useful are *polling-type questions,* questions which ask the audience for a show of hands: "How many of you have suffered through a boring lecture?" "How many of you intend to continue school after graduating college?" "How many of you have suffered from loneliness?"

Questions like these gain attention because they involve the audience; they tell the audience that you are talking directly to them and that you care about their responses. They are also useful because they focus the audience's attention on the subject of your talk.

Referring to audience members makes the audience perk up and pay attention, because they feel directly involved in the speech. Similarly, referring to recent happenings (for example, to a previous speech, recent event, or prominent person currently making news) gains attention because the audience is familiar with this and will pay attention to see how the speaker is going to approach it. Much as people are drawn to soap operas, so are we drawn to *illustrations and stories* about people. Here is an example from a speech by Brenda Dempsey (Boaz and Brey, 1988), a student from Eastern Michigan University, in a speech on genetic counseling:

> Mary Stewart was 23, happily married, and pregnant. A prenatal test showed it was a boy. But instead of the impending happiness which usually surrounds expectancy of a child, something was missing. You see, Mary's brother had been born with the crippling disease of Dishend's muscular dystrophy, a genetically inherited disease, which is passed on to boys from otherwise healthy mothers. Statistically, Mary stood a great chance of passing that disease to her unborn son.

People pay attention to what they feel is *important* to them and ignore what seems unimportant and irrelevant. For example, in addition to telling them that budget cuts will hurt education in the state (again, too general to relate to), the speaker tells them what this means to them specifically. For example:

> Budget cuts in the abstract mean little. So, let me tell you what these cuts will mean to us. First, our class size is going to be increased from thirty to fifty. Just think what that will mean in a course like Public Speaking. Second, all our laboratory courses will be eliminated. Those of us majoring in biology, chemistry, physics, physiology, and similar sciences will receive no practical experience. All these courses will be conducted purely as lecture courses. Third, our tuition—already too high to suit me and I'm sure most of you as well—will be increased by 30 percent!

Audiovisual aids are valuable because they are something new and different. They engage our senses, and thus our attention. When used in the introduction they serve to quickly secure the attention of the audience and let the audience know that this speech is going to be something special.

Telling the audience to pay attention is an obvious but effective means of securing attention. A simple, "I want you to listen to this frightening statistic," or "I want you to pay particularly close attention to. . . ," used once or twice in a speech, will help gain audience attention.

Quotations are useful because the audience is likely to pay attention to the brief and clever remarks of someone they have heard of or read about. Do make sure that the quotation is directly relevant to your topic. If you have to explain its relevance, it probably is not worth using.

Personal anecdotes gain attention because people enjoy hearing about other people's experiences or feelings. The popularity of tabloid journalism, television talk shows, and magazines like *People* and *US* provide ample evidence of this universal interest in people.

Little known facts or statistics will help perk an audience's attention. Headlines on unemployment statistics, crime in the schools, and political corruption sell newspapers because they gain attention.

Establish a Speaker-Audience-Topic Relationship   In addition to gaining attention, the introduction may help establish a connection among speaker, audience, and topic. The speaker tries to answer the listeners' inevitable question: Why should we listen to you speak on this topic? You can establish an effective speaker-audience-topic relationship in a number of ways.

The introduction is a particularly important time to *establish your competence, character, and charisma* (see Unit 20 for more detail).

Referring to others present will help gain attention and also help to establish an effective speaker-audience-topic relationship. Likewise, referring to the *reason the audience has gathered* establishes a speaker-audience-topic connection.

Expressing your pleasure in speaking effectively establishes a speaker-audience-topic relationship. *Paying the audience an honest and sincere compliment* makes them not only pay attention but also feel a part of your speech. In this example Eric Rubenstein (1992) compliments the audience directly by noting the group's accomplishments:

> Let me compliment your fine organization, Job Resources, on having counseled and job-trained more than 7,000 individuals, and having also obtained permanent employment for almost 2,000 men and women since 1979.

By *stressing similarity* with members of the audience the speaker creates a bond with them and become an "insider" instead of an "outsider."

Orient the Audience   The introduction should orient the audience in some way to what is to follow in the body of the speech. The orientation may be covered in a variety of ways.

Giving a general idea of the subject is probably the most common way:

Tonight I'm going to discuss atomic waste.
My concern today is with pollution.
I want to talk with you about the problems our society has created for the aged.

Sometimes a more *detailed preview* is needed:

I want to discuss three major problems confronting the economy. First, . . .

Conclusions

The conclusion is especially important because it is often the part of the speech that the audience remembers most clearly. It is the conclusion that in many cases determines what image is left in the minds of the audience. Generally, conclusions serve three major functions.

Summarize   The summary function is particularly important in an informative speech and less so in persuasive speeches or in speeches to entertain. A speaker may summarize the speech by restating the thesis or main assertion of the speech, by restating the importance of the topic or thesis, or by restating your major propositions (along with the thesis).

Motivate   A second function of the conclusion—most appropriate in persuasive speeches—is to motivate the audience. In the conclusion the speaker has the opportunity to give the audience one final push. Whether it is to buy stock, vote a particular way, or change an attitude, the conclusion serves effectively for a final motivation. One widely used motivation is the emotional appeal conclusion. Although widely used in religious speaking, it is often seen as inappropriate in, say, a classroom setting. On certain solemn occasions and with highly emotional issues, it may prove extremely effective.

Close   The third function of the conclusion is to provide closure. Often the summary will accomplish this, but in some instances it will prove insufficient. Speeches should end with a conclusion that is crisp and definite. The audience should know that the speech is definitely and clearly ended. Some kind of wrap-up, some sort of final statement, is helpful in providing this feeling of closure. Closure may be achieved through a variety of methods.

A quotation is often an effective means of providing this closure. Linda Reivitz (1985) uses a quotation in a humorous but pointed way to conclude her speech on women's equality:

I would like to close today with a salute to former President Grover Cleveland, who in 1905 said, "Sensible and responsible women do not want to vote." May all those who display equal enlightenment as that attain an equal place in history.

Summary

1. The *audience* is central to any conception of public speaking and must be analyzed carefully if an effective speech is to be constructed and if we are to understand the ways in which a speech has an effect.

2. A *sociological or demographic analysis* of the audience consists of analyzing age, gender, cultural factors, education and intellectual levels, occupation, income and status, and religion. In addition, your audiences' expectations, relational status, special interests, organizational memberships, and political affiliations often provide useful insight into who they are and what their attitudes and beliefs are.

3. The *size of the audience*, the *physical environment*, the *occasion*, the *time* of the speech, and the *sequence of events* are helpful in constructing and in relating a speech to the uniqueness of the situation.

4. In addition to its demographic characteristics, an audience needs to be examined in terms of its psychological *willingness* to hear the speech, its *favorableness*, its *knowledge* about the speech topic, and its *homogeneity*.

5. A speech consists of three main parts. They are *introduction*, *body*, and *conclusion*.

6. The *body* consists of a *thesis* and *propositions* which support the thesis.

7. The *introduction* gains attention, establishes a speaker-audience-topic relationship, and orients the audience as to what the speech will deal with.

8. The conclusion summarizes the thesis or the major arguments, motivates the audience, and provides crisp and clear closure for the speech.

Applications

21.1   ANALYZING A SPECIFIC AUDIENCE

This experience should familiarize you with some of the essential steps in analyzing an audience on the basis of relatively little evidence and in predicting their attidudes.

The class should be broken up into small groups of five or six members. Each group will be given a different magazine; their task is to analyze the audience (i.e., the readers or subscribers) of that particular magazine in terms of the characteristics discussed in Unit 7. The only information the groups will have about their audience is that they are avid and typical readers of the given magazine. Pay particular attention to the types of articles published in the magazine, the advertisements, the photographs or illustrations, the editorial statements, the price of the magazine, and so on.

Appropriate magazines for analysis are *Gentlemen's Quarterly, Movie Life, Ms., Playboy, Playgirl, Scientific American, Field and Stream, Family Circle, Good Housekeeping, Reader's Digest, National Geographic, Modern Bride, Gourmet, Architectural Digest, Christopher Street, Essence,* and *Personal Computing.* Magazines that differ widely from each other are most appropriate for this experience.

After the audience has been analyzed, try to identify at least three favorable and three unfavorable attitudes that they probably hold. On what basis do you make these predictions? If you had to address this audience advocating a position with which they disagreed, what adaptations would you make? That is, what strategies would you use in preparing and presenting this persuasive speech?

Each group should share with the rest of the class the results of their effort, taking special care to point out not only their conclusions but the evidence and reasoning they used in arriving at the conclusions.

21.2 IDENTIFYING AUDIENCE ATTITUDES

This exercise will enable you to deal with some of the issues involved in audience analysis and adaptation. Try to predict the attitudes of your class members toward each of the following propositions by indicating how you think the majority of the class members feel about each. Record the number of the attitude you predict the majority of the members hold. Use the following scale:

1 = strongly in favor of the proposition as stated
2 = mildly in favor of the proposition as stated
3 = neutral
4 = mildly against the proposition as stated
5 = strongly against the proposition as stated

After you have completed the predictions for all propositions, select one that you predicted the audience to be "strongly against" and indicate what kinds of adaptations you would make to get your audience to accept the proposition or at least to feel more positively toward it than they do now.

After all persons have completed both parts of this experience, the class as a whole or in small groups should discuss the following issues:

- The accuracy-inaccuracy with which the various attitudes were predicted
- The possible sources for the inaccurate and accurate guesses
- The appropriateness-inappropriateness of the adaptations proposed

1. Marijuana should be legalized for all persons over 18.
2. All required courses (general education requirements) should be abolished.
3. Parochial elementary and high schools should be tax supported.
4. NC-17-rated movies (even XXX movies) should be shown on television without time restrictions.
5. Prostitution (male and female) should be legalized.
6. Puerto Rico should be made the fifty-first state.
7. Members of minority groups that have been discriminated against should be given preferential treatment in entrance to graduate and professional schools.

Public Communication

Questions and Activities

1. How adequately does the model of public speaking describe public speaking as you understand it? Are there other elements you would add? Can you use the model to describe the classroom lecture?

2. What other differences would you identify between conversation and public speaking?

3. How would you describe your own speaker apprehension? Do you suffer from state apprehension? Trait apprehension? If state apprehension, what situations lead you to experience apprehension? What form does this apprehension take? That is, what behaviors do you engage in or not engage in as a result of this apprehension? What seems to help you to reduce it to a manageable level?

4. How does your apprehension in public speaking compare to your apprehension in conversations, small groups, and meetings? How might you account for these differences?

5. Of the five factors that account for speaker apprehension (perceived novelty, subordinate status, conspicuousness, dissimilarity, and prior history), which would influence you the most in giving a speech in your human communication class?

6. What standard of criticism would you use to evaluate an instructor's lecture? A politician's campaign speech? A religious leader's sermon? A classroom speech?

7. Apply each of the different standards of criticism (effectiveness, conformity to the principles of the art, universality, historical justification, and ethical merit) to the speeches identified in Unit 19, page 360. What problems does each standard create? What insights does each standard provide?

8. Create an evaluation form for rating a public speech. Include all the elements that you consider significant to the effectiveness of a public speech.

9. What principle of informative speaking do you think is the most important? Which principle do you see violated most often? What consequences do such violations have?

10. Can you identify any of the principles of informative speaking on television commercials?

11. Can you identify specific instances in which you use the principle of selective exposure? What effects does this have?

12. Can you identify those of your own beliefs for which you feel you are in-

oculated? Can you identify uninoculated beliefs? How does your inocula-
tion-uninoculation influence the way in which you respond to messages?

13. Has either the foot-in-the-door or the door-in-the-face technique ever
been used on you? Was it successful in gaining your compliance? If it was
successful, did you then or do you now resent it?

14. Select one of the following propositions: (a) Cigarette advertising should
be banned from all media; (b) AIDS awareness courses should be instituted in elementary schools; (c) Social security benefits should be discon-
tinued for those who earn over $100,000 per year. Construct an argu-
ment from specific instances, from analogy, from causes and effects, and
from signs for or against any one of these propositions.

15. What motives most influence your own behaviors, for example, your
studying, your work habits, and your relationship interactions?

16. Examine the list of motive appeals presented in Unit 20, pages 379–380.
In what ways do these motives influence your behaviors? Are there any
motives listed that are totally irrelevant to you?

17. Who do you think is the most credible person today on international politics? Religion? Self-awareness? Economics? Education?

18. In which areas would you ascribe high credibility to Madonna? Bill Clinton? Betty Friedan? Al Gore? Jesse Jackson? Michael Jackson? Ross Perot?
Martin Scorsese? Meryl Streep? Oprah Winfrey?

19. In what ways did issues of credibility influence the Anita Hill–Clarence
Thomas confrontation? Ross Perot's 1992 presidential campaign? The results of the last presidential election?

20. Examine your own credibility. In what ways and in what situations are
you perceived as credible? In what ways and in what situations do you
lack credibility?

21. Overall, would you generally be perceived as most credible in terms of
competence, character, or charisma? In which area would you be weakest?

22. Identify two of your most important attitudes, beliefs, and values. Which
attitudes, beliefs, and values do you maintain but which you would consider relatively unimportant? In what ways do the important ones differ
from the unimportant ones?

23. Are there other audience factors that you would consider important to
the persuasive speaker? Other context characteristics?

24. Can you formulate at least one generalization that might be useful to the
persuasive speaker on the basis of the audience's age; gender; culture; education or intellectual level; occupation, income, and status; and religion? Can you identify instances in which this generalization would not
hold?

25. What factors other than willingness, favorableness, knowledge, and homogeneity would you consider in drawing a psychological profile of your
audience?

26. What was the thesis of the last movie you saw? The last novel or short story you read?

27. Is it possible for a speech to have no introduction or no conclusion?

28. What other organizational patterns might be useful for organizing the major propositions in a public speech?

Skill Check

_____ 1. I understand the ways in which public speaking differs from conversation and can adjust my messages accordingly. (Unit 19)

_____ 2. I understand my own level of speaker apprehension and the major factors that influence it. (Unit 19)

_____ 3. I can apply a variety of standards in the evaluation of public communications. (Unit 19)

_____ 4. In communicating information, I follow the principles of information load, relevance, appropriateness, new to old, several senses, and levels of abstraction. (Unit 20)

_____ 5. In persuading, I follow the principles of selective exposure, audience participation, inoculation, and magnitude of change. (Unit 20)

_____ 6. In persuasion where there are several attempts, I can develop strategies based on the foot-in-the-door and the door-in-the-face techniques. (Unit 20)

_____ 7. I can recognize when such techniques as foot-in-the-door and door-in-the-face are used on me. (Unit 20)

_____ 8. When confronted with evidence, I apply the general tests of recency, corroboration, and fairness. (Unit 20)

_____ 9. In evaluating reasoning from specific instances, I ask: Were enough specific instances examined? Were the specific instances representative? Were there significant exceptions? (Unit 20)

_____ 10. In evaluating reasoning from analogy, I ask: Are the two cases being compared alike in essential respects? Do the differences make a difference? (Unit 20)

_____ 11. In evaluating reasoning from causes and effects, I ask: Might other causes be producing the observed effect? Is the causation in the direction postulated? Is there evidence for a causal rather than merely a time-sequence relationship? (Unit 20)

_____ 12. In reasoning from sign, I ask: Do the signs necessitate the conclusion drawn? Are there other signs that point to the same conclusion? Are there contradictory signs? (Unit 20)

_____ 13. I understand the motives—their hierarchy, complexity, and interaction—that influence my behaviors. (Unit 20)

_____ 14. I can use a variety of motives in framing appeals to persuade others—for example, fear; power, control, and influence; achievement; and financial gain. (Unit 20)

_____ 15. In my communications, I seek to establish my credibility by displaying competence, stressing my character, and acting dynamic (charisma). (Unit 20)

_____ 16. I can analyze an audience's characteristics and draw inferences about their attitudes, beliefs, and values on a wide variety of issues while recognizing that these inferences are generalizations that may be false for any specific audience. (Unit 21)

_____ 17. I can analyze an audience's willingness, favorableness, knowledge, and degree of homogeneity for a wide variety of topics, speakers, and situations. (Unit 21)

_____ 18. I can analyze a message and identify its thesis. (Unit 21)

_____ 19. I can construct a unified message built around a single thesis. (Unit 21)

_____ 20. I can organize information into such standard patterns as topical, problem-solution, temporal, spatial, cause-effect, and motivated sequence. (Unit 21)

_____ 21. I can gain an audience's attention through a variety of methods, for example, asking questions, referring to audience members, relating relevant illustrations, and using audiovisual aids. (Unit 21)

_____ 22. I can establish a speaker-audience-topic relationship by, for example, establishing my competence, referring to others present, and expressing my pleasure in speaking. (Unit 21)

_____ 23. I can orient an audience by giving them a general idea of the subject or a detailed preview. (Unit 21)

_____ 24. I summarize the major points in a speech in my conclusion. (Unit 21)

_____ 25. I can use the principles of motivation to motivate an audience in the conclusion of my speech. (Unit 21)

_____ 26. I provide a crisp closure in my speeches so that the audience knows that I am concluding my speech. (Unit 21)

SUGGESTED READINGS

Cialdini, Robert B. *Influence: How and Why People Agree to Things.* New York: Morrow, 1984. A popular but scholarly account of persuasion.

Dawson, Roger. *Secrets of Power Persuasion.* Englewood Cliffs, NJ: Prentice-Hall, 1992. A lively, thorough, and sound introduction to the practical side of persuasion.

Rank, Hugh. *The Pep Talk: How to Analyze Political Language.* Park Forest, IL: The Counter Propaganda Press, 1984. An excellent guide to analyzing persuasive messages of all kinds.

Richmond, Virginia P. and James C. McCroskey. *Communication: Apprehension, Avoidance, and Effectiveness,* 3rd ed. Scottsdale, AZ: Gorsuch Scarisbrick, 1992. An excellent introduction to speaker apprehension, what it is and how to manage it.

Riggio, Ronald E. *The Charisma Quotient: What It Is, How to Get It, How to Use It.* New York: Dodd, Mead, 1987. A popular but academically sound review of credibility.

Smith, Lawrence J. and Loretta A. Malandro. *Courtroom Communication Strategies.* New York: Kluwer Law Book Publishers, 1985. Applies the principles of public speaking and persuasion to the courtroom.

Textbooks in public speaking and persuasion will offer much additional insight into the topics covered briefly in these units. See, for example, DeVito (1994), Gronbeck, McKerrow, Ehninger, and Monroe (1994), Sprague and Stuart (1988), Larson (1992), and Woodward and Denton (1992).

Popular books on public speaking are plentiful. See, for example, Axtell (1992), Leeds (1988), Brody and Kent (1993), Buckley (1988), and Leech (1992).

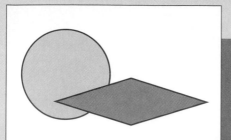

INTERCULTURAL COMMUNICATION

Unit 22. Preliminaries to Intercultural Communication: Importance, Difficulties, and Forms

Unit 23. Intercultural Communication: Principles, Barriers, and Gateways

Part 6. Feedback
Questions and Activities
Skill Check
Suggested Readings

The previous units stressed the importance of culture throughout human communication. This part of the text looks at intercultural communication as an area of study within human communication. Intercultural communication can occur in interpersonal, interviewing, small group, public, and mass communication. Its distinguishing characteristic is in the cultural differences among participants. The first unit (Unit 22) considers the importance of intercultural communication, the difficulties involved in mastering it, and its nature and forms. The second unit (Unit 23) explores the principles, barriers, and gateways to effective intercultural interaction.

Approaching Intercultural Communication

In approaching the study of intercultural communication, keep the following in mind:

- Try to see each culture's ways of behaving as one possible but arbitrary system. Avoid the tendency to evaluate the values, beliefs, and behaviors of your own culture as more positive than those of other cultures.

- Remember that the way you think about cultural differences when in a classroom or reading a textbook may not correspond with the way you behave. In a classroom your mindful state dominates. Outside the classroom you may communicate mindlessly—without thinking critically.

- Cultures differ within themselves. So a culture is to characterize its central concerns and not any absolute beliefs or behaviors. In fact, the failure to see differences within cultures will prove just as troublesome as the failure to see differences among cultures.

- More intercultural communication will not necessarily increase intercultural understanding; it is the quality, not the quantity, of communication that will make the difference.

PRELIMINARIES TO INTERCULTURAL COMMUNICATION

Importance, Difficulties, and Forms

UNIT CONTENTS

The Importance of Intercultural Communication

The Nature of Intercultural Communication

The Difficulty in Mastering Intercultural Communication

Summary

Application

   22.1 Dealing with Intercultural Obstacles

UNIT GOALS

After completing this unit, you should be able to

1. explain the factors accounting for the importance of intercultural communication

2. define *culture*, *enculturation*, and *acculturation*

3. define *intercultural communication* and its several forms and explain the model of intercultural communication presented in this unit

4. distinguish between collectivist and individualistic orientation and between low- and high-context cultures

5. explain ethnocentrism, mindfulness, and fear as contributors to intercultural communication difficulties

Before going into the specifics of this unit, consider your own willingness to engage in intercultural communication in interpersonal, small group, public, and mass communication situations. The self-test on pages 418 and 419 is designed to help you explore your openness to communication with members of other cultures.

THE IMPORTANCE OF INTERCULTURAL COMMUNICATION

Intercultural communication is more important today and more vital than at any other point in history (Dodd, 1991; Gudykunst & Kim, 1990, 1992; Samovar, Porter, & Jain, 1981). Factors such as mobility, economic and political interdependence, and communication technology contribute to this importance.

Mobility

The mobility of people throughout the world is at its height. Travel from one country to another and from one continent to another is at an all-time high. People now frequently visit other cultures for the pleasure of exploring new lands and different people and for promising economic opportunities. Your interpersonal relationships are becoming increasingly intercultural.

Another aspect of mobility is the changing immigration patterns. A walk through any major city in the United States will show that we are still a nation of immigrants (see Figure 22.1). Whether you are a long-time resident or a newly arrived immigrant,

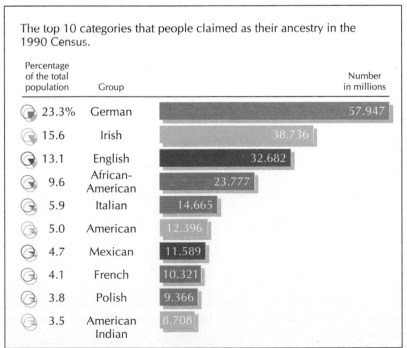

STATISTICAL PORTRAIT OF THE NATION

The top 10 categories that people claimed as their ancestry in the 1990 Census.

Percentage of the total population	Group	Number in millions
23.3%	German	57.947
15.6	Irish	38.736
13.1	English	32.682
9.6	African-American	23.777
5.9	Italian	14.665
5.0	American	12.396
4.7	Mexican	11.589
4.1	French	10.321
3.8	Polish	9.366
3.5	American Indian	8.708

FIGURE 22.1 Ancestry of United States resident.

How Open Are You Interculturally?

Select a specific culture (national, racial, or religious) different from your own, and substitute this culture for the phrase *culturally different person* in each of the questions below. Indicate how open you would be to communicate in each of these situations, using the following scale:

5 = very open and willing
4 = open and willing
3 = neutral
2 = closed and unwilling
1 = very closed and unwilling

___ 1. Talk with a culturally different person while alone waiting for a bus.

___ 2. Talk with a culturally different person in the presence of those who are interculturally similar to you.

___ 3. Have a close friendship with a culturally different person.

___ 4. Have a long-term romantic relationship with a culturally different person.

___ 5. Participate in a problem-solving group that is composed predominantly of culturally different people.

___ 6. Openly and fairly observe an information-sharing group consisting predominantly of culturally different people.

___ 7. Lead a group of culturally different people through a problem-solving or information-sharing group.

___ 8. Participate in a consciousness-raising group in which half the participants are culturally different people.

___ 9. Listen openly and fairly to a speech by culturally different person.

___ 10. Give a speech to an audience composed primarily of culturally different people.

you are living, going to school, and working with people very different from you. Your day-to-day experiences are becoming increasingly intercultural.

Economic and Political Interdependence

Today, most countries are economically dependent on other countries. At one time, not too long ago, the economic life of the United States was tied to Europe whose cultures were in many ways similar to those in the United States. Today, however, for much of our trade and technological equipment we have turned to East Asia—Japan, Korea, and Taiwan—cultures very different from the European-based cultures that were previously our dominant trade partners. Our economic lives depend on our ability to communicate effectively across different cultures.

Similarly, our political well-being greatly depends on that of other cultures. Polit-

SELF-TEST (continued)

_____ 11. Listen fairly to a public speaker describing this different cultural group.

_____ 12. Ascribe a level of credibility for a culturally different person identical to that ascribed to an culturally similar person—all other things being equal.

_____ 13. Listen fairly and openly to a television show favorable to the culturally different people.

_____ 14. Listen fairly and openly to a television program favorable to the culturally different people and at the same time unfavorable to your own culture.

_____ 15. Peruse on a fairly regular basis a newspaper or magazine addressed exclusively to culturally different people (written in a language you understand).

_____ 16. Attend to a variety of media in an effort to learn more about the culturally different people.

Scoring   This test was designed to raise questions rather than to provide answers. Questions 1 through 4 refer to your interpersonal communication behaviors; 5 through 8 to your small group communication behaviors; 9 through 12 to your public communication behaviors; and 13 through 16 to your mass communication behaviors. To calculate your scores, simply add your scores for each of these subsets of four questions; that is, to obtain your interpersonal openness score add your responses to questions 1, 2, 3, and 4. High scores for any subset (say above 14) indicate considerable openness; low scores for any subset (say below 10) indicate a lack of openness. Use these numbers for purposes of responding to the following questions rather than to indicate any absolute level of openness or closedness.

● Did you select the group on the basis of whether your attitudes were positive or negative? Why? What group would you be most open to interacting with? Least open? Why?

● In which form of communication are you most open? Least open? Why?

● How open are you to learning about the importance of greater intercultural understanding and communication?

● How open are you to learning what members of other groups think of your cultural groups?

ical unrest in any part of the world—South Africa, Eastern Europe, and the Middle East, to take a few examples—affects our own security. Intercultural communication and understanding seem now more crucial than ever.

Communication Technology

The rapid spread of communication technology has brought foreign and sometimes strange cultures right into your living rooms. From the television miniseries *Shogun* you learned about Japanese customs and history. From *The Immigrants* you learned about the many cultures that passed through Ellis Island on their way to a new life in the United States. News from foreign lands is commonplace. You see nightly—in vivid color—what is going on in "remote" countries: the starvation in Somalia, the eth-

Here is a street in Toronto, Canada, which has changed dramatically because of recent immigration. Note, too, Figure 22.1, which identifies the ancestry of people in the United States as reported in the 1990 census. How will your city look (culturally) 10 years from now? 30 years from now? How will a chart of ancestry for the United States look for the census from the year 2000? From the year 2020? How will this change the nature of your interactions? How might you best prepare yourself for those changes?

nic and religious war in Bosnia, and the political and economic changes in Russia, China, and so many other areas. And you can—as phone companies say repeatedly—dial direct to just about anywhere in the world.

Technology has made intercultural communication easy, practical, and inevitable.

Daily the media bombard you with evidence of racial tensions, religious disagreements, sexual bias and, in general, the problems caused when intercultural communication fails.

THE NATURE OF INTERCULTURAL COMMUNICATION

Culture refers to the relatively specialized life-style of a group of people—consisting of their values, beliefs, artifacts, ways of behaving, and ways of communicating—that is passed on from one generation to the next. Included in culture would be all that members of a social group have produced and developed—their language, modes of thinking, art, laws, and religion.

This culture is transmitted from one generation to another through a process known as enculturation. Culture is transmitted through learning, not through genes. Parents, peer groups, schools, religious institutions, and government agencies are the main teachers of culture.

Acculturation refers to the processes by which a person's culture is modified through direct contact with or exposure to (say, through the mass media) another culture. For example, when immigrants settle in the United States (the host culture), their own culture becomes influenced by the host culture. Gradually, the values, ways of behaving, and beliefs of the host culture become more and more a part of the immigrants' culture. At the same time, of course, the host culture changes too. Generally, however, the culture of the immigrant changes more. As Young Yun Kim (1988) puts it, "a reason for the essentially unidirectional change in the immigrant is the difference between the number of individuals in the new environment sharing the immigrant's original culture and the size of the host society."

The acceptance of the new culture depends on a number of factors (Kim, 1988). Immigrants who come from cultures similar to the host culture will become acculturated more easily. Similarly, those who are younger and better educated become acculturated more quickly than do older and less well-educated persons. Personality factors are also relevant. Persons who are risk takers and openminded, for example, have a greater acculturation potential. Also, persons who are familiar with the host culture prior to immigration—whether through interpersonal contact or mass media exposure—will be acculturated more readily.

Intercultural communication refers to communication between persons who have different cultural beliefs, values, or ways of behaving. The model in Figure 22.2 further explains this concept. The larger circles represent the culture of the individual communicator. The inner circles identify the communicators (the sources/receivers). In this model each communicator is a member of a different culture. In some instances the cultural differences are relatively slight—say, between persons from Toronto and New York. In other instances the cultural differences are great—say, between persons from Borneo and Germany, or between persons from rural Nigeria and industrialized England.

All messages originate from a specific and unique cultural context, and that context influences their content and form. You communicate as you do largely as a result of your culture. Culture (along with the processes of enculturation and acculturation) influences every aspect of your communication experience.

You receive messages through the filters imposed by your cultural context. That context influences what you receive and how you receive it. For example, some cultures rely heavily on television or newspapers and trust them implicitly. Others rely on face-to-face interpersonal interactions, distrusting many of the mass communication systems.

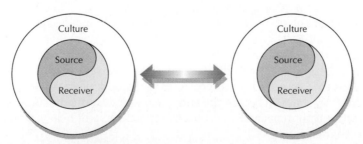

FIGURE 22.2 A model of intercultural communication.

The Forms of Intercultural Communication

The term *intercultural* refers broadly to all forms of communication among persons from different groups as well as to the more narrowly defined area of communication between different cultures. The model of intercultural communication presented in Figure 22.2 includes all of the following. As you read through these forms try to imagine a specific intercultural interaction you have had or might have for each one.

1. Communication between cultures—for example, between Chinese and Portuguese, or between French and Norwegian.
2. Communication between races (sometimes referred to as **interracial communication**)—for example, between blacks and whites.
3. Communication between ethnic groups (sometimes referred to as **interethnic communication**)—for example, between Italian-Americans and German-Americans (Kim, 1986).
4. Communication between religions—for example, between Roman Catholics and Episcopalians, or between Moslems and Jews.
5. Communication between nations (sometimes referred to as **international communication**)—for example, between the United States and Mexico, or between France and Italy.
6. Communication between cultures within cultures—for example, between doctors and patients, or between the blind and the sighted.
7. Communication between different cultural groups, both belonging to the same general culture—for example, between homosexuals and heterosexuals, or between teenagers and senior citizens.
8. Communication between the sexes—between men and women (Pearson, Turner, & Todd-Mancillas, 1991; Tanner, 1990; Elgin, 1993).

The Ways Cultures Differ

Examining the ways in which cultures differ will help us understand the intercultural communication differences. Following Gudykunst (1991) and Hall and Hall (1987) we can single out two ways in which cultures differ that have a major impact on their members' communications: individual and collective orientation and high- and low-contexts (see also Table 22.1).

Individual and Collective Orientation   Cultures differ in the extent to which an individual's goals and desires or the group's goals and desires are given precedence. Individual and collective tendencies are not mutually exclusive; this is not an all-or-none orientation but rather one of emphasis. Thus, you may, for example, compete with other members of your basketball team for most baskets or most valuable player award (and thus emphasize individual goals). At the same time, however, you will—in a game—act in a way that will benefit the entire team (and thus emphasize group goals). In actual practice both individual and collective tendencies will help you and your team each achieve your goals.

At times, however, these tendencies may come into conflict. For example, do you shoot for the basket and try to raise your own individual score or do you pass the ball to another player who is better positioned to score the basket and thus benefit your team?

Table 22.1   Some Cultural Differences

Individual (Low-Context) Cultures	Collective (High-Context) Cultures
The individual's goals are most important	The group's goals are most important
The individual is responsible for himself or herself and to his or her own conscience	The individual is responsible for the entire group and to the group's values and rules
Success depends on the individual's surpassing others	Success depends on the individual's contribution to the group
Competition is emphasized	Cooperation is emphasized
Clear distinction is made between leaders and members	Little distinction is made between leaders and members; leadership would normally be shared
In-group versus out-group distinctions are of little importance	In-group versus out-group distinctions are of great importance
Information is made explicit; little is left unsaid	Information is often left implicit and much is often omitted from explicit statement
Personal relationships are less important; hence, little time is spent getting to know each other in meetings and conferences	Personal relationships are extremely important; hence, much time is spent getting to know each other in meetings and conferences
Directness is valued; face-saving is seldom thought of	Indirectness is valued and face-saving is a major consideration

Source: This table is based on the work of Hall (1983) and Hall and Hall (1987) and the interpretations by Gudykunst (1991) and Victor (1992).

You make this distinction in popular talk when you call someone a team player (collectivist orientation) or an individual player (individualistic orientation).

In an individualistic-oriented culture members are responsible for themselves and perhaps their immediate family. In a collectivist culture members are responsible for the entire group. Success, in an individualistic culture, is measured by the extent to which you surpass other members of your group; you would take pride in standing out from the crowd. And your heroes—in the media, for example—are likely to be those who are unique and who stand apart. In a collectivist culture success is measured by your contribution to the achievements of the group as a whole; you would take pride in your similarity to other members of your group. Your heroes, in contrast, are more likely to be team players who do not stand out from the rest of the group's members.

In an individualistic culture you are responsible to your own conscience and responsibility is largely an individual matter; in a collectivistic culture you are responsible to the rules of the social group and responsibility for an accomplishment or a failure is shared by all members. Competition is fostered in individualistic cultures while cooperation is promoted in collectivist cultures.

In an individualistic culture you might compete for leadership in a small group setting and there would likely be a very clear distinction between leaders and members. In a collectivist culture leadership would be shared and rotated; there is likely to be little distinction between leader and members.

Distinctions between in-group members and out-group members are extremely important in collectivist cultures. In individualistic cultures, where the person's individuality is prized, the distinction is likely to be less important.

Here a group of Bolivians march in native costume in the Columbus Day Parade in New York
City. How would you describe your own culture
in terms of individual and collective orientation
and high and low context? How do those characteristics influence your own communications?

High- and Low-Context Cultures   A high-context culture is one in which
much of the information in communication is in the context or in the person—for example, information that is shared through previous communications, through assumptions about each other, and through shared experiences. The information is not explicitly stated in the verbal message.

A low-context culture is one in which most of the information in communication
is explicitly stated in the verbal message, and in formal transactions in written (contract) form.

To appreciate the distinction between high and low context, consider giving directions ("Where's the voter registration center?") to someone who knows the neighborhood and to a newcomer to your city. To someone who knows the neighborhood (a
high-context situation) you can assume that he or she knows the local landmarks. So,
you can give directions such as "next to the laundromat on Main Street" or "the corner
of Albany and Elm." To the newcomer (a low-context situation), you could not assume
that he or she shares any information with you. So, you would have to use only those
directions that even a stranger would understand, for example, "make a left at the next
stop sign" or "go two blocks and then turn right."

High-context cultures are also collectivist cultures (Gudykunst, Ting-Toomey, &
Chua, 1988; Gudykunst & Kim, 1992). These cultures (Japanese, Arabic, Latin American, Thai, Korean, Apache, and Mexican are examples) place great emphasis on personal relationships and oral agreements (Victor, 1992). Low-context cultures are also
individualistic cultures. These cultures (German, Swedish, Norwegian, and the United
States are examples) place less emphasis on personal relationships and more emphasis
on the written, explicit explanation and, for example, on the written contracts in business transactions.

It is interesting to note that as relationships become more intimate, they come to resemble high-context interactions. The more you and your partner know each other, the less you have to make verbally explicit. Truman Capote once defined love as "never having to finish your sentences" which is an apt description of high-context relationships. Because you know the other person so well, you can make some pretty good guesses as to what the person will say.

Members of high-context cultures spend lots of time getting to know each other interpersonally and socially before any important transactions take place. Because of this prior personal knowledge a great deal of information is shared and therefore does not have to be explicitly stated. Members of low-context cultures spend a great deal less time getting to know each other and hence do not have that shared knowledge. As a result everything has to be stated explicitly. High-context members rely more on nonverbal cues in reducing uncertainty (Sanders, Wiseman, & Matz, 1991).

We noted earlier (in our discussion of small group communication) that the Japanese spend lots of time getting to know each other before conducting actual business, whereas the Americans will get down to business very quickly. The reason for this difference may be explained in terms of contexting. The Japanese (and other high-context cultures) want to get to know each other because important information is only made implicit. They have to know you so they can read your nonverbals, understand when no means no and when it means yes. The American can get right down to business because all important information will be stated explicitly.

To high-context cultural members what is omitted or assumed is a vital part of the communication transaction. Silence, for example, is highly valued (Basso, 1972). To low-context cultural members what is omitted creates ambiguity. And to this person this ambiguity is simply something that will be eliminated by explicit and direct communication. To high-context cultural members ambiguity is something to be avoided; it is a sign that the interpersonal and social interactions have not proved sufficient to establish a shared base of information (Gudykunst, 1983).

When this simple difference is not understood, intercultural misunderstandings can easily result. For example, the directness characteristic of the low-context culture may prove insulting, insensitive, or unnecessary to the high-context cultural member. Conversely, to the low-context member, the high-context cultural member may appear vague, underhanded, or dishonest in his or her reluctance to be explicit or engage in communication that a low-context member would consider open and direct.

Another frequent source of intercultural misunderstanding that can be traced to the distinction between high- and low-context cultures can be seen in face-saving (Hall & Hall, 1987). High-context cultures place a great deal more emphasis on face-saving. For example, they are more likely to avoid argument for fear of causing others to lose face whereas low-context members (with their individualistic orientation) will use argument to win a point. Similarly, in high-context cultures criticism should only take place in private to enable the person to save face. Low-context cultures may not make this public-private distinction. Low-context managers who criticize high-context workers will find that their criticism causes interpersonal problems and does little to resolve the original difficulty that led to the criticism in the first place (Victor, 1992).

High-context cultures are reluctant to say no for fear of offending and causing the person to lose face. And so, for example, it is necessary to be able to read in the Japanese executive's yes when it means yes and when it means no. The difference is not in the words used but in the way in which they are used. It is easy to see how the low-context individual may interpret this reluctance to be direct—to say no when you mean no—as a weakness or as an unwillingness to confront reality.

THE DIFFICULTY IN MASTERING INTERCULTURAL COMMUNICATION

Intercultural communication is a difficult area to study and research and even more difficult to master. Three major difficulties are ethnocentrism, mindlessness, and fear.

Ethnocentrism

One difficulty is the tendency to see others and their behaviors through your own cultural filters. **Ethnocentrism** is the tendency to evaluate the values, beliefs, and behaviors of your own culture as being more positive, logical, and natural than those of other cultures. Ideally, you would see both yourself and others as different but equal, with neither being inferior nor superior.

Ethnocentrism exists on a continuum. People are not either ethnocentric or not ethnocentric; rather, most are somewhere between these polar opposites. And, of course, your degree of ethnocentrism varies depending on the group on which you focus. For example, if you are Greek American, you may have a low degree of ethnocentrism when dealing with Italian Americans but a high degree when dealing with Turkish Americans or Japanese Americans. Most important for our purposes is that your degree of ethnocentrism (and we are all ethnocentric to at least some degree) will influence your interpersonal, group, public, and mass communication behaviors.

Table 22.2, drawing from a number of studies (Gudykunst, 1991; Gudykunst & Kim, 1984; Lukens, 1978), summarizes some of the interconnections. Five degrees of

Table 22.2 The Ethnocentrism Continuum

Degree of Ethnocentrism	Communication Distance	Communications
Low	Equality	Treats others as equals; views different customs and ways of behaving as equal to your own.
	Sensitivity	Wants to decrease distance between self and others.
	Indifference	Lacks concern for others; prefers to interact in a world of similar others.
	Avoidance	Avoids and limits communications, especially intimate ones, with interculturally different others.
High	Disparagement	Engages in hostile behavior; belittles others; views different cultures and ways of behaving as inferior to his/her own.

ethnocentrism are identified; in reality, of course, there are as many degrees as there are people. The "communication distances" are general terms that highlight the attitude that dominates that level of ethnocentrism. Under "communications" are some of the major ways people might interact given their particular degree of ethnocentrism.

Mindlessness and Mindfulness

We can see a second difficulty by considering the distinction between mindless and mindful states (Langer 1978, 1989). When you are in a mindless state, you operate with assumptions that would not normally pass intellectual scrutiny. For example, we know that cancer is not contagious and yet we often avoid touching cancer patients. Similarly we often avoid touching those who are crippled or who have AIDS. Researchers exploring such unrealistic behaviors found that approximately one-third of participating college students said that they would not go swimming in a pool used by mental patients (Wheeler, Farina, and Stern, 1984). They also said that they would wash their hands after touching a mental patient. When the discrepancies between available evidence and our behavioral tendencies are pointed out and our mindful state is awakened, we realize that these behaviors are not logical or realistic.

When we deal with people from other cultures we are often in our mindless state and we therefore function nonrationally, in many ways. When our mindful state is awakened, as it is in academic discussions such as this one, we quickly resort to a more logical and rational mode of thinking. You recognize that other people and other cultural systems are different but not inferior or superior to yours. Thus, the barriers and gateways we discuss in the next unit may appear quite logical to your mindful state. You often ignore them, however, when in your mindless state.

Langer (1989) offers several suggestions for increasing mindfulness which are especially useful in intercultural communication. Try to provide a specific example or application for each of these suggestions.

- Create and recreate categories. See an object, event, or person as belonging to a wide variety of categories. Avoid storing in memory an image of a person, for example, with only one specific label; it will be difficult to recategorize it later.
- Be open to new information even if it contradicts your most firmly held stereotypes.
- Be open to different points of view. This will help you avoid the tendency to blame outside forces for your negative behaviors ("that test was unfair") and internal forces for the negative behaviors of others ("Pat didn't study," "Pat isn't very bright"). Be willing to see your own and others' behaviors from a variety of perspectives.
- Be careful of relying too heavily on first impressions, what psychologists call "premature cognitive commitment" (Chanowitz and Langer 1981; Langer 1989). Treat your first impressions as tentative, as hypotheses.

Fear

Another factor that stands in the way of mastering intercultural communication is fear (Gudykunst, 1990; Stephan & Stephan, 1985). You may wish to think of your responses to the self-test ("How Open Are You Interculturally?") as you consider these specific types of fear.

You may fear for your self-esteem. You may become anxious about your ability to control the intercultural situation or you may worry about your own level of discomfort.

You may fear that you will be taken advantage of by the member of this other culture. Depending upon your own stereotypes you may fear being lied to, financially duped, or made fun of.

You may fear that members of this other group will react to you negatively. You may fear, for example, that they will not like you or may disapprove of your attitudes or beliefs or they may even reject you as a person. Conversely, you may fear negative reactions from members of your own group. They might, for example, disapprove of your socializing with the culturally different.

These fears—coupled with the greater effort that intercultural communication takes and the ease with which you communicate with those who are culturally similar—can easily create sufficient anxiety to make some people give up.

Because your ways of communicating are largely culturally determined, persons from different cultures will communicate differently. Take special care, therefore, to see that cultural differences do not prevent meaningful interaction, but instead serve as sources for enriching your communication experiences. If communication is to be effective, these differences need to be understood and appreciated. Equally important is the understanding of the common barriers and effectiveness principles for communication between different cultures. We turn to this topic in the next unit.

Summary

1. *Intercultural communication* has become increasingly important because of increased mobility of people throughout the world, the economic interdependence of most countries, advances in communication technology, changing immigration patterns, and the political interdependence among countries.

2. *Culture* refers to the relatively specialized life-style of a group of people, consisting of their values, beliefs, artifacts, ways of behaving, and ways of communicating, that is passed on from one generation to the next.

3. *Enculturation* refers to the process by which culture is transmitted from one generation to the next.

4. *Acculturation* refers to the processes by which one culture is modified through contact with or exposure to another culture.

5. Culture influences the messages you send and how you send them and the messages you receive and how you receive them. *Communication rules and customs* are culturally determined.

6. Intercultural communication encompasses a broad range of communication and includes at least the following: *communication between cultures, between races, between ethnic groups, between religions,* and *between nations*.

7. Cultures differ in terms of the degree to which they teach individualistic or collectivist orientations.

8. High-context cultures are those in which much of the information is in the context or in the person's nonverbals; low-context cultures are those in which most of the information is explicitly stated in the message.

9. *Ethnocentrism* refers to the tendency to evaluate other cultures negatively and our own culture positively.

10. Distinguishing between states of *mindfulness* and *mindlessness* is helpful in understanding why intercultural communication may appear simple on the surface but may be extremely difficult in actual practice.

11. *Cultivate mindfulness* by creating and recreating categories, being open to new information, being open to different points of view, and avoiding too heavy an emphasis on first impressions.

12. *Fear* for your self-esteem, that you will be taken advantage of, or that members of your own group will react negatively toward you may contribute to further difficulties in intercultural interaction.

Application

22.1   DEALING WITH INTERCULTURAL OBSTACLES

How might you deal with each of the following obstacles to intercultural understanding and communication?

1. Your friend makes fun of Radha, who comes to class in her native African dress. You feel you want to object to this.

2. Craig and Louise are an interracial couple. Craig's family treat him fairly but virtually ignore Louise. They never invite Craig and Louise as a couple to dinner or to partake in any of the family affairs. The couple decide that they should confront Craig's family and ask your advice.

3. Malcolm is a close friend and is really an open-minded person. But he has the habit of referring to members of other racial and ethnic groups with derogatory language. You decide to tell him that you object to this way of talking.

4. Tom, a good friend of yours, wants to ask Pat out for a date. Both you and Tom know that Pat is a lesbian and will refuse the date and yet Tom says he's going to have some fun and ask her anyway—just to give her a hard time. You think this is wrong and want to tell Tom you think so.

5. Your parents persist in holding stereotypes about other religious, racial, and ethnic groups. These stereotypes come up in all sorts of conversations. You are embarrassed by these attitudes and feel you must tell your parents how incorrect you think these stereotypes are.

6. Lenny, a colleague at work, recently underwent a religious conversion. He now persists in trying to get everyone else—yourself included—to undergo this same religious conversion. Every day he tells you why you should convert, gives you literature to read, and otherwise persists in trying to convert you. You decide to tell him that you find this behavior offensive.

INTERCULTURAL COMMUNICATION

Principles, Barriers, and Gateways

UNIT CONTENTS

Principles of Intercultural Communication

Barriers to Intercultural Communication

Gateways to Intercultural Communication

Summary

Application

23.1   Responding to Intercultural Difficulties

UNIT GOALS

After completing this unit, you should be able to

1. explain three principles of intercultural communication
2. explain the five barriers to intercultural communication
3. define *culture shock* and explain how this may function as a communication barrier
4. explain how the characteristics of effective conversation apply to intercultural communication

Nacirema culture is characterized by a highly developed market economy which has evolved in a rich natural habitat. While much of the people's time is devoted to economic pursuits, a large part of the fruits of these labors and a considerable portion of the day are spent in ritual activity. The focus of this activity is the human body, the appearance and health of which loom as a dominant concern in the ethos of the people. While such a concern is certainly not unusual, its ceremonial aspects and associated philosophy are unique.

The fundamental belief underlying the whole system appears to be that the human body is ugly and that its natural tendency is to debility and disease. Incarcerated in such a body, man's only hope is to avert these characteristics through the use of the powerful influences of ritual and ceremony. Every household has one or more shrines devoted to this purpose. The more powerful individuals in the society have several shrines in their houses and, in fact, the opulence of a house is often referred to in terms of the number of such ritual centers it possesses. Most houses are of wattle and daub construction, but the shrine rooms of the more wealthy are walled with stone. Poorer families imitate the rich by applying pottery plaques to their shrine walls.

While each family has at least one such shrine, the rituals associated with it are not family ceremonies but are private and secret. The rites are normally only discussed with children, and then only during the period when they are being initiated into these mysteries. I was able, however, to establish sufficient rapport with the natives to examine these shrines and to have the rituals described to me.

The focal point of the shrine is a box or chest which is built into the wall. In this chest are kept the many charms and magical potions without which no native believes he could live. These preparations are secured from a variety of specialized practitioners. The most powerful of these are the medicine men, whose assistance must be rewarded with substantial gifts. However, the medicine men do not provide the curative potions for their clients, but decide what the ingredients should be and then write them down in an ancient and secret language. This writing is understood only by the medicine men and by the herbalists who, for another gift, provide the required charm.

From these observations of anthropologist Horace Miner (1956) you might conclude that the Nacirema are a truly strange people. But, look more carefully and you will see that we are the Nacirema and the rituals are our own. *Nacirema* is *American* spelled backwards. In the excerpt quoted, Miner describes the bathroom and the doctor writing prescriptions for the druggist. This excerpt is important because it brings into clear focus the fact that cultural customs (your own as well as those of others) are not logical or natural. Rather, they are better viewed as useful or not useful to the members of that particular culture. The excerpt is a timely reminder against ethnocentric thinking (your customs are right and others are wrong). The excerpt also awakens our mindful state and encourages us to think more objectively about our own customs and values.

This unit continues the discussion of intercultural communication and examines the underlying principles of intercultural communication, the most common barriers to intercultural communication and understanding, and some guidelines (*gateways*) for making intercultural communication more effective and satisfying.

As a preface to this discussion, consider the cases in the self-test on pages 434 and 435 (Axtell, 1990a, 1990b; Jensen, 1985). They are designed to awaken your mindful state about intercultural communication and to introduce just a few ways in which cultural differences may hinder effective communication (Samovar & Porter, 1988).

PRINCIPLES OF INTERCULTURAL COMMUNICATION

We may gain added insight into intercultural communication by examining three general principles. These principles derive largely from language and communication theories that are now being applied to intercultural communication.

Language Relativity

The general idea that language influences thought and ultimately behavior got its strongest expression from linguistic anthropologists. In the late 1920s and throughout the 1930s, the view was formulated that the characteristics of language influence the way you think (Carroll, 1956; Fishman, 1960; Hoijer, 1954; Miller & McNeill, 1969; Sapir, 1929). Since the languages of the world differ greatly in semantics and syntax (or structure), it was argued that people speaking widely different languages would also differ in how they viewed and thought about the world.

Subsequent research and theory, however, did not support the extreme claims made by linguistic relativity researchers. A more modified hypothesis seems currently supported: The language you speak helps to structure what you see and how you see it. As a result, people speaking widely differing languages will see the world *somewhat* differently. Thus, the Eskimo who has many words for snow may notice nuances that might escape an English speaker's attention (at least initially).

If communication stopped here (at the naming stage), language differences would make effective intercultural communication impossible. Fortunately, communication doesn't stop here. In conversation, for example, you explain yourself, ask questions, and ask for feedback ("Am I making myself clear?" "Do you know what I mean by. . . ?"). These efforts quickly erase the differences between most languages. In short, language differences do not make for very important differences in perception, thought, or behavior. Difficulties in intercultural understanding are not due to language differences but to ineffective communication.

Uncertainty Reduction

The greater the cultural differences, the greater the general uncertainty and ambiguity in communication will be (Berger & Bradac, 1982; Gudykunst, 1989). All relationships involve uncertainty. Much of your relational communication tries to reduce this uncertainty so you can better describe, predict, and explain the behaviors of others. Because of this greater uncertainty and ambiguity, it is necessary to take more time and effort to reduce this uncertainty and communicate meaningfully.

Further, in situations of great uncertainty the techniques of effective communication (for example, active listening, perception checking, being specific, and seeking feedback) take on added importance in intercultural situations.

Active listening and perception checking techniques, for example, help you to check on the accuracy of your perceptions and allow you the opportunity to revise and amend any incorrect perceptions. Being specific reduces ambiguity and the chances of misunderstandings. Misunderstanding is a lot more likely when talking about neglect (a highly abstract concept) than when talking about forgetting your last birthday (a specific event).

Seeking feedback helps you to correct any possible misconceptions almost immediately. Seek feedback on whether you are making yourself clear ("Does that make

SELF-TEST

What Do You Know About Intercultural Differences?

In each of the following six cases, something went wrong. What was it? Try to identify, individually or in a group, at least one possible explanation for the ineffective communication in each situation. (Following custom, the term *American* designates a person from the United States, although technically all persons from North and South America are "Americans." Most, however, prefer to be designated more specifically by their country of origin—for example, *Canadian, Argentinean,* and *Mexican.* And most persons from the United States prefer to be referred to as *American.*)

1. An American and an Arab are talking in an open yard. After a brief discussion the American concludes that the Arab was pushy and overly familiar; the Arab concludes that the American was cold and "standoffish."

2. An American and a Latin American are having dinner in a Latin American restaurant. The American raises his hand and tries to catch the waiter's eye, to no avail. The Latin American hits the water glass with a fork. The waiter comes to take the order. The Latin American concludes that the American is shy and unassertive. The American concludes that the Latin American is rude and overly aggressive.

3. An American couple living in Europe invites another couple (co-workers) to dinner at their home. All goes well. Several weeks later the European couple invites the American couple to dinner but at a local restaurant. The American couple feels somewhat insulted, concluding that the European couple did not wish to share the intimacy of their home and that they therefore did not really want to become friends.

4. An American teacher gives a lecture in Beijing to a group of Chinese college students. The students listen politely but make no comments and ask no questions. The teacher concludes that her lecture was uninteresting. A colleague consoles her by saying that the students didn't understand her lecture and suggests that on future occasions she attempt to simplify some of the more complex material.

5. An Arabian college student leaves the windows of his dormitory room open and blasts his stereo. The American students overhearing the stereo can't understand how this normally polite and considerate student could suddenly act so inconsiderate.

sense?" "Do you see where to put the widget?") as well as on whether you understand what the other person is saying ("Do you mean that you will never speak with them again? Do you mean that literally?")

Intercultural differences are especially important in initial interactions and gradually decline in importance as the relationship becomes more intimate (Taylor and Altman 1987; Gudykunst 1989).

Although you are always in danger of misperceiving and misevaluating another person, you are in special danger in intercultural situations. Therefore, try to resist your natural tendency to judge others quickly and permanently. A judgment made early is likely to be based on too little information. Because of this, be flexible and be willing to revise opinions you may have made on the basis of too little information. Prejudices

SELF-TEST (continued)

6. A politician is scheduled to give a 20-minute speech on economic trends. He speaks for exactly 20 minutes. The American listeners conclude that the speaker had prepared well and was considerate of his audience. The Latin American listeners conclude that the speaker was not really interested in his topic or his audience.

Here are some *possible* answers, since we can only guess at what went wrong in these examples.

1. Arabs generally maintain shorter distances in their interpersonal interactions than do Americans. As a result, the Arab is often considered too forward, while the American is considered too cold.
2. Calling the waiter by hitting a glass with a utensil is a common and expected custom among many Latin Americans.
3. Many Europeans who live in small apartments feel that it is more courteous to entertain in a restaurant. This difference is probably exaggerated by the reputation many Americans have of being wealthy and of expecting to be entertained "in style."
4. Chinese students generally do not ask questions; to do so would imply that the teacher has not been clear or that they do not know what they should know. Their silence does not at all reflect on the clarity of the professor's lecture or on their interest in the lecture.
5. In some parts of the world, radios and stereos are relatively rare and those who have such equipment often share it with others by playing it overly loud and opening the windows so that others may also enjoy the music. In the United States, where just about everyone can have access to radios and stereos, this behavior is considered inconsiderate and rude.
6. Americans are extremely time-conscious. A 20-minute speech should last 20 minutes. If it does not, it is a sign that the speaker has not prepared adequately or recognized the time restraints of the audience. To many Latin Americans, speakers build up steam with time: The longer a speaker speaks, the more involved, interested in the topic and audience, and interesting he or she is seen to be.

and biases when combined with high uncertainty are sure to produce judgments you'll want to revise.

As you learn about each other you will lose this self-consciousness and gain in confidence and spontaneity. These, in turn, will increase the satisfaction you get from your communication. The real problem is in not keeping with the interaction and working toward mutual understanding. It is so easy to give up after initial misunderstandings.

Maximizing Outcomes

In intercultural communication—as in all communication—you try to maximize the outcomes of your interactions (Sunnafrank, 1989). You try to gain the greatest rewards while paying the least costs. For example, you probably interact with those you predict will contribute to positive results; for example, you seek conversations that will prove satisfying, enjoyable, exciting, and so on. Because intercultural communication is difficult and positive outcomes may seem unlikely (at first at least), you may avoid it. And so, for example, you talk with the person in class who is similar to rather than different from you. However, extending and stretching yourself may actually result in greater satisfaction in the long run.

Also, consider that when you have positive outcomes, you continue to engage in communication and increase your communications. When you have negative outcomes, you begin to withdraw and communicate less. The implication here is obvious: Don't give up easily, especially in intercultural settings.

Since intercultural communication may be new or different from your usual communications, you will probably be more mindful about it (Gudykunst, 1989; Langer, 1989). This has both positive and negative consequences. On the positive side, this increased awareness probably keeps you more alert. It prevents you from saying things that might appear insensitive or inappropriate. On the negative side, it leads to guardedness, lack of spontaneity, and lack of confidence.

In your mindful state you probably make predictions about which types of communication will result in positive outcomes; you try to predict the results of, for example, the choice of topic, the positions you take, the nonverbal behaviors you display, the amount of talking versus listening that you do, and so on. You then do what you think will result in positive outcomes and avoid doing what you think will result in negative outcomes. To do this successfully, however, you will have to learn as much as you can about the other person's system of communication signals. This will help you predict the outcomes of your behavior more accurately.

BARRIERS TO INTERCULTURAL COMMUNICATION

Murphy's law ("If anything can go wrong, it will") is especially applicable to intercultural communication. Knowing some of the more likely barriers may help you avoid them or at least counteract their effects. Intercultural communication is, of course, subject to all the same barriers and problems as are the other forms of communication that were discussed throughout this volume. Drawing on a number of intercultural researchers, we cover here the barriers that are unique to intercultural communication (Burna, 1991; Ruben, 1985; Spitzberg, 1991).

Ignoring Differences Between Yourself and the Culturally Different

Perhaps the most prevalent barrier occurs when you assume that similarities exist and that differences do not. This is especially true in the area of values, attitudes, and beliefs. You might easily accept different hairstyles, clothing, and foods. In basic values and beliefs, however, you may assume that deep down everyone is really alike. We aren't. When you assume similarities and ignore differences, you implicitly communicate to others that your ways are the right ways and that their ways are not important to you. Take a simple example. An American invites a Filipino coworker to dinner. The Filipino politely refuses. The American is hurt and feels that the Filipino does not want to be friendly. The Filipino is hurt and concludes that the invitation was not extended sincerely. Here, it seems, both the American and the Filipino assume that their customs for inviting people to dinner are the same when, in fact, they are not. A Filipino expects

Although difficulties can be caused as a result of ignoring differences between yourself and culturally different others, difficulties can also be caused by emphasizing or focusing too heavily on differences. Can you give a specific example of the difficulties that might arise from either too little or too much concentration on differences?

to be invited several times before accepting a dinner invitation. When an invitation is given only once it is viewed as insincere.

Ignoring Differences
Among the Culturally Different Group

Within every cultural group there are wide and important differences. As all Americans are not alike, neither are all Indonesians, Greeks, Mexicans, and so on. When we ignore these differences we are guilty of stereotyping. We assume that all persons covered by the same label (in this case a national or racial label) are the same. A good example of this is seen in the use of the term "African American." The term stresses the unity of Africa and those who are of African descent and is analogous to "Asian American" or "European American." At the same time, it ignores the great diversity within this continent when, for example, it is used as analogous to "German American" or "Japanese American." "Nigerian American" or "Ethiopian American" would be analogous to, say, "German American."

Another case in point was seen during the furor over the film *The Last Temptation of Christ*. Among Roman Catholics, for example, there were wide variations in their feelings about this film. While Cardinal O'Connor, Archbishop of New York, condemned the film, Father Andrew Greeley, novelist and professor of sociology, praised it and considered it "a profound religious challenge" (1988). Both are Roman Catholic and both are priests, but each sees the same message quite differently.

Recognize that within each culture there are smaller cultures that differ greatly from each other and from the larger culture.

Ignoring Differences in Meaning

Earlier, we pointed out that meaning does not exist in the words used but in the person using the words. Be especially sensitive to this simple principle in intercultural communication. Consider, for example, the differences in meaning for such words as *woman* to an American and a Moslem, *religion* to a born-again Christian and an atheist, and *lunch* to a Chinese rice farmer and a Wall Street executive. Even though the same word is used, its connotative meanings will vary greatly depending on the listeners' cultural definitions.

With nonverbal messages, the potential differences seem even greater. Thus, the over-the-head clasped hands that signify victory to an American may signify friendship to a Russian. To an American, holding up two fingers to make a *V* signifies victory. To certain South Americans, however, it is an obscene gesture that corresponds to our extended middle finger.

A left-handed American who eats with the left hand may be seen by a Moslem as obscene. To the Moslem, the left hand is not used for eating or for shaking hands but to clean oneself after excretory functions. So, using the left hand to eat or to shake hands is considered insulting and obscene.

Violating Cultural Rules and Customs

Each culture has its own rules for communicating. These rules identify what is appropriate and what is inappropriate. Thus, for example, in American culture you would call a person you wish to date three or four days in advance. In certain Asian cultures, you might call the person's parents weeks or even months in advance. In our culture we say, as a general friendly gesture, "come over and pay us a visit." To members of other cultures, this comment is sufficient for the listeners actually to come to visit at their convenience.

In some cultures, people show respect by avoiding direct eye contact with the person to whom they are speaking. In other cultures this same eye avoidance would signal disinterest. If a young American girl is talking with an older Indonesian man, for example, she is expected to avoid direct eye contact. To an Indonesian, direct eye contact in this situation would be considered disrespectful. In some southern European cultures men walk arm in arm. Other cultures (the United States, for example) consider this inappropriate.

Obviously, if you don't know the rules and customs of the culture of the people with whom you are communicating, your efforts are likely to be ineffective. For example, examine the "Ten Commandments for Communicating with People with Disabilities" in Table 23.1. Have you violated any of these suggestions or seen any of them violated? Were you explicitly taught any of these principles?

Evaluating Differences Negatively

Even when you notice the differences between cultures, you must still be careful to avoid evaluating them negatively. Consider, for example, the simple act of spitting (LaBarre, 1964). In most Western cultures spitting is a sign of disgust and displeasure and is not to be performed in public. However, for the Masai of Africa it is a sign of affection, and for the American Indian it may be an act of kindness. For example, the

Table 23.1 Ten Commandments for Communicating with People with Disabilities

1. Speak directly rather than through a companion or sign language interpreter who may be present.

2. Offer to shake hands when introduced. People with limited hand use or an artificial limb can usually shake hands and offering the left hand is an acceptable greeting.

3. Always identify yourself and others who may be with you when meeting someone with a visual impairment. When conversing in a group, remember to identify the person to whom you are speaking.

4. If you offer assistance, wait until the offer is accepted. Then listen or ask for instructions.

5. Treat adults as adults. Address people who have disabilities by their first names only when extending that same familiarity to all others. Never patronize people in wheelchairs by patting them on the head or shoulder.

6. Do not lean against or hang on someone's wheelchair. Bear in mind that disabled people treat their chairs as extensions of their bodies.

7. Listen attentively when talking with people who have difficulty speaking and wait for them to finish. If necessary, ask short questions that require short answers, a nod, or shake of the head. Never pretend to understand if you are having difficulty doing so. Instead repeat what you have understood and allow the person to respond.

8. Place yourself at eye level when speaking with someone in a wheelchair or on crutches.

9. Tap a hearing-impaired person on the shoulder or wave your hand to get his or her attention. Look directly at the person and speak clearly, slowly, and expressively to establish if the person can read your lips. If so, try to face the light source and keep hands, cigarettes, and food away from your mouth when speaking.

10. Relax. Don't be embarrassed if you happen to use common expressions such as "See you later," or "Did you hear about this?" that seem to relate to a person's disability.

Source: United Cerebral Palsy Associations, Inc.

medicine man spits on the sick to cure them. Sticking out the tongue provides another example. To Westerners it is an insult. To the Chinese of the Sung dynasty, it was a symbol to make fun of the anger of another individual. To the modern southern Chinese it expresses embarrassment over some social mistake. In the United States men are (stereotypically) not supposed to show emotions and display affective; nor are men expected to rely on intuition rather than logic. In Iran, however, men are expected to show emotion and to rely on intuition. Women, on the other hand, are expected to be practical and logical rather than intuitive (Hall, 1959).

In an objective sense, spitting and sticking out the tongue are neither negative nor positive actions. When you see them as naturally or inherently negative (if you're a Westerner) or naturally positive (if you're a Masai or Native American), you are guilty of ethnocentric thinking. When you use such thinking, you put the other person on the defensive. You create a relationship in which you are superior and others are inferior. Cultural variations are learned behaviors. They are not natural or innate behaviors. As a result we need to view these culturally determined behaviors nonevaluatively, as different but equal.

Take the example of an American college student who hears the news that her favorite uncle has died. She bites her lip, pulls herself up, and politely excuses herself

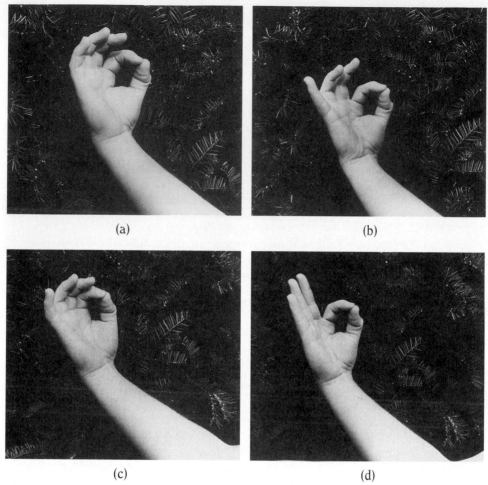

(a)   (b)

(c)   (d)

What do these nonverbal gestures mean to you? Do they all mean the same thing? Actually, they are all slightly different, and mean different things depending on their cultural context. (a) is American for "OK." (b) is from the Mediterranean, and means "zero." (c) is from Japan, and means "money." (d) is from Tunisia, and means "I will kill you."

from the group of foreign students with whom she is having dinner. The Russian thinks: "How unfriendly." The Italian thinks: "How insincere." The Brazilian thinks: "How unconcerned." To many Americans, it is a sign of bravery to endure pain (physical or emotional) in silence and without any outward show of emotion. To members of other groups, such silence is often interpreted negatively to mean that the individual does not consider them friends who can share such sorrow. To members of other cultures, people are expected to reveal to friends how they feel.

Culture Shock

Culture shock refers to the psychological reaction one experiences at being in a culture very different from one's own (Furnham & Bochner, 1986). Culture shock is normal. Most people experience it when entering a new and different culture. Nevertheless, it can be unpleasant and frustrating. Part of this results from the feelings of alien-

With which person in this photo do you think you would have the most difficulty communicating? The least difficulty? Why? With which person do you think you would have the most interesting conversation? Why?

ation, conspicuousness, and difference from everyone else. When you lack knowledge of the rules and customs of the new society, you cannot communicate effectively. You are apt to blunder frequently and seriously.

The person experiencing culture shock may not know some very basic things:

- how to ask someone for a favor or pay someone a compliment
- how to extend or accept an invitation for dinner
- how early or how late to arrive for an appointment or how long to stay
- how to distinguish seriousness from playfulness and politeness from indifference
- how to dress for an informal, formal, or business function
- how to order a meal in a restaurant or how to summon a waiter

Anthropologist Kalervo Oberg (1960), who first used the term *culture shock*, notes that it occurs in stages. These stages are useful for examining many encounters with the new and the different. Going away to college, getting married, or joining the military, for example, can all result in culture shock.

Stage One: The Honeymoon At first there is fascination, even enchantment, with the new culture and its people. *You finally have your own apartment. You're your own boss. Finally, on your own!* When in groups of people who are culturally different, this stage is characterized by cordiality and friendship among these early and superficial relationships. Many tourists remain at this stage because their stay in foreign countries is so brief.

Stage Two: The Crisis   Here, the differences between your own culture and the new one create problems. *No longer do you find dinner ready for you unless you do it yourself. Your clothes are not washed or ironed unless you do them yourself.* Feelings of frustration and inadequacy come to the fore. This is the stage at which you experience the actual shock of the new culture.

Stage Three: The Recovery   During this period you gain the skills necessary to function effectively. *You learn how to shop, cook, and plan a meal. You find a local laundry and figure you'll learn how to iron later.* You learn the language and ways of the new culture. Your feelings of inadequacy subside.

Stage Four: The Adjustment   At this final stage, you adjust to and come to enjoy the new culture and the new experiences. You may still experience periodic difficulties and strains, but on a whole, the experience is pleasant. *Actually, you're now a pretty decent cook. You're even coming to enjoy it. You're making a good salary so why learn to iron?*

People may also experience culture shock when they return to their original culture after living in a foreign culture. Consider, for example, the Peace Corps volunteers who work in a rural and economically deprived area. Upon returning to Las Vegas or Beverly Hills they too may experience culture shock. Sailors who served long periods aboard ship and then return to an isolated farming community might also experience culture shock. In these cases, however, the recovery period is shorter and the sense of inadequacy and frustration is less.

GATEWAYS TO INTERCULTURAL COMMUNICATION

Everything said about communication throughout this book relates to intercultural communication. So, in a sense, we have already identified the principles or guidelines for effective intercultural communication. I take this opportunity, however, to reiterate these suggestions within the context of intercultural communication.

Avoiding Barriers

Perhaps the first step in identifying the gateways or guidelines to intercultural communication is to note that the barriers just identified need to be avoided:

1. Recognize the differences between yourself and the culturally different person. When in doubt, ask questions; avoid assuming similarities. At the same time, however, do recognize the value of seeking out similarities and emphasizing these points of contact.
2. Recognize that differences exist within any group. Do not stereotype, overgeneralize, or assume that differences within a group are not important.
3. Remember that meaning is in the person and not in the words or in the gestures used. Check your meanings with those of the other person. Make sure that any assumed similarity (or difference) in meaning really exists.
4. Be aware of the cultural rules operating in any intercultural communication context. Recall our example in the Self-Test on page 434 of the American and

What barriers do you feel are the most important in your own communication with members of different cultures? With the opposite sex?

the Arab who each follow a different rule for interpersonal space. Become sensitive to the rules that the other person is following. Be careful not to assume that your rules are the only valid or logical ones. When in doubt, ask.

5. Avoid negative evaluation of cultural differences, both verbally and nonverbally. See cultural customs and rules (your own as well as those of others) as arbitrary and convenient rather than as natural and logical.

6. Guard against culture shock by learning as much as possible about the culture you will enter. Read, talk with natives and those who have had experience in the culture, and view films, for example.

Using the Principles of Effective Conversation

In Unit 11 we noted the characteristics of effective conversation, both the metaskills and the more specific skills. These characteristics are especially significant in intercultural communication and may be profitably considered within the cultural context.

These qualities would not be considered effective in all cultures, nor would the specific verbal and nonverbal behaviors carry the same meanings in all cultures. For example, Maria Rodriguez (1988) has shown that blacks and Hispanics evaluate assertiveness differently. Similarly, Hecht and Ribeau (1984) have shown that whites, blacks, and Hispanics define what is satisfying communication in different ways. What we present here, then, are general suggestions that should be useful most of the time. Always go to the specific culture for specific recommendations.

Metaskills   The metaskills of flexibility, mindfulness, and cultural sensitivity are, of course, paramount in helping you communicate in intercultural situations. Remember that each transaction is different, so be flexible. Each situation, especially new ones, calls for conscious thought, so be mindful about this uniqueness and also about the normal tendency to be ethnocentric. And, of course, each culture is unique, so be sensitive to the differences and especially to evaluations of behaviors that will differ from your own.

Openness   Be open to the differences existing among people. Be especially open to the different values, beliefs, and attitudes, as well as ways of behaving. This does not mean that you have to adopt these ways, but only that you recognize that people are different.

Empathy   Put yourself into the position of the person from another culture. Try to see the world from this different perspective. This practice will enable you to communicate more effectively and give you a new perspective on your own culture. And let the person know that you do feel as he or she is feeling. Signal this empathy with facial expressions, an attentive and interested body posture, and understanding and agreement responses.

Positiveness   Communicate positive regard. This is especially important in an intercultural setting because there are so many unknowns. As a result, you are unable to predict what the other person is thinking and feeling. Therefore, put the other person at ease by communicating positive regard.

Immediacy   Immediacy unites people. It helps to overcome the differences between individuals. In intercultural communication this quality takes on special importance because of the obvious and great differences between you and others. Communicate a sense of togetherness to counteract the obvious intercultural differences. When there are great age or status differences, however, realize that a display of immediacy may be seen as presumptuous.

Interaction Management   Be especially sensitive to the differences in turn taking. Many Americans, especially those from large urban centers, have the habit of interrupting other people or of completing their sentences. Some cultures consider this especially rude. Some cultures consider this a sign of an exciting interaction.

Expressiveness   When differences are great, some people feel uneasy and unsure of themselves. Counteract this by communicating genuine involvement in the interaction. Let the other person know that you are enjoying the interaction: Smile!

Other-Orientation   Recognize that each person has a share in the interaction. Do not monopolize the conversation by talking only of yourself, choosing the topics to talk about, and relating only your experiences. Instead, orient the conversation to the other. Use the skills of effective and active listening and show interest in the things that interest the other.

Summary

1. *General principles* of intercultural communication are: (1) Language helps to structure what you see and how you see it but does not impose any serious barriers to meaningful communication; when the language differences are great, use perception checking, active listening, feedback, and the general skills of communication. (2) The greater the intercultural differences, the greater the uncertainty and ambiguity, and the greater the communication difficulty. (3) Intercultural communication will be guided by the goal of maximizing the outcomes of such interactions; it often requires more effort and more time to achieve the desired outcomes.

2. Among the *barriers* to intercultural communication are: ignoring differences between yourself and the culturally different, ignoring differences among the culturally different (stereotyping), ignoring meaning differences in verbal and nonverbal messages, violating cultural rules and customs, evaluating differences negatively, and culture shock.

3. *Culture shock* is a psychological reaction to being placed in a culture different from one's own. It is a feeling of alienation and conspicuousness over being different.

4. Achieving *effective intercultural communication* involves the avoidance of the common barriers: Recognize differences between self and other; recognize differences among group members; remember that meaning is in the person, not in the words or gestures; be aware of the cultural rules operating in any intercultural context; avoid negative evaluation; and guard against culture shock.

5. *Effective intercultural communication* may be further enhanced (generally) by employing the characteristics of effective conversation—namely, the metaskills of flexibility, mindfulness, and cultural sensitivity as well as the more specific skills of openness, empathy, positiveness, immediacy, interaction management, expressiveness, and other-orientation.

Application

23.1 RESPONDING TO INTERCULTURAL DIFFICULTIES

For each of the following situations, identify the potential difficulties that may be encountered. How would you respond to the potential difficulties if you were the person in each of these situations?

1. A Mexican family—husband, wife, and four children between the ages of 6 and 13—moves into a white middle-class suburban neighborhood in Texas.

2. A gay male couple moves into an Irish Catholic family community in Boston.

3. A black male high school honor student tries to make friends with the

neighborhood males (a mixture of races and nationalities) who view students who do well in school as sissies.

4. A foreign student attending the University of Illinois who has been a fraternity member for four years and a member of the Liberal Coalition announces to his fraternity brothers that his bride, who he has never seen, will arrive next week.

5. A Jewish woman of 33 plans to marry a Moslem from Iraq. She is planning to tell her orthodox family of her intentions at dinner tonight.

6. A female college teacher of 42 and a 23-year-old male college student (who is not in any of the teacher's classes) fall in love and have intentions of moving in together. She plans to tell her department colleagues of her intentions at a faculty party.

7. Iris has just been offered a job at Gracious Publications as executive editor. She will supervise five male editors, all of whom are significantly older than Iris.

8. A teacher from Iowa has been invited to teach a history course (Twentieth-Century America in War and Peace) at the University of Moscow. At the same time a teacher from Moscow has been invited to teach a similar course (Twentieth-Century Russia in War and Peace) at the University of Iowa.

9. Yashimo is a Japanese businessman who has just purchased a McDonald's franchise in a town that was once supported by an auto plant that recently went bankrupt.

10. Cira is a young Latin American college student who wants to date a wide variety of men. Her parents, however, think this is immoral and want her to have only few—highly selected and carefully screened—dates. They want her home by midnight and insist on meeting everyone she goes out with.

Intercultural Communication

Questions and Activities

1. Look through your daily newspaper or a weekly news magazine like *Time, Newsweek,* or *US News and World Report.* Identify the 10 top news items. How many of these concern intercultural issues? What kinds of intercultural communication do they involve?

2. What role or part does intercultural communication play in your personal, social, and professional life? Has this changed in the last 10 years? Is it likely to change in the next 10 years? How?

3. How might you benefit from expanding your intercultural communications?

4. A large number of colleges are currently in the process of incorporating a multicultural component into the required curriculum for all students. How do you feel about this? What do you think would be the ideal course(s) for increasing the average United States college student's multicultural awareness and sensitivity?

5. Review the various forms of intercultural communication identified in Unit 22. With which form do you have the most difficulty? Why? With which form do you have the least difficulty? Why?

6. How would you describe your own culture in terms of collectivist-individualistic focus? In terms of high-context and low-context orientation? Can you explain how these orientations influence your communications?

7. How would you describe your own level of ethnocentrism? In what ways does your ethnocentrism influence your communications? How satisfied are you with this?

8. Of the three difficulties in mastering intercultural communication—ethnocentrism, mindlessness, and fear—which most influences your intercultural communications?

9. Review the introductory excerpt from "Body Ritual Among the Nacirema." What other rituals might have been noted? What ritual behaviors do you engage in? Is there a ritual behavior of your own culture that you find "silly"?

10. Formulate one principle of intercultural communication effectiveness. Why do you consider it so important?

11. Which barrier to intercultural communication do you think creates the most difficulties? Why?

12. Have you ever experienced a communication breakdown in intercultural communication? Describe it in as much detail as possible.

13. Has college given you culture shock? In what ways? Do the four stages

described here adequately describe your own experience? What additional insights can you add?

14. Sheba has just come to your college from another galaxy. Sheba asks for your help in learning the rules of your culture, especially those rules concerning interpersonal interaction. For example, Sheba isn't quite sure about the following four issues: (1) Is it considered correct to interrupt someone who is speaking, and if so when is it permissible? (2) How do you begin a conversation with someone you have never met before? (3) How long do you maintain eye contact when talking with someone? How long do you maintain eye contact when listening to someone? (4) What do you do with your hands and feet when you are sitting in a chair talking with someone? Would these rules differ depending on whether Sheba is male or female? What interpersonal communication rules can you give Sheba for dealing with these four communication situations?

15. Etiquette, the rules for what is considered proper and what is considered improper in "polite society," is largely culturally determined. The rules that regulate polite society in the United States are not necessarily the same rules that regulate polite societies elsewhere in the world. Martian, a young man, and Venusian, a young woman, have just come to the United States and are now trying to learn the rules of etiquette, especially the etiquette rules for (1) eating in expensive restaurants, (2) sending and responding to written invitations, and (3) dressing for a job interview. What advice would you offer Martian? What advice would you offer Venusian? If you offer different advice to Martian and Venusian, explain your reasons.

Skill Check

_____ 1. I avoid evaluating my own cultural values, beliefs, and ways of behaving as being more positive than others simply because they are my own. (Unit 22)

_____ 2. I distinguish between states of mindlessness and mindfulness especially when in intercultural situations. (Unit 22)

_____ 3. I build my communications with the recognition that the cultural groups one belongs to will also influence the form and substance of one's communications. (Unit 22)

_____ 4. I use the general principles of intercultural communication to help me understand the messages of others and to construct messages that will communicate my intending meanings. (Unit 23)

_____ 5. I acknowledge (when appropriate) the differences between myself and the culturally different. I avoid assuming similarities. (Unit 23)

_____ 6. I acknowledge (when appropriate) the differences among group members. (Unit 23)

_____ 7. I avoid stereotyping and overgeneralizing. (Unit 23)

_____ 8. Whenever I'm in doubt about the meaning of a message, I check with the person for his or her intended meaning. (Unit 23)

_____ 9. I avoid assuming that the rules of my culture will operate in other cultures also. (Unit 23)

_____ 10. I avoid expressing negative evaluation of cultural differences. (Unit 23)

_____ 11. I actively guard against culture shock by learning as much as I can about any new culture I will enter. (Unit 23)

_____ 12. I am open to different values, beliefs, and attitudes as well as ways of behaving. (Unit 23)

_____ 13. I see the world from the cultural perspective of the other person, and communicate this to the other person. (Unit 23)

_____ 14. I use the metaskills of flexibility, mindfulness, and cultural sensitivity in regulating my communications, especially in intercultural situations. (Unit 23)

_____ 15. I regulate openness appropriately and am open to the communications of others. (Unit 23)

_____ 16. I am empathic and communicate this empathy to culturally different others. (Unit 23)

_____ 17. I communicate positive regard for others, especially those from different cultures. (Unit 23)

_____ 18. I communicate immediacy—a sense of togetherness—to counteract the obvious intercultural differences. (Unit 23)

_____ 19. I practice effective interaction management skills. I am especially sensitive to cultural differences in turn taking. (Unit 23)

_____ 20. I communicate genuine involvement in the interaction through smiling, leaning forward, and expressing interest and attention. (Unit 23)

_____ 21. I orient the conversation to the other person by asking questions, practicing the skills of effective and active listening, and demonstrating interest in what interests the other. (Unit 23)

SUGGESTED READINGS

Gudykunst, William B. _Bridging Differences: Effective Intergroup Communication._ Newbury Park, CA: Sage, 1991. An excellent introduction to the theories and skills of intercultural communication.

Kim, Young Yun, ed. _Interethnic Communication: Current Research._ Newbury Park, CA: Sage, 1986. A collection of 12 original essays on communication between different ethnic groups focusing on the analysis of message decoding patterns, language and verbal/nonverbal behavior in interethnic interaction, and ethnicity in the development of interpersonal relationships.

Kim, Young Yun and William B. Gudykunst, eds. _Theories in Intercultural Communi-_

cation. Newbury Park, CA: Sage, 1988. The major theories of intercultural communication are reviewed in 13 original essays covering such areas as culture and meaning, intercultural behavior, and intercultural adaptation.

Kochman, Thomas. *Black and White: Styles in Conflict.* Chicago: University of Chicago Press, 1981. A detailed study of the differences in conflict styles of blacks and whites.

Samovar, Larry A. and Richard E. Porter, eds. *Intercultural Communication: A Reader,* 5th ed. Belmont, CA: Wadsworth, 1988. A collection of readings on such aspects of intercultural communication as socio-cultural backgrounds, taking part in intercultural interaction, and improving our intercultural communications.

Textbooks in intercultural communication are increasing as this area takes on greater importance. See, for example, Condon and Yousef (1975); Dodd (1991); Gudykunst (1991); Gudykunst, Ting-Toomey with Chua (1988); Samovar, Porter, and Jain (1980); and Singer (1987).

Popular works on intercultural communication include the classics by Edward T. Hall, *The Silent Language* (1959), *The Hidden Dimension* (1966), *Beyond Culture* (1976), and Hall and Hall's *Hidden Differences* (1987); Morris (1977); Morris, Collett, Marsha, and O'Shaughnessy (1980); and Aylesworth and Aylesworth (1978).

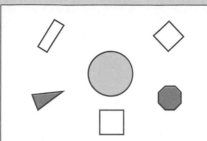

PART

P A R T   7

MASS COMMUNICATION

Unit 24. **Preliminaries to Mass Communication: Components, Forms, and Functions**

Unit 25. **Theories of Mass Communication**

Part 7. **Feedback**
  Questions and Activities
  Skill Check
  Suggested Readings

In this final part of the text, we consider mass communication. In Unit 24 we cover the nature of mass communication, its major forms (for example, radio, television, newspapers) and functions. In Unit 25 we discuss the major theories of mass communication and how they explain the influence that mass communications have on you as an individual and on society as a whole.

Unlike many of the previous topics throughout this book, the area of mass communication is approached from the point of view of the consumer rather than of the originator or sender. The emphasis here is on understanding the role of the media in contemporary society, how you are influenced by the media (and how you in turn may influence the media), and how you can improve your skills as intelligent users of the media.

Approaching Mass Communication

In approaching the study of mass communication, keep the following in mind:

- Media presentations do not represent reality. And yet the media help create the personal reality for many people and probably influence to some extent everyone's perception of reality. Understanding how and why this happens is crucial to learning to control the media rather than have the media control you.

- The media influence you in complex (and often subtle) ways, not merely with the obvious commercials but in their presentation of news, their depiction of relationships, and their endorsement of various political, economic, and religious beliefs and attitudes.

- Unlike conversations, where there is a simultaneous exchange of messages, the media largely serve the sender role and you serve the receiver role. You can, however, influence the media. The media will listen if you talk back.

PRELIMINARIES TO MASS COMMUNICATION

Components, Forms, and Functions

UNIT CONTENTS

A Definition of Mass Communication

Forms of Mass Communication

The Functions of Mass Communication

   Summary

   Application
     24.1   Television and Values

UNIT GOALS

After completing this unit, you should be able to

1. explain mass communication's five components

2. explain the major forms of mass communication and their major functions

3. explain the six functions of mass communication and illustrate how the media perform each one

4. distinguish between functional and dysfunctional media effects

The mass media are all around you. To live even one day without mass communication would be impossible for most people.

We need our morning newspaper, stereo, television, movies, and CDs. Without these, life would be drastically different and, for most of us, extremely difficult. And yet many know little of how the media work and how they influence our lives. Before beginning your study of mass communication, you might want to take the media awareness test on page 456.

In this unit, we introduce the topic of mass communication and define this form of communication by offering a definition of its essential characteristics. Second, we examine selected mass communication forms. Third, we explore the varied functions the mass media serve.

A DEFINITION OF MASS COMMUNICATION

We can best define mass communication by focusing on the five variables involved in any communication act and showing how these operate in the mass media.

Source

The mass communicator is a complex organization that goes to great expense to construct and transmit messages. Although mass communications cost a great deal to produce, they cost the receiver or consumer very little, at least directly. Books are perhaps the most expensive media products because the consumer must pay the entire cost of production. It costs us nothing to watch a broadcast television program or to listen to a radio show. We pay for these shows indirectly by purchasing the advertisers' products. The advertiser assumes the direct cost through the purchase of airtime for commercials.

Audience

Mass communications address the masses—an extremely large audience. Because of the vastness of the audience and because it is essential for the media to give the audience what it wants, the messages of mass communication must focus on some typical or average viewer. In this way, the media secures the largest number of possible receivers as their audience.

However, this works only for certain widely used products and hence certain programs. More and more, the media and the advertisers carefully research and divide the mass audience into smaller, more clearly defined targets. After all, the audiences for Hanes panty hose, Flintstone vitamins, and Budweiser beer are quite different. This process of segmenting a large audience (for example, the television audience) into more narrowly defined small groups (for example, children from 6 to 10, women from 25 to 40, or teenage boys) is referred to as **demassification** by academics and as *audience segmentation* by the industry (Williams, 1992). Through demassification, advertisers can direct their appeals to the specific group they wish to reach. *Family Circle* magazine has a circulation around 5 million, but an ad for a motorcycle would probably be less effective there than in *Cycle* (circulation 331,266) or *Road and Track* (circulation 703,899), which have fewer but more interested readers.

SELF-TEST

What Do You Know About Media?

Test yourself on what you know about the media and especially the way in which they exert influence. Record T (true) if you think the statement is always or usually true and F (false) if you think the statement is always or usually false.

_____ 1. Heavy television viewers are not different from those who watch little television in the way in which they see the world.

_____ 2. People can be easily persuaded directly by the media.

_____ 3. Advertisers should place their ads in newspapers or magazines with the largest audience.

_____ 4. Newspapers are still the primary means for people to get the national and local news.

_____ 5. Television programs that make fun of bigotry and prejudice help reduce prejudice in viewers.

_____ 6. The more a person attends to the media, the more actively he or she will participate in society.

_____ 7. Although television tries to make its characters appear realistic, viewers know quite clearly where reality begins and illusion ends.

_____ 8. In a democracy media present us with information rather than conclusions, and it is up to the viewers or readers to draw their own conclusions.

_____ 9. We listen to and are persuaded most by people who are most like us.

_____ 10. Unlike editors of newspapers who decide what should be printed and what should not be, teachers present information without any such "editorial censorship."

Scoring   This test was designed to raise some issues that we will discuss in this and the next unit. It was also designed to highlight some of the misconceptions that people have about mass communication. As you will discover in these two units, all statements are false.

Messages

The entire mass communication experience is a public one. Everyone has access to the messages of the mass media. Unlike a talk at a bar or a classroom lecture, anyone may receive mass communications.

The communication is also rapid; the messages are sent to an audience with very little delay. This characteristic—speed—has several qualifications, however. A novel may take years to write and a television series years to put together, yet once they are completed, there is little time lost in the transmission of the message. This rapid nature of mass communication refers most specifically to the broadcasting of news items and events. We can see fires, robberies, political rallies, and speeches while they are in progress. This, to use Marshall McLuhan's term, has turned us into a *global village*, where world events are common knowledge.

Process

In one sense mass communication is a one-way process. It goes from source to receivers. In contrast, in interpersonal communication, communication goes from source to receiver and then from receiver back to source. In mass communication the messages flow from the media to the receivers but not back again, except in the form of feedback—letters to the editor, audience ratings, box office receipts, and the like.

In another sense, however, mass communication is also a two-way process. Both media and audience make selections. First, the media select the portion of the total population that they will try to reach. Next, the receiver selects, from all the media available, particular messages to attend to. Some will read *Photoplay*, while others will read *Personal Computing*, *Time*, *Discover*, and so on.

Context

Mass communications operate in a social context. The media influence the social context and the social context influences the media. There is, in other words, a transactional relationship between the media and the society. Each influences the other. Thus, for example, the media influence the economic conditions of the society. But, economic conditions also influence the media. Similarly, the media influence the political environment and at the same time the political environment influences the media.

At one time the media, especially television, reinforced only the values and the attitudes of the dominant culture. With the proliferation of a wide variety of cable channels, however, there is today considerable cultural diversity. There are now numerous foreign language programs directed largely at newly arrived immigrants, as well as programming aimed at gays and lesbians, senior citizens, the politically conservative and the politically liberal, and the religious of varied faiths.

FORMS OF MASS COMMUNICATION

Another approach to the definition of mass communication is to define its most significant forms: television, radio, newspapers, magazines, films, books, and records/tapes/cassettes/discs (see Figure 24.1).

Before reading about these forms, consider your own media behavior:

- How much time do you spend watching television? What types of programs do you spend most time watching? Why do you watch them?
- For what purposes do you turn on the radio? What types of programming do you listen to?
- What newspaper(s) do you read? What purposes do newspapers serve for you?
- What magazines do you read on a fairly regular basis?
- How often do you attend the movies? What kinds of movies do you see most often? Why do you go to the movies?
- What kinds of books (other than textbooks) do you read?
- How much do you spend on tapes and CDs? What kinds of music do you spend most time listening to? Why do you listen to music?

Television

Television is the most pervasive and the most popular of all mass media. The televisionless world is shrinking rapidly and will soon be gone completely.

In the United States the average television set is on about seven hours per day. This is a total of over 2500 hours per year, or about 106 complete days per year. Each week this comes to 47 hours, more than the amount of time people work or sleep.

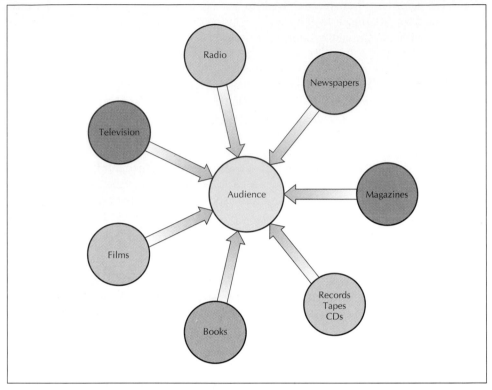

FIGURE 24.1 The mass media. Marshall McLuhan, perhaps the most widely quoted of all media theorists, saw the audience at the center of numerous attacks by the different media. McLuhan referred to this phenomenon as a *media implosion*: The media are directed toward the audience and bombard the audience with all sorts of sensory stimulation.

Although we might argue over whether this is for better or for worse, we would have to agree that American life without television would be drastically different.

Over the past 10 or 15 years television has changed drastically. During the next 10 or 15 years it will change a great deal more. Cable TV, originally designed to provide improved reception, now provides specialized programming and is found in over 50 million homes (Hickey, 1989). X-rated movies, counterculture programming, and shows directed at small groups would have been impossible without cable television. Channel One, the educational channel available in most (but not all) states is sure to account for major educational changes.

Communication satellites are now essential components of television and will in the next several years increase in influence. Intelsat or Early Bird goes back only to 1965, but today the entire world is connected through satellite television.

Videocassette recorders (VCRs), which provide viewers with control over the television, are in about 66 percent of U.S. homes (Hickey, 1989), a percentage that will surely increase in the coming years. Because VCRs can tape shows at preset times even when the viewer is not at home, the viewer now can watch shows at any time and can watch them repeatedly. The fact that the viewer may edit out commercials has created considerable difficulty for the advertising industry. In the next few years, high-definition television, large screens, and screens that show two or more channels at the same

What would the entertainment center of the average person in your culture (if such a person could be found) look like? If money, space, and time were unlimited, what would your ideal entertainment center look like?

time will be commonplace. Allready developed and soon to become a part of everyday experience are interactive compact disks (for game playing or scholarly research) and "smart boxes" that will enable you to choose your program, rent a movie, or buy a watch all at the touch of a button or movement of a joystick (*New York Times*, October 27, 1993, C1, C8).

Radio

Before the advent of television, radio was the dominant mass communication system. As families now gather to watch television shows, families used to gather to listen to *Jack Benny, Charlie McCarthy, The Shadow*, and *The Lone Ranger.*

Television has usurped the dominant role of radio. As a result, radio has had to redirect its focus. Instead of appealing to the large audience that television has permanently won over, radio has concentrated on smaller audiences. It tries to cater to specialized interests—for example, opera and symphonic music lovers, news enthusiasts, country/western or rock and roll fans, and so on. At the same time, radio serves as a kind of background noise while one is resting on the beach, working in the office, or driving to school.

Newspapers

Although newspapers are clearly a form of mass communication, they are less "mass" than, say, radio or television. While almost everyone listens to the radio and watches television, more educated and older people are the primary readers of newspapers. Only about 50 percent of people between the ages of 21 and 35 read newspapers regularly.

SELF-TEST

Why Do You Watch Television?

Here are some of the reasons people give for watching television. Circle the numbers of those which apply to you on a fairly regular basis.
I watch television:

1. so I can learn about things happening in the world.
2. so I can learn how to do things I haven't done before.
3. when I have nothing better to do.
4. because it passes the time away.
5. so I won't be alone.
6. because it makes me feel less lonely.
7. so I can get away from the rest of the family.
8. so I can get away from what I'm doing.
9. because it's thrilling.
10. because it excites me.
11. because it relaxes me.
12. because it's a pleasant rest.

This test is an abbreviated version of one used by mass media researcher Alan Rubin (1979) to investigate the reasons people watch television. Rubin discovered six major reasons, each of which is represented by two of the above statements: *to learn* (statements 1 and 2), *to pass the time* (3 and 4), *for companionship* (5 and 6), *to forget* (7 and 8), *for stimulation or arousal* (9 and 10), and *for relaxation* (11 and 12). Why do you watch television?

Newspapers serve two general functions. First, they are sources of information about what is happening throughout the world and locally. Older and more educated readers use newspapers for this function. Part of this news is presented to persuade us to a particular point of view. This function is *not* limited to the editorial page. Some news deals with important political, economic, and social issues. Some deals with "unimportant" gossip about TV and Hollywood stars, advice to the lovelorn, and human interest stories about lost dogs and kindly old people. And some tries to persuade us to buy everything from stocks and bonds to underwear, cologne, and meat and potatoes.

The second major function is to entertain, and it is for this function that the young and the less educated use newspapers—whether that entertainment is in the arts, in sports, or in comics.

Many newspapers today are faced with declining readership. When this happens, advertisers put their money elsewhere. This loss of revenue forces the newspaper to cut back on various features or coverage, which further reduces readership, which further cuts down advertising revenues. The result of this spiral is the closing of the paper—a common event today. Among the reasons people give for their declining readership are that television news serves their needs in an easier and more efficient way; newspapers contain too much politics and too much crime; and newspapers are not personalized enough to serve their individual needs.

This declining readership does not mean that newspapers are not influential. They are. Over 60 million copies of daily newspapers are sold each day. That represents a lot of news, a lot of advertisements, and, in general, a lot of influence.

Magazines

Magazines are both general and specialized. The general magazines include *Reader's Digest, TV Guide,* and *Family Circle.* But much as cable television programs focus on specialized audiences, many magazines are now directed at small specialized audiences. For example, *Science* appeals to that relatively small group of persons concerned with sophisticated scientific developments. *Scientific American* appeals to a similar audience but is somewhat less specialized. *Gentlemen's Quarterly* appeals to fashion-conscious men; *Vogue* to fashion-conscious women. *Sports Illustrated, Modern Bride, Stereo Review, Travel & Leisure, Field and Stream,* and similar magazines, as their titles imply, likewise appeal to specialized interests and audiences.

Magazines are big business and, in fact, most of the larger magazines are owned and controlled by major corporations. Time Warner, for example, owns *Time, Life, Fortune, Sports Illustrated, People,* and *Money.* The Hearst Corporation owns *Good Housekeeping, Cosmopolitan, Harper's Bazaar, Popular Mechanics,* and *House Beautiful.* The Johnson Publishing Corporation owns *Ebony, Jet,* and *Tan,* and Condé Nast owns *Glamour, Vogue, Architectural Digest,* and *Mademoiselle.* Thus, although there are many different magazines, they are actually controlled by relatively few corporations. So, the points of view—on significant political, social, and economic issues—are likewise relatively few.

Films

Television and film have developed a relationship in which one feeds off the other. For example, television talk shows frequently highlight the lives and problems of movie stars and provide advanced publicity for new movies. And, of course, people now go to the movies to see their favorite television stars. Current television stars like Damon Wayans and Dana Carvey are relatively new to films but may well become so identified with film that we forget their television beginnings. Clint Eastwood, Bruce Willis, Michael J. Fox, and Danny Devito are good examples of performers who got their start in television but are now so identified with movies that we think of them only as film stars.

Further, where once television cut into the income of the film industry, television now is one of the major supporters of film making and film makers. The large Hollywood studios now produce more films for television than they do for movie theaters. The typical film now earns more from television sales (cable and network showings, videocassette sales, and pay-per-view hookups) than from box office receipts.

Today, most films (especially the big money makers) are youth-oriented and constitute one of the most convenient places for the social activities of today's young. They are relatively inexpensive and easily accessible. At the same time they afford the young a judicious mixture of the company of peers and yet an opportunity to maintain sufficient privacy. Over the past several years, however, statistics show that the film audience is getting older. A large part of this audience is grown women, who probably account in large part for the success of such films as *A League of Their Own, The Joy Luck Club,* and *The Age of Innocence.*

Although we often think of film as synonymous with entertainment, many films serve other functions. Even the entertainment film does more than "just entertain." Films like *The Deer Hunter*, *Platoon*, and *Gettysburg* showed us how horrible war really is. *Norma Rae* showed us how unskilled workers are often exploited. The *Rocky* movies tried to demonstrate that the American dream can be a reality. *Boyz N the Hood* showed us the lives of inner city youth and the problems of racism, *Bob Roberts* the contradictions within the political process, and *Hoffa* the extent of corruption.

Other films, of course, function primarily to influence and persuade. The film of information is being used with considerable success in schools and business organizations. Concepts such as nonverbal communication, conference and public speaking techniques, and anatomical and physiological aspects of speech and hearing—to name just a few in the area of communication—are so much easier to teach and learn with the help of films.

Books

Of all the mass media, books are the most elitist. They are read by the intelligentsia of the mass communication audience. This holds true even when we add the popular pornographic or romance pocket books to this list. People who read books earn higher incomes, have attained a higher level of education, and are more likely to live in the city than in rural areas compared to people who do not read books.

Books are both entertainment and education. They offer a historical record of the past, guidance for the present, and direction for the future. About 50,000 trade books (non-textbooks) are issued each year. Only about 5 percent (around 2,500) will sell over 5,000 copies. The vast majority will fail to secure an audience and to make money.

Tapes and Compact Discs

Tapes and compact discs are becoming increasingly important in entertainment and education. College students spend more money on these recordings than on books. The periodic lags in such spending seem always to be countered by some new technology—stereo, cassette tapes, CDs, and, more recently, digital tapes and minidisks—that encourages even greater spending, now counted in the billions of dollars. Their combination with videos, first popularized beyond all industry expectations by Michael Jackson's "Thriller," have added a new dimension to audio recordings. Even when only listening, you can now visualize the video.

The popularity of recording artists can be measured, at least in part, by the enormous amounts of money they are paid. In 1992 Prince headed the list with contracts totaling $100 million; Madonna's contracts totaled $60 million; and Janet Jackson's $50 million.

Like film, tapes and CDs are designed primarily to entertain. At the same time they influence attitudes and values. This dual function is seen most clearly during times of political and social turmoil. The Vietnam War, for example, spawned numerous records directed at influencing attitudes and behaviors. Joan Baez and Buffy Sainte-Marie, for example, had considerable impact during this time, particularly with college students.

Today, the persuasive agents and their messages are somewhat different. Large groups have banded together to popularize and raise money for a variety of humanitarian causes. The Live Aid concert in 1985, for example, which raised some $70 million for Africa's poor, was perhaps the most widely publicized and the most successful. With Live Aid and various similar concerts, huge organizations had to be formed to coordinate the efforts of hundreds of recording stars and to collect and distribute the monies raised.

Live Aid and, for example, Willie Nelson's concerts to raise money for farmers, gave a new dimension to the role of concerts and of musicians generally. The Woodstock concert of 1969 represented drugs and antiwar and antigovernment sentiment, and freedom from society's rules and regulations. The concerts of the 1980s seemed more to represent participating actively in changing the world, helping the less fortunate, and, in general, using music and the musician's fame and talent as social forces. The theme of the 1990s has yet to be written. Any guesses?

THE FUNCTIONS OF MASS COMMUNICATION

The popularity and pervasive influence of the mass media can be maintained only by their serving a variety of significant functions. Six of the most important functions are discussed here (Figure 24.2).

To Entertain

The media design their programs to entertain. In reality, of course, they entertain to secure the attention of the largest possible group so they may sell this attention to

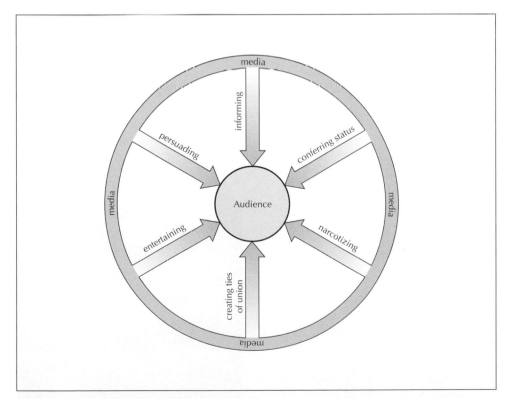

FIGURE 24.2 The functions of the mass media.

advertisers. This is the major reason why mass communications exist. In societies where the state supports the media or where advertising is banned from various media the process is different. In the United States and in most democracies, however, if the media did not entertain, they would no longer have viewers or readers and would quickly be out of business.

To Persuade

While the most obvious media function is to entertain, the most important function is to persuade. Persuasion comes in a number of forms: (1) reinforcing or strengthening a person's attitudes, beliefs, or values; (2) changing a person's attitudes, beliefs, or values; (3) activating the person to do something; and (4) ethicizing or providing the person with a system of values.

Reinforcing   It is difficult for anyone to convert someone from one attitudinal extreme to another (see Unit 20). And the media, with all the resources and power at their disposal, are no exception. More often, the media reinforce or make stronger our beliefs, attitudes, values, and opinions. Democrats will expose themselves to democratic persuasion and will emerge reinforced from the experience. Similarly, religious people will expose themselves to messages in line with their beliefs and will emerge reinforced or stronger in their convictions.

Even those communications we think are changing attitudes often only reinforce existing ones. Studies show, for example, that such programming may actually reinforce rather than reduce racial and ethnic prejudice. For example, in their study of *All in the Family,* media researchers Neil Vidmar and Milton Rokeach (1974) write: "The

What cultural values do the media reinforce? How do they do it? Can you provide examples from newspapers (comic strips, advice columns, hard news stories, entertainment news features, and so on) and television (situation comedies, dramas, advertisements, news shows, talk shows, and so on) that demonstrate that the media are in the business of transmitting cultural values?

data seem to support those who have argued that the program is not uniformly seen as satire and those who have argued that it exploits or appeals to bigotry."

Changing   The media will convert some people who are undecided on any issue. Thus, those who are torn between the Republicans and the Democrats may well find themselves converted to one side or the other on the basis of media messages.

The media also produces lots of changes that we would consider trivial. For example, changes in our toilet-paper buying behavior may well be greatly or even totally influenced by the media. Except to toilet paper manufacturers, our choice of toilet paper is unimportant. Political preferences, religious attitudes, and social commitments—especially those about which we feel strongly—are not so easily changed.

Activating   From the advertiser's point of view, the most important function of the media is to activate—to move consumers to action. The media try to get the viewer or reader the buy Wonder bread, to use Gillette, to choose Brut instead of Old Spice. Once an attitude is formed or a behavior pattern is established, the media function to channel it in specific directions. For example, once the pattern of paying $60 for a pair of jeans is established, the media can channel that behavior relatively easily to Guess?, Calvin Klein, Sasson, or in fact to any jean with a high price tag, preferably a tag that can be easily seen.

Ethicizing   Another persuasive function is that of **ethicizing** (Lazarsfeld and Merton, 1951). By making public certain deviations from the norm (for example, the Jim Bakker affair), the media arouse people to change the situation. They provide viewers with a collective ethic. For example, without the media coverage of Watergate, it seems unlikely that there would have been such a public outcry over the events that eventually led Richard Nixon to resign.

To Inform

Most of our information has been learned not from school, but from the media. You have learned music, politics, film, art, sociology, psychology, economics, and a host of other subjects from the media. You learn about other places and other times from seeing a good movie as well as from reading a history textbook.

A special type of information is communicated through the ever-increasing television talk shows. From these we learn about co-dependency, child abuse, plastic surgery, drug and alcohol addiction, racism, sexism, and homophobia. One of the main appeals of such shows is that they claim to offer (and in some cases probably do) usable skills for dealing with ordinary but perplexing daily problems that viewers do not have the time, money, or education to learn about in books or in therapy. A glance through *TV Guide* shows a wide array of such issues being discussed by Oprah Winfrey, Phil Donahue, Sally Jesse Raphael, Jenny Jones, Maury Povich, and various others.

One type of education (or persuasion) is to teach the viewers the values, opinions, and rules that society judges to be proper and just. That is, part of the educational function of the media is directed at socializing the audience. They do this in dramas, sitcoms, stories, discussions, articles, comics, and advertisements and commercials. In all these situations, the values of the society are expressed in an unspoken manner. We are taught how to dress for different occasions, what it means to be a good citizen, what a proper meal should consist of, how to hold a discussion or conversation, how to respond to people of different national and racial groups, how to behave in strange places, and so on.

Even when you turn to the media for "pure information" you are clearly being influenced. Two recent examples, presented in Figure 24.3, should illustrate the difficulty (perhaps the impossibility) of presenting information without persuasion.

To Confer Status

Your personal list of the 100 most important people in the world would almost certainly consist of people to whom the media give a great deal of exposure. Without such exposure the people would not in fact be important—at least not in the popular mind. Paul Lazarsfeld and Robert Merton (1951), in their influential *Mass Communication, Popular Taste, and Organized Social Action*, put it this way: "If you really matter, you will be at the focus of mass attention and, if you are at the focus of mass attention, then surely you must really matter." Conversely, of course, if you do not get mass attention, then you do not matter.

To Narcotize

One of the most interesting and most overlooked functions of the media is the narcotizing function. This means that when the media provide information about something the receiver believes that some action has been taken. As a result, the viewer is drugged into inactivity as if under the influence of a narcotic. As Lazarsfeld and Merton (1951) explain it:

> The individual reads accounts of issues and problems and may even discuss alternative lines of action. But this rather intellectualized, rather remote connection with organized social action is not activated. The interested and informed citizen can congratulate himself on his lofty state of interest and information and neglect to see that he has abstained from decision and action . . . . He comes to mistake *knowing* about problems of the day with *doing* something about them.

Lazarsfeld and Merton term this *dysfunctional* rather than functional "on the assumption that it is not in the interest of modern complex society to have large masses of the population politically apathetic and inert." And with seven hours of television viewing each day, there is little wonder that we confuse knowledge of problems and issues with action.

To Create Ties of Union

One of the functions of mass communication few people ever think of is its ability to make its viewers feel like members of a group. Consider the lone television viewer, sitting in his or her apartment watching television while eating dinner. The television programs make this lone soul feel a part of some larger group, for example, the soap opera family, the fans at a stadium, or the contestants on a quiz show. The media also function to create ties among viewers who can feel greater similarity with one another and who have a common base of information (Becker & Roberts, 1992).

Privatization   The media, however, also establish the opposite of union and relationships—namely, **privatization**. This is the tendency for an individual to retreat from social groups into a world of his or her own. Some theorists have proposed that

TURMOIL AT *TIMES* OVER JESSE JAB

Some New York *Times* staffers are furious over the way the paper covered Jesse Jackson's speech at the Democratic National Convention.

The city's three other general-interest dailies had positive front-page stories on the speech, but in a largely negative page-one article, B. Drummond Ayres Jr. wrote that Jackson "is not the commanding force he once was . . . and for much of his address . . . his voice reflected it." The article was labeled NEWS ANALYSIS in late editions, but that didn't mollify staffers. "The change was a tacit admission that the story was originally misjudged," says a source. "Even if it's analysis, you have to have evidence. . . . It's not just the reporters of color who are upset. It's one of the few things around here that we're united on." Says Ayres, "No one has complained to me. The story speaks for itself."

"Our editors feel the piece accurately reflected the perception of delegates and politicians on the convention-hall floor," says a *Times* spokeswoman. "In retrospect, it might have included more about how the speech was received by those watching it on television. The piece continued to be edited and further reported throughout the press run, so several versions appeared in the newspaper. The news analysis [label] was appropriate in the late edition. In hindsight, it may have been appropriate in the first edition as well."

HOW TV COVERED BUSH'S HECKLERS

Special to The New York Times

WASHINGTON, July 24—Was President Bush humiliated today by scores of angry hecklers or was it merely the sort of slight disruption that every politician endures now and then? It depends on which television network you watched.

All three major networks reported the incident in the first five minutes of their evening broadcasts.

On CBS and NBC, the episode came off as far more serious than on ABC. Both CBS and NBC devoted more time to Mr. Bush's angry retorts and to the pictures of furious people. NBC said there were "scores" of hecklers. CBS said that there were "about two dozen."

On the "NBC Nightly News," Mr. Bush appeared enraged as he was being shouted down, though he was shown later in the day looking relaxed as he insisted that "I didn't blow my cool."

On the "CBS Evening News," the reporter said the protest "drowned out the President's message and overshadowed his entire campaign day."

But ABC's "World News Tonight" played down the episode, mentioning it only at the end of a segment that showed Mr. Bush at a campaign rally later in the day.

FIGURE 24.3   Information or persuasion? [*Sources:* "Turmoil at Times Over Jesse Jab." Copyright © 1992 K-III Magazine Corporation. All rights reserved. Reprinted with the permission of *New York* Magazine. "How TV Covered Bush's Hecklers" in *The New York Times,* July 25, 1992. Copyright © 1992 by The New York Times Company. Reprinted by permission.]

the tremendous quantities of information almost forced upon us by the media overwhelm us and make us feel inadequate. Intense reports on wars, inflation, crime, and unemployment make some people feel so helpless that they retreat into their own private worlds. In many cases, this takes the form of concentrating on trivial issues—deciding which pair of designer jeans to buy and what restaurant to go to.

Parasocial Relationships   Many viewers develop **parasocial relationships** with media personalities and even with dramatic characters (Rubin & McHugh, 1987). They see these characters as friends and advisers. As a result, viewers may write to a television doctor or lawyer for medical or legal advice or send warning letters to their "friends" who are about to be murdered on a soap opera. As can be expected, these parasocial relationships are most important to those who spend a great deal of time with the media and who have few interpersonal relationships (Rubin, Pearse, & Powell, 1985).

Evaluating Media Functions

In evaluating and analyzing these functions of the media, keep in mind at least three related issues. First, each time you turn on the television or radio or read a newspaper, you do so for a unique set of reasons. Each mass communication event serves a unique set of functions. Second, every mass communication event serves a different function for each individual viewer. The same television program may entertain one person, educate another, and narcotize still another. Third, the functions served by any mass communication event for any person differ from one time to the next. Where a particular record once entertained, it may now socialize or create ties of union.

Earlier we noted that the narcotizing function of the media is detrimental to the social system. It hinders rather than fosters development and needed change. Actually, all six functions may be viewed from a functional-dysfunctional perspective. For example, the media as entertainment are generally viewed as functional or positive. The media provide viewers with convenient, inexpensive entertainment much needed after a day's work. On the other hand, the steady and constant flow of entertainment may prove dysfunctional and discourage people from engaging in interpersonal communication, studying, learning, working, and so on.

The media's conferral of status is functional if those who gain status prove deserving and socially productive. It is dysfunctional if they prove undeserving and socially unproductive. Note, for example, that those who get the most media coverage are for the most part sports stars and film and television actors. By giving these people extensive coverage, the media tell us they really matter. Scientists and educators, for example, get much less media coverage. In its present mode of operation, the conferral of status is frequently dysfunctional.

Summary

1. The *source of mass communications* is generally a complex organization that goes to great expense to construct and transmit messages.

2. The *audience of mass communication* is extremely large and varied, making it difficult for advertisers to target their messages to a specific audience. As a result, this large and heterogeneous audience is segmented into more narrowly defined small groups.

3. *Mass communication messages* are public ones; everyone has access to them.

4. The *process by which mass communication messages travel* is largely one-way. The messages go from source to receiver but seldom from receiver to source. The process of selection is two-way. The media sources select the group to which they wish to appeal and the receivers select the media to which they wish to attend.

5. The media operate within a social *context* and both influence and are influenced by that context.

6. The major forms of mass communication are *television, radio, newspapers, magazines, films, books*, and *records/tapes/cassettes/compact discs*.

7. Mass communications serve a variety of *functions:* to entertain, persuade, inform, confer status, narcotize, and create ties of union.

Application

24.1 TELEVISION AND VALUES

Listed below are eight values found to be significant among college students in a Daniel Yankelovich survey and reported in Tarshis (1979). The percentage figures represent the proportion of the respondents who identified the value as "very important."

1. Self-fulfillment, 87 percent
2. Education, 76 percent
3. Family, 68 percent
4. Hard work, 43 percent
5. Having children, 31 percent
6. Religion, 28 percent
7. Money, 20 percent
8. Patriotism, 19 percent

Examine the list of values and next to each value identify one, two, or three television characters who seem best to exemplify that value. After you have identified at least one character for each value, the entire class should pool their results and discuss them, considering some or all of the following questions. It may facilitate discussion if the values are written on the chalk-board and some of the more frequently named characters are listed next to the value. Do not read any further until you have identified the several characters requested.

1. Are there any sex differences? That is, do male and female characters ex-emplify the same or different values? What are the implications of these similarities or differences for television serving an educational function? Reinforcing function? Persuasive function?

2. Are there any differences based on age, race, religion, nationality? Again, what are the implications of these similarities or differences?

3. What type of character would you like to see achieve some prominence on television? For example, at the least, identify the sex, race, nationality, reli-gion, occupation, affectional preference, age, intelligence level, marital sta-tus, and general physical condition of the character you would like to see on television. What values would you like to see this character embody? What media functions would you particularly like to influence?

4. What type of character would you like to see less of on television? Identify specific characters. Why?

5. Are the characters in the movies similar to those on TV? Explain the rea-sons for the differences (if any).

6. Television characters seem not to have achieved the kind of prominence that many characters in novels and dramas have. For example, Scarlett O'Hara, Huck Finn, Willy Loman, and George and Martha have achieved a level of prominence television characters rarely, if ever, achieve. What fac-tors might account for these differences in universal and lasting fame? One possible exception that comes quickly to mind is Archie Bunker. Are there other "exceptions"?

THEORIES OF MASS COMMUNICATION

UNIT CONTENTS

Step Theories

Diffusion of Innovations Theory

Cultivation Theory

Uses and Gratification Theory

Agenda-setting Theory

Reversing the Process: Influencing the Media

   Summary

   Applications

      25.1   Exploring the Theories of Mass Communication

      25.2   The Talk Show and Human Communication

UNIT GOALS

After completing this unit, you should be able to

1. explain the step theories of mass communication

2. explain the diffusion of innovations theory

3. explain cultivation theory

4. explain the uses and gratification approach to mass communication

5. explain how agenda setting and gatekeeping work in mass communication

6. explain the ways you can influence the media

In this final unit we examine some theories of mass communication. The theories we examine will give considerable insight into how the mass media work and how they exert their influence. But all communication—even media—is a two-way process and so we conclude this unit with suggestions for how you can influence the media.

STEP THEORIES

Some theories view the effects of the media in terms of steps. We look at how each of these theories explains the way in which messages from the media eventually get through to and influence you and me.

The One-Step Theory

The one-step theory holds the influence of the media to be direct and immediate (Figure 25.1). You read a newspaper and are persuaded by what you read. As a result, you change your thoughts and behaviors in accordance with the media's injunctions. Messages go through only one step—from the media to the reader.

A variant of this theory has been called the *silver bullet theory* by theorist Wilbur Schramm (Schramm & Porter, 1982). This theory holds that the media work like bullets aimed at a target. If the gun is loaded correctly and aimed accurately, the bullet will penetrate the target. That is, the media will have the desired effect on their target audience. In this view the audience, like the target, is passive and offers no resistance. As the target cannot resist being penetrated, neither can the audience.

This bullet theory developed largely from the fear people had of wartime propaganda. People assumed that enemy governments would be able to change basic values and beliefs simply by firing the right messages. But receivers are active, not passive participants. Receivers mold, shape, alter, and otherwise recreate the messages they receive. Further, listeners are selective in what they expose themselves to and what they remember. The receiver has to buy the newspaper, turn on the television, or go to the movie. The receiver decides whether to read the morning's editorial, chooses to watch one station rather than another, and sees one movie but avoids ten others. Similarly, we remember largely what we want to remember and what is important to us.

Perhaps the major inadequacy with this one-step theory is its neglect of interpersonal interaction. Before we internalize an opinion or change an attitude, we seek support and confirmation from other people. The one-step approach neglects this crucial

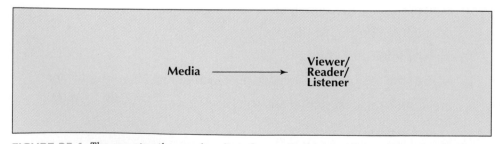

FIGURE 25.1 The one-step theory of media influence. In this view the media exert a direct—one-step—influence on the audience.

element and other interpersonal dynamics. This neglect of interpersonal influence led researchers to modify the one-step into a two-step theory.

The Two-Step Theory

A more sophisticated proposal was presented in *The People's Choice* (Lazarsfeld, Berelson, & Gaudet, 1944; see also Katz, 1957). In this study of the voters in the 1940 presidential election, these researchers found that people were influenced more by other people than by the mass media (then, primarily newspapers and radio). Those who did the influencing were **opinion leaders** (Figure 25.2). Mass communications, the researchers proposed, do not affect people directly. In this view messages from the media influence opinion leaders. Then these opinion leaders influence the general population in more interpersonal situations.

The two-step concept, although useful and revealing, is too simple (Schramm & Porter, 1982). For one thing, it is not always true. Much of our information comes right from the media. Further, the media today, especially television, enjoy extremely high credibility. Many people accept as true what they see and hear on the tube without need of local opinion leaders.

Second, the concept of an opinion leader must be examined in more detail. Generally, opinion leaders have more formal education, greater wealth, higher social status, and more exposure to mass communications than those they influence. They also participate in social activities to a greater extent and are more innovative, cosmopolitan, competent, and accessible than those they influence.

Some opinion leaders, however, are more influential than others. Some are leaders of leaders, whereas others are leaders of followers. Some leaders therefore get their information from the media. Others get their information from other leaders. Recognize, too, that many of the opinion leaders you turn to today are themselves media personalities—the Sam Donaldsons and the Ted Koppels, for example. You let these people into your homes every day, and you trust them implicitly. You have today, therefore, much less need of the local opinion leader. Also, you are less likely to turn to opinion leaders because you now have access to the same information they do. Why look to the local leader, for example, when you too can go directly to the network anchorperson?

The Multistep Theory

Developed largely out of the criticism of the two-step theory, the multistep theory holds that influence moves back and forth from the media to the people (who also in-

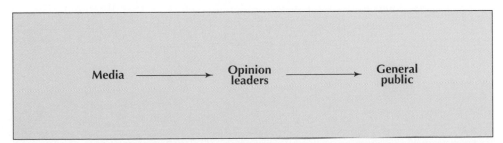

Media   ⟶   Opinion leaders   ⟶   General public

FIGURE 25.2 The two-step theory of media influence. In this view the media influence opinion leaders, who in turn influence the general public.

teract with each other), then back to the media, then back to the people, and so on (Figure 25.3). There are, in short, many steps that must be examined before we can begin to explain the effects of the media.

This back-and-forth process seems especially true today, with media so much a part of our lives. It also seems logical in view of the finding that people who expose themselves to one medium will often expose themselves to others as well. Inevitably the same issues and news items will be covered in the different media. We must further assume that interpersonal interaction occurs in between media exposures. Throughout these exposures (to both media and interpersonal interactions), we are influenced and we influence others. For example, you might hear on the radio in the morning that the stock market will go down. A friend at work might then strengthen your belief. The evening newspaper may cast some doubt on your belief or perhaps give you sufficient reason to change your attitude completely. Discussion with your family might lead you to reconsider your original beliefs, and so on.

This multistep theory seems more accurate in describing what happens in opinion and attitude formation. And it is particularly valuable in illustrating that each person is influenced by both the media and interpersonal interactions, and in turn influences the media and others. This does not mean that the issue of media effects is now solved. We still know very little about media influence. We need to combine this multistep theory with the insights provided by a number of other theories.

DIFFUSION OF INNOVATIONS THEORY

A theory directed at a somewhat different aspect of media influence is the **diffusion of innovations theory** (Rogers, 1983). This theory focuses on the way communications, especially mass communications, influence people to adopt something new or different (Mayer, Gudykunst, Perrill, & Merrill, 1990).

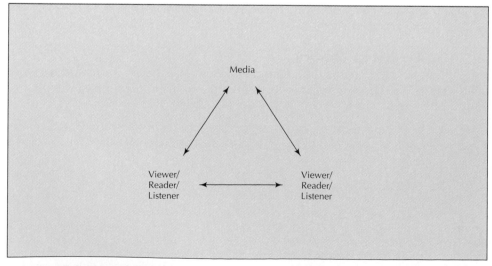

FIGURE 25.3 The multistep theory of media influence. In this view the media influence audience members, who also influence each other and in turn influence the media.

Diffusion refers to the passage of new information, the innovation, or the new process through society. The innovation may be of any type—for example, contact lenses, computers, food processors, behavioral objectives in teaching, experiential learning, or multimedia instruction—although the research has focused largely on news events (DeFleur, 1987; Rosengren, 1987). *Adoption* refers to people's positive reactions to and use of the innovation. In the process of adoption, William McEwen (1975) identifies three general stages:

1. At the *information acquisition* stage the person acquires and understands the information about the innovation. For example, a teacher learns about a new approach to teaching large lecture classes.
2. At the *information evaluation* stage the person evaluates the information about the innovation. For example, the teacher recognizes that the new method is more effective than the old one.
3. At the *adoption or rejection* stage the person adopts or rejects the innovation. For example, the teacher begins to teach with this new method.

Obviously all people do not choose to adopt or reject the innovation at the same time. Researchers in the area of information diffusion distinguish five types of adopters (Figure 25.4).

Innovators, the first to adopt the innovation, are not necessarily the originators of the new idea, but they are the ones who introduce it on a reasonably broad scale. *Early adopters*, sometimes called "the influentials," legitimize the idea and make it acceptable to people in general. The *early majority* follows the influentials and further legitimizes the innovation.

The *late majority* adopts the innovation next. People in this group may follow either the influentials or the early majority. Finally, *laggards*, the last group to adopt the innovation, may take the lead from people in any of the previous three groups.

These five groups constitute almost 100 percent of the population. The remaining portion are the "diehards." These are the ones who never adopt the innovation. These are the cooks who never use a blender or food processor, the teachers who refuse to use

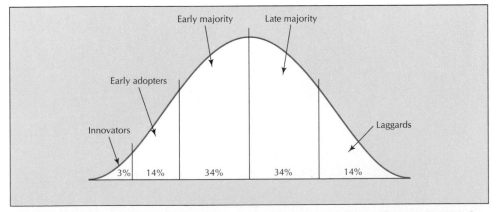

FIGURE 25.4 The five types of adopters as represented in the population. (*Source:* Reprinted with the permission of The Free Press, a Division of Macmillan, Inc. from *The Diffusion of Innovations,* third edition, by Everett M. Rogers. Copyright © 1962, 1971, 1983 by The Free Press.)

new instructional techniques, and so on. There are some instances in which there are no diehards. For example, teachers may wish to continue using a particular textbook. But if it goes out of print, they are forced to change and join the group of laggards.

In general, early adopters—the innovators compared with the laggards—are younger than late adapters and of a higher socioeconomic status. They have more specialized occupations, are more empathic, and are less dogmatic. They are more oriented toward change and make more use of available information. They have a more cosmopolitan orientation and are generally opinion leaders.

CULTIVATION THEORY

According to cultivation theory, the media, especially television, are the primary means by which you learn about your society and your culture (Gerbner, Gross, Morgan, & Signorielli, 1980). It is through your exposure to television (and other media) that you learn about the world, its people, its values, its customs.

Cultivation theory argues that heavy television viewers form an image of reality that is inconsistent with the facts (Potter, 1986; Potter & Chang, 1990). For example, heavy viewers see their chances of being a victim of a crime to be 1 in 10. In reality it is 1 in 50. The difference, according to cultivation theorists, is due to the fact that television presents crime to be significantly higher than it really is. That is, crime is highlighted on television dramas as well as in news reports. Rarely does television devote attention to the absence of crime.

What have you learned about other specific cultures from the media? Can you identify three or four beliefs about different cultures that you learned from the media? Did you acquire (or revise) beliefs about your own culture from reading or viewing the various media?

Heavy viewers think that 20 percent of the world's population lives in the United States. In reality it is 6 percent. Heavy viewers believe that the percentage of workers in managerial or professional jobs is 25 percent. In reality it is 5 percent. Frederick Williams (1989), commenting on these same studies, observes:

> People who are heavy viewers of television often have stereotyped attitudes about sex roles, physicians, doctors, gangsters, or the usual inhabitants of television shows. . . . In their world, housewives may be more concerned with keeping the "bathroom bowl" clean than anything else. Husbands are bumblers who exist in situation comedies. Police officials have minute-by-minute exciting days. People "die" without all the agonies of death, and gangsters are all evil-looking.

Of course, not all heavy television viewers are cultivated in the same way or to the same extent. Some are more susceptible to the influence of television than others (Hirsch, 1980). For example, the influence will depend not only on how much a person watches television but also on the person's education, income, and sex. For example, low income light viewers see crime as a serious problem but high income light viewers do not. Similarly, female heavy viewers see crime as a more serious problem than do male heavy viewers. That is, factors other than the amount of television viewing influence our perception of the world and how ready we are to take the world television portrays as the real world.

Thus, although television is not the only means by which our view of the world is created—other factors like income and sex are also important—it surely is one of the most potent. This seems especially true when exposure to television is heavy and when it occurs over a long period of time.

USES AND GRATIFICATION THEORY

In any given situation, we may reasonably ask why an audience chooses to select a particular medium. Wilbur Schramm, in his *Men, Women, Messages, and Media* (1982) proposes a formula:

$$\text{promise of reward/effort required} = \text{probability of selection}$$

Under the promise of reward, Schramm includes both immediate and delayed rewards. *Rewards* satisfy the needs of the audience. That is, you watch a particular television program because it satisfies your need for information or entertainment. The *effort required* for attending to mass communications depends on the availability of the media and the ease with which we may use them. Effort also includes the expense involved. For example, there is less effort required—less expense, less time lost—in watching television than in going to a movie. There is less effort in going to a movie than in going to a play. When we divide the *effort required* into the *promise of reward*, we obtain the *probability of selection* of a particular mass communication medium.

This approach to media has come to be referred to as the *uses and gratifications approach*. We can understand people's interaction with the media by (1) the uses they put the media to and (2) the gratifications they derive. Typical gratifications are escape from everyday worries, relief from loneliness, emotional support, acquisition of information, and social contact. The main assumption of this approach is that audience members actively and consciously link themselves to certain media to gain gratification. The media are seen in this approach as competing with other sources (largely interpersonal) to serve the needs of the audience.

AGENDA-SETTING THEORY

Another approach to media effects is *agenda-setting theory* (McCombs & Shaw, 1977). When you set up an agenda, you list the things you must attend to. In a similar way, the media establish our agenda by focusing attention on certain people and events. (This, of course, is similar to media's function of conferring status discussed in Unit 24.) These are the people and events to which we should give our attention. Or, so the media tell us.

This theory, as Agee, Ault, and Emery (1988) put it, refers to the "ability of the media to select and call to the public's attention both ideas and events." The media tell us what is and what is not important. The media "do not tell people 'what to think' but 'what to think about'" (Edelstein, 1993). Notice that the things you think are important and the things you talk about interpersonally. They are in fact the very things on which the media concentrate. In fact, we may argue that nothing important can happen without media coverage. If the media don't cover it, then it isn't important. But, does the media concentrate on events because they are important, or does media concentration make them important?

Surely the media lead you to focus attention on certain subjects. Although there is clearly no one-to-one relationship between media attention and popular perception of importance (interpersonal factors are also operating), the media do probably set your agendas to some significant degree.

Recognize too that most media are controlled by persons of enormous wealth and power (network owners and executives, advertisers, or directors of multimillion-dollar corporations). These people want to retain and increase such wealth and power. What gets attention from the media and influences what the media present is dictated largely by this small but extremely influential group. The media exist to make profit for this group. Of course, there are public service media which do not focus on financial gain. But they too have agendas. All communicators have agendas, and the messages from any person or organization establish agendas for the receiver.

Gatekeepers

Any consideration of agenda-setting theory needs to give special attention to gatekeepers (Hiebert, Ungurait, & Bohn, 1974). In the passage of a message from the source of mass media to the viewer, there a *gatekeeper* intervenes. The term *gatekeeping* was originally used by Kurt Lewin in his *Human Relations* (1947). It refers to (1) the process by which a message passes through various gates, as well as to (2) the people or groups that allow the message to pass (gatekeepers).

Gatekeepers may be individuals or a group through which a message passes in going from sender to receiver. A gatekeeper's main function is to filter the messages an individual receives. Teachers are perfect examples of gatekeepers. Teachers read the various books in an area of study. They read journal articles and listen to convention papers. They share information among themselves and conduct their own research in the field. From all this information, they pass *some* of it on to their students. Editors of newspapers, magazines, and publishing houses are also gatekeepers. They allow certain information to get through and not other information.

Everyone functions to some extent as a gatekeeper. For example, of all the messages that come to you during the day, you select certain of these to pass on to, say, your parents, friends, teachers, and so on. In passing them on, you may modify them in many ways for many reasons. You may choose not to pass on certain other messages at all.

The gatekeeper, then, limits the messages we receive. The teacher, for example, limits the information the students receive. However, the teacher enables the students to learn a great deal more by distilling, organizing, and analyzing information for them. That is, without gatekeepers we would not get half the information we now receive.

We might diagram the gatekeeping process as in Figure 25.5. Note that the messages (M_1, M_2, M_3) received by the gatekeeper come from different sources (S_1, S_2, S_3). So, one of the gatekeeper's functions is to select the messages to be communicated. The gatekeeper then selectively transmits numerous messages (M_A, M_B, M_C) to different receivers (R_1, R_2, R_3). Teachers, for example, do not pass on the same messages to advanced classes as to elementary classes. Perhaps the most important aspect to note about this process is that messages received by the gatekeeper (M_1, M_2, M_3) are not the same as the messages the gatekeeper sends (M_A, M_B, M_C).

You may find it interesting to translate this relatively abstract discussion into concrete reality by asking yourself how the following people function as gatekeepers:

- your communication instructor
- your *Human Communication* text author
- your parents
- the editor of your local or college newspaper
- Phil Donahue and Oprah Winfrey
- your best friend

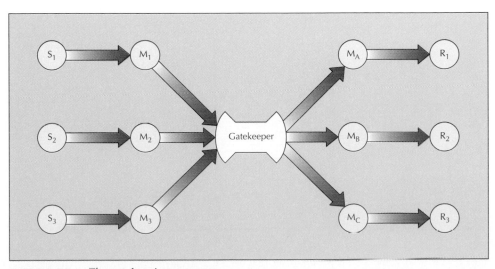

FIGURE 25.5 The gatekeeping process.

- your romantic partner (past or present)
- the president of the United States

REVERSING THE PROCESS: INFLUENCING THE MEDIA

Although the media are generally analyzed for their effects on the individual, recognize that viewers and readers also exert influence on each other and may ultimately effect the media. For example, you may influence your friends or your family. They, in turn, will influence others who will influence still others. Through these interpersonal channels, the influence of one person can be considerable. The larger and more influential these groups become, the more influence they will exert on the media through their selective attention and their buying habits.

You may also influence the media more directly. Kathleen Hall Jamieson and Karlyn Kohrs Campbell, in their perceptive *Interplay of Influence* (1991), for example, suggest that you can effectively influence the media in several important ways (see also Postman & Powers, 1992).

Register Individual Complaints   For example, you may write letters to (or call) a television station or to an advertiser expressing your views on the content of a program or topics to which you think more attention should be given. You can also write letters to a public forum such as letters to the editor of a newspaper or call in to a television talk show. And, of course, you can write letters to the Federal Communica-

How do the media present the cultures of which you are a member? Are the treatments generally fair? Unfair? If you had the power to change one thing about the media's portrayal of any culture to which you belong, what would you choose?

tion Commission or to other regulatory agencies that in turn will exert pressure of the media.

These letters and phone calls count a great deal more than most people think. Because most people do not write or call, the media give such messages considerable weight. Letters and phone calls, for example, may also help other audience members crystalize their own thinking and, depending on your persuasiveness, may even convince them to believe and to act as you do.

Group Pressure   When you join with others who think the same way, group pressure can be brought to bear on television networks, newspapers, advertisers, and manufacturers. Threatening a boycott or legal action (and potentially at least damage the economic base of an organization) can quickly gain attention and often some measure of compliance.

Protest Through an Established Organization   Obviously the larger the organization you use to influence the media, the better. Similarly, the more economically powerful, the more persuasive your appeal will be. The AIDS epidemic has led to the creation of a wide variety of organizations that have exerted pressure for increased research funding and services to people with AIDS. ACT UP (AIDS Coalition to Unleash Power) is perhaps the most visible of such organizations.

Protesting with a Social Movement   This technique has been used throughout history to gain civil rights for minority groups and for women. Forming such movements or aligning yourself with an established movement can enable you to secure not only a large number of petitioners but is almost sure to secure media coverage which would enable you to put forth your own position.

Create Legislative Pressure   You can exert influence on the state or federal level by influencing your local political representatives (through your own voting, calls, and letters), who will in turn influence representatives on higher levels of the political hierarchy. And of course you can help to influence the groups to which you belong to exert influence.

Summary

1. The *one-step theory* holds that mass communications influence the audience directly and immediately. One variant of this theory is the silver bullet theory, which holds that the media's messages work much as do bullets aimed at a target.

2. The *two-step theory* holds that the media influence opinion leaders, who in turn influence the general population.

3. The *multistep theory* holds that the influence process is reciprocal. It goes back and forth from the media to the people, then back to the media, then back to the people, and so on.

4. The *diffusion of innovations theory* focuses on the role of the media in influencing people to adopt something new. Three stages are identified: information acquisition, information evaluation, and adoption or rejection of the innovation.

5. *Cultivation theory* argues that the media, especially television, provide viewers with an unrealistic view of the world but one that many take to be reality.

6. The *uses and gratifications theory* explains people's interaction with the media by the uses to which they put the media and the gratifications they derive from the media.

7. The *agenda-setting theory* holds that the media exert their effects by establishing what is and what is not important.

8. *Gatekeepers* are those persons or institutions that receive messages and then pass them on to others or prevent such messages from reaching others. Often the messages are changed (most often in the direction of simplification) by the gatekeepers before they are passed on.

9. Individuals can influence the media by registering individual complaints, exerting group pressure, protesting through established organizations, protesting with a social movement, and creating legislative pressure on the local or national level.

Applications

25.1 EXPLORING THE THEORIES OF MASS COMMUNICATION

Each person should design a small experiment to provide preliminary answers to any one of the following questions. Survey at least ten people, but more is better.

1. Do people act in accordance with the predictions of the one-step theory? The two-step theory? The multistep theory?

2. To what group as defined in the diffusion of innovations theory do _____ belong? [Insert any group—for example, college athletes, college debaters, college professors, blue-collar workers, white-collar workers. Select any specific innovation you wish.]

3. In what situation(s) do you find support for cultivation theory?

4. Does the theory of uses and gratifications explain the television view behavior of _____ ? [Insert any group—for example, college men or women, children under 10, people who live alone.]

5. In what ways do the media influence your evaluation of what is and who is important or unimportant?

Discuss with the class as a whole the way in which you conducted your study, the results you obtained, and the conclusions you would be willing to draw on the basis of these results.

25.2 THE TALK SHOW AND HUMAN COMMUNICATION

This exercise brings together the several areas of communication discussed in this text: interpersonal communication, interviewing, small group communication, public speaking, intercultural communication, and mass communication. It should serve as a useful refresher of some central issues discussed in the text.

Either of two general procedures should prove effective.

1. The class may watch a videotape of part or all of a talk show. (An hour show can easily be edited to about 30 minutes.) Small groups may each be assigned one of the six areas (or five if interpersonal and interviewing are combined) to analyze. After viewing the show, each group should discuss the questions posed here and report its findings to the class as a whole.

2. Each student may watch a talk show of his or her choice and respond to any one of the six areas and report back to the class as a whole. Students who select the same content area or the same talk show might be grouped together for group presentations.

Interpersonal communication

- What three qualities of interpersonal communication effectiveness does the host most clearly display? Choose from those considered in the units on interpersonal communication (Part 3).

- What one quality should the host try harder to master?

- Which of the several talk show hosts whom you have seen displays the greatest empathy toward guest and audience? Which host communicates the greatest positiveness? Which host conveys the greatest confidence? Which host is the most expressive? What *specific* behaviors of the host(s) convey these qualities?

Interviewing

- How does the host deal with audience questions? supportively or defensively? Critically or with acceptance? With what *specific* behaviors does the host communicate this supportiveness or defensiveness, this criticalness or acceptance?

Small group communication

- What qualities or leadership does the host display? Would you describe the host as authoritarian? Democratic? Laissez-faire? What *specific* behaviors lead to your conclusions?

Public speaking

- How would you rate the host's credibility? Complete the following rating scale for the talk show host you observed.

Talk Show Host

Knowledgeable	7	6	5	4	3	2	1	Unknowledgeable
Experienced	7	6	5	4	3	2	1	Inexperienced
Confident	7	6	5	4	3	2	1	Not confident
Informed	7	6	5	4	3	2	1	Uninformed
Fair	7	6	5	4	3	2	1	Unfair
Concerned	7	6	5	4	3	2	1	Unconcerned
Consistent	7	6	5	4	3	2	1	Inconsistent
Similar	7	6	5	4	3	2	1	Dissimilar
Positive	7	6	5	4	3	2	1	Negative
Assertive	7	6	5	4	3	2	1	Unassertive
Enthusiastic	7	6	5	4	3	2	1	Unenthusiastic
Active	7	6	5	4	3	2	1	Passive

The first four qualities refer to *competence,* the second four to *character,* the last four to *charisma.*

- Compare your ratings with those of others. How similar are they? How different are they?

- What *specific* behaviors contributed to your ratings in each of the three major categories (competence, character, and charisma)?

Intercultural communication

- Were any of the barriers to intercultural communication evdenced durring the show? For each barrier, explain what went wrong and how the barrier might have been avoided.

Mass communication

- Usually, the media serve a variety of functions at the same time. What functions did this talk show serve?

Mass Communication

Questions and Activities

1. How would you distinguish interpersonal communication from mass communication? What are some of the similarities?

2. Throughout this text we stressed the intercultural nature of communication. In what ways is mass communication intercultural?

3. To which medium would you turn to learn today's weather forecast? Yesterday's baseball scores? The current movies? The president's latest speech? Yesterday's stock market's performance?

4. Are certain media more credible (in general) than others, or do you consider certain media credible for some issues and not credible for others? How would you rank the various media in terms of their credibility in reporting international news? In reporting local news? In reporting Hollywood "news"?

5. How much time do you spend with each of the media discussed in Unit 24? That is, of the 100 percent of the time you spend with media, how much do you spend with television? Radio? Newspapers? Magazines? Films? Books? Records and Tapes? How has this changed over the last several years? How do you suppose this will change over the next five to 10 years? What accounted for the change? What will account for the changes to come?

6. Of the functions of the media discussed in Unit 24, which are the most important to you? Why?

7. Do you attribute status to people who are given media attention because they are given media attention? What other bases do you use in attributing status to another person?

8. Do you or any of your friends or associates have parasocial relationships? Describe these relationships? What needs do these relationships serve? Do you think these relationships are generally beneficial? Generally dangerous? Explain.

9. Watch television for one evening; watch any programs you would normally watch. What ethical principles are espoused in the various programs? How are these principles communicated?

10. Are you ever influenced directly by the media? On what issues? Which medium is most likely to exert such influence? Can you give a specific example of such one-step influence?

11. Can you give an example of the two-step or multistep influence of media?

12. How would you describe your own behavior in terms of the diffusion of innovations theory?

13. Have you been cultivated by the media? Can you cite any personal anecdotes that might support or refute the cultivation theory of media influence?

14. What gratifications do you derive from the media? Can you identify specific gratifications from each of the seven major media highlighted in Unit 24?

15. In what ways do the various media establish your own agendas? In what ways can you argue you are totally independent of media influence in establishing what you consider important and what you consider unimportant?

16. How might the following people function as gatekeepers: (a) your communication instructor, (b) your *Human Communication* text author, (c) your parents, (d) the editor of your local or college newspaper, (e) Phil Donahue and Oprah Winfrey, (f) your best friend, (g) your romantic partner (past or present), (h) your neighbor, (i) your barber or hairdresser, and (j) your enemy.

17. Is there a particular issue on which you would like to influence the media? How might you go about exerting this influence?

Skill Check

_____ 1. I use a variety of media to secure relevant information. (Unit 24)

_____ 2. I exert influence over the media through buying or not buying the advertised product, writing letters to the media, and exercising interpersonal influence. (Unit 24)

_____ 3. I see the several functions of the media and recognize the messages that attempt to influence my values, attitudes, and beliefs about a wide variety of economic, social, and political issues. (Unit 24)

_____ 4. I am especially alert to the ways in which the media (especially television) may influence my views of minority groups and women. (Unit 24)

_____ 5. I make a distinction between media education and objective education. (Unit 24)

_____ 6. I avoid confusing media popularity with social significance. (Unit 24)

_____ 7. I do not allow the media to narcotize me—to drug me into inactivity. (Unit 24)

_____ 8. I distinguish between real interpersonal relationships and parasocial relationships—imagined relationships with media personalities. (Unit 24)

_____ 9. I analyze and evaluate the media's ethicizing function before internalizing the values and beliefs that the media attempt to instill. (Unit 24)

_____ 10. I distinguish clearly between information that is supported by evidence and research, and information presented as entertainment, propaganda, or advertisements. (Unit 25)

_____ 11. I use the media (ideally, several media) and interpersonal interactions to develop and refine my ideas about local, national, or international events. (Unit 25)

_____ 12. I recognize that what the media present as important may not necessarily be important to my own life and my own values. (Unit 25)

_____ 13. I evaluate what I receive (from television, radio, and even the best newspapers) in light of the media's gatekeeping function. I distinguish between the information the media present and what really happened. (Unit 25)

_____ 14. I understand the general ways to exert influence on the media and am able to use these as appropriate: registering individual complaints, exerting group pressure, protesting through established organizations, protesting with a social movement, and creating legislative pressure. (Unit 25)

SUGGESTED READINGS

Agee, Warren K., Phillip H. Ault, and Edwin Emery, eds. *Maincurrents in Mass Communications,* 2nd ed. New York: Harper & Row, 1989. A collection of 72 readings on the media's role in society, ethical and legal challenges, the technology revolution, the communicators, media trends and techniques, and living in the information society.

Schramm, Wilbur. *The Story of Human Communication: Cave Painting to Microchip.* New York: Harper & Row, 1988. An insightful history of communication with an emphasis of mass media.

Schramm, Wilbur and William E. Porter. *Men, Women, Messages, and Media: Understanding Human Communication,* 2nd ed. New York: Harper & Row, 1982. An easy to read, interesting, and insightful look at the world of media.

Severin, Werner J. with James W. Tankard, Jr. *Communication Theories: Origins, Methods, Uses,* 2nd ed. New York: Longman, 1988. An excellent review of theories in human communication with major attention to theories of mass communication.

Williams, Frederick. *The New Communications,* 3rd ed. Belmont, CA: Wadsworth, 1992. An introduction to all areas of communication, with a heavy emphasis on mass communication.

Textbooks in mass communication are plentiful and generally excellent. Some of the best include Agee, Ault, and Emery (1988), Hunt and Ruben (1993), Dominick (1991), and Merrill, Lee, and Friedlander (1990).

Popular books in the area of mass communication include Cross (1983), Williams (1983, 1991), Postman and Powers (1992), and, of course, the classic by Marshall McLuhan (1964).

BIBILIOGRAPHY

Adams, Linda with Elinor Lenz (1989). *Be Your Best*. New York: Putnam.

Addeo, Edmond G. and Burger, Robert E. (1973). *Egospeak: Why No One Listens to You*. New York: Bantam.

Adler, Mortimer J. (1983). *How to Speak, How to Listen*. New York: Macmillan.

Adler, Ronald B. (1977). *Confidence in Communication: A Guide to Assertive and Social Skills*. New York: Holt, Rinehart and Winston.

Adler, Ronald B. (1989). *Communicating at Work: Principles and Practices for Business and the Professions,* 3rd ed. New York: McGraw-Hill.

Adler, Ronald B., Lawrence B. Rosenfeld, and Neil Towne (1992). *Interplay: The Process of Interpersonal Communication,* 5th ed. New York: Holt, Rinehart and Winston.

Agee, Warren K., Phillip H. Ault, and Edwin Emery (1988). *Introduction to Mass Communications*, 9th ed. New York: Harper & Row.

Ailes, Roger (1988). *You Are the Message*. New York: Doubleday.

Akinnaso, F. Niyi (1982). On the Differences between Spoken and Written Language. *Language and Speech* 25(Part 2):97–125.

Akmajian, A., R. A. Demers, & R. M. Harnish (1979). *Linguistics: An Introduction to Language and Communication*. Cambridge, MA: MIT Press.

Alisky, Marvin (1985, January 15). *Vital Speeches of the Day* 51, 208–210.

Allen, Richard K. (1977). *Organizational Management Through Communication*. New York: Harper & Row.

Altman, Irwin and Dalmas Taylor (1973). *Social Penetration: The Development of Interpersonal Relationships*. New York: Holt, Rinehart and Winston.

Andersen, Peter A. and Ken Leibowitz (1978). The Development and Nature of the Construct Touch Avoidance. *Environmental Psychology and Nonverbal Behavior* 3:89–106.

Argyle, Michael (1988). *Bodily Communication,* 2nd ed. New York: Methuen & Co.

Argyle, Michael and R. Ingham (1972). Gaze, Mutual Gaze and Distance. *Semiotica* 1:32–49.

Arliss, Laurie P. (1991). *Gender Communication*. Englewood Cliffs, NJ: Prentice-Hall.

Arnold, Carroll C. and John Waite Bowers, eds. (1984). *Handbook of Rhetorical and Communication Theory*. Boston: Allyn & Bacon.

Aronson, Elliot (1980). *The Social Animal,* 3rd ed. San Francisco: W. H. Freeman.

Asch, Solomon (1946). Forming Impressions of Personality. *Journal of Abnormal and Social Psychology* 41:258–290.

Authier, Jerry and Kay Gustafson (1982). Microtraining: Focusing on Specific Skills. In Eldon K. Marshall, P. David Kurtz, and Associates, *Interpersonal Helping Skills: A Guide to Training Methods, Programs, and Resources* (pp. 93–130). San Francisco: Jossey-Bass.

Aylesworth, Thomas G. and Virginia L. Aylesworth (1978). *If You Don't Invade My Intimate Zone or Clean Up My Water Hold, I'll Breathe in Your Face, Blow on Your Neck, and Be Late for Your Party*. New York: Condor.

Axtell, Roger E. (1990a). *Do's and Taboos Around the World, 2nd ed*. New York: Wiley.

Axtell, Roger E. (1990b). *Do's and Taboos of Hosting International Visitors*. New York: Wiley.

Ayres, Joe (1986). Perceptions of Speaking Ability: An Explanation for Stage Fright. *Communication Education* 35:275–287.

Ayres, Joe (1990). Situational Factors and Audience Anxiety. *Communication Education* 39:283–291.

Ayres, Joe and Janice Miller (1986). *Effective Public Speaking,* 2nd ed. Dubuque, IA: Wm. C. Brown.

Bach, George R. and Ronald M. Deutsch (1979). *Stop! You're Driving Me Crazy*. New York: Berkley.

Bach, George R. and Peter Wyden (1968). *The

Intimacy Enemy. New York: Avon.

Backrack, Henry M. (1976). Empathy. *Archives of General Psychiatry* 33:35–38.

Baird, John E., Jr. (1977). *The Dynamics of Organizational Communication*. New York: Harper & Row.

Bales, Robert F. (1950). *Interaction Process Analysis: A Method for the Study of Small Groups*. Cambridge, MA: Addison-Wesley.

Barbato, Carole A. and Elizabeth M. Perse (1992). Interpersonal Communication Motives and the Life Position of Elders. *Communication Research* 19:516–531.

Barker, Larry, R. Edwards, C. Gaines, K. Gladney, and F. Holley (1980). An Investigation of Proportional Time Spent in Various Communication Activities by College Students. *Journal of Applied Communication Research* 8:101–109.

Barna, LaRay M. (1991). Stumbling Blocks in Intercultural Communication. In Larry A. Samovar and Richard E. Porter, eds., *Intercultural Communication: A Reader*, 6th ed. (pp. 345–352). Belmont, CA: Wadsworth.

Barnard, Chester (1938). *The Functions of the Executive*. Cambridge, MA: Harvard University Press.

Barnlund, Dean C. (1970). A Transactional Model of Communication. In J. Akin, A. Goldberg, G. Myers, and J. Stewart, eds., *Language Behavior: A Book of Readings in Communication*. The Hague, Netherlands: Mouton.

Barnlund, Dean C. (1975). Communicative Styles in Two Cultures: Japan and the United States. In A. Kendon, R. M. Harris, and M. R. Key, eds., *Organization of Behavior in Face-to-Face Interaction*. The Hague, Netherlands: Mouton.

Baron, Robert A. and Donn Byrne (1984). *Social Pscyhology: Understanding Human Interaction*, 4th ed. Boston: Allyn and Bacon.

Barrett, Karen (1982). Date Rape. *Ms.* (Sept):48–51.

Bartholomew, Kim (1990). Avoidance of Intimacy: An Attachment Perspective. *Journal of Social and Personal Relationships* 7:147–178.

Basso, K. H. (1972). To Give Up on Words: Silence in Apache Culture. In Pier Paolo Giglili, ed., *Langauge and Social Context*. New York: Penguin.

Bateson, Gregory (1972). *Steps to an Ecology of Mind*. New York: Ballantine.

Baxter, Leslie A. (1983). Relationship Disengagement: An Examination of the Reversal Hypothesis. *Western Journal of Speech Communication* 47:85–98.

Beatty, Michael J. (1988). Situational and Predispositional Correlates of Public Speaking Anxiety. *Communication Education* 37:28–39.

Becker, Samuel L. and Churchill L. Roberts (1992). *Discovering Mass Communication*, 3rd ed. New York: HarperCollins.

Beebe, Steven A. and John T. Masterson (1990). *Communicating in Small Groups: Principles and Practices*, 3rd ed. Glenview, IL: Scott, Foresman.

Beier, Ernst (1974, October). How We Send Emotional Messages. *Psychology Today* 8:53–56.

Bell, Robert A. and John A. Daly (1984). The Affinity-Seeking Function of Communication. *Communication Monographs* 51:91–115.

Benne, Kenneth D. and Paul Sheats (1948). Functional Roles of Group Members. *Journal of Social Issues* 4:41–49.

Bennis, Warren and Burt Nanus (1985). *Leaders: The Strategies for Taking Charge*. New York: Harper & Row.

Berg, John H. and Richard L. Archer (1983). The Dislcosure-Liking Relationship. *Human Communication Research* 10:269–281.

Berger, Charles R. and James J. Bradac (1982). *Language and Social Knowlege: Uncertainty in Interpersonal Relations*. London: Edward Arnold.

Berger, Charles R. and Steven H. Chaffee, ed. (1987). *Handbook of Communication Science*. Newbury Park, CA: Sage.

Bernstein, W. M., W. G. Stephan, and M. H. Davis (1979). Explaining Attributions for Achievement: A Path Analytic Approach. *Journal of Personality and Social Psychology* 37:1810–1821.

Berscheid, Ellen and Elaine Hatfield Walster (1978). *Interpersonal Attraction*, 2nd ed. Reading, MA: Addison-Wesley.

Bettinghaus, Erwin P. and Michael J. Cody (1987). *Persuasive Communication*, 4th ed. New York: Holt, Rinehart and Winston.

Bineham, Jeffrey L. (1988). A Historical Account of the Hypodermic Model in Mass Communication. *Communication Monographs* 55:230–246.

Birdwhistell, Ray L. (1970). *Kinesics and*

Context: Essays on Body Motion Communication. New York: Ballantine.

Blankenship, Jane (1968). *A Sense of Style: An Introduction to Style for the Public Speaker.* Belmont, CA: Dickenson.

Blumstein, Philip and Pepper Schwartz (1983). *American Couples: Money, Work, Sex.* New York: Morrow.

Bochner, Arthur (1978). On Taking Ourselves Seriously: An Analysis of Some Persistent Problems and Promising Directions in Interpersonal Research. *Human Communication Research* 4:179–191.

Bochner, Arthur (1984). The Functions of Human Communication in Interpersonal Bonding. In Carroll C. Arnold and John Waite Bowers, eds., *Handbook of Rhetorical and Communication Theory* (pp. 544–621). Boston: Allyn and Bacon.

Bochner, Arthur and Clifford Kelly (1974). Interpersonal Competence: Rationale, Philosophy, and Implementation of a Conceptual Framework. *Communication Education* 23:279–301.

Bok, Sissela (1978). *Lying: Moral Choice in Public and Private Life.* New York: Pantheon.

Bok, Sissela (1983). *Secrets.* New York: Vintage Books.

Bormann, Ernest G., William S. Howell, Ralph G. Nichols, and George L. Shapiro (1982). *Interpersonal Communication in the Modern Organization,* 2nd ed. Englewood Cliffs, NJ: Prentice-Hall.

Borisoff, Deborah and Lisa Merrill (1985). *The Power to Communicate: Gender Differences as Barriers.* Prospect Heights, IL: Waveland Press.

Bosmajian, Haig (1974). *The Language of Oppression.* Washington, DC: Public Affairs Press.

Bourland, D. D., Jr. (1965–66). A Linguistic Note: Writing in E-prime. *General Semantics Bulletin* 32–33:111–114.

Boyd, Stephen D. and Mary Ann Renz (1985). *Organization and Outlining: A Workbook for Students in a Basic Speech Course.* New York: Macmillan.

Bradac, James J., John Waite Bowers, and John A. Courtright (1979). Three Language Variables in Communication Research: Intensity, Immediacy, and Diversity. *Human Communication Research* 5:256–269.

Bradley, Bert E. (1988). *Fundamentals of Speech Communication: The Credibility*

of Ideas, 5th ed. Dubuque, IA: Wm. C. Brown.

Bravo, Ellen and Ellen Cassedy (1992). *The 9-to-5 Guide to Combating Sexual Harassment.* New York: Wiley.

Brilhart, John and Gloria Galanes (1992). *Effective Group Discussion,* 7th ed. Dubuque, IA: Brown & Benchmark.

Brody, Marjorie and Shawn Kent (1993). *Power Presentations: How to Connect with Your Audience and Sell Your Ideas.* New York: Wiley.

Brommel, Bernard (1990). Personal communication.

Brougher, Toni (1982). *A Way with Words.* Chicago, IL: Nelson-Hall.

Bruneau, Tom (1985). The Time Dimension in Intercultural Communication. In Larry A. Samovar and Richard E. Porter, eds. (1985), *Intercultural Communication: A Reader,* 4th ed. (pp. 280–289). Belmont, CA: Wadsworth.

Bruneau, Tom (1990). Chronemics: The Study of Time in Human Interaction. In Joseph A. DeVito and Michael L. Hecht, eds., *The Nonverbal Communication Reader* (pp. 301–311). Prospect Heights, IL: Waveland Press.

Buckley, Reid (1988). *Speaking in Public.* New York: Harper & Row.

Bugental, J. and S. Zelen (1950). Investigations into the 'Self-Concept,' I. The W-A-Y Technique. *Journal of Personality* 18:483–498.

Burgoon, Judee K., David B. Buller, and W. Gill Woodall (1989). *Nonverbal Communication: The Unspoken Dialogue.* New York: Harper & Row.

Burns, David D. (1985). *Intimate Connections.* New York: Morrow.

Cate, R., J. Henton, J. Koval, R. Christopher, and S. Lloyd (1982). Premarital Abuse: A Social Psychological Perspective. *Journal of Family Issues* 3:79–90.

Cathcart, Robert S. and Larry A. Samovar, eds. (1988). *Small Group Communication: A Reader,* 5th ed. Dubuque, IA: Wm. C. Brown.

Camden, Carl, Michael T. Motley, and Ann Wilson (1984). White Lies in Interpersonal Communication: A Taxonomy and Preliminary Investigation of Social Motivations. *Western Journal of Speech Communication* 48:309–325.

Cappella, Joseph N. (1987). Interpersonal Communication: Definitions and Fundamental Questions. In Charles R. Berger and Steven H. Chaffee, eds., *Handbook of Communication Science* (pp. 184–238). Newbury Park, CA: Sage.

Carroll, John B., ed. (1956). *Language, Thought and Reality: Selected Writings of Benjamin Lee Whorf*. New York: Wiley.

Carroll, John B. and Joseph B. Casagrande (1958). The Functions of Language Classifications in Behavior. In Eleanor E. Maccoby, Theodore M. Newcomb, and Eugene L. Hartley, eds. *Readings in Social Pscyhology,* 3rd ed. (pp. 18–31). New York: Holt, Rinehart and Winston.

Carter, L. F. (1953). On Defining Leadership. In M. Sherif and M. O. Wilson, eds., *Group Relations at the Crossroads* (pp. 262–265). New York: Harper & Row.

Chadwick-Jones, J. K. (1976). *Social Exchange Theory: Its Structure and Influence in Social Psychology*. New York: Academic.

Chesebro, James, ed. (1981). *Gayspeak*. New York: Pilgrim Press.

Chisholm, Shirley (1978, August 15). *Vital Speeches of the Day* 44.

Cialdini, Robert T. (1984). *Influence: How and Why People Agree to Things*. New York: Morrow.

Cialdini, Robert T. and K. Ascani (1976). Test of a Concession Procedure for Inducing Verbal, Behavioral, and Further Compliance with a Request to Give Blood. *Journal of Applied Psychology* 61:295–300.

Clark, Herbert (1974). The Power of Positive Speaking. *Psychology Today* 8:102, 108–111.

Clement, Donald A. and Kenneth D. Frandsen (1976). On Conceptual and Empirical Treatments of Feedback in Human Communication. *Communication Monographs* 43:11–28.

Cline, M. G. (1956). The Influence of Social Context on the Perception of Faces. *Journal of Personality* 2:142–185.

Coalition Commentary, a Publication of the Illinois Coalition against Sexual Assault (1990). Urbana, IL (Spring):1–7.

Coates, Jennifer (1986). *Women, Men and Language*. New York: Longman.

Cody, Michael J., P. J. Marston, and M. Foster (1984). Paralinguistic and Verbal Leakage of Deception as a Function of Attempted Control and Timing of Questions. In R. M. Bostrom, ed., *Communication Yearbook 7* (pp. 464–490). Newbury Park, CA: Sage.

Collier, Mary Jane (1991). Conflict Competence Within African, Mexican, and Anglo American Friendships. In *Cross-Cultural Interpersonal Communication*, ed. Stella Ting-Toomey and Felipe Korzenny. Newbury Park, CA: Sage, pp. 132–154.

Comadena, Mark and Diane Prusank (1988). Communication Apprehension and Academic Achievement among Elementary and Middle School Students. *Communication Education* 37:270–277.

Condon, John C. and Fathi Yousef (1975). *An Introduction to Intercultural Communication*. Indianapolis: Bobbs-Merrill.

Connors, Tracy Daniel (1982). *Longman Dictionary of Mass Media and Communication*. New York: Longman.

Cook, Mark (1971). *Interpersonal Perception*. Baltimore: Penguin.

Cooper, Martha (1989). *Analyzing Public Discourse*. Prospect Heights, IL: Waveland Press.

Cozby, Paul (1973). Self-Disclosure: A Literature Review, *Psychological Bulletin* 79:73–91.

Cragan, John F. and David W. Wright (1986). *Communication in Small Group Discussions: A Case Study Approach,* 2nd ed. St. Paul, MN: West.

Cross, Donna Woolfolk (1983). *Mediaspeak: How Television Makes Up Your Mind*. New York: New American Library.

Curtis, Dan B., James J. Floyd, and Jerry L. Winsor (1992). *Business and Professional Communication*. New York: HarperCollins.

D'Angelo, Frank J. (1980). *Process and Thought in Composition,* 2nd ed. Cambridge, MA: Winthrop.

Davis, Flora (1973). *Inside Intuition*. New York: New American Library.

Davis, Keith (1977). The Care and Cultivation of the Corporate Grapevine. In Richard Huseman, Cal Logue, and Dwight Freshley, eds., *Readings in Interpersonal and Organizational Communication,* 3rd ed. (pp. 131–136). Boston: Holbrook.

Davis, Keith (1980). Management Communication and the Grapevine. In Stewart Ferguson and Sherry Devereaux Ferguson, eds., *Intercom: Readings in Organizational Communication* (pp. 55–66). Rochelle Park, NJ: Hayden Book.

Davis, Murray S. (1973). *Intimate Relations*. New York: Free Press.

Davis, Ossie (1967). The English Language Is

My Enemy. *American Teacher,* pp. 13–15. Reprinted in DeVito (1973), pp. 164–170.

Davitz, Joel R., ed. (1964). *The Communication of Emotioanl Meaning.* New York: McGraw-Hill.

Deal, James E. and Karen Smith Wampler (1986). Dating Violence: The Primacy of Previous Experience. *Journal of Social and Personal Relationships* 3:457–471.

deBono, Edward (1987). *The Six Thinking Hats.* New York: Penguin.

DeFleur, Melvin (1987). The Growth and Decline of Research on the Diffusion of the News: 1945–1985. *Communication Research* 14:109–130.

DeFleur, Melvin L. and Sandra Ball-Rokeach (1989). *Theories of Mass Communication,* 5th ed. New York: Longman.

DeFrancisco, Victoria (1991). The Sound of Silence: How Men Silence Women in Marital Relations. *Discourse and Society* 2:413–423.

DeJong, W. (1979). An Examination of Self-Perception Mediation of the Foot-in-the-Door Effect. *Journal of Personality and Social Psychology* 37:2221–2239.

Derlega, V. J., B. A. Winstead, P. T. P. Wong, and S. Hunter (1985). Gender Effects in an Initial Encounter: A Case Where Men Exceed Women in Disclosure. *Journal of Social and Personal Relationships* 2:25–44.

Derlega, Valerian J., Barbara A. Winstead, Paul T. P. Wong, and Michael Greenspan (1987). Self-Disclosure and Relationship Development: An Attributional Analysis. In Michael E. Roloff and Gerald R. Miller, eds., *Interpersonal Processes: New Directions in Communication Research* (pp. 172–187). Newbury Park, CA: Sage.

DeStephen, R. and R. Hirokawa (1988). Small Group Consensus: Stability of Group Support of the Decision, Task Process, and Group Relationships. *Small Group Behavior* 19:227–239.

Detruck, Mark A. (1987). When Communication Fails: Physical Aggression as a Compliance-Gaining Strategy. *Communication Monographs* 54:106–112.

DeVito, Joseph A. (1965). Comprehension Factors in Oral and Written Discourse of Skilled Communicators. *Communication Monographs* 32:124–128.

DeVito, Joseph A. (1969). Some Psycholinguistic Aspects of Active and Passive Sentences. *Quarterly Journal of Speech* 55:401–406.

DeVito, Joseph A. (1970). *The Psychology of Speech and Language: An Introduction to Psycholinguistics.* New York: Random House.

DeVito, Joseph A. (1974). *General Semantics: Guide and Workbook,* rev. ed. DeLand, FL: Everett/Edwards.

DeVito, Joseph A. (1976). Relative Ease in Comprehending Yes/No Questions. In Jane Blankenship and Herman G. Stelzner, eds., *Rhetoric and Communication* (pp. 143–154). Urbana: Unviersity of Illinois Press.

DeVito, Joseph A. (1986). *The Communication Handbook: A Dictionary.* New York: Harper & Row.

DeVito, Joseph A. (1986, June). Teaching as Relational Development. In Jean Civikly, ed., *Communicating in College Classrooms (New Directions for Teaching and Learning),* No. 26 (pp. 51–60). San Francisco: Jossey-Bass.

DeVito, Joseph A. (1989). *The Nonverbal Communication Workbook.* Prospect Heights, IL: Waveland Press.

DeVito, Joseph A. (1992). *The Interpersonal Communication Book,* 6th ed. New York: Harper & Row.

DeVito, Joseph A. (1993). *The Elements of Public Speaking,* 5th ed. New York: HarperCollins.

DeVito, Joseph A. (1993). *Messages: Building Interpersonal Communication Skills,* 2nd ed. New York: HarperCollins.

DeVito, Joseph A., Jill Giattino, and T. D. Schon (1975). *Articulation and Voice: Effective Communication.* Indianapolis: Bobbs-Merrill.

DeVito, Joseph A. and Michael L. Hecht, eds. (1990). *The Nonverbal Communication Reader.* Prospect Heights, IL: Waveland Press.

Dindia, K. (1987). The Effects of Sex of Subject and Sex of Parner on Interruptions. *Human Communication Research* 13:345–371.

Dindia, Kathryn and Mary Anne Fitzpatrick (1985). Marital Communication: Three Approaches Compared. In *Understanding Personal Relationships: An Interdisciplinary Approach.* Steve Duck and Daniel Perlman, eds., 137–158. Newbury Park, CA: Sage.

Dodd, Carley H. (1991). *Dynamics of Intercultural Communication,* 3rd ed.

Dubuque, IA: Wm. C. Brown.

Dodd, David H. and Raymond M. White, Jr. (1980). *Cognition: Mental Structures and Processes*. Boston: Allyn and Bacon.

Dominick, Joseph R. (1974). The Portable Friend: Peer Group Membership and Radio Usage. *Journal of Broadcasting* 18:161–170.

Dominick, Joseph R. (1991). *The Dynamics of Mass Communication,* 3rd ed. New York: McGraw-Hill.

Downs, Cal W., G. Paul Smeyak, and Ernest Martin (1980). *Professional Interviewing.* New York: Harper & Row.

Dreyfuss, Henry (1971). *Symbol Sourcebook.* New York: McGraw-Hill.

Duck, Steve and Robin Gilmour, eds. (1981). *Personal Relationships. 1: Studying Personal Relationships*. New York: Academic Press.

Duncan, Barry L. and Joseph W. Rock (1991). *Overcoming Relationship Impasses: Ways to Initiate Change When Your Partner Won't Help.* New York: Plenum Press [Insight Books].

Duran, Robert L. and L. Kelly (1988). The Influence of Communicative Competence on Perceived Task, Social, and Physical Attractiveness. *Communication Quarterly* 36:41–49.

Edelstein, Alex S. (1993). Thinking About the Criterion Variable in Agenda-Setting Research. *Journal of Communication* 43:85–99.

Egan, Gerard (1970). *Encounter: Group Processes for Interpersonal Growth*. Belmont, CA: Brooks/Cole.

Eisen, Jeffrey with Pat Farley (1984). *PowerTalk: How to Speak It, Think It, and Use It*. New York: Simon & Schuster.

Eisenberg, Nancy and Janet Strayer, eds. (1990). *Empathy and its Development*. New York: Cambridge University Press.

Ekman, Paul (1965). Communication through Nonverbal Behavior: A Source of Information about an Interpersonal Relationship. In S. S. Tomkins and C. E. Izard, eds., *Affect, Cognition and Personality.* New York: Springer.

Ekman, Paul. *Telling Lies* (1985). New York: W. W. Norton.

Ekman, Paul and W. V. Friesen (1969). The Repertoire of Nonverbal Behavior: Categories, Origins, Usage, and Coding. *Semiotica* 1:49–98.

Ekman, Paul, Wallace V. Friesen, and Phoebe Ellsworth (1972). *Emotion in the Human Face: Guidelines for Research and an Integration of Findings*. New York: Pergamon Press.

Ekman, Paul, Wallace V. Friesen, and S. S. Tomkins (1971). Facial Affect Scoring Technique: A First Validity Study. *Semiotica* 3:37–58.

Elgin, Suzette Haden (1993). *Genderspeak: Men, Women, and the Gentle Art of Verbal Self-Defense.* New York: Wiley.

Ellis, Albert and Robert A. Harper (1975). *A New Guide to Rational Living*. Hollywood: Wilshire Books.

Exline, R. V., S. L. Ellyson, and B. Long (1975). Visual Behavior as an Aspect of Power Role Realtioships. In P. Pliner, L. Krames, and T. Alloway, eds., *Nonverbal Communication of Aggression*. New York: Plenum.

Faber, Adele and Elaine Mazlish (1980). *How to Talk so Kids Will Listen and Listen so Kids Will Talk*. New York: Avon.

Filley, Alan C. (1975). *Interpersonal Conflict Resolution*. Glenview, IL: Scott, Foresman.

Fisher, B. Aubrey (1980). *Small Group Decision Making: Communication and the Group Process,* 2nd ed. New York: McGraw-Hill.

Fishman, Joshua A. (1972). *The Sociology of Language*. Rowley, MA: Newbury House.

Fiske, Susan T. and Shelley E. Taylor (1984). *Social Cognition*. Reading, MA: Addison-Wesley.

Floyd, James J. (1985). *Listening: A Practical Approach*. Glenview, IL: Scott, Foresman.

Folger, Joseph P. and Marshall Scott Poole (1984). *Working Through Conflict: A Communication Perspective.* Glenview, IL: Scott, Foresman.

Foss, Sonja K. (1989). *Rhetorical Criticism: Exploration and Practice.* Prospect Heights, IL: Waveland Press.

Freedman, Jonathan (1978). *Happy People: What Happiness Is, Who Has It, and Why*. New York: Ballantine Books.

Freedman, J. and S. Fraser (1966). Compliance Without Pressure: The Foot-in-the-Door Technique. *Journal of Personality and Social Psychology* 4:195–202.

French, J. R. P., Jr., and B. Raven (1968). The Bases of Social Power. In *Group Dynamics: Research and Theory,* 3rd ed. Dorwin Cartwright and Alvin Zander, eds., pp. 259–269. New York: Harper & Row.

Frentz, Thomas (1976). A General Approach to Episodic Structure. Paper presented at the Western Speech Association Convention, San Francisco. Cited in Reardon (1987).

Frye, Jerry K. (1980). *FIND: Frye's Index to Nonverbal Data*. Duluth: University of Minnesota Computer Center.

Furnham, Adrian and Stephen Bochner (1986). *Culture Shock: Psychological Reactions to Unfamiliar Environments*. New York: Methuen.

Gabor, Don (1989). *How to Talk to the People You Love*. New York: Simon & Schuster.

Galvin, Kathleen and Bernard J. Brommel (1991). *Family Communication: Cohesion and Change,* 3rd ed. New York: Harper-Collins.

Garner, Alan (1981). *Conversationally Speaking*. New York: McGraw-Hill.

Gelles, R. (1981). The Myth of the Battered Husband. In *Marriage and Family 81/82,* R. Walsh and O. Pocs, eds. Dushkin: Guilford.

Gelles, R. and C. Coarnell (1985). *Intimate Violence in Families*. Newbury Park, CA: Sage.

Gerbner, George, L. P. Gross, M. Morgan, and N. Signorielli (1980). The 'Mainstreaming' of America: Violence Profile No. 11. *Journal of Communication* 30:10–29.

Gergen, K. J., M. S. Greenberg, and R. H. Willis (1980). *Social Exchange: Advances in Theory and Research*. New York: Plenum.

Gibb, Cecil A. (1969). Leadership. In G. Lindsey and E. Aronson, eds. *The Handbook of Social Psychology,* 2nd ed., vol. 4 (pp. 205–282). Reading, MA: Addison-Wesley.

Gibb, Jack (1961). Defensive Communication. *Journal of Communication* 11:141–148.

Gill, Mary M. and William J. Wardrope (1992). To Say or Not: To Do or Not—Those Are the Questions: Sexual Harassment and the Basic Course Instructor. *Basic Communication Course Annual,* Vol. 4 (June), ed. Lawrence W. Hugenberg. Boston: Academic.

Gilmour, Robin and Steve Duck, eds. (1986). *The Emerging Field of Personal Relationships*. Hillsdale, NJ: Lawrence Erlbaum.

Glucksberg, Sam and Joseph H. Danks (1975). *Experimental Psycholinguistics: An Introduction*. Hillsdale, NJ: Lawrence Erlbaum.

Goffman, Erving (1967). *Interaction Ritual: Essays on Face-to-Face Behavior*. New York: Pantheon.

Goffman, Erving (1971). *Relations in Public: Microstudies of the Public Order*. New York: Harper Colophon.

Goldhaber, Gerald (1990). *Organizational Communication,* 5th ed. Dubuque, IA: Wm. C. Brown.

Gonzalez, Alexander and Philip G. Zimbardo (1985). Time in Perspective. *Psychology Today* 19:20–26.

Goodale, James G. (1992). *One to One: Interviewing, Selecting, Appraising, and Counseling Employees*. Englewood Cliffs, NJ: Prentice-Hall.

Gordon, Thomas (1975). *P.E.T.: Parent Effectiveness Training*. New York: New American Library.

Goss, Blaine (1989). *The Psychology of Communication*. Prospect Heights, IL: Waveland Press.

Goss, Blaine, M. Thompson, and S. Olds (1978). Behavioral Support for Systematic Desensitization for Communication Apprehension. *Human Communication Research* 4:158–163.

Gratus, Jack (1988). *Successful Interviewing: How to Find and Keep the Best People*. New York: Penguin.

Greeley, Andrew (1988, August 14). Letter to the Editor. *The New York Times,* p. 21.

Greenberg, J. H., ed. (1963). *Universals of Language*. Cambridge, MA: MIT Press.

Gronbeck, Bruce E., Raymie E. McKerrow, Douglas Ehninger, and Alan H. Monroe (1994). *Principles and Types of Speech Communication,* 12th ed. Glenview, IL: Scott, Foresman.

Grove, Theodore G. (1991). *Dyadic Interaction: Choice and Change in Conversations and Relationships*. Dubuque, IA: Wm. C. Brown.

Gudykunst, William B., ed. (1983). *Intercultural Communication Theory: Current Perspectives*. Newbury Park, CA: Sage.

Gudykunst, William B. (1989). Culture and the Development of Interpersonal Relationships. In *Communication Yearbook 12,* J. A. Andersen, ed. (pp. 315–354). Newbury Park, CA: Sage.

Gudykunst, W. B. (1991). *Bridging Differences: Effective Intergroup Communication*. Newbury Park, CA: Sage.

Gudykunst, William B., and Y. Y. Kim (1990). *Communicating with Strangers: An Ap-*

proach to Intercultural Communication, 2nd ed. New York: McGraw-Hill.

Gudykunst, W. B. and Y. Y. Kim, eds. (1992). Readings on Communication with Strangers: An Approach to Intercultural Communication. New York: McGraw-Hill.

Gudykunst, W. B. and Stella Ting-Toomey with Elizabeth Chua (1988). Culture and Interpersonal Communication. Newbury Park, CA: Sage.

Haggard, E. A., and K. S. Isaacs (1966). Micromomentary Facial Expressions as Indicators of Ego Mechanisms in Psychotherapy. In L. A. Gottschalk and A. H. Auerbach, eds., Methods of Research in Psychotherapy. Englewood Cliffs, NJ: Prentice-Hall.

Hall, Edward T. (1959). The Silent Language. Garden City, NY: Doubleday.

Hall, Edward T. (1963). System for the Notation of Proxemic Behavior. American Anthropologist 65:1003–1026.

Hall, Edward T. (1966). The Hidden Dimension. Garden City, NY: Doubleday.

Hall, Edward T. (1983). The Dance of Life: The Other Dimension of Time. New York: Doubleday.

Hall, Edward T. and Mildred Reed Hall (1987). Hidden Differences: Doing Business with the Japanese. New York: Doubleday [Anchor Books].

Hambrick, Ralph S. (1991). The Management Skills Builder: Self-Directed Learning Strategies for Career Development. New York: Praeger.

Hamlin, Sonya (1988). How to Talk so People Listen. New York: Harper & Row.

Haney, William (1973). Communication and Organizational Behavior: Text and Cases, 3rd ed. Homewood, IL: Irwin.

Hart, R. P. and D. M. Burks (1972). Rhetorical Sensitivity and Social Interaction. Communication Monographs 39:75–91.

Hart, R. P., R. E. Carlson, and W. F. Eadie (1980). Attitudes Toward Communication and the Assessment of Rhetorical Sensitivity. Communication Monographs 39:75–91.

Hashimoto, I. (1986). The Myth of the Attention-Getting Opener. Written Communication 3:123–131.

Hastorf, Albert, David Schneider, and Judith Polefka (1970). Person Perception. Reading, MA: Addison-Wesley.

Hatfield, Elaine and Jane Traupman (1981). Intimate Relationships: A Perspective from Equity Theory. In Steve Duck and Robin Gilmour, eds., Personal Relationships. 1: Studying Personal Relationships (pp. 165–178). New York: Academic Press.

Hayakawa, S. I., and A. R. Hayakawa (1989). Language in Thought and Action, 5th ed. New York: Harcourt Brace Jovanovich.

Hecht, Michael (1978a). The Conceptualization and Measurement of Interpersonal Communication Satisfaction. Human Communication Research 4:253–264.

Hecht, Michael (1978b). Toward a Conceptualization of Communication Satisfaction. Quarterly Journal of Speech 64:47–62.

Hecht, Michael and Sidney Ribeau (1984). Ethnic Communication: A Comparative Analysis of Satisfying Communication. International Journal of Intercultural Relations 8:135–151.

Heinrich, Robert et al. (1983). Instructional Media: The New Technologies of Instruction. New York: Wiley.

Heiskell, Thomas L. and Joseph F. Rychiak (1986). The Therapeutic Relationship: Inexperienced Therapists' Affective Preference and Empathic Communication. Journal of Social and Personal Relationships 3:267–274.

Hellweg, Susan A. (1992). Organizational Grapevines. In Kevin L. Hutchinson, ed., Readings in Organizational Communication (pp. 159—172). Dubuque, IA: Wm. C. Brown.

Henley, Nancy M. (1977). Body Politics: Power, Sex, and Nonverbal Communication. Englewood Cliffs, NJ: Prentice-Hall.

Hersey, P. and K. H. Blanchard (1982). Management of Organizational Behavior, 4th ed. Englewood Cliffs, NJ: Prentice-Hall.

Hersey, Paul and Ken Blanchard (1988). Management of Organizational Behavior: Utilizing Human Resources. Englewood Cliffs, NJ: Prentice-Hall.

Hess, Ekhard H. (1975). The Tell-Tale Eye. New York: Van Nostrand Reinhold.

Hewitt, John and Randall Stokes (1975). Disclaimers. American Sociological Review 40:1–11.

Hickey, Neil (1989, December 9). Decade of Change, Decade of Choice. TV Guide 37:29–34.

Hickson, Mark L. and Don W. Stacks (1993). NVC: Nonverbal Communication: Studies and Applications, 3rd ed. Dubuque, IA: Wm. C. Brown.

Hiebert, Ray Eldon, Donald F. Ungurait, and

Thomas W. Bohn (1974). *Mass Media: An Introduction to Modern Communication*. New York: David McKay.

Hirsch, P. (1980). The 'Scary World' of the Nonviewer and Other Anomalies: A Reanalysis of Gerbner et al.'s Findings on Cultivation Analysis. *Communication Research* 7:403–456.

Hocker, Joyce L. and William W. Wilmot (1985). *Interpersonal Conflict,* 2nd ed. Dubuque, IA: Wm. C. Brown.

Hockett, Charles F. (1977). *The View from Language: Selected Essays*, 1948–1974. Athens: University of Georgia Press.

Hoijer, Harrry, ed. (1954). *Language in Culture*. Chicago: University of Chicago Press.

Hollender, Marc and Alexander Mercer (1976). Wish to Be Held and Wish to Hold in Men and Women, *Archives of General Psychiatry* 33:49–51.

Hopper, Robert, Mark L. Knapp, and Lorel Scott (1981). Couples' Personal Idioms: Exploring Itnimate Talk. *Journal of Communication* 31:23–33.

Huffines, Launa (1986). *Connecting with All the People in Your Life*. New York: Harper & Row.

Hunt, Todd and Brent D. Ruben (1993). *Mass Communication: Producers and Consumers*. New York: HarperCollins.

Huseman, Richard C. (1977). The Role of the Nominal Group in Small Group Communication. In Richard C. Huseman, Cal M. Logue, and Dwight L. Freshley, eds., *Readings in Interpersonal and Organizational Communication,* 3rd ed. (pp. 493–502). Boston: Holbrook Press.

Hutchinson, Kevin L., ed. (1992). *Readings in Organizational Communication*. Dubuque, IA: Wm. C. Brown.

Hymes, Dell (1974). *Foundations in Sociolinguistics: An Ethnographic Approach*. Philadelphia: University of Pennsylvania Press.

Infante, Dominic A. (1988). *Arguing Constructively*. Prospect Heights, IL: Waveland Press.

Infante, Dominic A. and Andrew S. Rancer (1982). A Conceptualization and Measure of Argumentativeness. *Journal of Personality Assessment* 46:72–80.

Infante, Dominic A. and C. J. Wigley (1986). Verbal Aggressiveness: An Interpersonal Model and Measure. *Communication Monographs* 53:61–69.

Infante, Dominic A., Andrew S. Rancer, and Deanna F. Womack (1993). *Building Communication Theory,* 2nd ed. Prospect Heights, IL: Waveland Press.

Insel, Paul M. and Lenore F. Jacobson, eds. (1975). *What Do You Expect? An Inquiry into Self-fulfilling Prophecies*. Menlo Park, CA: Cummings.

Jaksa, James A. and Michael S. Pritchard (1988). *Communication Ethics: Methods of Analysis*. Belmont, CA: Wadsworth.

Jamieson, Kathleen Hall and Karlyn Kohrs Campbell (1992). *The Interplay of Influence,* 3rd ed. Belmont, CA: Wadsworth.

Janis, Irving (1983). *Victims of Group Thinking: A Psychological Study of Foreign Policy Decisions and Fiascoes,* 2nd ed., rev. Boston: Houghton Mifflin.

Jassem, Harvey and Roger Jon Desmond (1984). Theory Construction and Research in Mass Communication: The Implications of New Technologies. Paper delivered at the Eastern Communication Association Convention, Philadelphia, Pennsylvania.

Jecker, Jon and David Landy (1969). Liking a Person as a Function of Doing Him a Favor. *Human Relations* 22:371–378.

Jensen, J. Vernon (1985). Perspectives on Nonverbal Intercultrual Communication. In *Intercultural Communication: A Reader,* 4th ed., ed. Larry Samovar and Richard E. Porter. Belmont, CA: Wadsworth, pp. 256–272.

Johannesen, Richard L. (1991). *Ethics in Human Communication,* 4th ed. Prospect Heights, IL: Waveland Press.

Johnson, Wendell (1951). The Spoken Word and the Great Unsaid. *Quarterly Journal of Speech* 37:419–429.

Jones, E. E. and K. E. Davis (1965). From Acts to Dispositions: The Attribution Process in Person Perception. In L. Berkowitz, ed. *Advances in Experimental Social Psychology,* vol. 2. New York: Academic Press, pp. 219–266.

Jones, E. E., et al. (1984). *Social Stigma: The Psychology of Marked Relationships*. New York: W. H. Freeman.

Jones, Stanley (1986). Sex Differences in Touch Communication, *Western Journal of Speech Communication* 50:227–241.

Jones, Stanley and A. Elaine Yarbrough (1985). A Naturalistic Study of the Meanings of Touch, *Communication Monographs* 52:19–56.

Jourard, Sidney M. (1966). An Exploratory Study of Body-Accessibility. *British Journal of Social and Clinical Psychology* 5:221–231.

Jourard, Sidney M. (1968). *Disclosing Man to Himself*. New York: Van Nostrand Reinhold.

Jourard, Sidney M. (1971a). *Self-disclosure*. New York: Wiley.

Jourard, Sidney M. (1971b). *The Transparent Self,* rev. ed. New York: Van Nostrand Reinhold.

Kanner, Bernice (1989). Color Schemes. *New York Magazine* (April 3):22–23.

Katz, Elihu (1957). The Two-Step Flow of Communication: An Up-to-Date Report on an Hypothesis. *Public Opinion Quarterly* 21:61–78.

Kelley, H. H. (1967). Attribution Theory in Social Psychology. In D. Levine, ed., *Nebraska Symposium on Motivation* (pp. 192–240). Lincoln: University of Nebraska Press.

Kelley, H. H. (1973). The Process of Causal Attribution. *American Psychologist* 28:107–128.

Kelley, H. H. (1979). *Personal Relationships: Their Structures and Processes*. Hillsdale, NJ: Erlbaum.

Kelley, H. H. and J. W. Thibaut (1978). *Interpersonal Relations: A Theory of Interdependence*. New York: Wiley/Interscience.

Kemp, Jerrold E. and Deane K. Dayton (1985). *Planning and Producing Instructional Media,* 5th ed. New York: Harper & Row.

Kennedy, C. W. and C. T. Camden (1988). A New Look at Interruptions. *Western Journal of Speech Communication* 47:45–58.

Kersten, K. and L. Kersten (1988). *Marriage and the Family: Studying Close Relationships*. New York: Harper & Row.

Kesselman-Turkel, Judi and Franklynn Peterson (1982). *Note-Taking Made Easy*. Chicago: Contemporary Books.

Kim, Young Yun, ed. (1986). *Interethnic Communication: Current Research*. Newbury Park, CA: Sage.

Kim, Young Yun (1988). Communication and Acculturation. In In Larry A. Samovar and Richard E. Porter, eds., *Intercultural Communication: A Reader,* 4th ed. (pp. 344–354).

Kim, Young Yun (1991). Intercultural Communication Competence. In *Cross-Cultural Interpersonal Communication,* ed.

Stella Ting-Toomey and Felipe Korzenny. Newbury Park, CA: Sage, pp. 259–275.

Kim, Young Yun and William B. Gudykunst, eds. (1988). *Theories in Intercultural Communication*. Newbury Park, CA: Sage.

Klein, Jeremy, ed. (1992). Special Issue: The E-Prime Controversy: A Symposium. *Etc.: A Review of General Semantics* 49, No. 2.

Kleinfield, N. R. (1992). The Smell of Money. *New York Times* (October 25), 9:1, 8.

Kleinke, Chris L. (1978). *Self-Perception: The Psychology of Personal Awareness*. San Francisco, CA: W. H. Freeman.

Kleinke, Chris L. (1986). *Meeting and Understanding People*. New York: W. H. Freeman.

Knapp, Mark L. and Anita L. Vangelisti (1992). *Interpersonal Communication and Human Relationships,* 2nd ed. Boston: Allyn and Bacon.

Knapp, Mark and Judith Hall (1992). *Nonverbal Behavior in Human Interaction,* 3rd ed. New York: Holt, Rinehart and Winston.

Knapp, Mark L., Roderick P. Hart, Gustav W. Friedrich, and Gary M. Shulman (1973). The Rhetoric of Goodbye: Verbal and Nonverbal Correlates of Human Leave-Taking. *Communication Monographs* 40:182–198.

Kochman, Thomas (1981). *Black and White: Styles in Conflict*. Chicago: University of Chicago Press.

Korzybski, Alfred (1933). *Science and Sanity*. Lakeville, CT: The International Society for General Semantics.

Kossen, Stan (1983). *The Human Side of Organizations,* 3rd ed. New York: Harper & Row.

Kramarae, Cheris (1974a). Folklinguistics. *Psychology Today* 8:82–85.

Kramarae, Cheris (1974b). Stereotypes of Women's Speech: The Word from Cartoons. *Journal of Popular Culture* 8:624–630.

Kramarae, Cheris (1977). Perceptions of Female and Male Speech. *Language and Speech* 20:151–161.

Kramarae, Cheris (1981). *Women and Men Speaking*. Rowley, MA: Newbury House.

Kramer, Ernest (1963). Judgment of Personal Charactistics and Emotions from Nonverbal Properties. *Psychological Bulletin* 60:408–420.

Kreps, Gary L. (1990). *Organizational Com-*

munication, 2nd ed. New York: Longman.

Krivonos, P. D. and M. L. Knapp (1975). Initiating Communication: What Do You Say When You Say Hello? *Central States Speech Journal* 26:115–125.

LaBarre, W. (1964). Paralinguistics, Kinesics, and Cultural Anthropology. In T. A. Sebeok, A. S. Hayes, and M. C. Bateson, eds. *Approaches to Semiotics,* pp. 191–220. The Hague, Netherlands: Mouton.

LaFrance, M. and C. Mayo (1978). *Moving Bodies: Nonverbal Communication in Social Relationships.* Monterey, CA: Brooks/Cole.

Laing, Ronald D., H. Phillipson, and A. Russell Lee (1966). *Interpersonal Perception.* New York: Springer.

Lambdin, William (1981). *Doublespeak Dictionary.* Los Angeles, CA: Pinnacle Books.

Langer, Ellen J. (1978). Rethinking the Role of Thought in Social Interaction. In J. H. Harvey, W. J. Ickes, and R. F. Kidd, eds., *New Directions in Attribution Research,* vol. 2 (pp. 35–58). Hillsdale, J.J.: Lawrence Erlbaum.

Langer, Ellen J. (1989). *Mindfulness.* Reading, MA: Addison-Wesley.

Larson, Charles U. (1992). *Persuasion: Reception and Responsibility,* 6th ed. Belmont, CA: Wadsworth.

Lazarsfeld, Paul F., Bernard Berelson, and Helen Gaudet (1944). *The People's Choice.* New York: Duell, Sloan and Pearce.

Lazarsfeld, Paul F. and Robert K. Merton (1951). Mass Communication, Popular Taste, and Organized Social Action. In Lyman Bryson, ed., *The Communication of Ideas* (pp. 95–118). New York: Harper & Row.

Leathers, Dale G. (1986). *Successful Nonverbal Communication: Principles and Applications.* New York: Macmillan.

Lederer, William J. (1984). *Creating a Good Relationship.* New York: Norton.

Lederman, Linda (1990). Assessing Educational Effectiveness: The Focus Group Interview as a Technique for Data Collection. *Communication Education* 39:117–127.

Leech, Thomas (1992). *How to Prepare, Stage, and Deliver Winning Presentations.* New York: American Management Association.

Leeds, Dorothy (1988). *Powerspeak.* New York: Prentice Hall Press.

LeVine, R. and K. Bartlett (1984). Pace of Life, Punctuality and Coronary Heart Disease in Six Countries. *Journal of Cross-Cultural Psychology* 15:233–255.

Lewin, Kurt (1947). *Human Relations.* New York: Harper & Row.

Likert, Rensis (1967). *The Human Organization.* New York: McGraw-Hill.

Littlejohn, Stephen W. (1992). *Theories of Human Communication,* 4th ed. Belmont, CA: Wadsworth.

Littlejohn, Stephen W. and David M. Jabusch (1987). *Persuasive Transactions.* Glenview, IL: Scott, Foresman.

Loftus, Elizabeth F. and J. C. Palmer (1974). Reconstruction of Automobile Destruction: An Example of the Interaction Between Language and Memory. *Journal of Verbal Learning and Verbal Behavior* 13:585–589.

Luft, Joseph (1969). *Of Human Interaction.* Palo Alto, CA: Mayfield Publishing Co.

Luft, Joseph (1984). *Group Processes: An Introduction to Group Dynamics,* 3rd ed. Palo Alto, CA: Mayfield Publishing Co.

Lund, Philip R. (1974). *Compelling Selling: A Framework for Persuasion.* New York: American Management Association.

Lurie, Alison (1983). *The Language of Clothes.* New York: Vintage.

Lyman, Stanford M. and Marvin B. Scott (1967). Territoriality: A Neglected Sociological Dimension. *Social Problems* 15:236–249.

MacLachlan, John (1979, November). What People Really Think of Fast Talkers. *Psychology Today* 13:113–117.

Mahl, George F. and Gene Schulze (1964). Psychological Research in the Extralinguistic Area. In T. A. Sebeok, A. S. Hayes, and M. C. Bateson, eds., *Approaches to Semiotics.* The Hague, Netherlands: Mouton.

Malandro, Loretta A., Larry Barker, and Deborah Ann Barker (1989). *Nonverbal Communication,* 2nd ed. New York: Random House.

Malinowski, Bronislaw (1923). The Problem of Meaning in Primitive Languages. In C. K. Ogden and I. A. Richards, *The Meaning of Meaning.* New York: Harcourt Brace Jovanovich, pp. 296–336.

Marshall, Evan (1983). *Eye Language: Understanding the Eloquent Eye.* New York: New Trend.

Marshall, Linda L. and Patricia Rose (1987).

Gender, Stress, and Violence in the Adult Relationships of a Sample of College Students. *Journal of Social and Personal Relationships* 4:299–316.

Martel, Myles (1989). *The Persuasive Edge.* New York: Fawcett.

Mayer, Michael, William Gudykunst, Norman Perrill, and Bruce Merrill (1990). A Comparison of Competing Models of the News Diffusion Process. *Western Journal of Speech Communication* 54:113–123.

Maynard, Harry E. (1963). How to Become a Better Premise Detective. *Public Relations Journal* 19:20–22.

McCombs, Maxwell E. and Donald L. Shaw (1972). The Agenda-Setting Function of Mass Media. *Public Opinion Quarterly* 36:176–185.

McCombs, Maxwell E. and Donals L. Shaw (1993). The Evolution of Agenda-Setting Research: Twenty-five Years in the Marketplace of Ideas. *Journal of Communication* 43:58–67.

McCormack, Steven A. and Malcolm R. Parks (1990). What Women Know That Men Don't: Sex Differences in Determining the Truth Behind Deceptive Messages. *Journal of Social and Personal Relationships* 7:107–118.

McCroskey, James C. (1986). *An Introduction to Rhetorical Communication,* 5th ed. Englewood Cliffs, NJ: Prentice-Hall.

McCroskey, James, Virginia P. Richmond, and Robert A. Stewart (1986). *One on One: The Foundations of Interpersonal Communication.* Englewood Cliffs, NJ: Prentice-Hall.

McCroskey, James and Lawrence Wheeless (1976). *Introduction to Human Communication.* Boston: Allyn and Bacon.

McEwen, William (1975). Communication, Innovation, and Change. In G. Hannenman and W. McEwen, eds., *Communication and Behavior* (pp. 197–217). Reading, MA: Addison-Wesley.

McGill, Michael E. (1985). *The McGill Report on Male Intimacy.* New York: Harper & Row.

McGregor, Douglas (1960). *The Human Side of Enterprise.* New York: McGraw-Hill.

McGuire, William J. (1964). Inducing Resistance to Persuasion: Some Contemporary Approaches. In Leonard Berkowitz, ed., *Advances in Experimental Social Psychology,* vol. 1 (pp. 191–229). New York: Academic Press.

McLaughlin, Margaret L. (1984). *Conversation: How Talk Is Organized.* Newbury Park, CA: Sage.

McLuhan, Marshall (1964). *Understanding Media: The Extensions of Man.* New York: McGraw-Hill.

McMahon, Ed (1986). *The Art of Public Speaking.* New York: Ballantine.

Medley, H. Anthony (1978). *Sweaty Palms: The Neglected Art of Being Interviewed.* Belmont, CA: Wadsworth Lifetime Learning Publications.

Megginson, Leon C., Donald C. Mosley, and Paul H. Pietri, Jr. (1992). *Management: Concepts and Applications,* 4th ed. New York: HarperCollins.

Mehrabian, Albert (1968). Communication Without Words. *Psychology Today* 2:53–55.

Mehrabian, Albert (1976). *Public Places and Private Spaces.* New York: Basic Books.

Mehrabian, Albert (1978). *How We Communicate Feelings Nonverbally* (A *Psychology Today* Cassette). New York: Ziff-Davis.

Mella, Dorothee L. (1988). *The Language of Color.* New York: Warner.

Mencken, H. L. (1971). *The American Language.* New York: Knopf.

Merrill, John C., John Lee, and Edward Jay Friedlander (1990). *Modern Mass Media.* New York: Harper & Row.

Merrill, John C. and Ralph L. Lowenstein (1979). *Media, Messages, and Men: New Perspectives in Communication.* New York: Longman.

Merton, Robert K. (1957). *Social Theory and Social Structure.* New York: Free Press.

Miller, George A. and David McNeill (1969). Psycholinguistics. In Gardner Lindzey and Elliot Aronson, eds. *The Handbook of Social Psychology,* 2nd ed. Vol. III (pp. 666–794). Reading, MA: Addison-Wesley.

Miller, Gerald R. (1978). The Current State of Theory and Research in Interpersonal Communication. *Human Communication Research* 4:164–178.

Miller, Gerald R. and Malcolm R. Parks (1982). Communication in Dissolving Relationships. In Steve Duck, ed., *Personal Relationships. 4: Dissolving Personal Relationships.* New York: Academic Press.

Miller, Sherod, Daniel Wackman, Elam Nunnally, and Carol Saline (1982). *Straight Talk.* New York: New American Library.

Miner, Horace (1956). Body Ritual Among the Nacirema. *American Anthropologist*

58:503–507.

Molloy, John (1975). *Dress for Success*. New York: P. H. Wyden.

Molloy, John (1977). *The Women's Dress for Success Book*. Chicago: Follet.

Montagu, Ashley (1971). *Touching: The Human Significance of the Skin*. New York: Harper & Row.

Montana, Patrick (1991). *Management*. New York: Barron's.

Morris, Desmond (1967). *The Naked Ape*. London: Jonathan Cape.

Morris, Desmond (1972). *Intimate Behaviour*. New York: Bantam.

Morris, Desmond (1977). *Manwatching: A Field Guide to Human Behavior*. New York: Abrams.

Morris, Desmond (1985). *Bodywatching*. New York: Crown.

Morris, Desmond, Peter Collett, Peter Marsh, and Marie O'Shaughnessy (1980). *Gestures: Their Origins and Distribution*. New York: Stein and Day.

Mulac, A., J. M. Wiemann, S. J. Widenmann, and T. W. Gibson (1988). Male/Female Language Differences and Effects in Same-Sex and Mixed-Sex Dyads: The Gender-Linked Language Effect. *Communication Monographs* 55:315–335.

Naifeh, Steven and Gregory White Smith (1984). *Why Can't Men Open Up? Overcoming Men's Fear of Intimacy*. New York: Clarkson N. Potter.

Naisbitt, John (1984). *Megatrends: Ten New Directions Tranforming Our Lives*. New York: Warner.

Napier, Rodney W. and Matti K. Gershenfeld (1981). *Groups: Theory and Experience*, 2nd ed. Boston: Houghton Mifflin.

Nichols, Ralph (1961). Do We Know How to Listen? Practical Helps in a Modern Age. *Communication Education* 10:118–124.

Nichols, Ralph and Leonard Stevens (1957). *Are You Listening?* New York: McGraw-Hill.

Nierenberg, Gerald and Henry Calero (1971). *How to Read a Person Like a Book*. New York: Pocket Books.

Nierenberg, Gerald and Henry Calero (1973). *Metatalk*. New York: Simon and Schuster.

Oberg, Kalervo (1960). Cultural Shock: Adjustment to New Cultural Environments. *Practical Anthropology* 7:177–182.

O'Hair, Dan and Gustav W. Friedrich (1992). *Strategic Communication in Business and the Professions*. Boston: Houghton Mifflin.

O'Hair, Dan, M. J. Cody, B. Goss, and K. J. Krayer (1988). The Effect of Gender, Deceit Orientation and Communicator Style on Macro-Assessments of Honesty. *Communication Quarterly* 36:77–93.

Osborn, Alex (1957). *Applied Imagination*, rev. ed. New York: Scribners.

Osborn, Michael and Suzanne Osborn (1991). *Speaking in Public*, 2nd ed. Boston, MA: Houghton Mifflin.

Ouchi, William (1980). *Theory Z*. New York: Avon.

Patton, Bobby R., Kim Giffin, and Eleanor Nyquist Patton (1989). *Decision-Making Group Interaction*, 3rd ed. New York: Harper & Row.

Pearce W. Barnett and Steward M. Sharp (1973). Self-Disclosing Communication. *Journal of Communication* 23:409–425.

Pearson, Judy C. (1980). Sex Roles and Self-Disclosure. *Psychological Reports* 47:640.

Pearson, Judy C. (1993). *Communication in the Family: Seeking Satisfaction in Changing Times*, 2nd ed. New York: HarperCollins.

Pearson, Judy C. and B. H. Spitzberg (1990). *Interpersonal Communication: Concepts, Components, and Contexts*, 2nd ed. Dubuque, IA: Wm. C. Brown.

Pearson, Judy C., Lynn H. Turner, and William Todd-Mancillas (1991). *Gender and Communication*, 2nd ed. Dubuque, IA: Wm. C. Brown.

Pease, Allen (1984). *Signals: How to Use Body Language for Power, Success and Love*. New York: Bantam Books.

Penfield, Joyce, ed. (1987). *Women and Language in Transition*. Albany: State University of New York Press.

Peplau, Letitia Anne and Daniel Perlman, eds. (1982). *Loneliness: A Sourcebook of Current Theory, Resarch and Therapy*. New York: Wiley/Interscience.

Perlman, Daniel and Letitia Anne Peplau (1981). Toward a Social Psychology of Loneliness. In Steve Duck and Robin Gilmour, eds., *Personal Relationships. 3: Personal Relationships in Disorder* (pp. 31–56). New York: Academic Press.

Peters, Thomas J. and Robert H. Waterman, Jr. (1982). *In Search of Excellence: Lessons from American's Best-Run Companies*. New York: Harper & Row.

Pilkington, Constance J. and Deborah R. Richardson (1988). Perceptions of Risk in

Intimacy. *Journal of Social and Personal Relationships* 5:503–508.

Pilotta, Joseph J., Timothy Widman, and Susan A. Jasko (1988). Meaning and Action in the Organizational Setting: An Interpretive Approach (with commentaries by Stanley Deetz and Sue DeWine). In Anderson, James A., eds., *Communication Yearbook/11* (pp. 310–355). Newbury Park, CA: Sage.

Pittenger, Robert E., Charles F. Hockett, and John J. Danehy (1960). *The First Five Minutes*. Ithaca, NY: Paul Martineau.

Postman, Neil and Steve Powers (1992). *How to Watch TV News*. New York: Penguin.

Potter, W. James (1986). Perceived Reality and the Cultivation Hypothesis. *Journal of Broadcasting and Electronic Media* 30:159–174.

Potter, W. James and Ik Chin Chang (1990). Television Exposure Measures and the Cultivation Hypothesis. *Journal of Broadcasting and Electronic Media* 34:313–333.

Prather, Hugh and Gayle Prather (1988). *A Book for Couples*. New York: Doubleday.

Pratkanis, Anthony and Elliot Aronson (1991). *Age of Propaganda: The Everyday Use and Abuse of Persuasion*. New York: W. H. Freeman.

Putnam, Linda and M. Pacanowsky, eds. (1983). *Communication and Organizations: An Interpretive Approach*. Newbury Park: CA: Sage.

Qubein, Nido R. (1986). *Get the Best from Yourself*. New York: Berkley.

Rank, H. (1984). *The PEP Talk: How to Analyze Political Language*. Park Forest, IL: Counter Propaganda Press.

Rankin, Paul (1929). Listening Ability. *Proceedings of the Ohio State Educational Conference's Ninth Annual Session*.

Raven, R., C. Centers, and A. Rodrigues (1975). The Bases of Conjugal Power. In R. E. Cromwell and D. H. Olson, eds., *Power in Families*. New York: Halstead Press, pp. 217–234.

Reardon, Kathleen K. (1987). *Where Minds Meet: Interpersonal Communication*. Belmont, CA: Wadworth.

Reed, Warren H. (1985). *Positive Listening: Learning to Hear What People Are Really Saying*. New York: Franklin Watts.

Reik, Theodore (1944). *A Psychologist Looks at Love*. New York: Rinehart.

Reivitz, Linda (1985). *Vital Speeches of the Day* 52 (November 15):88–91.

Rich, Andrea L. (1974). *Interracial Communication*. New York: Harper & Row.

Richards, I. A. (1951). Communication Between Men: The Meaning of Language. In Heinz von Foerster, ed., *Cybernetics, Transactions of the Eighth Conference*.

Richmond, Virginia P. and James C. McCroskey (1992). *Communication: Apprehension, Avoidance, and Effectiveness*, 3rd ed. Scottsdale, AZ: Gorsuch Scarisbrick.

Richmond, Virginia, James McCroskey, and Steven Payne (1987). *Nonverbal Behavior in Interpersonal Relationships*. Englewood Cliffs, NJ: Prentice-Hall.

Riggio, Ronald E. (1987). *The Charisma Quotient*. New York: Dodd, Mead.

Robinson, W. P. (1972). *Language and Social Behavior*. Baltimore: Penguin Books.

Rodriguez, Maria (1988). Do Blacks and Hispanics Evaluate Assertive Male and Female Characters Differently? *Howard Journal of Communication* 1:101–107.

Rogers, Carl (1970). *Carl Rogers on Encounter Groups*. New York: Harrow Books.

Rogers, Carl and Richard Farson (1981). Active Listening. In Joseph A. DeVito, *Communication: Concepts and Processes*, 3rd ed. Englewood Cliffs, NJ: Prentice-Hall, pp. 137–147.

Rogers, Everett M. (1983). *Diffusion of Innovations*, 3rd ed. New York: Free Press.

Rogers, Everett M. and Rekha Agarwala-Rogers (1976). *Communication in Organizations*. New York: Free Press.

Rosenfeld, Lawrence (1979). Self-disclosure Avoidance: Why I Am Afraid to Tell You Who I Am. *Communication Monographs* 46:63–74.

Rosenfeld, Lawrence, Sallie Kartus, and Chett Ray (1976). Body Accessibility Revisited. *Journal of Communication* 26:27–30.

Rosengren, Karl (1987). Introduction to "A Special Issue on News Diffusion." *European Journal of Communication* 2:135–142.

Rosenthal, Peggy (1984). *Words and Values: Some Leading Words and Where They Lead Us*. New York: Oxford Unviersity Press.

Rosenthal, Robert and L. Jacobson (1992). *Pygmalion in the Classroom*, rev. ed. New York: Irvington.

Rossiter, Charles M., Jr. (1975). Defining

"Therapeutic Communication." *Journal of Communication* 25:127–130.

Rothwell, J. Dan (1982). *Telling It Like It Isn't: Language Misuse & Malpractice/What We Can Do About It.* Englewood Cliffs, NJ: Prentice-Hall.

Rothwell, J. Dan (1992). *In Mixed Company: Small Group Communication.* Fort Worth, TX: Harcourt Brace Jovanovich.

Ruben, Brent D. (1985). Human Communication and Cross-Cultural Effectiveness. In Larry A. Samovar and Richard E. Porter, eds., *Intercultural Communication: A Reader,* 4th ed. (pp. 338–346). Belmont, CA: Wadsworth.

Ruben, Brent D. (1988). *Communication and Human Behavior,* 2nd ed. New York: Macmillan.

Rubenstein, Eric (1992). *Vital Speeches of the Day* (April 15):401–404.

Rubenstein, Carin and Philip Shaver (1982). *In Search of Intimacy*. New York: Delacorte.

Rubin, Alan, (1979). Television Use by Children and Adolescents. *Human Communication Research* 5:109–120.

Rubin, Theodore Isaac (1983). *One to One: Understanding Personal Relationships*. New York: Viking.

Rubin, Zick (1973). *Liking and Loving: An Invitation to Social Psychology*. New York: Holt.

Rubin, Rebecca and Michael McHugh (1987). Development of Parasocial Interaction Relationships. *Journal of Broadcasting and Electronic Media* 31:279–292.

Rubin, Zick and Elton B. McNeil (1985). *Psychology: Being Human,* 4th ed. New York: Harper & Row.

Rubin, Alan, Elizabeth Pearse, and Robert Powell (1985). Loneliness, Parasocial Interaction, and Local Television News Viewing. *Human Communication Research* 12:155–180

Rubin, Rebecca B., Elizabeth M. Perse, and Carole A. Barbato (1988). Conceptualization and Measurement of Interpersonal Communication Motives. *Human Communication Research* 14:602–628.

Ruesch, Jurgen and Gregory Bateson (1951). *Communication: The Social Matrix of Psychiatry*. New York: Norton.

Ruggiero, Vincent Ryan (1987). *Vital Speeches of the Day* 53:671–672.

Sabatelli, Ronald M. and John Pearce (1986). Exploring Marital Expectations. *Journal of Social and Personal Relationships* 3:307–321.

Samovar, Larry A., Richard E. Porter, and Nemi C. Jain (1981). *Understanding Intercultural Communication*. Belmont, CA: Wadsworth.

Samovar, Larry A. and Richard E. Porter, eds. (1988). *Intercultural Communication: A Reader,* 5th ed. Belmont, CA: Wadsworth.

Sanders, Judith A., Richard L. Wiseman, and S. Irene Matz (1991). Uncertainty Reduction in Acquaintance Relationships in Ghana and the United States. In *Cross-Cultural Interpersonal Communication,* ed. Stella Ting-Toomey and Felipe Korzenny. Newbury Park, CA: Sage, pp. 79–98.

Sargent, J. F. and Gerald R. Miller (1971). Some Differences in Certain Communication Behaviors of Autcratic and Democratic Leaders. *Journal of Communication* 21:233–252.

Sashkin, Marshall and William C. Morris (1984). *Organizational Behavior: Concepts and Experiences*. Reston, Va.: Reston Publishing/Prentice-Hall.

Schaefer, Charles E. (1984). *How to Talk to Chidlren about Really Important Things*. New York: Harper & Row.

Schatski, Michael (1981). *Negotiation: The Art of Getting What You Want*. New York: New American Library.

Scherer, K. R. (1986). Vocal Affect Expression. *Psychological Bulletin* 99:143–165.

Schramm, Wilbur (1988). *The Story of Human Communication: Cave Painting to Microchip*. New York: Harper & Row.

Schramm, Wilbur and William E. Porter (1982). *Men, Women, Messages and Media: Understanding Human Communication*. New York: Harper & Row.

Schultz, Beatrice G. (1989). *Communicating in the Small Group: Theory and Practice*. New York: Harper & Row.

Seidler, Ann and Doris Bianchi (1988). *Voice and Diction Fitness: A Comprehensive Approach*. New York: Harper & Row.

Seidman, I. E. (1991). *Interviewing as Qualitative Research: A Guide for Researchers in Education and the Social Sciences*. New York: Teachers College, Columbia University.

Severin, Werner J. with James W. Tankard, Jr. (1988). *Communication Theories,* 2nd ed. New York: Longman.

Shaw, D. L. and M. E. McCombs, eds. (1977). *The Emergence of American Political Issues: The Agenda-Setting Function of the Press*. St. Paul, Minn.: West.

Shaw, Marvin (1955). A Comparison of Two Types of Leadership in Various Communication Nets. *Journal of Abnormal and Social Psychology* 50:127–134.

Shaw, Marvin (1981). *Group Dynamics: The Psychology of Small Group Behaviors*, 3rd ed. New York: McGraw-Hill.

Shimanoff, Susan (1980). *Communication Rules: Theory and Research*. Newbury Park, CA: Sage.

Shockley-Zalabak, Pamela (1991). *Fundamentals of Organizational Communication: Knowlede, Sensitivity, Skills, Values*, 2nd ed. White Plains, New York: Longman.

Sillars, Alan L. and Michael D. Scott (1983). Interpersonal Perception Between Intimates: An Integrative Review. *Human Communication Research* 10:153–176.

Sincoff, Michael Z. and Robert S. Goyer (1984). *Interviewing*. New York: Macmillan.

Singer, Marshall R. (1987). *Intercultural Communication: A Perceptual Approach*. Englewood Cliffs, NJ: Prentice-Hall.

Skopec, Eric William. *Situational Interviewing*. Prospect Heights, IL: Waveland Press, 1986.

Snyder, Mark (1987). *Public Appearances, Private Realities*. New York: W. H. Freeman.

Sommer, Robert (1969). *Personal Space: The Behavioral Basis of Design*. Englewood Cliffs, NJ: Prentice-Hall/Spectrum.

Spitzberg, Brian H. (1991). Intercultural Communication Competence. In Larry A. Samovar and Richard E. Porter, eds., *Intercultural Communication: A Reader*. Belmont, CA: Wadsworth, pp. 353–365.

Spitzberg, Brian H. and William R. Cupach (1984). *Interpersonal Communication Competence*. Beverly Hills, CA: Sage.

Spitzberg, Brian H. and William R. Cupach (1989). *Handbook of Interpersonal Comptence Research*. New York: Springer-Verlag.

Spitzberg, Brian H. and Michael L. Hecht (1984). A Component Model of Relational Competence. *Human Communication Research* 10: 575–599.

Sprague, Jo and Douglas Stuart (1988). *The Speaker's Handbook*, 2nd ed. San Diego: Harcourt Brace Jovanovich.

Staines, Graham L., Kathleen J. Pottick, and Deborah A. Fudge (1986). Wives' Employment and Husbands' Attitudes Toward Work and Life. *Journal of Applied Psychology* 71:118–128.

Steil, Lyman K., Larry L. Barker, and Kittie W. Watson (1983). *Effective Listening: Key to Your Success*. Reading, MA: Addison-Wesley.

Steiner, Claude (1981). *The Other Side of Power*. New York: Grove.

Stevenson, William (1967). *The Play Theory of Communication*. Chicago: University of Chicago Press.

Stewart, Charles J. and William B. Cash, Jr. (1988). *Interviewing: Principles and Practices*, 4th ed. Dubuque, IA: Wm. C. Brown.

Stewart, Lea P., A. D. Stewart, S. A. Friedley, and P. J. Cooper (1990). *Communication Between the Sexes*, 2nd ed. Scottsdale, AZ: Gorsuch Scarisbrick.

Stillings, Neil A., et al. (1987). *Cognitive Science: An Introduction*. Cambridge, MA: MIT Press.

Strauss, George and Leonard R. Sayles (1980). *Behavioral Strategies for Managers*. Englewood Cliffs, NJ: Prentice-Hall.

Summer, Robert (1969). *Personal Space: The Behavioral Basis of Design*. Englewood Cliffs, NJ: Prentice-Hall.

Sunnafrank, Michael (1989). Uncertainty in Interpersonal Relationships: A Predicted Outcome Value Interpretation of Gudykunsts's Research Program. *Communication Yearbook/12*, ed. James A. Anderson. Newbury Park, CA: Sage.

Swets, Paul W. (1983). *The Art of Talking so That People Will Listen*. Englewood Cliffs, NJ: Prentice-Hall/Spectrum.

Tannen, Deborah (1990). *You Just Don't Understand: Women and Men in Conversation*. New York: Morrow.

Taylor, Dalmas A. and Irwin Altman (1987). Communication in Interpersonal Relationships: Social Penetration Processes. In M. E. Roloff and G. R. Miller, eds., *Interpersonal Processes: New Directions in Communication Research*, pp. 257–277. Newbury Park, CA: Sage.

Taylor, Frederick W. (1911). *The Principles of Scientific Management*. New York: Harper & Brothers.

Tersine, Richard J. and Walter E. Riggs

(1980). The Delphi Technique: A Long-Range Planning Tool. In Stewart Ferguson and Sherry Devereaux Ferguson, eds., *Intercom: Readings in Organizational Communication* (pp. 266–373). Rochelle Park, NJ: Hayden Book.

Thibaut, John W. and Harold. H. Kelley (1986). *The Social Psychology of Groups*. New Brunswick, NJ: Transaction Books.

Thorne, Barrie, Cheris Kramarae, and Nancy Henley, eds. (1983). *Language, Gender and Society*. Rowley, MA: Newbury House Publishers.

Ting-Toomey, Stella and Felipe Korzenny, eds. (1991). *Cross-Cultural Interpersonal Communication*. Newbury Park, CA: Sage.

Tolhuizen, James H. (1989). Communication Strategies for Intensifying Dating Relationships: Identification, Use and Structure. *Journal of Social and Personal Relationships* 6:413–434.

Trager, George L. (1958). Paralangauge: A First Approximation. *Studies in Linguistics* 13:1–12.

Trager, George L. (1961). The Typology of Paralanguage. *Anthropological Linguistics* 3:17–21.

Trenholm, Sarah (1991). *Human Communication Theory,* 2nd ed. Englewood Cliffs, NJ: Prentice-Hall.

Truax, C. (1961). *A Scale for the Measurement of Accurate Empathy*, Wisconsin Psychiatric Institute Discussion Paper No. 20. Madison: Wisconsin Psychiatric Institute.

Tubbs, Stewart L. (1988). *A Systems Approach to Small Group Interaction,* 3rd ed. New York: Random House.

Ullmann, Stephen (1962). *Semantics: An Introduction to the Science of Meaning*. New York: Barnes & Noble.

Ulschak, Francis L., Leslie Nathanson, and Peter G. Gillan (1981). *Small Group Problem Sovling: An Aid to Organizational Effectiveness*. Reading, MA: Addison-Wesley.

Uris, Auren (1986). *101 of the Greatest Ideas in Management*. New York: Wiley.

Valenti, Jack (1982). *Speaking Up with Confidence: How to Prepare, Learn, and Deliver Effective Speeches*. New York: William Morrow.

Van Fleet, James K. (1984). *Conversational Power*. Englewood Cliffs, NJ: Prentice-Hall.

Veenendall, Thomas L. and Marjorie C. Feinstein (1990). *Let's Talk About Relationships: Cases in Study*. Prospect Heights, IL: Waveland Press.

Verderber, Kathleen S. and Rudolph F. Verderber (1989). *Inter-Act: Using Interpersonal Communication Skills*. Belmont, CA: Wadsworth.

Victor, David (1992). *International Business Communication*. New York: Harper-Collins.

Vidmar, Neil and Milton Rokeach (1974). Archie Bunker's Bigotry: A Study in Selective Perception and Exposure. *Journal of Communication* 24:36–47.

Walster, E. and G. W. Walster (1978). *A New Look at Love*. Reading, MA: Addison-Wesley.

Walster, Elaine, G. W. Walster, and Ellen Berscheid (1978). *Equity: Theory and Research*. Boston: Allyn and Bacon.

Wardhaugh, Ronald (1985). *How Conversation Works*. New York: Basil Blackwell.

Watson, Arden K. and Carley H. Dodd (1984). Alleviating Communication Apprehension through Rational Emotive Therapy: A Comparative Evaluation. *Communication Education* 33:257–266.

Watzlawick, Paul (1977). *How Real Is Real? Confusion, Disinformation, Communication: An Anecdotal Introduction to Communications Theory*. New York: Vintage Books.

Watzlawick, Paul (1978). *The Language of Change: Elements of Therapeutic Communication*. New York: Basic Books.

Watzlawick, Paul, Janet Helmick Beavin, and Don D. Jackson (1967). *Pragmatics of Human Communication: A Study of Interactional Patterns, Pathologies, and Paradoxes*. New York: Norton.

Weinstein, Eugene A. and Paul Deutschberger (1963). Some Dimensions of Altercasting. *Sociometry* 26:454–466.

Wells, Theodora (1980). *Keeping Your Cool Under Fire: Communicating Non-Defensively*. New York: McGraw-Hill.

Werner, Elyse K. (1975). A Study of Communication Time. M. A. thesis, University of Maryland, College Park. Cited in Wolvin and Coakley (1982).

Wessells, Michael G. (1982). *Cognitive Psychology*. New York: Harper & Row.

Wheeless, Lawrence R. and Janis Grotz (1977). The Measurement of Trust and Its Relationship to Self-Disclosure. *Human Communication Research* 3:250–257.

White, Ralph and Ronald Lippitt (1960). *Autocracy and Democracy*. New York: Harper & Row.

Whitman, Richard F. and John H. Timmis (1975). The Influence of Verbal Organizational Structure and Verbal Organizing Skills on Select Measures of Learning. *Human Communication Research* 1:293–301.

Wiemann, John M. (1977). Explication and Test of a Model of Communicative Competence. *Human Communication Research* 3:195–213.

Wiemann, John M. and Philip Backlund (1980). Current Theory and Research in Communicative Competence. *Review of Educational Research* 50:185–199.

Wiemann, John M., A. Mulac, D. Zimmerman, and S. K. Mann (1987). Interruption Patterns in Same-Gender and Mixed-Gender Dyadic Conversations. Paper presented at the Third International Conference on Social Psychology and Language, Bristol, England. Cited in Mulac, Wiemann, Widenmann, and Gibson (1988).

Williams, Andrea (1985). *Making Decisions*. New York: Zebra.

Williams, Frederick (1983). *The Communications Revolution*. New York: New American Library.

Williams, Frederick (1987). *Technology and Communication Behavior*. Belmont, CA: Wadsworth.

Williams, Frederick (1991). *The New Telecommunications*. New York: Free Press.

Williams, Frederick (1992). *The New Communications*, 3rd ed. Belmont, CA: Wadsworth.

Wilmot, William W. (1987). *Dyadic Communication*, 3rd ed. New York: Random House.

Wilson, R. A. (1989). Toward Understanding E-prime. *Etc.: A Review of General Semantics* 46:316–319.

Wilson, Glenn and David Nias. *The Mystery of Love*. New York: Quadrangle/The New York Times Book Co., 1976.

Winhahl, Sven and Benno Signitzer with Jean T. Olson (1992). *Using Communication Theory: An Introduction to Planned Communication*. Newbury Park, CA: Sage.

Wolf, Florence I., Nadine C. Marsnik, William S. Tacey, and Ralph G. Nichols (1983). *Perceptive Listening*. New York: Holt, Rinehart and Winston.

Wolvin, Andrew D. and Carolyn Gwynn Coakley (1982). *Listening*. Dubuque, IA: Wm. C. Brown.

Won-Doornink, Myong Jin (1991). Self-Disclosure and Reciprocity in South Korean and U.S. Male Dyads. In Stella Ting-Toomey and Felipe Korzenny, eds., *Cross-Cultural Interpersonal Communication* (pp. 116–131). Newbury Park, CA: Sage.

Woodward, Gary C. and Robert E. Denton (1992). *Persuasion and Influence in American Life,* 2nd ed. Prospect Heights, IL: Waveland Press.

Wright, Charles (1986). *Mass Communiction: A Sociological Perspective,* 3rd ed. New York: Random House.

Zima, Joseph P. (1983). *Interviewing: Key to Effective Management*. Chicago: Science Research Associates, Inc.

Zimmer, Troy A. (1986). Premarital Anxieties. *Journal of Social and Personal Relationships* 3:149–159.

Zunin, Leonard M. and Natalie B. Zunin (1972). *Contact: The First Four Minutes*. Los Angeles, CA: Nash.

GLOSSARY

A

Abstraction. A general concept derived from a class of objects; a part representation of some whole.

Abstraction process. The process by which a general concept is derived from specifics; the process by which some (never all) characteristics of an object, person, or event are perceived by the senses or included in some term, phrase, or sentence.

Accent. The stress or emphasis placed on a syllable when pronounced.

Active listening. A process of putting together into some meaningful whole the listener's understanding of the speaker's total message—the verbal and the nonverbal, the content and the feelings.

Acculturation. The processes by which a person's culture is modified or changed through contact with or exposure to another culture.

Adaptors. Nonverbal behaviors that, when emitted in private or in public without being seen, serve some kind of need and occur in their entirety—for example, scratching one's head until the itch is eliminated.

Adjustment principle. The principle of verbal interaction claiming that communication can take place only to the extent that the parties communicating share the same system of signals.

Affect displays. Movements of the facial area and body that convey emotional meaning—for example, anger, fear, and surprise.

Affinity-seeking strategies. Behaviors designed to increase your interpersonal attractiveness and make another person like you more.

Agape. A selfless, altruistic love.

Agenda-setting. The effect of the media in focusing attention on certain issues and problems. This media attention or inattention influences people to see various issues as important or unimportant; gen-erally, the more media attention given an issue, the more will people think it is important.

Aggressiveness. See **Verbal aggressiveness.**

Allness. The assumption that all can be known or is known about a given person, issue, object, or event.

Altercasting. A statement the places the listener in a specific role for a specific purpose and asks that the listener consider the question or problem from this role's perspective.

Ambiguity. The condition in which a word or phrase may be interpreted as having more than one meaning.

Analogy, reasoning from. A type of reasoning in which you compare like things and conclude that since they are alike in so many respects that they are also alike in some previously unknown respect.

Appeals for the suspension of judgment. A type of **disclaimer** in which the speaker asks listeners to delay their judgments.

Appraisal interview. A type of interview in which the interviewee's performance is assessed by management or by more experienced colleagues.

Apprehension. See **Speaker apprehension.**

Arbitrariness. The feature of human language that refers to the fact that there is no real or inherent relationship between the form of a word and its meaning. If we do not know anything of a particular language, we could not examine the form of a word and thereby discover its meaning.

Argot. A kind of **sublanguage;** the sublanguage of a particular class, generally an underworld or criminal class, which is difficult and sometimes impossible for outsiders to understand.

Argument. Evidence (for example, facts or statistics) and a conclusion drawn from the evidence.

Argumentativeness. A willingness to argue for a point of view, to speak your mind. Distinguished from **verbal aggressiveness.**

Articulation. The physiological movements

of the speech organs as they modify and interrupt the air stream emitted from the lungs.

Artifactual communication. Communication that takes place through the wearing and arrangement of various artifacts—for example, clothing, jewelry, buttons, or the furniture in your house and its arrangement.

Assertiveness. A willingness to stand up for your rights but with respect for the rights of others.

Assimilation. The process of message distortion in which messages are reworked to conform to your own attitudes, prejudices, needs, and values.

Attention. The process of responding to a stimulus or stimuli.

Attitude. A predisposition to respond for or against an object.

Attraction. The state or process by which one individual is drawn to another, by having a highly positive evaluation of that other person.

Attraction theory. A theory holding that we form relationships on the basis of our attraction for another person.

Attribution. A process through which we attempt to understand the behaviors of others (as well as our own), particularly the reasons or motivations for these behaviors.

Audience participation principle. A principle of persuasion stating that persuasion is achieved more effectively when the audience participates actively.

Authoritarian leader. A group leader who determines the group policies or makes decisions without consulting or securing agreement from group members.

Avoidance. An unproductive conflict strategy in which we take mental or physical flight from the actual conflict.

B

Backchanneling cues. Responses made by a listener during a conversation that acknowledge the speaker or the speaker's message rather than request a turn as speaker.

Behavioral approach to organizations. An approach to organizations holding that increases in worker satisfaction lead to increases in productivity; the function of management is to keep workers happy and satisfied so that workers, in turn, will be productive; also referred to as "humanistic" or "organic."

Behavioral synchrony. The similarity in the behavior, usually nonverbal, of two people. Generally, behavioral synchrony is an index of mutual liking.

Belief. Confidence in the existence or truth of something; conviction.

Beltlining. An unproductive conflict strategy in which we hit the other person with insults below his or her level of tolerance—that is, below the belt.

Blame. An unproductive conflict strategy in which we attribute the cause of the conflict to the other person or devote our energies to discovering who is the cause and avoid tackling the issues causing the conflict.

Blind self. The part of the self that contains information about the self that is known to others but unknown to oneself.

Boundary markers. **Markers** separating territories—for example, the armrests in a theater that separate one person's space from another's.

Brainstorming. A technique for generating ideas among people.

Breadth. The number of topics about which individuals in a relationship communicate.

Bypassing. A pattern of misevaluation in which people fail to communicate their intended meaning. Bypassing may take either of two forms: (1) when two people use different words but give them the same meaning, resulting in apparent disagreement that hides the underlying agreement; and (2) when two people use the same words but each gives them different meanings, resulting in apparent agreement that hides the underlying disagreement.

C

Cant. A kind of **sublanguage**; the conversational language of any nonprofessional (usually noncriminal) group, which is generally understood only by its own members.

Causes and effects, reasoning from. A form of reasoning in which you reason that certain effects are due to specific causes or that specific causes produce certain effects.

Central markers. Items placed in a territory that are intended to reserve it for us—for example, a jacket left on a library chair.

Certainty. An attitude of closed-mindedness that creates a defensiveness among communication participants; opposite to **provisionalism.**

Channel. The vehicle or medium through which signals are sent.

Character. One of the qualities of **credibility;** the individual's honesty and basic nature; moral qualities.

Charisma. One of the qualities of **credibility;** the individual's dynamism or forcefulness.

Cherishing behaviors. Small behaviors that we enjoy receiving from a relational partner—for example, a kiss, a smile, or being given flowers.

Chronemics. The study of communicative nature of time—how we treat time and how we use it to communicate. Two general areas of chronemics are usually distinguished: cultural time and psychological time.

Civil inattention. Polite ignoring of others so as not to invade their privacy.

Clearance. The quality that identifies the other person as being available for an interpersonal interaction.

Cliché. Overused phrase that has lost its novelty and part of its meaning, and that calls attention to itself because of its overuse.

Closed-mindedness. An unwillingness to receive certain communication messages.

Code. A set of symbols used to translate a message from one form to another.

Coercive power. **Power** dependent on one's ability to punish or to remove rewards from another person.

Cognitive disclaimer. A **disclaimer** in which the speaker seeks to confirm his or her cognitive capacity, for example, "You may think I'm drunk, but I'm as sober as anyone here."

Cohesiveness. The property of togetherness. Applied to group communication situations, it refers to the mutual attractiveness among members; a measure of the extent to which individual members of a group work together as a group.

Collective orientation. A cultural orientation in which the group's rather than the individual's goals and preferences are given greater importance. Opposed to **individual orientation.**

Colloquy. A small group format in which a subject is explored through the interaction of two panels (one asking and one answering questions) or through the panel members responding to questions from audience members.

Communication. (1) The process or act of communicating; (2) the actual message or messages sent and received; and (3) the study of the processes involved in the sending and receiving of messages. The term **communicology** (q.v.) is suggested for the third definition.

Communication network. The pathways of messages; the organizational structure through which messages are sent and received.

Communicology. The study of communication and particularly that subsection concerned with human communication.

Competence. In communication, the rules of the more social or interpersonal dimensions of communication, often used to refer to those qualities that make for effectiveness in interpersonal communication; one of the qualities of **credibility** which encompasses a person's ability and knowledge.

Complementarity. A principle of **attraction** holding that one is attracted by qualities one does not possess or one wishes to possess and to people who are opposite or different from oneself; opposed to **similarity.**

Complementary relationship. A relationship in which the behavior of one person serves as the stimulus for the complementary behavior of the other; in complementary relationships, behavior differences are maximized.

Compliance-gaining strategies. Tactics that are directed to gain the agreement of others; behaviors designed to persuade others to do as we wish.

Compliance-resisting strategies. Tactics used to resist or refuse to do as asked. Nonnegotiation, negotiation, identify management (positive or negative), and justification are four types of compliance-resisting strategies.

Confidence. The absence of social anxiety; the communication of comfortableness in social situations. One of the qualities of effective interpersonal communication.

Confirmation. A communication pattern in which we acknowledge the presence of the other person and also indicate our acceptance of this person, this person's definition of self, and our relationship as defined or viewed by this other person. Opposite of **disconfirmation**.

Conflict. An extreme form of competition in which a person tries to bring a rival to surrender; a situation in which one person's behaviors are directed at preventing, interfering with, or harming another individual. *See* Interpersonal conflict.

Connotation. The feeling or emotional aspect of meaning, generally viewed as consisting of the evaluative (for example, good-bad), potency (strong-weak), and activity (fast-slow) dimensions; the associations of a term. *See* Denotation.

Consciousness-raising group. A supportive group in which people discuss their feelings and in doing so raise their level of intrapersonal and interpersonal awareness.

Consensus. A principle of attribution through which we attempt to establish whether other people react or behave in the same way as the person on whom we are now focusing. If the person is acting in accordance with the general consensus, then we seek reasons for the behavior outside the individual; if the person is not acting in accordance with the general consensus, then we seek reasons that are internal to the individual.

Consistency. (1) A perceptual process that influences us to maintain balance among our perceptions; a process that influences us to see what we expect to see and to be uncomfortable when our perceptions contradict our expectations; (2) a principle of attribution through which we attempt to establish whether this person behaves the same way in similar situations. If there is consistency, we are likely to attribute the behavior to the person, to some internal motivation; if there is no consistency, we are likely to attribute the behavior to some external factor.

Contact. The first stage of an interpersonal relationship in which perceptual and interactional contact occurs.

Contamination. A form of **territorial encroachment** that renders another's territory impure.

Content and relationship dimensions. A principle of communication holding that messages refer both to content (the world external to both speaker and listener) and to relationship dimensions (the relationship existing between the individuals interacting).

Context of communication. The physical, social-psychological, and temporal environment in which communication takes place.

Controllability. One of the factors considered in judging whether or not a person is responsible for his or her behavior. If the person was in control, then you judge that he or she was responsible. *See* Attribution theory.

Conversation. Relatively informal talk in which the roles of speaker and listener are exchanged freely and frequently.

Conversational turns. The changing (or maintaining) of the speaker or listener role during a conversation. These turns are generally signaled nonverbally. Four major types of conversational turns may be identified: turn-maintaining, by which we indicate our desire to continue in the role of speaker; turn-yielding, by which we indicate our desire to change roles from speaker to listener; turn-requesting, by which we indicate our desire to speak; and turn-denying, by which we indicate our desire not to assume the role of speaker.

Cooperation principle. An implicit agreement between speaker and listener to cooperate in trying to understand what each is communicating.

Counseling interview. A type of interview in which the interviewer tries to learn about the interviewee in an attempt to provide some form of guidance, advice, or insight.

Credentialing. A type of **disclaimer** in which the speaker acknowledges that what is about to be said may reflect poorly on himself or herself but will say it nevertheless (usually for quite positive reasons).

Credibility. The degree to which a receiver perceives the speaker to be believable.

Critical thinking. Reasoned and reasonable thinking and decision-making.

Critical thinking hats technique. A technique developed by Edward deBono in which a problem or issue is viewed from six distinct perspectives.

Criticism. The reasoned judgment of some work; although often equated with faultfinding, criticism can involve both positive or negative evaluations.

Cultivation theory. A theory of mass communication effects which claims that the media, largely television, teaches us our culture.

Cultural time. The communication function of time as regulated and as perceived by a particular culture. Generally, three types of cultural time are identified: *technical time* refers to precise scientific time; *formal time* refers to the divisions of time that a culture makes (for example, dividing a semester into 14 weeks); and *informal time* refers to the rather loose use of such time terms as *immediately*, *soon*, and *right away*.

Cultural transmission. The feature of language referring to the fact that human languages (at least in their outer surface form) are learned. Unlike various forms of animal language, which are innate, human languages are transmitted traditionally or culturally. This feature of language does not deny the possibility that certain aspects of language may be innate. Also referred to as *cultural transmission*.

Culture. The relatively specialized life-style of a group of people—consisting of their values, beliefs, artifacts, ways of behaving, and ways of communicating—that is passed on from one generation to the next.

Culture shock. The psychological reaction one experiences at being placed in a culture very different from one's own or from what one is used to.

D

Date. An extensional device used to emphasize the notion of constant change and symbolized by a subscript: for example, Joan Smith 1991 is not Joan Smith 1994.

Decoder. What takes a message in one form (for example, sound waves) and translates it into another code (for example, nerve impulses) from which meaning can be formulated. In human communication, the decoder is the auditory mechanism; in electronic communication, the decoder is, for example, the telephone earpiece. *See* Encoder.

Decoding. The process of extracting a message from a code—for example, translating speech sounds into nerve impulses. *See* Encoding.

Defensiveness. An attitude of an individual or an atmosphere in a group character-

ized by treats, fear, and domination; messages evidencing evaluation, control, strategy, neutrality, superiority, and certainty are assumed to lead to defensiveness. Opposed to supportiveness.

Delphi method. A type of problem-solving group in which questionnaires are used to poll members on several occasions so as to arrive at a group decision on, say, the most important problems a company faces or activities a group might undertake.

Demassification. The process of segmenting the general audience mass communication into smaller, more clearly defined groups. This is primarily done so that media and advertising may be more precisely targeted to a more homogeneous audience.

Democratic leader. A group leader who stimulates self-direction and self-actualization of the group members.

Denotation. Referential meaning; the objective or descriptive meaning of a word. *See* Connotation.

Depenetration. A reversal of penetration; a condition where the *breadth* and *depth* of a relationship decreases. *See* Social penetration theory.

Depth. The degree to which the inner personality—the inner core of an individual—is penetrated in interpersonal interaction.

Deterioration. A state in an interpersonal relationship in which the bonds holding the individuals together are weakened.

Dialogue. A form of communication in which each person is both speaker and listener; communication characterized by involvement, concern, and respect for the other person; opposed to *monologue*.

Diffusion of innovations theory. A theory of media that concentrates on how the media influence people to adopt something new or different.

Direct speech. Speech in which the speaker's intentions are stated clearly and directly. *See* Indirect speech.

Disclaimer. Statements that ask listeners to receive what the speaker says as intended without it reflecting negatively on the speaker's image or reputation.

Disconfirmation. A communication pattern in which we ignore the presence of the other person as well as this person's communications. Opposed to *confirmation*.

Dissolution. The breaking of the bonds holding an interpersonal relationship together.

Distinctiveness. A principle of attribution in which we ask whether this person reacts in similar ways in different situations. If the person does, there is low distinctiveness and we are likely to conclude there is an internal cause or motivation for the behavior; if there is high distinctiveness, we are likely to seek the cause in some external factors.

Double-bind message. A particular kind of contradictory message possessing the following characteristics: (1) The persons interacting share a relatively intense relationship; (2) two messages are communicated at the same time, demanding different and incompatible responses; (3) at least one person in the double bind cannot escape from the contradictory messages; (4) there is a threat of punishment for noncompliance.

Downward communication. Communication in which the messages originate at the higher levels of an organization or hierarchy and are sent to lower levels—for example, management to line worker.

Dyadic communication. Two-person communication.

Dyadic consciousness. An awareness of an interpersonal relationship or pairing of two individuals, distinguished from situations in which two individuals are together but do not perceive themselves as being a unit or twosome.

Dyadic effect. The tendency for the behavior of one person in a dyad to influence a similar behavior in the other person. Used most often to refer to the reciprocal nature of self-disclosure.

Dysfunctional effects of mass communication. Effects of the media that are not in the interest of society.

E

Ear markers. Identifying marks that indicate that the territory or object belongs to you—for example, initials on an attache case.

Effect. The outcome or consequence of an action or behavior; communication is assumed always to have some effect.

Emblems. Nonverbal behaviors that directly translate words or phrases—for example, the signs for okay and peace.

Emotion. The feelings we have; for example, of guilt, anger, or sorrow.

Empathy. A quality of effective interpersonal communication that refers to the ability to feel another's feelings as that other person does and the ability to communicate that similarity of feeling.

Employment interview. A type of interview in which the interviewee is questioned to ascertain his or her suitability for a particular job.

Encoder. Something that takes a message in one form (for example, nerve impulses) and translates it into another form (for example, sound waves). In human communication the encoder is the speaking mechanism; in electronic communication the encoder is, for example, the telephone mouthpiece. *See* **Decoder.**

Encoding. The process of putting a message into a code—for example, translating nerve impulses into speech sounds. *See* **Decoding.**

Enculturation. The process by which culture is transmitted from one generation to another.

E-Prime. A form of the language that omits the verb *to be* except when used as an auxiliary or in statements of existence. Designed to eliminate the tendency toward *projection,* or assuming that characteristics that one attributes to a person (for example, "Pat is brave") are actually in that person instead of in the observer's perception of that person.

Equality. A quality of effective interpersonal communication in which the equality of personalities is recognized, and both individuals are seen as worthwhile, valuable contributors to the total interaction.

Equity theory. A theory claiming that we experience relational satisfaction when there is an equal distribution of rewards and costs between the two persons in the relationship.

Erotic love. A sexual, physical love; a love that is ego- centered and given because of an anticipated return.

Etc. An extensional device used to emphasize the notion of infinite complexity; since one can never know all about anything, any statement about the world or event must end with an explicit or implicit *etc.*

Ethicizing function of communication. The media's function of providing viewers with a collective ethic or ethical system.

Ethics.   The branch of philosophy that deals with the rightness or wrongness of actions; the study of moral values.

Ethnocentrism.   The tendency to see others and their behaviors through our own cultural filters, often as distortions of our own behaviors; the tendency to evaluate the values and beliefs of one's own culture more positively than those of another culture.

Euphemism.   A polite word or phrase used to substitute for some taboo or otherwise offensive term.

Evaluation.   A process whereby a value is placed on some person, object, or event.

Exit interview.   A type of interview designed to establish why an employee (the interviewee) is leaving the organization.

Expert power.   *Power* dependent on a person's expertise or knowledge; knowledge gives an individual expert power.

Expressiveness.   A quality of effective interpersonal communication referring to the skill of communicating genuine involvement in the interpersonal interaction.

Extemporaneous speech.   A speech that is thoroughly prepared and organized in detail and in which certain aspects of style are predetermined.

Extensional devices.   Those linguistic devices proposed by Alfred Korzybski for keeping language as a more accurate means for talking about the world. The extensional devices include the *etc., date,* and *index*—the working devices; and the *hyphen* and *quotes*—the safety devices.

Extensional orientation.   A point of view in which the primary consideration is given to the world of experience and only secondary consideration is given to the labels. *See* **Intensional orientation.**

F

Fact-inference confusion.   A misevaluation in which one makes an inference, regards it as a fact, and acts upon it as if it were a fact.

Factual statement.   A statement made by the observer after observation, and limited to the observed. *See* **Inferential statement.**

Feedback.   Information that is fed back to the source. Feedback may come from the source's own messages (as when we hear what we are saying) or from the receiver(s) in the form of applause, yawning, puzzled looks, questions, letters to the editor of a newspaper, increased or decreased subscriptions to a magazine, and so forth.

Feedforward.   Information sent prior to the regular messages telling the listener something about future messages.

Field of experience.   The sum total of an individual's experiences, which influences his or her ability to communicate. In some views of communication, two people can communicate only to the extent that their fields of experience overlap.

Focus group.   A group designed to explore the feelings and attitudes of a its individuals and which usually follows a question and answer format.

Force.   An unproductive conflict strategy in which one attempts to win an argument by physical force or threats of force.

Forum.   A small group format in which members of the group answer questions from the audience; often follows a *symposium.*

Free information.   Information about a person that one can see or that is dropped into the conversation, and that can serve as a topic of conversation.

G

Gatekeeping.   The process of filtering messages from source to receiver. In this process some messages are allowed to pass through, and others are changed or not allowed to pass at all.

General semantics.   The study of the relationships among language, thought, and behavior.

Gossip.   Communication about someone not present, some third party, usually about matters that are private to this third party.

Grapevine.   The informal lines through which messages in an organization may travel; these informal lines resemble the physical grapevine, with its unpredictable pattern of branches.

Group.   A collection of individuals related to each other with some common purpose and with some structure among them.

Group norm.   Rules or expectations of appropriate behavior for a member of the group.

Groupthink.   A tendency observed in some groups in which agreement among members becomes more important than the exploration of the issues at hand.

Gunnysacking. An unproductive conflict strategy in which we store up grievances against the other person and unload these during a conflict encounter.

H

Haptics. Touch or tactile communication.

Hedge. A type of *disclaimer* in which the speaker disclaims the importance of what he or she is about to say.

Heterosexist language. Language that assumes all people are heterosexual and thereby denigrates lesbians and gay men.

Hidden self. The part of the self that contains information about the self known to oneself, but unknown to and hidden from others.

High-context culture. One in which much of the information in communication is in the context or in the person rather than explicitly coded in the verbal messages. Opposed to *low-context culture*.

Home territories. Territories for which individuals have a sense of intimacy and over which they exercise control—for example, a child's club house.

Humanistic model of interpersonal effectiveness. An approach to interpersonal communication effectiveness based on the qualities that should characterize meaningful interpersonal interaction. Five such qualities are identified: *openness, empathy, supportiveness, positiveness,* and *equality*.

Hyphen. An *extensional device* used to illustrate that what may be separated verbally may not be separable on the event or nonverbal level; although one may talk about body and mind as if they were separable, in reality they are better referred to as body-mind.

I

Idea-generation group. A group whose purpose is to generate ideas; see *Brainstorming*.

Illustrators. Nonverbal behaviors that accompany and literally illustrate the verbal messages—for example, upward movements that accompany the verbalization "It's up there."

I-messages. Messages in which the speaker accepts responsibility for personal thoughts and behaviors; messages in which the speaker's point of view is stated explicitly. Opposed to *you-messages*.

Immediacy. A quality of effective interpersonal communication referring to the creation of a feeling of togetherness and oneness with another person.

Implicit personality theory. A theory of personality that each individual maintains, complete with rules or systems, and through which others are perceived.

Impromptu speech. A speech given without any direct prior preparation.

Inclusive talk. Communication which includes all people; communication which does not exclude certain groups, for example, women, lesbians and gays, or members of certain races or nationalities.

Index. An *extensional device* used to emphasize the notion of nonidentity (no two things are the same) and symbolized by a subscript—for example, politician$_1$ is not politician$_2$.

Indirect speech. Speech that hides the speaker's true intentions; speech in which requests and observations are made indirectly.

Indiscrimination. A misevaluation caused by categorizing people or events or objects into a particular class and responding to specific members only as members of the class; a failure to recognize that each individual is an individual and is unique; a failure to apply the *index*.

Individual orientation. A cultural orientation in which the individual's rather than the group's goals and preferences are given greater importance. Opposed to *collective orientation*.

Inevitability. A principle of communication referring to the fact that communication cannot be avoided; all behavior in an interactional setting is communication.

Inferential statement. A statement that can be made by anyone, is not limited to the observed, and can be made at any time. *See* **Factual statement**.

Information. That which reduces uncertainty.

Information power. *Power* dependent on one's information and one's ability to communicate logically and persuasively. Also called "persuasion power."

Informative interview. A type of interview in which the interviewer asks the interviewee, usually a person of some reputation and accomplishment, questions designed to elicit his or her views, predictions, perspectives, and the like on specific topics.

Information overload. That condition in which the amount of information is too great to be dealt with effectively; the condition in which the number or complexity of messages is so great that the individual or organization is not able to deal with them.

In-group talk. Talk about a subject or in a vocabulary that only certain people understand, often in the presence of someone who does not belong to this group and therefore does not understand.

Inoculation principle. A principle of persuasion stating that persuasion will be more difficult to achieve when beliefs and attitudes that have already been challenged previously are attacked, because the individual has built up defenses against such attacks in a manner similar to inoculation.

Insulation. A reaction to *territorial encroachment* in which we erect some sort of barrier between ourselves and the invaders.

Intensional orientation. A point of view in which primary consideration is given to the way in which things are labeled and only secondary consideration (if any) to the world of experience. *See* **Extensional orientation.**

Interaction management. A quality of effective interpersonal communication referring to the ability to control the interpersonal interaction to the satisfaction of both participants.

Interaction process analysis. A content analysis method that classifies messages into four general categories: social emotional positive, social emotional negative, attempted answers, and questions.

Intercultural communication. Communication that takes place between persons of different cultures or who have different cultural beliefs, values, or ways of behaving.

Interethnic communication. Communication between members of different ethnic groups.

International communication. Communication between nations.

Interpersonal communication. Communication between two persons or among a small group of persons and distinguished from public or mass communication; communication of a personal nature and distinguished from impersonal communication; communication between or among intimates or those involved in a close relationship; often, intrapersonal, dyadic, and small group communication in general.

Interpersonal conflict. A conflict or disagreement between two persons; a conflict within an individual caused by his or her relationships with other people.

Interpersonal perception. The perception of people; the processes through which you interpret and evaluate people and their behaviors.

Interracial communication. Communication between members of different races.

Interview. A particular form of interpersonal communication in which two persons interact largely by question-and-answer format for the purpose of achieving specific goals.

Intimacy. The closest interpersonal relationship; usually used to denote a close primary relationship.

Intimate distance. The shortest proxemic distance, ranging from touching to 6 to 18 inches.

Intrapersonal communication. Communication with oneself.

Involvement stage. That stage in an interpersonal relationship that normally follows contact in which the individuals get to know each other better and explore the potential for greater intimacy.

Irreversibility. A principle of communication referring to the fact that communication cannot be reversed; once something has been communicated, it cannot be uncommunicated.

Invasion. The unwarranted entrance into another's territory that changes the meaning of the territory. *See* **Territorial encroachment.**

J

Jargon. A kind of *sublanguage;* the language of any special group, often a professional class, which is unintelligible to individuals not belonging to the group; the "shop talk" of the group.

Johari window. A diagram or model of the four selves: *open, blind, hidden,* and *unknown self.*

K

Kinesics. The study of the communicative dimension of face and body movements.

L

Laissez-faire leader. A group leader who allows the group to develop and progress or make mistakes on its own.

Language relativity hypothesis. The theory that the language we speak influences our perceptions and our behaviors of the world, and that therefore persons speaking widely differing languages will perceive and behave differently as a result of the language differences. Also referred to as the *Sapir-Whorf hypothesis* and the *Whorfian hypothesis*.

Lateral communication. Communication among equals—for example, manager to manager, worker to worker.

Leadership. That quality by which one individual directs or influences the thoughts and/or the behaviors of others. *See* **Laissez-faire leader, Democratic leader,** and **Authoritarian leader.**

Legitimate power. *Power* dependent on the belief that a person has a right, by virtue of position, to influence or control another's behavior.

Leveling. A process of message distortion in which a message is repeated, but the number of details is reduced, some details are omitted entirely, and some details lose their complexity.

Level of abstraction. The relative distance of a term or statement from the actual perception; a low-order abstraction would be a description of the perception, whereas a high-order abstraction would consist of inferences about inferences about descriptions of a perception.

Linguistic collusion. A reaction to *territorial encroachment* in which we speak in a language unknown to the intruders and thus separate ourselves from them.

Listening. An active process of receiving aural stimuli consisting of five phases: receiving, understanding, remembering, evaluating, and responding.

Logic. The science of reasoning; the study of the principles governing the analysis of inference making.

Looking-glass self. The *self-concept* that results from the image of yourself that others reveal to you.

Loving. An interpersonal process in which one feels a closeness, a caring, a warmth, and an excitement for another person.

Low-context culture. One in which most of the information in communication is explicitly stated in the verbal messages.

Ludus love. Love as a game, as fun; the position that love is not to be taken seriously and is to be maintained only as long as it remains interesting and enjoyable.

M

Magnitude of change principle. A principle of persuasion stating that the greater and more important the change desired by the speaker, the more difficult its achievement will be.

Manic love. Love characterized by extreme highs and extreme lows; obsessive love.

Manipulation. An unproductive conflict strategy in which open conflict is avoided; instead, attempts are made to divert the conflict by being especially charming and getting the other person into a noncombative frame of mind.

Manuscript speech. A speech designed to be read from a script verbatim.

Markers. Devices through which we signal to others that a particular territory belongs to us.

Mass communication. Communication addressed to an extremely large audience, mediated by audio and/or visual transmitters, and processed by gatekeepers before transmission.

Matching hypothesis. The assumption that persons date and mate people who are approximately the same as they are in terms of physical attractiveness.

Mere exposure hypothesis. The theory holding that repeated or prolonged exposure to a stimulus may result in attitude change toward the stimulus object, generally in the direction of increased positiveness.

Message. Any signal or combination of signals that serve as *stimuli* for a receiver.

Metacommunication. Communication about communication.

Metalanguage. Language used to talk about language.

Metaskills. Skills for regulating more specific skills, for example, the skills of interpersonal communication such as openness and empathy must be regulated by the metaskills of flexibility, mindfulness, and cultural sensitivity.

Micromomentary expressions. Extremely brief movements that are not consciously perceived and that are thought to reveal a person's real emotional state.

Mindfulness and mindlessness. States of relative awareness. In a mindful state we are aware of the logic and rationality of our behaviors and the logical connections existing among elements. In a mindless state we are unaware of this logic and rationality.

Minimization. An unproductive conflict strategy in which we make light of the other person's disagreements or of the conflict as a whole.

Mixed messages. Messages that contain contradictory meanings, a special type of which is the *double bind message.*

Model. A physical representation of an object or process.

Monologue. A communication form in which one person speaks and the other listens; there is no real interaction among participants; opposed to *dialogue.*

Motivated sequence. An organizational pattern for arranging the information in a discourse to motivate an audience to respond positively to one's purpose.

Multi-step flow of communication. A theory of mass communication which assumes that media influence interacts with influences from other sources (for example, interpersonal interactions).

N

Narcotizing function of communication. The media's function of providing receivers with information, the knowledge of which is, in turn, confused by receivers with doing something about something.

Negative feedback. *Feedback* that serves a corrective function by informing the source that her or his message is not being received in the way intended. Negative feedback serves to redirect the source's behavior. Looks of boredom, shouts of disagreement, letters critical of newspaper policy, and the teacher's instructions how to better approach a problem are examples of negative feedback.

Noise. Anything that distorts or interferes with the message in the communication system. Noise is present in communication to the extent that the message sent differs from the message received. *Physical noise* interferes with the physical transmission of the signal or message— for example, the static in radio transmission. *Psychological noise* refers to distortions created by such psychological processes as prejudice and biases. *Semantic noise* refers to distortions created by a failure to understand each other's words.

Nominal group. A collection of individuals who record their thoughts and opinions which are then distributed to others. Without direct interaction, the thoughts and opinions are gradually pared down until a manageable list (of solutions or decisions) is produced. When this occurs the nominal group (a group in name only) may restructure itself into a problem-solving group that analyzes the final list.

Nonallness. An attitude or point of view in which it is recognized that one can never know all about anything and that what we know or say or hear is only a part of what there is to know, say, or hear.

Nonnegotiation. An unproductive conflict strategy in which the individual refuses to discuss the conflict or the disagreement, or to listen to the other person.

Norm. *See* **Group norm.**

O

Olfactory communication. Communication by smell.

Openness. A quality of effective interpersonal communication that refers to (1) the willingness to engage in appropriate self-disclosure, (2) the willingness to react honestly to incoming stimuli, and (3) the willingness to own one's own feelings and thoughts.

Open self. The part of the self that contains information about the self that is known to oneself and to others.

Opinion leader. Persons looked to for opinion leadership; those who mold public opinion.

Oral style. The style of spoken discourse that, when compared with *written style,* consists of shorter, simpler, and more familiar words; more qualification, self-reference terms, allness terms, verbs and adverbs; and more concrete terms and terms indicative of consciousness of projection—for example, *as I see it.*

Organization. A group of individuals organized for the achievement of specific goals.

Other-orientation. A quality of effective interpersonal interaction referring to one's ability to adapt to the other person's needs and desires during the interpersonal encounter.

Owning feelings. The process by which you take responsibility for your feelings instead of attributing them to others.

P

Panel or round table. A small group format in which participants are arranged in a circular pattern and speak without any set pattern.

Paralanguage. The vocal (but nonverbal) aspect of speech. Paralanguage consists of voice qualities (for example, pitch range, resonance, tempo), vocal characterizers (for example, laughing or crying, yelling or whispering), vocal qualifiers (for example, intensity, pitch height), and vocal segregates (for example, *uh-uh* meaning "no," or *sh* meaning "silence").

Parasocial relationship. Relationships between a real and an imagined or fictional character, usually used to refer to relationships between a viewer and a fictional character in a television show.

Pause. A silent period in the normally fluent stream of speech. Pauses are of two major types: filled pauses (interruptions in speech that are filled with such vocalizations as *-er* or *-um*) and unfilled pauses (silence of unusually long length).

Perception. The process of becoming aware of objects and events from the senses.

Perceptual accentuation. A process that leads us to see what we expect to see and what we want to see; for example, we see people we like as better looking and smarter than people we do not like.

Personal distance. The second-shortest proxemic distance, range from one and a half to four feet.

Personal growth group. A group designed to gain greater awareness of themselves and an improved ability to deal with their experiences.

Personal rejection. An unproductive conflict strategy in which the individual withholds love and affection, and seeks to win the argument by getting the other person to break down under this withdrawal.

Persuasion. The process of influencing attitudes and behavior.

Persuasive interview. A type of interview in which the interviewer attempts to change the interviewee's attitudes or behavior.

Phatic communion. Communication that is primarily social; communication designed to open the channels of communication rather than to communicate something about the external world; "Hello," and "How are you?" in everyday interaction are common examples.

Pitch. The highness or lowness of the vocal tone.

Polarization. A form of fallacious reasoning by which only the two extremes are considered; also referred to as "either-or" thinking.

Positive feedback. *Feedback* that supports or reinforces behavior along the same lines as it is proceeding—for example, applause during a speech.

Positiveness. A quality of effective interpersonal communication referring to the communication of positiveness toward the self, the other, and the communication situation generally, and willingness to stroke the other person as appropriate.

Power. The ability to control the behaviors of others.

Power play. A type of game or manipulative strategy by which someone repeatedly tries to control another's behavior.

Pragma love. Practical love; love based on compatibility; love that seeks a relationship that will satisfy each person's important needs and desires.

Primacy effect. The condition by which what comes first exerts greater influence that what comes later or more recently. *See* **Recency effect.**

Primary affect displays. The communication of the six primary emotions: happiness, surprise, fear, anger, sadness, and disgust/contempt. *See* **Affect displays.**

Privatization. A function of the mass media; the tendency for an individual to retreat from social groups into a world of one's own.

Problem-solving group. A group whose primary task is to solve a problem, but more often to reach a decision.

Problem-solving sequence. A logical step-by-step process for solving a problem frequently used by groups and consisting of defining and analyzing the problem, establishing criteria for evaluating solutions, identifying possible solutions, evaluating solutions, selecting the best solution, and testing the selected solutions.

Process. Ongoing activity; nonstatic; communication is referred to as a process to emphasize that it is always changing and always in motion.

Productivity. The feature of language that makes possible the creation and understanding of novel utterances. With human language we can talk about matters that have never been talked about before, and we can understand utterances we have never heard before. Also referred to as *openness.*

Projection. A psychological process whereby we attribute characteristics or feelings of our own to others; often used to refer to the process whereby we attribute our own faults to others.

Pronunciation. The production of syllables or words according to some accepted standard, as presented, for example, in a dictionary.

Provisionalism. An attitude of open-mindedness that leads to the creation of *supportiveness;* opposite to *certainty.*

Proxemics. The study of the communicative function of space; the study of how people unconsciously structure their space—the distance between people in their interactions, the organization of space in homes and offices, and even the design of cities.

Proximity. As a principle of *perception*, the tendency to perceive people or events that are physically close as belonging together or representing some unit; physical closeness; one of the qualities influencing interpersonal *attraction.*

Public communication. Communication in which the source is one person and the receiver is an audience of many persons.

Public distance. The longest proxemic distance, ranging from 12 to over 25 feet.

Public speaking. Communication that occurs when a speaker delivers a relatively prepared, continuous address in a specific setting to a large audience that provides little immediate feedback.

Punctuation of communication. The breaking up of continuous communication sequences into short sequences with identifiable beginnings and endings, or stimuli and responses.

Pupillometrics. The study of communication through changes in the size of the pupils of the eyes.

Pragmatic model of interpersonal effectiveness. An approach to interpersonal communication effectiveness that stresses the behaviors that speakers should focus on to gain their desired goal. Generally, five characteristics are identified: *confidence, immediacy, interaction management, expressiveness, other-orientation.*

Psychological time. The importance that we place on past time, in which particular regard is shown for the past and its values and methods; present time, in which we live in the present for the enjoyment of the present; and future time, in which we devote our energies to planning for the future.

Public speaking. A form of communication in which a speaker addresses a relatively large audience with a relatively continuous discourse, usually face to face.

Purr words. Highly positive words that express the feelings of the speaker rather than refer to any objective reality; opposite to *snarl words.*

Pygmalion effect. The condition in which one makes a prediction and then proceeds to fulfill it; a type of self-fulfilling prophecy but one that refers to others and to our evaluation of others rather than to ourselves.

R

Racist language. Language that denigrates a person or group because of their race.

Rapid fading. The evanescent or impermanent quality of speech signals.

Rate. The speed with which we speak, generally measured in words per minute.

Receiver. Any person or thing that takes in messages. Receivers may be individuals listening or reading a message, a group of persons hearing a speech, a scattered television audience, or a machine that stores information.

Recency effect. The condition in which what comes last (that is, most recently) exerts greater influence than what comes first. *See* **Primacy** effect.

Redefinition. An unproductive conflict strategy in which the conflict is given another definition so that the source of the conflict disappears.

Referent power. *Power* dependent on one's desire to identify with or be like another person.

Reflexiveness.   The feature of language referring to the fact that human language can be used to refer to itself; that is, we can talk about our talk and create a *metalanguage*—a language for talking about language.

Regulators.   Nonverbal behaviors that regulate, monitor, or control the communications of another person.

Reinforcement/packaging, principle of.   The principle of verbal interaction holding that in most interactions, messages are transmitted simultaneously through a number of different channels that normally reinforce each other; messages come in packages.

Rejection.   A response to an individual that rejects or denies the validity of an individual's self-view.

Relationship communication.   Communication between or among intimates or those in close relationships; term used by some theorists as synonymous with interpersonal communication.

Relationship deterioration.   The stage of a relationship during which the connecting bonds between the partners weaken and the partners being drifting apart.

Relationship repair.   Attempts to reverse the process of relationship deterioration.

Reward power.   *Power* dependent on one's ability to reward another person.

Rigid complementarity.   The inability to change the type of relationship between oneself and another even though the individuals, the context, and a host of other variables have changed.

Role.   The part an individual plays in a group; an individual's function or expected behavior.

S

Scientific approach to organizations.   An approach to organizations holding that scientific methods should be applied to the organization to increase productivity; through the use of scientifically controlled studies, management can identify the ways and means for increasing productivity and ultimately profit.

Selective exposure principle.   A principle of persuasion stating that listeners will actively seek out information that supports their opinions and actively avoid information that contradicts their existing opinions, beliefs, attitudes, and values.

Self-attribution.   A process through which we seek to account for and understand the reasons and motivations for our own behaviors.

Self-awareness.   One's level of intrapersonal knowledge.

Self-concept.   An individual's self-evaluation; an individual's self-appraisal.

Self-disclosure.   The process of revealing something significant about ourselves to another individual or to a group—something that would not normally be known by them.

Self-esteem.   The value one places on oneself.

Self-fulfilling prophecy.   The situation in which we make a prediction or prophecy and fulfill it ourselves—for example, expecting a class to be boring and then fulfilling this expectation by perceiving it as boring.

Self-monitoring.   The manipulation of the image that we present to others in our interpersonal interactions. High self-monitors carefully adjust their behaviors on the basis of feedback from others so that they can project the desired image. Low self-monitors do not consciously manipulate their images.

Self-serving bias.   A bias that operates in the self-attribution process and leads us to take credit for the positive consequences and to deny responsibility for the negative consequences of our behaviors.

Sexist language.   Language derogatory to one sex, generally women.

Sexual harassment.   Behavior that proves annoying or is offensive in a sexual way.

Sharpening.   A process of message distortion in which the details of messages, when repeated, are crystallized and heightened.

Shyness.   The condition of discomfort and uneasiness in interpersonal situations.

Sign, reasoning from.   A form of reasoning in which the presence of certain signs (clues) are interpreted as leading to a particular conclusion.

Silence.   The absence of vocal communication; often misunderstood to refer to the absence of any and all communication.

Silencers.   Unproductive conflict strategies that literally silence the other person—for example, crying, or feigning emotional or physical disturbance.

Sin licenses.   A *disclaimer* in which the

speaker acknowledges that he or she is about to break some normally operative rule; the speaker asks for a license to sin (that is, to break a social or interpersonal rule of behavior).

Slang. The language used by special groups, which is not considered proper by the general society; the language made up of the *argot, cant,* and *jargon* of various subcultures, known by the general public.

Small group communication. Communication among a collection of individuals, small enough in number that all members may interact with relative ease as both senders and receivers, the members being related to each other by some common purpose and with some degree of organization or structure among them.

Snarl words. Highly negative words that express the feelings of the speaker rather than refer to any objective reality; opposite to *purr words.*

Social comparison processes. The processes by which we compare ourselves (for example, our abilities, opinions, and values) with others and then assess and evaluate ourselves.

Social distance. The third proxemic distance, ranging from 4 to 12 feet; the distance at which business is usually conducted.

Social exchange theory. A theory claiming that we develop and maintain relationships in which the rewards or profits are greater than the costs.

Social penetration theory. A theory concerned with relationship development from the superficial to the intimate levels and from few to many areas of interpersonal interaction.

Source. Any person or thing that creates messages. A source may be an individual speaking, writing, or gesturing or a computer solving a problem.

Speaker apprehension. A fear of engaging in communication transactions; a decrease in the frequency, strength, and likelihood of engaging in communication transactions.

Specific instances, reasoning from. A form of reasoning in which several specific instances are examined and then a conclusion about the whole is formed.

Speech. Messages utilizing a vocal-auditory channel.

Static evaluation. An orientation that fails to recognize that the world is characterized by constant change; an attitude that sees people and events as fixed rather than as constantly changing.

Status. The relative level one occupies in a hierarchy; status always involves a comparison, and thus one's status is only relative to the status of another. In our culture, occupation, financial position, age, and educational level are significant determinants of status.

Step theories of mass communication. A group of theories holding that the media have their effects on viewers and listeners in steps. The one-step theory holds that the media influence people directly; the two-step theory holds that the media influence opinion leaders, who in turn influence the majority of others; the multistep theory holds that the media's influence is a reciprocal one, a process that goes back and forth, from the media to the people, then back to the media, then back to the people, and so on.

Stereotype. In communication, a fixed impression of a group of people through which we then perceive specific individuals; stereotypes are most often negative (Martians are stupid, uneducated, and dirty), but may also be positive (Venusians are scientific, industrious, and helpful).

Storge love. Love based on companionship, similar interests, and mutual respect; love that is lacking in great emotional intensity.

Strategy. The use of some plan for control of other members of a communication interaction that guides one's own communications; encourages *defensiveness.*

Sublanguage. A variation from the general language used by a particular subculture; *argot, cant,* and *jargon* are particular kinds of sublanguages.

Supportiveness. A quality of effective interpersonal communication in which one is descriptive rather than evaluative, spontaneous rather than strategic, and provisional rather than certain.

Symmetrical relationship. A relation between two or more persons in which one person's behavior serves as a stimulus for the same type of behavior in the other person(s). Examples of such relationships include situations in which anger in one person encourages or serves as a stimulus for anger in another person, or in which a critical comment by one person leads the other to respond in like manner.

Symposium. A small group format in which each member of the group delivers a relatively prepared talk on some aspect of the topic. Often combined with a *forum.*

Systems approach to organizations. An approach to organizations that stresses the interaction of all parts of the organization; each part influences each other part. The organization should be seen as an open system in which the physical and physiological factors and the social and psychological factors interact, each influencing the other.

T

Taboo. Forbidden; culturally censored. Taboo language is what is frowned upon by "polite society." Themes and specific words may be considered taboo—for example, death, sex, certain forms of illness, and various words denoting sexual activities and excretory functions.

Tactile communication. Communication by touch; communication received by the skin.

Territorial encroachment. The trespassing on, use of, or appropriation of one's territory by another. The major types of territorial encroachment are *violation, invasion,* and *contamination.*

Territoriality. A possessive or ownership reaction to an area of space or to particular objects.

Theory. A general statement or principle applicable to a number of related phenomena.

Thesis. The main assertion of a message— for example, the theme of a public speech.

Touch avoidance. The tendency we have to avoid touching and being touched by others.

Transactional. The relationship among elements in which each influences and is influenced by each other element; communication is a transactional process, since no element is independent of any other element.

Turf defense. The most extreme reaction to territorial encroachment through which one defends one's territory and expels the intruders.

Two-step flow of communication. A hypothesis stating that the influence of the media occurs in two steps: (1) The media influence opinion leaders, and (2) the opinion leaders influence the general population through interpersonal communication.

Two-valued orientation. A point of view in which events are seen or questions are evaluated in terms of two values—for example, right or wrong, good or bad. Often referred to as the fallacy of black-and-white and *polarization.*

U

Uncertainty reduction. The process by which uncertainty or ambiguity about another person is reduced.

Universal of communication. A feature of communication common to all communication acts.

Unknown self. That part of the self that contains information about the self that is unknown to oneself and to others, but that is inferred to exist on the basis of various projective tests, slips of the tongue, dream analyses, and the like.

Upward communication. Communication in which the messages originate from the lower levels of an organization or hierarchy and are sent to upper levels—for example, line worker to management.

Uses and gratifications. A theory of mass media that seeks to explain the influence of the media in terms of the uses to which people put the media and the gratifications they derive from those uses.

V

Value. Relative worth of an object; a quality that makes something desirable or undesirable; ideals or customs about which we have emotional responses, whether positive or negative.

Verbal aggressiveness. A method of winning an argument by attacking the other person's *self-concept.*

Violation. Unwarranted use of another's territory. *See* Territorial encroachment.

Volume. The relative loudness of the voice.

W

Withdrawal. (1) A reaction to *territorial encroachment* in which we leave the territory. (2) A tendency to close oneself off from conflicts rather than confront the issues.

Written style. *See* Oral style.

Y

You-messages. Messages in which the speaker denies responsibility for his or her thoughts and behaviors; messages that attribute what is really the speakers' perception to another person; messages of blame; opposed to I-messages.

CREDITS

Photographs

Unless otherwise acknowledged, all photographs are the property of Scott, Foresman and Company

2   David Young-Wolff/Photo Edit
10   David R. Frazier Photolibrary
12   Tibor Bognar/The Stock Market
27   Bob Daemmrich/The Image Works
34   David Young-Wolff/Photo Edit
44   Rhoda Sidney/The Image Works
51   Myrleen Ferguson/The Image Works
62   Bill Anderson/Monkmeyer Press Photo Service
66   Art Montes De Oca/FPG
82   Joel Gordon Photography
89   M. Douglas/The Image Works
96   Jim Whitmer
101   Owen Franken/Stock Boson
105   Rick Whitmer
117   Roger Tulley/Tony Stone Images
120   Shinichi Kanno/FPG
130   Jim Whitmer
133   Bob Daemmrich/The Image Works
139   Charles Gatewood/The Image Works
150   Jim Whitmer
154   Bob Daemmrich/The Image Works
161   Jim Whitmer
165   Karen Leeds/The Stock Market
172   Anna E. Zuckerman/Photo Edit
182   Jon Riley/Tony Stone Images
188   Milt & Joan Mann/Cameramann International, Ltd.
202   Shirley Rosicke/The Stock Market
209   Jim Whitmer
215   T. Clark/The Image Works
218   Bob Daemmrich/The Stock Market
226   Milt & Joan Mann/Cameramann International, Ltd.
233   Allford Trotman
235   Jim Whitmer
243   Jim Whitmer
249   Howard Dratch/The Image Works
250   Dick Luria/FPG
262   Jim Whitmer
263   Joseph A. DeVito
265   Chuck Savage/The Stock Market
282   Geer/Mink/Tony Stone Images
287   Jim Whitmer
295   Jean-Marc Giboux/Gamma-Liaison
303   Kit Latham/FPG

330 Jim Whitmer
333 Joseph Nettis/Tony Stone Images
335 AP/Wide World
338 Richard Laird/FPG
348 Bob Daemmrich/Tony Stone Images
352 Jay Wiley/Monkmeyer Press Photo Service
356 Bob Daemmrich/Stock Boston
370 McLaughlin/The Image Works
376 Richard Hutchings/Photo Edit
391 Milt & Joan Mann/Cameramann International, Ltd.
395 Bob Daemmrich/Stock Boston
414 Arlene Collins/Monkmeyer Press Photo Service
420 David R. Frazier Photolibrary
424 Rogers/Monkmeyer Press
437 Renato Rotolo/Gamma-Liaison
440 Grunnitus Studios/Monkmeyer Press
441 Carl Young/FPG
443 Dave Bartruff/FPG
452 Robert Clay
459 Jim Whitmer
464 Jeff Isaac Greenberg/Photo Researchers
476 Laima Druskis/Stock Boston
480 Al Michaud/FPG

Text

187 Reprinted by permission of Rod Hart.
362 From *Championship Debates and Speeches*. Copyright © 1989 by the American Forensic Association. Reprinted by permission.
405 "I Have a Dream" by Martin Luther King, Jr. Copyright © 1963 by Martin Luther King, Jr., copyright renewed 1991 by Coretta Scott King. Reprinted by arrangement with the Heirs of the Estate of Martin Luther King, Jr., c/o Joan Daves Agency as agent for the proprietor.

INDEX

Abstraction principle, and informative
  speaking, 368
Abstractions, 119
Acceptance, in conflict management, 249
Acculturation, 420–421
Achievement, and psychological appeals,
  379–380
Active listening, 87–89
  functions of, 88
  methods of, 88–89
Adaptors, body movements, 148
Affinity seeking, strategies for, 217
Agape, 211
Age of audience, 390
Agenda-setting theory, mass communi-
  cation, 478–480
Aggressiveness, verbal, 250–251
  nature of, 250–251
  test of, 252–253
All-channel pattern, communication net-
  works, 332
Allness, 118–119
  and communication problems, 118–119
  correction of, 119
  meaning of, 118
Altercasting, meaning of, 14
Altruism, and psychological appeals, 379
Analogy
  figurative, 373
  literal, 373
  reasoning from, 373
Anecdotes, use in speech, 400
Appraisal interview, 261
Appropriateness principle, and informative speaking, 367
Argumentativeness
  cultivation of, 251–252
  positive aspects of, 251
  test of, 254–255
Artifactual communication, 162–166

body adornment, 164
clothing, 163–164
color, 162–163
smell, 165–166
space decoration, 164–165
Assertiveness training groups, 296
Attention-gaining, and introduction of
  speech, 399–400
Attitudes, nature of, 389, 394
Attraction theory, 215–217
  affinity-seeking strategies in, 217
  complementarity in, 217
  personality of other in, 215–216
  physical attraction in, 215–216
  proximity in, 216
  reinforcement in, 216
  similarity in, 216
Attribution
  effect on perception, 66–67
  negative effects of, 69–70
  principles in use for, 68–69
Audience
  attitudes/beliefs/values of, 389–390, 394
  context characteristics of, 393
  demographic aspects
    age, 390
    cultural factors, 391
    educational levels, 392
    gender, 390–391
    socioeconomic status, 392
  favorability of, 394
  homogeneity of, 394–395
  knowledgeability of, 394–395
  in mass communication, 455
  and public communication, 351
  willingness of, 393–394
Audience participation principle of persuasive communication, 369
Audiovisual aids, use in speech, 400
Authoritarian leader, 313, 314

Authority, decision making by, 293
Avoidance, and conflict, 245–246

Backchanneling cues, conversation, 184–185
Balanced communication, nature of, 127
Behavioral approach, organizational communication, 327–328
Behavioral management approach, organizations, 327
Beliefs, nature of, 389
Blame, and conflict, 247
Blind self, 45
Body adornment, 164
Body movements, 147–148
    adaptors, 148
    affect displays, 148
    emblems, 147–148
    illustrators, 148
    regulators, 148
Books, 462
    functions of, 462
Boundary markers, of territory, 168
Brainstorming, 294, 295
Bypassing, 116–118
    and communication problems, 118
    correction of, 118
    meaning of, 116–117

Cause and effects
    organization of speech, 398
    reasoning from, 374
Chain pattern, communication networks, 332
Channels, 11–12
    and public communication, 353
Character, and credibility of speaker, 382
Charisma, and credibility of speaker, 382
Circle structure, communication networks, 331
Closing, in conversations, 180–181, 186
Closure, and conclusion of speech, 401
Clothing, 163–164
    communication aspects of, 163–164
Coercive power, 288–289
Color communication, 162–163
    color and perception, 163

positive/negative messages of color, 163
Communication apprehension, 355–358
    affecting factors, 358
    degrees of, 357
    in interpersonal conversations, 228
    normal, 357–358
    positive, 358
    prevalence of, 356
    in small groups, 286
    state, 356–357
    test of, 357
    trait, 356
Communication barriers
    allness, 118–119
    bypassing, 116–118
    fact-inference confusion, 115–116
    indiscrimination, 120–121
    intensional orientation, 114–115
    in intercultural differences, 436–442
    polarization, 113–114
    static evaluation, 119
Communication competence
    meaning of, 11
    and self-disclosure, 50
Communication networks, 331–334
    all-channel pattern, 332
    chain pattern, 332
    characteristics of, 331
    circle structure, 331
    morale and participation, 332–333
    wheel structure, 331, 332
    Y pattern, 332
Communication process
    channels in, 11–12
    messages in, 11–14
    noise in, 14–15
    source-receivers in, 10–11
Communication technology, and intercultural experiences, 419–420
Competence, and credibility of speaker, 381
Complementarity, and attraction, 216
Complementary relationships, 30
Conclusions, of speech, 401
Confidence, at employment interview, 269–271
Confidentiality

principle of, 133
and self-disclosure, 55
Confirmation
meaning of, 135, 136
self-test for, 134
Conflict management. *See* Interpersonal conflict management
Connotative meaning, of message, 102–103
Consciousness-raising groups, 296
Consensus, for decision making, 294
Consistency
and attribution, 68
as barrier to perception, 65
Contact stage, in interpersonal relationships, 207, 228–229
Content conflict, interpersonal conflict, 242
Context of communication, 8–10, 99–104
cultural, 9
in mass communication, 457
and meaning, 103–104
physical, 8–9
social-psychological, 9
and space communication, 162
temporal, 9
Control, and touch, 169
Conversation
backchanneling cues, 184–185
business stage in, 180
closing of, 180, 186
cultural sensitivity, 187
empathy in, 189–190
expressiveness, 193–194
feedback in, 180
feedforward in, 180
flexibility, 187
immediacy in, 190–191
initiation of, 181–183
interaction management, 191–193
maintenance of, 183–185
mindfulness in, 186
opening in, 179–180, 181–183
opening lines, types of, 182–183
openness, 188–189
other-orientation in, 194
positiveness in, 190

turn-denying cues, 184
turn-maintaining cues, 183–184
turn-requesting cues, 184
turn-yielding cues, 184
Counseling interview, 262
Credibility of speaker, 380–382
and character, 382
and charisma, 382
and competence, 381
impression, formation of, 380–381
Critical feedback, 13
Critical listening, 85–86
guidelines for, 85–86
Criticism
in public speaking, 359–361
standards of, 359–360
value of, 359
Cultivation theory, mass communication, 476–477
Cultural approach, organizational communication, 328–330
Cultural context, of communication, 9
Cultural sensitivity, in conversation, 187
Cultural time, 171–172
types of, 171
Culture
acculturation, 420–421
and audience, 391
communication rules of, 438
high-context, 423, 424–425
low-context, 423, 424–425
meaning of, 420
and nonverbal communication, 104–105
and self-disclosure, 50
and space communication, 161–162
and touch communication, 170
transmission of, 420
Culture shock, 440–442
meaning of, 440–441
stages of, 441–442

Decision-making methods, 293–294
consensus, 294
decisions by authority, 293
majority rule, 293–294
Decoding, meaning of, 11

Delivery, and public communication, 354–355
Delphi method, 293
Democratic leader, 313, 314
Demographic aspects, of audience, 392
Denotative meaning, of message, 102–103
Depth listening, 86–87
  guidelines for, 86–87
Deterioration stage, in interpersonal relationships, 211
Diffused time orientation, 171
Diffusion of innovations theory, of mass media, 474–476
Disabled persons, communication with, 440
Disclaimers, 87
  purpose of, 14, 180
Disconfirmation
  heterosexism as, 139–140
  meaning of, 134–135, 136
  racism as, 135–136
  sexism as, 137–139
Displaced time orientation, 171
Dissolution stage, in interpersonal relationships, 211
Door-in-the-face technique, persuasive communication, 371
Double-bind messages, 24–27
  example of, 25
  interactive requirements in, 25–26
Downward communication, 336
  characteristics of, 336
  guidelines for, 336
  problems with, 336
Downward talk, 127–129
  interrupting as, 127
  power plays as, 128–129
  verbosity as, 127
Dyadic effect, and self-disclosure, 50

Earmarkers, of territory, 168
Effect-cause pattern, speech, 398
Emblems, body movements, 147–148
Emotions. See also Psychological appeals
  affect blends, 149
  affect displays, 148
  and conflict, 248

and facial expressions, 149
and touch, 169
and voice, 153
Empathic listening, 84–85
  guidelines for, 84–85
Empathy
  in conflict management, 247–248
  in conversation, 189–190
  and intercultural communication, 444
Employment interview, 265–273
  common questions for, 268
  confidence, guidelines for, 269–270
  conversational behavior during, 269, 270
  failure of interviewee, reasons for, 270
  follow-up for, 271
  lawfulness of questions, 271–273
  objectives of, 267
  preparation of, 265–266
  questions, preparation of, 267–258
Encoding, meaning of, 11
Encounter groups, 296
Encroachment, of territory, 167–168
Entertainment function, of mass communication, 463–464
Equal Employment Opportunity Commission, 271
Equity theory of relationships, 219
Erotic love, 210
Ethical merit standard, 360
Ethicizing, and mass media, 465
Ethics
  and communication, 16–17
  gossip, 133
  and lying, 131
  and public communication, 355
Ethnocentrism, 426–427
  barrier to intercultural communication, 426–427
  meaning of, 426
Evaluation
  and listening, 81
  static evaluation, 119
Evidence
  and reasoning, 371
  tests of, 372–373
Exit interview, 261–262

Expert power, 289
Expressiveness
    in conversation, 193–194
    methods for communication of, 193
    nonverbal communication of, 193
Eye communication, 150–152
    eye contact avoidance, 152
    functions of, 151–152
    pupil dilation, effects of, 152
    visual dominance behavior, 151
Eye contact, 228
    cultural aspects, 104–105
Eye movements, 150–152

Face saving, and culture, 425
Facial Affect Scoring Technique, 149
Facial movements, 149–150
    affect displays, 148
    emotions communicated by, 149
    encoding-decoding of, 149
    micromomentary expressions, 149–150
Fact-inference confusion, 115–116
    and communication problems, 115
    correction of, 115–116
    test for fact-inference ability, 116
Fear
    barrier to intercultural communication, 427–428
    and psychological appeals, 379
Feedback messages, 12–13
    in conversation, 180
    critical, 13
    and eye communication, 151
    immediate and delayed, 13
    low and high monitored, 13
    self-feedback, 13
Feedforward messages, 13–14
    in conversation, 180
    disclaimers, 14, 180
    functions of, 14
    as metamessages, 14
Feelings of speaker
    and active listening, 89
    and empathic listening, 84
Fighting
    active, and conflict, 246
    below/above belt, 249–250

Figurative analogy, 373
Films, 461–462
    audience of, 461
    functions of, 462
    relationship to TV, 461
Financial difficulties, and relationship deterioration, 231
Financial gain, and psychological appeals, 380
Flexibility, in conversation, 187
Focus groups, 297, 299
Foot-in-the-door technique, persuasive communication, 371
Formal time, 171
Furnishings, communication aspects of, 164–165

Gatekeepers, 478–480
    characteristics of, 479–480
    functions of, 479
Gender, as audience characteristic, 390–391
Gender differences
    relationship messages, 29–30
    and self-disclosure, 51
    and space communication, 162
    touch communication, 170
Gender-free language, 138
General Semantics, 119
Global village, 456
Gossip, 132–133
    ethical aspects, 133
    problems created by, 132
Grapevine, 337–339
    events associated with, 338
    guidelines for, 339
    origin of term, 337–338
    problems with, 338–339
Greetings
    in conversation, 179–180
    functions of, 179–180
Group size, and self-disclosure, 48–49
Groupthink, 307–308
    characteristics of, 308
    signs of, 308
Gunnysacking, and conflict, 248

Hairstyle, communication aspects of, 164
Halo effect
    meaning of, 62
    reverse halo effect, 62
Heterosexist language, 139–140
    meaning of, 139
    subtle forms of, 139–140
Hidden self, 45
High-context cultures, 423, 424–425
Historical justification standard, 360
Honesty, effects of, 132
Human communication
    as adjustment process, 27
    areas of, 6–7
    content aspect of, 28
    context of, 8–10
    effective versus ineffective, 5–6
    ethical questions in, 16–17
    irreversible nature of, 34–35
    purposes of, 17–20
    relational aspects of, 28–30
    sequences of, 30–32
    as transactional process, 32–33

Idea-generation groups, 294–295
    brainstorming, 294
    rules for, 294–295
Illustrations, use in speech, 399
Illustrators, body movements, 148
Immediacy
    in conversation, 190–191
    nonverbal communication of, 191
    verbal communication of, 191
Implicit personality theory
    effect on perception, 61–62
    and halo effect, 62
Inclusive talk, 126–127
Indirect messages, 105–107
Indiscrimination, 120–121
    correction of, 121
    meaning of, 120
Individuality, and psychological appeals, 379
Inequity, and relationship deterioration, 232, 233
Informal time, 171
Information, and mass media, 465–466

Information interview, 262–264
    appointment with interviewee, 263–264
    closing, 264
    follow-up of, 264
    open-ended questions, 264
    rapport with interviewer, 264
    selection of interviewee, 263
    taping, 264
Information load principle, and informative speaking, 367
Information overload, 339–340
    causes of, 339–340
    guidelines for dealing with, 340
    problems with, 340
Information-sharing groups, 297–299
    focus, 297, 299
    learning, 297
Informative speaking, 367–368
    abstraction principle, 368
    appropriateness principle, 367
    information load principle, 367
    relevance principle, 367
    several senses principle, 368
In-group talk, 126–127
    nature of, 126
    self-talk, 126–127
Innovation, diffusion of innovations theory, 474–476
Inoculation principle, of persuasive communication, 369–370
Intensional orientation, 114–115
    and communication problems, 114–115
    correction of, 115
    meaning of, 114
Interaction management, in conversation, 191–193
Intercultural communication
    barriers to, 436–442
        ethnocentrism, 426–427
        fear, 427–428
        mindfulness, 427
        mindlessness, 427
    and culture shock, 440–442
    definition of, 421
    and differences in cultures, 422–425
    effective communication guidelines, 443–444

ethical issues, 17
forms of, 422
importance of, 417–420
intercultural openness self-test,
    418–419
knowledge about intercultural differ-
    ences, test of, 434–435
meaning of, 6
nature of, 420–421
principles of, 433–436
Interpersonal communication
apprehension test, 228
definitions of, 205–206
    componential, 205
    developmental, 205–206
    relational, 205
ethical issues, 17
and explanatory knowledge of other, 206
meaning of, 6
rules of interaction, 206
Interpersonal conflict
and aggressiveness, 250–251
and argumentativeness, 251–252
content, 242
myths about, 242–243
negative aspects of, 244
positive aspects of, 244–245
preconflict situation, 253–254
relationship, 242
Interpersonal conflict management,
    245–255
avoidance versus active fighting,
    245–246
blame versus empathy, 247–248
fighting below versus above belt,
    249–250
force versus talk, 246–247
gunnysacking versus present focus, 248
manipulation versus spontaneity,
    248–249
personal rejection versus acceptance,
    249
postconflict situation, 254–255
in relationship repair, 235
silencers versus facilitators of open ex-
    pression, 248
unproductive strategies, 245

Interpersonal relationships
attraction theory, 215–217
deterioration of, 211, 229–233
    causes of, 230–232
    communication related to, 232–233
development of, 226–229
    first encounters, 227–229
    reasons for, 226–227
equity theory, 219
love, types of, 210–211
reasons for, 226–227
repair of, 211, 233–237
    self-repair and dissolved relationship,
        236–237
    steps in process, 234–236
social exchange theory, 218–219
social penetration theory, 213–215
stages of, 207–212
    contact, 207, 228–229
    deterioration, 211, 229–233
    dissolution, 211
    intimacy, 208–211
    involvement, 207–208
    movement along, 212
    repair, 211, 233–237
Interrupting, in conversation, 127
Interview
appraisal, 261
counseling, 262
employment, 265–273
exit, 261–262
goals of, 260
information, 262–264
persuasive, 261
structure of, 261
Intimacy, 208–211
fear of, 209–210
intensifying relationships, methods of,
    208
and love, 210–211
stages of, 208
Intimate distance, 159–160
Intrapersonal communication, meaning
    of, 6
Introduction, of speech, 399–401
Involvement stage, in interpersonal rela-
    tionships, 207–208

Jewelry, communication aspects of, 164
Johari Window, components of self-aware-
    ness, 43–45

Laissez-faire leader, 313
Language, and public communication,
    354
    relativity of, 433
Lateral communication, 336–337
    characteristics of, 336–337
    guidelines for, 337
    problems with, 337
Leaders, 308–317
    functions of, 314–317
    leadership evaluation form, 316
    leadership style test, 310–311
    qualities of effective leader, 315
    situational leadership, 308, 312
Leadership styles, 313–314
    authoritarian, 313, 314
    democratic, 313, 314
    laissez-faire, 313
    and leader effectiveness, 313–314
Learning groups, 297
Legitimate power, 288
Listening
    active, 87–89
    benefits of effective, 79
    critical, 85–86
    depth, 86–87
    effectiveness test, 77
    empathic, 84–85
    evaluation in, 81
    nonjudgmental, 85–86
    objective, 84–85
    participatory, 83
    passive, 83
    receiving in, 78–79
    remembering in, 80–81
    responding in, 81–82
    surface, 86–87
    understanding in, 79–80
Literal analogy, 373
Logic, and public speaking, 371–375. See
    also Reasoning
Loneliness
    and end of relationship, 236–237

    and need for relationships, 226–227
Looking-glass self, 42
Love
    agape, 211
    erotic, 210
    ludus, 210
    manic, 210
    pragma, 210
    and psychological appeals, 379
    self-test for, 212–213
    storge, 210
Low-context cultures, 423, 424–425
Ludus love, 210
Lying, 107–108, 129–132
    effectiveness of, 131–132
    ethical aspects, 131
    gray areas related to, 131
    meaning of, 129
    nonverbal messages in, 107–108, 131
    reasons for, 130–131
    and relationship deterioration, 232
    and social disapproval, 132
    verbal responses in, 107–108

Magazines, 461
    general and specialized types, 461
Magnitude of change principle, of persua-
    sive communication, 370–371
Majority rule, for decision making,
    293–294
Managers, Theory X and Theory Y, 329
Manic love, 210
Manipulation, and conflict, 248–249
Markers, of territory, 168
Marriage, premarital anxieties, 209–210
Mass communication
    agenda-setting theory, 478–480
    audience in, 455
    books, 462
    compact discs, 462–463
    context in, 457
    cultivation theory, 476–477
    diffusion of innovations theory,
        474–476
    entertainment function of, 463–464
    ethical issues, 17
    films, 461–462

influences on media, 480–481
information-giving function of,
    465–466
magazines, 461
meaning of, 6
messages in, 456
multistep theory, 473–474
narcotizing function of, 466
newspapers, 459–461
one-step theory, 472–473
persuasive function of, 19–20, 464–465
process in, 456–457
radio, 459
relationships created by, 466–468
source in, 455
tapes, 462
television, 457–459
two-step theory, 473
uses and gratification theory, 477–478
Mass media. *See* Mass communication
Meaning
    and communication process, 100
    context-based nature of, 103–104
    denotative and connotative, 102–103
    and receiver of message, 101–102
    unique, 102
Messages, 11–14, 104–109
    believability of, 107–108
    double-bind, 24–27
    feedback, 12–13
    feedforward, 13–14
    indirect, 105–107
    and mass communication, 456
    metacommunicational statements,
        108–109
    and nonverbal communication, 104
    and public communication, 353
    regulation by rules, 104
    types of, 12
Metacommunication, 108–109
    meaning of, 108
    metamessages, 14
    nonverbal messages as, 108–109
Mindfulness
    barrier to intercultural communication,
        427
    in conversation, 186

Mind reading, 247
Mobility, and intercultural experiences, 417
Motivated sequence pattern, speech,
        398–399
Motivation
    complexity of motives, 379
    and conclusion of speech, 401
    degrees of intensity of motives, 378
    and human needs, 376–377
    and individual differences, 378
    interaction of motives, 378
Multistep theory, mass communication,
        473–474

Narcotizing function, of mass media, 466
Needs, hierarchy of, 376–377
Networks. *See* Communication networks
Newspapers, 459–461
    declining readership, 460–461
    functions of, 460
Noise, 14–15
    and public communication, 351–352
    types of, 14–15
Nominal group method, 292–293
    advantages/disadvantages of, 293
Nonjudgmental listening, 85–86
Nonverbal messages
    and body movements, 147–148
    of expressiveness, 193
    and eye movements, 150–152
    and facial movements, 149–150
    gift giving, 167
    greetings, 179
    of immediacy, 191
    and lying, 107–108, 131
    as metacommunication, 108–109
    of other orientation, 194
    and rules, 104–105
    stroking, 190
    use with verbal messages, 99
Norms, group, 285, 287

Objective listening, 84–85
One-step theory, mass communication,
        472–473
Open-ended questions, in information in-
        terview, 264

Openness, in conversation, 188–189
Open self, 43–45
Organization
    characteristics of, 323, 325
    formal and informal structure of, 323
    goals of, 323, 325
Organizational communication
    behavioral approach, 327–328
    cultural approach, 328–330
    downward, 336
    formal, 325
    grapevine, 337–339
    informal, 325
    information overload, 339–340
    lateral, 336–337
    meaning of, 6
    networks. *See* Communication networks
    scientific approach, 327
    sexual harassment, 325–326
    systems approach, 328
    upward, 334–336
Organizations
    behavioral management approach, 327
    characteristics of excellent companies,
        330–331
    participatory management, 327
    scientific management, 327
    systems approach to, 328
Other-orientation
    communication methods of, 194
    in conversation, 194
    nonverbal communication of, 194

Panel format, small groups, 299
Paralanguage, 153–155
    judgments about people from, 153
    rate of speech, effects of, 154–155
    vocal characteristics of, 153
Paraphrasing, in active listening, 88
Parasocial relationships, with media fig-
        ures, 467–468
Parent-Effectiveness-Training (P-E-T), 87
Participatory listening, 83
Participatory management, 327
Passive listening, 83
    benefits of, 83
    guidelines for, 83–84

Perception
    improving accuracy of, 70–71
    influencing factors
        attribution, 67–70
        consistency, 65
        implicit personality theory, 61–62
        perceptual accentuation, 63–64
        primacy-recency, 64–65
        self-fulfilling prophesy, 62–63
        stereotyping, 66–67
    and sensory stimulation, 59–60
    steps in perceptual process, 59–60
Perceptual accentuation, 63–64
    meaning of, 63
    negative effects of, 64
Personal distance, 160
Personal growth group, 295–296
    assertiveness training, 296
    consciousness-raising, 296
    encounter, 296
    rules/procedures of, 296
Personality, and attraction, 215–216
Persuasion power, 289
Persuasive communication, 368–371
    audience participation principle, 369
    door-in-the face technique, 371
    foot-in-the door technique, 371
    inoculation principle, 369–370
    magnitude of change principle,
        370–371
    and mass communication, 464–465
    and rate of speech, 154
    selective exposure principle, 368–369
Persuasive interview, 261
Physical attractiveness, 215–216
Physical context, of communication, 8–9
Play
    and communication, 20
    and touch, 169
Polarization, 113–114
    and communication problems, 113
    meaning of, 113
Positive apprehension, communication,
        358
Positiveness
    in conversation, 190
    in relationship repair, 236

and stroking, 190
Power
  coercive, 288–289
  definition of, 288
  expert, 289
  legitimate, 288
  persuasion, 289
  and psychological appeals, 379
  referent, 288
  reward, 288
  in small groups, 288–289
Power plays, 128–129
  management of, 128–129
  types of, 128, 129
Pragma love, 210
Primacy-recency
  effect on perception, 64–65
  negative effects of, 65
Privatization, and mass media, 466–467
Problem-solution pattern, speech, 397
Problem-solving groups, 289–294
  decision-making methods, 293–294
  Delphi method, 293
  nominal group method, 292–293
  steps in problem solving, 289–292
Problem-solving steps
  criteria for evaluation of solutions, 291
  definition of problem, 289–290
  evaluation of solutions, 291
  identification of possible solutions, 291
  selection of solution, 292
  testing of solution, 292
  thinking hats in, 291–292
Proxemics, 159–162
  influences in communication, 161–162
  intimate distance, 159–160
  personal distance, 160
  public distance, 160–162
  social distance, 160
  spatial distances, 159–161
Proximity, and attraction, 216
Psychological appeals, 375–380
  forms of, 379–380
  motivational aspects, 377–380
  nature of, 375–377
  power of, 375
Psychological time, 172–175

future orientation, 173–175
past orientation, 172
present orientation, 172, 175
self-test for, 173–174
Public communication
  apprehension, 355–358
  context in, 352–353
  credibility of speaker, 380–382
  criticism of, 358–361
    standards of, 359–361
    value of, 358–359
  delivery of speaker, 354–355
  ethical aspects, 355
  ethical issues, 17
  informative speaking, principles of,
    367–368
  language for, 354
  listeners in, 351
  meaning of, 6
  messages/channels in, 353
  noise in, 351–352
  persuasive communication, 368–371
  psychological appeals, 375–380
  reasoning principles in, 371–375
  speaker in, 351
Public distance, 160–162
Pygmalion effect, nature of, 63

Qualifiers, in interpersonal relationships,
  227
Questioning, in active listening, 89
Quotations, use in speech, 400, 401

Racist language, 135–136
  effect of, 136–137
  inherently, 137
Radio, 459
  focus of programming, 459
Rape, 247
Reasoning
  from analogy, 373
  from causes and effects, 374
  general tests of evidence in, 371–372
  from sign, 374–375
  from specific instances, 372–373
Receiving, and listening, 78–79
Referent power, 288

Regulators, body movements, 148
Reinforcement, and attraction, 216
Rejection, and conflict, 249
Relationship messages, 28–30
  gender differences, 29–30
Relationships
  complementary, 30
  and eye communication, 151–152
  interpersonal. *See* Interpersonal relationships
  symmetrical, 30
Relevance principle, and informative speaking, 367
Remembering, and listening, 80–81
Repair stage, in interpersonal relationships, 211, 233–237
Responding, and listening, 81–82
Reverse halo effect, 62
Reward power, 288
Ritualistic touching, 169
Roles of group members, 303–305
Round table format, small groups, 299

Scientific approach, organizational communication, 327
Scientific management, 327
Selective exposure principle, of persuasive communication, 368–369
Self-actualization, and psychological appeals, 380
Self-awareness, 43–47
  blind self in, 45
  hidden self in, 45
  increasing, 46–47
  open self in, 43–45
  unknown self in, 45
Self-concept, 42–43
  development of, 42–43
  meaning of, 43
Self-disclosure, 48–55
  dangers of, 53
  guidelines for, 53–54
  influencing factors in, 48–51
  nature of, 48
  nondisclosers, 127
  and relationship deterioration, 232
  responding to, 54–55

rewards of, 52–53
test for, 49
Self-esteem, 47–48
  enhancement of, 47–48
  and failed relationships, 237
  and lying, 130
  and psychological appeals, 379
Self-fulfilling prophesy
  effect on perception, 62–63
  meaning of, 62–63
  negative effects of, 63
  Pygmalion effect as, 63
  steps in, 63
Self-knowledge, and interpersonal relationships, 227
Self-monitoring, 191–193
  high self-monitors, 192–193
  low self-monitors, 192–193
  test of, 192
Self-orientation, communication in, 194
Self-talk, 126–127
Sensory stimulation, and perception, 59–60
Sequences of communication, 30–32
Sex, and relationship deterioration, 230–231
Sexist language, 137–139
  examples of, 137–138
  gender-free language, 138
  and sex role stereotyping, 139
Sexual harassment, 325–326
  definition of, 325–326
  prevention of, 326
Sign, reasoning from, 374–375
Silencers, and conflict, 248
Similarity, and attraction, 216
Situational leadership, 308, 312
Small group communication
  barriers to, 317
  communication apprehension test, 286
  ethical issues, 17
  groupthink, 307–308
  interaction process analysis, 305–306
  leaders in, 308–317
    functions of, 314–317
    situational leadership, 308, 312
    styles, 313–314

meaning of, 6
members in, 303–305
  group-building roles, 304, 305
  group orientation of, 306–307
  group task roles, 303–304
  individual roles, 304–305
open-mindedness of members, 307
understanding of members, 307
Small groups
  characteristics of, 285
  idea-generation, 294–295
  information-sharing, 297–299
  norms, 285, 287
  panel format, 299
  personal growth, 295–296
  power in, 288–289
  problem-solving, 289–294
  round table format, 299
  symposium format, 299
  symposium-forum format, 299
Smell, communication aspects of, 166
Social distance, 160
Social exchange theory, 218–219
  comparison level in, 219
  rewards and costs in, 218–219
Social penetration theory, 213–215
  breadth/depth of relationships, 213–213
  depenetration in, 214–215
Social-psychological context, of commu-
    nication, 9
Sound, 152–155. *See also* Voice
Source-receivers, 10–11
  communication competence, 11
  encoding-decoding of, 10–11
Space
  artifactual communication, 162–166
  decoration, 164–165
    communication aspects of, 164–165
  proxemics, 159–162
  territoriality, 166–168
  touch communication, 168–171
Spatial pattern, speech, 398
Speech, 395–401
  body of, 396–399
  cause-effect pattern, 398
  conclusions, functions of, 401
  effect-cause pattern, 398

introduction, functions of, 399–401
motivated sequence pattern, 398–399
problem-solution pattern, 397
spatial pattern, 398
speaker-audience-topic relationship,
    400–401
temporal pattern, 397–398
thesis of, 396
topical organization, 397
Standards
  in criticism of public speaking, 359–360
  ethical merit, 360
  historical justification, 360
  universality, 360
State apprehension, communication,
    356–357
Static evaluation, 119
  and communication problems, 119
  correction of, 119
  meaning of, 119
Statistics, use in speech, 400
Status
  conferred by mass media, 466
  and psychological appeals, 380
  and space communication, 161
  and temporal communication, 175
  and time orientation, 174–175
Steamrolling, 246
Stereotyping
  common stereotypes, 67
  effect on perception, 66–67
  negative effects of, 67
  and sexist language, 139
Stimulation, and interpersonal relation-
    ships, 227
Storge love, 210
Stroking
  nature of, 190
  verbal and nonverbal, 190
Success, and self-esteem, 48
Surface listening, 86–87
Symmetrical relationships, 30
Symposium format, small groups, 299
Symposium-forum format, small groups,
    299
Systems approach, organizational com-
    munication, 328

Tapes, 462
Technical time, 171
Television, 457–459
    increasing use of, 458–459
Temporal communication, 171–175
    and appropriateness, 175
    cultural time, 171–172
    psychological time, 172–175
    and status, 175
Temporal context, of communication, 9
Temporal pattern, speech, 397–398
Territoriality, 166–168
    encroachment, types of, 167–168
    markers of territory, 168
    theories of, 166
Theory X and Theory Y managers, 329
Thesis, of speech, 396
Time
    clocks, cultural differences, 172
    diffused, 171
    displaced, 171
    formal, 171
    informal, 171
    psychological, 172–175
    technical, 171
Time-and-motion studies, 327
Topical organization, speech, 397
Touch communication, 168–171
    avoidance, 171
    and culture, 170
    gender differences, 170
Trait apprehension, communication, 356
Transactional process, communication as, 32–33
Turn-denying cues, conversation, 184
Turn-maintaining cues, conversation, 183–184

Turn-requesting cues, conversation, 184
Turn-yielding cues, conversation, 184
Two-step theory, mass communication, 473

Understanding, and listening, 79–80
Universality standard, 360
Unknown self, 45
Upward communication, 334–336
    characteristics of, 334
    guidelines for, 335–336
    problems with, 334–335
Uses and gratification theory, mass communication, 477–478

Values, nature of, 390
Verbal messages
    downward talk, 127–129
    inclusive talk, 126–127
    in-group talk, 126–127
    and lying, 107–108
    use with nonverbal messages, 99
Violence, in relationships, 246–247
Voice
    and emotional state, 153
    judgments about people from, 153
    and paralanguage, 153
    rate of speech, effects of, 154–155

Wheel structure, communication networks, 331, 332
Win-lose situations, 106
Win-win situations, 106–107
Withdrawal, and relationship deterioration, 232
Work, and relationship deterioration, 231

Y pattern, communication networks, 332